Alternatives for teaching exceptional children

Essays from Focus on Exceptional Children

by Edward L. Meyen,
University of Kansas

Glenn A. Vergason,
Georgia State University

Richard J. Whelan,
University of Kansas Medical Center

LOVE PUBLISHING COMPANY
Denver, Colorado 80222

EDUCATIONAL SERIES

Copyright © 1975 Love Publishing Company
Printed in the U.S.A.
ISBN 0-89108-047-3
Library of Congress Catalog Card Number 75-10937

3 /75/77 Beekers Tyler 8.80

Contents

PREFACE   7

The Alternative Movement in Special Education   9
    Edward L. Meyen, *University of Kansas, Lawrence*
    Glenn A. Vergason, *Georgia State University*
    Richard J. Whelan, *University of Kansas Medical Center*

PART 1   RATIONALE   21

Rationale for Alternative Programming: A Perspective   23
    B. K. Tilley, *Madison Public Schools, Wisconsin*

Mainstreaming: Toward an Explication of the Construct   35
    Martin J. Kaufman, Jay Gottlieb, Judith A. Agard,
    Maurine B. Kukic, *Intramural Research Program,*
    Bureau of Education for the Handicapped,
    U. S. Office of Education

Recent Influences of Law Regarding the Identification
and Educational Placement of Children   55
    Frederick J. Weintraub
    The Council for Exceptional Children, Reston, Virginia

Special Education for the Mildly Retarded: Servant or Savant   73
    Donald L. MacMillan, *University of California, Riverside*

Alternatives to Special Class Placement for Educable
Mentally Retarded Children   92
    Robert H. Bruininks, John E. Rynders
    University of Minnesota

Crosscultural Evaluation of Exceptionality   112
    Jane R. Mercer, *University of California, Riverside*

Strategies for Culturally Different Children
in Classes for the Retarded   122
    Oliver L. Hurley, *University of Georgia, Athens*

Career Education for the Mildly Handicapped   135
    Gary M. Clark, *University of Kansas, Lawrence*

PART 2   MODELS — 151

Models for Alternative Programming: A Perspective — 153
  Richard A. Johnson, *Minneapolis Public Schools*

Will the Real "Mainstreaming" Program Please Stand Up!
(or . . . Should Dunn Have Done It?) — 173
  Jerry D. Chaffin, *University of Kansas, Lawrence*

Observation Systems and the Special Education Teacher — 205
  Melvyn I. Semmel, Sivasailam Thiagarajan
  Indiana University

Responsive Teaching: Focus on Measurement and Research
in the Classroom and the Home — 225
  R. Vance Hall
  Juniper Gardens Children's Project, Kansas

Developing Programs for Severely Handicapped Students:
Teacher Training and Classroom Instruction — 236
  Lou Brown, Robert York
  University of Wisconsin, Madison

An Educational Solution: The Engineered Classroom — 255
  Robert J. Stillwell, Alfred A. Artuso, Frank D. Taylor
  Santa Monica School District, California
  Frank M. Hewett
  University of California, Los Angeles

Integration of Exceptional Children into Regular Classes:
Research and Procedure — 275
  Judith K. Grosenick, *University of Missouri, Columbia*

A Learning Center Plan for Special Education — 290
  Frank D. Taylor, Alfred A. Artuso, Robert J. Stillwell,
  Michael M. Soloway, *Santa Monica School District*
  Frank M. Hewett, *University of California, Los Angeles*
  Herbert C. Quay, *Temple University*

Planning Resource Rooms for the Mildly Handicapped — 301
  J. Lee Wiederholt, *University of Texas, Austin*

The Classroom as an Ecosystem — 318
  Anne W. Carroll, *University of Denver*

Mainstreaming: A Problem and an Opportunity for General Education — 338
  Keith E. Beery, *Institute for Independent Educational
  Research, San Rafael, California*

PART 3   APPROACHES   351

Approaches for Alternative Programming: A Perspective   353
    Nettie R. Bartel, Diane Bryen, Helmut W. Bartel
    Temple University

Creating and Evaluating Remediation for the Learning Disabled   365
    Esther H. Minskoff, *Groves School, Hopkins, Minnesota*

Inductive Teaching Techniques for the Mentally Retarded   383
    George S. Mischio, *University of Wisconsin, Whitewater*

Facilitating Educational Progress by Improving Parent Conferences   400
    Roger L. Kroth, *University of New Mexico, Albuquerque*

The Consulting Teacher Approach to Special Education:
Inservice Training for Regular Classroom Teachers   419
    Lu S. Christie, Hugh S. McKenzie, Carol S. Burdett
    University of Vermont

Teacher Attention to Appropriate and Inappropriate Classroom
Behavior: An Individual Case Study   436
    Hill M. Walker, *University of Oregon, Eugene*
    Nancy K. Buckley
    Spanish Peaks Mental Health Center, Pueblo, Colorado

Procedures for Developing Creativity in Emotionally
Disturbed Children   446
    Patricia A. Gallagher
    University of Kansas Medical Center

Curriculum and Methods in Early Childhood Special Education:
One Approach   461
    Merle B. Karnes, R. Reid Zehrbach
    University of Illinois, Urbana

Curriculum for Early Childhood Special Education   480
    David P. Weikart
    High Scope Educational Research Foundation, Ypsilanti, Michigan

AUTHOR INDEX   493

Preface

Books of readings and essay collections serve professionals in a number of ways. Basically, they make their contribution by organizing literature around a circumscribed theme highly relevant to a particular professional group. Such collections retrieve selections from the literature which cover a broad time span. This particular essay collection represents a planned effort, beginning two years ago, to commission manuscripts related to the movement toward alternative educational programming for handicapped children which was emerging at that time. The result is a collection of highly interrelated essays central to the current major issue of alternative programming in public education. The purpose of this book is to place the alternative movement in perspective and to cite emerging areas of concern.

The Alternative Movement in Special Education

Edward L. Meyen
University of Kansas, Lawrence

Glenn A. Vergason
Georgia State University

Richard J. Whelan
University of Kansas Medical Center

The delivery of educational services to exceptional children is in the process of unprecedented change. Legislation mandating publicly supported education for a full spectrum of handicapped persons has been enacted in many states (Abeson, 1973; Ross, DeYoung & Cohen, 1971; Weintraub, 1972). Litigation involving individual rights such as the right to treatment, the right to education, the right to due process, and class action suits has resulted in a challenge to placement of handicapped children in isolated and segregated educational settings, e.g., special classes, routinely employed in special education service programs (Dailey, 1974; Kuriloff, True, Kirp & Buss, 1974; Stafford, 1974). There has also been a definite trend toward establishing alternatives to the popular self-contained, special class model. State departments of education have responded by implementing regulations and financial aid programs which allow for and encourage alternate delivery systems. Local districts, while varying in structure and rate of change, have established programs which exercise the new options available to them (Birch, 1974; Chaffin, 1974; Mann, 1974).

The primary alternative model being promulgated is popularly referred to as "mainstreaming." If program implementation can be interpreted as proof of acceptance, mainstreaming, in many varieties and forms, is indeed gaining substantial acceptance. Many local school districts are responding to the cues of legislators, state agencies, parents, and major professional voices by implementing programs under the guise of mainstreaming or alternative programs. Even though many mainstreaming program options have been implemented, several reports have been published which suggest considerable variance in scope,

9

objectives, and relative value of programs operational at the district level (Beery, 1972; Birch, 1974; Chaffin, 1974).

In general, the following principles underlie most mainstreaming programs. The manner in which these principles are operationalized into programs varies by district.

1. The mildly handicapped child's primary educational placement should be in a regular class setting.
2. Instructional support personnel and services such as diagnostic and prescriptive resource personnel, consulting teachers, itinerant teachers, resource rooms, and special therapy should be made available to each child requiring such assistance, but they should not function to remove a child from a regular class setting for a major portion of the school day.
3. Placement and instructional decisions are collaborative decisions made by a team of regular and special education personnel.
4. No placement is considered final; options must be held open pending evidence which dictates placement change.
5. An individually prescribed educational plan is developed and implemented.
6. Instructional responsibility is no longer vested solely with the special education teacher but is shared with regular teachers and other specialists who may be involved in the instructional process.

Operationally, the typical mainstreaming program takes the form of an arrangement in which a group is involved in the total process by which a placement decision is made. The program is primarily based in the regular class. In addition, resource personnel are made available to provide direct support or remediation for a child's academic and social excesses or deficits and to give assistance to the teacher in curriculum, behavior management, and other instructional aspects. Practical restraints on local resources have a tendency to shape what is actually implemented in mainstreaming programs; therefore, not all of the basic principles are applied or followed. The consequence is a wide variance in the quality and quantity of support services.

In contrast to educational trends which occur as a result of new research findings on the development of more effective instructional strategies, the impetus given to the alternative model (mainstream) movement has emerged from a social base couched in litigation and legislative action. For the most part, this is a logical add-on to the civil rights movement which has been receiving public support. The extension of the civil rights influence to include the handicapped has made passage of legislation a less difficult task. The consequence has been the creation of a set of circumstances which requires public schools to respond without the instructional and curricular strategies needed to effectively implement the proposed alternatives. This is not to imply that research challenging the efficiency of the traditional self-contained, special class model, as implemented in the United States, is not sufficient; however, it is clearly evident that the current mainstreaming movement is not based on systematic research design, curriculum improvements, or instructional strategies which *assure* resolvement of the pedagogical problems facing the education of exceptional children.

AREAS OF CONCERN

As is true in many educational movements, the initial progress is in operationalizing experimental or demonstration programs. Frequently, these early efforts are couched in compromise. To a degree this is the case with alternative programming. Insufficient numbers of appropriately trained personnel exist for the new and additional support roles. Although legislative mandates can dictate the establishment of program options, the attitude change required by many regular educators toward their responsibility to handicapped children cannot be legislated. The movement is young, but the rate of growth has been substantial. Consequently, areas of concern which are difficult to deal with and currently unresolved in alternative programming will have to be dealt with in the future. Certainly, initial research and program experimentation with a variety of mainstreaming organizational structures will yield new knowledge.

This chapter will attempt to describe some elements of alternative programming for which literature does not now exist. These omissions may well be the topic of a future collection of essays.

Curriculum Concerns

A primary goal of the current emphasis on change in the education of exceptional children is to increase programming options through alternative delivery systems. Operationally, at the local level, this means establishing program arrangements such as itinerant teachers and/or resource rooms, assessment-prescriptive services, and tutorial instruction in combination with partial placement in regular classes. The establishment of an array of options allows for more choice in matching program options with pupil needs. The underlying assumption is that these increased options will also result in more precision in meeting the specific needs of handicapped children. However, from a curriculum perspective a case can be made that the process of increasing program options, i.e., alternative placements and models, results in restricting instructional placements and curriculum options. This consequence is best illustrated by a comparison between the parameters of the self-contained, special class model and the parameters of the alternative model.

The parameters of the self-contained, special class model are explicit. The parameters of alternative models are definable; but, because they are more sensitive to local variables, they vary more in design. In spite of the design consistency of the special self-contained model versus the variableness of the alternative model, there are unique features common to most alternative models. They serve to illustrate how a movement from the self-contained model to the broader approach based on alternative models restricts instructional/curriculum options.[1]

Figure 1 presents a comparison of basic characteristics of the self-contained model and those generally characteristic of alternative models. In essence, the more elemental the alternatives, i.e., more teachers, settings, and varied time-frames, the greater the restrictions on instructional/curriculum options. The self-contained class for homogeneous groups allows for maximum instructional and curriculum options. It allows for the vast majority of the options not allowable within existing alternative models. In other words, the grouping of children by some instructional criterion, assignment to a single teacher, and allocating to this arrangement a full day time-frame allows for maximum flexibility in terms of curriculum and instruction.

This is not a value statement intended as support for either approach. The comparison is made to point out that attention needs to be given to determining the specific characteristics, i.e., conditions of alternative programs, which dictate specific design features of curricula and/or instructional materials. Questions arise such as: If a comprehensive curriculum is developed which integrates a broad spectrum of skills and is found to be highly effective, will it be applicable for resource rooms? The questions which emerge regarding the applicability of particular kinds of materials to teaching handicapped children in regular class settings are even more numerous.

From a curriculum/material development perspective, problems and probable solutions need to be made explicit. It is apparent, with only surface information, that many materials and currently available curricula are not appropriate for emerging alternative models. This is true even though their effectiveness with handicapped children has been demonstrated in circumscribed settings. The most obvious restraint is that some materials are group oriented and/or too comprehensive to be effectively employed in resource room settings or for handicapped children placed in regular classes.

---

1. Instructional options are herein defined to include the use of prepared instructional materials and/or the employment of teaching methodologies, while curriculum options are herein defined to include instructional programs in a subject matter area or areas inclusive of instruction covering substantial periods of time.

From a curriculum perspective, the transition to mainstream alternatives may be more significant for the mildly mentally retarded than for other mildly handicapped populations. The history of relying primarily on the self-contained special class model for the delivery of educational services to this group has tended to institutionalize certain instructional practices, administrative expectations, and curriculum assumptions which work against effective mainstreaming implementation. The assumptions which have underlined the development of curriculum for special class settings do not hold when the characteristics of existing alternative models are concerned.

Because of the curriculum/instructional implications of moving from a self-contained model to a model which varies instructional time-frames, settings, and teaching personnel, it could be assumed that in establishing alternative programs major attention would be given to determining curriculum and instructional variables which must be considered in the new delivery models. This does not appear to be the case. The program and project reviews to date (Birch, 1974; Mann, 1974) suggest that they have been concerned with principles of staff development, i.e., inservice to regular and special education personnel, social status of handicapped children in regular class settings, procedures for establishing and coordinating needed support services, and for assessment and prescriptive procedures which facilitate employment of particular remediation strategies.

There is a paucity of data and discussion in the literature regarding the criteria which curricula or materials must meet in order to be applicable to alternative settings. The net result is that some materials and curricula are not used because they are presumably inappropriate for differential instructional settings, and those which are used are selected on the same basis, i.e., without validation. In any event, the recycling of curricula in accordance with evaluative criteria must occur before the effectiveness of their use in alternative settings can be verified.

Population Concerns

The sequence of class action suits, civil cases involving individuals, and legislative enactments focusing on equal rights for the handicapped has tended to have a generalized influence across the rationale for alternative programs. As one reads the literature and attends conferences, there is an implied assumption that the full spectrum of handicapped individuals are candidates for alternative programs approaching mainstream designs. At least there is a hesitancy to question the application to particular populations.

The major emphasis in mainstreaming at the present time involves the mildly handicapped at the elementary level. While the experience with this population has been encouraging, it is not reasonable, based on these success examples, to

13

Figure 1
MODEL CHARACTERISTICS—CURRICULUM CONSEQUENCES

Self-Contained	Feature	Alternative Models	Curriculum Consequence
1. One teacher has primary responsibility for instruction.	*Teacher Variable*	1. Responsibility for instruction is shared among at least two teachers.	1.1. Each teacher has a different area of instructional responsibility.
			1.2. Coordination in programming and material selection is essential.
			1.3. One teacher is always a regular class teacher who must make changes in his/her regular curriculum to the degree possible.
			1.4. Control of curriculum variances are more difficult to accomplish.
2. Placement is basically full-time.	*Time Variable*	2. Placement is part-time for designated periods of time.	2.1. Decisions must be made on what instruction takes place where and when.
			2.2. Time restraints preclude use of curricula in resource rooms which are integrated and require large time-frames.
			2.3. Restricted time-frame reduces the teacher's option for reinforcing skills and concepts throughout the day which were previously introduced through specific lessons.

Self-Contained	Feature	Alternative Models	Curriculum Consequence
3. Focus is on a total instructional program.	*Curriculum Variable*	3. Focus is more on specific skills and concepts with instructional responsibility shared among teachers.	3.1. Local curriculum planning and development are more complicated because of having to relate areas of instruction to different settings and teachers. 3.2. Need for teachers to gain access to instructional activities within curricula or materials which relate to specific skills and concepts increases.
4. Administrative control more aligned with Special Education Director or person designated responsible for Special Education.	*Administrative Variable*	4. Administrative responsibility more directly aligned with building principal.	4.1. More control of curriculum by regular education. 4.2. Loss of flexibility for applied instruction such as field trips, etc.
5. Reasonable homogeneity of pupil characteristics in class.	*Pupil Variable*	5. Broad heterogeneity of pupil characteristics in regular class; more resources specific to the instructional problems of children served.	5.1. Decision-making of regular class teacher increases and becomes more significant. Resource teacher requires more diagnostic information.

15

project that alternative program designs approaching mainstreaming at the secondary level for the mildly handicapped will be equally or more successful. The implementation of career education, academic preparation, teaching of life skills, and basic social development instruction required by many mildly handicapped adolescents must be carefully studied relative to delivery systems. It would be risky to discount the unique instructional needs of this group in deference to structuring interaction with normal peers.

Operational alternative programs for the severely handicapped are conspicuous by their absence on the local scene. The low incidence of this population probably accounts for this. The tendency to generalize the spirit of alternative programming dictates that serious attention be given to options appropriate to particular populations. Certainly, as the extent of learning and behavioral problems increases, models designed for the extensive integration of the severely handicapped become less applicable.

Considerable research is necessary to answer those pervasive questions which pertain to the matching of alternative models with the characteristics of individuals.

Personnel Preparation Concerns

Implementation of alternative programs for handicapped children did not immediately follow the conceptualization of differential models or the philosophical base supporting the rationale for alternative instructional strategies. The various alternative programs are designed to provide instructional opportunities in accordance with the desired goal of individualizing instruction. Discrimination of unique learner needs, and differential instruction to serve those needs, are the philosophical roots of individualized instruction. Therefore, the many operational alternative service delivery systems represent means to attain the desired goal of individualized instruction.

At the present time, alternative programs reflect variety in administrative arrangements. As such, these arrangements appear to be consistent with the strategy of providing a continuum of services based upon individual child needs. However, administrative arrangements are only structures within which specific child based instruction should be facilitated. These structures merely set the stage for, but do not guarantee, relevant learning activities. If instructional processes and child-teacher relationship variables are not designed or changed in a manner which the administrative organization purportedly makes possible, then it is doubtful that changes in learner behavior will be observed. Since learner behavior is largely elicited by teacher behavior, then changes in teacher behavior should occur as unique child instructional needs are encountered. Effectiveness of various alternative models is dependent upon the skills and knowledge of instructional personnel. Teachers must be prepared to assume roles which are unique to each administrative arrangement. If alternative instructional systems are to be efficient and effective, personnel preparation must occur prior to or simultaneously with implementation of the systems.

Successful alternative instructional models cannot be achieved by simply mandating changes in administrative arrangements. Changes in pupil-teacher interaction must also occur; thus, teacher behavior must be responsive to child needs. Personnel preparation which focuses upon, and includes attention to, interpersonal relationships, attitudes, understanding, as well as cognitive knowledge of materials, media, and methods is required before handicapped children will be assured full access to society's educational resources (Martin, 1974).

Issues. There are two issues or concerns related to personnel preparation. The issues are interrelated and, therefore, cannot be separated for the purposes of policy planning and program implementation.

One cogent issue pertains to certification standards for the variety of instructional roles assigned to regular and special educators. The movement toward alternative programs requires more intensive commitment and involvement of regular educators in the provision of instructional services for handicapped children. Yet, present regular teacher and administrator certification requirements do not require or include academic and practicum experiences with the handicapped. As a result, the opportunities to acquire new knowledge and revise long-ingrained attitudes toward individual variance or handicapping conditions are neither available nor planned for in preparation programs. By contrast, special educators, even though most of them were trained to function as regular educators, must learn again to appreciate and understand the unique problems regular educators have in devising individualized instructional experiences in a large group setting. In addition, special educators must adapt to a situation in which cooperative program development with regular educators is a necessity if alternative programs are to be successful. Previous approaches in which the regular educator relinquished, and the special educator assumed, full responsibility for the handicapped child will not suffice for implementing effective alternative programs. Therefore, contemplated changes in regular educator certification requirements must include the mandate for realistic and desirable experiences with the handicapped, as well as experiences in developing child instructional programs in cooperation with special education support personnel. Conversely, the special educator must learn to function in cooperation with regular educator colleagues in developing and managing instructional programs for the handicapped. Changing certification requirements is a type of administrative arrangement and, as such, does not necessarily specify the substantive areas of content and experiences in a preparation program.

The preparation curriculum, the second issue or concern, must be systematically designed and operated for preservice and inservice activities. This curriculum should include opportunities to change attitudes toward handicapping conditions, gain insight, understanding, and appreciation for individual variances, and obtain instructional knowledge and skills. Adding a course or two to a basic teacher education curriculum will not be sufficient to attain desirable levels of understanding, appreciation, and skills. Rather, attention to the problems and needs of all children, including the handicapped, should permeate all coursework and practica provided for regular educators at preservice and inservice levels of preparation. For example, an educational foundation course can be designed to include an objective analysis of society's attitudes and beliefs about individuals who differ from what is thought to be normal. Instructional methods courses can include opportunities for students to learn precise skills in tailoring learning experiences for the handicapped. In all probability, these two examples, plus others, could function to improve instruction for all children and, therefore, for the handicapped. Regular education and special education faculty members, just as their colleagues in alternative child instructional systems must do, will need to cooperatively plan for a general reform of preservice and inservice preparation sequences. Indeed, the preparation curriculum cannot be developed in isolation from ongoing instructional programs for children. What is taught to educators should develop out of what is needed by children.

Educators, as well as those who prepare them, must learn from children. If that occurs, instructional programs will become responsive and relevant to the needs of *all* children. Alternative educational programs are means to the common goal of appropriate instructional experiences, but the goal can only be reached through the efforts of well prepared, competent, humanistic educators who are committed to the precise formulation and implementation of means.

TOPICAL SECTIONS

The book is divided into three major sections. These sections represent the sequential phases which most new programs must consider before systematic implementation can become a reality. Alternative programs for the education of handicapped children are currently at various stages of development within the phases of program rationales, models, and approaches. At the present time, these three phases, as represented by the three sections of this book, are characterized by divergence in philosophy, objectives, and activities. This is as it should be. Such divergence, diversity, and variance will function to create a climate in which various issues and perplexing problems can be discussed, clarified, evaluated, and resolved. Out of this productive foment, improved educational programs for handicapped children will be initiated. The children will be the winners; after all, that is what it is all about.

The *rationale* section contains a portion of the background and trends which have focused attention upon the need for change in special education services, training, and research. While one collection of essays cannot begin to identify all change variables, the rationale portion of the book does provide a comprehensive and representative overview of relevant educational issues.

Identification of issues usually leads to the development of a rationale for action. Action, though, requires a base or a model to provide direction. Therefore, the *models* section provides descriptions of a variety of systems, or models, which special educators have developed and tried as alternatives to the status quo and, more precisely, with the hope that educational programs for the handicapped would be improved.

Activities are required to implement models and to verify if the basic rationale for action has merit or not. The *approaches* section focuses upon processes, activities, and tactics which may be used to implement models.

There are many rationales, models, and approaches for improving the education programs available to handicapped children. Some programs overlap extensively, some represent differences in semantics rather than substance, and some contain only few points of agreement with others.

This book, then, should stimulate further discussion, contemplation, and action relevant to educational programs for the handicapped. As such, the book is merely a starting point. It can never be completed since each day, week, month, and year should bring to visibility more effective and varied programs. But this book is a start, a beginning and, as such, will contribute a share to the creative and productive processes which are needed now in educational programs for handicapped children.

REFERENCES

Abeson, A. "Recent Developments in the Courts." *The Right to an Education Mandate.* Leadership Series in Special Education, University of Minnesota, Vol. 3, 1973.

Beery, K. E. *Models for Mainstreaming.* San Rafael, California: Dimensions Publishing Co., 1972.

Birch, J. W. *Mainstreaming: Educable Mentally Retarded Children in Regular Classes.* University of Minnesota, Leadership Training Institute/Special Education, 1974.

Chaffin, J. D. "Will the Real 'Mainstreaming' Program Please Stand Up! (or. . . Should Dunn Have Done It?)." *Focus on Exceptional Children, 6* (5), 1974.

Dailey, R. F. "Dimensions and Issues in '74: Tapping into the Special Education Grapevine." *Exceptional Children, 40,* 1974 (503-507).

Kuriloff, P., True, R., Kirp, D. & Buss. "Legal Reform and Educational Change: The Pennsylvania Case." *Exceptional Children, 41,* 1974 (35-42).

Mann, P. H. (Ed.). *Mainstream Special Education.* Proceedings of the University of Miami Conference on Special Education in the Great Cities, Council for Exceptional Children, 1974.

Martin, E. W. "Some Thoughts on Mainstreaming." *Exceptional Children, 41,* 1974 (150-153).

Ross, S. L. DeYoung, H. G. & Cohen, J. S. "Confrontation: Special Education." *Exceptional Children, 38,* 1971 (5-12).

Stafford, R. T. "The Handicapped: Challenge and Decision." *Exceptional Children, 40,* 1974 (485-488).

Weintraub, F. J. "Recent Influences of Law Regarding the Identification and Educational Placement of Children." *Focus on Exceptional Children, 4* (2), 1972.

Part I
Rationale

Rationale for Alternative Programming: A Perspective

B. K. Tilley
Madison Public Schools, Wisconsin

Since Dunn's (1968) classic article boldly questioning the integrity of segregated special classes as *the* model for serving retarded children, there has been an inexorable move to explore and develop alternative administrative and programmatic arrangements for children with handicaps of all types and severities. Full discussions of this phenomenon can be found in several places within this anthology (Chaffin, Bruininks & Rynders).

In many of the discussions and articles, the term "alternatives" is used quite synonymously with "mainstreaming," leading to some confusion as to what the two terms mean. For the purpose of this discussion, some clarification will be undertaken so as not to add to an already confusing situation.

MAINSTREAMING

More than an alternative or set of alternatives, mainstreaming refers to a philosophical position—a guiding concept designed to direct the efforts of program designers and developers toward enhancing the coping ability of the individual and stretching the tolerance and understanding of society as manifested in the general education program.

In the truest sense, mainstreaming should not be considered a special education concept. Philosophically, it is much broader and encompasses the notion of prevention: educational actions and programs that keep children from ever becoming handicapped or labeled as such. The term is heuristic for a single simplified definition and deserves to be discussed from more than one perspective.

Preventive Mainstreaming

From this particular perspective, mainstreaming becomes a descriptive term for all activities and programs that are developed to keep children from becoming labeled and treated as handicapped. Most of the programs or activities covered under this meaning are or should be under the responsibility and control of regular education (with special education consultant help, of course).

Examples of programs that may be included under this definition are Head Start, Montessori programs, junior primary programs, Individually Guided Education, Individually Prescribed Instruction, ungraded arrangements, unitized structures, remedial and developmental reading instruction, and counseling.

Reintegrative Mainstreaming

This perspective refers to the systematic movement of children from specialized educational settings into regular program settings. This occurs after special programming has been progressing for some more or less extensive period. Usually the children have been assessed, diagnosed, and labeled as a condition for special placement, and consequently the reintegration of the child into the mainstream involves quite different programming strategies and considerations than preventive mainstreaming. Typically, after a child has been placed in a special setting, the awareness on the part of regular teachers that the child has been labeled "special" makes it more difficult to mainstream the child. The problems associated with labeling and teacher expectations come into play, requiring a careful planning and educational effort if the child is to be successfully accepted into a more normalized program.

Proximity Mainstreaming

This concept refers to the institutionalization and desegregation of special facilities. Increasingly, parents of moderately and severely handicapped children are demanding that their children be served, in some fashion, along with "normal" children in a normal setting. Institutions for the handicapped are also under pressure to return many clients to their home communities to be served locally, in order to prevent the development of certain negative behaviors associated with long institutional stays.

While serving the more seriously handicapped child within regular classrooms seems untenable and professionally inappropriate at this point, many school and institutional programs are moving intact groups of such children into regular school settings, bringing about a certain limited contact between the normal child and the handicapped child. This move is considered by advocates as beneficial to both groups of children since it provides models of appropriateness for the handicapped child and awareness and understanding for the normal children. Whether or not this actually occurs is yet to be substantiated, although some preliminary evidence does tend to suggest mutual positive benefits (Tilley & Webster, 1975).

Essentially, then, mainstreaming is an organizing or philosophical concept that ties together these concepts with others which promote multiple relationships of handicapped children to the entire realm of societal activities and, particularly, with educational activities.

ALTERNATIVES

Alternatives in education appear to have developed as creative attempts to meet the individual needs of school children. It appears also likely that a strong element of frustration with traditional models of education is present in the alternative movement.

Fantini (1973) traces the genesis of the alternative movement to the civil rights developments of the 1960s when "freedom schools" were set up in homes, churches, and store fronts by parents and teachers to protest the racial integration of schools. This has been followed by a "free school" explosion over the past few years as a response to the perceived inflexibility, impersonality, and repressiveness of the traditional public school.

In one sense, the free school movement has been a failure. The combined problems of funding, lack of public sanction, and high teacher and student turnover have taken their toll. The average life span for free schools is about two years (Fantini, 1973).

But, in another sense, the free school movement has had lasting and significant impact. This movement as an attempt at radical reform outside public education appears to have failed, but it has stimulated more progressive, although certainly less radical, reform within the public school system.

In the general education area, school districts have developed and are continuing to develop multiple structural and programmatic alternatives for meeting the diverse needs of a pluralistic society. In one school district, Madison (Wisconsin) Public Schools, some of the alternatives currently operating include:

1. Shabazz High School—an open, highly flexible, self-governed alternative
2. City High School—a school-without-walls concept emphasizing community involvement
3. Diploma Completion Program—a night school program which allows school dropouts to complete their high school education during the evening while they work during the day
4. Open Classroom Alternatives—elementary classrooms that emphasize informality and student choice in directing learning activities
5. British Primary Option—a more classic open education model based upon specific British educational principles

25

6. Montessori Classroom Model
7. Pre-Vocational Thrust—a program emphasizing career development, choice, and heavy involvement of members of trade and industry in the community
8. University Work Internship—an option that allows students to pursue university course work
9. Computer Managed Instruction—a program utilizing the computer in the classroom as a tool for learning
10. Independent Studies Program—an option allowing students to choose an area of individual study and learning
11. S.A.M. Program—an option for school age mothers
12. Continuous Progress Programs
13. IGE Programs.

It seems clear, then, that some school systems have gone to great lengths in their attempt to individualize instruction for the differing needs of children. Madison is used here as an example, but many additional alternatives are offered in school systems all across the nation—alternatives that attest to the impact of the original free school movement.

From this discussion one can see that the concept of alternatives encompasses a broad range of options in education, including organizational structures and options as well as specific programmatic choices. Organizational or structural options are designed to modify the traditional classroom structure to allow a different kind of activity to occur within the program, but they may not necessarily describe the kind of program which does occur within the new structure. Examples of organizational options are unitized schools and ungraded programs. On the other hand, programmatic options often combine a structure with a specific curricular program. Examples of these kinds of options would include the Individually Guided Education program and the Montessori option, which not only specify how the learning is to be organized and structured but also deal with the content and curricular variables.

Clearly, the term alternatives must be used to refer to a whole continuum of programs, structures, and activities which differ from the traditional educational structures and programs and which are designed to specifically meet the needs of a wide variety of children from a wide variety of backgrounds with a wide variety of abilities and interests.

SPECIAL EDUCATION IN TRANSITION

The changes being contemplated now as a result of incisive self-examination by the professional special educator are just short of revolutionary. Practically every assumption upon which our past models were based is under scrutiny. The result is the evolution of a whole new vision of what special education should be. An appropriate analogy may serve to illustrate the changing role and purpose of the profession.

The Historical Model: A Sanitation Analogy

The power of special education, historically, has derived from a willingness to take children who do not fit in the general education system and develop a segregated, parallel educational system to serve them. This situation has led to a relationship between the general and special elements of the system, having some characteristics of a garbage collection model.

The profession of garbage collection is dependent upon society's recognition of certain materials as waste which needs to be removed to some distant place. There it is treated in some fashion out of the sight, interest, and understanding of the majority of society. Occasionally, through the process of recycling, some of the original waste finds its way back into the mainstream of society. However, it always returns in a different form and is never recognizable as the original waste material. For recycled waste material to be accepted, it must have different essential or distinguishing traits than when it was rejected.

It would be economic suicide for the garbage collector (or the sanitation engineer as he is more popularly called today) to suggest that the client take back some waste material in its original form and consider modifying his values and practices in a way that the material could be put to fuller, more productive use. What would happen if the garbage collection company suddenly refused to remove garbage at all and instead became a firm of consultants or resource specialists dedicated to helping the customer keep his garbage and to learn to make better use of it by modifying his habits?

The garbage consultant might set up inservice programs for whole neighborhoods on such topics as garbage management and development, the rights of garbage, how to prevent garbage failure, learning to live with garbage, garbage as a debilitating label, and finally, the effect of expectations on the behavior of you and your garbage.

Obviously, the empire of garbage collection would collapse in waste and ruin were such a radical approach to the problem of waste material taken.

However, the sanitation engineer knows how to keep his empire growing and thriving. He supports advertising campaigns to clean up the environment and to deposit waste in special containers so it may be quickly and easily processed. He brings his delivery system right to the customer's door so it is maximally convenient to remove the waste, and he is very liberal as to the kind of waste he will accept for processing. Over time he has expanded his operation to be able to handle new kinds of waste and is now quite capable and willing to process as much as 15% of all material as waste.

And to further encourage the empire, the Environmental Protection Agency has provided federal funds for innovative garbage service projects. Consequently, the garbage company has refined its delivery system with new trucks and a systems approach to collection. The company has also experimented with new processing systems and has learned to successfully process 85% of all waste material and to recycle 90% of it.

This makes the customer happy, but less creative. He used to save some waste material as a challenge to himself. He used coffee cans to make small musical drums for his children and to store small nuts and bolts (which are now under consideration as possible garbage). He saved bottles as an excuse to buy the new bottle-cutting kit and to encourage his wife's creative talents. He saved broken toys to repair for needy children. But, no longer. Since the garbage company takes all the waste products possible, the customer has lost interest in putting out the effort to reclaim some of the waste. It is much easier just to set it out and let the truck haul it away. The waste is soon forgotten, and the man doesn't recognize the loss of some skills and creativity since he no longer has use for them.

Similarly, special education has developed its empire. The profession has grown and thrived by developing a highly sophisticated symbiotic relationship with general education. General education has encouraged our profession to develop in order to serve a "surplus population" which they find difficult to assimilate. And special education has been very willing to serve this surplus population. We have developed increasingly exotic techniques of assessment, diagnosis, and identification to aid the general system in locating more surplus children. Our rewards for such activities have been increased power, increased federal and state funds, increased staff and other resources and, very importantly, a highly visible identity.

Our profession has been built on the notions of defective children, segregated direct services, and separate but parallel organizational structures. In fact, the special education department in many school systems operates almost as a completely separate school system with its own money, rules, children, and even buildings.

The Tide of Change

With the empire doing so well, one might question the interest in such ideas as mainstreaming, alternatives, new models, and more cooperation with general education. Why risk co-optation by the larger general system, why run the risk of loss of control, why share the power so carefully acquired and protected by legislation, parent coalitions, and our own ingenious machinations?

The answer is actually an altruistic one. Even though special education is painted rather darkly in this analogy for the part it played in creating the dual system, the fact is that separate-but-parallel services were felt to be in the best interests of the children. Prior to the development of special classes and schools these children were completely excluded from educational opportunities and any efforts on their behalf were steps in the right direction.

Although the profession may have been a trifle opportunistic, it has not been heartless or unethical in its pursuit of good programs for children. When the professional literature consistently questioned the status quo, special educators began to react in a concerned and constructive way. If what was being done was not helping children (and, indeed, possibly harming them), new ways had to be considered even at considerable cost to the empire.

The Efficacy Studies

The first clues that there might be something wrong with what the profession was doing with children could be found as early as 1932 in Bennett's study indicating that retarded children in regular classes with little or no help performed better academically than those in special classes. This study was followed by many others supporting essentially the same thesis. [The reader is referred to Cegelka and Tyler (1970) for a full review of the efficacy studies.] For a long while these studies were ignored due to numerous design weaknesses, but Goldstein, Moss, and Jordan (1965) remedied many of the design problems and came to essentially similar conclusions, especially with relation to the mildly retarded. The seeds of professional doubt were sown.

Labeling and Expectations

Much has been written recently on the debilitating effects of negative labels and expectations on the behavior of children and their teachers. Much of the interest in this area was stimulated by Rosenthal and Jacobson's study (1966) demonstrating the negative effect of labels on teacher behavior. Edgerton (1967), Becker (1963), Hurley (1969), and Beez (1968) have also considered various aspects of labeling, expectations, and the self-fulfilling prophecy of negative labels.

Generally, the frightening conclusions drawn from the literature on these topics provides the special educator ample justification for seeking creative new ways to serve children to prevent labeling them as deviant.

Legislation and Litigation

Many states have passed comprehensive laws related to the handicapped which incorporate a policy encouraging mainstream programming, a range of

29

services, and stiff due process provisions for parents and children. Consequently, there is strong legislative inducement for school districts to develop creative alternatives to meet the individual needs of children.

Court cases dealing with the civil and constitutional rights of handicapped children have had an increasing impact on the alternatives thrust. Litigation has been completed or is pending in over half the states, and the overwhelming trend is toward supporting the rights of handicapped children to an *appropriate* education which reduces negative labeling and categorization of children. This movement is so significant that the Council for Exceptional Children has established a project to continuously review and publish litigation cases completed or pending.

The reader may gain a complete perspective on the impact of court interventions in special education by reviewing Johnson, Gross, and Weatherman (1973).

Societal Variables

In addition to the above factors, social and economic influences have contributed to the alternative movement in special education. The rate of technological change occurring today really challenges educators to create new ways of preparing the handicapped child for living in a time and situation where his skills may become obsolete overnight. Recession and economic uncertainty forces the profession to rethink the idea that there may be an economic place in society for many of the handicapped. Perhaps there will be no place for them. Then what? Perhaps we need to consider a stronger emphasis on leisure and recreation as alternatives for fulfilling the adult lives of many of the handicapped. The recent legislative interest in a guaranteed income and a total welfare system may make this a reality in the near future.

New Thrusts

It is obvious that the challenge is great and that the motivation is ample. It may be that the greatest barrier to the creation of new programs and alternatives in special education is the fear of change by the profession itself. If we are to move from the sanitation model of organizing and delivering services, some very important changes in attitudes and practices will need to be made—at considerable risk.

The profession of special education should regard itself as a catalytic agent as well as a direct service agent. It is doubtful that the profession can ever muster enough resources to provide direct service to every child who deviates from normal. Even if resources could be found to do this, it would be very unwise considering what the literature tells us. What seems to be needed is an organizational restructuring that brings the field into closer harmony and cooperation with general education—essentially, the mainstreaming of the organization itself.

The success of such a restructuring depends on a number of considerations. First, in order for special education to be able to influence regular education, it must operate from a position of power sufficient to get the attention of the regular system. When I speak of "mainstreaming" the organization, I do not mean either the co-optation of special education by general education or the merging of special education with regular education. What I do mean is the process of consciously moving away from a parallel system and creating, with general education, joint programs for the whole continuum of children utilizing a broad spectrum of alternatives.

To accomplish this, special education should occupy a position in the hierarchy similar to that of general education departments, control its own budget and personnel, and become a member of the top policy making groups in the system. It is only when the position, autonomy, and sovereignty of the profession is safe that real cooperation and joint decision making can be successful. Many special educators shy away from liaisons with general education; their power base is often so tenuous that cooperation for them is tantamount to capitulation. With both systems on an equal footing, however, joint operations can proceed freely.

One organizational structure showing great promise of promoting the joint planning of alternatives is the range-of-services concept described by Deno (1970). Essentially, the model suggests a range of services based on the severity of the handicap experienced by the child, with increasing mainstream involvement as the handicapping condition becomes less severe.

Tilley (1973) has described a model of joint planning and program development between regular and special education that culminates in a specific contract between parties. The contract specifies the intent of the effort, expected behavioral outcomes, procedures to be followed, specification of mutual responsibilities, and the system of evaluation to be followed.

Some interesting alternatives have been mutually negotiated through the contracting system.

1. Mainstreaming of orthopedic students within a regular middle school
2. Development of a team teaching model involving special and regular teachers in elementary, middle, and high school
3. Development of adaptive classes in vocational subjects for the mildly and moderately handicapped designed to develop specific skills to ensure successful mainstreaming, taught by regular education teachers with support from the special teachers

4. Adaptive physical education programs developed and run by the general physical education department with consultant help from special education

5. Creation of a highly innovative community-based approach for socially maladjusted middle-school students staffed by regular and special staff

6. Development of a kindergarten screening program utilizing the kindergarten teacher as the central figure and aimed at gaining information for curricular change, not at identifying "ready" or "unready" children.

There are many more, but none of these alternatives would have been possible without the expectation of joint planning and the availability of a structure to assure an orderly and successful process.

It should be noted that practically all the alternatives outlined above involve both special and regular educational staff. This is a key concept if we are to be successful as catalytic agents in creating or influencing noncategorical, nonlabeling alternatives that enhance the uniqueness of each child regardless of the degree or level of his handicap. Regular teachers are beginning to realize they can be successful with a broader range of individual differences, particularly when they have the material, professional, and moral support of special education. Our ultimate power in effecting the mainstreaming of children depends upon influencing general education to create an array of alternatives to include as many children as possible, while realizing that some children will continue to require "special" education.

Evaluation

It is very important that evaluation mechanisms be developed concurrently with alternatives or we may doom ourselves to unnecessary duplication of efforts. We also need to protect ourselves from our own enthusiasm. It is important to avoid another era similar to the period of the special class.

IMPLICATIONS FOR THE PROFESSION

The development of joint planning between special and general education for meeting the needs of all children has multiple implications for the profession.

Both preservice and inservice training will need to be developed differently than in the past. New roles will be demanded of special education personnel in order to implement various alternatives. Resource teachers, consultant teachers, noncategorical teachers, and specialists in curriculum, behavior, and other areas will need to be trained. Teachers will have to learn interactive and consultation skills as well as management of instructional settings and programs rather than provision of direct service. Universities, public school systems, and state education agencies will have to cooperate in joint planning for these eventualities. University training programs will need to be validated in field settings, and certification practices will have to reflect this work.

Legislation will have to be pursued to allow and encourage flexible program alternatives based on the needs of children. New laws which discourage labeling and segregation need to be passed. Fortunately, many states are now moving in this direction.

A definition of successful matches between child characteristics and alternative program elements will have to be researched. Reynolds and Balow (1972) write of an aptitude-by-treatment interaction system for making program decisions for children. Research further defining such an approach promises to be more productive than typical group experimental methods of conducting program research.

Finally, the profession will need to revitalize its curiosity and creativity if the alternative movement is to be successful. We need to question all of our practices, examine our assumptions, and think new thoughts. The rewards will be great. This could be an opportunity to help children and society at the same time. Only when improvements in children are matched with concern and tolerance toward them by society can we achieve lasting progress in our field. The alternative movement may give us our best chance yet. Let us hope that we have the wisdom, courage, and talent to make it a successful venture.

REFERENCES

Becker, H. S. *Outsiders: Studies in the Sociology of Deviance.* New York: Free Press of Glencoe, 1963.

Beez, W. V. "Influence of Biased Psychological Reports on Teacher Behavior." Doctoral dissertation, Indiana University, 1968.

Bennett, A. *A Comparative Study of Subnormal Children in the Elementary Grades.* New York: Teachers College, Columbia University Bureau of Publications, 1932.

Cegelka, W. J. & Tyler, J. J. "The Efficacy of Special Class Placement for the Mentally Retarded in Proper Perspective." *Training School Bulletin, 67,* 1970 (33-68).

Deno, E. N. "Special Education as Developmental Capital." *Exceptional Children, 37,* 1970 (229-40).

Dunn, L. M. "Special Education for the Mildly Retarded—Is Much of It Justifiable?" *Exceptional Children, 35,* 1968 (5-22).

Edgerton, R. B. *The Cloak of Competence: Stigma in the Lives of the Retarded.* Berkeley: University of California Press, 1967.

Fantini, M. D. "The What, Why, and Where of the Alternatives Movement." *The National Elementary Principal, 52,* 1973 (14-22).

Goldstein, H., Moss, J. W. & Jordan, L. J. *The Efficacy of Special Class Training on the Development of Mentally Retarded Children.* U.S. Office of Education, Cooperative Research Program Project No. 619. Urbana, Illinois: Institute for Research on Exceptional Children, 1965.

Hurley, R. *Poverty and Mental Retardation: A Causal Relationship.* New York: Random House, 1969.

Johnson, R. A., Gross, J. C. & Weatherman R. (Eds.) *Decategorization and Performance Based Systems, Special Education in Court,* Audio Visual Library Service, University of Minnesota, 1973.

Reynolds, M. C. & Balow, B. "Categories and Variables in Special Education." *Exceptional Children, 38,* 1972 (357-366).

Rosenthal, R. & Jacobson, L. "Teachers Expectancies: Determinants of Pupils' IQ Gains." *Psychological Reports, 19,* 1966 (115-118).

Tilley, B. K. "The Madison Plan for Organizing and Delivering Specialized Educational Services." In R. A. Johnson, J. C. Gross & R. F. Weatherman (Eds.), *Decategorization and Performance Based Systems, Special Education in Court,* Audio Visual Library Service, University of Minnesota, 1973.

Tilley, B. K. & Webster, C. "The Effects of Integrating Orthopedically Handicapped Students in a Middle School." Unpublished Working Paper, Madison Public Schools, Madison Wisc., 1975.

Dr. Kaufman et al., in addition to focusing on those conditions which have contributed to the mainstream movement, have addressed a number of significant questions frequently overlooked. The article is not a general discussion based on philosophical commitments. Rather, it is a detailed analysis of the literature and of the conceptual implications. The authors drew upon research and literature from disciplines outside of special education in building their construct. In general, the article represents a serious attempt at synthesizing the state of the art and at focusing the reader's attention on areas of concern.

Mainstreaming: Toward an Explication of the Construct

Martin J. Kaufman, Jay Gottlieb, Judith A. Agard, Maurine B. Kukic
Intramural Research Program, Bureau of Education for the Handicapped, U. S. Office of Education

A fifty-year history of self-contained special education classes as the predominant organizational arrangement for mentally retarded children is rapidly coming to a close. During the past six years, thousands of children who had previously attended special classes have been returned to regular grades, usually with more educational support than is traditionally offered to nonhandicapped children. Furthermore, many educable mentally retarded children who would have been placed in segregated classes are no longer being removed from their regular class program. Instead, they are receiving special services in a manner which permits them to remain members of a regular classroom.

THE IMPETUS FOR MAINSTREAMING

There have been three major influences providing the impetus for special education to implement mainstreaming services: professional educators, court

35

decisions, and state governmental policies. Each of these will be examined briefly.

Educators' Influence

Concern by educators regarding the most appropriate class placement for mentally retarded children is not new; it began appearing in the literature at least 40 years ago when Bennett (1932) conducted the first of the so-called "efficacy" studies. The efficacy research consisted of a number of studies which compared the desirability of special and regular classes for educating mildly retarded children. Kirk (1964) concluded from the results of these studies that mentally retarded children achieved more academically in the regular grades but appeared to be better adjusted socially in special classes. Educators have used these results as a "scientific" basis for the promotion of mainstreaming efforts. The paradox of the efficacy research data was raised when Johnson (1962) questioned why mentally retarded children achieved more academically in regular classes than in special classes when the latter had fewer pupils, supposedly better trained teachers, and more financial resources available on a per capita basis. Johnson's report, however, had little impact in modifying the organization or orientation of special education. It was not until Dunn (1968, p. 5) exhorted special educators to " . . .stop being pressured into a continuing and expanding special education program (*special classes*) that we know now to be undesirable for many of the children we are dedicated to serve" that other educators began, en masse, to voice their concerns about the inadequacies of segregated classes. Labeling and stigma were the most frequently cited concerns as to why self-contained classes were thought to be deleterious to children. To illustrate, Dunn (p. 9) claimed that "removing a child from the regular grades for special education probably contributes significantly to his feelings of inferiority and problems of acceptance."

Educators responded to criticisms such as Dunn's by altering the focus of special education from a predominantly alternative program approach to include a more general service orientation. The rationale for this alteration was based on the belief that it would

1. Remove the stigma that is associated with special class placement
2. Enhance the social status of mentally retarded children with their nonhandicapped peers
3. Facilitate the modeling of appropriate behavior as exhibited by nonhandicapped peers
4. Provide a more cognitively stimulating peer environment
5. Provide the mentally retarded child with competitive situations which the mildly impaired must eventually experience

6. Provide a more flexible vehicle from which to deliver educational services
7. Enable more children to be served, thereby providing a more cost-effective education
8. Provide decentralized services, avoiding the need to transport mentally retarded children out of the neighborhood
9. Avoid the legal issues involved in segregated classes
10. Be more likely to be acceptable to the public, especially among minority groups.

Finally, as a result of the general pressure placed on special education administrators to change the structure of special education, they rapidly began to implement those services they perceived to require only slight modification in orientation or delivery to be considered as mainstreaming.

Influence of Court Decisions

A second impetus for the trend toward mainstreaming services has been the courts. Concern for the appropriate placement of mentally retarded children is embedded in the larger issue of discrimination and basic civil rights. To date, at least 36 cases have appeared before state and federal courts which have been focused on guaranteeing the exceptional child the right to an education, the right to appropriate treatment, and the opportunity for appropriate placement (NSPRA, 1974; Abeson, 1974). Of particular importance to the development of the mainstreaming movement was a 1971 opinion by the U.S. District Court for the Eastern District of Pennsylvania that " . . .placement in a regular school class is preferable to placement in a special public school class." This opinion as well as other court rulings have influenced several state legislative bodies to enact laws specifying regular class placement as preferable to special class placement (Tennessee 1972, Wisconsin 1973). Given this precedent, it is not surprising that mainstreaming services are expanding.

Influence of State Governmental Policies

In certain states, policies of the state education agency concerned with allocating fiscal resources to establish and deliver educational services to exceptional children have either reinforced or discouraged local education agencies in implementing mainstreaming services. Three alternative funding formulas for special education are illustrative of the influence fiscal policies have on the implementation of mainstreaming services. The first fiscal procedure to be presented encourages mainstreaming by permitting the mentally retarded child to be included in the funding formula for regular education (Georgia, Texas). The second example of fiscal policy relates to the effects of funding procedures which employ a weighted equivalency formula (Florida Stats., Sec. 236.081). The final example is indicative of fiscal policies which permit the mentally retarded child to be eligible either for special or regular education funding, but not for both (New Mexico Stats., Sec. 77-18.4).

Several states (e.g., Georgia, Texas) employ different pupil accounting procedures for exceptional children depending on whether or not the child is receiving mainstreaming services. Fiscal reimbursement policies have operationally defined mainstreaming on a temporal basis. As an example, Georgia fiscally defines a mainstreamed child as one who spends more than half of the school day integrated with nonhandicapped children (Ga. 30-1100-30-1110). The differential pupil accounting procedures for mainstreamed or segregated mentally retarded children depend on whether they are eligible for inclusion in the funding formula for regular education programs. The mainstreamed mentally retarded child is eligible for inclusion in the formula for regular education program funding whereas the segregated mentally retarded child is not. Differential pupil accounting procedures for mainstreamed children not only provide funding for special education costs but also provide fiscal incentives to support regular education programs by allowing the mentally retarded child to be included in that funding formula too. The mainstreamed mentally retarded child thus generates fiscal resources not only for special education but also for regular education. Consequently, mainstreaming is encouraged through an incentive which provides additional fiscal resources to regular education which are usually unavailable under other funding formulas.

A second type of funding practice for special education is characterized by a weighted equivalency formula (Florida Stats., Sec. 236.081). Under such a paradigm, local education agencies are reimbursed on a computed cost per category of exceptionality multiplied by percent of time in special education. Thus the greater the amount of time in special education, the greater the amount of reimbursement. It is apparent that mainstreaming is discouraged by states utilizing the weighted equivalency method of reimbursement.

Another state fiscal policy which discourages mainstreaming occurs when special education programs are funded on the basis of a specific number of predetermined eligible retarded children being identified, while at the same time regular programs are funded on the basis of a fixed number of nonhandicapped children per classroom unit (New Mexico Stats., Sec. 77-18.4). This funding arrangement lacks the fiscal incentive to encourage mainstreaming because it permits an identified eligible mentally retarded child to be considered only as part of the regular or special education pupil accounting procedure, but not both. Funding for mentally retarded children is provided to special education programs while no additional funds are provided to regular education for serving the retarded child. As a result, little mainstreaming of mentally retarded children occurs. This is in contradistinction to the first funding paradigm discussed above where the mentally retarded child is eligible for inclusion in both special and regular education funding formulas.

In summary, three forces have been identified as the primary levers in affecting the evolution of the mainstreaming movement. The empirical and philosophical influences of professional educators, the influence of judicial decisions and opinions, and the effects of state fiscal funding policies have operated, singularly or interactively, to influence the development of mainstreaming services. Unfortunately, neither the professional educators, the courts, nor the states have developed a comprehensive conceptual structure of mainstreaming upon which to base the various aspects of the services implied by the construct. Perhaps this omission reflects a lack of understanding of the mainstreaming concept.

WHAT IS MAINSTREAMING?

The provision of equal educational opportunities for mentally retarded children requires the establishment and delivery of high quality comprehensive educational programs and services. Mainstreaming may be regarded as a range of administrative and instructional options available as part of the comprehensive educational services provided for mentally retarded children. It has not evolved as a single option but as a range of instructional directives as well as an array of organizational arrangements and staff utilization patterns. The multiple service options inherent in mainstreaming efforts are in contrast to the initial conceptualization and organization of special education as an educational program separate from regular education.

Although the term "mainstreaming" permeates much of the recent literature in special education, a precise definition of the term has remained elusive. For example, in his definition of mainstreaming Birch (1974) incorporated 14 descriptors, not to mention a panoply of related nomenclature, that have resulted from mainstreaming practices. Beery (1972), while not defining mainstreaming directly, suggested that it be critically examined for three elements: that it provides for a continuum of programs for children who are experiencing difficulty, that it accomplishes a reduction of "pull-out" programs, and that it calls for specialists to work in the regular classrooms as much as possible.

Perhaps the one common denominator in definitions of mainstreaming is that they include a provision that mentally retarded children should be educated, at least in part, in the regular classroom (e.g., Massachusetts, 1974). How much education mentally retarded children should receive in regular classes has been the subject of some controversy. Lilly (1970) advocated a "zero-reject model" which implied that no mentally retarded child should be

39

"rejected" from the general education program and placed in special classes. The CEC Policies Commission (1973, p. 494) adopted a policy that "children should spend only as much time outside regular classroom settings as is necessary to control learning variables." In order to modulate the pendulum swing and decrease the emphasis on integrating mentally retarded children into regular programs, Adamson and Van Etten (1972) indicated that no single educational progam is beneficial to all children and that some children may benefit from special class placement.

It is noteworthy that definitions and comments pertaining to mainstreaming which appear in the literature have focused more on administrative considerations (e.g., the amount of time spent in regular classrooms) than on instructional variables (e.g., the instructional activities in which the child should participate when he attends the regular class). Quite possibly, the emphasis on administrative concerns reflects the prevailing view among researchers and practitioners that mainstreaming is primarily an administrative arrangement and is only secondarily, if at all, an instructional approach.

Focus on the administrative aspects of integrating mentally retarded children into regular grades has led to the predominant view of mainstreaming as a temporal dichotomy. From this perspective, mainstreaming occurs when mentally retarded children spend an arbitrarily established portion of their school time enrolled in regular classes. When mentally retarded children do not spend the required minimum amount of time in regular grades, mainstreaming is not occurring.

It becomes readily apparent, however, that this view of mainstreaming as a temporal dichotomy is simplistic. Mainstreaming must take into account not only the amount of time that a mentally retarded child spends in regular classes but also the instructional activities in which the child partakes as well as his social involvement with nonhandicapped peers. Johnson's (1950) admonition that mentally retarded children in regular classes may be physically integrated but socially and psychologically isolated must be seriously weighed in any discussion of mainstreaming. A concise definition of mainstreaming that incorporates the many complexities inherent in describing the interrelationships between a mentally retarded child's educational needs and the educational experiences offered in the regular classroom is clearly necessary.

Mainstreaming Defined

In an effort to provide a conceptual framework of mainstreaming that encompasses its various complexities, the following definition is offered:

Mainstreaming refers to the temporal, instructional, and social integration of eligible exceptional children with normal peers based on an ongoing, individually determined, educational planning and programming process and requires clarification of responsibility among regular and special education administrative, instructional, and supportive personnel.

Thus, the definition of mainstreaming encompasses three major components which require elaboration: *integration, educational planning and programming process,* and *clarification of responsibility.*

Integration

Within our definitional framework, integration is a necessary component of mainstreaming; it is not synonymous with it. There are at least three elements of integration that could affect a mentally retarded child's educational experience: *temporal integration,* which refers to the amount of time that a child spends in regular classrooms with nonhandicapped peers; *instructional integration,* which refers to the extent to which the mentally retarded child shares in the instructional environment of his classroom; and *social integration,* which refers to the mentally retarded child's physical proximity, interactive behavior, assimilation, and acceptance by his classmates.

Temporal Integration. The underlying assumption of temporal integration is that the greater the amount of time the mentally retarded child spends with normal peers, the more positive will be the social and/or instructional outcomes expected for him. Support for this contention may be obtained from several sources. Carroll (1963) advanced a model of school learning in which the time variable was the critical dimension. Specifically, the school related time dimension included opportunities such as time allowed for learning. Carroll advanced a formula that degree of learning could be conceptualized as a function of time spent in learning divided by the time needed for learning. Additional support for considering time as a critical factor is provided by Wiley (1974, p. 3) who suggested that "under ordinary circumstances, we will value the effect of a given amount of schooling the more, the larger it is." The question which can now be posed then is, what effect does a particular amount of schooling have on a mentally retarded child's social and/or instructional outcomes?

It is generally assumed that temporal integration will benefit the mentally retarded child. Temporal integration should be beneficial to the retarded child because it provides opportunities for him to become familiar to his nonhandicapped peers and, hopefully, more socially acceptable (Christoplos & Renz, 1969). In addition, the more time mentally retarded children are integrated into regular classes, the greater should be the opportunity for them to model appropriate behavior exhibited by nonhandicapped peers. Finally, the more time mentally retarded children spend in regular classes, the more they will be exposed to the cognitive stimulation generated by the regular class.

Consideration of temporal integration as a treatment is given additional credence when viewed from an administrative vantage point. As previously mentioned, certain state education agency fiscal policies employ amount of time mentally retarded children are integrated into regular programs as the criterion for determining pupil accounting procedures. Mainstreaming has been defined in the fiscal policies of several state education agencies as occurring when the retarded child spends 50% or more of the school year with nonhandicapped children (e.g., Georgia, Texas).

Thus, conceptually and administratively, temporal integration should be considered as one element of integration and as an independent variable which in and of itself may affect child outcomes.

Instructional Integration. The second element of the integration component of mainstreaming concerns the extent to which the mentally retarded child shares in the instructional environment of the regular class. For instructional integration to occur, three conditions of compatibility must exist. First, a retarded child's learning characteristics and educational needs must be compatible with the learning opportunities provided to nonhandicapped peers in the regular classroom. Second, compatibility must exist between a mentally retarded child's learning characteristics and educational needs and the regular classroom teacher's ability and willingness to modify his instructional practices. Third, the special education services provided to a mentally retarded child (such as resource room help) must be compatible with and supportive to the regular classroom teacher's instructional goals for the child.

Instructional integration is perhaps the most critical component of mainstreaming, because it addresses the issue of how to coordinate and implement an effective educational program for a mentally retarded child. Not surprisingly, it is probably the most difficult component of mainstreaming to execute properly. The difficulties can best be illustrated by referring back to the three compatibility conditions that form the foundation for instructional integration and observing some of the potential impediments that could interfere with their implementation.

The first compatibility condition is between the child's needs and the learning opportunities that are available in the regular classroom. Inherent in this first condition is the assumption that the mentally retarded child's educational needs are best fulfilled by emphasizing those areas of academic skill and content acquisition that are emphasized for nonhandicapped children. Historically, however, there has not been consensus on what the mentally retarded child should be taught. Considerable attention has traditionally been focused on the social and occupational needs of mentally retarded children (e.g., Gunzberg, 1965; Kolstoe, 1970). The practice of watering down the regular class curricula (Innskeep, 1926) to accommodate the abilities of retarded children has been criticized (Kirk & Johnson, 1951). Appropriate implementation of instructional integration must address the question of what instructional experiences are appropriate for mentally retarded children.

The second compatibility condition concerns the mentally retarded child's learning characteristics and educational needs, and the regular classroom teachers's ability and willingness to modify his instructional practices. There is little specific evidence, however, as to the willingness of regular teachers to modify their instructional practices to accommodate mentally retarded children in their classes. If one assumes that teachers' attitudes toward retarded children reflect their willingness to modify their instructional practices, there is reason to doubt that the necessary modifications will be made. The literature related to regular classroom teachers' attitudes toward mentally retarded children indicates a generally nonaccepting pattern of response (Gottlieb, 1974). Clearly, the regular classroom teacher's receptivity and instructional adaptability to mentally retarded children are critical considerations when integrating for instructional purposes.

The third compatibility condition requires that regular and special education personnel provide the mentally retarded child with an appropriately coordinated and well-articulated educational program. Historically, however, special education has been characterized by organizational arrangements and staff utilization patterns having a segregated program focus. Mainstreaming requires the development and implementation of new organizational arrangements and staff utilization patterns which permit appropriate interfacing of regular and special education personnel. The evolution of special education from a segregated alternative program focus to include a coordinated service orientation with regular education will undoubtedly necessitate considerable knowledge, attitude, and behavioral changes on the part of both regular and special education personnel. How these changes are to be effected is still largely unknown, although many efforts in this regard are currently being studied (e.g., Chaffin, 1974). An inability to produce compatibility between regular and special education services would result in an ineffective, segmented educational program with different instructional goals and objectives being provided for a mentally retarded child.

Instructional integration, then, occurs when regular and special education services are coordinated to offer compatible instructional goals and objectives so that the mentally retarded child is neither isolated from the regular class activities nor required to perform beyond his level of ability.

Social Integration. Social integration refers to the relationship between eligible retarded children and their normal peer group. Social integration may be described in terms of physical proximity, interactive behavior, assimilation, and acceptance. The inclusion of four dimensions to define social integration avoids the circumscribed idea of socialization as being a one-dimensional construct confined to social acceptance. The four elements composing social integration do not represent a stage-dependent hierarchy. They are conceptualized, however, as having differential values. Thus, physical proximity, interactive behavior, assimilation, and acceptance are posited as a value hierarchy of attitudes and/or behaviors. The nature of the relationships among the four elements of social integration requires clarification.

Physical proximity refers to the spatial distance between the retarded child and his nonhandicapped peer group. Interactive behavior, assimilation, and acceptance may or may not require a minimum level of physical proximity. Underlying the inclusion of physical proximity as a separate element of social integration is the assumption that the closer the proximity of the retarded child to his peer group, the more likely he is to have interactions, be assimilated, and/or be accepted to the extent that he exhibits appropriate behavior.

However, there are many situations where physical proximity is not a prerequisite condition to social acceptance. It is well known that many individuals are attracted to others without ever having been in contact or obtaining any information about them; that is, attraction occurs prior to physical proximity or interactive behavior. For example, the physically attractive person may be immediately accepted by his peers regardless of physical proximity, social interaction, or assimilation (Kleck, Richardson & Ronald, 1974). Also, various personality traits affect responsiveness to others, such as need for affiliation (Byrne, 1962). Thus, physical proximity should be considered as a separate element of social integration warranting investigation.

Social interactive behavior as an element of social integration refers to verbal, gestural, and/or physical communication between two or more people. Social interactive behavior requires attending, assessment of potential for involvement, overt behavioral expression, and the evaluation of the consequences of the overt behavioral expression. In terms of a social integration value hierarchy, social interactive behavior is a higher order index of social integration than is physical proximity. Social interactive behavior is assumed to be related to the attainment of peer assimilation and acceptance but is not necessarily a prerequisite to it. The complex nature of the relationship between social interaction and social acceptance has been noted elsewhere (Bryan, 1974; Gottlieb & Budoff, 1973). Therefore, social interaction behavior is considered a second element of social integration warranting attention.

Social assimilation refers to the inclusion of the retarded child in the ongoing social milieu of the peer group. Social assimilation occurs when the retarded child is acknowledged and actively included as a participant in the activities of his peer group. Social assimilation is a more valued index of social integration than social interactive behavior because it denotes a willingness to include the mentally retarded child in the extant social milieu, whereas social interactive behavior denotes only the behavioral act of communication. Social assimilation is considered as a third element of social integration, distinct from physical proximity and social interactive behavior.

Social acceptance is the fourth and final element of social integration. It denotes peer approval of the retarded child. Social acceptance is distinct from social assimilation because being acknowledged and actively included as a participant in the peer group does not necessarily imply peer approval. Social acceptance is the most valued element in the hierarchy of social integration because it more directly fulfills one of the child's most basic needs—the need for approval (Jones, 1974).

In summary, although integration has been discussed as a triad of distinct elements, in reality they are mutually interdependent. The temporal, instructional, and social integration elements of mainstreaming are child- and situation-specific. The nature of a child's academic and social needs will greatly influence the appropriate integration opportunities which he is provided. Further, each element of integration affects and is affected by the others, depending on the specific ecology of a classroom. Thus, integration represents countless potential interactive effects in the mainstreaming gestalt.

Educational Planning and Programming Process

The complex interactions between the academic, social, and emotional characteristics of the mentally retarded child and the ecology of the regular classroom require coordinated planning and programming for providing appropriate and effective mainstreaming services. The purpose of implementing an ongoing, individually determined educational planning and programming process is to ensure an effective and efficient means for providing equal educational opportunities for each mentally retarded child.

Educational planning and programming is an ongoing cyclical process consisting of two elements—planning and programming. Planning refers to the assessment of a child's educational needs and the determination of goals and objectives related to the educational services required by the child. Programming refers to the identification and selection of regular and special education human, fiscal, and material resource alternatives available to provide the educational services required by a mentally retarded child. The cyclical process requires the synthesis of planning and programming information for developing an educational plan representing the educational services and resource allocations determined to be appropriate to meet the child's educational needs. The implementation of educational services and the commitment of resources consonant with the educational plan represents the child's educational program. Finally, the planning and programming process requires ongoing evaluation of the appropriateness and effectiveness of the mentally retarded child's educational plan and program. While this total process has applicability for providing educational services to all children, it will be discussed only in relation to the provision of mainstreaming to mentally retarded children.

Assessment of Educational Needs. The first step in the planning and programming process is the assessment of the mentally retarded child's educational needs. An educational needs assessment implicitly assumes the existence of a frame of reference in which to compare the mentally retarded child's educational performance. The frame of reference for considering provision of mainstreaming services should be the child's ability to benefit from the instructional activities and social milieu provided in the regular classroom. Specifically, the educational needs assessment should provide information concerning the child's academic, social, and emotional development. This information is necessary to determine appropriate strategies for effective instruction of the mentally retarded child.

Educational Goals and Objectives. Goals and objectives should be formulated in terms of the educational services required to meet the needs of the mentally retarded child. The nature and extent of the discrepancy between the educational needs of the mentally retarded child and the opportunities available in the regular classroom provide an index from which to determine the *intensity, content* and *location* of educational services required. The educational goals and objectives provide the basis for development of the child's educational plan.

Goals and objectives related to the *intensity* of educational services refer to both the amount of time special education services are required and the extent of individual academic and behavioral attention required by the mentally retarded child. The greater the discrepancy between the child's educational needs and the instructional activities and practices of the regular classroom, the greater the intensity of special education services which will be required.

Goals and objectives related to the *content* of educational services reflect the academic and behavioral skills to be taught as well as the strategies necessary for providing effective instruction. To the extent that the content of service goals and objectives of a mentally retarded child are incompatible with the instructional activities and practices of the regular classroom, modifications and/or alternatives to the regular instructional program will be required.

Establishment of educational goals and objectives related to intensity and content of services required by the mentally retarded child should provide the parameters necessary to determine goals and objectives concerning the appropriate *location* for delivery of educational services. Location refers to both regular and special education organizational arrangements (self-contained classroom, departmentalized classes, open classroom, resource room) and staff utilization patterns (resource teacher, helping teacher, itinerant teacher) which are necessary to deliver the child's educational services. The complexities inherent in determining the appropriate physical location for the delivery of educational services emanate in part from the lack of criteria for selecting appropriate potential organizational arrangements and staff utilization patterns.

Identification and Selection of Resources. The provision of appropriate educational services for each mentally retarded child requires the educational system to maintain information describing the availability and location of regular and special education resources, including instructional and supportive personnel, organizational arrangements, physical facilities, equipment, media, and materials. Within practical and political limitations, an educational system can manipulate time, assignment, use, access and/or availability of human, fiscal, and material resources. These resources, singularly or in combination, represent resource allocation alternatives for delivery of educational services.

The intensity, content, and location of services required by the mentally retarded child should be the basis for identifying all appropriate resource alternatives available within the educational system. Selection of appropriate resource allocations will necessitate determining whether current allocation of resources is consonant with the educational services required by a child or whether reallocation of resources must be considered. Having identified all appropriate resource allocation alternatives, a selection of *the* most appropriate one(s) is required. In order to provide appropriate mainstreaming services, educational decision makers must conceptualize and utilize available resources in a creative and flexible manner, consonant with meeting the educational service needs of each mentally retarded child.

Development of Educational Plan. The synthesis of the planning elements (educational needs assessment, determination of educational goals and objectives) with the programming elements (identification and selection of resource allocation alternatives) results in the formulation of an educational plan for each mentally retarded child. The individually determined educational plan represents a written commitment of *intent* by educational decision makers regarding the type of educational services and resources to be provided a mentally retarded child.

Establishment of Educational Program. Implementation of educational services and *commitment* of resources consonant with the intent of the educational plan represent a mentally retarded child's educational program. The child's educational program will differ from his educational plan to the extent that decision makers having authority and responsibility for operationally implementing educational services and committing resources are unable to provide the services and resources required by the child's educational plan.

Evaluation of educational plan and program. The educational plan and program for a mentally retarded child should be responsive to the educational services he requires at any given point in time. Therefore, the educational plan and program provided a child necessitates *ongoing evaluation* in order to assess

47

changes in pupil academic and behavioral performance. Evaluation information will provide the basis for determining the continued appropriateness and effectiveness of the educational plan and program for the mentally retarded child and ensure a means for providing continuous direction to the cyclical educational planning and programming process.

An ongoing, individually determined educational plan and program for the mentally retarded child can only be maintained when information is provided to educational decision makers who have authority and responsibility for mainstreaming mentally retarded children. Such information is necessary for promoting the coordination of planning and programming by regular and special education administrative, instructional, and supportive personnel.

Clarification of Responsibilities

The final component of the mainstreaming definition is the clarification of responsibilities. Clarification refers to the delineation and assignment of responsibilities necessary for effecting coordinated planning and programming by regular and special education administrative, instructional, and supportive personnel. The ongoing individual determination of educational plans and programs for mentally retarded children occurs within the context of a complex organizational structure.

The organizational structure in which mainstreaming services are provided is characterized by vertical and horizontal levels of independent, intradependent, and interdependent authority and responsibility (Braybooke & Lindblom, 1963). Vertical organization refers to the existence of multiple levels within the educational hierarchy. To illustrate, differential authority and responsibility for the education of mentally retarded children is assigned to the superintendent, director of special education, principals, and teachers. In contrast, horizontal organization refers to a single level within the educational system. For example, both regular and special education instructional personnel represent a single horizontal level within the educational system having authority and/or responsibility to provide educational services to mentally retarded children.

Mainstreaming requires not only definition of administrative, instructional, and supportive responsibilities but also delineation of the manner in which responsibilities are assigned or assumed. Basically, the assignment or assumption of responsibilities can occur within three types of jurisdiction: exclusive, alternating, and consensual. *Exclusive* responsibility refers to those situations in which an individual or program has independent jurisdiction. Exclusive responsibility is exemplified when either regular or special education has been given total responsibility for the overall educational planning and programming for a mainstreamed mentally retarded child. *Alternating* responsibilities occur when two or more individuals or programs have jurisdiction which is exercised interchangeably. For example, regular and special education instructional personnel may alternate responsibility for mainstreamed mentally retarded children, each assuming responsibility only for that segment of the child's educational plan and program which they directly deliver. The inherent limitation to alternating jurisdiction is that no individual or program has been assigned or has assumed total responsibility for the child's overall educational plan and program. Finally, *consensual* responsibility refers to jurisdictional areas which two or more individuals or programs jointly maintain. Consensual responsibility implies that although jurisdiction alternates between regular and special education instructional personnel, overall responsibility for the educational planning and programming of the mentally retarded child is shared. In order for regular and special education instructional personnel to exercise consensual responsibility for the overall educational plan and program of a mentally retarded child, formalized procedures must be implemented for communication, coordination, and cooperation.

Clarification of responsibilities and the nature of their assignment or assumption—exclusive, alternating, or consensual—is critical to the effective implementation of an ongoing individually determined educational planning and programming process. Whereas most educational functions are organizationally delimited to a single line of authority, mainstreaming requires an interfacing of regular and special education administrative, instructional, and supportive services.

Currently, many different organizational authority and responsibility patterns characterize the allocation of resources as well as the establishment and delivery of special education services. While separation and segmentation of authority and responsibility for any educational function may result in operational discordance, mainstreaming may magnify this effect. Often, educational decision makers who have authority for providing special education services are not the same individuals who have been assigned the responsibility for providing the services. For example, the director of special education is assigned the authority and the responsibility for establishing special education arrangements (e.g., self-contained classes, resource rooms) but the principal often maintains authority related to the allocation of space. Consequently, the principal, not the director of special education, may determine whether space will be provided for the delivery of special education services. The lack of clarity in responsibilities is often evidenced by different decision makers having responsibility for educational planning and programming. To illustrate, responsibility for planning—assessing the child's educational needs and establishing appropriate educational objectives—is often assigned to appraisal and/or instructional personnel. However, responsibility for programming— the allocation of human, fiscal, and material resources required to implement the educational plan—is typically assigned to administrative personnel. The potential result of the differential assignment of responsibility for planning and programming may be a discrepancy between the mentally retarded child's educational plan and his educational program. Thus the delineation and assignment of responsibilities among regular and special education administrative, instructional, and supportive personnel is essential to the provision of appropriate and high-quality educational services to facilitate mainstreaming.

In summary, mainstreaming refers to the temporal, instructional, and social integration of eligible mentally retarded children with normal peers, based on an ongoing, individually determined educational planning and programming process and requires clarification of responsibility among regular and special education administrative, instructional, and supportive personnel. Each component of mainstreaming—integration, planning and programming, and clarification of responsibilities—is composed of several elements. The question of for whom and under what conditions mainstreaming is a viable educational alternative is only answerable when information is available concerning all of its components and elements. The definitional framework discussed above elucidates some of the complexities inherent in developing appropriate mainstreaming services. In addition, the framework provides a conceptual model from which to study the effectiveness of mainstreaming services. What, then, are the implications of the definition of mainstreaming for research?

DEFINITIONAL IMPLICATIONS FOR RESEARCH

The goal of experimental design and inferential statistical analysis in scientific investigations is to obtain the least ambiguous information as to whether a "treatment" affected, in some manner, particular outcomes. Unlike laboratory research where the treatment variables are known, can be controlled, manipulated, and examined in microscopic fashion, most educational research conducted in situ cannot control treatment variables with any degree of precision. Most often, in situ educational research cannot even identify precisely what the treatment variables were because the variables themselves are macroscopic and loosely defined. Therefore, educational research that poses the question of whether one in situ treatment is more effective than another may be necessary but is hardly sufficient. Of greater importance is the identification of particular aspects of the treatment that are responsible for producing the outcomes of interest.

Mainstreaming research, which until now has been viewed primarily as an administrative arrangement, has typically been studied in a *between-groups* paradigm (e.g., Walker, 1972; Budoff & Gottlieb, 1974). That is, mainstream programs and segregated programs have been compared and conclusions made that one or the other treatment was more effective. The between-groups approach assumes a homogeneity within each treatment group. Put another way, this paradigm assumes that segregated and mainstreamed special educational services will reflect greater variation between than within treatment conditions. The between-groups approach for studying the effects of mainstreaming, however, appears overly simplistic within the context of the multidimensional definition proposed in this paper.

Given the complexity of mainstreaming constructs, a between-groups research paradigm provides information of very limited utility for decision-making purposes. This paradigm only provides superficial information that global administrative distinctions (e.g., special classes versus mainstreaming services) produced differential pupil outcomes. The information obtained from a between-groups paradigm provides little insight regarding specific aspects of either the segregated or the mainstreaming treatments which differentially affect pupil outcomes. The conceptualization of mainstreaming as a multidimensional treatment involving numerous administrative and instructional options requires the use of a research paradigm which does not concentrate only on between-group variance.

Mainstreaming has evolved as an array of administrative and instructional options, each one of which may be conceptualized as a treatment variable. The diversity of philosophies and values regarding educational needs of mentally retarded children has resulted in extensive variability in the intent and implementation of mainstreaming services. The selection of a particular mainstreaming option has resulted from administrators' varying conceptualizations of special education services, availability of human, fiscal, and material resources, and differential emphasis given to the learning characteristics and educational needs of mentally retarded children. Mainstreaming options have also reflected differing organizational influences related to authority and responsibility. The broad range of practices that have been subsumed under the label "mainstreaming" is partially attributable to the inadequacy of available definitions which have not established parameters for what is or is not to be considered as mainstreaming.

The proposed definition suggests that mainstreaming is a proxy variable for integration, the educational planning and programming process, and the clarification of responsibilities for mainstreaming services provided by regular and special education personnel. Each component of mainstreaming must be clearly delineated and must be comprised of operationally defined constructs that are meaningful and measurable. Thus, the extensive variability possible within the suggested definitional framework requires research paradigms which will permit results to be attributed to the effects of specific *within-treatment* variations.

Treatment variables that are both meaningful and measurable have never been easy to isolate and historically have confounded special education research. It may be recalled that one of Kirk's (1964) criticisms of the efficacy research was that

> there has not been a clear-cut definition of a special class, the curriculum, or the qualifications of special teachers. Special classes vary widely in organization and in curriculum and teaching methods. Qualifications of teachers vary from well-trained teachers to those subjected to short-term summer courses taught largely by instructors who have had little training or experience with special classes. The administrative labeling of a group of retarded children as a special class for the purpose of receiving state subsidy does not assure it being a special class for experimental purposes. (p. 62-63)

The difficulties involved in specifying meaningful and measurable treatment variables in mainstreaming research are even more formidable than they have been for research on segregated special classes. Not only are all of Kirk's criticisms regarding the efficacy research applicable to mainstreaming research, but in addition mainstreaming has its own unique complexities. To illustrate, mainstreaming services present the researcher with a perplexing problem regarding the teacher as a treatment variable. Typically, the special education teacher fulfills a variety of concurrent roles and functions regardless of the descriptive label assigned—education statistician (Buffmire, 1973), diagnostic/prescriptive teacher (Prouty & McGarry, 1973), or consulting teacher (McKenzie, 1972). Specifically, these multiple functions include direct instruction to children, instructional assistance to the regular classroom teacher, assessment, and/or prescription. In addition, the special education teacher's direct instruction of children differs in both intensity and content depending on the child's educational needs. Moreover, delivery of the instructional service may occur in a variety of locations, such as a resource classroom or regular classroom.

Given the variability of roles and functions performed by regular and special education personnel providing mainstreaming services, researchers must employ designs which would enable them to specify and isolate aspects of mainstreaming treatments that affect pupil outcomes. The proposed definition provides one framework from which to specify potentially relevant variables. Research related to the effectiveness of mainstreaming must examine its many aspects that operate either singularly and/or interactively to affect the education of the mentally retarded child.

CONCLUSION

Mainstreaming, as defined in this paper, represents one of the most complex educational service innovations undertaken to date by the educational system. The integration, educational planning and programming, and clarification of responsibilities components of mainstreaming, independently and interactively, represent perplexing and sometimes conflicting conceptual constructs requiring operational definition and implementation by educational decision makers. The organizational, administrative, and instructional complexities inherent in providing mainstreaming services will require attention, not circumvention. The benefits of mainstreaming services to the educational system in general, and the mentally retarded child in particular, are likely to occur to the extent that responsible leadership is exercised by regular and special education administrative, instructional, and supportive personnel.

REFERENCES

Abeson, A. "Movement and Momentum: Government and the Education of Handicapped Children—II." *Exceptional Children, 41,* 1974 (109-116).

Adamson, G. & Van Etten, G. "Zero-Reject Model Revisited: A Workable Alternative." *Exceptional Children, 38,* 1972 (735-738).

Beery, K. *Models for Mainstreaming.* San Rafael, Ca.: Dimensions Publishing Co., 1972.

Bennett, A. *A Comparative Study of Subnormal Children in the Elementary Grades.* New York: Teachers College, Columbia University, Bureau of Publications, 1932.

Birch, J. *Mainstreaming: Educable Mentally Retarded Children in Regular Classes.* Leadership Training Institute/Special Education, University of Minnesota, 1974.

Braybrooke, D. & Lindblom C. *A Strategy of Decision.* New York: The Free Press, 1963.

Bryan, T. "An Observational Analysis of Classroom Behaviors of Children with Learning Disabilities." *Journal of Learning Disabilities, 7,* 1974 (26-34).

Budoff, M. & Gottlieb, J. "A Comparison of EMR Children in Special Classes with EMR Children Who Have Been Reintegrated into Regular Classes." *Studies in Learning Potential, 3,* No. 50, 1974.

Buffmire, J. A. "The Stratistician Model." In E.N. Deno (Ed.), *Instructional Alternatives for Exceptional Children.* Arlington, Va.: Council for Exceptional Children, 1973.

Bryne, D. "Response to Attitude Similarity-Dissimilarity as a Function of Affiliation Need." *Journal of Personality, 30,* 1962 (164-177).

Carroll, J. B. "A Model of School Learning." *Teachers College Record, 64,* 1963 (723-733).

CEC Policies Commission. "Proposed CEC Policy Statement on the Organization and Administration of Special Education." *Exceptional Children, 39,* 1973 (493-497).

Chaffin, J. "Will the Real "Mainstreaming" Program Please Stand Up! (Or. . .Should Dunn Have Done It?)." *Focus on Exceptional Children, 6,* No. 5, 1974.

Christoplos, F. & Renz, P. "A Critical Examination of Special Education Programs." *Journal of Special Education, 3,* 1969 (371-380).

Dunn, L. M. "Special Education for the Mildly Retarded—Is Much of It Justifiable?" *Exceptional Children, 34,* 1968 (5-22).

Georgia Board of Education and State Superintendent of Schools. *Policies and Executive Procedure.* Atlanta, Georgia.

Gottlieb, J. "Public, Peer and Professional Attitudes toward Mentally Retarded Persons." Paper presented at conference, "The Mentally Retarded and Society: A Social Science Perspective," National Institute of Child Health and Human Development and the Rose Kennedy Center for Research in Mental Retardation and Human Development, Niles, Michigan, 1974.

Gottlieb, J. & Budoff, M. "Classroom Behavior and Social Status." *Studies in Learning Potential, 3,* No. 53, 1973.

Gunzberg, H. "Educational Problems in Mental Deficiency." In A. M. Clarke & A. D. Clarke (Eds.), *Mental Deficiency: A Changing Outlook* (rev. ed.). New York: The Free Press, 1965.

Innskeep, A. *Teaching Dull and Retarded Children.* New York: The Macmillan Co., 1926.

Johnson, G. O. "Social Position of Mentally Handicapped Children in Regular Grades." *American Journal of Mental Deficiency, 55,* 1950 (60-89).

Johnson, G. O. "Special Education for the Mentally Handicapped—A Paradox." *Exceptional Children, 29,* 1962 (62-69).

Jones, S. "Psychology of Interpersonal Attraction." In C. Memeth (Ed.), *Social Psychology: Classic and Contemporary Integrations.* Chicago: Rand McNally, 1974.

Kirk, S. "Research in Education." In H. A. Stevens & R. Heber (Eds.), *Mental Retardation: A Review of Research.* Chicago: University of Chicago Press, 1964.

Kirk, S. & Johnson, G. O. *Educating the Retarded Child.* Cambridge, Ma.: Riverside Press, 1951.

Kleck, R., Richardson, S. & Ronald, L. "Physical Appearance Cues and Interpersonal Attraction in Children. *Child Development, 45,* 1974 (305-310).

Kolstoe, O. *Teaching Educable Mentally Retarded Children.* New York: Holt, Rinehart & Winston, 1970.

Lilly, M. S. Special Education: A Teapot in a Tempest. *Exceptional Children, 37,* 1970 (43-48).

Massachusetts Teachers Association. *Puzzled About 766? Evaluation and Planning.* Boston: Massachusetts Department of Education Grant No. D74-000-034, 1974.

McKenzie, H. S. "Special Education and Consulting Teachers." In F. Clark, D. Evans & L. Hammerlynk (Eds.), *Implementing Behavioral Programs for Schools and Clinics.* Champaign, Ill.: Research Press, 1972.

National School Public Relations Association (NSPRA). *Educating Children with Special Needs: Current Trends in School Policies and Programs.* Arlington, Va.: National School Public Relations Association, 1974.

Prouty, R. W. & McCarry, F. M. "The Diagnostic/Prescriptive Teacher." In E. N. Deno (Ed.), *Instructional Alternatives for Exceptional Children.* Arlington, Va.: Council for Exceptional Children, 1973.

TENN. CODE ANN. Z 49-2913(B) (Supp. 1973).

Texas Education Agency. *Administrative Guide and Handbook for Special Education.* Austin: Texas Education Agency Bulletin 711.

U.S. District Court for the Eastern District of Pennsylvania. *Pennsylvania Association for Retarded Children, Nancy Beth Bowman et al.* v. *Commonwealth of Pennsylvania, David H. Kurtzman et al.* CA 71-42 (Penn., 1971).

Walker, V. *The Resource Room Model for Educating Educable Mentally Retarded Children.* Unpublished doctoral dissertation. Temple University, 1972.

Wiley, D. E. & Harnischfeger, A. *Explosion of a Myth: Quantity of Schooling and Exposure to Instruction, Major Educational Vehicles.* Report No. 8, Systems Development Corporation, Santa Monica, California, 1974.

Wisconsin. Ch. 89, Z 1(4), [1973] Laws of Wis. [Wis. Legislative Service 256, ch. 89, Z 1(4) (West 1973)].

The rights of the exceptional child have been the focus of considerable litigation since the late 1960s. Weintraub discusses the implications of recent as well as historical cases. Particular attention is given to assisting the reader in interpreting legal decisions as they pertain to special education. Of special interest is the author's review of litigation pertaining to professional liability. This selection represents an attempt to provide special and regular educators with a meaningful reference on current efforts to enhance the rights of exceptional children.

Recent Influences of Law Regarding the Identification and Educational Placement of Children

Frederick J. Weintraub
The Council for Exceptional Children, Reston, Virginia

Special education, as an institution of the American educational enterprise, has had a proud history of being that one element of the enterprise which has been an advocate for the learning needs of children. Law has been used by special educators and parents of handicapped children as a "sword of Damocles" to force an unwilling educational system to direct resources to the establishment of special programs for handicapped children (Weintraub, 1969).

However, only recently has this "sword" been found to have a second cutting edge; for, in the zeal to provide for children, it has become apparent that in some cases the basic rights of these children and their families have been violated. In recent years, this realization has resulted in numerous court proceedings, corrective legislation, media condemnations, confrontations, and a general sense of bewilderment on the part of the professional community.

A review of the historical and philosophical development of special education, in terms of the major legal developments pertaining to identification

55

and placement, and the implications of these developments to special education is presented.

DEVELOPMENTAL OVERVIEW

While the United States Constitution charges government to promote "the general welfare," such purpose has been inherent to all governments at all times, with varying perceptions of "the general welfare." The Greeks of Sparta placed their cripples on the mountain sides; and the U.S. state governments, since the early 1800s, have placed their handicapped in institutions. Even today, "the general welfare" is often construed to legally sanction coercive methods of protecting society from the deviant.

In 1919, the Supreme Court of Wisconsin ruled in *Beattie* v. *State Board of Education* (172 N.W. 153) that "the rights of a child of school age to attend the public schools of the state cannot be insisted upon, when his presence therein is harmful to the best interests of the school." It was shown that the child in question was not a physical threat and could compete in the academic environment. The major argument presented by the school district for exclusion was that his physical condition (cerebral palsy) produced a "depressing and nauseating effect on the teachers and school children" and that he required an undue portion of the teacher's time and attention.

Historically, American public education, as conceived by its founders, thought that it would be enough to open the schools to everyone, to rich and pool alike, and then let the youngsters make the most of their opportunities. It was assumed that in a free-for-all contest the prizes would go to those who have the most brains, industry, ambition, and character (Mann, 1968). The Georgia populist, Tom Watson, expressed this philosophy most clearly (Woodward, 1938):

> Close no entrance to the poorest, the weakest, the humblest. Say to ambition everywhere, "the field is clear, the contest fair; come, and win your share if you can!"

However, for many, this limited concept of equality of educational opportunity, coupled with the legal sanctions of cases such as *Beattie* v. *State Board of Education,* closed the educational door to those who could not compete in the fair race.

By the early 1900s, a growing concern for these children developed (Coleman, 1968):

> As families lost their economic production activities, they also began to lose their welfare functions, and the poor or ill or incapacitated became more nearly a community

56

responsibility. Thus the training which a child received came to be of interest to all in the community, either as his potential employers or as his potential economic supports if he became dependent.

While public school special education classes for the deaf received their impetus in the 1860s, the first public school class for the mentally retarded was established in 1896 in Providence, Rhode Island. By 1922, there were 191 public school programs for children with varying handicapping conditions in cites with populations over 100,000 (Weintraub, 1971).

The major stimulus to this growth was an increasing base of state legislation requiring and/or providing financial incentive for the development of such programs. Legislation in New Jersey in 1911, New York in 1917, and Massachusetts in 1920 made it mandatory for local boards of education to determine the number of handicapped children within their school districts and, in the case of the mentally retarded, to provide special classes when there were 10 or more such children. In 1915 Minnesota provided state aid in the amount of $100 for each child attending a special class and also required that teachers hold special certificates (Weintraub, 1971).

By 1948, 1,500 school systems reported special education programs; 3,600 in 1958; and 5,600 in 1963. Mackie (1965) reported that as many as 8,000 school districts contracted for special education services from neighboring districts. Today, it is estimated that 40% of the nation's six million handicapped children of school age are receiving special education services.

Of the 60% of the handicapped children not receiving special education services, approximately one million are excluded totally from a publicly supported education. These children languish in homes or institutions or receive private education paid for by their parents or charity. While over half of the states mandate through statutes for education of the handicapped (Abeson and Weintraub, 1971), presently no state is meeting this obligation.

Recent court decisions, however, may portend a dramatic change. In 1969, Judge Wilkens, Third Judicial District Court of Utah, required that two mentally retarded children excluded from education and placed under the Department of Welfare be provided education as a part of the public education system. In his ruling (*Fred G. Wolf, et al.* v. *The Legislature of the State of Utah*, Div. No. 182646, 1969), he noted:

Today it is doubtful that any child may reasonably be expected to succeed in life if he is denied the right and opportunity of an education. In the instant case the segregation of the plaintiff children from the public school system has a detrimental effect upon the children as well as their parents. The impact is greater when it has the apparent sanction of the law. The policy of placing these children under the Department of Welfare and segregating them from the educational system can be and probably is usually interpreted as denoting their inferiority, unusualness, and incompetency. A sense of inferiority and not belonging affects the motivation of a child to learn. Segregation, even though perhaps well intentioned, under the apparent sanction of law and state authority has a tendency to retard the educational, emotional, and mental development of the children.

In January, 1971, the Pennsylvania Association for Retarded Children on behalf of the parents of thirteen retarded children brought suit in the United States District Court for the Eastern District of Pennsylvania against the state of Pennsylvania, its agencies, and school districts for failure to provide their children and other retarded children a publicly supported education. The plaintiffs argued that the denial of such education was a violation of the equal protection clause of the Fourteenth Amendment of the Constitution of the United States. Or more simply, if education is provided by government to some, it must be made available to all. In October of 1971, a consent agreement was reached between the parties; the court ordered the state to provide education to all mentally retarded children including those living in state institutions within one year (*Pennsylvania Association for Retarded Children et al.* v. *Commonwealth of Pennsylvania, David H. Kurtzman, et al.,* Civil Action No. 71-42).

While there may be many social and professional issues related to the task of identifying and placing children in special education programs, the existing body of law addresses itself to four major issues: (1) the acceptability of present standardized achievement tests as a criterion for placement for minority group children; (2) the liability of the evaluator; (3) the placement process, (4) the grouping of children by ability.

ACCEPTABILITY OF ACHIEVEMENT TESTS FOR MINORITY CHILDREN

All state education codes contain a definition or enumeration of the types of handicapped children entitled to receive special education services. The statutes vary greatly ranging from New York's (Laws of New York, Article 89, Section 4401) broad statement,

One who, because of mental, physical, or emotional reasons cannot be educated in regular classes, but can benefit by special services.

to New Mexico's (77-11-3) disability enumerations,

'Handicapped children' includes all persons of school age to twenty-one years of age inclusive who require special education in order to obtain the education of which they are capable because they are educable mentally handicapped, trainable mentally handicapped, blind, partially sighted, deaf, hard of hearing, speech defective, crippled or neurological and other health impaired or are emotionally maladjusted to the extent that they cannot make satisfactory progress in the regular school program.

to California's (6901) definition by disability approach,

'Mentally retarded minors' means all minors who because of retarded intellectual development as determined by individual psychological examination are incapable of being educated efficiently and profitably through ordinary classroom instruction.

to Georgia's (H.B. No. 453) highly specified definition by disability approach,

Exceptional Children: are those who have emotional, physical, communicative, and/or intellectual deviations to the degree that there is interference with school achievements or adjustments, or prevention of full academic attainment, and who require modifications or alterations in their educational programs. This definition includes children who are mentally retarded, physically handicapped, speech handicapped, multiple handicapped, autistic, intellectually gifted, hearing impaired, visually impaired, and any other areas of exceptionality which may be identified.

State statutes proceed in similar varying fashion in specifying the procedures for certifying a child to be handicapped and placing such child in a special program. However, when statutes are combined with regulations, a general consistency can be observed among the states.

All states serve a classification of children generally referred to as "mentally retarded" or "mentally handicapped." The major criterion for certification is an intelligence quotient derived from an individual psychological test administered by a state-approved, certified, or licensed psychologist or psychometrist. The most commonly recognized tests are the Stanford-Binet and the WISC. Other tests sometimes mentioned include the Bender Gestalt, the Draw-A-Person, and the Wide Range Achievement Test. The I.Q. ceiling is usually 75-79. Many states require additional data for certifying a child to be educable mentally retarded. These often include physical examinations, social work case studies, and school counselor and teacher reports.

Recent Decisions

In the last several years, there have been four major cases directed at challenging the legality of placement of children in classes for the mentally retarded on the basis of I.Q. tests which are prejudicial to the children in regard to their native language, cultural background, and normative standardization. The most significant case to date is *Diana* v. *State Board of Education* (c-70 37 R F R).

In January, 1970, a suit was filed in the District Court of Northern California on behalf of nine Mexican-American students, ages 8 to 13. The children came from homes in which Spanish was the major, if not the only, language spoken. All had been placed in classes for the mentally retarded in Monterey County, California. Their IQs ranged from 30 to 72 with a mean score of 63½. They were retested bilingually; seven of the nine scored higher than the IQ cutoff line, and the lowest score was three points below the cutoff line. The average gain was 15 IQ points.

The plaintiffs charged that the testing procedures utilized for placement were prejudicial in that the tests place heavy emphasis on verbal skills requiring facility with the English language, the questions are culturally biased, and the tests are standardized on white, nativeborn Americans. The plaintiffs further pointed out that in "Monterey County, Spanish surname students constitute about 18½% of the student population, but nearly one-third (33 1/3%) of the children in EMR classes."

Studies conducted by the California State Department of Education corroborated the inequity. In 1966-67, of 85,000 children in EMR classes, children with Spanish surnames comprised 26% while they accounted for only 13% of the total school population.

The plaintiffs sought a class action on behalf of all bilingual Mexican-American children then in EMR classes and all such children in danger of inappropriate placement in such classes. On February 5, 1970, a stipulated agreement order was signed by both parties. The order required that:

1. Children are to be tested in their primary language. Interpretors may be used when a bilingual examiner is not available.
2. Mexican-American and Chinese children in EMR classes are to be retested and evaluated.
3. Special efforts are to be extended to aid misplaced children readjust to regular classrooms.
4. The state will undertake immediate efforts to develop and standardize an appropriate IQ test.

In 1968, a case very similar to *Diana* was initiated in the Superior Court of Orange County, California, on behalf of eleven Mexican-American students, ages 5 to 18 (*Arreola* v. *Board of Education,* Santa Ana School District, No. 160 577). The status of the charges are questionable due to the changes occasioned by *Diana.*

A third case, *Covarrubias* v. *San Diego Unified School District,* is also similar in argument to the *Diana* case except for two distinctions. First, twelve of the seventeen student plaintiffs are black; secondly, the plaintiffs seek $400,000 in punitive damages for the period they spent in EMR classes. The suit was filed with the school district in April, 1970.

The California cases have resulted in several amendments to the California statutes and substantial amendments to the state's regulations. Senate Bill 1317 was the major substantive legislation passed by the California legislature. The following is the Legislative Counsel's digest of the statute:

Requires verbal or nonverbal individual intelligence testing of minors in specified primary home language prior to admission to a special education program for the mentally retarded.

Prohibits placement of minor in special education class for the mentally retarded if he scores higher than two standard deviations below the norm on a specified individual intelligence test.

Prohibits placement of minor in special education program for the mentally retarded if, when being tested in a language other than English, he scores higher than two standard deviations below the norm on a nonverbal intelligence test or on nonverbal portion of an individual intelligence test including both verbal and nonverbal portions.

Permits placement of minor in such program if he scores two standard deviations, or more, below the norm on specified individual intelligence tests and after examination by credentialed school psychologist.

Prohibits placement of minor in such class without parents' written consent obtained after complete explanation of special education program.

Requires Department of Education to submit annual report to Legislature on testing and placement of minors in programs for mentally retarded minors.

Provides for termination of act two years following its enactment.

The cases have also had impact at the federal level. On May 25, 1970, an HEW memorandum was sent from J. Stanley Pottinger, Director of HEW's Office for Civil Rights, to 1,000 school districts with large numbers of bilingual children. The memo noted that schools would not be in compliance with Title VI of the Civil Rights Act if students whose predominant language is other than English were assigned to classes for the mentally retarded on the basis of criteria which essentially measure or evaluate English language skills.

Stewart et al. v. *Phillips et al.* (70-1199-F), filed in October, 1970, before the Federal District Court of Massachusetts on behalf of seven black students and parents, took another major step in the attack on IQ testing and EMR placement. As in *Diana,* the children were tested adjudged mentally retarded, and placed in Boston EMR classes. Private retesting found the students were not retarded. Several retesting studies of minority group EMR children in Boston have found 50% to be misclassified. The plaintiffs sought class action to enjoin further testing or placement until a Commission on Individual Needs is appointed to oversee testing and classification. Two of the Commission's members would be parents of children in the schools. The plaintiffs also seek $20,000 per individual for damages.

LIABILITY OF THE EVALUATOR

On the basis of recent findings of large numbers of children misclassified as mentally retarded by school psychologists or other examiners, the question has been raised as to whether such persons may be sued for libel or slander. None of the aforementioned cases have brought such action, and no ruling has yet been given on punitive damages. However, two tangential cases may help to understand this issue.

In *Iverson* v. *Frandsen* (237 F. 2d 898, Idaho, 1956), suit was brought by the parents of a nine-year-old girl against a psychologist at a state hospital for the mentally ill. The child had been taken to the hospital for treatment of fear of enclosed places. Hospital regulations required a psychological examination. A Stanford-Binet test showed the girl to be a "high grade moron." Upon request by the school guidance counselor, the findings were forwarded to school officials.

The U.S. Court of Appeals ruled that "where a psychologist, as a public official, made a professional report on plaintiff's mental level. . .in good faith, and as representing his best judgment, such report was free from actionable malice and was not libelous."

A case quite different (*Kenny* v. *Gurley*, 94 So. 34) in nature does provide helpful thinking regarding libel and misclassification. In 1923 in Alabama, a girl was sent home from college after the school doctor had diagnosed her as having venereal disease. A letter was sent by the doctor to the parents explaining her dismissal. Further medical examination disproved the doctor's original diagnosis of venereal disease. Suit was then brought against the doctor for slander. The court ruled that the doctor behaved without malice, that the action of dismissal was justifiable to his responsibility to maintain the health of the general student body, and that his letter was privileged communication to a legitimate recipient.

PLACEMENT PROCESS

Until recently, very little was said in the statutory or regulatory provisions of the states regarding the process of placing a child in a special education program. There does appear to be a trend toward the requirement for admissions committees to review the child's records (Alabama, 1965):

> A placement committee appointed by the local superintendent shall be established for determining the eligibility of exceptional children for placement in special classes. Such a committee should be composed of representation from medicine, education, and psychology, if possible.

> This committee, after the study of all data available on each child, shall make recommendations concerning each child's admission to the special class on a trial basis.

A second trend is for the requirement of parental involvement and/or approval in the placement of a child in an EMR program (Colorado statutes 123-22-7 [2] ; Arizona ARS 15-1013 [e]).

> The determination of the mental handicap of a child shall be made by individual examination conducted by a psychologist with the consent of the parent or guardian of the child. In the event that the parents or guardian of the child disagree with the determination of the psychologist or the placement of the child, they may refer the

child to a psychologist of their own choice, and at their own expense, and submit such evaluation to the Board of Education. The Board of Education shall have the ultimate right of placement of children attending the public schools within their jurisdiction.

The Chief Administrative Official of the school district or county or such person as designated by him as responsible for special education shall place the child, except that no child shall be placed or retained in a special education program without the approval of his parent or guardian.

The following cases may help clarify some of the considerations when preserving the rights of children in the placement process.

In the 1961 New York case, *Van Allen* v. *McCleary* (211 NYS 2d 501), the plaintiff sought a court order requiring the board of education to release the school records on his son, particularly the psychological report to a private physician who was treating his son. The court ruled in favor of the plaintiff noting that "the parent's right (to the records) stems from his relationship with the school authorities as a parent who, under compulsory education, has delegated to them the educational authority over his child."

An old but pertinent case is *State ex. rel. Kelley* v. *Ferguson* (95 Neb. 63, 144 N.W. 1059) in which in 1914 the Supreme Court of Nebraska ruled in favor of the right of a parent to select courses for his child. The plaintiff had for some time instructed his daughter not to attend a required domestic science course provided at a neighboring school one mile away, since such attendance would conflict with her music course. As a result, the daughter was expelled from school. The court, in its wisdom, ruled:

But no pupil attending the school can be compelled to study any prescribed branch against the protest of the parent that the child shall not study such branch, and any rule or regulation that requires the pupil to continue such studies is arbitrary and unreasonable. There is no good reason why the failure of one or more pupils to study one or more prescribed branches should result disastrously to the proper discipline, efficiency, and well-being of the school. Such pupils are not idle but merely devoting their attention to other branches; and so long as the failure of the students, thus excepted, to study all the branches of the prescribed course does not prejudice the equal rights of other students, there is no cause for complaint.

The state is more and more taking hold of the private affairs of individuals and requiring that they conduct their business affairs honestly and with due regard for the public good. All this is commendable and must receive the sanction of every good citizen. But in this age of agitation, such as the world has never known before, we want to be careful lest we carry the doctrine of governmental paternalism too far, for, after all is said and done, the prime factor in our scheme of government is the American home.

A 1950 Iowa Supreme Court decision may qualify the principle established in *Kelly*. The case *Petty in re* (41 N.W. 2d 672) concerned the refusal of the parents of a deaf child to send their child to a state school for the deaf after evidence was shown that the child could not be educated adequately in a local school. The court ruled against the parent, stating that:

> To obtain an education for a normal child with facilities presented in an average school means one thing, but to obtain an education for a handicapped child, particularly one who is deaf, would mean another thing. A child who has a physical defect necessarily must receive a different type of instruction than one who is not handicapped.

In 1967, the Supreme Court of the United States in *In re Gault* (887 U.S. 1, 87 S. Ct. 1428, 18 L. Ed 2d 527) established that children and their parents are entitled to counsel and to be furnished counsel if they are unable to afford it in matters which could lead to commitment to an institution for delinquency. *Madera* v. *Board of Education of City of New York* (267 F. Supp. 356, 386 F. 2d 778) expanded the *Gault* principle to situations more closely related to the placement of children in special education programs. The child of the plaintiff had been suspended from school. The parents were required to appear before the "superintendent's guidance conference" comprised of various school personnel. The purpose of the meeting was to review alternatives for meeting the educational needs of the child. Among the alternatives considered were reinstatement, placement in a special school for maladjusted children, referral to the Bureau of Child Guidance which would evaluate the child and recommend appropriate placement, and referral to the Bureau of Attendance for court action. The parents were denied the opportunity to be represented by counsel.

The U.S. District Court ruled that the guidance conference could result in a loss of personal liberty for the child and that the parents as a result of the "conference" would be in jeopardy of legal proceedings for child neglect. The court concluded

> that the due process clause of the Fourteenth Amendment to the Federal Constitution is applicable to a District Superintendent's Guidance Conference. More specifically, this court concludes that 'enforcement by defendants of the 'no attorneys provision'. . .deprives plaintiffs of their right to a hearing in a state initiated proceeding which puts in jeopardy the minor plaintiff's liberty and right to attend the public schools.

The U.S. Court of Appeals reversed the findings of the lower court noting that the guidance conference is preliminary conference and not an adjudication. The court did note, however, that

> what due process may require before a child is expelled from public school or is remanded to a custodial school or other institution which restricts his freedom to come and go as he pleases is not before us.

One of the most significant aspects of the Pennsylvania Association for Retarded Children case discussed earlier (*Pennsylvania Association for Retarded Children et al.,* v. *Commonwealth of Pennsylvania, David H. Kurtzman, et al.,* Civil Action No. 71-42) was the court's stipulations regarding due process rights of children and their parents in regard to education. In examining the question of whether children had the right to an education, the court was disturbed by the fact that the schools were totally autonomous in their decisions to place or not to place. The court ordered the state to adopt regulations regarding procedures for "change in educational status" of mentally retarded children. These are to include the following:

Whenever any mentally retarded or allegedly mentally retarded child, aged five years, six months, through twenty-one years, is recommended for a change in educational status by a school district, intermediate unit or any school official, notice of the proposed action shall first be given to the parent or guardian of the child.

Notice of the proposed action shall be given in writing by registered mail to the parent or guardian of the child (N.B. being changed to certified mail).

The notice shall describe the proposed action in detail, including specification of the statute or regulation under which such action is proposed and a clear and full statement of the reasons therefor, including specification of any tests or reports upon which such action is proposed.

The notice shall advise the parent or guardian of any alternative education opportunities, if any, available to his child other than that proposed.

The notice shall inform the parent or guardian of his right to contest the proposed action at a full hearing before the Secretary of Education, or his designee, in a place and at a time convenient to the parent, before the proposed action may be taken.

The notice shall inform the parent or guardian of his right to be represented at the hearing by legal counsel, of his right to counsel, of his right to examine before the hearing his child's school records including any tests or reports upon which the proposed action may be based, of his right to present evidence of his own, including expert medical, psychological, and educational testimony, and of his right to confront and to cross-examine any school official, employee, or agent of a school district, intermediate unit or the department who may have evidence upon which the proposed action may be based.

The notice shall inform the parent or guardian of the availability of various organizations, including the local chapter of the Pennsylvania Association for Retarded Children, to assist him in connection with the hearing and the school district or intermediate unit involved shall offer to provide full information about such organization to such parent or guardian upon request.

The notice shall inform the parent or guardian that he is entitled under the Pennsylvania Mental Health and Mental Retardation Act to the services of a local center for an independent medical, psychological, and educational evaluation of his child and shall specify the name, address, and telephone number of the MH-MR center in his catchment area.

The notice shall specify the procedure for pursuing a hearing, which procedure shall be stated in a form to be agreed upon by counsel, which form shall distinctly state that the parent or guardian must fill in the form and mail the same to the school district or intermediate unit involved within 14 days of the date of notice.

If the parent or guardian does not exercise his right to a hearing by mailing in the form requesting a hearing within 14 days of receipt of the aforesaid notice, the school district or intermediate unit unvolved shall send out a second notice in the manner prescribed above, which notice shall also distinctly advise the parent or guardian that he has a right to a hearing as prescribed above, that he had been notified once before about such right to a hearing and that his failure to respond to the second notice within 14 days of the date thereof will constitute his waiver to a right to a hearing. Such second notice shall also be accompanied with a form for requesting a hearing of the type specified above.

The hearing shall be scheduled not sooner than 20 days nor later than 45 days after receipt of the request for a hearing from the parent or guardian.

The hearing shall be held in the local district and at a place reasonably convenient to the parent or guardian of the child. At the option of the parent or guardian, the hearing may be held in the evening and such option shall be set forth in the form requesting the hearing aforesaid.

The hearing officer shall be the Secretary of Education, or his designee, but shall not be an officer, employee or agent of any local district or intermediate unit in which the child resides.

The hearing shall be an oral, personal hearing, and shall be public unless the parent or guardian specifies a closed hearing.

The decision of the hearing officer shall be based solely upon the evidence presented at the hearing.

The local school district or intermediate unit shall have the burden of proof.

A stenographic or other transcribed record of the hearing shall be made and shall be available to the parent or guardian or his representative. Said record may be discarded after three years.

The parent or guardian or his counsel shall be given reasonable hearing by legal counsel of his choosing.

The parent or guardian or his counsel shall be given reasonable access prior to the hearing to all records of the school district or intermediate unit concerning his child, including any tests or reports upon which the proposed action may be based.

The parent or guardian or his counsel shall have the right to compel the attendance of, to confront and to cross-examine any witness testifying for the school board or intermediate unit and any official, employee, or agent of the school district, intermediate unit, or the department who may have evidence upon which the proposed action may be based.

The parent or guardian shall have the right to present evidence and testimony, including expert medical, psychological or educational testimony.

No later than 30 days after the hearing, the hearing officer shall render a decision in writing which shall be accompanied by written findings of fact and conclusions of law and which shall be sent by registered mail to the parent or guardian and his counsel.

Pending the hearing and receipt of notification of the decision by the parent or guardian, there shall be no change in the child's educational status.

GROUPING BY ABILITY

The final issue to which an increasing body of legal examination is being given is the placement of children in self-contained special classes limited to children of a single ability classification.

Traditionally, special education meant special classes. This is not so today. There is a distinct movement to encourage other program options such as resource aides to the regular classroom teachers, resource rooms, itinerant services, etc. This trend is not meant to discredit the special class, but rather to view it as a more extreme placement on a continuum of special education services that should be used with caution.

Slowly, this trend is being reflected in changes in state statutes and regulations. One major deterrent to the swing from the special class is the structure of state financial incentive to administrative practices which may be in conflict with appropriate educational practice. The Analytic Study of State Legislation for Handicapped Children (Ackerman & Weintraub, 1971) found that local school districts often use the state funding procedures as the prime source of planning for the educational needs of handicapped children. This reality is diminishing as more comprehensive legislative authorities are created; however, the situation nationally is far from healthy. A number of recent cases have bearing on this issue.

In 1962, a woman was taken into custody by police in the District of Columbia after being found wandering about the city in a state of confusion. After psychiatric observation which indicated the woman was suffering from senility, the woman was committed to a mental hospital. The psychiatrist noted that the woman was not a threat to the community, only a threat to herself. The woman filed a writ of habeas corpus. The trial court denied her petition (*Lake* v. *Cameron*, 364 F. 2d 657). The U.S. Court of Appeals reversed the trial court and in doing so laid down a most important principle:

> Deprivations of liberty soley because of dangers to the ill persons themselves should not go beyond what is necessary for their protection. . . .

> Appellant may not be required to carry the burden of showing the availability of alternatives. . .(She) does not know and lacks the means to ascertain what alternatives, if any, are available, but the Government knows or has the means of knowing and should therefore assist the court in acquiring such information. . . .

From this ruling, it would seem that when there exists a continuum of treatments varying in degree of deprivation of individual liberty that government can only require that appropriate treatment which is least delimiting to the individual's rights. It is also important to note that the court placed the burden on the government to be familiar and make known the alternative treatments.

In two school desegregation cases, *McLaughlin* v. *Florida* (379 U.S. 184, 1964) and *Loving* v. *Virginia* (388 U.S. 1, 1967), the Supreme Court established a "yardstick" for determing when a procedure was constitutionally offensive. The high court ruled that racial distinctions, differentiations, and classifications are constitutionally offensive, unless the state is able to justify them as essential to the accomplishment of an otherwise permissible state policy. As in the *Lake* case, the court emphasized that when alternatives were available, it would be difficult to justify a practice that limited or discriminated individual liberty.

Track System

The most cited case by protagonists of traditional special education programming is *Hobson* v. *Hansen* (269 F. Supp, 401) from the U.S. District Court of the District of Columbia in 1967. The case centered around the question whether the "track system" utilized in the Washington, D.C. public schools which separated children into five ability groupings (honors track for gifted students, regular track for college preparation; general track, vocational or commercial program for most students; the special or basic track for those with IQs below 75; junior primary track for readiness before first grade) was an illegal, discriminating practice. Judge Wright noted that "the track system was based on three asumptions."

> First, a child's maximum educational potential can and will be accurately ascertained. Second, tracking will enhance the prospects for correcting a child's remediable educational deficiences. Third, tracking must be flexible so as to provide an individually tailored education for students who cannot be pigeon-holed in single curriculum (p. 446).

> The track system. . .translates ability into educational opportunity. When a student is placed in a lower track, in a very real sense his future is being decided for him; the kind of education he gets there shapes his future progress not only in school but in society in general. Certainly, when the school system undertakes this responsibility it incurs the obligation of living up to its promise to the student that placement in a lower track will not simply be a shunting off from the mainstream of education, but rather will be an effective mechanism for bringing the student up to his true potential (p. 473).

> None of this is to suggest either that a student should be sheltered from the truth about his academic deficiencies or that instruction cannot take account of varying levels of ability. It is to say that a system that presumes to tell a student what his ability is and what he can successfully learn incurs an obligation to take account of the psychological damage that can come from such an encounter between the student and the school; and to be certain that it is in a position to decide whether the student's deficiencies are true, or only apparent (p. 492).

> . . .It should be made clear that what is at issue here is not whether defendants are entitled to provide different kinds of students with different kinds of education. Although the equal protection clause is, of course, concerned with classifications which result in disparity of treatment, not all classifications resulting in disparity are unconstitutional. If classification is reasonably related to the purposes of the governmental activity involved and is rationally carried out, the fact that persons are thereby treated differently does not necessarily offend (p. 511).

As in *Diana*, Judge Wright emphasized the prejudicial nature of present standardized aptitude tests, which are based on the white norms, when applied in school systems such as Washington, D.C., with a black student population in excess of 90%.

Judge Wright further noted

.. any system of ability grouping which, through failure to include and implement the concept of compensatory education for the disadvantaged child or otherwise, fails in fact to bring the great majority of children into the mainstream of public education denies the children excluded equal educational opportunity and thus encounters the constitutional bar (p. 515).

Judge Wright's final remarks reflect the difficulty faced by the court in its decision and portend the possible future nature of such court decisions.

It is regretable, of course, that in deciding this case this court must act in an area so alien to its expertise. It would be far better indeed for these social and political problems to be resolved in the political arena by other branches of government.

The *Hobson* v. *Hansen* decision was appealed in *Smuck* v. *Hobson* (F08 F. 2d 175) in 1969 and upheld on a four to three decision by the U.S. Court of Appeals. The appeal was complex since two new dimensions had been initiated. First, the Congress had established a board of education for the District, elected by the people and given full responsibility for educational policy. Second, the board had accepted the findings and recommendations of the Passow Report, an independent study of the D.C. schools conducted by Teachers College, Columbia University. The report provided remedies to many of the discriminatory issues raised in the initial case. The appellants argued that the sweeping ban on the "track system" was no longer necessary. While the majority upheld Judge Wright's decision, latitude was provided for the board to bring alternative plans before the court for consideration.

Judge Burger (now Chief Justice of the Supreme Court) delivered a dissenting opinion. In his dissent, Judge Burger cited the following comment from the Harvard Law Review:

[T]he limits upon what the judiciary can accomplish in an active role are an additional reason for circumspection, particularly in an area where the courts can offer no easy solutions.

...A court applying the Hobson doctrine must necessarily resolve disputed issues of educational policy by determining whether integration by race or class is more desirable; whether compensatory programs should have priority over integration; whether equalization of physical facilities is an efficient means of allocating available resources for the purpose of achieving overall equal opportunity. There is a serious danger that judicial prestige will be committed to ineffective solutions, and that expectations raised by *Hobson*-like decisions will be disappointed. Furthermore, judicial intervention risks lending unnecessary rigidity to treatment of the social problems involved in foreclosing a more flexible, experimental approach.

The *Hobson* doctrine can be criticized for its unclear basis in precedent, its potentially enormous scope, and its imposition of responsibilities which may strain the resources and endanger the prestige of the judiciary.

In *Swann* v. *Charolette-Mecklenburg Board of Education* (300 F. Supp. 1358) the U.S. District Court of North Carolina ruled in 1969 that:

There is no legal reason why fast learners in a particular subject should not be allowed to move ahead and avoid boredom while slow learners are brought along at their own pace to avoid frustration. It is an educational, rather than a legal, matter to say whether this is done with the students all in one classroom or separated into groups.

CONCLUSIONS

As mentioned in the beginning of this paper, law has been the "sword of Damocles" that has forced an unwilling educational enterprise to develop a system of educating handicapped children, and it is this same law that is now being used to rectify the injustices in that system. Law is the corrective method of a democratic society when assurances of good conduct have not been forthcoming from citizens' groups (Berger, 1967).

Today there are many who question whether law can command the behaviors its seeks; if it cannot, then its role as a teacher of the citizenry must be enhanced through every vehicle possible. Perhaps the true value of the cases mentioned in this paper and others yet to come will not be measured by volume of litigation, but rather by the educational community's implementing strategies to prevent further injustices. I would hope that some of the following points will be given serious consideration.

1. Perhaps the best motto for education would be "to each child, in his own way, in his own time." Philosophically, education has long accepted this motto; however, its conscience has gotten lost in administrative realities. And so we took the tool—the intelligence test, for example—overworked it, legalized it, and made it become, against our own warnings, a weapon of discrimination. The recent court decisions must be construed as saying, in a fashion similar to gun control legislation, that if you cannot control these tools they will have to be taken away. The court has not banned intelligence testing for the purpose of placement; it has said, clean your own house. In doing so, caution will have to be utilized to assure that children are measured on tests that are consistent with their major language, that reflect their environment and cultural heritage, and that are standardized on similar children.

2. Throughout our history, children have not been considered citizens having the basic freedoms granted by the Constitution. Numerous cases in recent years, reaching far beyond the scope of this paper, have granted American youth the rights of American citizenship. One of the most cherished of

these rights is the entitlement to due process of law in our interactions with the varying elements of government.

The importance of this right was stressed at a White House Conference on Children (Forum 22, 1970);

Unfortunately, procedures initially designed to be rehabilitative but not retributive, informed but not abusive, enlightened but not willful, have too frequently become the opposite of their intent. Children have been forced to seek redress from their presumed benefactors.

For those of us concerned about the education of handicapped children, the cases relating to due process offer several important guidelines (Weintraub, Abeson & Bradock, 1971):

Evaluation on the basis of norms consistent with the culture of the child.

Evaluation conducted in the primary language of the child.

Parental right to obtain an independent evaluation of their child at public expense if necessary.

A due process hearing in which the parents meet with school officials to determine appropriate placement. In this regard, parents should be entitled to advance notification, access to appropriate school records, representation by legal counsel and provision of additional evidence concerning their child.

Official transcripts of the due process hearing should be maintained, and parents should have the right to appeal decisions resulting from such hearings to the state education agency or directly to the appropriate court.

3. One of our most important legal rights is privacy and maintenance of our personal dignity. In a radio speech (SRS, 1969) in 1968, President Richard M. Nixon noted that government must "do more than help a human body survive, it must help a human spirit revive, to take a proud place in the civilization that measures its humanity in terms of every man's dignity." Often in our zeal, we deny those we are trying to help. We do not need to go far beyond these cases, our schools, or our institutions to affirm this reality.

A review of the major cases on libel or slander has been presented. Very little can be learned from this review other than the fact that professionals are safe in their judgments (whether they be correct or incorrect) as long as they did not have malice in their hearts and did not circulate information beyond appropriate channels. However, we can anticipate greater litigation and protective legislation in this regard.

The tragedy is that many professionals see the growing rights movement as a threat. Instead, the movement should be seen as enabling the professional to behave in a professional rather than a bureaucratic manner. But the message must be clear—individual rights must transcend bureaucratic and professional needs or limitations.

We have institutionalized many persons knowing that an unavailable, less harsh treatment would have been more appropriate. Similarly, we have accepted many children into special classes for the lack of an alternative. Thus, in many ways, we have allowed ourselves to aid the education system avoid its responsibility to offer children the wide range of services needed. Those concerned with identification and placement of handicapped children can settle for no less than what is appropriate.

REFERENCES

Abeson, Alan R. & Weintraub, Frederick J. "State Law for the Handicapped." *Compact, 5* (4), August, 1971, 19-22.

Ackerman, Paul & Weintraub, Frederick. *Final Report*, Analytic Study of State Legislation (Office of Education Project No. 6-2650), Council for Exceptional Children, 1971.

Alabama, State of. *Manual for Psychological Evaluation of Children for Placement in Special Classes*, Bulletin 1965, Number 9, State Department of Education, Montgomery, Alabama, 1965.

Berger, Morroe, *Equality by Statute: The Revolution in Civil Rights.* New York: Doubleday, 1967.

Coleman, James. "The Concept of Equality of Educational Opportunity." *Harvard Educational Review.* 38:(1), Winter, 1968, 7-22.

Mackie, Romaine. "Spotlighting Advances in Special Education." *Exceptional Children.* The Council for Exceptional Children, 1965.

Mann, Arthur. "A Historical Overview: The Lumpen Proletariat, Education, and Compensatory Action." *The Quality of Inequality: Urban and Suburban Public Schools* (Charles U. Dah, ed.), University of Chicago Press, Chicago, 1968.

Nixon, Richard M. *SRS Newsletter*, January-February, 1969.

Weintraub, Frederick J. "Government and Special Education." *Encyclopedia of Education,* MacMillan Company, 1971.

Weintraub, Frederick J. "The People, Yes, Revisited." *Exceptional Children,* The Council for Exceptional Children, 1969.

Weintraub, Frederick J.; Abeson, Alan R.; & Bradock, David. L. *State Law and Education of Handicapped Children; Issues and Recommendations,* The Council for Exceptional Children, 1971.

White House Conference on Children. Report of Forum 22, The Rights of Children, draft copy, December, 1970.

Woodward, C. Vann. *Tom Watson, Agrarian Rebel,* New York, 1938.

Dunn's 1968 article became a classic in special education literature, and Dunn set into motion most of the current special education trends. However, his article evoked a variety of responses; and while many found the published message reinforcing, others disagreed. Nevertheless, it became the paper to quote; Dunn's thesis was used to support a variety of views. MacMillan is one of the few people to invest the required effort to respond from a scholarly position. He challenges several positions postulated by Dunn, but he also supports many of Dunn's observations. MacMillan draws upon his own research and an analysis of research by others to present his views. The paper is not an emotional response to the contrasting views of a colleague. Instead, it is a carefully written response based on substantive information. He argues that the problem is extremely complex and should not be oversimplified by polarizing special class placement against regular class placement. MacMillan's discussion on cognitive adjustment is particularly noteworthy.

Special Education for the Mildly Retarded: Servant or Savant

Donald L. MacMillan
University of California, Riverside

Seldom, if ever, has one single article had an impact on the field of special education comparable to that of Professor L. M. Dunn (1968) regarding special education for minority children labeled as educable mentally retarded (EMR). The debate stimulated by that article has been extensive. Some school districts have wholeheartedly endorsed what they perceive Dunn's position to be, and have moved toward total integration of EMR-labeled children into regular classes. In addition, state departments of education have made policy decisions designed to prevent misidentification of minority children as EMR. Clearly, Dunn has been an important influence in reversing a trend toward the

73

proliferation of self-contained special classes for the EMR, which he sensed and spoke out against.

For years preceding the publication of the Dunn article, concern was expressed by many special educators as well as increasingly militant minority groups about the overrepresentation of minority children in special classes for the EMR. However, it took someone of Dunn's stature to stimulate the field into action by recommending a plan for change in an attempt to ameliorate this social problem.

I do not agree with some professionals who apparently interpret Dunn's article as "proof" that EMR classes should be totally abolished—though admittedly nowhere does Dunn himself call for such a move. Certainly, some special educators have seen EMR classes as *the* way to educate children with IQs from 50-70, and this restrictive view has proven stifling (see MacMillan, 1969). Nevertheless, total abolition of these classes seems to me premature. For these reasons it seems time for the issues regarding special class placement to be clarified and for someone to re-evaluate the evidence on which the case was made by Dunn (1968).

In stating the reasons for a change, Professor Dunn presents *evidence* which supports his contention that special classes have proven a disservice to the mildly retarded. In the course of this paper that evidence will be re-examined, and other evidence of which Dr. Dunn was either unaware or chose to ignore will be presented. Hopefully, the discussion can bring to light the complexity of the issues presented which must be considered in deciding the most efficacious administrative arrangement for a particular child. Finally, an attempt is made to restate the problem as I see it and make recommendations regarding it. Specifically, the issues raised, and the bases on which my case is built, are as follows:

1. Though self-contained classes fail to promote academic and personal growth of the dimensions originally expected, such classes are still useful for some low-IQ children.
2. The method of identifying children as mentally retarded described by Dunn (1968) reflects a strict psychometric definition of mental retardation and thereby ignores the consensus AAMD definition.
3. Evidence on the effects of placement and labeling is sorely lacking; hence, these effects must not be considered as a sole *cause* of achievement and adjustment problems.
4. Adjustments in the environment which are strictly cognitive in nature are unlikely to aid learning in low-IQ children whose problems are emotional or motivational—a description which probably fits many minority children of low IQ.

5. The real issue is not whether special classes or regular classes are better for the mildly retarded, but rather the extent to which a wider range of individual differences can be accommodated in the regular class.

One point must be clarified before moving on. In no way am I arguing that homogeneous classes for children with IQs ranging between 50-70 or 75 is the best arrangement. Rather, on the basis of the evidence uncovered so far, I would contend that a self-contained special class may well be the best placement for certain low-IQ children.

SELF-CONTAINED SPECIAL CLASSES

A given administrative arrangement is neither good nor bad. As Goldberg et al. (1961) pointed out with regard to the gifted, what really counts is what is done with the group once it is established. The argument applies equally well when applied to the lower end of the intellectual distribution; hence, poor implementation should not be interpreted to invalidate the administrative organization. Indeed, a debate over which administrative arrangement, special class or regular class, for low-IQ children categorically degenerates into an academic exercise with no meaning for the real world.

For any given case, the better placement depends on many variables unspecified in the question of the efficacy of special or regular classes for low IQ children. Among the questions which must be raised are the following: (1) How competent are the teachers in each setting for dealing with the specific characteristics of the child in question? (2) To what extent has the child developed prerequisite readiness skills in the regular class? (3) How does the child respond to the consequences likely to be used in the regular class? (4) What is the general level of functioning of other children in the regular class, or to what degree will that child deviate from the other children? (5) Does the regular class teacher have the time needed to accommodate this child? Therefore, what is needed is an interaction model which includes, at least *administrative arrangement x child x teacher x children in alternate placements*, perhaps the least important of which is the administrative arrangement.

EFFICACY STUDIES

As Dunn suggests (1968, p. 8), an examination of studies on the efficacy of special classes is in order. Such an examination should, however, begin with the methodology utilized, not with the results. With few exceptions (e.g., Goldstein, Moss & Jordan, 1965) these studies could be described as poorly designed,

75

replete with sampling biases which render the results uninterpretable. For example, in both the Cassidy and Stanton (1959) and Thurstone (1960) studies, the investigators failed to randomly assign subjects to the self-contained and regular class placements. Therefore, the finding that EMR children in the regular classes exceeded the EMR children in the self-contained classes on some achievement measures is difficult, if not impossible, to interpret. More specifically, were those EMR children who were allowed to remain in the regular class left there *because* they were, in fact, academically advanced by comparison?

At the same time, the means of assessing "adjustment" in these two studies are questionable. Cassidy & Stanton (1959) used teacher ratings as one measure, while the Thurstone (1960) study used a sociometric device. In the former case the validity of the teacher's ratings is questionable due to variable frames of reference, while the latter procedure makes the results difficult to compare since acceptance within a special class is hardly comparable to acceptance in a class with higher ability children.

In the one study where EMR subjects were randomly assigned to the treatments (Goldstein, Moss & Jordan, 1965), EMRs in the regular class were found to achieve significantly better in reading at the end of a two-year period. However, by the end of four years the EMR children in the self-contained classes had caught up to the former group. Post hoc comparisons of low-IQ children within each group revealed that this subsample achieved significantly better on certain achievement measures than did the low-IQ subsample placed in regular classes.

Hence, the best controlled of the studies concerned with efficacy of special classes does little to undermine Dunn's contention that special classes have failed to live up to original expectancies. Raised as an empirical question, the fact that such classes have not been found to result in superior achievement or adjustment *must not* be interpreted to mean that there are no differences in the two placements. In the cases where significantly superior performance was found for the regular class placement (Cassidy & Stanton, 1959; Thurstone, 1960), the sampling bias renders the results questionable.

Using different criteria (i.e., social competence and economic efficiency) than typical achievement and adjustment measures, Porter and Milazzo (1958) concluded that the post-school adjustment of children who had been enrolled in special classes was markedly superior to that of equally retarded children who had remained in regular classes. Again, the small sample size (twelve in each group) and the sampling procedures render definite conclusions hazardous.

While Dunn (1968) cites Kirk's (1964) review as supportive of his contention that retarded pupils make as much or more progress in regular grades as they do in special education, he fails to include Kirk's mention of the pitfalls inherent in the studies which deal with the special-versus-regular class debate:

1. Problems in sampling—taking *in situ* groups to compare.
2. No control over the length of time spent in special classes prior to the evaluation.
3. Lack of a delineation of a special class, the curriculum, or the teacher qualifications.
4. Measurement instruments used in the studies were often improvised and, therefore, of questionable validity and reliability.

Kirk goes on to conclude that "until we obtain well-controlled studies of a longitudinal nature, our opinions about the benefits or detriments of special classes will remain partly in the realm of conjecture" (Kirk, 1964, p. 63).

The teacher variable has defied educational researchers in evaluating curricula and administrative arrangements since the beginning of educational research. Likewise, the failure to control this variable has plagued the attempts at evaluating special classes. Any particular low-IQ child placed with the "right" teacher, regardless of the administrative arrangement, is likely to benefit. Unfortunately, the reverse is just as true. In a recent article, Davis (1970) argues that because of the demand for more and more teachers in classes for the mentally retarded, requirements for specific credentials are frequently modified or postponed. While one *would not* consider being operated on by a surgeon operating on a "postponement of requirements" or being defended in a court of law by a lawyer operating on a "partial fulfillment of requirements," we seem satisfied to allow children identified as needing special teaching skills to learn under the direction of a teacher whose preparation fails to meet *minimal* standards as set by a particular state. Is it any wonder, then, that the children assigned to such a setting have not progressed at a rate considered appropriate? To what extent are the "failures" of special classes attributable to the administrative arrangement *per se*, and to what extent attributable to the teacher's inadequacies?

Related to the above discussion is the possibility that teachers of the mentally retarded enjoy little status in the schools. A study by Jones and Gottfried (1966) had teachers rate the prestige of teachers of various exceptionalities (e.g., severely retarded, blind, gifted, orthopedically handicapped). They found that teachers of the EMR enjoy little status among colleagues and individuals in teacher-training. The most dramatic finding, however, was that the teachers of the EMR rated themselves lower than they were rated by regular classroom teachers. Hence, not only are they assigned little prestige in the schools, but they appear to accept the lack of prestige as being justified. If the above findings are taken at face value, they well might support Dunn; however, it may also reflect a phenomenon related to the *type* of teacher attracted to this phase of special education. If we attract those threatened by regular classes or those who are not as capable, then the failure of special classes must not be interpreted as a failure of the administrative arrangement *per se*, but rather a failure of implementation. If we cannot determine how to individualize in a setting where there is one teacher for 15-18 students, are we ready to advise on how individualization can occur in a setting with 30 children and one teacher?

IDENTIFICATION PROCESS

On the point that numerous minority children are inappropriately labeled as EMR, I find myself in complete agreement with Professor Dunn. The stigma attached to this lable very probably operates in direct opposition to the potential advantages attributed to reduced pupil/teacher ratio. Of course, special educators tend not to participate in the identification procedure, often deferring judgment instead to the psychologist, psychometrist, or physician— and in most cases it is the latter upon whom the focus of this criticism should probably be directed.

The precise reason so much consideration went into the development of a flexible definition of mental retardation by the American Association on Mental Deficiency (AAMD) with the support of the National Institute of Mental Health was to deal with the borderline cases (Heber, 1959; revised, 1961). Severely and profoundly retarded individuals are identified with a minimum of difficulty, but borderline cases require careful attention. The definition agreed upon was "Mental retardation refers to subaverage general intellectual functioning which originates during the developmental period and is associated with impairment in adaptive behavior" (Heber, 1961, p. 3).

Clearly, three specific criteria must be met before an individual is to be considered retarded: (1) IQ is at least one standard deviation below the population mean, (2) mental retardation must occur prior to age 16, and (3) there must be evidence indicating impaired adjustment. The absence of any one of the three criteria should preclude placement in a special class. In practice, an intelligence test may on occasion be used to "justify the label 'mentally retarded' " (Dunn, 1968, p. 9); however, such a practice goes on in violation of criteria constituted to determine the presence of the condition or state labeled as mentally retarded.

Most professionals in the field of mental retardation feel somewhat uneasy about the reliance upon IQ in diagnosing retardation, particularly when dealing with borderline cases involving minority children from culturally different backgrounds. Clausen (1967) stated what many others have come to realize when attempting to use the AAMD classification system: namely, that there are few guidelines for determining an impairment in adaptive behavior. As a result, one makes extremely subjective evaluations of "social adequacy"; hence, clinicians ignore social adequacy and make the diagnosis on the basis of general intellectual functioning alone.

Alternative tacks may be taken in attempts to deal with the above problem. Clausen (1967) suggests that cut-off be dropped from one standard deviation below the mean (i.e., IQ = 84-85) to two standard deviations (i.e., IQ = 68-70) for evidence of subaverage intellectual functioning. He contends that below IQ = 70 or 75 individuals tend to show evidence of impaired social adaptive behavior caused by the low level of intellectual functioning (Clausen, 1967, p. 743). This would appear to be Dunn's preference. In his recent address, Dunn (1970) set the following IQ cut-offs for EMR placement: Anglo children, IQ = 70; American Indian children, IQ = 65; and inner-city black children, IQ = 55. Such limits are arbitrary and still reflect a psychometric definition of retardation of which Dunn (1968) was critical.

Another approach would be to develop more objective means of assessing adaptive behavior which would be valid for use with borderline children of minority status. Such an attempt has been made by Mercer (1970) on an experimental basis. Her adaptive behavior scales and pluralistic norms provide an interesting and promising alternative to the strict psychometric classification system used by some.

It has been my experience that committees charged with considering EMR placement for a child approach the task with far more consideration than was implied by Dunn. Before such a conference is called, two pieces of information are already available. First, the child's performance in the regular class has been poor enough, by comparison to the class as a whole, to attract the teacher's attention. Second, an individual intelligence test (usually supplemented by an entire battery of tests) has been administered on which the child scores below the district cut-off for EMR (usually IQ of 70).

At this point, I must agree that minority children are at a particular disadvantage when it comes to taking an intelligence test. Specifically, I suspect emotional and motivational variables prevent many such children from performing near the level of which they are capable. Riessman (1962) refers to this as the issue of the relation of examiner to examined. When examiners who differ from the children on the basis of social class and ethnic origin see the child briefly, it is difficult to establish the type of rapport conducive to best functioning of the child (Pasamanick & Knobloch, 1955). Performance, then, becomes difficult to evaluate since it could reflect the effects of poor relations between the examiner and the examined or a true measure of a child's abilities and achievements. Psychologists and psychometrists charged with evaluating children from different social and/or ethnic backgrounds might find the procedures reported in Hertzig et al. (1968) or the "optimizing" test conditions used by Zigler and Butterfield (1968) as helpful in countering this source of bias.

One may argue that tests of intelligence in use are culturally biased and thereby discriminate against the minority child. However, they are biased in the same direction as are the schools. As a result, these instruments do have rather good predictive validity on a short term basis. Taken in combination (regular class problems plus low IQ), these bits of evidence tell us that this child is likely to continue encountering problems if he is left in the regular classroom and presented with a standard curriculum. In other words, this child needs something "special." In such a context, special education is not synonymous with self-contained class.

Among minority children meeting the two criteria specified above, there are at least several *types* of children:

1. Bilingual children (e.g., Chicano, Puerto Rican) in need of accommodation in the area of language but who, genotypically speaking, are not defective or retarded.
2. Children from environments described as impoverished, in that they are lacking in materials or experiences considered beneficial to a child in adjusting to the school. Again, these children are not genotypically retarded.
3. Children who have developed failure sets—i.e., who have poor self-concepts and expect to fail before they even attempt a task.
4. Children of dull-normal ability with so much emotional overlay that their performance in school and on the intelligence test is depressed below the district cut-off.
5. Children who simply received a poor genetic pool or suffered prenatal, paranatal, or postnatal damage resulting in lowered cognitive capacity. These children are genotypically retarded.

Obviously one could go on to specify greater numbers of types, and any typology suffers from ignoring within-type variance. However, the point to be made concerns the nature of the "something special" needed by each of the types of minority children of low IQ described. In what kind of administrative arrangement can an individual child maximally benefit? In some cases (such as those described in 2 and 3 above) a resource specialist, as described by Dunn, may be sufficient. In others (such as 1, 4, and 5) a more intensive program may be needed. Some, in fact, may be best off in a self-contained special class! In none of the cases should the child be allowed to flounder in a regular class with no ancillary services.

Before leaving the topic of placement, I should mention the fact that many minority children whose IQs alone would warrant EMR placement remain in regular classes. In her demographic study, Mercer (1970) identified a group of children she labelled as *eligibles*—IQ below 75 but for a variety of reasons not placed in EMR classes. Most of these eligibles were functioning adequately in the regular program. It should be noted, however, that IQ alone did not appear to automatically result in EMR placement. Rather, other variables in addition to IQ were considered; and those with low IQ but adequate functioning remained in regular classes.

EFFECTS OF PLACEMENT

While my suspicion coincides with Dunn's with respect to the operation of a self-fulfilling prophecy, the dynamics underlying such a phenomenon are complex and far from fully understood. If one could extrapolate so easily from the Rosenthal and Jacobsen (1968) work as is implied by Dunn, the problem could be solved immediately by simply labeling the children under considera-tion "gifted" and thereby increase the teachers' expectancy for them to succeed. Secondly, the methodology underlying research on expectancy appears to affect the results considerably (see Barber & Silver, 1968a, 1968b, and Rosenthal's response, 1968); and the hypothesis testing utilized is often inappropriate. Thirdly, using the Rosenthal and Jacobsen (1968) work to any extent as support for the operation of a self-fulfilling prophecy is hazardous in light of the telling critique of Thorndike (1968). In discussing the study he states:

> Alas, it is so defective technically that one can only regret that it ever got beyond the eyes of the original investigators! Though the volume may be an effective addition to educational propagandizing, it does nothing to raise the standards of educational research. [p. 708]

In addition to the self-fulfilling prophecy, the principal objection raised by Dunn concerns the effects of labels upon the child. Granted, the label "mentally retarded" is not a badge of distinction. Neither, however, is being called "dummy" by higher ability children in the regular class typically prescribed for such children. Again, the effects of such a label are likely to be varied. In discussing the concern over the negative effects of such labels, Goldstein (1963) writes:

> There are those who wish to avoid the false positives inherent in early placement. They express the very reasonable fear that some children will be tainted unjustifiably with the label "retarded" if they are admitted to a special class at age six and later gain intellectually beyond the upper limits for such classes. However, we must not overlook the fact that such a child, through his academic achievement in an appropriate regular class placement, stands an excellent chance of erasing the label.

> Instead of becoming preoccupied solely with labels and stigma, we might do well to look at the other side of the coin and ask what efforts delayed placement has on the

personality development of the child, the status he acquires among his regular class peers, and the pressures placed on the family. In all justice, we cannot close our eyes to the fact that the retarded child in the regular class can be and frequently is labeled by his peers in much the same way as children in special classes. [pp. 12, 52]

Some empirical evidence is available on the last point made by Goldstein. Johnson (1950) and Johnson and Kirk (1950) studied the social position of retarded children in regular classes. Unfortunately, the sampling problems discussed earlier regarding efficacy studies contaminates the findings of these studies as well. A type of psychological segregation was found typical for retardates in regular class placements in both studies. Johnson (1950) did, however, find approximately 5% of the retardates identified as "stars" on a sociometric device. It would be interesting to have descriptions of these children, in that it might indicate characteristics associated with high social standing in a regular class which could aid us in determining which EMR children might profit from such placements.

The evidence cited by Dunn as supportive of the negative impact of such labels warrants a closer look. Goffman (1961) does, in fact, discuss the stripping and mortification of the self—important concepts indeed in understanding the careers of inmates of institutions such as monasteries, military camps, prisons, and mental hospitals. Note, however, that the institutions mentioned do not even include institutions for the mentally retarded. Among the degrading experiences described (Goffman, 1957) are the removal of personal clothing and possessions, the restrictions on privacy, the reduction of independence of movement and decision, the restriction of communication with the outside world. These experiences are hardly typical in a special class for the EMR. Hence, extrapolation of findings from these settings to a setting (i.e., self-contained EMR class) which is not an institution and contains individuals who are labeled in an altogether different manner from the above groups seems risky at best. At the same time, Dunn failed to mention the work of Edgerton & Sabagh (1962) which did apply Goffman's constructs to patients in an institution for the mentally retarded. These investigators studied stripping and mortification as they applied to the careers of the mentally retarded and their findings were not consistent with those of Goffman (1961).

Edgerton and Sabagh (1962) suggest that the mortifications of the self may be fewer within institutions for the high-grade retardate than in the case of the outside. In fact, for the high-grade retardate there may be certain *aggrandizements* of the self accrued as a result of having low-grade retardates with whom to compare himself for greater social success within the institution, the support and approval from ward personnel, and the opportunity for validation of his normality provided by his peers. As noted by Cromwell (1963), these arguments are reminiscent of the rationale presented by Johnson & Kirk (1950) with regard to the EMR in special classes. That is, the social position of the EMR is improved when placed in a setting where the mean IQ is reduced.

The effect a label such as "mentally retarded" has on a given child depends on a whole host of variables. To begin with, it is necessary to examine his pre-identification career. To what extent has the child been labeled "dumb" or "stupid" by peers or others (e.g., parents, teachers, and other adults)? To what extent has he been isolated or rejected socially in the regular class and in other social situations? Answers to these questions provide clues to the extent to which the self has suffered mortification *before* he has been formally labeled and placed.

Secondly, one must assess whether or not the child accepts or rejects these external evaluations. If he rejects them, he is also likely to reject the "mentally retarded" label when the educators try to attach that to him. Edgerton and Sabagh (1962) describe children coming from minority families of low socioeconomic status as follows:

> This nonacceptance may have been facilitated by several circumstances. For instance, the entire family of the retarded person may have been rejected and mortified by the community at large and feel the need to protect its members against the onslaught of "authorities." Many of the mentally retarded come from families of low ethnic or socioeconomic status, and the family members may have had humiliating experiences with law enforcement or welfare agencies. Such a family will protect its members against those who "accuse" them of mental retardation and may not even believe that the accused actually is retarded, since his intellectual level may not be much below that of his relatives. To them, this may simply be another instance of discrimination against the whole family. [pp. 265-266]

In such an instance the child may be immunized against mortifications of the self, in which case the label may have far less effect than would be the case where the child accepts the label as accurate.

Once a child is identified, labeled, and placed in a special class, it would again be helpful to understand whether he accepts the label as accurate or whether he denies the accuracy of such a label. Should a child reject the label and find himself in a class with children of clearly inferior status, he is able to derive certain aggrandizements by means of comparision. Hence, he renews his attempt to define the self as adequate and rejects those things that challenge such a positive self-perception. It may be that for one type of low-IQ child the special class provides a haven which supports his denial of retardation, whereas a regular class would confront him with evidence and confirmation of his retardation in that his peers would be clearly superior academically. Such a situation would confirm the accuracy of such derogatory labels and disarm the child of his defense mechanisms.

Meyerowitz (1962, 1967) did study the effects of placement on personality characteristics of the mentally retarded, and it was done within the context of a study in which the subjects were randomly assigned to classes (i.e., Goldstein, Moss & Jordan, 1965). He did find more self-derogation in children placed in special classes; however, the findings are based on an instrument (Illinois Index of Self-Derogation) of unknown validity and reliability.

In conclusion, we do not yet understand the effects of placement on personality. On the one hand we find evidence (Meyerowitz, 1962) indicating that the child suffers in a special class, while on the other the evidence indicates that he suffers in a regular class (Johnson, 1950; Johnson & Kirk, 1950). In other words according to the evidence the child can't win—but all of the evidence is of questionable validity in terms of sampling bias, lack of control of pre-placement experiences, and the questionable nature of the criterion instruments.

COGNITIVE ADJUSTMENTS

Any discussion of grouping, of which special classes are one form, must ultimately consider the flexibility or inflexibility of a particular grouping arrangement. Special classes for low-IQ children came to be considered *the best way* to educate such children. Paradoxically, a field committed to individual differences appears to have assumed a homogeneity within the group labeled "mentally retarded." Despite the failure of evidence to conclusively support the special class arrangement, children achieving IQs in the EMR range have been placed in such classes and taught "the EMR curriculum" since it was assumed that they share common characteristics. About the only characteristic on which there is any commonality is IQ (see Berkson, 1966), while on virtually every other characteristic there is as great, if not greater, intragroup variability as among nonretarded children. Yet the adaptations which occurred have been principally cognitive adaptions of the environment.

In an earlier article, MacMillan (1971) argued that attempts to adapt the environment in special classes for low-IQ children have been basically cognitive adaptations. It is as if the line of reasoning went as follows: Since these children are *mentally* retarded, remediation must be designed that will ameliorate their *mental* deficits. Yet the literature abounds with evidence which indicates that for a high proportion of low socioeconomic status, low-IQ children, the problems in learning (or more accurately performance) originate in the *motivational* sphere rather than in the *cognitive* sphere (see Zigler & Butterfield, 1968; MacMillan, 1971). Hence, one of the reasons special classes have failed to achieve the degree of success hoped for may lie in the fact that these environments have tried to treat problems originating in the motivational sphere by adapting the environment to treat cognitive deficits. Such a lack of balanced emphasis would seem to doom a program to failure.

Zigler (1966) has summarized extensive evidence which indicates that motivational and emotional variables depress the performance of retardates below the level indicated on the basis of their cognitive development. In his American Educational Research Association address (1968), many of the findings with institutionalized patients were generalized to disadvantaged children. While space does not permit a comprehensive review of motivationally-related variables which probably affect academic performance (see MacMillan, 1971), three variables have been selected in order to show how such phenomena depress performance levels of disadvantaged children below what would be expected. The three variables are: expectancy for failure, positive and negative reaction tendencies, and outerdirectedness.

Expectancy of Failure. As a result of personal academic failure and social "histories of failure," many children develop problem-solving approaches characterized by the primary motivation to avoid failure rather than to achieve success. Failure occurs so often in their life space that such children approach a new task with an expectancy to fail before they even attempt the task (MacMillan & Koegh, 1971). The development of a failure set often results in a lowered level of aspiration which prevents a child from attempting tasks slightly beyond his present level of achievement.

Clearly, teachers must reverse this failure set if the child is to progress at the rate he is capable. Teachers cannot allow the child to avoid tasks which are slightly beyond him; yet, at the same time, they must protect the child from experiencing unnecessary additional failure. Techniques such as prompting, as opposed to confirmation, may provide a means to guarantee success while still "challenging" him with tasks which are not trivial and for which successful completion represents mastery.

Positive and Negative Reaction Tendencies. Zigler (1966) labeled the desire to interact with an approving adult as the "positive reaction tendency" and the wariness of adults as the "negative reaction tendency." Children who have experienced social deprivation desire to interact with an approving adult and at the same time are hesitant to do so because of their many negative encounters with adults (i.e., teachers). These two phenomena are thought to be positively related to the amount of social deprivation experienced and the amount of negative interaction with adults. In describing the operation of these two variables with disadvantaged children, Zigler (1968) writes:

Children who do not receive enough affection and attention from the important adults in their life space suffer in later years from an atypically high need for attention and affection. We find that such children, when faced with cognitive tasks, are not particularly motivated to solve the intellectual problems confronting them. Rather, those children employ their interactions with adults to satisfy their hunger for attention, affection, and yes, as unscientific as it may be, their need for love. [p. 21]

As the child expends energy protecting the self, less energy is available for solving cognitive or academic tasks. Hence, the teacher must cope with these motivational variables before the child can devote his energies toward the solution of academic tasks.

Related to the above discussion is the child's reinforcer hierarchy—a construct unique for each individual. Zigler (1968) contends that being correct is not as high on the hierarchy for disadvantaged and retarded children as it is on the hierarchy of a middle-class, nonretarded child. Therefore, one cannot assume that lower-class EMRs are putting forth a maximum effort in order to be correct. In fact, there is evidence to the effect that such children perform significantly better under extrinsic reward conditions than under intrinsic reward conditions (Keogh & MacMillan, 1971; Terrell, Durkin & Wiesley, 1959). Hence, it is essential that incentives be found on an individual basis which serve as reinforcers and which result in maximum effort on the part of the child.

Outerdirectedness. Repeated failure can also result in a problem-solving style characterized as outerdirected. Zigler (1966) described it as follows: ". . .the retarded child comes to distrust his own solutions to problems and therefore seeks guides to action in the immediate environment" (p. 99). As a result the child comes to over-rely on external cues, a tendency which runs counter to a normal developmental trend in which children become more innerdirected as cognitive development releases the child from his dependence on external cues.

MacMillan (1971) describes and suggests techniques for dealing with children exhibiting these motivational characteristics. As Dunn (1968) describes the role of the resource teacher, the adaptations of the environment are still primarily cognitive in nature. As such, the resource teacher arrangement for serving those low-IQ children whose performance deficts originate in the motivational sphere would seem as inappropriate as have those self-contained classes wherein the environmental adaptation has been cognitive in nature. Regardless of the administrative arrangement into which these children are placed, such children, in substantial numbers, are likely to manifest a high expectancy for failure, positive and negative reaction tendencies, and outer-directedness. Unless these motivational variables are dealt with by teachers, children of this type are unlikely to succeed in an integrated situation to any greater extent than they have in the special class.

RESTATEMENT OF THE PROBLEM

Special educators must not allow the present issue to become one of special classes versus regular class placement lest they find themselves in a quagmire analogous to that which resulted from the nature-nurture debates over intelligence. Yet, that is precisely what seems to be developing—polarization in which one group condemns special classes while another feels compelled to defend them. Implicit in the title of Dunn's (1968) article is the notion that special education and self-contained classes are synonymous, a notion which must be rejected.

The larger issue and one which if debated and researched could prove fruitful is *To what extent, and under what circumstances, can a wider range of individual differences be accommodated in the regular class than is presently the case?*

Attempts to answer this question would, first of all, have to determine the extent to which regular class teachers are accommodating the range of individual differences represented in their classes at present. Despite the new developments cited by Dunn, the evidence indicates that regular class teachers are unable to cope with the range of abilities they are presently faced with; hence, the introduction of children who deviate more markedly would seem inadvisable. While the list of characteristics (i.e., individual differences) related to success in school is long (e.g., achievement, behavior, language abilities, motivational characteristics), the IQ will be used for illustrative purposes because it is the one common variable on which EMR children differ from *most* children in the regular classes.

TMR Class, EMR Class		Regular Class		Gifted Class
IQ=25	IQ=50	IQ=75	IQ=125	IQ=150

At present, a regular class typically contains children with IQs between 75 and 125. Those children whose IQs fall below 75 or above 125 or 130 are thought to require "special" adaptations in order that they can maximally benefit from the educational experience. After all, that's virtually the definition of the exceptional child. Now the question becomes, how can we modify the regular class in such a way as to enable the child with an IQ below 75 to benefit maximally from that setting?

Hopefully, in attempts to modify the regular class in order to accommodate those children with an IQ below 75, a variety of educational models will be developed, implemented, and evaluated. Dunn (1968) outlines one such model in his article—i.e., the resource teacher to supplement the regular teacher. This model must not, however, come to be accepted as *the best* way to educate low-IQ children any more than the self-contained class has in the past been thought to be *the best* way. There should not be a proliferation of resource teachers, but rather a proliferation of different models all designed to provide for the accommodation of a wider range of individual differences in the regular class.

No one to date has advocated the integration of TMR children into regular classes. Obviously, they deviate too markedly on too many variables to make that arrangement feasible. So, however, do many EMR children; among their number will be some borderline cases of minority status. In the immediate future, the removal of large numbers of EMRs from special classes and replacement into regular classes would seem inadvisable in that the regular classes do not appear capable of handling them. For the time being, then, it seems desirable to focus our energies and resource on three fronts:

1. *Preventive Programs.* Rather than constantly focusing our resources on the remediation of problems once they exist, we might focus on the prediction and prevention of learning problems. For instance, one might look to the possibility that certain learning problems occur because of unfortunate environmental demands which the student cannot meet. One might be able to identify certain skills (e.g., high verbal ability, docile classroom behavior) which are essential if a child is to be successful in a given teacher's class. If a child does not possess these skills, he becomes a likely candidate for failure in that teacher's class. Hence, it may be possible to prevent failure (and subsequent EMR referral) for some children by matching their abilities with a teacher in whose class these abilities enhance the possibility for success.

2. *Transitional Programs.* Assuming that the misidentified children in special classes for the EMR can be identified, the next concern is how does one enable them to move back into the regular program. Clearly, if such children are thrust back unaided the likelihood for success is minimal. Even though such children may warrant reassignment on the basis of IQ and social adjustment, most curricula for EMR classes lag behind in the presentation of tool subjects. Therefore, intensive acceleration in tool subjects is essential if these children are to be placed in regular classes with their peers. How can transition be facilitated? A variety of transitional programs should be designed, implemented, and evaluated in attempts to answer the above question.

3. *Model Regular Programs.* At present, regular class teachers are unable to cope with the range of individual differences they find in their classes. Therefore, without rather radical modifications in the classroom organization and the development of teacher competencies not presently possessed, the feasibility of inserting children who deviate more markedly is questionable. The resource specialist described by Dunn (1968) may provide one model. Competency-based models, in which skills teachers must possess are specified, must be developed and evaluated. Subse-

quently, regular class teachers are going to have to be retrained or replaced. The former alternative will require inservice training of teachers, and this will require follow-up procedures to insure that the competencies taught are being developed and employed.

The innovations mentioned above will require development of many educational models, implementation of these models, and their evaluation. This means cooperation between researchers and school personnel. Without such cooperation, the results of such studies are likely to be invalidated by the lack of controls described earlier with regard to the special versus regular class studies. Unless the quality of the research is high, it will not provide us with the necessary information on which we must make educational decisions regarding children. School personnel will have to endure some inconveniences in order that variables known to affect dependent measures can be controlled (e.g., sampling, teacher variable). Conversely, researchers must involve school personnel from the earliest stages so that they can provide input on concerns of teachers and constraints opeating in the school setting. By working in concert researchers might control independent variables sufficiently to achieve tight research and, at the same time, research questions that will be seen as important by public school personnel.

REFERENCES

Barber, T. X. & Silver, M. J. "Facts, Fiction, and the Experimenter Bias Effect." *Psychological Bulletin Monograph*, 1968, 70, 1-29 (No. 6, pt. 2).

Barber, T. X. & Silver, M. J. "Pitfalls in Data Analysis and Interpretation: A Reply to Rosenthal." *Psychological Bulletin Monograph*, 1968, 70, 48-62.

Berkson, G. "When Exceptions Obscure the Rule." *Mental Retardation*, 1966, 24-27.

Cassidy, V. & Staton, J. "An Investigation of Factors in the Educational Placement of Mentally Retarded Children: A Study of Differences between Children in Special and Regular Classes in Ohio." U.S. Office of Education Cooperative Research Programs, Project No. 043, Columbus: Ohio State University, 1959.

Clausen, J. "Mental Deficiency: Development of a Concept." *American Journal of Mental Deficiency*, 1967, 71, 727-745.

Cromwell, R. L. "A Social Learning Approach to Mental Retardation." In N. R. Ellis (Ed.), *Handbook of Mental Deficiency*. New York: McGraw-Hill, 1963. pp. 41-91.

Davis, F. R. "Demand-Degradable Teacher Standards: Expediency and Professional Thantos." *Mental Retardation*, 1970, 8, 37-40.

Dunn, L. M. "Special Education for the Mildly Retarded—Is Much of It Justifiable?" *Exceptional Children*, 1968, 35, 5-22.

Dunn, L. M. "The 70s: A Decade of Restitution from Special Miseducation for the Retarded." AAMD Region II Annual Fall Conference, Los Angeles, California, Nov. 14, 1970.

Edgerton, R. B. & Sabagh, G. "From Mortification to Aggrandizement: Changing Self-Conceptions in the Careers of the Mentally Retarded." *Psychiatry*, 1962, 25, 263-272.

Goffman, E. "Characteristics of Total Institutions." *Symposium on Preventative and Social Psychiatry*. Washington, D.C.: U.S. Government Printing Office, 1957.

Goffman, E. *Asylums: Essays on the Social Situation of Mental Patients and Other Inmates.* Garden City, N.Y.: Anchor, 1961.

Goldberg, M., Justman, J., Parson, A. H. & Hage, J. "The Effects of Ability Grouping: A Comparative Study of Broad, Medium, and Narrow-Range Classes in the Elementary School." Horace-Mann-Lincoln Inst. Interim Report. New York: Teachers College, Columbia University, 1961.

Goldstein, H. "Issues in the Education of the Educable Mentally Retarded." *Mental Retardation,* 1963, 1, 10-12 52-53.

Goldstein, H., Moss, J. W. & Jordan, L. J. "The Efficacy of Special Class Training on the Development of Mentally Retarded Children." U.S. Department of Health, Education and Welfare, Office of Education, Cooperative Research Project No. 619. Urbana: Institute for Research on Exceptional Children, University of Illinois, 1965.

Heber, R. F. "A Manual on Terminology and Classification in Mental Retardation." *American Journal of Mental Deficiency,* Monograph Supplement (rev. ed. 1961), 64, 1959.

Hertzig, M. E., Birch, H. G., Thomas, A. & Mendez, O. A. "Class and Ethnic Differences in the Responsiveness of Preschool Children to Cognitive Demands." *Monographs of the Society for Research in Child Development,* 1968, 33, No. 1, Serial No. 117.

Johnson, G. O. "A Study of the Social Position of Mentally Handicapped Children in Regular Grades." *American Journal of Mental Deficiency,* 1950, 55, 60-89.

Johnson, G. O. & Kirk, S. A. "Are Mentally Handicapped Children Segregated in the Regular Grades?" *Journal of Exceptional Children,* 1950, 17, 65-68.

Jones, R. L. & Gottfried, N. W. "The Prestige of Special Education Teaching." *Exceptional Children.* 1966, 32, 465-468.

Keogh, B. K. & MacMillan, D. L. "Effects of Motivational and Presentation Conditions on Digit Recall of Children of Differing Socioeconomic, Racial, and Intelligence Groups. *American Educational Research Journal,* 1971, 8, 27-38.

Kirk, S. A. "Research in Education." In H. A. Stevens & R. Heber (Eds.), *Mental Retardation: A Review of Research.* Chicago: The University of Chicago Press, 1964, 57-99.

MacMillan, D. L. "An Examination of Developmental Assumptions Underlying Special Classes for Educable Retardates." *California Journal for Instructional Improvement,* 1969, 12, 165-173.

MacMillan, D. L. "The Problem of Motivation in the Education of the Mentally Retarded." *Exceptional Children,* 1971, 37, 579-586.

MacMillan, D. L., & Keogh, B. K. "Normal and Retarded Children's Expectancy for Failure." *Developmental Psychology,* 1971, 4, 343-348.

Mercer, J. R. "The Meaning of Mental Retardation." In R. Koch & J. Dobson (Eds.), *The Mentally Retarded Living in the Community.* Seattle, Wash.: Special Child Publishing Company, 1970.

Meyerowitz, J. H. "Peer Groups and Special Classes." *Mental Retardation,* 1967, 5, 23-26.

Meyerowitz, J. H. "Self Derogations in Young Retardates and Special Class Placement." *Child Development,* 1962, 33, 443-451.

Pasamanick, B. & Knobloch, H. "Early Language Behavior in Negro Children and the Testing of Intelligence." *Journal of Abnormal and Social Psychology,* 1955, 50, 401-402.

Porter, R. B. & Milazzo, T. C. "A Comparison of Mentally Retarded Adults Who Attended a Special Class with Those Who Attended Regular School Classes." *Exceptional Children,* 1958, 24, 410-412.

Riessman, F. *The Culturally Deprived Child.* New York: Harper, 1962.

Rosenthal, R. "Experimenter Expectancy and the Reassuring Nature of the Null Hypothesis Decision Procedure." *Psychological Bulletin Monograph,* 1968, 70, 30-47.

Rosenthal, R. & Jacobsen, L. *Pygmalion in the Classroom.* New York: Holt, Rinehart & Winston, 1968.

Terrell, G. Jr., Durkin, K. & Wiesley, M. "Social Class and the Nature of the Incentive in Discrimination Learning." *Journal of Abnormal and Social Psychology*, 1959, 59, 270-272.

Thorndike, R. L. "Review of Jacobsen, L. & Rosenthal, R. *Pygmalion in the Classroom.*" *American Educational Research Journal*, 1968, 5, 708-711.

Thurstone, T. G. "An Evaluation of Educating Mentally Handicapped Children in Special Classes and in Regular Grades." U.S. Office of Education Cooperative Research Program, Project No. OE-SAE-6452. Chapel Hill: University of North Carolina, 1960.

Zigler, E. "Research on Personality Structure in the Retardate." In N. R. Ellis (Ed.), *International Review of Research in Mental Retardation*, Vol. 1. New York: Academic Press, 1966.

Zigler, E. & Butterfield, E. "Motivational Aspects of Changes in IQ Test Performance of Culturally Deprived Nursery School Children." *Child Development*, 1968, 39, 1-14.

Since this manuscript was published in 1971, endless papers have been presented and published on alternatives to the special class model. This selection by Bruininks and Rynders, however, remains a current objective analysis of the special class concept as a model in need of revision if not replacement. In contrast to much of the current literature on alternatives, the authors are not promoting a particular model. Rather they have committed themselves to an objective review of the special class concept and of emerging alternatives. The summary section discusses the temptation of opting for alternatives without sufficient study. This type of article serves to remind educators that every program decision carries with it a long-term consequence on the lives of children and that such decisions should not be made hastily.

Alternatives to Special Class Placement for Educable Mentally Retarded Children

Robert H. Bruininks, John E. Rynders
University of Minnesota

Public schools first provided day school programs for educable mentally retarded (EMR) children in Providence, Rhode Island, in 1896. These initial attemps to provide special education services to retarded pupils assumed the form of special classes. Originally started as an effort to provide instruction for children who were typically excluded from the public schools, these special classes were felt to embody a more flexible approach to education than institutional placement, since they enabled slow learners to enjoy normal social intercourse with children in regular classroom programs. Considered controversial even in 1896, the opening of the first special class for retarded children was announced by a Providence columnist in a sarcastic article entitled "The Fool Class" (Kanner, 1964). None other than Binet and Simon (1905), inventors of the first widely used general intelligence scale, stated that "to be a member of a special class can never be a mark of distinction, and such as do not merit it must be spared the record" (p. 82). Even though early authorities recognized the limitations of such placements, special classes continued to develop as the primary means of providing special education assistance to retarded children.

Stimulated largely by support from parents' groups and professional organizations, special education provisions for retarded pupils have expanded dramatically in the past seventy-five years, particularly in the past twenty years. By 1966, more than 540,000 children were enrolled in programs for the mentally retarded (Mackie, 1969). Statistics indicate that by 1963 approximately 90 percent of the retarded children in special education programs were receiving instruction in self-contained special classes (Mackie, 1969). While the number of retarded children served by other organizational arrangements has undoubtedly increased since 1963, the self-contained classroom has continued to be the predominant pattern in special education for serving EMR children.

In recent years, disenchantment with practices in special education has been evidenced in the activities of a wide spectrum of individuals and agencies. A number of authors, for example, have discussed the inappropriateness of special class placement for educating many children classified as mentally retarded (cf. Christophos & Renz, 1969; Deno, 1970; Dunn, 1968; Johnson, 1962; Lilly, 1970). (Most of the present controversy has focused primarily on the issue of special class placement for borderline retarded children with IQs between approximately 70 and 85. The present authors believe that many of the arguments and issues in this area may be equally applicable to the problems of providing services to more seriously retarded children.) The growing disenchantment with prevailing practices in special education reflected in recent articles has resulted largely from the disappointing findings of empirical studies exploring the efficacy of special class placement for retarded children, and from the placement of disproportionate numbers of minority group children in special education classes (Chandler & Plakos, 1969; Dunn, 1968; MacMillan, 1971; Wright, 1967).

An article by Dunn (1968) has been a catalyst for much controversy and introspection among special educators over the issue of special class placement for retarded children. The central thesis of Dunn's paper is that special educators have been guilty of imposing special class placement on mildly retarded children, particularly minority group children from low socioeconomic status backgrounds. He further indicts special educators for their failure to develop viable administrative and curricular alternatives to special classes for mildly handicapped children. [The empirical support and logical rationale for the issues explicated by Dunn (1968) and others were thoroughly reviewed by MacMillan (1971)].

Empirical findings, legal pressures, and social consciousness have created heated debate over the issue of how the field of special education should respond to the needs of retarded children. Summarized in Table 1 are some of

Table 1
SELECTED POSITIONS ON SPECIAL CLASS PLACEMENT FOR EMR CHILDREN*

Pros	Cons
1. Research evidence indicates that mentally retarded children in regular classrooms are usually rejected by more able classroom peers.	1. Special class placement isolates retarded child from normal classroom peers.
2. Mentally retarded children in regular classrooms experience loss of self-esteem because of their inability to compete with more able classroom peers.	2. Special class placement results in stigmatizing the retarded child, resulting in a loss of self-esteem and lowered acceptance by other children.
3. It is logically absurd to assign children to instruction without considering differences in ability or achievement levels.	3. There is little evidence to support the practice of ability grouping for retarded or normal children.
4. Evidence on the efficacy of special classes is inconclusive since most studies possess significant flaws in research design.	4. Mildly retarded children make as much or more academic progress in regular classrooms as they do in special classrooms.
5. Criticisms of special classes are based ostensibly upon examples of poorly implemented programs.	5. There is little point in investing further energy in improving special classes, since this arrangement poorly serves the social and educational needs of children.
6. The alternatives to present practices are less desirable and would lead to a return to social promotion as an approach to dealing with mildly retarded children.	6. Other more flexible administrative and curricular arrangements should be developed to supplement or supplant special classes.
7. Properly implemented special classes are optimally suited to deal with the major learning problems of retarded children.	7. Special class arrangements inappropriately place the responsibility for academic failure on children rather than upon schools and teachers.
8. Special class arrangements should not be unfairly indicted for mistakes in diagnosis and placement.	8. The very existence of special classes encourages the misplacement of many children, particularly children from minority groups.
9. A democratic philosophy of education does not dictate that all children have the same educational experiences, but that all children receive an equal opportunity to learn according to their individual needs and abilities.	9. Special class placement is inconsistent with the tenets of a democratic philosophy of education because it isolates retarded from normal children, and vice versa.

*Most of the positions summarized in this table are based on recent articles by Dunn (1968), Milazzo (1970), Kidd (1970), Johnson (1962), Lilly (1970), and Christophos and Renz (1969).

the more common arguments advanced for and against special class placement for EMR children. While the validity of certain arguments on both sides of the present controversy appears beyond dispute, our contention is that much of the present debate over special class placement for retarded children has tended to result in the development of extreme positions—either unqualified endorsement of present practices or strident calls for their total abolition.

It is time to discontinue the needless squandering of professional energy on the dialectics of the special class issue. Unqualified endorsement of arguments for radical change or complete obeisance to conventional patterns contributes little to resolving the current challenges of providing equal educational opportunity to all children.

Little improvement in services to children is likely to accrue from demands to replace one form of organizational inflexibility with another, equally rigid pattern. What is required is not simply that children in special classes be returned to regular classrooms with no further assistance, but rather that a wide array of flexible service arrangements, intervention strategies, and support systems be designed to serve both handicapped children and their teachers. A focus on alternatives might reduce the present conflict by bringing the forces of change and those of conservation into closer juxtaposition.

The primary purpose of this article is to outline and discuss possible alternatives to special classes for serving the educational and social needs of EMR children. Along with an explication of various administrative and curricular alternatives, descriptions of selected programs will be provided which present a broader range of curricular options for children and teachers than are presently available through special class arrangements. However, to provide context for a discussion of administrative alternatives to special class placement, the following section presents a brief discussion of research findings and selected assumptions bearing on the controversy over special class placement for retarded children.

GENERAL FINDINGS AND ASSUMPTIONS

George Santayana once wrote that "those who do not remember the past are condemned to relive it." Special educators might in the future avoid many of the difficulties that have beset the development of past programs by examining the history of research and implementation of special classes for EMR children. Presented below are brief discussions of research findings and persistent assumptions related to this controversy.

The Evidence

During the past forty years over twenty studies employing a variety of research designs, instruments, and samples have reported findings concerning the efficacy of special class placement for EMR children. [The reader is directed to writings of Cegelka & Tyler (1970), Goldstein (1967), Guskin & Spicker (1968), Johnson (1962), Kirk (1964), and MacMillan (1971) for thorough discussions of the research findings in this area.] Early efforts focused on contrasting retarded children enrolled in regular classes with those in special classes within the same school systems. These studies typically found special class enrollees inferior to their regular class counterparts in academic areas, but comparable or slightly superior on measures of classroom adjustment and personality (Cegelka & Tyler, 1970; Kirk, 1964).

95

Since children are typically referred for special class placement for severe behavior problems as well as learning difficulties, retarded children in regular classes probably enjoyed advantages in achievement and may have possessed higher motivation to succeed in school-relevant tasks. This obvious selection bias favoring regular class children, along with the inadequate instrumentation employed to measure classroom adjustment and personality, rendered these early findings invalid.

Later studies sought to control sampling bias by using regular class comparison groups in school districts without special education classes (Blatt, 1958; Cassidy & Stanton, 1959). The findings of these studies were equivocal, with one study reporting no significant differences between regular and special class groups in achievement (Blatt, 1958), while the other reported differences favoring the regular class sample (Cassidy & Stanton, 1959). Again a sampling bias was present favoring the regular class retardates, since the regular class samples probably included a greater number of children who would not have been referred for placement in special classes (Goldstein, 1967).

Goldstein, Moss, and Jordan (1965) attempted to control for problems of selection bias by randomly assigning retarded children to regular or special class placements upon entrance to the first grade. Attempts were also made in this study to avoid the methodological shortcomings of previous studies by improving instrumentation, by standardizing the special class curricula, and by employing recently certified special class teachers. After four years there were no significant differences between the two groups in either IQ gains or academic achievement. *Post hoc* analyses of small numbers of low-IQ (below 81) and high-IQ (above 80) children revealed that the low-IQ children profited more academically from a special class placement, while the high-IQ children achieved more in the regular classroom setting.

Evidence from studies on the efficacy of special classes is largely inconclusive and provides little information on the effects of such placements upon children. Moreover, findings on the effects of placement on the personality development and personal adjustment of the retarded are particularly contradictory, leading MacMillan (1971) to conclude:

> . . . We do not yet understand the effects of placement on personality. On the one hand we find evidence . . . indicating that the child suffers in a special class, while on the other the evidence indicates that he suffers in a regular class. . . . In other words, . . the child can't win—but all of the evidence is of questionable validity in terms of sampling bias, lack of control of preplacement experiences, and the questionable nature of the criterion measures. [p. 1]

Inadequacies in research designs and problems of interpreting the findings of studies concerned with ascertaining the efficacy of special classes for EMR children lead inevitably to the conclusion that *available evidence is less than conclusive, it is basically uninterpretable.* As Nelson and Schmidt (1971) have noted, "statements about the efficacy of special classes presuppose a number of prior statements such as efficacy for whom, efficacy under what circumstances, efficacy at what times, and efficacy for what goal ..." (p. 382-383). Until issues cited by Nelson and Schmidt are considered in efficacy studies of special classes, generalization of available data beyond sample populations is extremely hazardous. Equally evident is that knowledge about the efficacy of special classes contributes little toward resolving the present controversy. Available data can be applied with equal validity to arguments favoring the maintenance of special classes as well as to those recommending the abolition of such placements. The polemical arguments, in short, remain more political than educational (Engel, 1969) and gather little or no support from the nearly forty years of reported research.

One need that becomes painfully evident from a review of past research efforts is that researchers have chosen to ignore the possibility that existing administrative arrangements in special education may affect individual children in different ways. Furthermore, the validity of extant findings is based on a number of unproven assumptions regarding the nature of special class programs. The following section explores a few of the persistent assumptions which have guided the expansion of services for retarded children.

Persistent Assumptions

Throughout the past sixty years several persistent assumptions regarding the nature and purposes of special classes have been invoked to defend program expansion. It will be instructive to examine these assumptions in order to extend our perspective on the present controversy, as well as to improve our understanding of the issues involved in the development of programs for handicapped children.

Homogeneous grouping. Special class programs for retarded children were considered for instructional purposes as a means of narrowing the range of intragroup differences in children. The supposition was that children with IQ scores between 50 and 80 who were placed in special classes possessed highly similar instructional needs.

The contention that the range of IQ scores is reduced in special classes cannot be disputed. The range in special classes of individual differences on important educational characteristics, however, is not necessarily reduced correspondingly. In a large metropolitan area survey, the authors found that several special classes included children with reading achievement scores ranging from nonreading to sixth grade levels. The variability in other educationally relevant characteristics of these special classes was probably equally heterogeneous, resulting in groups of children with a wide rather than a narrow range of individual differences. Other studies have reported greater intragroup variability in performance on a variety of learning tasks among retardates than among normals (MacMillan, 1971). Thus, it appears that special classes do not necessarily contain children with highly similar learning needs and characteristics.

Concepts of diagnosis are in large part responsible for viewing children in special classes as homogeneous groups, defeating the intent to provide individualized instruction. Figure 1 depicts the tautological reasoning which underlies much of the diagnostic and testing efforts in special education. This figure suggests that children are referred initially for specialized services because of specific problems in learning and/or adjustment. (No assumption is being made regarding the cause of the child's problem.) Following the initial referral, an assessment of the child is conducted in the areas of intelligence and achievement. If the child scores low enough on the intelligence test, he is generally referred for special education assistance. By the end of the diagnostic sequence, however, mental retardation emerges as a causal explanation of the child's problem(s). This specious ascription of causation to correlated events often leads to the conclusion that the problems of children with similar IQ scores arise from the same source (Reynolds, 1970). Once an assignment is made to a special class there is a strong inclination to view children on the basis of group rather than individual criteria.

No available evidence supports the contention that special classes include children exhibiting similar educational needs, or that such placements lead to greater individualization of instruction. Unfortunately the assumption that children with similar intelligence quotients also resemble each other closely on other behavioral characteristics was seldom questioned in the development and implementation of programs.

Unique curriculum. Another persistent assumption in special education was that special classes afforded an opportunity to provide specialized curriculum for retarded children. While special educators publicly castigated the concept of the "watered-down" curriculum, programs in special classes actually closely resemble the types of experiences provided children in regular classes. In reviewing over 250 curriculum guides for mentally retarded children, Simches and Bohn (1963) were led to conclude:

> . . . The indication is that special educators feel, that although much work is yet to be done in regard to refinement, what exists are essentially different curricula. . . . What does exist is the rephrasing and reemphasizing of available courses of study used for normal children that do not even have the benefit of the form, structure, and sequence connected with standard curriculum development. [pp. 86. 115]

The conclusions of Simches and Bohn suggest that the assumption of differentiated, carefully sequenced curricula for mentally retarded pupils was rarely implemented in special class programs.

Figure 1
TYPICAL DIAGNOSTIC SEQUENCE IN SPECIAL EDUCATION

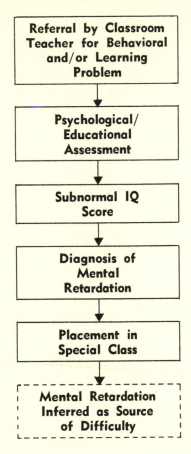

Specially trained teachers. With the development of special classes, certification standards for teachers were prescribed in most states. State, college and university training standards for special class teachers typically specified lists of courses for certification rather than competencies necessary to teach children. The only truly comprehensive survey concerned with determining the competencies necessary to teach retarded children was published by Mackie, Williams and Dunn (1957). For some unknown reason, however, the issue of what competencies special class teachers should possess was given only token consideration in professional literature or training programs in special education.

There is little evidence that training programs in special education have systematically evaluated the extent to which their trainees have mastered prescribed and agreed upon teaching skills. Instead, the stress in training programs has ostensibly been placed upon increasing the number of available teachers rather than on the quality of training, which leads to what Davis (1970) has characterized as a condition of "demand-degradable teacher standards" in special education. The assumption that specially trained teachers are necessary to teach retarded children in special classes remains untested. Moreover, there is little evidence that special educators have established unique training programs for teachers, or that they have evaluated the extent to which certified special education teachers possess the skills considered necessary to teach retarded children. While general educators may also stand indicted on these issues, the presumed advantages of specially trained teachers educating retarded children as yet remains unproven.

Summary. The persistent assumptions that special classes provided an optimal setting for individualized instruction, for providing differentiated curricula for retarded children, and for employing specially trained teachers remain untested. Ambiguity in goals and practices has resulted in a general failure to effectively implement special class programs (Brown, 1968; MacMillan, 1971). Considerable doubt exists, moreover, that special classes even if properly implemented are optimally suited to provide EMR children with individualized instruction, specialized curricula, or specially trained teachers.

The historical development of special classes provides instructive lessons to guide the future development of services for retarded children. The first lesson is that the tendency to grasp at convenient nostrums as complete solutions for complex educational problems should be resisted. The second and equally important lesson is that successful implementation of programs requires that the assumptions underlying program development be verifiable (Nelson & Schmidt, 1971), and that programs be continually examined to assess whether assumptions are being appropriately implemented. A third lesson is that programs in special education have evolved without the benefit of clearly stated goals and sound philosophical concepts. Because assumptions underlying the development of special classes have not been monitored, service arrangements have closely paralleled the educational program in regular classes. In short, very little of special education for retarded children could be considered either *special* or *specialized.*

EDUCATIONAL ALTERNATIVES

Over the past seventy-five years special classes have emerged as the primary vehicle for providing educational opportunity for retarded children. Unfortunately, during this period we have learned little about the precise effects of special education services upon children. The search for effective models for serving EMR children has been hindered significantly by the implementation of programs which exemplify unclarified purposes and assumptions, as well as by the general failure of special educators to develop service models based upon accepted philosophical tenets.

The search for viable educational alternatives for EMR children might be facilitated by applying general philosophical principles to efforts in program development. The *normalization principle* is gaining increasing acceptance among professionals in the field of mental retardation. When applied to problems of program planning and implementation, this concept appears to embody a philosophical principle of considerable potential. Developed in Scandinavian countries, "the normalization principle means making available to the mentally retarded patterns and conditions of everyday life which are as close as possible to the norms and patterns of the mainstream of society" (Nirje, 1969, p. 181). Application of the *normalization principle* to special education programs implies that retarded children should experience the educational and social activities generally provided normal children. Applying this principle to the problems of planning educational services for retarded children would lead to changes in existing service arrangements as well as in practices of allocating children to special education programs. If adopted, the *normalization principle* would encourage the development of an array of service systems, all designed to maximize the meaningful integration of EMR children into normal school routines. Under this principle no child would be placed directly into segregated service arrangements unless it was certified that he was unable to be served in normal settings, even with specialized assistance.

Another concept which might help guide program development is that of *individualization*. Considered as *raison d' etre* of special education, *individualization* more than any other word has served to symbolize special education. The concept is especially useful when defined as consisting of "planning and conducting, with each student, general programs of study and day-to-day lessons that are tailor-made to suit his learning needs and his characteristics as a learner" (Heathers, 1971, p. 1).

A commitment to the concepts of *normalization* and *individualization* might lead to overdue changes in the way children are assigned to special education services. Presently, children are allocated to special education services ostensibly on the basis of categories—i.e., mentally retarded, deaf, etc. (cf., Reynolds, 1970). While categorical designations such as mental retardation serve as indicators of educational problems, they provide little information of value for designing educational programs for children (Reynolds, 1970). Simply diagnosing children as mentally retarded accomplishes little. Instead, categorical approaches to planning instruction encourage practices of making qualitative rather than quantitative distinctions among children. Educational decisions about appropriate teaching strategies and organizational arrangements must be based upon relevant behavioral variables which predict differentially among contrasting instructional alternatives.

Stressing *normalization* and *individualization* in program development might clarify educational alternatives and identification procedures in assigning children to alternative, specialized programs. Perhaps a good way to gain some perspective on the matter of alternatives is to view the school as encompassing a variety of possible influences which contribute to each child's development. These influences take the form of (1) administrative arrangements, (2) instructional roles of staff, and (3) instructional materials. The impact of educational forces on the development of children, as depicted in Figure 2, can be conceptualized as representing thrusts of services in a school program.

Figure 2
EDUCATIONAL INFLUENCES ON THE DEVELOPMENT OF THE RETARDED CHILD

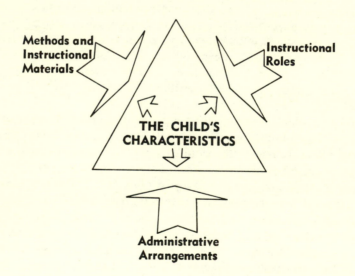

Implicit in Figure 2 is the contention that the educational difficulties experienced by children result from the complex interaction of several factors, including the child's characteristics, instructional content and quality, and administrative arrangements. [See Szasz (1970) and Clark (1970) for excellent discussions related to the causes of pupil failure]. If instructional alternatives shown in Figure 2 are viable, continuous, and sensitized to the needs of children, the retarded child is likely to thrive. On the other hand, if the options available are limited and insensitive to the individual needs of children, educational development of retarded children will most likely be impaired. The child's educational development is thus dependent on the personal-social-cognitive qualities he manifests in interaction with the personal-professional qualities of instructional staff with whom he comes into contact.

An expanded concept of educational alternatives to special classes emerges in Table 2. Implied is the need for increased sensitization to the needs of handicapped children through resources potentially available in both regular and special education programs. The material in Table 2 and in Figure 2 suggests that special education assistance need not be defined simply in terms of administrative arrangements, but may also be defined in terms of instructional roles and specialized curricula. The undue stress by special educators on the issue of administrative arrangements has tended to obscure the rich potential for achieving truly differentiated instruction for children through alterations in curricula and/or professional roles.

In this section, selected aspects of philosophy, instructional methods and materials, instructional roles, and administrative arrangements were presented as primary ingredients in developing and implementing special education programs for retarded children. In the following section several programs will be discussed which present interesting, contrasting alternatives to special classes.

PROGRAM PROFILES

Individually Prescribed Instruction (IPI). IPI is an instructional system which is based on specific objectives, interlinked with diagnostic tools and teaching materials (Scanlon, 1971). It stresses assessment of pupil abilities and the continuous monitoring of pupil progress. As the pupil enters a new instructional situation, the teacher diagnoses his abilities through a placement instrument and an achievement pretest representing the objectives within a learning unit. Based on this initial assessment and her knowledge of the child's learning characteristics, the teacher writes a learning prescription utilizing the set of objectives and complementary instructional materials produced for the program. The teacher's role in an IPI program becomes that of progress analyzer, tutor, and instructional manager, in contrast to the more conventional teaching role of dispenser of instruction.

The child's role is also somewhat different in an IPI classroom than in the traditional setting. Though he is in a standard classroom, the child acts as his own instructional agent by working toward mastery of objectives that have been prescribed for him. As he finishes a piece of work to his satisfaction, he turns it

Table 2

EDUCATIONAL SERVICES FOR EMR CHILDREN

Personnel Roles	Instructional Resources	Administrative Placements
1. Paraprofessionals—support and extend the capability of classroom teachers.	1. Programmed learning materials and other self-instructional programs.	1. Nongraded, open school arrangements—self-directed learning, individually prescribed instruction, etc.
2. Case managers—assume child advocacy roles, coordination of services, etc.	2. Instructional technologies—	2. Regular class — special education support to classroom teacher.
3. Child development specialists—expand the capability of classroom teachers to accommodate a wider range of individual differences.	a. teaching machines b. computer assisted instruction c. closed circuit TV d. listening centers e. language laboratories f. etc.	3. Regular class — special education assistance to classroom teacher; short-term ancillary services to child (tutoring, diagnosis, etc.).
4. Instructional specialists—serve regular and special education teachers in consultative roles.	3. Instructional materials centers.	4. Regular class—intensive special education assistance to children and classroom teachers.
5. Resource learning specialists—serve children directly and consult with classroom teachers; specialize in particular developmental areas (language development, mathematics, etc.)	4. Diagnostic and prescriptive instruction centers. 5. Specialized curriculum materials and remedial education systems.	5. Special class—some academic and non-academic instruction in regular classes.
6. Diagnostic specialists — diagnose educational problems; prescribe appropriate materials.		6. Special class—only non-academic contact in regular classes.
7. Special education tutorial personnel—provide short-term assistance to children.		7. Special class—little significant contact with children in regular classes.
8. Special class teachers — serve very small groups of children with severe educational handicaps.		8. Special day school for retarded pupils—no significant contact with children in regular school settings.
		9. Homebound instruction—individual instruction for children who are unable to attend school.
		10. Residential school—contact with pupils in nearby community programs.
		11. Residential school—no significant amount of contact with pupils in community programs.

in to a teacher aide who scores it and informs the teacher of the student's progress. The teacher then represcribes work for him which coincides with that performance. When appropriate, she administers unit tests to determine content mastery and curriculum-embedded tests which measure progress toward an objective.

Based on principles of reinforcement theory, IPI is an instructional system designed to facilitate classroom learning through careful specification of objectives, pacing of instruction, and reward for mastery. Since this system does not depend on the attainment of any prerequisite achievement level, it is not dependent upon homogeneous grouping for its implementation. In an IPI classroom, retarded children might work at their own pace with normal peers without revealing their inadequacies in school learning which are often amplified in group instructional settings.

Downriver Learning Disability Center. The Downriver Learning Disability Center is an example of another program which emphasizes pupil assessment as an approach to planning instruction (School District of the City of Wyandotte, Michigan, 1971). The Center, supported by a consortium of twelve school districts, is an outpatient facility for learning disabled children in which specially trained staff accept individual referrals. In contrast to IPI, which includes a complete program of assessment, instructional programming, management, and evaluation, the Downriver Center staff perform the assessment function only, relying on the child's home teacher and school to follow through with his instruction.

The classroom teacher initiates a referral to the Center by sending a request to the local district's special services department. The school psychologist for the district administers some preliminary tests to determine the child's eligibility for learning disability services. From the total number of children within each district, the local district or the private school selects their quota to be sent to the Center. This selection is usually based both on the child's needs and the teacher's ability to profit from the Center experience.

On an appointed day the child and his classroom teacher come to the Center. The teacher arrives before the child in order to participate in some preliminary discussion of the case and to attend a general orientation session in which the diagnostic tests are explained. The teacher observes the child being tested and views a slidetape presentation of a demonstration of materials likely to be recommended for her child.

Toward the end of the afternoon, a Center staff member coordinates a case staffing conference including the classroom teacher, building principal, remedial reading teachers, speech correctionist, school district diagnostician and other persons involved with the child. During this conference, particular attention is paid to recommendations involving instructional suggestions. The Center instructs the teacher in the use of the materials which have been recommended and provides her with materials if they are unavailable within the district.

Ten weeks after the assessment, a Center staff member pays a follow-up visit to the teacher to discuss the child's progress and to help update the recommendations. Center personnel are also constantly available to the teacher for consultation.

The Downriver Learning Disability Center offers a promising approach to augmenting the regular class teacher's assessment skills and knowledge of instructional strategies, thereby reducing the necessity for special class services.

The next two programs illustrate alternatives which emphasize the structuring of teacher roles and use of instructional materials.

The Educational Modulation Center. This program is aimed at the improvement of a child's specific educational skills so that he can remain in the regular class (Adamson & Van Etten, 1970; Van Etten, 1969). According to the authors of the program, selection of appropriate materials constitutes an important and complex problem. Therefore, the Center has developed a retrieval system which matches a child's learning characteristics with the attributes of instructional materials which have been analyzed for specific content. Here is how the system works using a hypothetical case: A child is evaluated and found to be functioning intellectually at a level comparable to a six-year-old child. The evaluation has also revealed that the student has a deficit in alphabet recognition and that he has been observed to respond best to auditory material.

What steps are required to retrieve the needed material? First the diagnostician, utilizing the prescriptive materials retrieval system, selects the descriptor card for alphabet recognition, the child's specific content disability. The second card selected is the descriptor card appropriate for an intellectual level of a six-year-old. The third descriptor card selected is for taped material suitable for alphabet recognition purposes. When these descriptor cards are placed over a light box, an illumination process refers the user to materials matching all these descriptors. By changing or eliminating various descriptor cards, large amounts of material can be searched in a short span of time.

Though materials prescription is the major thrust of the project, consultants are also provided who work in classrooms to assess a child's abilities and explore educational approaches in cooperation with his teacher. Other services include consultative help for schools wishing to use prescriptive teaching techniques and a research program to sharpen the use of instructional methods and materials.

The Educational Modulation Center represents an inroad toward solving one of the major problems that has plagued special educators for a long time, i.e., the matching of instructional materials to selected characteristics of children.

Harrison Resource Learning Center. This program is located in an inner-city school in Minneapolis, Minnesota. Co-sponsored by the Department of Special Education at the University of Minnesota and the Minneapolis Public Schools, the Center has two purposes: (1) to provide direct prescriptive instruction to intellectually subnormal children enrolled in regular classes, and (2) to train special education students from the University in the skills of prescriptive teaching.

The Harrison Resource Learning Center is one example of how a school can alter the roles of its teaching staff by installing an educational alternative which can become an integral part of the school's teaching program. The resource teacher assumes direct responsibility for some daily instruction of children in areas of greatest educational need, as well as for assisting the child's classroom teacher in designing appropriate educational experiences.

Perhaps a brief case history would be helpful in illustrating the resource teacher's role. Charles (IQ = 68) has been in a special class for retarded children for almost a year. When the Resource Center opened, Charles was one of the first children recommended for placement back into a regular class with support from the resource teacher. At first, Charles spent most of the school day in the Resource Learning Center. The resource teacher began by emphasizing experiences designed to improve his self-confidence, while gradually increasing the demands placed upon him for achievement in basic school subjects. Over a period of two months, the length of time that Charles spent in regular class was gradually increased except for those periods in the regular class schedule when the material was beyond his skill level. During this period he gained more than one grade level in reading and almost two grade levels in arithmetic. His teachers and mother also reported a marked improvement in his attitude toward school.

Charles presently spends forty-five minutes per day in the Resource Center, receiving help primarily in reading. His resource and regular class teachers hope to reduce this out-of-regular-class time even further by designing instructional content that will permit him to progress without requiring an inordinate amount of the regular class teacher's attention.

In the first year of the program, eight special class children were returned to regular classes and an additional twelve out of twenty-eight regular class children who were on the waiting list for placement in special classes also received help. None of these children have been re-recommended for special class placement in the two years of the Center's operation.

Summary. The programs described above were chosen for discussion because they offer interesting and contrasting alternatives to special class placement for EMR children. Widespread adoption of these programs would be ill-advised, however, since there is insufficient evidence to judge their efficacy at the present time. Nevertheless, it appears that these programs are attempting to employ the principle of *normalization* by providing alternatives minimizing the perceived differences between the instructional experiences of retarded and normal children; these programs appear to embody the principle of *individualization* by customizing instructional roles, instructional materials, and administrative arrangements to suit the learner's perceived needs and characteristics.

SUMMARY

The central thesis of this article is that polemical arguments for and against special class placement for EMR children have achieved their intended purpose of making special educators sensitive to the inadequacies of current practices. Now is the time to begin the painstaking development, implementation, and evaluation of a range of viable alternatives. As an antidote to the present controversy that grips the field of special education, it is further recommended is that less emphasis be placed upon conceptualizing the educational difficulties of handicapped children in terms of categories (Reynolds, 1970) unless such classifications can be translated into effective educational treatments.

If the principles of normalization and individualization are to become realities in the education of EMR children, general education must also become more accommodative to individual differences in children. Fortunately, there are examples where this accommodation is occurring such as the Differentiated Staffing Program of Temple City (Stoner, 1969) in which teachers assume differing roles because of their competencies in specific instructional areas and strengths in dealing with particular learning attributes of children; ungraded schools which promote children on the basis of achievement and not on the basis of chronological age; open classrooms where young children play a major role in determining their instructional experiences (Silberman, 1970).

Special educators must invest greater resources in efforts to enhance the capability of general education to better accommodate the educational and social needs of handicapped children. Perhaps this point can be sharpened by viewing special education as developmental capital (Deno, 1970). Deno (1970) has recommended that special education serve as a vehicle for setting the general education system in competition with itself, initiating an internal challenge that will generate and sustain creative tension. In her words:

> The special education system is a unique position to serve as developmental capital . . . to upgrade the effectiveness of the total public education effort. It has the motivation and the justification to enter into cooperative competition with regular education, to act as advocate for those children who fall out or are squeezed out of the educational mainstream's sieve-like bottom half. [p. 231]

Attempts to improve present services for handicapped children should be firmly rooted in sound philosophical tenets. All too often special education programs have developed without proper consideration for statements of purpose and tests of assumptions. Ambiguity of purpose and failure to test the validity of assumptions have led to the practice of judging program effectiveness by the simple, expedient metric of program expansion. Special education services must be judged by their effects on the development of children as well as by the extent to which these services approximate those afforded children in general education.

At this time hasty attempts to abolish special classes seem unwise and premature. Instead, special class programs for EMR children should be restructured to serve only those children who cannot remain in a regular classroom, even with specialized assistance.

One major caveat must be considered in developing programs: *special educators should avoid impetuous implementation of alternatives to replace special classes.* Sudden implementation of programs without the necessary safeguards of objective evaluation leads inevitably toward institutionalizing program models without validating their effectiveness. The rush in many areas to replace special classes with resource rooms seems as premature and unwise as persistent recommendations to abolish special classes. Before any special education program is implemented, a number of prior questions must be pondered: (1) What are the goals of the program? (2) Whom should the program serve? (3) What are the major constitutents of the program? (4) What services (curricula) should be provided in the program? (5) Upon what assumptions is the program based? (6) What are the roles of special and regular education personnel in the program? (7) What criteria should be employed to judge the effectiveness of the program? (8) Under what conditions is the program effective?

Above all special educators must shed their preoccupation with the special class issue and develop comprehensive research and development programs designed to increase the quality, variety, and availability of services to handicapped children. Further attempts to provide instructional alternatives to special classes for EMR children will likely lead to trivial results unless such efforts are accompanied by careful planning and evauation. The interests of children we serve require that future research contribute to the development of programs by yielding information on the efficacy of services for individual children, rather than by focusing on the effects of treatments upon groups of children differing in a variety of school-relevant behaviors. This approach to research and evaluation in special education assumes that no program is best for all children, but that program effectiveness varies depending upon the characteristics of children, settings and personnel. An approach to research focusing on individual differences rather than group characteristics might lead to both accretions in knowledge and improvements in services to handicapped children.

REFERENCES

Adamson, G. & Van Etten, C. "Prescribing via Analysis and Retrieval of Instructional Materials in the Educational Modulation Center." *Exceptional Children*, 1970, *36*(7), 531-533.

Binet, A., & Simon T. "Upon the Necessity of Establishing a Scientific Diagnosis of Inferior States of Intelligence." *L' Année Psychologique*, 1905, *11*, 163-191. Reprinted in J. J. Jenkins & D. G. Patterson (Eds.), *Studies in Individual Differences.* New York: Appleton-Century-Crofts, 1961, pp. 81-90.

Blatt, B. "The Physical, Personality, and Academic Status of Children Who Are Mentally Retarded Attending Special Classes as Compared with Children Who Are Mentally Retarded Attending Regular Classes." *American Journal of Mental Deficiency*, 1958, *62*, 801-818.

Brown, L. F. "The Special Class: Some Aspects for Special Educators to Ponder." *Education and Training of the Mentally Retarded*, 1968, *3*, 11-16.

Cassidy, V. M. & Stanton, J. E. "An Investigation of Factors Involved in the Educational Placement of Mentally Retarded Children: A Study of Differences between Children in Special and Regular Classes in Ohio." *Cooperative Research Project No. 043.* Columbus, Ohio: Ohio State University, 1959.

Cegelka, W. J. & Tyler, J. L. "The Efficacy of Special Class Placement for the Mentally Retarded in Proper Perspective." *Training School Bulletin*, 1970, *65*, 33-68.

Chandler, J. T. & Plakos, J. *Spanish-Speaking Pupils Classified as Educable Mentally Retarded.* Sacramento: California State Department of Education, 1969.

Christophos, F. & Renz, P. "A Critical Examination of Special Education Programs." *Journal of Special Education,* 1969, *3*(4), 371-380.

Clark, K. B. "Fifteen Years of Deliberate Speed." *Saturday Review*, 1970, *53*(12), 59-70.

Davis, F. R. "Demand-Degradable Teacher Standards: Expediency and Profession Thanatos." *Mental Retardation*, 1970, *8*(1), 37-39.

Deno, E. "Special Education as Developmental Capital." *Exceptional Children*, 1970, *37* (3), 229-237.

Dunn, L. M. "Special Education for the Mildly Retarded—Is Much of It Justified?" *Exceptional Children*, 1968, *35*, 5-22.

Engel, M. "The Tin Drum Revisited." *Journal of Special Education,* 1969, *3*(4), 381-384.

Goldstein, H. "The Efficacy of Special Classes and Regular Classes in the Education of Educable Mentally Retarded Children." In J. Zubin & G. A. Jervis (Eds.), *Psychopathology of Mental Development.* New York: Grune & Stratton, 1967, pp. 580-602.

Goldstein, H., Moss, J. W., & Jordan, L. J. "The Efficacy of Special Class Training on the Development of Mentally Retarded Children." *Cooperative Research Project No. 619.* Washington, D. C.: U.S. Office of Education, 1965.

Guskin, S. L. & Spicker, H. H. "Educational Research in Mental Retardation." In N. R. Ellis (Ed.), *International Review of Research in Mental Retardation, Vol. 3.* New York: Academic Press, 1968.

Heathers, G. "A Definition of Individualized Instruction." Paper presented at Annual Meeting of American Educational Research Association, New York, 1971.

Johnson, G. O. "Special Education for the Mentally Handicapped—A Paradox." *Exceptional Children*, 1962 (Oct.), 62-69.

Kanner, L. *A History of the Care and Study of the Mentally Retarded.* Springfield, Ill.: Charles C. Thomas, 1964.

Kidd, J. W. "Pro—the Efficacy of Special Class Placement for Educable Mental Retardates." Paper presented at the 48th Annual Convention of the Council for Exceptional Children, Chicago, April 1970.

Kirk, S. A. "Research in Education." In H. A. Stevens & R. Heber (Eds.), *Mental Retardation: A Review of Research.* Chicago: University of Chicago Press, 1964, pp. 57-99.

Lilly, M. S. "Special Education: A Teapot in a Tempest." *Exceptional Children*, 1970, *37*(1), 43-49.

Mackie, R. P. *Special Education in the United States: Statistics 1948-1966.* New York: Teachers College Press, 1969.

Mackie, R. P., Williams, H. M. & Dunn, L. M. *Teachers of Children Who Are Mentally Retarded.* Washington, D. C.: U.S. Government Printing Office (O.E. Bulletin, No. 3), 1957.

MacMillan, D. L. "Special Education for the Mildly Retarded: Servant or Savant?" *Focus on Exceptional Children,* 1971, *2*(9), 1-11.

Milazzo, T. C. "Special Class Placement or How to Destroy in the Name of Help." Paper presented at the 48th Annual Convention of the Council for Exceptional Children, Chicago, April 1970.

Nelson, C. C., & Schmidt, L. J. "The Question of the Efficacy of Special Classes." *Exceptional Children*, 1971, *37*(5), 381-384.

Nirje, B. "The Normalization Principle and Its Human Management Implications." In R. B. Kugel & W. Wolfensberger (Eds.), *Changing Patterns in Residential Services for the Mentally Retarded.* Washington, D. C.: President's Committee on Mental Retardation, 1969, pp. 179-188.

Reynolds, M. C. "Categories and Variables in Special Education." In *Exceptional Children in Regular Classrooms.* Minneapolis, Minn.: University of Minnesota, 1970, pp. 30-38.

Scanlon, R. G. "Individually Prescribed Instruction: A System of Individualized Instruction." Unpublished paper. Philadelphia, Penn.: Research for Better Schools, Inc., 1971.

School District of the City of Wyandotte. " The Downriver Learning Disability Center." Application for continuation grant. Wyandotte, Michigan, 1971.

Silberman, C. E. *Crisis in the Classroom.* New York: Random House, 1970.

Simches, G. & Bohn, R. "Issues in Curriculum: Research and Responsibility." *Mental Retardation,* 1963, *1,* 84-87.

Stoner, M. *Temple City Story.* Temple City, Calif.: Temple City Unified School District, 1969.

Szasz, T. S. *The Manufacture of Madness.* New York: Harper & Row, 1970.

Van Etten, G. "Modulations Systems Research: A Proposed Model." Unpublished working paper of the Educational Modulation Center. Olathe, Kansas, 1969.

Whitehead, A. N. *Science and the Modern World.* New York: Macmillan, 1925.

Wright, J. S. *Hobson vs. Hansen: Opinion by Honorable J. Skelly Wright, Judge, United States Court of Appeals for the District of Columbia,* Washington, D. C.: West Publishing, 1967.

111

Mercer challenges traditional assessment practices used to place children in programs for exceptional children. She supports her position with data resulting from her own research with minority group children in California schools. A multicultural pluralistic assessment system is proposed. The system departs from primary reliance on formal intelligence tests to a focus on the child and his/her social situation. Special inventories are used to assure consideration of information relevant to the child's cultural background.

Crosscultural Evaluation of Exceptionality

Jane R. Mercer
University of California, Riverside

Although the United States is a pluralistic society consisting of persons from large numbers of different cultural backgrounds, the issue of cultural diversity and clinical assessment has been given relatively little attention. During the past decade, there has been a rising tide of protest from the Black community, the Mexican-American community, and other cultural groups over the disproportionate assignment of children from non-European cultural backgrounds to special education programs designed for subnormal children. Although difficulties in crosscultural assessment using standardized "intelligence" tests have been recognized since the 1930s, the issue generally has been ignored in actual clinical practice and training (Eells et al., 1951).

In a study of the process by which persons are labeled as mentally retarded in a southern California community of 100,000, we found that most agencies were relying primarily on IQ tests in making diagnoses. For example, 99% of the persons in classes for the mentally retarded in the public schools had been administered an individual IQ tests but only 13% had been given a medical examination. We found no evidence that school psychologists were making allowances for cultural differences in interpreting individual scores. In fact, Black and Mexican-American children who scored below 79 on an individually administered IQ tests were slightly more likely to be recommended by school psychologists for placement in special education classes than Euro-American children with similar scores. Such practices resulted in a disproportionately large number of minority children being labeled as mentally retarded and placed in programs designed for children who are assumed to have subnormal biological potential.

Various approaches have been suggested for crosscultural assessment: developing "culture-free" tests; modifying existing tests by translating them into other languages; changing administration procedures in order to vary the speed vs. power components of a test; differential weighting of verbal and nonverbal portions of tests; and developing culture-specific tests for each major cultural group in American society. Some of the limitations of each of these approaches have been discussed elsewhere (Mercer, 1971). We are developing an approach which differs significantly from any of these methods, a system of multicultural pluralistic assessment. This system is based on a set of assumptions which differ markedly from the assumptions of traditional assessment.

TRADITIONAL VS. MULTICULTURAL ASSUMPTIONS

Traditional assessment procedures are based on the implicit, unstated assumptions of the "melting pot" theory of society. Historically, public policy and public education in the United States have been based on the assumption that all persons from diverse cultures who migrated to the United States should become "Americanized." Americanization meant that persons from non-Anglo cultural backgrounds would relinquish their linguistic, emotional, and cultural ties to their culture of origin and conform to the predominantly Anglo-American core culture by learning English and accepting the values and traditions of Anglo-American institutions. The public schools have been the primary social institution for implementing the Americanization process. All instruction has, traditionally, been in English; and the curriculum has focused primarily on the study of Anglo-American history, literature, and social institutions.

Assessment has always been closely tied to educational institutions. Starting with Binet, the criterion for the validity of tests which purport to measure "intelligence" has been their ability to predict which persons will succeed in school. Because the public schools in the United States are the culture bearers for the Anglo-American culture, the content of "intelligence" tests inevitably has been selected from the Anglo cultural materials found in the curriculum of the school because such materials best predict academic success in the schools. Thus, clinical assessment has reinforced the "melting pot" process by defining persons who are not "melting" as subnormal. Assessment procedures have implemented a monocultural social policy.

Some cultural groups have attempted bicultural socialization for their children by sending them to private schools or developing supplementary educational programs outside the public schools. Such efforts are difficult to maintain in the face of a monocultural public school system. Although a child who can speak two languages and is familiar with more than one cultural tradition has a greater breadth of experience than the monocultural child, he may be assessed by standard clinical procedures as inferior to the child who is totally immersed in the Anglo-American cultural tradition and, consequently, may be more proficient in that single language and culture.

We believe that assessment procedures should be modified so that the bicultural child is not penalized for his biculturality by being defined as subnormal. To accomplish this end, we are proposing that multiple norms be developed so that the performance of the bicultural child can be evaluated *both* in terms of the dominant Anglo culture and in terms of the cultural milieu in which he is being socialized by his family.

Another assumption of traditional assessment as practiced by clinicians and psychologists is that evaluation of the academic skills needed to succeed in the public school provides a sufficient basis for making a diagnosis of mental retardation. The American Association for Mental Deficiency's definition of mental retardation defines a mental retardate as one who is subnormal in intelligence and adaptive behavior (Heber, 1961). We found little evidence that clinicians in the community were systematically evaluating adaptive behavior in reaching a diagnosis of mental retardation. The system of pluralistic assessment which we are developing is based on two behavioral dimensions—academic readiness as measured by a standard test and a systematic measure of adaptive behavior.

We also believe that any systematic assessment, whether done by the schools or a medical clinic, should include information about the child's health history and should include a preliminary screening for possible physiological problems. Thus, we believe that vision, hearing, and manual dexterity should be screened as part of the regular public school assessment process.

SYSTEM OF MULTICULTURAL PLURALISTIC ASSESSMENT

Our system of multicultural pluralistic assessment requires securing information from two sources, the child's mother or principal caretaker and the child himself. An interviewer secures systematic information from the mother about the child's adaptive behavior, the socialization milieu in which the child is being reared, and the child's health history and present impairments. The child is administered a standard, individual "intelligence" test (WISC, 1973 revision) and is also screened for vision, hearing, and manual dexterity. Each of these procedures will be described briefly.

Adaptive Behavior Inventory for Children (ABIC)

A child's success in learning the roles expected of him in his family, neighborhood, peer group, school, and community is the basis on which his social adequacy is judged by persons playing reciprocal roles in those systems. As the child matures, the behavioral expectations of society become more demanding and the number and complexity of social roles he is expected to play increases. His ability to cope with these increasing expectations constitutes his adaptive behavior. The child's ability to perform successfully in the social roles considered appropriate for his age and sex forms the basis of our Adaptive Behavior Inventory for Children (ABIC).

Our construct of adaptive behavior incorporates the sociological concept of the social role as a unifying focus. Adaptive behavior is conceptualized both as the development of skills in interpersonal relations and as an expanding, age-graded dimension in which the child gradually increases the number of social systems in which he participates and the number and complexity of the roles he plays in those systems. Increasing societal expectations revolve around three underlying dimensions: increasing complexity of the performance expected; the expectation that role performance will be progressively more motivated by internal than external controls; and increasing independence and freedom from adult supervision in role performance.

We are in the process of developing an Adaptive Behavior Inventory for Children (ABIC) based on these concepts which will be appropriate for children five through eleven years of age. This age span was selected because it is the period in life when children are most carefully scrutinized and are subject to the highest risk of being labeled as deviant. Items were designed so that very simple as well as very complex social role behavior can be evaluated. Items appropriate for children three through fifteen years of age are included in the inventory in order to provide a low enough floor to evaluate subnormal five-year-old children and a high enough ceiling to evaluate supranormal eleven-year-old children.

Question content for the inventory was collected from a variety of sources. The Adaptive Behavior scales developed for the Riverside epidemiology of mental retardation served as one source of items in all spheres of behavior (Mercer, 1973). Information from follow-up interviews with 268 mothers whose children had been placed in classes for the educable mentally retarded provided extensive information on the performance of children at home. Additional items were developed in consultation with Black, Mexican-American and Anglo parents of all socioeconomic levels who described in detail the typical activities of their children at home and in the community. Insofar as possible, behaviors were included that appeared to apply equally to all socioeconomic levels and all ethnic groups. Four social role spheres were covered:

Family Role Performance
> Care of own and family belongings
> Responsibility for younger children
> Care, dressing, and health of own body
> Preparation of food and use of equipment
> Family communication, decision-making, and scheduling of own time

Neighborhood Role Performance
> Independence in movement about the neighborhood
> Neighborhood play and peer group activities
> Work in neighborhood to earn money
> Neighborhood social affairs and activities
> Volunteer services to neighbors

Student Role Performance
> Learning and study habits
> Responsibilities assigned by teachers
> Responsibilities conferred by peers
> Social and athletic activities
> Academically-oriented activities

Community Role Performance
> Consumer-spender behavior
> Worker-earner behavior
> Independence in movement about the community
> Social, political, religious, and recreational activities
> Community service and volunteer activities

To pre-test the 500 items, mothers and fathers of children five through eleven years of age from all ethnic and socioeconomic levels were contacted. Pre-test questionnaires were completed by 250 Black parents, 230 Mexican-American parents, and 814 Anglo parents. To determine the approximate age placement for each question and the sequence in which questions should be placed in the age series, a least-squares, two-way analysis of variance was used. Responses to each item were compared for seven age groups (five through eleven years) by sex, by three ethnic groups (Anglo, Black, and Mexican-American), and by two socioeconomic groups (white-collar and blue-collar). Questions with significantly different patterns of response by sex, ethnic group, or socioeconomic status were discarded or modified. Redundant questions were eliminated or rewritten. Questions that respondents reported as ambiguous, inappropriate, unanswerable or unclear were either discarded or modified.

The question format adopted for the final version of the adaptive behavior inventory currently being standardized allows for three levels of response: nonperformance of the role behavior described, emergent behavior, and mastery. The interviewer enters the question sequence at the chronological age of the child and works backwards to establish a floor below which role behaviors have been "mastered." The questioning then proceeds forward in the chronological age sequence until a ceiling is reached beyond which role behaviors have not been performed by the child. A separate series of questions deals with non-age graded behaviors and focuses on interpersonal behaviors.

It is anticipated that the Adaptive Behavior Inventory will yield three additional measures that can be used to describe the socialization milieu of each child: a Level of Information Scale, an Opportunity Scale, and a Restrictiveness Scale. The Level of Information Scale will be based on the number of questions, both in the ABIC and the Health History and Impairment Inventories, to which the respondent gives a "Don't Know" response. Children being reared in foster homes or by persons other than biological parents or relatives may experience a type of anonymity in which the significant adults in their lives know very few of their personal historical details. The Level of Information Scale should provide a means of identifying anonymous children, and this factor can be taken into account in interpreting the meaning of a particular set of clinical scores.

During the pre-test, we found that some parents, especially in rural areas, were reporting that their children did not have the opportunity to perform certain social roles. Distance from populated centers meant that their children had not learned certain role behaviors because those particular roles were not a part of the socialization setting in which the child was being reared. The Opportunity Scale will be developed from these responses to provide a measure of environmental limitations on role performance. These limitations can also be taken into account when interpreting scores on clinical measures.

During the pre-test we found some parents reporting that they did not permit their children to perform certain types of roles because these roles were not culturally permissable for a person of the child's age and/or sex. For example, in the traditional Mexican-American home, an unmarried girl is not permitted to stay overnight with friends or relatives unless her parents are present. Consequently, all role behaviors which involve a girl's unchaperoned absence from the home after nightfall are culturally prohibited. A Restrictiveness Scale will be developed based on the "Not Allowed" responses. This information will also be used to help describe the socialization milieu in which each child is being reared.

Health History and Impairment Inventories

The system of pluralistic assessment also includes a Health History Inventory and an Impairment Inventory. Each of these measures consists of a systematic set of questions which the child's mother or principal caretaker answers concerning the child's health history and present inpairments. The inventories are designed as standardized instruments which can be used by a school nurse, a welfare worker, a school psychologist or other agency persons wishing to secure a brief health history or report of impairments in order to identify those children who may need further medical evaluation or special educational resources. The inventories are *not* medical evaluations. They depend entirely upon the report of the mothers and are subject to all the errors found in such reports.

The Health History Inventory covers four dimensions: prenatal and postnatal complications, serious acute illnesses, chronic conditions, and major operations and/or injuries. The inventory consists of a series of funnel questions. An affirmative answer to a lead question is followed by a systematic set of probing questions designed to reveal the nature and extent of the health problem as understood by the mother.

The Impairment Inventory covers six dimensions: vision, hearing, speech, use of members, activity limitations, and need for home care. In general, response categories covering each dimension are arranged in ordinal fashion from the least to the most severe. The respondent is asked to indicate which of the descriptive phrases best describe the current functioning of the child.

Sociocultural Modality Index

The third section of the mother interview covers the characteristics of the socialization setting in which the child is being reared. The index secures information concerning family structure; the socioeconomic level and education of adults in the family; information about the environment settings in which the parents were reared; a series of questions dealing with parental participation in community activities; questions on parental values; and questions on the use of Spanish in the home. Responses to these items together with information yielded by the Level of Information Scale, the Opportunity Scale, and the Restrictiveness Scale will be developed into a measure of the socialization milieu in which the child is being reared. This measure will be the basis for developing multiple normative frameworks within which the performance of a child can be interpreted.

Individual Evaluation of the Child

The test session with the child includes two primary measures: a measure of general academic readiness based on his performance on the Weschler Intelligence Scale for Children (1973 revision) and a Physical Dexterity Battery. The Physical Dexterity Battery includes the Bender-Gestalt Test for Young Children and a selected group of fine and gross motor-coordination tasks, height and weight data, and the psychometrist's ratings of the child's response to the test situation.

The Motor Coordination Screening includes short exercises that ask the child to touch the tip of the nose with an extended index finger, to hop, to tandem walk, and to tiptoe walk along a line of the floor. Use of the hands is observed for dominance and coordination with foot tapping. Other items include observation of the child following verbal directions using normal conversational tones. All of the performances evaluated in this battery are tasks which require a minimal amount of equipment and can be performed by a school psychologist in his office. Standardization data will provide important information which can be used in clinical evaluations.

Prognosis vs. Diagnosis

The use of the multicultural pluralistic assessment system requires rigorous differentiation between prognosis and diagnosis. A fundamental confusion in traditional clinical procedures has been one of mistaking prognosis for diagnosis. A *prognosis* is a clinician's estimate of the probable future course of any given condition and is his prediction of the probable outcome. *Diagnosis*, on the other hand, is an investigation of the probable cause or nature of a given condition. In medical practice, the physician ordinarily makes a diagnosis first and, on the basis of his diagnosis, then makes a prognosis.

Binet's original test was designed specifically for making a prognosis, that is, a prediction concerning which children would succeed in the regular school program without supplementary help. Although Binet's test was designed for prognosis, he gave it a name which had a diagnostic rather than a prognostic connotation. He named it a test of "intelligence." Today, testmakers usually name a test according to the type of behavior it predicts, statistically. That is, testmakers name a test for the kind of prognostic statements they can make based on the test score. If Binet had followed this principle, he would have named his test a test of general academic readiness because academic performance is the type of behavior his test predicted. Instead, he chose to give his test a name with diagnostic rather than prognostic implications and called it a test of "intelligence." Thus, educators, clinicians, researchers, and lay persons have come to view the IQ test as a diagnostic measure, a measure of the individual's "raw resources," his biological potential. They forget that the criterion used for establishing the validity of "intelligence" is no different from that used for establishing the validity of an "achievement" test. Both are designed to predict the child's academic performance. Both are prognostic measures.

If a child scores 75 on an IQ test, the school can predict with a high degree of accuracy that that child will need special help beyond the program offered in the regular classroom. This prognosis holds regardless of the child's race, ethnic group, physical disabilities, or socialization milieu. A similar prognosis could also be made from performance on an academic achievement test. Such predictions are useful information for educational programming. It identifies those children who will need supplementary assistance. However, it is essential that we recognize that a child's score relative to the standard norms on either a so-called test of "intelligence" or a test of academic achievement provides only prognostic information. The standard norms, alone, cannot provide diagnostic information for any child. They cannot tell us *why* a child's score is low.

The psychologist usually wants to go beyond prognostic statements. He wants to understand *why* a child has achieved a particular score. In other words, he wants to use an IQ test score not only for prognosis but also for diagnosis. There are many reasons why a particular child might achieve a low score on an IQ test. He may be emotionally disturbed by stress at home or school. He may have undetected problems in vision, hearing, or other physical handicaps that interfere with his learning the material in the test or with his test-taking performance. He may be excessively anxious in the test situation because of fears generated in the school situation. He may have been socialized in a sociocultural setting in which he had little opportunity to learn the kinds of cultural materials contained in the test. He may have less biological potential for learning than other children. Any or all of these factors may explain why a particular child received a low score on an IQ test. The task of the psychologist is to make a differential diagnosis and to determine which of these factors probably explain the child's score. The type of educational program prescribed for the child will depend upon this diagnosis.

In the past, public school testing programs and psychological practices have been based on the assumption that the primary reason for a low score on an IQ test is low biological potential. It has been assumed that the other factors listed above have relatively little effect on a child's score and can be ignored, except in those cases in which a child has suffered serious physical trauma or emotional disturbances. The system of multicultural pluralistic assessment will provide the psychologist with culturally relevant norms so that he can make a diagnosis as well as a prognosis for a particular child.

PLURALISTIC ASSESSMENT

In pluralistic assessment, the clinician begins his evaluation by identifying the sociocultural milieu in which the child is being socialized. We anticipate that five to eight sociocultural settings will encompass the major variations to be found among the elementary school children in California on whom the system is being standardized. In order to make a *prognosis*, the clinician will compare the child's performance with the socioculturally appropriate norms for the WISC and the ABIC. He will also examine information from the child's Health History, Impairment Inventory, and Motor-Coordination Screening to determine the extent to which the child's performance may be influenced by organic problems or physical disabilities. If the child's performance on the prognostic norms (i.e., standard norms) is subnormal but his performance on the diagnostic norms (i.e., socioculturally relevant norms) is normal and there is no indication of organic problems, then the clinician would conclude that the child's performance is reflecting cultural differences rather than individual subnormality. The child's educational program would be designed accordingly. Thus, pluralistic assessment would make it possible to distinguish between individual subnormality and cultural difference and would alleviate some of the monocultural biases resulting from exclusive reliance on standard, prognostic norms.

REFERENCES

Eells, K. et al. *Intelligence and Cultural Differences.* Chicago, Ill.: University of Chicago Press, 1951.

Heber, R. F. "A Manual on Terminology and Classification in Mental Retardation." *American Journal of Mental Deficiency*, 64 Monograph Supplement (2nd ed.), 1961.

Mercer, Jane R. "Institutionalized Anglocentrism: Labeling Mental Retardation in the Public Schools in *Race, Change, and Urban Society.*" In P. Orleans & W. R. Ellis (Eds.), *Urban Affairs Annual Reviews.* Vol. V. Beverly Hills, Calif.: Sage Publications, Inc., 1971.

Mercer, Jane R. *Labeling the Mentally Retarded.* Berkeley, Calif.: University of California Press, 1973.

Hurley focuses on the complexity of language problems experienced by "culturally" different children. He draws on his background in language and mental retardation to synthesize research results and the perspectives of theoreticians. Inductive teaching is presented as an appropriate methodology for the needs of the "culturally" different child. The author successfully integrates a conceptual discussion with suggestions for practitioners.

Strategies for Culturally Different Children in Classes for the Retarded

Oliver L. Hurley
University of Georgia, Athens

During the past few years there has been increasing concern over the misplacement of children in special classes for the educable mentally retarded. Most such children are minority group members, poor, or both. The President's Committee on Mental Retardation (1970, 1971a, 1971b, 1972) has documented this problem in recent years and made recommendations.

The fact remains, however, that a sizeable percentage of our special class children are culturally different; that the special class must meet their needs and teach them so that they can fulfill their own potentials rather than our predictions. The fact remains that proportionately few in special education have heard the expression, "The Six-Hour Retarded Child," and even fewer are attempting to do anything about it at the local level. The purpose of this article, therefore, is to suggest some methods that may help us work with these children.

THE INDUCTIVE APPROACH

One of the things that can be done is to teach the youngsters in special classes in such a way that their specific pedagogic needs are met and their potential released.

First of all, there should be a general methodology used within special classes that has as its ultimate objective the development of independent learners. One such method is the inductive approach described by Goldstein (1969) and used as a guiding assumption in the development of the Social Learning Curriculum. This Curriculum assumes that "materials should be presented systematically so that while a child is learning facts, skills, and concepts he is also learning how to learn" (p. 24). In order to accomplish this "learning how to learn," the Curriculum focuses at all times on the questions asked by the teacher and suggests a sequence of questioning based upon the five steps of the inductive method. It should be pointed out here that classroom verbal interaction research supports the soundness of this emphasis on teacher questions. Research with both the gifted (Gallagher, 1965) and the EMR (Minskoff, 1967) reveals that children produce the kinds of responses called for by the teacher's questions. This point will be returned to later. One implication from the data is that certain kinds of thinking are fostered if appropriate questions are asked.

The inductive process includes the following steps:

1. Labeling
2. Detailing
3. Inferring
4. Predicting
5. Generalizing

Labeling is the naming or identification of parts of a problem, elements in a picture. Labeling questions enable the teacher to diagnose areas of experiential or vocabulary deficiency.

Detailing is closely akin to labeling but requires finer discriminations and closer observation of stimuli. A response to a labeling question might elicit the words "orange" and "apple." A detailing question might call for attention to similarities and dissimilarities in color, shape, texture, location if in a picture or physically present, or any peculiarities specific to the stimuli present. Detailing is an elaboration of the label. Detailing questions serve to focus the students' attention on relevant and irrelevant characteristics. Detailing is the basis for categorization and multiple categorization of the same stimulus item.

Inferring is the process of applying the data collected in the first two processes. It is a step in the direction of going beyond the concrete. For example, if a picture of fruit also shows a few fruit flies buzzing around, the teacher might ask, "Why do you think the fruit flies are buzzing around?"—which requires the inference that the fruit is a bit overripe. Inferences are guarded predictions. They are tentative statements made with the option to withdraw or change them. Once an inference is made, a check of the data is necessary—that is, returning to the detailing phase to see if any cues were missed

123

or misinterpreted. If the recheck of the data reveals that some relevant cues (details) were not taken into account, then one can draw another inference. If the data support the inference, then one can move on to the next step.

Predicting is using the information collected to conjecture about what will happen in the future. For example, "What will happen to the fruit if it is not eaten soon?" Predictions should be verifiable to some degree. There are various ways of verifying: reading the next paragraph, performing an experiment, teacher or other pupil confirmation from previous experience, looking at the next picture, reassessment of the data. Sometimes, of course, exact verification of the prediction is not possible. This happens when the data is sparse or alternatives are possible. In such cases, the teacher should discuss the alternatives and their ultimate, probable, and possible outcomes with the class. For example, a discussion of "bullies" can lead to making predictions about the outcomes relative to the bully—"He'll get beat up by my big brother," "No one will like him," "He'll get sent to the Principal," etc.—or relative to those bullied—"They'll be unhappy," "They'll be afraid to come to school," "They'll cry," etc. Each of these predictions can be pursued—e.g., "If they cry, what will the bully do next?" The prediction, thus, becomes another detail added to the others and becomes data for further inferences, predictions, and generalizations. It is important to free children from the belief that there is only one right answer in all situations; therefore, it is important for us to accept and work with alternatives.

Generalizing, of course, is the development of principles or rules that have application beyond the immediate situation—for example, "Do fruit flies always show up when overripe fruit is left exposed?" "When don't they show up?" "What precautions should we take when we see them buzzing around fruit stands?"

The first two processes can be called data collection and the last three data processing. The assumption is that, if a child—guided by his teacher's questions—is required to do the kind of thinking involved in these processes often enough and whenever appropriate, he will learn not only the knowledge the teacher wishes to convey but also how to learn.

Practice Is Necessary

Minskoff's (1967) study revealed that teacher-questions in EMR classes are preponderantly the cognitive-memory (labeling, detailing) type, with a very small percentage of questions requiring productive thinking (inference, prediction, generalization). These classes failed to provide the opportunity for the pupils to learn how to manipulate and use information (i.e., to think) since memorization and regurgitation were sufficient. In order to learn how to learn, one must learn not only how to collect information but also how to process that information. Furthermore, one learns how to collect and process information by being required to do so again and again, week after week, year after year. In other words, practice is necessary.

The inductive method as described provides this practice. After a certain amount of such directed practice (research does not tell how much), the learner will begin to follow the procedure by himself. This will free him from a dependence on the teacher, for he will have learned how to collect information and what to do with it once he has collected it. Thus, he is now free to pursue areas of interest to him, to ask appropriate questions, etc. above and beyond what may be the current topic of instruction in the classroom.

In such a situation a six-hour retardate will be able to reveal his potential, especially if the teacher listens to the content of his responses rather than the grammatical form (this will be discussed in the next section). Likewise, then, if a child does indeed become an independent learner, he is limited by his own motivation rather than by our predictions, so often based on insufficient data collection.

Teaching inductively is extremely hard work for the teacher and class, especially initially. Usually, there is much cycling back to the detailing phase because of missed or misinterpreted relevant cues or because of the intrusion of irrelevant cues. The proper wording of questions is difficult because of the necessity for the right amount of cuing within the question itself. Often, rewording a question without giving away the answer seems impossible. Further, most teachers have developed the habit of asking questions requiring only a "yes," "no," or other one word response. We have been imbued with the notion that teachers "teach" (which, translated, means "lecture"), and too often this means regurgitating what has been said by the lecturer. Overcoming this habit is very difficult.

The students, on the other hand, initially will produce so few and such impoverished responses—thus forcing the teacher to rephrase and rethink the question often—that frustration results: it is easier to lecture. It must be remembered, however, that the situation is new for the student too. He is not sure of the ground rules. No one has ever asked him to think before. Even simple questions become difficult because the student has been conditioned to look for the "trick" in questions. Constantly responding to thought questions is hard work because it is an active process, whereas listening to a lecture is a passive process. But with time and perseverance on the part of the teacher, the process becomes easier. This is true with college classes—how much more so with EMR classes that have had so little practice in productive thinking! Teaching inductively is, indeed, hard work; but the rewards are more than compensatory.

LANGUAGE AND LANGUAGE TEACHING

In the sixties much of the work with culturally different children dealt with language differences. The work of Bernstein (1961) influenced thinking concerning the language characteristics of disadvantaged students and the evaluation of them by educators and linguists. The assumption behind compensatory programs was that the culturally different child spoke a language deficient in many respects (Bereiter & Englemann, 1966). Most literature of the early and middle sixties spoke of deficiencies. More recently, linguists have maintained that the language of minority group children is different rather than deficient. Much of the work was done with Black English (Cazden, 1972; Houston, 1971) which has been shown to possess all the characteristics of any language system. Thus, there has been a slow change in mental attitudes toward children and the language they bring to school within regular education as well as an attempt by some to use the children's language as a vehicle for instruction.

The current view of many linguists is reflected by Houston (1971) who presented evidence and arguments for the following propositions: that the language of disadvantaged children is not deficient, although it may differ from "Standard English;" that within their language system disadvantaged children do use words properly, contrary to the "Giant-Word Syndrome" hypothesis advanced by Bereiter and Englemann (1966); that the language of the disadvantaged child does provide him with an adequate vehicle for thinking, contrary to the Bernstein (1961) and Lawton (1968) assumptions, since "the innate ability to abstract, generalize, conceptualize, and so forth is necessary in order for language, generally speaking, to be present" (p. 244); that the disadvantaged child is verbal. Unlike some other linguists, Houston also believes that the child should be taught the language of the schools. Her discussion of the concept of "register" is of value to special class teachers. In her research she found that disadvantaged children possessed and used at least two language registers—a "school register" and a "nonschool register"—i.e., styles of language that appear in different social situations or environments. Thus, these youngsters speak one way to teachers and other authority figures and another way to their peers, friends, and family. Whereas the school register possesses many of the characteristics termed deficient by previous researchers, the nonschool register showed all of the syntactic patterns expected of any language as well as the abilities of any language to specify events and relationships in the environment. Labov (1972) presents a discussion which is relevant at this point. He reproduced the transcripts of two conversations with the same child. The first involved only the boy and the interviewer; the second involved the boy, his friend, and the interviewer. Labov showed the difference in content, level of linguistic performance, and use of logic between the two social settings by the same child. He discussed how easy it would have been to decide that the child was relatively "dull" after the first interview when, in reality, he was a perceptive and thinking child. This research is interesting, and anyone working with disadvantaged children in special classes should become familiar with it.

In spite of the evidence which Labov and Houston presented, it is this writer's belief that some children who do get labeled and placed in EMR classes may have language deficiencies even in their nonschool registers. Many disadvantaged children are tested, but all do not score low enough to be labeled EMR. Those who do score below 75-80 on the Stanford-Binet or WISC fall into two groups. One group, like Labov's boy, will appear dull because the children fail to respond adequately in the testing situation (thus failing to provide a more accurate picture of their competence); the other group will consist of those youngsters who, indeed, have language deficiencies in both registers. Thus, what the teacher does must accommodate and meet the needs of both these groups.

One thing a teacher can do is listen to the children and allow them to speak. More strongly, she should encourage them to use their nonschool register in school. This will not happen, however, if the teacher pays attention only to form (Standard English) and not to content and if she criticizes the child's natural language. Use of the inductive approach will help the teacher stay focused on the content, the concepts under study. Turning social learning lessons, for example, into language or reading lessons discourages participation by the children.

Potential Problems

By listening to her pupils, the teacher can begin to identify those who are thinkers. However, there still must be some instruction in the language of the school since there are three potential sources of problems for the children and the teacher: phonological, lexical, and syntactical (Channon, 1968).

Phonological

Phonological problems arise from the sounds of the language. Thus, a child may view the words *foal* and *fold* or *pin* and *pen* as homonyms. Channon (1968, pp. 6, 7, and 11) describes vividly how phonology can sometimes interfere with communication. In one case she describes a lesson rhyming words with *old* (pronounced by the children as *ole*). The children produce *fole* (fold), *bole* (bold or bowl?), *cole* (cold), *pole, sole* (sold), and *role*. In a confounding of spelling and sound (and a failure to realize that the class has not once produced the final *-d* sound), the teacher rejects *pole, role,* and *bole* if, by using it in a sentence, the child indicates *bowl*. The resulting confusion and tension on the part of the children is described. Enough experiences of such misunderstanding may lead to a view of school as a useless exercise that makes no sense. In her other example, Channon describes the resulting confusion when children heard the words *meadow, medal,* and *metal* as homonyms. Cazden (1972) points out that dialects and Black English differ phonologically from Standard English in important ways. She suggests that some teachers may expect a higher degree of auditory perceptual competence from children than they expect of themselves, since teachers often expect children to understand their dialect but excuse their own imcompetence in understanding the children's dialect: "It's so hard to understand them!"

Lexical

Lexical problems are, of course, vocabulary problems. The child may not know the work *pen*, meaning an enclosure, although he knows what a writing *pen* is. Children cannot make sense out of material they cannot decode meaningfully. In cases such as the different meanings of the word *pen*, children will often try to change the sentence so that it does convey some meaning to them. For example, the sentence, "The pig is in the pen," may be changed to "The pig is *on* the pen" or "The pig *ate* the pen" or to some more creative statement. Such changes should serve as cues to possible problems for us.

Syntactical

Syntactical differences are variations in the structure of sentences or the use of certain morphological structures to indicate tense or time. For example, speakers of Black English often omit the final *-s* in the third person singular verb form; the copulative is often but not always omitted. At the same time, the word *be* is used in ways not found in Standard English. The linguists tell us that there are rules which govern these productions and that they are accompanied with different meanings. For example, consider the two statements, "He gone" and "He be gone." The latter represents a tense not found in Standard English; it means that he is *usually* (habitually) gone. The former means simply that he is gone *at the present time.* Syntactical differences give rise to problems when the successful completion of a task or the successful answering of a question relies on the information imbedded in the morphology of a sentence or in function words (prepositions, conjunctions, etc.) that would not occur in the children's natural language (nonschool register).

The teacher can deal with these potential problems by being aware of them and recognizing when communication is being interferred with. Language education should occur not only during the language arts period but should permeate the whole day.

Guidelines

In an earlier report, Hurley (1967) commented on the lack of opportunity in special classes for children to use the language they do have during instructional periods. He noted the lack of variety and complexity in the children's school language and suggested that Stearns's (1967) guidelines be adopted. These were guidelines for specific language lessons dealing with the school register and for general teacher behavior throughout the school day. (It is important to reiterate that all lessons should not become language lessons.) Since these are general, they will be discussed before discussing more specific ways of dealing with the problems identified by Channon.

Stearns's guidelines focus on three areas which he calls verbal definition, verbal feedback, and response elaboration.

Verbal Definition

Verbal definition refers to the teacher's supplying the children with the correct responses and talking through her own actions. This technique provides a model for the children to imitate and demonstrates the relationship between the school register and behavior—a relationship such children are already aware of in terms of the nonschool register. In addition, there is research (Galperin, 1957; Salvina, 1957) that indicates such verbal self-monitoring is a necessary step in the learning of a new skill.

Verbal Feedback

Verbal feedback is the conscious use of the reduction and expansion of the child's responses into the grammatically correct form of the school register. This technique reproduces the processes in children's normal acquisition of language as described by Brown and Bellugi (1964). In the course of learning any language, children and parents participate in verbal interactions in which the child imitates and reduces the parent's longer productions to a manageable length, and parents imitate and expand children's two or three word sentences into longer and correct statements or questions. This reduction and expansion is done without judgments of rightness or wrongness; it is simply done. Nor are all child productions expanded. Some are, some are not; the situation does not become stilted. Such expansions (verbal feedback) by the teacher may serve the same purpose as the mother's—to aid the child in acquisition of syntax. Such expansion of incomplete productions of the child provides a model for him to imitate. Note should be taken that syntactically incomplete productions by a child are not necessarily cognitively incomplete. For example, consider the following sequence:

Teacher: "What are two things that a busboy does?"
Student: "Pick up dishes and wipe the table..."
Teacher: "Yes, the busboy picks up the dirty dishes when people leave the table, and he washes the table so it will be clean for the next customer."

The student's answer is informationally complete. The subject is understood of conversations and unless the teacher has established a condition—everyone must speak in complete sentences for the next one-half hour—she should expect and accept them. The teacher, in the sequence above, has expanded the child's statement. Notice what she has done! She has introduced a qualifier ("dirty") and two dependent clauses. Thus, she has provided a model of the use of such subordinate clauses with content she is fairly certain he knows and indirectly encouraged him and the class to elaborate their responses. This is important encouragement, if she is also using the inductive approach. Lastly, without making a big deal out of it and putting the child on the defensive, she has added the morphological -s onto the verbs. If, in the vernacular, it is acceptable to omit the -s on third person singular verbs, comment about it may produce a defensive reaction. By simply accepting his response as correct and expanding it in the school register, she avoids a potential source of conflict while also teaching. This is not to say that at some time in her direct language teaching lessons she may not want to deal specifically with this difference between the school and nonschool registers. Lastly, it should be noted that the expansion is not a simple parroting-back of the child's statement. Neither simple repetition nor the expansion of every child production should be practiced. This means that the teacher must be continually alert and selective in the verbal feedback she gives.

Response Elaboration

Stearns's last guideline is response elaboration. Two facets of this are important and dovetail nicely with the use of inductive teaching. During some time of the day the teacher should insist on the use of syntactically complete productions by the children. As stated before, it is unreasonable to expect such productions all day, for it is not natural. The second facet is requiring more than just a naming response. Requiring detailing of the important and unimportant features of an item is important as is requiring the children to vocalize their categorizations and discriminations, their inferences, etc. The child gets practice using school language, and the teacher learns something about his cognitive style.

These guidelines combined with the inductive style will help the child to learn the school language, to use his natural language, to trust his own thinking ability, *provided* the general classroom atmosphere is nonpunitive and one of trust and mutual respect.

Specific Strategies

These guidelines can be considered general techniques useful for reinforcing and providing opportunities to practice what has been taught. A little thought would indicate that the use of verbal definition, verbal feedback, and response elaboration would help alleviate some of the problems that Channon identifies. But, there are still more specific things a teacher can do.

Phonological differences require that the teacher tune in. Since she is the adult, she must bear the major portion of the responsibility for being sensitive to sound (as sound) without confusing it with spelling. This confusion is normal. Classes of college students have been asked to orally give words rhyming with *ole* while the instructor wrote *old* on the board. In every case, one-half to three-fourths of the class confused the two. Eventually, a perceptive student will ask for clarification. We must be aware of the possibilities of confusion and correct them before they result in the "tuning-out" of the pupils.

Care must be taken to avoid making negative value judgments about the children's phonological patterns simply because they differ from ours. In the same way that Northerners moving South and Southerners moving North must work at attuning their ears to regional differences, so the teacher of culturally different children must work at tuning in on differences.

Vocabulary is developed through experiences. Since, ultimately, words must have a reality base, use of trips, films, pictures, and other media becomes necessary. Vocabulary building is an area most teachers are skilled in and requires no further elaboration. It is worth noting, however, that children learn those words that are necessary to learn in order to cope with the reality of their own lives. Thus, words we use in our instruction and words in reading material should be scrutinized and possible sources of confusion pinpointed and handled appropriately.

Local idiomatic use of words or expressions must be learned. This means listening to children, noting such usages and asking them for an explanation if the meaning is unclear. Also important is the establishment of a classroom climate in which the children feel free to ask us what we mean by a word, phrase or expression. An example comes to mind. A graduate student from a Northern state was working in a Southern state as a house painter during the summer. His boss told him, "Get shut of those cans!" The student, never having heard this expression before, proceeded to put the lids back on all of the empty cans, wondering why the cans needed to be recovered. The boss, of course, had serious doubts about the "college student's" intelligence, since "everyone" knows he was told to discard them.

Syntax is best learned through the methods described previously which serve to provide a model for the children. Direct teaching may focus on comparisons between school and nonschool language. Channon insists that pattern practice is necessary. Certainly this is so if we consider that learning another dialect shares many of the same difficulties as learning a foreign language's syntactical particularities. Thus, the use of materials, such as *Distar Language* (Englemann et al., 1969), which incorporate a certain amount of practice of the syntactical

131

patterns of Standard English has been found useful in special classes. Such practice during designated time periods should be verbal so that the teacher can hear what is being said since research (Anastasiow, no date; Torrey, 1969) reveals that children will recode into their own dialects what they hear or read. Without self-correction and teaching-correction procedures, the child will not learn to spontaneously produce the syntactical patterns being taught.

With reference to Standard English syntax, it is necessary to realize that the children understand more than they spontaneously produce. The reconstruction of sentences reveals this. Anastasiow's subjects recoded the sentence, "Joe is good when he feels like it," to "Joe be good when he feel like it." Notice that the sense of the sentence is retained; that the original sentence was understood. With children like Anastasiow's, the teaching job is not to teach them what the sentence means but to get them to *produce* those morphological parts when the situation demands it.

READING

The concern for language differences is related to the question of teaching reading. That language skill and learning to read are related is unquestioned. The nature of the relationship, however, is unclear. It seems logical to say that children find it difficult to learn to read material which is not written in natural (for them) language and hence, in some degree, is incomprehensible. Cazden (1972) indicates that even though research on this point is inconclusive there are several attempts to develop beginning reading materials written in the Black dialect. These are basal reading books written in nonstandard dialects, some with the Standard English beside them, some with the Standard English in a companion book—content and pictures identical (see Cazden, 1972, pp. 158-159) which special class teachers may find useful.

Even though research does not clarify whether the use of dialect readers or regular readers is better, it is certain that children can learn to read (crack-the-code) using any dialect. The use of experience stories, dictated by the children themselves, as reading material is a viable technique, especially with older children whose interest level exceeds that of most materials on their reading level—the Fernald (1943) approach with or without the kinesthetic tracing. Initially, certain rules need to be followed. First, write the story the way it is dictated. If grammar is corrected, vocabulary changed, etc., it is no longer the child's story and some motivation is lost. Secondly, be sure to have the typed story ready the day after dictation.

By minimizing problems in comprehension, this approach avoids the problem of syntactical differences impeding the learning of reading. Most special class teachers have been trained in the use of experience charts, stories, etc. However, often the training has included the automatic simplification, correction, or other change of the children's product. What is being said here is to write the children's production the way they said it. If the objective is to teach code-cracking skills, why confound it with possible comprehension problems. This approach places greater responsibility on the teacher to understand the child's dialect. Further, it attaches a certain amount of legitimacy to the child's natural language, adds to the teacher's credibility in the eyes of the children, and reinforces or develops the notion that reading is talking written down. If there is a straightforward approach to the child's natural language, the teacher can always say something like "Yes, you're right! How would we say that in school language?"

CONCLUSION

This paper has recommended the use of inductive teaching with classes of EMR children. The language of culturally different children and some techniques for dealing with these differences have been discussed.

The difficulty of dealing with differences in a positive way is intensified by the fact that not all Black, Indian, Puerto-Rican, Chicano, or poor children speak a dialect; that there are dialectical variations within these groups. The difficulty is further compounded by the children's perceptions of the nature of school and of teachers and the attitudes engendered by these perceptions. Some of these attitudes can vitiate any methods or techniques used. Therefore, this article has focused on those methods which may serve to establish a climate or opportunity for child self-expression and to alert the teacher to possible sources of difficulty.

Perhaps—by encouraging the culturally different child to use his nonschool language in school, by using natural language as a vehicle for teaching skills, by teaching the school language as an alternative (second) language, by focusing on content and ideas—it may become possible to gradually eliminate the placement of the six-hour retardate in special classes.

REFERENCES

Anastasiow, N. J. "Language Reconstruction Patterns of Kindergarten, First and Second Graders as Indicators of the Development of Cognitive Processes: A Study Exploring the Difference-Deficit Explanations of Language Behavior." Bloomington: Indiana University, Institute for Child Study, (no date). Mimeo.

Bereiter, C. & Englemann, S. *Teaching Disadvantaged Children in the Preschool*. Englewood Cliffs, N. J.: Prentice-Hall, 1966.

Bernstein, B. "Social Class and Linguistic Development: A Theory of Social Learning." In A. H. Halsey, J. Floud, & C. A. Anderson (Eds.), *Education, Economy, and Society*. New York: Free Press, 1961 (288-314).

Brown, R. & Bellugi, V. "Three Processes in the Child's Acquisition of Syntax." In E. H. Lenneberg (Ed.), *New Directions in the Study of Language.* Cambridge, Mass.: MIT Press, 1964. (131-161).

Cazden, C. B. *Child Language and Education.* New York: Holt, Rinehart & Winston, 1972.

Channon, G. "Bulljive—Language Teaching in a Harlem School." *The Urban Review, 2* (4), 1968 (5-12).

Englemann, S., Osborn, J., & Englemann, T. *Distar Language I, II: An Instructional System.* Chicago: Science Research Associates, 1969.

Fernald, G. M. *Remedial Techniques in Basic School Subjects.* New York: McGraw-Hill, 1943.

Gallagher, J. J. "Productive Thinking of Gifted Children." U. S. Office of Education, Cooperative Research Project No. 965, Final Report. Urbana, Ill.: University of Illinois, Institute for Research on Exceptional Children, 1965.

Galperin, P. Y. "An Experimental Study in the Formation of Mental Actions." In B. Simon (Ed.), *Psychology in the Soviet Union.* Stanford, Calif.: Stanford University Press, 1957 (213-225).

Goldstein, H. "The Social Learning Curriculum: How to Use, Evaluate and Field Test." New York: Yeshiva University, 1969 (mimeo).

Houston, S. H. "A Reexamination of Some Assumptions about the Language of the Disadvantaged Child." In S. Chess & A. Thomas (Eds.), *Annual Progress in Child Psychiatry and Child Development 1971.* New York: Brunner/Mazel, 1971 (233-250).

Hurley, O. L. "Teacher Language: Key to Learning?" *Education and Training of the Mentally Retarded, 2,* 1967 (127-133).

Labov, W. "Academic Ignorance and Black Intelligence." *The Atlantic Monthly, 229* (6), 1972 (59-67).

Lawton, D. *Social Class, Language and Education.* London: Routledge & Kegan Paul, 1968.

Minskoff, E. H. "An Analysis of the Teacher-Pupil Verbal Interaction in Special Classes for the Mentally Retarded." U. S. Office of Education, Project No. 6-8092, Final Report. New York: Yeshiva University, 1967.

President's Committee on Mental Retardation. *The Six-Hour Retarded Child.* Wash., D. C.: U. S. Government Printing Office, 1970.

President's Committee on Mental Retardation. *Placement of Children in Special Classes for the Retarded: Background Position Papers.* Wash., D. C.: P.C.M.R. 1971a.

President's Committee on Mental Retardation. *A Very Special Child.* Wash., D. C.: U. S. Government Printing Office, 1971b.

President's Committee on Mental Retardation. *MR 71: Entering the Era of Human Ecology.* Wash., D. C.: U. S. Government Printing Office, 1972.

Slavina, L. S. "Specific Features of the Intellectual Work of Unsuccessful Pupils." In B. Simon (Ed.), *Psychology in the Soviet Union.* Stanford, Calif.: Stanford University Press, 1957 (205-212).

Stearns, K. E. "The Effectiveness of a Language Development Program for Disadvantaged Children." Paper read at the Annual Convention of the Council for Exceptional Children, St. Louis, March 1967.

Torrey, J. W. "Learning to Read without a Teacher: A Case Study." *Elementary English, 46,* 1969 (550-556).

Embedded in the trends of the 1970s is a growing concern on the part of educators for career education. For several years special educators have pushed for the establishment of secondary-level programs for exceptional children. However, in general the emphasis has been on a rather circumscribed approach to job preparation. Little systematic attention has been given at the elementary level to preparation for the world of work, and even less attention has been given to the post-high school needs of exceptional children. Clark's paper provides a major contribution to special education literature. He discusses the concept of career education within the context of relating special to general education. He concedes that confusion exists regarding the future of career education and what should constitute career education for the handicapped. However, he takes advantage of the existing literature by incorporating into it his own ideas. Clark presents a clear approach to career education which is worthy of consideration by special educators.

Career Education for the Mildly Handicapped

Gary M. Clark
University of Kansas, Lawrence

Whether one sees it as another "movement" in education, a passing fad, or a reflex action to a rap on the American education system's patella, career education is something to be acknowledged as an increasingly potent force in education today demanding study and evaluation. Its proponents are following the lead of former U.S. Commissioner of Education, Sidney P. Marland, Jr., and are spurred on by public statements or endorsements by former President Nixon, the National Association of Secondary School Officers, the U.S. Chamber of Commerce, and with some qualifications the educational leadership of AFL-CIO. Members of Congress have placed financial support behind their verbal endorsements in the passage of The Occupational and Adult Education Act of 1972 to further encourage the leadership for career education.

135

The past two years have been active ones for educators who have seen career education as a focus around which all education can be developed. This has been especially true for educators of the handicapped who not only have advocated the basic principles of career education for the education of the handicapped for some time but also currently see it as a desirable change within the mainstream of education that may permit greater accommodation of mildly handicapped children. Since many of the concepts of career education have been advocated for the handicapped in public schools for some time (DeProspo & Hungerford, 1946; Hungerford, 1941; Kirk & Johnson, 1951; Martens, 1937), one might ask why educators of the handicapped should be drawn into the movement of career education—especially when it appears that it is so nearly the same as current emphases in secondary special education.

This paper will attempt to clarify the scope and sequence of career education and the vital relevance it has for the education of the mildly handicapped, not only as a means of improving career education curricula and instruction but also in the benefits derived from an understanding of it as a movement within the mainstream of education. An effort will be made to define career education, delineate its goals, focus on the key concepts, describe current conceptualizations of its evolving structure, and stress the implications of it for the education of all handicapped.

WHAT IS CAREER EDUCATION?

There is no single definition of career education that has been universally accepted or endorsed. This has been by design in hopes that a lack of definition would result in disparate and divergent groups coming to grips with the problem and contributing to a body of knowledge yielding a definition. In essence, a definition of this type would be a descriptive statement of a concept after it has been studied, debated, applied, analyzed, and evaluated, rather than a definitive statement to which all study, debate, application, analysis, and evaluation must conform.

Hoyt (Budke, Bettis & Beasley, 1972) has formulated one definition that appears to be receiving considerable attention as one of the first attempts at a formal definition since career education was launched as a movement in 1971:

> Career education represents the total effort of public education and the community to help all individuals become familiar with the values of a work oriented society, to integrate those values into their personal value structure, and to implement those values in their lives in ways that make work possible, meaningful, and satisfying to each individual. [p. 3]

Hoyt (General Learning Corporation, 1972) has qualified one aspect of this definition by pointing out that there is an inherent assumption that the term "work values" encompasses a variety of work motivations including, but not limited to, the Protestant work ethic. This is an important assumption because, if one were to interpret this definition in terms of the work values of the traditional Protestant work ethic, there could be a line of argument made against the concept of career education that would detract from its major thrust. Green (McClure & Buan, 1973), for example, has challenged the "fulfillment of personal identity" notion inherent in the Protestant work ethic by asserting that many jobs do not provide people either with an adequate sense of self-identity or any satisfactory central life interest. Gordon (McClure & Buan, 1973) also raises the question of the importance of work in personal fulfillment in his observation that work may no longer be central in the new social order.

The implications of this definition for the handicapped are more easily described with the perspective provided by Hoyt's clarification and the issues raised by Green and Gordon. For those educators of the handicapped and (re)habilitation workers who have had to acknowledge that their own limitations, their perceptions of the limitations of some handicapped persons, and the availability of employment opportunities have resulted in placement of handicapped in jobs that provide little challenge or dignity, there is some attraction to the interpretation of career education which holds that there are motivations for work other than personal fulfillment or identity realization. The very structure of many of our work institutions in modern American society promote alienation from work and perpetuate anti-work attitudes among those who are more interested in "survival" and "security" than in "self-actualization," if one uses Maslow's (1954) terminology and his theory of basic human needs.

The important issue in interpreting this definition of career education, in light of the needs of the handicapped, is not to judge career education on the basis of one definition, but rather to see in it the possibilities of providing a common understanding of what the primary purposes of it might include and to accept it as an idealistic statement of intent. Rejection of career education should be a consequence of the unacceptability of specific applications of it in community settings rather than based on a philosophical position statement that may or may not reflect the intent of its advocates.

Some Goals of Career Education

For the benefit of those educators of (re)habilitation personnel who have been led to perceive career education as a new name for vocational education in special education, the following summary of goals for career education are presented. These goals were initially established by the Bureau of Adult, Vocational, and Technical Education, U.S. Office of Education (1971):

1. To make all instructional subject matter more personally relevant through restructuring and focusing it around a career development theme when possible.
2. To provide all persons the guidance, counseling, and instruction needed to (a) develop self-awareness and self-direction, (b) expand occupational awareness and aspirations, (c) develop appropriate attitudes about the personal and social significance of work.
3. To assure all persons an opportunity to gain an entry level marketable skill prior to their leaving school if termination is necessary or a desirable option.
4. To prepare all persons completing secondary school with the knowledge and skills necessary to become employed or to pursue more training.
5. To provide placement services for every person in his preparation for a career, whether it be placement assistance in employment or further education.
6. To build into the educational system greater involvement and coordination of all possible resources in the community.
7. To facilitate entry and re-entry, either into the world of work or the educational system, for all persons through a flexible educational system which continually reviews and expands educational and occupational options.

Key Concepts in Career Education

As one reads between the lines in these formally stated goals, some dynamic, sweeping changes in education become apparent as consequences-of efforts to implement them. Some key concepts that emerge, and that further clarify what career education is about, include the following:

1. Preparation for successful working careers shall be a key objective of *all* education. This implies that it is assumed to be appropriate for all persons pursuing an instructional program at all levels of education, beginning in pre-school and extending through adult education. It is appropriate for youth and adults, boys and girls, those who are academically talented and those who are handicapped, those who choose college and those who make other choices.
2. Preparation for careers will encompass the mutually important aspects of
   a. work attitudes
   b. human relations
   c. orientation to the realities of working environments
   d. exposure to alternatives in choice of occupations
   e. acquisition of actual job skills

3. Every teacher in every subject matter area that has career relevance will emphasize the contribution that academics can make to a successful career.

4. "Hands-on" occupationally oriented experiences will be used as a standard method of teaching and motivating the learning of abstract academic concepts.

5. Instruction and guidance for career education will not be limited to the boundaries of a classroom, but will be expanded into the home, community, and employing establishments.

6. Career education will seek to extend its time boundaries, beginning in early childhood and continuing through the regular school years and adult years, allowing the flexibility for an individual to leave school for some work experience and return to school for further education or training when he chooses. In addition, it would include opportunities for adults to upgrade and/or update their skills or, if needed, change occupational roles. Further, it would give attention to the productive use of leisure time and the years of retirement.

7. Career education in no way conflicts with other legitimate educational objectives, e.g. basic education, citizenship, culture, and family responsibility. It is, however, a basic and pervasive approach to all education that provides a focus and unifying theme to which young and old, advantaged and disadvantaged, and intellectually and physically able and disabled can relate.

These key concepts are elaborations of the ideas, assumptions, and objectives that have been generated thus far regarding the concept of career education. Career education, like any other conceptual notion, does have some idealized statements describing a proposed structure which would move it from theory into practice. A discussion of these statements is appropriate at this point.

CAREER EDUCATION—A PROPOSED STRUCTURE

The U.S. Office of Education has formulated four models of career education or, rather, four alternative ways of facilitating career education goals. It is making substantial efforts in supporting research and development of career education through the National Center for Educational Research and Development by concentrating resources on the following four models or delivery systems:

1. School-Based Model
2. Employer-Based Model

3. Home/Community-Based Model
4. Residential-Based Model

Each of these, in a unique way, can provide handicapped youth and adults some of the advantages of career education. Since many educators of handicapped may tend to be familiar with only the School-Based Model, each of the four will be described briefly to establish a perspective for the complete structure of career education.

School-Based Career Education Model

The School-Based Model for career education is being developed through a grant to the Center for Vocational and Technical Education at the Ohio State University in Columbus, Ohio. Marland (1971) has presented one version of this model (see Figure 1) which describes the vertical and horizontal progression of career education as a pyramid that begins with "career awareness" in the elementary grades and moves from the general to the specific concerning an orientation to the world of work as the student progresses through school.

If one were to evaluate the School-Based Career Education Model on the basis of what appears to be the major thrust of this version of the model, it would be basically an occupational guidance and skill acquisition program which is a thinly disguised effort by vocational educators to infuse its objectives into a K-12 curriculum sequence. A major criticism thus far of career education as a movement has been the continued difficulty for some in separating out vocational education from career education. The traditional conceptions and misconceptions of the goals of vocational and technical education become enmeshed in the schema to the point where parents, teachers, academicians, and students themselves lose sight of the complete scope of career education objectives. Figure 2 provides some clarification as to how each of the models relates to vocational education.

The School-Based Model is intended to develop in students not only a comprehensive awareness of career options and the ability to enter employment in a selected occupational area or to go on for further education but also a concept of self in relation to work, personal characteristics (such as initiative, resourcefulness, pride in work, etc.), and a realistic understanding of the relationships between the world of work and education. The emphasis being placed on career awareness, career exploration, and entry level job skill acquisition in this model reflect the most unique thrusts of the movement but, in the process, may be leaving the concept of career education vulnerable to undue criticism.

Keller (1972) has provided a summary of specific goals of the School-Based Career Education Model by educational level which include some helpful ideas

Figure 1
CAREER EDUCATION

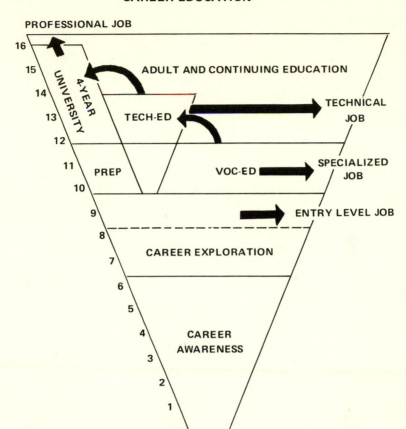

in demonstrating the balance needed in career education concept and skill development:

Elementary School

1. Encourage development of work habits and realistic attitudes toward occupations and work.

2. Identify occupational groupings or clusters and integrate them into basic educational skill instruction.

3. Involve children in self-discovery activities.

4. Introduce instruction in problem-solving and decision-making.

5. Provide opportunities for pupils to render services to others.

6. Provide opportunities for pupils to observe and/or interact with selected community workers.

Junior High School

1. Orient students to (a) society and work, (b) occupational information, (c) self-knowledge, (d) career planning, (e) basic technology, and (f) occupational training through guidance and instructional activities in the subject matter areas.

2. Expose students to a wide range of occupations through exploration of clusters.

3. Provide for "hands-on" experiences in simulated work environments and personal identification with role models from the community.

4. Organize career development instructional centers for discretionary and prescriptive learning experiences.

5. Provide extensive career guidance activities.

Figure 2

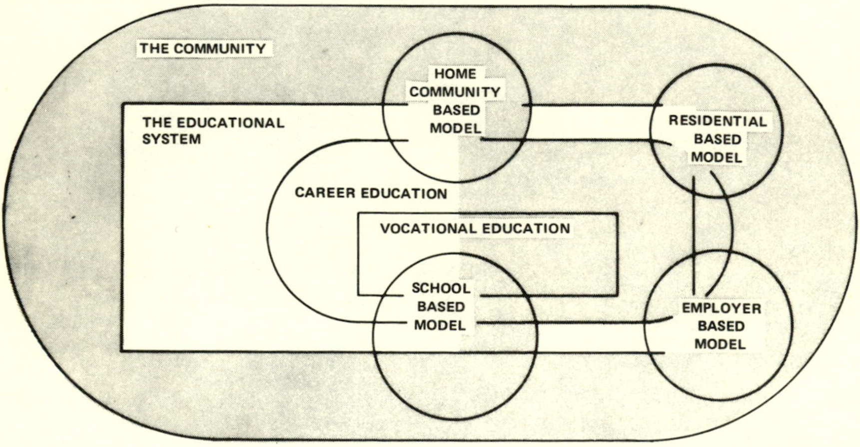

6. Provide appropriate occupational preparation for students who have decided to leave school prior to completing junior high school.

Senior High School

1. Provide students with activities that unify basic subject areas with career development concepts and skills to make academic instruction more relevant.

2. Provide every student with intensive preparation in a selected occupational cluster or in a specific occupation in preparation for job entry and/or further training.

3. Provide extensive guidance and counseling services for every student.

4. Provide placement services for all students, upon termination of schooling, in (a) a job, (b) a postsecondary occupational training program, or (c) a four-year college program.

The occupational "clusters" referred to in the goals of all three levels cited above are clusters or groupings of occupations that may be accomplished on any logical organizational base. The most common cluster system suggested in career education programs is that developed by the U.S. Office of Education (see Figure 3).

Figure 3
U.S. OFFICE OF EDUCATION—OCCUPATIONAL CLUSTERS

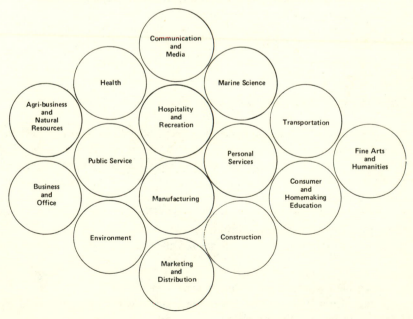

Employer-Based Career Education Model

This model is being developed, operated and supported primarily by business and industry in cooperation with school systems. The target population for this model is the thirteen to twenty age group primarily and, as one might expect for an out-of-school option, many of the target population will be characterized as "unmotivated, alienated, and disaffected." However, it is intended to be a legitimate, viable option for any student. Its primary goal is to provide a comprehensive set of personalized educational experiences to junior or senior high school students who *voluntarily* choose to participate in this approach to education instead of the traditional classroom approach.

Two key elements of this model include defining individual learning needs and locating actual work situations in which those needs can be met. A special attempt is made to allow each student to participate in the definition of those needs and in the selection of his own work situation from a variety of opportunities. The model provides for the completion of high school graduation requirements.

Budke, Bettis, and Beasley (1972) report that Employer-Based Career Education projects are planned to be developed and operated by consortia of businesses and other public or private organizations. These consortia are being sponsored by selected agencies across the country who are under contract with the U.S. Office of Education to develop and field test this model. Some of these agencies include Research for Better Schools, Inc., Philadelphia; the Far West Laboratory for Educational Research and Development, Berkeley, California; the Northwest Regional Educational Laboratory, Portland, Oregon; and the Appalachia Educational Laboratory, Charleston, West Virginia.

Home/Community-Based Career Education Model

The Home-Based Model is designed to reach individuals who have left the traditional school environment but who need or desire further education. The population for which this model is designed would range in age from eighteen to twenty-five and would include those who spend most of their time at home. This could include women during pregnancy or during preschool child-rearing years, unemployed persons, or handicapped persons with short-term or relatively permanent disabling conditions.

The primary objectives of the Home-Based Model generally are stated as follows:

1. To provide new career education programs for adults
2. To establish a guidance and career placement system to assist individuals in occupational and personal decision-making

3. To develop more competent workers
4. To enhance the efficacy of the home as a learning environment.

The delivery of this model will take several approaches. One will follow a mass media approach with an emphasis on motivating individuals to study for career development. Television and radio will be the most frequently used media. Another approach will involve direct instruction to individuals at home via cable television, correspondence programs, telephone hook-ups, audio cassettes, radio, and instructional kits designed for specific content areas. A third approach to supplement the first two will be the establishment of career clinics in the community or neighborhood centers to provide personal career guidance and counseling, referral services, and information on relevant career-oriented education programs that are or will be available.

Rural Residential Career Education Model

A typical criticism of many new education and training programs is that the only people who can benefit from them are those who live in urban environments or are close enough to them to be able to take advantage of such opportunities. The Rural Residential Model is proposed as a partial solution to this problem and offers what is perhaps the boldest, most imaginative model for the delivery of career education opportunities yet described.

It is presently designed to serve isolated, disadvantaged families or unmarried individuals from a geographical region covering no more than six states. It will attempt to provide rural residents with the development and/or improvement of employment capabilities appropriate for the area, provide stimulation for economic development of the area by introducing new occupational possibilities and training for them, and improving family living generally.

The model at this point is a research and demonstration project testing the hypothesis that entire families from disadvantaged or isolated areas can improve their economic and social situations through an intensive program at a residential center. This approach involves moving individuals and families from their home environments to a setting which is designed to provide a comprehensive array of services for accomplishing the objectives stated. Services will include day care, kindergarten, elementary and secondary education, career and technical education, adult education, parent/family assistance, medical and dental services, welfare services, counseling and guidance, and cultural and recreational opportunities for both single and married participants and their families.

IMPLICATIONS FOR THE HANDICAPPED

The implications of career education for mentally and physically handicapped individuals depend somewhat on the success of the movement within general education. As a concept, it has served to corroborate the proposals for occupational education and prevocational training for the handicapped which have existed for some time. However, as a movement, it will have varying degrees of impact on the handicapped as a group, depending upon the extent of its implementation.

At this point in time, most efforts at career education development appear to be concentrating on general programming and implementation procedures for regular education programs. Secondary special education programs based on a work-study concept are so compatible with the concept of career education that their teachers and coordinators may not see the advantages of incorporation into the entire model. On the other hand, career education leadership personnel may see high school work-study programs as areas that can be claimed as career education activities, but do not see them as being included in the total program to any greater degree than they already are included in the education system.

A more specific analysis of the implications of career education for the handicapped may be accomplished better by consideration of each of the career education models. The following sections will briefly evaluate the School-Based Model, Employer-Based Model, Home/Community-Based Model, and Rural Residential Model as they relate to handicapped children, youth, and adults.

The School-Based Career Education Model

The most obvious disability groups to benefit from this career education model are the mildly retarded and the learning disabled. Since these two groups are the largest within the public schools, it is to be expected that they will be accommodated as groups to fit into a career education program of some kind. Budke, Bettis, and Beasley (1972) reviewed twenty-six career education programs in twenty-two states and found that only about one-third (nine) claimed to have any special instruction for handicapped youth in career education and less than ten percent of the twenty-six programs provided a component for the educable retarded. It is not clear whether this information reflects lack of inclusion of special education programs in career education programming or whether the mildly handicapped in public schools are becoming "invisible" to the extent that they are included in regular programs without labels and are consequently not treated as a special group.

The learning disabled children identified at the ages of nine or ten are now being recognized as students with assets as well as liabilities during their adolescent years and some special programs that de-emphasize academics are being provided. The Part D funds of the Vocational Education Amendments of 1968 set aside for "special needs" students are increasingly being used to support programs for students who may or may not be defined as handicapped, but who need a program different from those available through regular or vocational options and those available through special education. Programs of this type include dropout-prone youth, learning disabled, educationally handicapped, socially maladjusted, and some who are or have been classified as educable retarded.

The School-Based Model emphasizes a sequential approach to career education that should influence programs for the partially sighted, hard of hearing, mildly developmentally disabled, and mildly orthopedically handicapped. These programs should feel the impact of what is being taught in the regular grades at the elementary and junior high school levels and make some curricular revisions to insure that students are receiving a comparable foundation in career preparation.

The goals of "career awareness which leads to career identity" and "self-awareness which leads to self-identity" developed for the School-Based Model by the Center for Vocational and Technical Education at Ohio State University (Budke, Bettis & Beasley, 1972, p. 10) are vital to career development for the handicapped. These two goals are especially crucial to the level of employment the handicapped may eventually attain. Career identity and self-identity are demonstrated by what an individual allows himself to be guided into—by parents, teachers, counselors, friends, or circumstances. Handicapped persons have enough problems in dealing with the stereotyped career identity and preconceived ideas of the identity of the handicapped by the nonhandicapped to have questions about these themselves. The implications of this model on the long-term pursuit of these two goals by the handicapped are exciting when contrasted to what has been provided in the past.

Employer-Based Model

The Employer-Based Model could be instrumental in solving a major employment problem for many handicapped—exclusion from union membership. Legal obstacles and employment problems related to mobility and architectural barriers are problems best solved from within. The involvement of business and industry in career preparation on a contractual basis may prove to be one of the best things that has happened for the handicapped in some time. When business and industry are committed to a program that embodies the concept that career preparation is for *all* individuals, they can provide political and economic persuasion that can go a long way in alleviating problems that educators and rehabilitation personnel have not been able to solve.

This model could have significant effect on the type of training and subsequent employment opportunities for those handicapped youth who receive most, if not all, of their high school vocational training in a state school, particularly schools for the auditorially and visually impaired. With some exceptions, the variety and level of vocational training in these settings are limited. Training in many instances is dependent upon obsolete and/or inadequate equipment or inadequately trained instructors who do the best with what they have. The possibility of going directly to potential work environments to obtain career preparation from highly skilled craftsmen or technicians using modern equipment is an encouraging development for the handicapped and those who have been frustrated in attempts to provide quality career preparation.

Home/Community-Based Model

A large number of handicapped persons find themselves employed seasonally or part-time, or unemployed due to pregnancy, small children at home, or mobility problems. Much of their time is spent in the home or immediate neighborhood and efforts to venture out are either too threatening, too expensive, or too much trouble. It is for this group that the Home/Community-Based Model is ideal.

The use of mass media may be effective in stimulating interest in the possibilities of further career preparation. Beyond that, however, contacts and initiation of an educational program must be formalized if credit for completion is to be obtained. It is at this point that the neighborhood or mobile guidance centers should be able to assist the handicapped in making tentative occupational choices and arranging for appropriate home/community instruction.

Rural Residential Model

This model has basically the same implications for handicapped persons as nonhandicapped persons in rural areas. It is admittedly designed for the disadvantaged rural population; but where persons from rural areas are both handicapped and disadvantaged, as is so frequently the case, the service is available and a unique possibility.

SUMMARY

Career education, as a concept, is rapidly evolving into a movement with structure and definable parameters. It is still misunderstood by some as to its intent, its scope, and its structure; but, increasingly, more information is being made available to educators and the general public to respond to these misconceptions. As it evolves into what it is to be, there need to be continuous reminders of what it is *not*:

—Career education is *not* vocational education with a new name.

—Career education is *not* a new educational movement to replace or downgrade academic education.

—Career education is *not* a system bound to traditional school ages.

—Career education is *not* a program to be limited to any one environment.

—Career education is *not* training for a single occupation.

—Career education is *not* a program for one educational population.

When one defines "career" as Gordon (McClure & Buan, 1973, p. 59) does "...the course by which one develops and lives a responsible and satisfying life," there is a distinction made in the term that differentiates it from the traditional meaning—e.g., a succession of jobs or occupational roles. Career education based on Gordon's definition concerns itself with a merging of liberal education and vocational development such that it facilitates the *process of living* and is not limited to facilitating the *process of making a living*.

The mildly handicapped fit into the schema of career education as readily as any group and stand to gain from its offerings. Those interested in their welfare, however, must move aggressively into the arena of career education development if there is to be a significant impact from the movement on the careers of the handicapped.

REFERENCES

Budke, W. E., Bettis, G. E. & Beasley, G. F. *Career Education Practice.* Columbus, Ohio: ERIC Clearinghouse on Vocational and Technical Education, December, 1972.

Bureau of Adult, Vocational, and Technical Education, "Career Education: Description and Goals." Division of Vocational and Technical Education, BAVTE, U.S. Office of Education, Washington, D.C., 1971.

Career Education: A Handbook for Implementation. Washington, D.C.: U.S. Department of Health, Education and Welfare, February, 1972.

DeProspo, C. J. & Hungerford, R. H. "A Complete Social Program for the Mentally Retarded." *American Journal of Mental Deficiency, 51,* 1946 (115-122).

Dunn, Charleta J. & Payne, B. F. *World of Work.* Dallas, Texas: Leslie Press, 1971.

General Learning Corporation. *Career Education Resource Guide.* Morristown, New Jersey: General Learning Corporation, 1972.

Hungerford, R. H. The Detroit plan for the occupational education of the mentally retarded. *American Journal of Mental Deficiency,* 1941, 46, 102-108.

Keller, Louise J., *Career Education In-Service Training Guide.* Morristown, New Jersey: General Learning Corporation, 1972.

Kirk, S. A. & Johnson, G. O. *Educating the Retarded Child.* Cambridge, Massachusetts: Riverside Press, 1951.

Marland, S. P., Jr. "Career Education Now." Speech presented to the Convention of the National Association of Secondary School Principals in Houston, Texas, January 23, 1971.

Martens, E. H. "Occupational Preparation for Mentally Handicapped Children." *Proceedings and Addresses of the Sixty-first Annual Session of the American Association on Mental Deficiency, 42,* 1937 (157-65).

Maslow, A. H. *Motivation and Personality.* New York: Harper and Row, 1954.

McClure, L. & Buan, Carolyn. *Essays on Career Education.* Portland, Oregon: Northwest Regional Educational Laboratory, 1973.

Part 2
Models

Models for Alternative Programming: A Perspective

Richard A. Johnson
Minneapolis Public Schools

Special educators are currently facing monumental challenges. No longer are we saviours of the lost; no longer are we separate or secure in our special status; no longer are we able, in good conscience, to justify the wholesale isolation and segregation of children. Today our business is not only very complex, but is also subject to the requirements of accountability—accountability for demonstrating that what we do with and for handicapped learners is productive. We also, as a profession, need to improve the way in which we communicate about what we do. Time is short and improvement of practice can no longer be considered an evolutionary process of natural selection. The courts have said so! The civil rights of children and parents will not wait for leisurely dissemination and adoption of current technology (and there *is* much existing technology and expertise already available). The difficulty is in organizing and delivering this technology and expertise so that the greatest productivity can be achieved in the least time with the least possible expenditure of resources.

The several excellent conceptual, philosophical, and programmatic efforts represented by contributions to this book (and in other resources), while constituting a substantial effort toward making an impact on current practices, are innovations which have never really come to fruition. Or, as some change theorists would say, never been "diffused" (Netzer & Eye, 1970). The so-called "engineered classroom" concept has been with us since the early 1960s, yet there are still thousands of school districts in the United States who either deliver almost no services at all to the handicapped or whose level of practice is still anchored in the early 1950s. As a matter of fact there are, in my experience of the past several years, relatively few school districts providing a full range of educational alternatives for the handicapped, and not many which have put to good use one or more of the several innovative practices and programs described here and elsewhere. For the few bright spots one observes there are hundreds of places just now stirring. Why?

153

There are many "good" reasons: No money. Lack of qualified leadership. Training programs are turning out the wrong kind of people. I can't get the superintendent interested. There hasn't been enough research to justify changing. No guts. No time. And others.

In my opinion, valid as some of these reasons are, the problems which hinder a more uniform advance in developing alternatives for exceptional children are related to the ability of both regular and special educators to make sense out of the many models available for public consumption. The list of those who have advocated, conceptualized, and practiced various alternatives is long. Reynolds (1962), Deno (1970), Lilly (1971), McKenzie (1970), Fox (1973), Hewett (1967), Miesgier (1971), Johnson & Gross (1973), Taylor (1972), and a host of others have developed special conceptualizations, programs, and practices which relate to the task of developing alternatives. There should be no one way, and these professionals all learn from one another and from testing models against reality.

However, few of these innovations (models) are effectively communicated in a manner which allows ready replication of practice, process, or structure. There have been many efforts to communicate—through journal articles, professional conference presentations, books, individual consultation, and organized efforts such as the University of Minnesota's National Leadership Training Institute. Clearly, many school districts have felt the impact of these communication efforts. Although dissemination has been extensive, the impact of existing model efforts could be greatly enhanced through a somewhat more rigorous use of the term "model," and through standardization of our professional communication system around some common reference base.

The purpose of this article is to (1) suggest that our many excellent philosophical, conceptual, and operational models for alternative programs and practices could have more replication effect; (2) establish a common definition for use of the term "model"; (3) suggest essential ingredients which programs and/or practices must include if they are to be considered models; (4) discuss several of these ingredients in more detail, and (5) suggest an alternatives-related taxonomy as a common reference base for use in understanding the relationship of any reported model or practice to a "levels-of-service" delivery system.

IMPACT FROM CURRENT MODELS

Existing model programs and practices and future innovations could be more effectively communiciated if models were communicated with replicability rather than "show and tell" as an essential goal, and if any given model could be identified in its contextual relationship to a levels-of-service or continuum-of-service delivery system and to other program models. In the past, communicating for the purpose of "show and tell" has been a valuable professional stimulant, and will continue to be. We do, however, need to be increasingly rigorous in our definitions and in our attempts to describe programs and practices with replicability in mind.

The dictionary defines "model" as a miniature representation of some existing object, as a preliminary pattern, as a tentative ideational structure used as a testing device, as an example to be emulated, and as a standard of excellence worthy of imitation.

For purposes of this article, the term "model" will be used in relation to either a tentative ideational structure or an example to be emulated. Deno's (1970) Cascade of Services delivery system model is an example of the former, and Taylor's (1972) Learning Center model is an example of the latter.

ESSENTIAL CHARACTERISTICS FOR ALTERNATIVES MODELS

One might examine several rather esoteric characteristics of models, such as stigma-neutral (replicable across all racial, ethnic, and cultural populations), ego-neutral (replicable outside the influence of the designer), situation-neutral (replicable outside the idiosyncracies of one setting), and others. However, the only way to determine if a model possesses these characteristics is to replicate the program or practice in various settings. In discussing specific characteristics deemed important to qualifying a program or practice as a model worthy of emulating or replicating, then, only clearly reportable characteristics will be discussed, and all characteristics will relate to models designed to create or improve systems, programs, and practices pertaining to education of the exceptional child.

Given the assumption that a model is a model only if it is replicable, I suggest that models in special education must, at a minimum,

1. adhere to, comply with, or complement the doctrine of least restrictive alternatives (Johnson & Vitolo, 1975; Burgdorf, 1975) and other legal requirements
2. provide for written rather than implied definition of all processes and procedures necessary to establish and conduct the model
3. define in writing the competencies expected of all actors significant to the conduct of the model
4. provide written role and function statements for all actors
5. define the target population in functional rather than categorical terms
6. specify underlying assumptions and/or theoretical approaches
7. specify objectives of the model in student-related terms
8. present existing outcome data on the target population

155

9. specify intended replication targets
10. specify necessary internal and external personnel and related resource needs
11. specify type and extent of superordinate support necessary in replication sites
12. specify an approximate activity schedule for the planning-organizing-implementing cycle
13. suggest degree of flexibility (i.e., which components of the model are essential to operation and which are peripheral or situational)
14. detail structural and contextual requirements such as physical space and configuration, needed school day definition, or treatment span
15. specify the type of internal client-related decision system required, such as the Pupil Progress Management System (Brown, 1974) or the Discrepancy Evaluation Model (Provost, 1969)
16. specify overall program goals
17. specify leadership and/or supervision structures required.

Models that are "real," when reported for public consumption and replication, will meet or address substantively these and other criteria. While some of these requirements may be of more importance than others, replication (emulation) depends in large part on the degree to which *all* essential characteristics are defined and effectively communicated. One possibility for communicating model systems, programs, and practices effectively is the User-Adopter Manual Approach utilized by USOE for disseminating successful Title III, E.S.E.A. programs.

While all of the characteristics listed above are important, three will be discussed in more detail: the doctrine of least restrictive alternatives, the need to define the target population in functional rather than categorical terms, and the type of internal client-related decision system.

The Doctrine of Least Restrictive Alternatives

The doctrine of least restrictive alternatives is a common sense idea related ι freedoms guaranteed by the U.S. Constitution. This doctrine, typically applied by the courts in non-education-related civil cases, has recently been applied and upheld as a defense against arbitrary and capricious placement and treatment practices. The doctrine is particularly germane to the development of model systems, programs, or practices since any program must establish procedures to insure that when a student is placed or a treatment applied, that placement or treatment is the least restrictive necessary.

In essence, this doctrine provides that, when government pursues a legitimate goal that may involve the restricting of fundamental liberty, it must do so using the least restrictive alternative available. Applied to education, courts have ruled in principle that special education systems or practices are inappropriate if they remove children from their expanded peer group without benefit of constitutional safeguards. Placement in special environments for educational purposes can, without appropriate safeguards, become a restriction of fundamental liberties.

It is required, then, that substantive efforts be made by educators to maintain handicapped children with their peers in a regular education setting, and that the state (as represented by individual school districts) bear the burden of proof when making placements or when applying treatments which involve partial or complete removal of handicapped children from their normal peers.

This doctrine represents, for handicapped children, the right to be educated in the regular class, however defined, unless clear evidence is available that partial or complete removal is necessary. Factors idiosyncratic to school districts (such as organizational arrangements, technological differences in delivery systems, agency jurisdictional problems, and/or lack of adequate local, state, or federal financial support) may not be considered as reasons for abrogating the right of an individual child to the least restrictive alternative necessary to meet his/her unique educational needs.

The doctrine of least restrictive alternatives has been a primary reference in court decisions involving the right of handicapped children to both treatment and education. Among these cases are *Mills* vs. *Board of Education, PARC* vs. *Commonwealth of Pennsylvania, Wyatt* vs. *Stickney, Lake* vs. *Cameron,* and *Welsh* vs. *Likens.* Ideas expressed in these decisions include the following:

> No person shall be admitted to the institution unless a prior determination shall have been made that residence in the institution is the least restrictive habilitation setting feasible for that person. No mentally retarded person shall be admitted to the institution if services in the community can afford adequate habilitation to such person.

> Residents shall have a right to the least restrictive conditions necessary to achieve the purposes of habilitation. To this end, the institution shall make every attempt to move residents from (1) more to less structured living; (2) larger to smaller facilities; (3) larger to smaller living units; (4) group to individual residence; (5) segregated from the community to integrated into the community living; (6) dependent to independent living. *(Wyatt* vs. *Stickney)*

> Each member of the plaintiff class is to be provided with a publicly supported educational program suited to his needs, within the context of a presumption that among the alternative programs of education, placement in a regular public school class with appropriate ancillary services is preferable to placement in a special school class. *(Mills* vs. *Board of Education)*

> It is the Commonwealth's obligation to place each mentally retarded child in a free, public program of education and training appropriate to the child's capacity, within the context of a presumption that, among the alternative programs of education and training required by statute to be available, placement in a regular public school class is preferable to placement in a special public school class and placement in a special

public school class is preferable to placement in any other type of program of education and training. (*PARC* vs. *Commonwealth of Pennsylvania*)

State legislation on education of the handicapped has begun to incorporate appropriate legislative safeguards which require application of the doctrine, as in recently enacted Iowa legislation:

> To the maximum extent possible, children requiring special education shall attend regular classes and shall be educated with children who do not require special education. Whenever possible, hindrances to learning and to the normal functioning of children requiring special education within the regular school environment shall be overcome by the provision of special aids and services rather than by separate programs for those in need of special education. Special classes, separate schooling or other removal of children requiring special education from the regular education environment shall occur only when and to the extent that the nature or severity of the educational handicap is such that education in regular classes, even with the use of supplementary aids and services, cannot be accomplished satisfactorily. (SF 1163–Iowa 5/28/74)

Thus, schools or persons planning and developing alternative programs for the handicapped must define those strategies, processes, procedures, timetable and resource requirements necessary to deliver special education programs and services in a manner consistent with the least restrictive alternative doctrine. Several characteristics are important to consider in structuring program models to comply with this doctrine:

1. Anticipated changes in placement, or assignment to treatments must be governed by either (a) informed parent/student consent, or (b) application of full procedural due process.
2. Programs and practices should relate to a continuum-of-services delivery system.
3. Processes and procedures must be defined and implemented which would result in student needs being defined (a) individually and (b) through an interdisciplinary team process. These teams should define and implement procedures necessary to generate written individual educational plans.
4. Processes and procedures must be defined which would ensure periodic reassessment of student behaviors on (a) an individual basis determined by unique student needs *and* (b) a mandatory fixed interval schedule.
5. Processes and procedures must provide for fluidity of movement through and between alternative placement or treatment options, and decisions to place students in a more restrictive environment or to move to a less restricting environment must be data-based.
6. Processes and procedures must be established which would create a formal appeal process for parents and students through which professional decisions to move away from or closer to a less restrictive placement or

treatment alternative can be appealed. Procedures should be defined to ensure that parents are informed that they have the legal right to question and if necessary appeal the placement or transfer of their child to a special education program or to another placement or treatment option.

Application of the doctrine of least restrictive alternatives to education of handicapped children requires, in defining model program and practices, not only the use of a continuum-of-services delivery system, but also requires safeguards related to team decision making, due process and/or parent consent, and periodic reassessment. This doctrine must be specifically addressed in the development of model programs for the handicapped.

Functional Descriptors

Reynolds and Balow (1972), Deno (1970), Gallagher (1972), Jones (1972), Lilly (1970, 1971), Johnson and Gross (1973), and others have all discussed the importance of describing the client population, whenever possible, in terms which relate to performance (observable behaviors) rather than to categories or labels such as the "mentally retarded" or the "emotionally disturbed." Common problems observed with use of categories or clinical labels have included the stigma associated with the label, the influence of the label on expectations of significant others, the application of labels and clinical categories without constitutional safeguards, and the lack of relevance of labels and/or categories to the actual day-to-day teaching/learning process.

The use of clinical categories in future attempts to design or communicate model programs or practices should be minimized as a counterproductive practice. First, there is no clear agreement on criteria for determining assignment of a child to any given category or use of a particular label for a child. Second, any group of children, regardless of how rigorously identified, is likely to contain multiple clinical categories. Third, the range of behaviors or performance within categories of children is so great that the clinical category as a descriptor actually describes little other than administrative practice.

Replication of promising programs and/or practices, then, is confounded if the program or practice is touted as appropriate for one or more disability categories, rather than for a client population described along functional characteristics. Functional behaviors related to language performance, psycho-social performance or motor performance, to name a few, provide a more relevant means of defining the clientele than do the typical categories. The Vermont Consulting Teacher Program (McKenzie et al., 1970), for example, defines its clientele without reference to clinical category and utilizes measured educational performance deficits as a means of identifying clients.

Client-Related Decision System

Alternative models for provision of services to handicapped students are all organized and delivered with the basic goal of providing meaningful and effective instruction and services for the individual handicapped learner. Clear definition of the way in which decisions about clients (handicapped learners) are made is extremely critical to ensure meaningful and effective instruction.

Several decision classes are important, including decisions related to *assessment* (what instruments, techniques, and/or procedures are necessary to determine entry status or baseline); decisions related to *acceptance* (if assessment is conducted to determine eligibility for some predefined program or service, is this particular learner eligible and is he/she accepted or rejected for service); decisions related to *treatment of choice* (what interventions should be applied to modify the learner's performance or behavior); decisions related to *evaluating outcome* (how and when the impact of the interventions on the learner's behavior or performance will be assessed); and decisions related to *modifying or terminating intervention*. In defining a client-related decision system, these decision classes should not necessarily be thought of as discrete, but as elements of a total decision system which is simply a cycle composed of assessment of the learner, selection and application of intervention, outcome evaluation, reassessment, and reprogramming or exiting.

Several types of decision systems are already available, such as the "Input-Output Systems Model for Process Sub-systems for Service to Handicapped Learners" (Case & Moore, 1974), the Pupil Progress Management System (Brown, 1974), the Vermont Consulting Teacher Minimum Objectives/Discrepancy Evaluation System (Christie & McKenzie, 1975), the Minneapolis Diagnostic-Prescriptive Process (Johnson & Grismer, 1975) and others.

Many of these systems utilize principles of applied behavior analysis (Baer, Wolf & Risley, 1968; Bandura, 1969; Ramp & Hopkins, 1971), an approach which is disability category neutral and thus compatible with models which describe clients and desired outcomes (behaviors) in functional terms. Decision systems utilizing principles of applied behavior analysis have been applied at all levels of service and to students with all degrees of handicap, including very severely handicapped youth (Brown & York, 1974).

The purpose of this discussion is not to elaborate on any one of the existing client decision system efforts, nor is the case being made here for singular use of principles of applied behavior analysis in the design of such decision systems. The important point is that one cannot purport to be delivering special education instruction and services—no matter what the program effort is called—unless a data-based client decision system has been defined and is operational. Any model program effort, whether developed as a total service delivery system for a school district or as a single teacher-based prescriptive teaching effort, must operate within the context of a defined client decision system.

The Remaining Characteristics

The doctrine of least restrictive alternatives, the need to identify clients in functional rather than categorical terms, and the need for a defined client decision system are not necessarily the most important of the tentative list of characteristics necessary if any given effort is to be called a "model." Other characteristics are also important, but space will not permit even a brief discussion of each.

There is, however, one characteristic which needs brief reference, especially in light of the national concern with decategorizing and delabeling, and in light of the trend in schools to move to alternatives-based delivery systems.

In this respect, a very important essential for any program effort is that of *leadership* or, more narrowly defined, administration and supervision. As programs move to develop total delivery systems based on a levels-of-service system, the categorical model of leadership becomes an albatross. Johnson and Gross (1973), in reporting on the reorganization of Minneapolis' special education leadership resources, state that

> Obviously, these new programming models and systems harbinger the need for leadership systems organized much differently than those now extant. It will be very difficult for school systems to advocate, much less effectively operate, non-categorical, multiple option programs with categorically defined leadership systems. Not only is there a clear need to minimize the use of categories in structuring tomorrow's special education leadership resources, but the new demands of mainstreaming and of court-required full service to all handicapped will require new leadership dimension and structure. Clearly then, given current program direction, most public school leadership systems for the handicapped need extensive redefinition in both form and substance.

New or existing model systems, programs, or services must not only specifically define their leadership structures and requirements, but should also ensure that leadership structures are consistent with program design and goals. Noncategorical, performance-based service systems will be seriously restricted by categorical leadership structures.

A COMMON REFERENCE BASE

In addition to improving our communications and understandings base by specifying characteristics (criteria) which model programs or efforts must meet, it would be helpful if the proliferation of programs, services, and strategies which are legitimate models for replication purposes could be organized within some type of established taxonomy.

While there are obviously many ways of classifying various types of program efforts, one might consider using a system which relates quite directly to an alternatives-based conception of a special education service delivery system. It should be possible to organize all of the program and service models reported in this book, for example, in relationship not only to one another, but also to a levels- or continuum-of-services delivery system.

Figure 1 illustrates a classification schema which could be utilized in this manner and which takes into account three critical dimensions: *type* of model, *focus* of model, and *comprehensiveness* of model.

In this schema, the comprehensiveness dimension consists of the several criteria or characteristics defined earlier; the type dimension includes ideational, experimental, and applied; and the focus dimension includes delivery system direct and delivery system indirect. The vertical dotted line running through the comprehensiveness dimension section illustrates that the several compre-

Figure 1

**SPECIAL EDUCATION MODELS CLASSIFICATION SCHEMA
BY TYPE, FOCUS, AND COMPREHENSIVENESS OF MODEL**

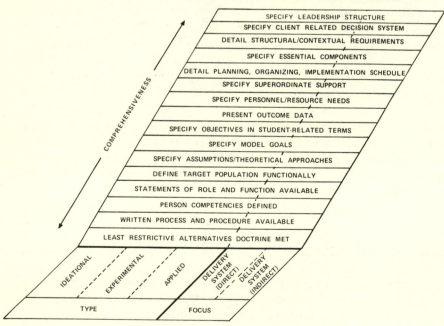

hensiveness criteria apply regardless of whether the model is ideational, experimental, or applied, or whether the focus is delivery system direct or indirect. The principal exception within this otherwise generic comprehensiveness dimension is the "present outcome data" criterion. While one could expect experimental and applied models to both generate and present outcome data, models at the ideational level generally will not have generated outcome data. Also, the criteria would need to be revised for evaluating models which are delivery system indirect. The model is applicable, but the names and number of criteria would change.

Of the several types of models, an ideational model, for purposes of definition, is a model which has been conceptualized around some theoretical framework but has not yet been subjected to either field experimentation and validation or to direct field application without experimental controls. An experimental model is essentially an ideational model in some process of defined experimentation in either a field or controlled setting. An applied model is either an ideational or experimental model which is in full scale application in several school settings and has become accepted as a legitimate and efficacious practice or program.

Model focus, the third dimension of the models schema, is organized around the concept of "delivery system." Delivery system in this respect applies to arrangements of programs, practices, and resources designed to provide special educational services for the handicapped. Some models have as their direct focus one or more components or elements of a service delivery system, such as models for resource teacher programs, for leadership configurations, for prescriptive instruction, etc. For purposes of determining model focus, these are considered delivery system *direct*. Delivery system *indirect* refers to models which involve service delivery, but which are less directly focused on actual programs and practices as applied in the school setting. Models for preservice training, organizational change, legislation, and policy development are examples of indirect focus models. A model for a competency-based training program for special education resource teachers, for example, may eventually have an impact on services to the handicapped, but is less direct in application than is a model for use of a minimum objectives approach to evaluating performance of the handicapped learner.

An important element of this models classification schema is the relationship of the comprehensiveness dimension to the type and focus dimensions. Figure 2 illustrates the relationship of comprehensiveness criteria to type of model and is illustrative of the fact that, regardless of whether the model in question is ideational, experimental, or applied, these criteria obtain. An ideational model, for example, should be more than a vaguely defined concept, and the degree to which it is more than that is measured by how completely the originator addresses each of the several comprehensiveness criteria. Even without actual experimentation or field application, then, an ideational model needs structuring and specificity.

Figure 2 also represents the perspective that criteria against which to evaluate the comprehensiveness of any given model can expand beyond those examples listed, and requirements related to other doctrines, functions, systems, and procedures can be added or substituted.

Figure 2 illustrates, by arrow in the center, the reality that models can be either prospective (proceeding from ideation to application) or post hoc (proceeding from practice to ideation). In this latter instance, models for replication purposes often begin with practice and then gain credibility through

Figure 2
RELATIONSHIP OF "COMPREHENSIVENESS" DIMENSION TO "TYPE OF MODEL" DIMENSION

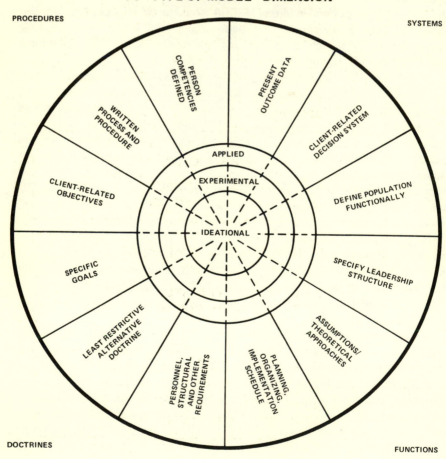

experimentation and/or conceptual definition (ideation). Regardless of the origin of the model, however, a program or practice can lay claim to the designation "model" only if it meets comprehensiveness criteria.

Figure 3 illustrates the models classification schema or taxonomy in outline form. The purpose of organizing the taxonomy in this manner is to allow for classification of any model program or practice according to the three dimensions of model type, model focus, and model comprehensiveness. Obviously, classification of models as to type of model can vary with time. Deno's Cascade of Services model (1970) initially would have been classified as ideational (1.1), delivery system direct (2.1), and, on the comprehensiveness dimension, ideational and delivery system direct (3.1.1). Today, in 1975, the Cascade of Services model is applied rather than ideational, and there is much

Figure 3
OUTLINE OF MODELS CLASSIFICATION SCHEMA

	MODEL TYPE	
	1.1	IDEATIONAL
1.0	1.2	EXPERIMENTAL
	1.3	APPLIED

	MODEL FOCUS	
2.0	2.1	DELIVERY SYSTEM (DIRECT)
	2.2	DELIVERY SYSTEM (INDIRECT)

	MODEL COMPREHENSIVENESS	
	3.1	IDEATIONAL
		3.1.1 DELIVERY SYSTEM (DIRECT)
		3.1.2 DELIVERY SYSTEM (INDIRECT)
3.0	3.2	EXPERIMENTAL
		3.2.1 DELIVERY SYSTEM (DIRECT)
		3.2.2 DELIVERY SYSTEM (INDIRECT)
	3.3	APPLIED
		3.3.1 DELIVERY SYSTEM (DIRECT)
		3.3.2 DELIVERY SYSTEM (INDIRECT)

Figure 4
MODELS TAXONOMY — Focus Section

2.0 MODEL FOCUS
  2.1 Delivery system, direct focus
    2.1.1 Total delivery system model
      2.1.1.1 Alternatives related system
        2.1.1.1.1 Noncategorical system
        2.1.1.1.2 Categorical system
        2.1.1.1.3 Generic
      2.1.1.2 Non-alternatives related system
        2.1.1.2.1 Noncategorical system
        2.1.1.2.2 Categorical system
        2.1.1.2.3 Generic
    2.1.2 Delivery system service level or component
      2.1.2.1 Consultation/technical assistance/inservice training
        2.1.2.1.1 Noncategorical system
        2.1.2.1.2 Categorical
          2.1.2.1.2.1 EMR
          2.1.2.1.2.2 TMR
          2.1.2.1.2.3 ED/SOC MAL
          2.1.2.1.2.4 PH
          2.1.2.1.2.5 MH
          2.1.2.1.2.6 Speech
          2.1.2.1.2.7 HI
          2.1.2.1.2.8 VI
          2.1.2.1.2.9 OHI
          2.1.2.1.2.10 OH
          2.1.2.1.2.11 LD
        2.1.2.1.3 Generic
      2.1.2.2 Resource teacher or tutoring program—direct service model
        2.1.2.2.1 Noncategorical
        2.1.2.2.2 Categorical
          2.1.2.2.2.1 EMR
          2.1.2.2.2.2 TMR
          2.1.2.2.2.3 ED/SOC MAL
          2.1.2.2.2.4 PH
          2.1.2.2.2.5 MH
          2.1.2.2.2.6 Speech
          2.1.2.2.2.7 HI
          2.1.2.2.2.8 VI
          2.1.2.2.2.9 OHI
          2.1.2.2.2.10 OH
          2.1.2.2.2.11 LD
        2.1.2.2.3 Generic
      2.1.2.3 Resource teacher program—indirect service model
        2.1.2.3.1 Noncategorical
        2.1.2.3.2 Categorical
          2.1.2.3.2.1 EMR
          2.1.2.3.2.2 TMR
          2.1.2.3.2.3 ED/SOC MAL
          2.1.2.3.2.4 PH
          2.1.2.3.2.5 MH
          2.1.2.3.2.6 Speech
          2.1.2.3.2.7 HI
          2.1.2.3.2.8 VI
          2.1.2.3.2.9 OHI
          2.1.2.3.2.10 OH
          2.1.2.3.2.11 LD
        2.1.2.3.3 Generic
      2.1.2.4 Itinerant service program
        2.1.2.4.1 Noncategorical
        2.1.2.4.2 Categorical
          2.1.2.4.2.1 EMR
          2.1.2.4.2.2 TMR
          2.1.2.4.2.3 ED/SOC MAL
          2.1.2.4.2.4 PH
          2.1.2.4.2.5 MH
          2.1.2.4.2.6 Speech
          2.1.2.4.2.7 HI
          2.1.2.4.2.8 VI
          2.1.2.4.2.9 OHI
          2.1.2.4.2.10 OH
          2.1.2.4.2.11 LD
        2.1.2.4.3 Generic
      2.1.2.5 Part-time special class program
        2.1.2.5.1 Noncategorical

2.1.2.5.2 Categorical
    2.1.2.5.2.1   EMR
    2.1.2.5.2.2   TMR
    2.1.2.5.2.3   ED/SOC MAL
    2.1.2.5.2.4   PH
    2.1.2.5.2.5   MH
    2.1.2.5.2.6   Speech
    2.1.2.5.2.7   HI
    2.1.2.5.2.8   VI
    2.1.2.5.2.9   OHI
    2.1.2.5.2.10 OH
    2.1.2.5.2.11 LD
2.1.2.5.3 Generic
2.1.2.6 Full-time special class program
  2.1.2.6.1 Noncategorical
  2.1.2.6.2 Categorical
    2.1.2.6.2.1   EMR
    2.1.2.6.2.2   TMR
    2.1.2.6.2.3   ED/SOC MAL
    2.1.2.6.2.4   PH
    2.1.2.6.2.5   MH
    2.1.2.6.2.6   Speech
    2.1.2.6.2.7   HI
    2.1.2.6.2.8   VI
    2.1.2.6.2.9   OHI
    2.1.2.6.2.10 OH
    2.1.2.6.2.11 LD
  2.1.2.6.3 Generic
2.1.2.7 Special school program
  2.1.2.7.1 Noncategorical
  2.1.2.7.2 Categorical
    2.1.2.7.2.1   EMR
    2.1.2.7.2.2   TMR
    2.1.2.7.2.3   ED/SOC MAL
    2.1.2.7.2.4   PH
    2.1.2.7.2.5   MH
    2.1.2.7.2.6   Speech
    2.1.2.7.2.7   HI
    2.1.2.7.2.8   VI
    2.1.2.7.2.9   OHI
    2.1.2.7.2.10 OH
    2.1.2.7.2.11 LD
  2.1.2.7.3 Generic
2.1.2.8 Homebound and institution
2.1.2.9 Community residential program: school intake
2.1.2.10 Community residential program: agency intake
2.1.2.11 Other programs
2.1.3 Supportive subsystems/processes
  2.1.3.1 Leadership/administration/supervision
    2.1.3.1.1 Categorical
    2.1.3.1.2 Noncategorical or alternatives-related
    2.1.3.1.3 Generic
  2.1.3.2 Referral and placement
  2.1.3.3 Parent involvement
  2.1.3.4 Program evaluation
  2.1.3.5 Management information
  2.1.3.6 Staff development
  2.1.3.7 Child study/diagnostic-prescriptive process
  2.1.3.8 Budget and fiscal
  2.1.3.9 Personnel utilization
  2.1.3.10 Program planning and development
  2.1.3.11 Software/hardware/media development and
          utilization
  2.1.3.12 Ancillary services: social work, psychology, health
  2.1.3.13 Other
2.1.4 Delivery system clinical strategies
  2.1.4.1 Teaching/learning process and methods
  2.1.4.2 Organizational management
  2.1.4.3 Pupil assessment and prescription
  2.1.4.4 Teaming
  2.1.4.5 Communications
2.2 Delivery system: indirect focus
  2.2.1 Change models
    2.2.1.1 Process orientation
    2.2.1.2 Structural orientation
    2.2.1.3 Other
  2.2.2 Preservice training
  2.2.3 Legislation
  2.2.4 Regulation and guidelines
  2.2.5 Policy
  2.2.6 Other

more information available with which to judge the comprehensiveness, for replicability purposes, of the model. Clearly then, many model programs and practices go through an evolutionary process, and any classification must account for changes over time.

The outline presented in Figure 3 is not, however, sufficiently detailed for purposes of classification, especially in regard to the focus and comprehensiveness dimensions of a model. Figure 4 provides additional detail for the focus section of the taxonomy, and Figure 5 provides detail on the comprehensiveness section. Utilizing this additional detail, the Cascade of Services model now would be classified as:

Type 1.3	Applied
Focus 2.1.1.1.3	Direct focus, total delivery system model, alternatives related system, generic
Comprehensiveness 3.3.1.2	Applied, delivery system direct, meets most criteria

In this example, the term "generic" under the focus section indicates that this model of a total delivery system is designed not only for categorical or noncategorical purposes, but is applicable to either approach. This particular model is, however, an alternatives-related model in that levels of service (alternatives) are indigenous to the model, regardless of whether one chooses to create categorical, noncategorical, or both types of alternatives within the total delivery system.

The phrase "meets most criteria" under the comprehensiveness classification was selected because the "presents outcome data" classification criterion has not yet been to my knowledge fully met, nor have several other criteria been sufficiently explicated for replication purposes. The way in which one meets the requirements of the doctrine of least restrictive alternatives or the type of client-related decision system considered necessary to this model has not been addressed except as individual districts have struggled to add substance to the conceptual design. The point is not that the Cascade of Services model lacks value because it does not meet exactly this 1975 suggested classification schema, but rather, future ideational models should be defined with the comprehensiveness dimension and related criteria in mind.

As another example of the way in which this system is applied, the Responsive Teaching model (Hall, 1971) would be classified as follows:

Type 1.3	Applied
Focus 2.1.4.1	Direct focus, clinical strategies, teaching/ learning process and methods
Comprehensiveness 3.3.1	Applied, direct, meets most criteria

While Hall and others, in their contributions related to this model, have not specifically addressed each of the comprehensiveness criteria in turn, their description of this system reveals that clients are usually described in functional terms, outcome data is presented, that theoretical foundations are described, etc. Again, this model could be more clearly explicated and more readily replicated if all comprehensiveness criteria were specifically applied.

Figure 5
MODELS TAXONOMY — Comprehensiveness Section

3.0 MODEL COMPREHENSIVENESS
  3.1 Ideational
    3.1.1 Delivery system direct
      3.1.1.1 Meets all criteria
      3.1.1.2 Meets most criteria, exceptions specified
      3.1.1.3 Meets few or no criteria
      3.1.1.4 Insufficient information
    3.1.2 Delivery system indirect
      3.1.2.1 Meets all criteria
      3.1.2.2 Meets most criteria, exceptions specified
      3.1.2.3 Meets few or no criteria
      3.1.2.4 Insufficient information
  3.2 Experimental
    3.2.1 Delivery system direct
      3.2.1.1 Meets all criteria
      3.2.1.2 Meets most criteria, exceptions specified
      3.2.1.3 Meets few or no criteria
      3.2.1.4 Insufficient information
    3.2.2 Delivery system indirect
  3.3 Applied
    3.3.1 Delivery system direct
      3.3.1.1 Meets all criteria
      3.3.1.2 Meets most criteria, exceptions specified
      3.3.1.3 Meets few or no criteria
      3.3.1.4 Insufficient information
    3.3.2 Delivery system indirect
      3.3.2.1 Meets all criteria
      3.3.2.2 Meets most criteria, exceptions specified
      3.3.2.3 Meets few or no criteria
      3.3.2.4 Insufficient information

This classification system for developing and communicating replicable models is offered as an initial suggestion only. Not only are more detail and refinement required, but also professional consensus supporting the need for such a taxonomy is necessary.

SUMMARY

This article has discussed several issues related to the development and utilization of models for programs related to education of the handicapped. One of these issues is the need for more definition and scientific rigor in designing and communicating model programs and practices, with emphasis for communication purposes on potential for replicability rather than on "show and tell."

Another issue relates to the urgency of the task. The profession is being pressed to provide full service to all the handicapped and to provide that service with major emphasis on documenting that what we do makes a difference. Also, services must be given not only to create improved learner status, but also to ensure that the doctrine of least restrictive alternatives and other court-mandated safeguards are applied. Given the urgency, we must not only refine and clinically define model programs and practices, but we must also aggressively communicate and disseminate these programs and practices in some understandable manner.

A third issue discussed in this article is the need to standardize our professional communications base. Model programs, practices, and systems are reported everywhere but always come in different size containers, and with either limited or confusing packaging directions. There are hundreds of useful programs and practices available, but there is no commonly-agreed-on understandable means for organizing and communicating these to potential users. This article suggests a classification schema which might be helpful in standardizing our professional communications base. This schema is based on the assumption that certain types of information would be helpful to the potential consumer (director of special education, school superintendent, teacher etc.) and that three of the most important are model type, model focus, and model comprehensiveness. Of these, model comprehensiveness is critical. Comprehensiveness of a model is established by analysis of the degree to which a particular model program or practice meets several criteria, including the presence of a defined client decision system, the use of functional descriptors in defining client population, and others. All major comprehensiveness criteria must be accounted for if, strictly speaking, a program or practice is to be considered an example to be emulated.

To date, we have made do without a cognitive road map or models classification schema. However, as special education (in its thrust to develop alternatives necessary to meet the infinite variation of need in individual handicapped learners) becomes more complex and as various ideas and practices increase geometrically, we will need to have some means of sorting out model programs and practices for replication purposes and will need to standardize our professional communications base. "Show and tell" will still perform a useful professional function and will continue to be necessary. I do not wish to suggest replacement of existing professional communications via journal articles and other means nor to denigrate such efforts. Not every program and practice thus reported is a model, however, and some commonly defined means of sorting out true models and of targeting or replicability is needed.

REFERENCES

Baer, D. M., Wolf, M. M. & Risley, T. R. "Some Current Dimensions of Applied Behavior Analysis." *Journal of Applied Behavior Analysis, 1* (1), 1968.

Bandura, A. *Principles of Behavior Modification.* New York: Holt, 1969.

Brown, Judith. The Pupil Progress Management System, 1974 (unpublished).

Brown, Lou & York, Robert. "Developing Programs for Severely Handicapped Students: Teacher Training & Classroom Instruction." *Focus on Exceptional Children, 6* (2), April, 1974.

Burgdorf, R. L. Jr. "The Doctrine of the Least Restrictive Alternative." In R. Johnson, J. Gross, R. Weatherman (Eds.), Leadership Series in Special Education, Volume IV. Minneapolis, MN: University of Minnesota AV Publishing Service, in press.

Case, Charles W. & Moore, John W. "The Problem Oriented Educational Record: A Systems Analysis, Design, and Implementation Process." University of Vermont, 1974 (unpublished).

Chaffin, Jerry D. "Will the Real 'Mainstreaming' Program Please Stand Up! (or . . . Should Dunn Have Done It?)." *Focus on Exceptional Children, 6,* (5), October, 1974.

Christie, L. S. & McKenzie, H. S. "Minimum Objectives: A Measurement System to Provide Evaluation of Special Education in Regular Classrooms." In *Exceptional Children Educational Abstract,* Reston, VA: Education Resource Information Center, National Institute of Education, 1975.

Deno, E. "Special Education as Developmental Capital." *Exceptional Children, 37,* 1970 (229-240).

Fox, W. L., et al. "An Introduction to a Regular Classroom Approach to Special Education." In Deno, E. (Ed.), *Instructional Alternatives for Exceptional Children.* Arlington, VA: The Council for Exceptional Children, January, 1973.

Gallagher, J. J. "The Special Education Contract for Mildly Handicapped Children." *Exceptional Children, 38,* 1972 (527-536).

Hall, R. Vance. "Responsive Teaching: Focus on Measurement and Research in the Classroom and the Home." *Focus on Exceptional Children, 3* (7), December, 1971.

Johnson, R. A. & Grismer R. "Diagnostic Prescriptive Processes: The Minneapolis Model." Gainesville, FL: LTI Institute, February, 1975.

Johnson, R. A. & Grismer, R. "The Harrison School Center: A Public School-University Cooperative Resource Program." In Deno, E. (Ed.), *Instructional Alternatives for Exceptional Children.* Arlington, VA: The Council for Exceptional Children, January, 1973.

Johnson, R. A. & Vitolo, R. "The Doctrine of Least Restrictive Alternatives and Education of the Handicapped." Unpublished monograph, 1975.

Johnson, R. A. & Gross, J. C. "Restructuring Special Education Leadership Systems: The Minneapolis Plan." In R. Johnson, J. Gross & R. Weatherman (Eds.), *Special Education in Court*. Minneapolis, MN: University of Minnesota AV Publishing Service (Leadership Series in Special Education), 1973.

Johnson, R. A., Gross, J. C., Weatherman, R. F. Leadership Series in Special Education, Volumes I and II. Minneapolis, MN: University of Minnesota AV Publishing Service, 1973.

Jones, R. L. "Labels and Stigma in Special Education." *Exceptional Children, 38,* 1972 (553-564).

Lilly, M. S. "A Training Based Model for Special Education." *Exceptional Children, 37,* 1971, (747-749).

Lilly, M. S. "Special Education: A Teapot in a Tempest." *Exceptional Children, 37,* 1970 (43-49).

McKenzie, H. S.; Egner, A.; Knight, M.; Perelman, P.; Schneider, B.; & Garvin, J. "Training Consulting Teachers to Assist Elementary Teachers in the Management and Education of Handicapped Children." *Exceptional Children, 37,* 1970 (137-143).

Meisgeier, Charles. "The Houston Plan: A Proactive Integrated Systems Plan for Education." In E. Deno, (Ed.), *Instructional Alternatives for Exceptional Children*. Arlington, VA: The Council For Exceptional Children, January, 1973.

Mills vs. *Board of Education* of D.C., C.A. No. 1939-71 (D.D.C.).

Morris, William (Ed.). *The American Heritage Dictionary of the English Language*. Boston, MA: American Heritage Publishing Co. and Houghton Mifflin Company, 1970 (p. 843).

Netzer, Lanore A. & Eye, Glen G. (Eds.). *Education, Administration and Change*. New York: Harper & Row, 1970 (chapters 1 and 7).

Pennsylvania Association of Retarded Citizens vs. *Commonwealth of Pennsylvania*, C.A. No. 334 S. Supp. 1257 (E.D. PA. 1971).

Provos, M. *Discrepancy Evaluation for Educational Program Improvement and Assessment*. Berkeley: McCutchan Publishing, 1971.

Ramp, Eugene & Hopkins, Bill. *A New Direction for Education: Behavior Analysis*. Lawrence, KS: Support and Development Center for Follow-Through, Department of Human Development, University of Kansas, 1971.

Reynolds, M. "A Framework for Considering Some Issues in Special Education." *Exceptional Children, 28,* 1962 (367-370).

Reynolds, M. & Balow, B. "Categories and Variables in Special Education." *Exceptional Children,* January, 1972.

SF 1163, Iowa State Legislature, May 28, 1974.

Taylor, F. D., et al. "A Learning Center Plan for Special Education." *Focus on Exceptional Children, 4* (3), May, 1972.

Wyatt vs. *Stickney*, 325 F. Supp. 781, 784 (M.D. Ala. 1971).

This chapter is a most significant contribution to the past, present, and future of the movement to place handicapped children in instructional settings which are facilitative of learning and least restrictive in opportunities for interactions with the mainstream of educational programs. Chaffin has placed the cogent issues into perspective through a critical review of the precursors to present mainstreaming efforts. This is important since an understanding of the present and planning for the future require a critical review of what has occurred in the past. From historical roots, Chaffin then proceeds to describe and compare current mainstreaming programs within a framework that includes philosophy, administrative arrangements, type of children served, etc. This aspect allows the reader to discern differences and similarities among the various programs even though program titles indicate some purported variance.

The final portion of the chapter is devoted to a comprehensive description of a mainstreaming project which Chaffin and his doctoral students have conducted over a period of several years. This chapter is indeed a landmark, a must for any serious professional who wishes to plan a mainstreaming program for handicapped children.

Will the Real "Mainstreaming" Program Please Stand Up! (or . . . Should Dunn Have Done It?)

Jerry D. Chaffin
University of Kansas, Lawrence

Since the turn of the century when the first special classes were established in the United States, segregated special classroom environments have been the most popular means for educating mildly and moderately retarded children. However, during the past decade, increasing discontent with segregated classes has emerged among special educators, and a variety of alternative delivery systems have been proposed and implemented. These alternative educational programs are characterized by the retention of the mildly retarded child in the

173

regular education classroom with supplemental instructional support being provided to the regular classroom teacher—this practice is popularly referred to as "mainstreaming."

The present emphasis on mainstreaming programs for mildly and moderately retarded children was brought about in part by:

1. The equivocal results of research dealing with the effectiveness of special classes for the mildly retarded.
2. The recognition that many of the diagnostic instruments used for identifying retarded children were culturally biased, which often resulted in inappropriate diagnosis and placement of children into special classes for the retarded.
3. The realization on the part of special educators that the effects of "labeling" a child may be more debilitating than the diagnosed handicap.
4. Court litigation in special education related to placement practices and the rights of children to appropriate educational treatment.

The above factors (and others) which have led to the current practice of "mainstreaming" exceptional children have been amply reviewed and expanded upon in other sources (Tilley, 1970; Kolstoe, 1972; Iano, 1972; Dunn, 1968; Dunn, 1973; Garrison & Hammill, 1971) and will not be reviewed here. Instead, the purpose of this paper is (1) to provide the reader with a brief historical overview of the debate in the literature among special educators regarding the appropriateness of special class placement for the retarded; (2) to highlight briefly several theoretical proposals describing alternative delivery systems; (3) to present a variety of "mainstreaming" models currently being implemented in the public schools; and (4) to establish guidelines for special education administrators who may initiate mainstreaming programs in the future.

"TO SEGREGATE OR NOT TO SEGREGATE"

Professional dialogue related to the validity of segregated special classes, as a viable means of intervention for the problems of exceptional children, has been carried on among special educators for more than 30 years. Efficacy research on special class placement prior to 1940 (Bennett, 1932; Pertsch, 1936) must have prompted some special educators to question seriously the appropriateness of special class placement, and the Twenty Second Annual Meeting of the International Council for Exceptional Children (in 1944) featured a panel of administrators and professors who presented their views on *Segregation versus Non-Segregation of Exceptional Children*. A summary of the panelists' comments is reported by Shattuck (1946). The views of several of the panelists would be quite current today, for they emphasized a need for training regular classroom teachers to work with handicapped children and also expressed

For example, Bess Johnson, then principal of Smouse Opportunity School in Des Moines, Iowa, argued ". . .dumping a handicapped child into a pool of normal children where he must sink or swim should not be permitted until all teachers have been trained to be lifesavers" (Shattuck, 1946, p. 236). On this same panel, Harley Wooden, then Superintendent of the Michigan School for the Deaf, reminded the audience that the environment selected for a child's development ". . .must . . .be based on a thorough understanding of the particular child involved rather than on an administrative expediency of segregation or a blind ideal of nonsegregation" (Shattuck, 1946, p. 236). Wooden indicated that the real concern, when placing an exceptional child, is with creating an environment in which he can satisfactorily grow and develop. He stressed that

> neither the ordinary unmodified normal environment nor the unmodified segregated environment is suitable for growth and development of a markedly exceptional child. The normal environment must be appreciably modified to provide for his deviation from the normal group and for his acceptance into it, while the segregated environment, which is designed to meet his exceptional condition, must be appreciably modified to meet his social needs. [p. 239]

The views expressed by this panel in 1944 appear not so much against segregation as for integration where possible—a philosophy not inconsistent with views of many special educators today.

Nearly two decades later, Johnson (1962) reviewed some 14 research studies dealing with various aspects of the efficacy question. Finding no strong supportive evidence in favor of special class placement, he noted:

> It is indeed paradoxical that mentally handicapped children having teachers especially trained, having more money (per capita) spent on their education, and being enrolled in classes with fewer children and a program designed to provide for their unique needs should be accomplishing the objectives of their education at the same or at a lower level than similar mentally handicapped children who have not had these advantages and have been forced to remain in the regular grades. [p. 66]

Johnson postulated, as a possible explanation of this seemingly paradoxical situation, that the removal of exceptional children from regular classrooms had also removed much of the competition and pressure to learn which is present in most school situations. Citing several selected research studies which supported his position, Johnson then proposed that educators consider the introduction of "realistic stress" in special classes as a means of enhancing the learning outcomes of children.

In a rebuttal of Johnson's suggestion, Steigman (1964) suggested that Johnson had inaccurately interpreted the research dealing with the effects of stress on learning. Steigman then presented his own interpretation of this research which in actuality, he said, supports a position related to simplifying "the tasks to be learned and to reduce stress in the learning situation" (p. 68)—a position nearly opposite that of Johnson.

Though Johnson's article resulted in considerable controversial discussion among professional educators, the fact that it did not result in a major reversal of practices in special education may have been partially due to Steigman's lethal critique of his proposal.

During the next few years, the professional dialogue regarding the validity of special class placement expanded from the efficacy question to include concern about the effects of labeling children and the recognition that some of the measurement tools used for identification and placement of children into segregated environments were unfair to minority-group children. Later dialogue included the potential ramifications of court litigation on some practices in special education. Dunn (1968) reviewed the research associated with the above concerns in his now familiar essay "Special Education for the Mildly Retarded—Is Much of It Justifiable?" and called for a moratorium on the placement of mildly retarded children in special classes. The timeliness of Dunn's comments or his prominence among special educators (possibly both) influenced significantly the thinking and action of special educators. MacMillan (1971) acknowledged this influence by noting, "Clearly, Dunn has been an important influence in reversing a trend toward the proliferation of self-contained special classes. . ." (p. 1).

MacMillan went on to take issue not with Dunn's recommendations, but rather with the apparent misinterpretation of Dunn's findings by some school districts. The wholehearted endorsement by some school districts of what they perceive Dunn's position to be has resulted in many schools moving "toward total integration of EMR-labeled children into regular classrooms" (p. 12). MacMillan maintains that an abrupt and unorderly change from self-contained classrooms to total integration can be dangerous. Instead, he argues, what is needed is a systematic development of preventive, transitional, and regular classroom models whereby programs are developed cooperatively by university and public school personnel so that they evolve as a result of controlled research. He emphasized that "unless the quality of research is high, it will not provide us with the necessary information on which we must make educational decisions regarding children" (p. 10).

After carefully reviewing the evidence presented by Dunn, MacMillan added his own interpretation and concluded that "the larger issue and one which if debated and researched could prove fruitful is: to what extent and under what circumstances can a wider range of individual differences be accommodated in the regular class than is presently the case?" (p. 9).

MacMillan's concern for the systematic development and evaluation of alternative programs for the retarded is undoubtedly shared by a majority of special educators. The extent to which that shared concern is actually reflected in practice will be noted later in this paper.

THEORETICAL PROPOSALS FOR MAINSTREAMING

Dunn's (1968) forceful critique of special classes for the retarded resulted in a number of proposals for alternative delivery systems. Four such models are presented below. Each model, though prompted by concern for programs for the retarded, describes a system which would be applied across most areas of exceptionality—in most cases without attention to labels.

Deno's Cascade of Services: Evelyn Deno (1970) has proposed that special education "conceive of itself primarily as an instrument for facilitation of educational change. . ." (p. 229). Deno argues that successful industries invest a part of their resources in research and development, resulting in the improvement and development of new products. Deno perceives special education as the research-and-development arm of regular education, thus providing "Developmental Capital" to improve all education. To assume such a role, special education must be inseparably linked to regular education; Deno proposes a cascade of education services (see Figure 1) to illustrate this linkage. Deno describes this system as one which "facilitates tailoring of treatment to individual needs rather than a system for sorting out children so they will fit conditions designed according to group standards not necessarily suitable for the particular case" (p. 235). In summary, Deno's cascade of services recognizes the individuality of exceptional children by providing a wide variety of service options.

Lily—A Training Based Model: Steve Lilly (1970) has argued that, for too long, the focus of educational intervention has been on the child and not on the educational system. He then offers a new definition of exceptionality which emphasizes the characteristics of the school situation and not the characteristics of the child (p. 48). In a later paper, Lilly (1971) outlines the Training Based Model for providing services to exceptional children, which model he emphasizes must meet several criteria. The first criterion to be met is that the model must be a zero-reject system. Inherent in the zero-reject system is the policy that ". . .once a child is enrolled in a regular education program within a school, it must be impossible to administratively separate him from that program for any reason" (p. 745). Lilly notes that the zero-reject system places responsibility for failure on the teacher and not on the child, and forces educators (both special and regular) to deal with educational problems in the regular classroom.

A second criterion is that the responsibility for ". . .rectification of difficult classroom situations" (p. 746) lies with the regular classroom teacher, with

177

Figure 1

CASCADE OF EDUCATION SERVICES

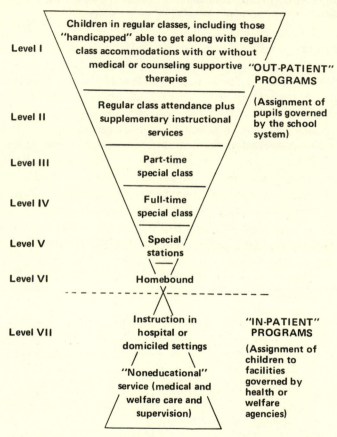

Level I — Children in regular classes, including those "handicapped" able to get along with regular class accommodations with or without medical or counseling supportive therapies

Level II — Regular class attendance plus supplementary instructional services

Level III — Part-time special class

Level IV — Full-time special class

Level V — Special stations

Level VI — Homebound

Level VII — Instruction in hospital or domiciled settings

"Noneducational" service (medical and welfare care and supervision)

"OUT-PATIENT" PROGRAMS

(Assignment of pupils governed by the school system)

"IN-PATIENT" PROGRAMS

(Assignment of children to facilities governed by health or welfare agencies)

The cascade system of special education service. The tapered design indicates the considerable difference in the numbers involved at the different levels and calls attention to the fact that the system serves as a diagnostic filter. The most specialized facilities are likely to be needed by the fewest children on a long term basis. This organizational model can be applied to development of special education services for all types of disability. (Deno, 1970, p. 235) Reprinted by permission of the publisher.

special education providing only a supportive role. As a corollary, Lilly's third criterion is that the major goal of special education is to develop the skills of regular classroom teachers to the point where they no longer need special education support. Lilly then goes on to describe a training-based approach.

> Upon referring a child, a teacher would be offered the services of an instructional specialist whose function would be to instruct that teacher in ways to handle the referred problem, as well as other identifiable problems within the regular classroom. The task of the instructional specialist would be to equip the teacher to deal with the class as it exists, to handle both behavioral and academic problems.

> While in the classroom, the instructional specialist would work with the teacher in such areas as diagnosis of problems in academic skill areas, specification of both individual and small-group study programs, behavior management procedures, and group and individual reinforcement patterns. In short, the instructional specialist would teach skills deemed necessary to enable the classroom teacher to cope effectively with the classroom situation. At no time during the period of service would the instructional specialist remove a child from the classroom for individual work, whether it be of a diagnostic or tutorial nature, *for this practice in no way contributes to preparing the teacher to perform this function in the future.* [p. 746]

Lilly emphasizes that the training based model would replace, not supplement, existing services and notes that many former special class teachers would be cast in new roles requiring that the district provide extensive inservice training. Lilly's model represents a major challenge to training institutions since the effective instructional specialists in Lilly's model, must be "experts in all areas of behavior and curriculum management, and at the same time, must develop interpersonal skills necessary to conduct successful teacher education" (p.748).

Gallagher's Contract Model: The Special Education Contract model proposed by Gallagher (1972) is directed mainly toward mildly retarded, disturbed, or learning-disabled primary-age children. This model involves the adoption of a signed formal contract between parents and school officials prior to the commitment of a mildly handicapped child to special education services. This formal contract would outline specific goals to be attained during the intervention program and would cover a time period of no longer than two years. The contract would be ". . .nonrenewable, or renewable only under a quasi-judicial type of hearing, with the parents represented by legal or child advocate counsel" (p. 532).

Gallagher emphasizes that the Special Education Contract is not a substitute for all current special education services and notes that it (the model) is only a

> . . .limited suggestion for dealing with two pressing problems facing special education today. The first problem is the difficulty of replacement of mildly handicapped children in regular education once they have been assigned to special education. The second and related problem is the tendency to overassign certain minority group children to special education. [p.527]

Gallagher also stresses that his proposal is not one to be adopted blindly without much discussion and pilot work in a number of communities.

Adamson's and Van Etten's Fail-Save Model: The fail-save model (Adamson & Van Etten, 1972) was published as a response to Lilly's (1971) proposed training-based model. The authors suggested that Lilly's model may be too limiting in not offering enough alternatives for exceptional children. They propose a plan incorporating at one level the training aspects emphasized by Lilly but including several alternatives. In the fail-save model:

> The "fail" represents the system's failure to meet all children's needs, not the child's. The "save" represents the adaptation of the system to the child's individual needs and "save" him. [p. 736]

Procedurally, the "fail-save" model begins with a referral from the regular classroom teacher. Upon receipt of the referral, a methods and materials consultant begins a 10-week evaluation and observation of the child. During this period, the consulting teacher conducts both formal and informal testing of the child, recommends trial procedures and materials to the regular classroom teacher, and makes regular observations of the child, as well as regular contacts with the teacher, in an attempt to determine the responsiveness of the child to the trial programs. "At no time does the methods and materials specialist become the tutor or the remedial teacher" (p. 737).

At the completion of the 10-week cycle a conference, attended by parents, teachers, administrators, and the methods and materials person, is held to decide on future action. At this point one of two decisions may be made. The child may either be retained in the initial treatment phase for an additional 10-week period, or he may be referred to a resource classroom/regular class placement. The resource placement extends for a period no longer than 90 days. During this period the child is assigned to regular class and attends the resource room for diagnostic instruction and tutoring as needed. The materials and methods consultant also continues to monitor the progress of the child. At the end of 90 days another evaluation conference is held, and one of three decisions is made: (1) the child is returned to the itinerant cycle for 10 weeks; (2) the child remains in the resource room/regular class program for an additional 90 days; or (3) the child is referred for special class/resource room placement. When the child is placed in the special class/resource room, his program is coordinated jointly by the special-class and resource-room teachers. This placement is made for a maximum of 9 months. Following an evaluation of the child's response to this level of instruction, the child may be returned to the resource room/regular class program or be referred for special-class placement. If the latter decision is made, the child must automatically be returned to a resource-room program after 2 years.

According to the authors, the fail-save model is based on ". . .experience and data gathered from implementing educational diagnosis, itinerant methods and materials consultant/teachers, resource rooms, materials laboratories and a teacher-based training model" (p. 735). They emphasize that such an administrative model better meets the needs of the exceptional because it offers greater instructional and program alternatives which the diverse exceptional population needs.

The four models described above represent the individual authors' particular approaches for improving delivery systems for handicapped children. The models are in some respects theoretical, though they have been implemented with some variation in a variety of applied settings. For example, Deno's concept of a service hierarchy is present (in some form) in nearly all applied programs; Lilly's emphasis on the inservice role of the special educator is also present in many applied models; and Gallagher's suggestions for formally contracted education plans for the individual child are also present in many programs, though admittedly most programs do not develop these plans in cooperation with parents nor with the formality urged by Gallagher. The "fail-save" model of Adamson and Van Etten has been implemented in the State of New Mexico (Pepe, 1973) with some minor changes being made in the model prior to implementation (Van Etten & Adamson, 1973).

MAINSTREAMING PROGRAMS IN THE PUBLIC SCHOOLS

Four recent publications have described a number of mainstreaming programs currently operational in the public schools. These publications are *Models for Mainstreaming,* by Keith Beery (1972); *Instructional Alternatives for Exceptional Children*, edited by Evelyn N. Deno (no publication date); *Configurations of Change: The Integration of Mildly Handicapped Children into Regular Classrooms,* edited by Nancy Kreinberg and Stanley H. Chou (1973); and *Mainstreaming: Educable Mentally Retarded Children in Regular Classes*, by Jack Birch (1974). These four publications contain a total of 30 different alternative systems for delivering special education services to exceptional children. A few of the models are descriptions of university training models, but most of the models represent descriptions of alternative programs that are currently being implemented in public school settings. Table 1 contains a listing of the programs, their location, and the source from which the information was obtained.

The programs in Table 1 were reviewed initially with the idea of comparing and contrasting each of the programs on such variables as program philosophy, administrative organization, staffing patterns, type and number of handicapped served, parent involvement, extent of inservice training, and attitudes of regular classroom teachers toward the program. However, the variations in format used

Table 1
MAINSTREAMING PROGRAMS IN THE SCHOOLS

	Program	Deno	Birch	Kreinberg & Chou	Beery
1.	Tacoma Board of Education (Tacoma, Washington)	X			
2.	Richardson Public Schools (Richardson, Texas)	X			
3.	Plano Independent School District (Plano, Texas)	X			
4.	Tucson Board of Education (Tucson, Arizona)	X			
5.	Louisville Public Schools (Louisville, Kentucky)	X			
6.	Kanawha County Schools (Kanawha County, West Virginia)	X			
7.	North Sacramento Project (Sacramento, California)				X
* 8.	The Diagnostic Prescriptive Teacher (Washington, D.C.)	X		X	X
9.	Helping or Crisis Teacher (Ann Arbor, Michigan)				X
10.	The Madison Plan (Santa Monica, California)	X		X	X
11.	Fail Save (Albuquerque, New Mexico)	X		X	
12.	Stratistician Model (Salt Lake City, Utah)	X			
* 13.	Learning Problems Approach (Miami, Florida)	X			
* 14.	Consulting Teacher Program (Burlington, Vermont)	X			
15.	Inservice Experience Plan (Storrs, Connecticut)	X			
16.	Improved Learning Conditions (Seattle, Washington)	X			
17.	Precision Teaching-Junior High (Seattle, Washington)	X			
* 18.	Harrison School (Minneapolis, Minnesota)	X			
* 19.	Seward University Project (Minneapolis, Minnesota)	X			
20.	Building Administrators- Individualized Instruction (Rockford, Illinois)	X			
21.	The Houston Plan (Houston, Texas)	X			
22.	Kindergarten-North Carolina Open Classroom (Raleigh, North Carolina)				X
23.	Northwest Colorado Learning Analysis Approach (Steamboat Springs, Colorado)				X
24.	Team Planning for Integration (Yuba City, California)				X
25.	Franklin Pierce Project (Tacoma, Washington Area)				X
26.	Parkway Elementary School (Tacoma, Washington Area)				X
27.	Diagnosis and Prescription: A Route to Individualization (Oak Grove School - San Jose, California)				X
28.	Brigadoon Elementary School- Individualized Instruction through Continuous Assessment (Federal Way, Washington)				X
29.	Project Catalyst (San Francisco, California)				X
30.	Santa Monica Plan (Santa Monica, California)				X

*University-Based Training Model

in describing the programs and the imprecise terminology used, made detailed comparisons between specific programs almost impossible. A careful reading of these programs is useful, however, in that the general nature of the program is described and usually the significant features of the program are quite clear. Following are the author's impressions of various programs on several variables.

Program Philosophy

The philosophical basis for mainstreaming usually was not stated explicitly in the program descriptions and, consequently, must be inferred from the overall description of the program. Inherent in the philosophy of most programs is the child's basic right to an equal educational opportunity—where equal means not the same educational experiences but rather "different" educational experiences based on the child's unique needs. Nearly all program descriptions expressed a belief that for a majority of exceptional children integration, not segregation, should be the first consideration in designing educational experiences. Most of the programs reflected a position that labeling and grouping of children into specific categories such as mentally retarded, emotionally disturbed, or learning disabled does not contribute significantly to the design of the instructional program (except perhaps for the severely handicapped). Finally, a number of the programs emphasize a position of decentralization of authority for program decisions to the individual school building level.

Administrative Organization

Although the various programs reviewed are similar in underlying philosophy, they vary greatly in the type of administrative organization adopted and the degree to which it is described—making comparative statements difficult. Team teaching is frequently referred to as sometimes involving a special education teacher with three or more regular teachers in an open, multigraded setting. In other cases team teaching refers to the combining of a special education person and her students with the students and teacher in one regular classroom. Team *planning* is also emphasized in several of the programs. Texas programs rely on an Admissions, Review, and Dismissal (ARD) Committee to admit, periodically review status, and dismiss children receiving special instruction. This team is chaired by the building principal. The remainder of the committee composition varies but could involve the sending and/or receiving regular and special education teachers, special education diagnostician or curriculum consultant, counselor, psychologist, and social worker. In contrast team planning in the Yuba City, California district refers to the cooperative weekly planning of individualized learning experiences for children by regular and special education teacher teams.

Other programs rely heavily on itinerant special education personnel. The Oak Grove School District (San Jose, California) combines an open space, team teaching (in this case 4 regular classroom teachers) arrangement with the services of a diagnostic/prescriptive strategist who consults with various teams on an itinerant basis. The Northwest Colorado Child Study Center provides itinerant support services of a psychologist, social worker, and speech therapist to support a special education resource person and regular classroom teacher in each building of the geographic area it serves in rural Colorado. The special education person in each building is referred to as a Child Study Teacher (CST) and provides resource services to the regular classroom teacher. The way a CST functions varies from building to building depending upon the administrative organization of the building, the needs and attitudes of the regular classroom teachers, and nature of the school population. Some CSTs may spend a considerable amount of time providing direct services to children, while others may spend most of their day in providing instructional support to regular classroom teachers.

A number of other programs also rely on the resource room model, such as Tucson, Arizona, and Tacoma, Washington, though both of these programs also provide self-contained classrooms for some children. The approach taken in the Richardson, Texas, program also relies mainly on a resource room arrangement, though self-contained classrooms, self-contained/integrated, and helping teacher arrangements are also utilized. A similar array of services exists in the Louisville, Kentucky, program.

In conclusion, although the terminology used in describing the various programs did not allow precise discrimination between many of the administrative arrangements, it is clear that programs across the country rely on a wide variety of administrative arrangements. These approaches range from open classrooms with regular and special education teachers participating in a team approach or team teaching with itinerant support to more common itinerant, self-contained, or resource room arrangements. While most programs emphasize one type of service arrangement, it is usually acknowledged in the program description that a wide variety of service options are available to exceptional children.

Type and Number of Handicapped Served

Since the programs reviewed usually claimed to provide services on a noncategorical basis, the type or severity of the handicapping condition usually was not clear. In many cases the programs reviewed were designed to serve mildly mentally handicapped, and others emphasized services to mildly learning disabled, emotionally disturbed, and other mildly handicapped children. The number of handicapped children served by the various programs was also unclear though some information was occasionally provided.

The Parkway Elementary School project indicated that the total student population of the school was about 400 and that the project served *all* of the mildly handicapped children in the school, but the specific number of handicapped children receiving services was not given. Other references to number of students served indicated what percent of the total student population were receiving services. These ranged from 8.6% in the Franklin Pierce project to 20% in the Richardson, Texas, program. The Tucson program provided information pertaining specifically to EMR children and noted that 95% of the EMR students were maintained in regular classes two-thirds or more of the school day. The description of the Tucson program also indicated that only 3 self-contained programs were operational in 1973 compared with 20 in 1969 when the mainstreaming emphasis was initiated. Similar kinds of data was provided by the Tacoma, Washington, and the Richardson, Texas, programs.

On the basis of the meager data provided it would appear that a variety of mildly handicapped children are being accommodated in the regular classroom with instructional support from special education personnel. This includes in some cases up to 90-95% of the mildly mentally handicapped population. The reader is urged to consider this information with caution as it will be noted later there is very little data which speaks strongly for the effectiveness of such services.

Parent Involvement

Parent involvement in the programs reviewed appeared to range from strong involvement to no mention of parents' role or interest in the program. In the Franklin Pierce project, for example, parents were encouraged to observe the program. In other programs, it was mandatory that parents be informed of the student's problem as well as the remedial method being used. In the Richardson, Texas, program the parents are part of the ARD committee and in Plano, Texas, the parents were used as volunteers. Parent volunteers were used in the Brigadoon Elementary School also. Other programs indicated involvement but did not specify how or the degree of involvement. Some programs only indicated favorable parental reaction to the program and others made no mention of parental involvement. The lack of information related to parental involvement in many of the programs may be attributed to reporting errors, since most states have now adopted "due process" legislation requiring parental involvement.

Inservice

For the most part, all of the programs examined indicated a need and interest in inservice. For example, in the Tucson program some inservice education was provided by staff from the University of Arizona with additional inservice training conducted informally by the Tucson Public School staff. The Tacoma, Washington, program operated a "micro-college" which provided short courses and workshops for their teachers. The Franklin Pierce Project provided inservice for its staff through summer institutes. The Houston Plan and other programs also reported extensive inservice efforts. Other programs reported that more systematic inservice training programs for regular and special education staff was needed.

Acceptance of Program by Regular Teachers

Acceptance of mainstreaming by regular classroom teachers was a topic frequently overlooked in the program descriptions; however, a few of the reports do supply such information. The Parkway Elementary School program and the Yuba City Plan indicated strong support of regular classroom teachers for mainstreaming. Other project reports note that the mainstreaming efforts received mixed teacher reaction, and one report noted that the responses ranged from outright rejection to only qualified acceptance. Since the projects varied considerably in number and type of handicapped children served, amount and kind of instructional support provided, and the amount of preparation and inservice provided, it is not unusual that the regular teacher reaction to the project would also vary considerably.

Cost Factors

If regular administrators anticipate that mainstreaming efforts will result in a substantial reduction of costs, it is not evident from the program descriptions reviewed that such reductions ensue. Some program reports noted that mainstreaming resulted in only nominal increased costs, while most programs reporting on the topic noted the costs were about the same as providing segregated classes, though some program descriptions noted that *more* children could be served in integrated programs than in segregated classes. One or two programs noted that if savings occurred it would be in the area of student transportation.

Program Evaluation

Of all the topics considered in reviewing the program reports listed in Table 1, the information pertaining to student evaluation proved to be the most disappointing. At least two-thirds of the 30 programs listed could be described as actual on-going programs in the public schools and, as such, might be reasonably expected to report some data on student achievement. Ten of these programs reported no evaluative information at all; three contained case studies or graphs as examples of student success; two relied on questionnaires to parents and/or teachers as a means of evaluating the effectiveness of the services provided; and two of the program reports indicated that evaluations were currently being planned. Four of the program descriptions contained minimally acceptable evaluation information. Three of the programs which presented data related to program effectiveness utilized some form of control groups as a means of interpreting the treatment effects of their particular program. Statistical comparison were usually made between the groups on standardized test scores, rating forms and/or behavioral observations. The fourth program providing information related to program effectiveness did not use a control population but instead compared the scores of the environmental group with the national norms of the tests used. In all of the above cases, the data presented *tended* to favor the experimental programs, but the results were not at all impressive. In fairness to the originators of the programs reviewed, the reader is reminded that the purpose of these programs was to develop new and innovative delivery systems for providing services to exceptional children. In this regard, the programs are of much value. It is indeed unfortunate that information related to the effectiveness of the services provided was not also collected on a systematic basis, since the professional literature contains very little data to support the varying administrative arrangements for serving handicapped children. This fact is particularly true regarding mainstreaming arrangements for the mildly mentally handicapped.

The following is a brief overview of other research relating to the mainstreaming issue. Thorsell (1964) studied the effects of an itinerant teacher arrangement for EMR pupils in several rural counties in Western Kansas. She identified a control group of EMR subjects in the same locale who were in regular classes but received no special education service and compared their performance with the experimental group (receiving itinerant services) on five criterion reference-like measures. The results favored the experimental group on two of the measures (calendar test and clock test), while no significant differences were found between the two groups on the remaining three measures (money test, common signs, and arithmetic combinations). However, in all cases the experimental subjects had higher adjusted means.

Carroll (1967) investigated the effects of partial integration of EMR students into regular classrooms. EMR pupils who attended special class half day and regular class half day were matched on IQ, age, and achievement with a group of EMR pupils who attended special class the entire day. The results indicated a significant decrease in self-derogatory statements as measured by the Illinois Index of Self-Derogation by the experimental group. The experimental group also made greater gains than the control group in reading. Flynn and Flynn (1970) compared the social adjustment of EMR pupils enrolled in special classes on a part-time basis (45 minutes daily) with a group of EMR pupils on a "waiting list." They found no differences in the two groups on social adjustment but noted that more of the EMR subjects on the "waiting list" (39%) were unconditionally promoted at the end of the year than the EMR pupils placed in part-time special classes (21%).

Studies dealing more directly with the differential effects of varying administrative arrangements of services for EMR pupils have been conducted by Tilley (1970) and Rodee (1971). Both Tilley and Rodee investigated the effects of three types of educational placement (itinerant, resource, self-contained) for mildly mentally handicapped pupils. Tilley essentially found no differences between the groups on measures of math, reading, self-concept, and behavior, while Rodee's investigation favored the resource group over the special class group in reading achievement but resulted in no differences between the groups on measures of word knowledge, word discrimination, arithmetic, behavior, or attendance. In contrast to the findings of Tilley and Rodee, Walker (1972) found that EMR subjects receiving instruction in resource rooms were significantly better academically and socially than a control group of special class students. Similar support for the resource room arrangement is noted by Hammill and Wiederholt (1972). They report that the measured growth in reading of a group of educable retarded pupils who attended noncategorical resource rooms had "...an average increase of .7 of a grade in seven months of attendance" (p. 34). Hammill and Wiederholt also report that a two year project involving the placement of 64 EMR pupils in resource rooms in Atlanta, Georgia (Barksdale & Atkinson, 1971) resulted in "...significant and impressive gains" (Hammill & Wiederholt, 1972, p. 34) in academic performance. A review of this study revealed that these "impressive" gains amounted to an average of about one and one-half years per student over a three year (not two) period from September 1967 to May 1970. While the gains may still be statistically significant, they do not appear to be impressive.

On the basis of the program reports and other research studies considered above, it is evident that there is little substantial data on which to state any firm conclusions regarding the effectiveness of various administrative arrangements for mildly mentally handicapped children. Nor does the data shed any light on the problem of what kind of services might be best for what kind of child? Even more important is the fact that MacMillan's (1971) plea for the systematic development of alternative models, designed, implemented, and evaluated cooperatively by public school and university personnel, seems to have gone unheeded. Though some of the projects reported on above do reflect the cooperative efforts of the university and public schools, the quality of the research does not always reflect this cooperative effort.

Currently, the most promising research and development effort related to the mainstreaming of exceptional children is Project PRIME—Programmed Reentry into Mainstream Education—(Kaufman, Semmel & Agard, 1974). This project was initiated in the spring of 1971 by the Bureau of Education for the Handicapped in cooperation with the Texas Education Agency. The project was designed to provide "...descriptive, comparative, explanatory, and predictive information of pupil academic, social, and emotional growth as they relate to comprehensive patterns of special and educational services" (p. 109). This project has a substantial funding base which allows for the collection of a wide array of standardized tests, observations, ratings, and other information related to variables being studied. The sample population encompasses more than 2,000 handicapped and nonhandicapped children in 650 classrooms. Some preliminary results from this project should be forthcoming in the near future.

TWO ADDITIONAL MAINSTREAMING PROJECTS

Two additional mainstreaming projects are described in some detail below. They are included here because they offer some promise as effective models which might be successfully replicated in other settings.

Children without Labels—Fountain Valley, California[1] : The mainstreaming of handicapped children in the Fountain Valley, California, School District is carried out in the midst of a decentralized enriched instructional environment involving team teaching, differentiated staffing, and individualized planning for every child in the district. All but a few severely handicapped pupils function within the regular education program and receive instructional support as needed by special education resource personnel. A brief explanation of the organization of the instructional resources in the Fountain Valley system follows since the regular education and special education programs are virtually inseparable.

The school district is comprised of 17 elementary (K-8) schools attended by about 11,000 children. Each of the schools has reorganized the use of space so that every six or eight classrooms are clustered around a Learning Center. All of the Learning Centers are well equipped with diagnostic and instructional materials. Each school has a primary (K-2), middle (3-5), and upper (6-8) Learning Center. The teachers of the 6-8 classrooms which surround the Learning Center are coordinated by a person designated as the Learning Coordinator. The Learning Coordinator does not have direct responsibility for a classroom of pupils but is assigned to the Learning Center with responsibilities for some individual and small group instruction particularly in remedial reading and math. This person is also responsible for coordinating the planning and instructional activities of the classroom teachers and support staff of the cluster team. The support staff consists of a special education resource teacher, speech clinician, and a school psychologist. Each of the 17 schools in the Fountain Valley School District have at least one special education resource teacher though several schools must share a speech teacher and psychologist with at least one other building. Several schools, designated as supplementary centers because they serve children with more severe handicaps, have two or more special education resource teachers.

---

1. The description of the Fountain Valley, California Special Education project was obtained from the Fountain Valley Title III ESEA Project (Project #1232) and from two visits to the district by the author. Principal contacts for these visits were Mr. Milo Bibleheimer, Director of Special Education, Fountain Valley Schools, and Mr. Carl Cunningham, Learning Coordinator, Fulton School.

The communication necessary among the teachers, support staff, and the Learning Coordinator for effective individualized planning requires a great deal of time. Extra time for this communication is provided through the Modified Teaching Day. One day each week, the school day is shortened for students, allowing the principals and their staff an uninterrupted afternoon for conferences, inservice, and individual planning.

Special Education Provisions: Prior to the 1969 school year the Fountain Valley School District provided special education services to exceptional children mainly through special classroom arrangements. About 50-60 EMH (educable mentally handicapped) students were bused to two centrally located schools and received instruction in four special classrooms. Some educationally handicapped pupils were also served in special classes. At this time parents, teachers, and administrators of the program were concerned by the poor academic progress of the students as well as their poor adaptive behavior.

With assistance provided through a Title III, ESEA Project (#1232) planning was begun in June 1969 on a new model to be implemented in the fall. During the subsequent school year the special class programs were gradually phased out, and by September 1970 the entire district-wide handicapped population was integrated into the regular classroom. Each school in the district was provided with a resource room teacher, and schools which accommodated more severely handicapped students were designated as supplementary centers and provided with additional resource teachers. Individual planning for the handicapped students was done in the same manner as for all students with the resource teachers providing planning and instructional assistance as indicated by the needs of the students and their regular classroom teachers. Most of the pupils were seen daily by Special Education Resource Personnel. After morning activities in the regular classroom, students were scheduled into the Learning Center to see the Resource Specialist where daily individual contracts were developed and implemented by either the regular teacher, the resource teacher, or both.

During the first project year the enrollment in the program consisted of 59 EMR and 31 EH students. The ages of the students in the EMR and EH program ranged from 6-2 to 14-5 and 6-8 to 13-2 respectively. The mean IQ for the EMR group was 71. The intelligence data for the EH group was not provided.

Evaluation: Objectives of the Fountain Valley program called for (1) increased academic achievement, (2) improved acceptance of handicapped children by the regular classroom teachers, and (3) improved self-concept of the project students.

Improved achievement for project students was based on whether or not the students maintained or exceeded their *expected gain. Expected gain* was computed by dividing the pretest grade equivalent score by the difference of the child's chronological age at time of pretest minus his chronological age upon entry in school. Eighty-one percent of the students met or exceeded their expected gains scores in reading, and 89% of the students met or exceeded their expected grade equivalency in mathematics.

A semantic differential test was used to determine the changes in acceptance of project students by regular classroom teachers. Although there were no statistically significant differences in the pre and posttest scores, the Title III report concludes that the overall acceptance by the regular classroom teachers was good and that lack of significant pretest/posttest differences was due to the high level of acceptance by teachers at the beginning and throughout the project. Similar conclusions were reached regarding the acceptance of the project students by their normal classroom peers.

The data, while minimally acceptable, does not afford undisputed support for the Fountain Valley approach to providing services for exceptional children. The author was told that approximately 20 TMR and severely emotionally disturbed students were provided services on a contract basis from other school districts. While this procedure is a good alternative for some students, it may be that other alternatives should be provided to the approximately 20% of the students who did not achieve the expected rate of gain in reading.

In the opinion of a respected colleague of the author—Carl Cunningham, who is a former special class teacher and now a Learning Coordinator in the Fountain Valley District—the current mainstreaming approach is far more rewarding to teachers, students and parents than the old special class arrangement. The author was also favorably impressed with the program and more particularly with the enthusiasm of the staff.

The Pinckney Project—A Full Service School[2] : The "Full Service"[3] education model resulted from the collective thought and effort of several faculty members and doctoral students at the University of Kansas and the professional staff assigned to the Pinckney Elementary School in Lawrence, Kansas.

The staff at Pinckney Elementary had been involved with University special education personnel in implementing a "Transitional" first grade room for children who experienced failure in kindergarten. An outgrowth of this work, which featured an "individualized" learning environment along with the present trend to "mainstream" EMR pupils, was a proposal by the staff at Pinckney and University personnel to integrate a number of EMR pupils into the regular primary grades at that school.

---

2. The following report of the Pinckney Project was adapted from a report prepared for the April 1974 CEC Convention in New York, New York by the author and three doctoral students in Special Administration: Bob Campbell, Fred Geer, and Betty Weithers.
3. The Pinckney program *does not* provide the service option of special class placement and thus technically does not provide a "full" range of services to exceptional children. Consequently, the name "Full Service" program is somewhat of a misnomer.

The basic concern of the people involved in the development of the project was to redesign the available instructional resources at Pinckney School so that a wide variety of optional instructional services could be provided which would maximize the possibility of success for children with mild to moderate handicapping conditions.

Setting of the Project: The Pinckney School is one of 16 elementary schools in the Lawrence, Kansas (District #497) public schools. Pinckney School is designated as a Title I school, which implies that a substantial portion of the population falls in the lower socioeconomic levels. Though the population of 224 children at Pinckney is predominately Caucasian (74%), the overall achievement level of the students in only slightly below the local norms. This does not imply that Pinckney is a "typical" elementary school, since the mean achievement level of the school is influenced by a sizeable number of children whose parents are faculty members or graduate students at the University of Kansas.

Staffing: The regular education staff assigned to Pinckney during the 1973-74 school year consisted of 9 regular classroom teachers grades K-6 and half-time specialists for physical education, music, and remedial reading. The principal was also assigned on a half-time basis but was assisted by an administrative intern. The school district special education office provided Pinckney and all Lawrence Schools with a school psychologist, a learning disabilities teacher, and an elementary counselor—each, one day per week.

One additional special education instructional support person was provided to the Pinckney project by reassigning a former self-contained special class teacher to the project. This person was not needed as a special class teacher since a number of primary EMR children from another elementary school in Lawrence were transferred from self-contained classes and reassigned to regular classrooms at Pinckney.

Selection of Subjects: The EMR students in the Pinckney project were selected from a pool of 34 subjects who were enrolled or on waiting lists for three self-contained primary special classes. The three special education classroom teachers, the school psychologist, and the principal of the building where the self-contained rooms were housed comprised the selection committee. The committee was first asked to identify EMR students who they felt had the potential for success in a regular class environment. Of the 34 students enrolled in the primary EMH classes, 19 were thought to have some potential for success by one or more members of the committee. Four of these students were excluded because they lived outside the Lawrence School District, leaving 15 possible candidates for the mainstreaming project. These 15 students were then rated individually by the committee members on a scale of 1-5 as most to least likely to meet success in a regular classroom. The ratings were averaged to produce a rank order list. The twelve highest rated students were designated as the experimental group to be transferred to the Pinckney School. Three of these children left the district during the summer and were replaced by the next highest ranked nominees. During the first semester one experimental student moved to another city, leaving a total group of eleven.

The Full Service Program: The basic purpose of the Pinckney Project was to create a comprehensive instructional support system for exceptional children which would allow them to be successfully accommodated in regular education classrooms. The essential program elements of the Full Service Instructional Support system are (1) a well-defined service hierarchy that clearly delineates the variety of service options that are available to the exceptional child, (2) a set of systematic procedures and prescriptive forms designed to enhance the communication between the regular classroom teacher and the instructional resource person(s), and (3) a system of accountability that focuses on (a) the effectiveness of the system in meeting the instructional needs of the children and (b) how well the components of the system are being implemented. These program elements are implemented within the broader philosophical stance that service for exceptional children should (1) be instructional based and (2) that the instructional alternatives for dealing with exceptional children should be developed at the building level.

Instructional Based Service: An instructional based service system requires that each child be provided our best instructional efforts within the regular class structure before removing the child to a "special education" environment. Thus instruction, not psychometrics, should serve as the basis for moving the child from one instructional arrangement to another. This procedure does not imply that the school psychologist's role is de-emphasized. It does imply that the school psychologist's role is re-directed from a formal evaluation function that often results in the separation of the child from the mainstream of educational activity to a function designed to help teachers and other support persons to better understand the child to assist in the redesigning of the child's educational environment.

Building Level Services: When services for exceptional children are designed at each school, the entire faculty and the principal of that building can participate in defining the alternative services and instructional support needed in their building. The nature of the student population in each building determines the variety of service alternatives needed. Other variables at each school include kind and number of instructional support persons available and attitude of the principal and teachers in the building toward exceptional children. Some district-level support personnel may be involved by providing itinerant services to the various school buildings. In this instance, the itinerant support person's role would be dictated by the prevailing philosophy in the individual building. The district special education director would control the qualitative level of the programs by annually reviewing the alternative systems at each school and requiring adherence to the essential program elements described in the next section.

Service Hierarchy: The first essential program element of the Full Service Instructional Support System is the service hierarchy. One of the major benefits of a carefully defined service hierarchy is enhanced communication between the regular and special education staff. Regular education staff know what kind of services are available and what functional behaviors of the special educators are associated with each service. The services provided in a hierarchy may vary, but it is essential that they be cooperatively developed and explicitly defined by the building staff and the assigned instructional support persons.

The hierarchy of services accepted by the Pinckney staff (see Figure 2) was designed to serve children with mild to moderate handicaps. The hierarchy does not contain a provision for special class placement, so a few handicapped children who live in the Pinckney attendance area must be provided to another school in the district. In descending order the services range from the least intensive support service a child might need to the most intensive that could be provided short of special class placement. The service options are characterized as either "indirect" or "direct."

The *indirect levels* of service provided by instructional support persons are limited to interactions between the resource person and the regular classroom teacher—that is, except for observation, *the resource person has no direct contact with the child*. An explanation of the indirect service follows:

I-1 Consultation and Observation: At this level of service it is assumed that the support persons have *experience and knowledge* which may be valuable to the regular teacher in working with children with learning problems. Support at this level may involve observation of the referred child in the classroom followed by *suggestions* of procedures or resources that are available to the teacher. The important concern at this level is that the help needed by regular classroom teachers comes from the *experience* of the support person.

I-2 Formal and Informal Testing Assistance: At this level the support person will provide assistance to the regular classroom teacher in conducting the formal or informal testing that may be necessary to plan a program for the referred student. The support person *does not* work with the child at this level. Instead, the support person will furnish test materials or suggestions of informal means of assessment that will provide both the teacher and the support person with helpful information about the child. This level of support is intended to help the regular classroom teacher become a better academic diagnostician. When the teacher has obtained the results of the testing, she will communicate these results to the support person for help in program planning. This level of service will be further differentiated by the amount of help the regular classroom teacher needs in order to administer the tests. Depending upon the number of

Figure 2

SERVICE HIERARCHY

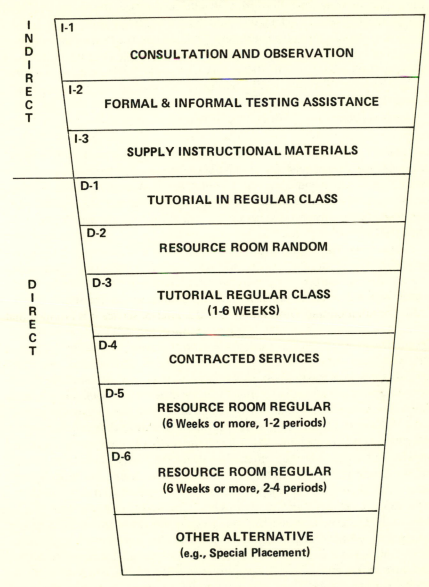

children in the class and heterogeneity of the pupils' ability level, some teachers may

    a. be able to administer the formal or informal tests during a regular class period while other children are working independently.

    b. need some help from the consultant or classroom aide to manage the class or some portion of the class while she is administering the tests.

    c. need the consultant to take over the class while tests are being administered. The important concern at this level of support is that the regular classroom teacher is responsible (with or without help from the support person) for the diagnostic work up.

I-3 Supply Instructional Resources: When the teacher and the outside support person have agreed on an instructional plan, the teacher may need assistance in locating and using the recommended resource materials. In the Pinckney project it is anticipated that by relying on local building, district, and university resources any material needed by a child can be made available within 24 hours. This level of support is different from I-1 in that the resource person may obtain or provide explanations regarding the use of a material. This level is different from I-2 in that it involves instructional rather than diagnostic resources. If a demonstration of the resource material is required with the child in order to help the teacher implement the program, the level of service *is not* I-3 but, instead, a form of direct service as described below.

In contrast to indirect service, the *direct levels* of service involve some direct interaction of the outside resource person with the child. Interaction with the regular classroom teacher must also continue at these levels of services.

D-1 Tutorial in Regular Class: This level of service provides for the support person to work directly with the student *in his regular classroom*. This service will vary as a function of the needs of the child and the regular classroom teacher but could include formal or informal evaluation, skill training in an instructional area, or helping the student learn to use prescribed resource materials. This level of service is intended to assist the regular classroom teacher in implementing a program for the student that will then be continued by her. Service to the child at this level is limited to approximately two weeks.

D-2 Resource Room Random: At this level of service the emphasis is on one specific task. The classroom teacher will send the student to the resource room for help that cannot be provided at that particular time by the classroom teacher. This is not a continued service and will be completed when the student leaves the resource room.

D-3 Tutorial, Regular Class (1-6 weeks): This level of service is different from D-1 primarily in the length of time allowed for assistance by the outside resource person. This level may also be different from D-1 in that the D-3 services may involve three or more children where as D-1 will probably (though not necessarily) involve only one or two. As in D-1 it is the intent of this level of service that the tutorial service be maintained in regular classroom instructional program. If it becomes apparent during this level of service that some kind of long term support is needed to maintain the child in the regular classroom, the outside support person begins to arrange for D-4 services.

D-4 Contracted Services: This level of service can be implemented at any time during D-3. The support person and the classroom teacher evaluate the duration of the tutorial services needed (during D-3). If services in the classroom are needed for an extended period, the support person locates and trains a tutor to carry out the program. In the Pinckney Project the tutors who carry out these services include parents, aides, and KU students.

D-5 Resource Room Regular Basis (6 weeks or more, 1-2 periods daily): This level of service will be used only when a combination of D-3 and D-4 are inadequate for the instruction needed by the student. Rarely will this level be used without first implementing lower level services in the classroom.

D-6 Resource Room Regular Basis (6 weeks or more, 2-4 periods daily): Service at this level is the highest level provided within the school. Direct referral will not be made to this level but will be preceded by referral to other levels of service.

The hierarchy of services as described above is essential to the program for two important reasons: *First*, the descriptions of each level of service enhances communication between the resource person(s) and the regular classroom teachers. Each party understands what service can be provided, thus reducing the possibility that a regular teacher might "expect" a particular service yet "receive" another service by the support person. *Second*, the defined hierarchy insures that a variety of service options remain available. Theoretically, any resource room teacher or itinerant teacher could provide the variety of service options contained on the Pinckney hierarchy. In practice, however, support persons are likely to provide those services from which they receive the most reinforcement—that is, some support persons enjoy working with teachers while others derive more satisfaction from working with children. The support person's preference should, of course, be honored as long as the best interests of the children they serve are also being considered. The presence of the hierarchy serves as a constant reminder to the regular classroom teacher and the instructional support persons that the needs of exceptional children may require a variety of instructional strategies.

Procedures and Forms: Initially the procedures for implementing the full-service model and service hierarchy began with a regular classroom teacher filling out a simple referral form concerning a student in her room who was experiencing difficulties. The referral form itself consisted of only the most essential information and required only a few minutes to complete. Unlike most referral systems where referrals are routed through the principal to a school psychologist or itinerant teacher, the referrals at Pinckney went to a *committee of three regular classroom teachers.* The committee membership changed weekly on a revolving basis with each teacher serving for three consecutive weeks. Each week one new teacher was added as another teacher finished her length of term. The senior member of the committee was designated the chairperson. After reviewing each referral, the teacher committee was to decide the service level option appropriate for the child and either support or modify the child's classroom teacher's recommendation.

The teacher referral committee was seen as an important means of enhancing communication, placing more responsibility with classroom teachers and educating regular teachers about how to meet individual student needs of exceptional children.

Though the above procedures appeared to be appropriate at the beginning of the Pinckney project, some aspects of the project were modified at midyear. It was intended that the teacher referral committee would gain sophistication about the needs of exceptional children via the decisions they were required to make in assigning service. Instead, the teachers felt unqualified to make such decisions and in most cases simply approved all services as requested. Consequently, the procedure for having referral routed through the teacher referral committee was discontinued, but it is expected that a modified version of this system may be reinstated during the coming year.

Currently, the referral and treatment procedure begins with the regular classroom teacher visiting informally with the instructional support person of her choice regarding a student exhibiting difficulties. This conversation is entered on a contact record as a consultative (I-1) level of service. At this time, the Instructional Resource Person puts the name of the student, name of the teacher, and a general statement of the student's problem on her *contact record.* If a service level other than I-1 is to be initiated, a formal *Instructional Service Plan* (ISP) is filled out jointly and maintained cooperatively by the chosen Instructional Resource Person and the regular classroom teacher. A new ISP is completed each week as long as the child is receiving service of an instructional support person. This procedure results in a continuous re-evaluation of the child's program by the instructional support person and the regular classroom teacher.

Evaluation: Of a total of 226 children enrolled in the Pinckney Elementary School, 64 were referred for service. Nine of the 64 referrals were EMR transfer students who were selected for mainstreaming. The remaining children were not labeled and represent children perceived by the regular classroom teacher as needing some kind of instructional support. It is interesting to note that only 9 of the 11 EMR children were referred for special education services. Two of the children were not referred, though their regular classroom teacher did refer other children from her class.

An attempt was made in the Pinckney project to collect data on how well the recommended system was being implemented as well as its overall effectiveness in terms of student achievement. Achievement data was available only for the EMR transfer students and was assessed with Peabody Individual Achievement Test (PIAT). Due to delays in organizing the project and the need to collect data for an April report, a total of only 5 months elapsed between the pretest (November 1973) and posttest (April 1974). Table 2 contains the results of achievement testing on the various subtests of the PIAT. The mean IQ of the Pinckney EMR students was 73 with a range from 63 to 83.

Table 2

ACHIEVEMENT GAINS OF MAINSTREAMING STUDENTS IN THE PINCKNEY PROJECT

PIAT Subtest	Pretest (Nov., 73)	Posttest (April, 74)	Gain
Math	1.1	1.6	.5
Reading Recognition	1.8	2.3	.5
Reading Comprehension	1.2	1.7	.5
Spelling	1.9	2.3	.4
General Information	1.4	2.3	.9
Total Test	1.5	2.0	.5

The mean gain on the total test of .5 represents an average gain of one month for each month the students were in school.

How accurately the service system was being implemented was examined by reviewing the number of instructional service contacts the children received at each of the levels of the service hierarchy. It was assumed that the services were arranged in descending order from the least intensive service (I-1) to the most intensive (D-6) and that more student contacts would be made at the upper levels than at the lower levels of the hierarchy. The project staff estimated that about 50% of the service contacts would be made at the top three levels of the service hierarchy, 35% at the middle three levels, and 15% at the lower three levels of the service hierarchy. An analysis of the services provided indicated that actual service contacts were 36%, 6%, and 58% at the top, middle, and bottom levels of service hierarchy respectively. Thus more services were being provided to children at the lower level (58%) where it was expected that fewer children would need service (15%). It is also interesting that few services (6%) were provided in the middle levels of the service hierarchy. The middle levels of the hierarchy generally require that the instructional support person be physically present in the regular teacher classroom for work with the child receiving service.

The discrepancy between the expected and actual service contacts could be due to faulty implementation of the project—that is, the support staff may have tended to provide services they felt most comfortable in providing rather than basing the kind of service on the needs of children. An alternate explanation is that the service hierarchy as defined in fact is not a hierarchy but simply a collection of unrelated and ill-defined services.

Table 3

REGULAR TEACHER RATINGS OF THE PINCKNEY PROJECT AND RESOURCE TEACHER SERVICES

Questions Pertaining to Overall Acceptance of the Project	Rating
1. I (regular teacher) feel comfortable working with the main-streaming kids.	1.46
2. I (regular teacher) feel the mainstreaming kids have made progress under my tutorage.	1.90
3. I feel the mainstreaming kids would be happier in a special education class.	4.64
4. I feel the mainstreaming kids got along with the other children as well as others in my class did.	2.00
5. I feel the mainstreaming kids held the rest of my class back.	4.70
6. In my opinion, the mainstreaming kids should spend more time in the resource room.	3.90

Questions Pertaining to the Communication and Interpersonal Relationship of the Resource Teacher	
1. Offers constructive suggestions for alternatives.	1.67
2. Gives sufficient support.	1.67
3. Expresses herself clearly.	1.75
4. Is available for consultation and sharing.	1.83
5. Supports teachers.	1.58
6. Is concerned for welfare of others.	1.50
7. Is enthusiastic.	1.50
8. Supplies enough materials.	1.75

A final aspect of evaluation of the Pinckney Project involved the assessment of the regular classroom teachers' general feelings about the project and its effectiveness with the EMR transfer students. The rating scale used for this purpose was constructed and administered by Lois Llewellyn, one of the instructional support persons in the project. Regular classroom teachers responded to the rating scale anonymously on a scale of 1 (strongly agree) to 5 (strongly disagree). The results of these ratings are presented in Table 3.

The results of the Pinckney project are encouraging but, as in the case of the results of other programs, are of limited usefulness in providing general support to the concept of mainstreaming. A more comprehensive evaluation of the Pinckney model is being conducted during the current school year.

SOME FINAL THOUGHTS

The content of the material reviewed for this paper is of such a nature that few if any definitive conclusions or recommendations can be stated. It is clear that a large number of mainstreaming programs are in operation; that the programs vary considerably regarding the administrative organization and services provided; and that in most cases the originators of the program are satisfied with the *subjective* results of their projects. It is also evident that the most notable omission of the various components of the programs reviewed is evaluation. In lieu of conclusions or specific recommendations, the following suggestions are offered to administrators who may be considering the initiation or expansion of a mainstreaming program. While the suggestions are generally reflective of the literature reviewed in this paper, they also reflect the bias of the author.

1. The decision to mainstream should be accompanied by a decision to provide a comprehensive instructional support system for the children involved and their teachers.
2. Not all handicapped children will benefit from mainstreaming. Selection of the children to be involved should be done carefully and should be based on the recommendations of persons thoroughly familiar with the educational and social needs.
3. Mainstreaming plans should be developed at the school building level. Many school buildings are substantially different in terms of the administrative style of the principal, the attitude of the teachers, and the student population in the building. Thus, different approaches to mainstreaming may be necessary depending on the particular climate in the building.
4. Participatory planning may be the most important element in mainstreaming efforts. All personnel (regular and special) who will be involved with

handicapped children should be allowed to participate in the planning of the program.

5. If regular classroom teachers are made responsible for exceptional children in their classroom, they should also be allowed to make decisions related to the kind and amount of special education support they, or the child, are to receive.

6. No mainstreaming effort should be attempted without serious attention given to providing inservice education. A systematic inservice education program will be needed by both the special and regular personnel.

7. The procedures for providing instructional support in each building should be carefully delineated. A detailed description of the kinds of support services provided in the building should also be developed. This practice not only enhances communication among the staff of a building but also provides a basis for a student accounting system.

8. Develop a pupil accounting system as a part of the mainstreaming plan. This accounting system should provide minimally a cumulative record of numbers of children served, type of service provided, who provided the service, and for what duration the service was provided. This form of accounting allows the building staff to monitor their own activities and to determine whether they are providing the kind of service they intended to provide. The accounting system is also useful to the Special Education person responsible for the administration of decentralized service systems.

9. Obtain data related to student progress and other important variables such as teachers' attitudes toward the program. It is not necessary to obtain data on every child receiving service. However, a sample of children (every 5th, 10th, or 20th) receiving service should be followed up to provide some feedback regarding the effectiveness of the services rendered.

10. Report the results obtained from the program to administrators, teachers, parents, and community. Even poor results can improve morale if proper steps are being taken to remedy problem areas.

Finally, it is necessary to relate to the request made in the title of this paper, "Will the real mainstreaming program please stand up?" On the basis of the material reviewed here, it is safe to say that it is too early for the real mainstreaming program to stand up. As yet there is an insufficient data base for determining the effectiveness of the mainstreaming programs, and consequently none of the programs (figuratively speaking) have a leg to stand on! And lastly. . .should Dunn have done it? Of course, he should have—although the present mainstreaming programs do not offer proof that they are an improvement over traditional delivery systems, they are certainly no worse and hold the promise of much more.

REFERENCES

Adamson, Gary & Van Etten, Glen. "Zero Reject Model Revisited: A Workable Alternative." *Exceptional Children, 38,* 1972 (735-738).

Beery, K. *Models for Mainstreaming.* Dimensions Publishing Co., (Box 4221, San Rafael, California 94903), 1972.

Bennett, Annette. *A Comparative Study of Subnormal Children in the Elementary Grades.* New York: Bureau of Publications, Teachers College, Columbia University, 1932;

Birch, J. W. *Mainstreaming: Educable Mentally Retarded Children in Regular Classes.* Leadership Training Institute/Special Education, University of Minnesota, 1974.

Carroll, A. W. "The Effects of Segregated and Partially Integrated School Programs on Self-Concept and Academic Achievement of Educable Mentally Retarded. *Exceptional Children, 34,* 1967 (93-96).

Deno, E. N. (Ed.) *Instructional Alternatives for Exceptional Children.* Council for Exceptional Children (no publication date).

Deno, E. N. "Special Education as Developmental Capital." *Exceptional Children, 37,* 1970 (229-240).

Dunn, Lloyd M. *Exceptional Children in the Schools: Special Education in Transition.* New York: Holt, Rinehart & Winston, 1973.

Dunn, Lloyd M. "Special Education for the Mildly Retarded–Is Much of It Justified?" *Exceptional Children, 35,* 1968 (5-22).

ESEA Title III Project 1232. "Handicapped Children in the Regular Classroom." Fountain Valley School District, Fountain Valley, California 92708.

Flynn, T. & Flynn, L. "Effects of a Part-Time Special Education Program of Adjustment of EMR Students." *Exceptional Children, 36,* 1970 (680-681).

Gallagher, James J. "The Special Education Contract for Mildly Handicapped Children." *Exceptional Children, 38,* 1972 (527-535).

Garrison, M. & Hammill, D. "Who Are the Retarded?" *Exceptional Children, 38,* 1971 (13-20).

Hammill, D. & Wiederholt, J. L. "Review of the Frostig Test and Training Program." In L. Mann & D. Sabatino (Eds.), *Review of Special Education.* Ft. Washington, Pa.: The *Journal of Special Education,* 1972, in press.

Iano, Richard P. "Shall We Disband Special Classes?" *The Journal of Special Education, 6,* 1972 (167-177).

Johnson, G. Orville. "Special Education for the Mentally Handicapped." *Exceptional Children, 29,* 1962 (62-69).

Kaufman, M., Semmel, M. & Agard, J. "Project PRIME–An Overview." *Education and Training of the Mentally Retarded, 9,* 1974 (107-112).

Kolstoe, Oliver P. "Programs for the Mildly Retarded: A Reply to the Crisis." *Exceptional Children, 39,* 1972 (51-56).

Kreinberg, N. & Chou, S. (Eds.). Configurations *of Change: The Integration of Mildly Handicapped Children into the Regular Classroom.* Far West Laboratory for Educational Research and Development, 1973.

Lilly, M. Stephen. "A Training Based Model for Special Education." *Exceptional Children, 37,* 1971 (745-749).

Lilly, M. Stephen. "Special Education: A Teapot in a Tempest." *Exceptional Children, 37,* 1970 (43-49).

MacMillan, Donald L. "Special Education for the Mildly Retarded: Servant or Savant." *Focus on Exceptional Children, 2,* 1971 (1-11).

Pepe, H. J. "A Comparison of the Effectiveness of Itinerant and Resource Room Model Programs Designed to Serve Children with Learning Disabilities." Unpublished doctoral dissertation. University of Kansas, 1973.

Pertsch, C. F. "A Comparative Study of the Progress of Subnormal Pupils in the Grades and in Special Classes." Unpublished doctoral dissertation. Teachers College, Columbia University, 1936.

Rodee, W. M. "A Study to Evaluate the Resource Teacher Concept When Used with High Level Educable Retardates at the Primary Level." Unpublished doctoral dissertation, University of Iowa, 1971.

Shattuck, Marquis. "Segregation versus Non-Segregation of Exceptional Children." *Journal of Exceptional Children, 12,* 1946 (235-240).

Steigman, Martin J. "Paradox in Special Education: A Critique of Johnson's Paper." *Exceptional Children, 31,* 1964 (67-68).

Thorsell, M. V. "The Education of Educable Mentally Retarded Children in Sparsely Populated Areas." Unpublished doctoral dissertation. University of Kansas, 1964.

Tilley, Bille Kay. "The Effects of Three Educational Placement Systems on Achievement, Self-Concept, and Behavior in Elementary Mentally Retarded Children." Unpublished doctoral dissertation, University of Iowa, 1970.

Van Etten & Adamson, "The Fail-Save Program: A Special Education Continuum." *Instructional Alternatives for Exceptional Children.* Council for Exceptional Children, 1973 (156-165).

Walker, V. "The Resource Room Model for Educating Educable Mentally Retarded Children." Unpublished doctoral dissertation. Temple University, 1972.

For a teacher to be effective as a facilitator of pupil performance or behavior change, a procedure to determine present pupil efforts must be devised and implemented. Effective teachers display many competencies which are important in enabling pupils to progress toward the acquisition of relevant social and academic behaviors. One of the most important of these competencies is the ability to observe pupil behavior in a precise manner. It is this ability to observe ongoing pupil behaviors and interpersonal interactions that enables teachers to plan and evaluate learning sequences. Precise observation, plus actions based upon them, eliminates redundant, inappropriate, and ineffective planning and implementation of learning programs.

The authors have provided an excellent description of several observational systems. More importantly, they have provided a concrete plan for teachers to use precise observations of pupil behavior. Following the authors' suggestions will function to improve classroom instruction.

Observation Systems
and the Special Education Teacher

Melvyn I. Semmel, Sivasailam Thiagarajan
Indiana University

It is a well-known phenomenon that eye witnesses differ in their descriptions of even a brief incident. A classroom is such a complex environment, swarming with actions and interactions of different kinds, that if we ask 10 observers to describe what is happening it is very likely that we will have 10 different reports. People's perceptions are based on their background experiences and philosophies; the description from a behavior-modification oriented teacher would differ from that of a diagnostic-prescriptive teacher. Given this fact of different people using different language and methodology to describe the same classroom event, it is no wonder that there is a lack of communication among teachers, supervisors, and other professional personnel. Unless there are a common terminology and common ground rules among educators for talking about teaching-learning interactions, there is bound to be confusion.

As early as 1914, Ernest Horn recognized this problem and established a systematic recording procedure to help him communicate with teachers. He was interested in measuring the extent to which teachers were reaching the individual child by allowing equal opportunities for participation in classroom recitations. Horn decided to disregard all other activities and concentrate on pupil responding behavior. He segmented this area into two categories: pupils reciting and pupils "responding in some other fashion" (e.g., writing on the chalkboard). For each category he devised a symbol: a circle for reciting and a square for responding in some other fashion. Using this system for recording what he saw in the classroom, Horn was able to record and report classroom events clearly and objectively.

Horn's work was one of the first reported uses of observation systems in a classroom context. During the last decade, the idea has attracted a number of investigators and trainers and has given rise to virtually hundreds of observation systems. Although these systems differ considerably from Horn's initial attempts and from each other, they share a number of common attributes. All observation systems provide shorthand techniques for describing specific aspects of classroom interaction and behavior within the teaching-learning process. Each system uses a set of categories for recording events of interest. At the same time, the system selectively ignores a number of other events outside its domain. Most observation systems are content-free, which enables them to describe what is happening under different classroom conditions. Observation systems do not normally imply value judgments; there are no "good" or "bad" categories. However, a supervisor or a researcher may define desirable patterns of teacher behaviors and interactions based on the observation categories.

WHOSE BEHAVIOR IS OBSERVED

Most observation systems in use today concentrate on the two important actors in the classroom drama—the teacher and the student. Some deal exclusively with the teacher and others with the student. In the latter case, some deal with the entire class of children while others concentrate on individual children.

The most frequently used observation system, the *Flanders' System of Interaction Analysis* (Flanders, 1970), is an excellent example of a system that records the behavior of both teacher and students. The categories of this system are listed in Table 1.

The Indiana Behavior Management System (Fink & Semmel, 1971) also deals with the behaviors of both teacher and students; however, it differs from the Flanders system in that the behavior of only one child is recorded at any given time. The categories of this system are given in Table 2. It will be noted that this system is primarily concerned with affective pupil behaviors and teacher behavior management techniques.

The Teacher Practices Observation Record (Brown, 1970) is an example of observation systems that concentrate exclusively on teacher behavior. Sample categories from this system are shown in Table 3.

Table 1
CATEGORIES FROM THE FLANDERS' SYSTEM
OF INTERACTION ANALYSIS*

Teacher Talk Categories

1. Accepts feelings
2. Praises or encourages
3. Accepts ideas
4. Asks questions
5. Lectures
6. Gives direction
7. Criticizes or justifies authority

Student Talk Categories

8. Student response
9. Student initiated talk
10. Silence or confusion

*Flanders, 1970.

Table 2
CATEGORIES FROM THE
INDIANA BEHAVIOR MANAGEMENT SYSTEM II (IBMS-II)*

Pupil Categories

1. On task
2. Self-involvement
3. Noise
4. Verbal interaction
5. Physical interaction
6. Verbal aggression
7. Physical aggression
8. Verbal resistance
9. Physical resistance

Teacher Categories

10. On task
11. Demand
12. Value-law
13. Conditioned stimulus
14. Criticism
15. Punishment
16. Empathy
17. Interpretive
18. Humor
19. Consequences
20. Redirection
21. Probing

*Fink & Semmel, 1971.

Table 3
SAMPLE CATEGORIES FROM THE
*TEACHER PRACTICES OBSERVATION RECORD**

I. **Nature of the Situation**
T occupies center of attention.
T makes p center of attention.
T makes some *thing* as a *thing* center of p's attention.

II. **Nature of the Problem**
T organizes learning around Q posed by T.
T organizes learning around p's own problem or Q.
T prevents situation which causes p doubt or perplexity.

III. **Development of Ideas**
T accepts only one answer as being correct.
T permits p to suggest additional or alternative answers.
T expects p to come up with answer T has in mind.

IV. **Use of Subject Matter**
T collects and analyzes subject matter for p.
T has p make his own collection and analysis of subject matter.
T provides p with detailed facts and information.

---

*Brown, 1970.

In contrast, the *Student Observational Form* (Lindvall, Yeager, Wang & Wood, 1970) deals exclusively with pupil behavior and that, too, of an individual pupil. This system is designed for use in individualized instructional settings. Sample categories are found in Table 4.

WHAT BEHAVIOR IS OBSERVED

Most observation systems deal with verbal behavior, which is not at all surprising when we remember that the predominant behavior in the classroom is verbal. Some systems include a few nonverbal categories; but those that deal exclusively with nonverbal communication are very few—e.g., Interpersonal Communication Behavior Analysis (Buehler & Richmond, 1963). Both verbal and nonverbal systems may deal with affective (emotional) or cognitive (intellectual) domains. Among other types of categories in observation systems are those of content, classroom climate, and physical environment.

One major variation among categories is the degree of abstraction. At the most general level, a system may have a single category for all teacher questions, requiring a simple discrimination between questions and all other types of

Table 4

SAMPLE CATEGORIES FROM THE STUDENT OBSERVATIONAL FORM*

I. **Independent Work**
   The student is reading independently.
   The student is working independently on a work sheet.
   The student is individually listening to a tape recorder.

II. **Teacher-Pupil Work**
   The pupil seeks assistance from the teacher.
   The pupil receives assistance from the teacher.
   The pupil discusses his progress with a teacher.

III. **Noninstructional Use of Pupil Time**
   Pupil spends time at desk not working.
   Pupil waits for teacher or clerk to provide lesson materials for him.
   Pupil waits for prescription.

IV. **Pupil-Pupil Activity**
   Pupil asks assistance from another pupil.
   Pupil receives assistance from another pupil.

V. **Group Activity**
   Pupil contributes to a group discussion.
   Pupil takes a group test under supervision.
   Pupil answers a question directed to him.

_____

*Lindvall, et al., 1970.

teacher statements. At the next level of specificity, the system may have categories of high-level and low-level questions, requiring the observer to differentiate between these two major classes of question-type categories (e.g., factual recall questions, problem-solving questions, etc.).

Figure 1 illustrates various possible levels of generality in a system used to observe behaviors of teachers. Definitions of each category in this figure are given in Table 5.

The degree of specificity of a system depends upon its purpose. The more general the categories are, the more parsimonious the system becomes—i.e., it is possible to reduce classroom interactions to a smaller set of codes. Such observation systems require less time to collect and record information. However, in this reduction process, much valuable information may be lost. Generally, it is easier to train observers on systems with very few specific behavioral categories (e.g., "raising hand"); reliability of such observation systems is higher than those which require the observers to make the more difficult discriminations among broadly inclusive and/or abstract categories.

209

Figure 1
FOUR LEVELS OF SPECIFICITY OF TEACHER BEHAVIOR CATEGORIES*

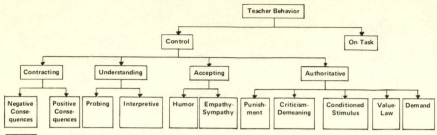

*Fink & Semmel, 1971.

Table 5
DEFINITIONS OF CATEGORIES IN FIGURE 1

1. Demand	Direct verbal commands to "cease and desist" in firm, authoritative tone. No pupil response expected—e.g., "Be quiet!"
2. Value Law	Teacher *explicitly* reminds pupil of the established rules of behavior in the classroom by describing or referring to a *norm* of behavior—e.g., "You know we raise our hands when we wish to speak."
3. Conditioned Stimulus	A "signal" for the pupil to stop misbehaving; short phrases and gestures like "O.K.," calling the pupil's name, "Sh," pauses, stares.
4. Criticism-Demeaning	Psychological degradation of pupil with verbal attack, criticism, or sarcasm—e.g., "I suppose you think you're being clever?""
5. Punishment	A direct, verbal or physical *application* of negative sanctions, including loss of privileges and restrictions on pupil freedoms.
6. Empathy-Sympathy	Teacher expression of his understanding of pupil's feelings.
7. Humor	Teacher efforts to reduce tension and control pupil behavior by means of jokes, clowning, asides, etc. No intent to criticize pupil.
8. Interpretive	Teacher statements which *explain* the reason for a pupil's misbehavior—e.g., "You're not paying attention because you don't get enough sleep at night."
9. Probing	Teacher questions to find out (or get the pupil to think about) the reason for his misbehavior. Teacher expects the pupil to answer.
10. Consequences	Verbal statements stating or implying consequences to behavior. Incentives, rewards, or promises are positive consequences; threats are negative consequences.

HOW BEHAVIOR IS OBSERVED AND RECORDED

In addition to specifying whose behavior and what types of behavior are to be observed, each observation system has a set of ground rules for observing and recording. Based on these ground rules, we may classify observation systems into two major types: (1) *category system* consisting of a small number of categories (usually from 5 to 15) memorized by codes, and (2) *sign system* consisting of a larger number of categories (usually from 50 to 200) in the form of a printed checklist.

Using Category Systems

A category system can be used in two different ways. A *behavior change unit* can be used to code every time the relevant behavior changes from one category to another. Another way is to use a *time unit* and record the relevant behavior once every three seconds (or some other time interval).

Let's assume that you are using the behavior change unit with the Indiana Behavior Management System (IBMS) categories listed in Table 2. You have a coding sheet listing all the categories of the system (see Figure 2). You get into the classroom before the lesson begins and locate your target student. (As you may remember, in the IBMS you code the behaviors of the teacher and one particular student.) You let the teacher go through the first few minutes of classroom activities and settle down. When you begin your observation period, you notice that the teacher is explaining something and the target student is listening attentively. You make a hash mark next to categories 1 and 10 on your coding sheet, indicating that both the teacher and the student are "on task." As long as these behaviors continue—i.e., as long as the teacher is teaching and the student is attending—you do not code anything else. However, after about five minutes you notice the student turning around and whispering something to his neighbor. You make a hash mark by number 4 (verbal interaction) on your coding sheet. The teacher notices this and yells, "John, be quiet!" You code this as an 11 (demand). The target student begins paying attention, and the teacher continues with his earlier activity. You indicate this by coding 1 and 10 again. You continue this process of making a hash mark every time the behavior of either the teacher or the student changes into some other category of the system. You stop coding at the end of a predetermined time—let's say, 10 minutes. Your coding sheet looks like Figure 2.

Figure 2
SAMPLE IBMS CODING SHEET

Student Category Number	Frequency	Teacher Category Number	Frequency
1	╫╫ ╫╫ IIII (14)	10	╫╫ ╫╫ ╫╫ (15)
2		11	╫╫ II (7)
3	IIII (4)	12	II (2)
4	╫╫ IIII (9)	13	
5	II (2)	14	╫╫ I (6)
6		15	
7		16	
8		17	
9		18	
		19	
		20	
		21	

From this sheet you get a summary picture of what happened in the classroom during these ten minutes within the categories of IBMS. You notice that John is inclined to verbal interaction and also makes noise by himself and physically interacts with other children. The teacher uses demand, value law, and criticism as major control techniques. Although this gives you an indication of the frequency of various categories of behavior, it does not give you the pattern of behavior nor an indication of how long each behavior lasted. It does not enable you to answer the questions, "Does the teacher use the same control technique with the same type of student 'off task' behavior?" or "How much time is John on task?"

We can use the *behavior change unit* method of coding with a slight difference to obtain a clearer picture of *patterns* of behavior. This involves the coder making a sequential list of different behaviors rather than merely making hash marks. A part of this type of sequential coding may look like Figure 3.

Figure 3
EXCERPT FROM SEQUENTIAL CODING ON IBMS

10, 1, 10, 4, 11, 1, 10, 4, 11, 1, 10, 4, 14, 6, ...

Going back to the list of categories, the cryptic numbers are translated in this classroom drama. At the beginning, both the teacher and the target student are on task (10-1). The target student talks to someone else, and the teacher demands that he return to task (10-4-11). The student does so but talks again after some time (1-10-4). The teacher makes another demand, but succeeds only temporarily in controlling the student (11-1-10-4). The teacher now criticizes the student and tries to get him back on task; the student talks back to the teacher aggressively (14-6). With a much lengthier code sheet, it will be possible for us to come up with such generalizations as "most of the time the teacher uses demand when the student talks to someone else," "if repeated demands fail, the teacher uses criticism," and "John doesn't take kindly to teacher criticism." Although this gives more information than the previous frequency table, there is still a major question about duration which is left unanswered. We do not know if John reverts to his verbal interaction behavior within one minute of the teacher demand or after 10 minutes. We do not know if the teacher's criticism is a brief remark or a lengthy sermon.

The *time unit* method of coding enables us to answer these questions. In this method, the coder records teacher and student behaviors every five seconds. Although this interval may seem to be impossibly short, many coders have been trained to make repeated records using a shorter interval. In using IBMS categories, the coder looks up every fifth second, notes what the teacher and the target student are doing *at that instant* and records those behaviors. The resulting coding sheets look like Figure 4. This record indicates that the student was talking for 30 seconds before the teacher intervened with a brief demand. This sent the student back on task for half a minute, after which he stopped attending to the lesson but did not interact with anyone else. After about a minute of this, the teacher emitted a demand and got the student back on task.

Figure 4
EXCERPT FROM TIME UNIT CODING ON IBMS

Five-Second Interval	1	2	3	4	5	6	7	8	9	10	11
Teacher Behavior	10	10	10	10	10	10	10	11	10	10	10
Student Behavior	1	4	4	4	4	4	4	1	1	1	1

12	13	14	15	16	17	18	19	20	21	22	23	24
10	10	10	10	10	10	10	10	10	10	10	10	10
1	1	2	2	2	2	2	2	2	2	2	2	2

25	26	27	28	29	30	31	32	33	34	35
10	11	10	10	10	10	10	10	10	10	10
2	1	1	1	1	1	1	1	1	1	1

In summary, a *category system* for classroom observation consists of a small number of categories of teacher and student behavior and a set of ground rules for coding. By tallying the number of times a relevant category of behavior occurs, we obtain a nonevaluative description of the classroom in terms of frequencies of behaviors. By keeping sequential records, we are also able to identify patterns of behaviors. By recording the category of behavior at brief and regular intervals, we obtain a picture of both the pattern and duration of different types of behaviors.

Using a Sign System

As we saw earlier, this second major type of observation system uses lengthy checklists of behaviors. The *Florida Climate and Control System* (FLACCS) (Soar, Soar & Ragosta, 1971), for example, is composed of 158 listed behaviors. In using this system, the coder may, for example, observe classroom interactions for periods of five minutes each. After each period s/he goes through the list of behaviors and checks off each item that was exhibited during that time frame,

S/he observes for five minutes, then rates, observes for another five minutes, then rates again, etc. S/he does not have to remember how many times a particular behavior occurs during each period because even if that behavior occurs more than once during any observation period, it is checked only once. Thus, a sign system merely indicates the type of behaviors that occur; it does not give any indications of the frequency, sequence, or duration of these behaviors. By summing across time periods for any listed behavior, the frequency of occurrence of that behavior can be estimated for the entire observation. Hence, sign systems permit the observer to record a larger number of behavior categories since s/he neither has to memorize them nor observe and code at the same time. Sign systems are similar to rating scales—the difference being that they demand many ratings replicated across time on some arbitrarily defined, fixed interval schedule.

Another type of observation system, called *point-time sampling systems,* is somewhat similar to the sign system. The *Student Activity Profile* (SAP) (Honigman & Stephens, 1969) referred to earlier is an example of this type used in individualized learning situations. The coder observes the student and records the first unambiguous behavior. S/he then moves on to the next student and records his/her behavior. This procedure is repeated until the behaviors of all students in the setting are repeatedly observed and recorded.

APPLICATIONS IN SPECIAL EDUCATION

Obviously, observation systems are useful in any situation which requires an objective and reliable description of interactive behaviors in the classroom. Although many systems were orginally designed as research instruments for studying teacher behavior, they are now finding increasing use in the training and supervision of teachers. In this section, six major areas of application in special education are discussed; the amount of detail provided corresponds to the relevance of each application to the teacher of exceptional children.

Research: Clarifying Variables

For a long time, research on teacher behavior and its effects has been inconclusive because of the vagueness of the variables studied. Although controlled experiments in laboratory situations offered a possible solution to this problem, these results seldom transferred to actual classroom conditions. It was in the classroom that observation systems first made their appearance and provided a method for specifying teacher and student variables in unambiguous terms. In special education, observation-system based research may take a number of different forms. In descriptive research settings, information on the interaction between the handicapped child and his/her teacher may be accumulated over a period of time and in different contexts. Analysis of these records should enable researchers to correlate teacher behaviors and student outcomes and eventually specify a theory of instruction of exceptional children (Minskoff, 1967). In another approach, exemplary special education programs may be identified because of their extremely positive or negative outcomes. Systematic observation of teacher and student behaviors in these settings should help us identify desirable competencies for teaching the handicapped (Semmel, Sitko & Kreider, 1973). Still another approach may provide more control over the teacher-learning situations. The teacher may be required to exhibit certain categories of behavior based on a specific observation system, and the effect of teacher behavior on student behavior may be identified. This type of research design permits more confident conclusions about teacher influence on pupil behavior (Semmel, 1972; Schmitt, 1969; Van Every, 1971).

Evaluation: Emphasis on the Process

Evaluation is similar to research except it involves an assessment of the relative worth of some material or method. In special education, a number of curricular and administrative innovations are being constantly evaluated. The usual design for such evaluations has been to take a pre-measure (of children, teachers, classroom climate, etc.), administer the new material or method, and take a post-measure of the same variables. Any gains between the pre- and post-measures are attributed to the intervention. In recent years, however, there has been a realization that in addition to measuring these input and outcome variables, measurement of *process* variables (which specify what happens between these measurements) is also equally important. The relative ineffectiveness of a new curricular package, as determined by the lack of pupil gains between pretest and posttest, may also be due to the inefficient use by teachers. Observation systems are used in these situations to measure process variables and identify the extent to which the actual behavior of teachers corresponds to the prescribed behavior in the teacher's manual. The same technique is also useful in measuring additional independent variables in evaluating administrative and legislative innovations. Project PRIME (Kaufman, Semmel & Agard, 1973) in Texas, for example, is currently attempting to answer the question, "Under what conditions and for what types of exceptional children is reintegration in regular classrooms a viable alternative?" This project makes extensive use of four different observation systems to collect data on pupil participation in classroom activities, behavior management techniques, types of questions, answers and feedback, and quality of the classroom climate. Data collected involve regular and special education teachers; normal, educable mentally retarded, and learning disabled children; and integrated and self-contained classrooms.

Supervision: More Objective Feedback

One purpose of supervision is to provide feedback to the teacher for the improvement of the quality of teaching. Unfortunately, the role of the supervisor is frequently taken to be evaluative rather than helping. A number of problems in teacher-supervisor interactions arise due to different interpretations of the same terms and the lack of clear distinction between facts and opinions expressed by the supervisor. The use of an objective observation system as a common communication mode greatly reduces these problems. Different terms now acquire the same meaning. The use of a nonevaluative system forces the supervisor to pay attention to what is happening rather than what is not happening. Information on actual student behaviors is more convincing than the supervisor's opinions about possible effects of the teacher's behavior. In a later section of this article, various methods for the use of observation systems for mutual professional development of teachers are outlined. A supervising teacher may find these suggestions useful in working with his/her teachers.

Student Training

Children, too, benefit from objective feedback about their behaviors. Handicapped students may be trained on relevant categories of an observation system, and the teacher may cooperatively establish various behavioral objectives in terms of these categories. Periodic feedback from the teacher or some other observer should help the student in his/her acquisition of suitable patterns of behavior. A token reinforcement system may be used in conjunction with this systematic feedback to accelerate his/her progress.

Preservice Teacher Training: A Curriculum Based on Observation Systems

Observation systems are finding increasing use in the preservice training of teachers. The following description of an experimental teacher-training program now being developed at the Center for Innovation in Teaching the Handicapped should give a clearer picture of this application.

The basic training model developed by the senior author for use in this program is shown in Figure 5. The model suggests that the trainee should first learn to discriminate among relevant teaching performances, then generate or produce each performance when required, and finally evaluate the appropriateness of a particular teaching performance for a given situation (Semmel, 1972; Shuster, 1973). Observation systems have an important role to play in each of these three phases of discrimination, generation, and evaluation. Categories from different systems provide the basis for the trainee to discriminate clearly between different performances. Hence, this phase consists mainly of training on coding methods for selected observation systems. In this process, the trainee learns how to discriminate, for example, between low-level and high-level questions or between criticism and threat. In the generation phase, the trainee sets up behavior objectives in terms of observation-system categories. For example, s/he may decide to acquire the skill of asking a large proportion of higher-level questions. During practice teaching session, trained observers provide feedback on how well s/he is doing in the selected category. Such feedback becomes a major training technique for attaining the specific competency. In the evaluation phase, observational data on both his/her performance and the students' behaviors are made available to the trainee. By analyzing this information, s/he determines which teacher behaviors are likely to obtain desired student behaviors in the given situation.

Figure 5
A MODEL FOR PRESERVICE TRAINING OF TEACHERS

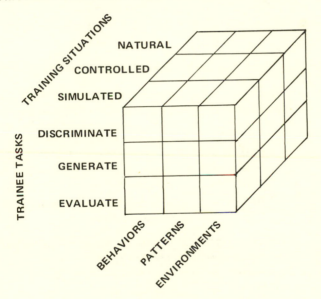

LEVELS OF ANALYSIS OF TEACHING PERFORMANCE

Another dimension of this teacher-training model is the continuity of discrimination, generation, and evaluation. As the figure indicates, the trainee moves from individual behaviors to patterns of behaviors and finally to the discrimination, generation and evaluation of teaching environments. For example, s/he may initially work on such individual categories as inference questions, probe, and positive feedback. Later s/he may combine them into

217

such patterns as inference question-probe-positive feedback. Still later, s/he may combine these patterns to create an inductive teaching environment. To offer another example from the behavior management area, such individual behaviors as demand, appeal to authority, criticism, and punishment in combination form sequences which constitute a pattern of teacher control behavior. A combination of these patterns constitutes an authoritarian environment.

The third dimension of the teacher-training model is the situation in which the trainee is required to perform different operations on different contents. As the figure indicates, this takes place initially under simulated conditions, later in laboratory-like controlled conditions, and finally in public school classrooms. Table 6 provides examples of different phases of training in each of these situations.

Inservice Teacher Training: Self-Evaluation and Mutual Development

Perhaps the most exciting application of observation systems in special education is in the area of inservice teacher training. Although such training

Table 6
SAMPLE TRAINING ACTIVITIES IN DIFFERENT SITUATIONS

	Simulated Situation	Controlled Situation	Natural Situation
Discrimination	Trainee codes interactions from a protocol (record of a classroom situation).	Trainee codes interactions in a special experimental classroom from behind a one-way mirror.	Trainee undertakes participatory observation during teaching in a public school classroom.
Generation	Trainee performs specific categories in a micro-teaching situation.	Trainee performs specific categories in a tutorial situation with an exceptional child.	Trainee performs specific categories during actual teaching in the classroom.
Evaluation	Trainee evaluates effects of teacher behavior in an instructional simulation game.	Trainee evaluates effects of teacher behavior when given immediate feedback from trained observers.	Trainee undertakes self-evaluation in actual classroom situations.

may begin in a workshop situation, the real learning and development takes place in the actual classroom. Whether the teacher works out a formal arrangement with his/her supervisor, or an informal one with his/her colleagues, or prefers to work alone, this on-the-job training involves receiving continuous observation data feedback and changing one's teaching behaviors until a prespecified teaching environment is created. The first time a teacher receives this type of feedback s/he is apt to say, "I didn't realize I do all those things!" Awareness of what one is doing (or not doing) in the classroom is the first step in bringing teaching behaviors under conscious control. Continuous feedback on one's progress in his/her pursuit of the goal is an essential and often sufficient condition for self-development.

In the developmental process, coding on observation systems may be done either directly in the classroom by one or more of the teacher's peers or by the teacher him/herself using audio- or videotape recordings of his/her classroom behavior. Each method has its advantages and disadvantages. Recordings preserve privacy and provide a base for leisurely and repeated coding. However, obtaining high-fidelity recordings, especially of the behavior of the entire class, is a complex process requiring specialized skills. In addition, self-analysis and self-confrontation require the highest degree of intellectual honesty and lack of bias. Coding of the "live" performance by a colleague is less biased and more detailed. However, there is no check on the reliability unless a recording is made at the same time or more than one person undertakes the coding.

Various steps in the self-development process are shown in Figure 6. Details of each step are given below so that you may apply the process to your own situation.

1. *Specification of goals.* In the first step the teacher decides upon the type of teaching-learning environment to be created in the classroom. The teacher may specify all details of this environment or concentrate on just one aspect such as the affective, cognitive, or sociological component. The exact nature of the environment depends upon personal preferences and philosophy. The teacher may decide, for example, to provide a discover-learning environment, a creative atmosphere, a cooperative climate, or an open-classroom situation. At this stage the goal may sound vague and nonbehavioral. However, this is intentional. Our experiences with teachers suggest that beginning with an environment-goal makes them aware of the total picture, whereas beginning with a single target behavior usually makes the effort isolated and trivial. This environment-goal provides an ideal which can be analyzed later into suitable indicators in terms of observation-system categories.

2. *Selecting and learning observation systems.* The environment-goal also helps the teacher select a suitable observation system or systems. In contrast to

Figure 6
STEPS IN TEACHER SELF-DEVELOPMENT USING OBSERVATION SYSTEMS

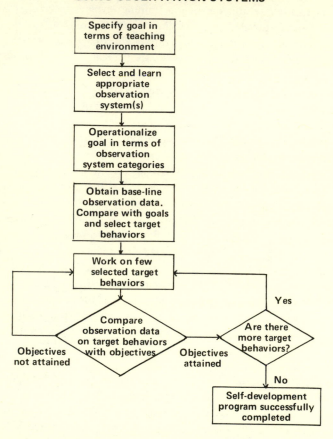

beginning with a system and setting up objectives in terms of its categories, this procedure insures that the "form" will not dictate the "functions" (goals). Unless the teacher is already familiar with a suitable system or has access to an expert, the best source of information is an anthology called *Mirrors for Behavior II* (Simon & Boyer, 1970). The 1970 edition of this anthology contains 79 different observation systems; it is extremely likely that whatever the goals may be, one or more existing systems described in this volume will prove appropriate. To simplify the selection process, *Mirrors for Behavior II* provides brief descriptions of the setting in which each system is used, subject of observation, number of subjects observed, uses of the system, data collection and coding procedures, and coding units. A list of categories of each system is also provided.

Having chosen a system, your next task is to learn it. Although the teacher may decide against coding his/her own behavior, he/she still must learn the system in order to effectively interpret somebody else's coding of his/her classroom. The best way to learn a system is to attend a workshop given by various groups from time to time. If no such workshop is available, locate suitable training materials through the appendix in *Mirrors for Behavior II*. The essential element in learning a system is to get as much practice in actual classroom coding as early as possible. A useful strategy is to work with a partner, code the same classroom, compare your records and discuss any discrepancies.

3. *Operationalizing environmental-goals in terms of system categories.* After learning the system, the teacher is ready to compare its categories with the established environment-goal and decide which ones are relevant. Some categories may describe behaviors which are irrelevant to the targeted environment; others may deal with behaviors which are to be reduced or eliminated; still others, with behaviors to be improved or increased. To give a specific example, let's assume that the teacher wishes to create a supportive classroom climate. After mastering the Indiana Behavior Management System (outlined in Table 5), the teacher may decide that the categories of empathy-sympathy, probing, and interpretive behaviors are to be increased; demand, criticism, conditioned stimulus, and value-law are to be decreased; and positive consequences and humor are of neutral value. Later he/she may ignore the neutral categories either during coding or during data analysis.

4. *Selecting target behaviors.* The next task is to obtain observation data on normal teaching performance. If the teacher is working with a partner, s/he begins by establishing some ground rules for observation. It is important to assure that the time and situation of observation are varied sufficiently to obtain an overall picture. This means that the teacher is not always coded the first thing in the morning or only during reading or mathematics lessons. If the teacher decides on coding him/herself, s/he must obtain recordings of his/her performances in a variety of situations. Depending upon whether s/he is primarily interested in verbal or nonverbal behaviors, s/he may obtain either audio- or videotape recordings. The former are fairly easy to do with cassette recorders. For videotape recording, some professional assistance is needed. If available, a classroom with a remote TV camera is ideal. Details on suitable recording equipment and its use are usually provided in books which deal with observation systems in the classroom (e.g., Flanders, 1970; Allen, Barnes, Reece & Roberson, 1970).

The "base-line" data, which is obtained from coding one's own teaching behavior or by having it coded by a colleague, are next compared with the list of categories relevant to the environment-goal. It may be discovered that in some categories the teacher is already performing at the desired level. From the remaining categories s/he may want to choose a few target behaviors to concentrate upon for improving (or reducing) in the near future. Which behaviors to begin with depends upon such factors as how important specific behaviors are to the creation of a targeted environment-goal and how close the teacher is to the desired level. It is generally better to begin with a small number of categories than to attempt a complete metamorphosis overnight.

5. *Working on target behaviors.* Control of teaching behaviors depends largely upon awareness and frequent feedback. Once the teacher has decided upon a set of target behaviors, s/he can consciously attempt to bring them under control. Immediately after specific lessons, at daily or weekly intervals, s/he codes the recorded behavior (or obtains a copy of coding of his/her behavior from a colleague) and evaluates his/her progress. If more improvement is suggested, concentrate upon a smaller number of specific behaviors during ensuing phases. Normally, this process of self-discipline and feedback results in noticeable progress toward the environment-goal in a very short period. If any specific behavior proves to be resistant to change, the teacher may need assistance from his/her supervisor or a master teacher. Once the teacher has reached the desired level of performance in a given set of target behaviors, s/he can move to other sets. Even after completing the entire set, taking monthly "maintenance checks" should insure that s/he has not reverted to earlier behavior patterns.

The Teacher Empiricist: Another Application of Observation Systems

Once a teacher completes the basic self-development program outlined above, s/he may want to move on to a slightly more complex use of observation systems in the classroom. In this procedure, the focus is shifted away from his/her own performance to that of the children. The teacher begins by setting a goal in terms of student behaviors which s/he wishes to elicit. For example, s/he may decide to increase the number of higher-level responses made by mildly handicapped students. Following this decision, s/he hypothesizes alternative behaviors which are likely to produce this student outcome. For example, the teacher may decide to increase the number of higher-level questions asked in the classroom or probe lower-level student responses until they are transformed to the higher level, or positively reinforce all higher-level responses while ignoring lower ones. The next task is to locate (or design) an observation system which will include categories for all alternative teacher behaviors and the desired student behaviors. Each of the alternative teacher behaviors are used for a given period of time (e.g., a week) and the classroom is coded. This observation data enables the teacher to check if s/he is really performing at the desired level and what effects the teacher behavior has on the desired student outcomes. After trying out alternative strategies, the coding will provide some evidence upon which to evaluate their relative effectiveness and to choose a technique or combination of techniques to elicit reliably the types of student outcomes desired.

The use of observation systems for self-development and exploration has to be actively experimented upon by the teacher. The mere use of observation systems will not make an individual a better teacher; however, the systems provide powerful and neutral tools for helping teachers reach their goals toward more effective instruction of exceptional children.

REFERENCES

Allen, P. M., Barnes, W. D., Reece, J. L. & Roberson, E. W. *Teacher Self-Appraisal: A Way of Looking over Your Own Shoulder.* Worthington, Ohio: Charles A. Jones Publishing Company, 1970.

Brown, B. B. "Teacher Practices Observation Record (TPOR)." In A. Simon & E. G. Boyer (Eds.), *Mirrors for Behavior II.* Philadelphia: Research for Better Schools, 1970.

Buehler, R. E. & Richmond, J. F. "Interpersonal Communication Behavior Analysis: A Research Method." *Journal of Communication, 13,* 1963, (146-55).

Fink, A. H. & Semmel, M. I. *Indiana Behavior Management System-II.* Center for Innovation in Teaching the Handicapped, Indiana University, Bloomington, Indiana, 1971.

Flanders, N. A. *Analyzing Teaching Behavior.* Reading, Mass.: Addison-Wesley Publishing Company, 1970.

Honigman, F. K. & Stephens, J. "Analyzing Student Functioning in an Individualized Instructional Setting." In *Final Report: Demonstration Project in the Processes of Educating Adult Migrants.* Fort Lauderdale, Florida: NeaRad, Inc., 1969.

Kaufman, M. J., Semmel, M. I. & Agard, J. A. *Project PRIME: An Overview.* United States Office of Education, Bureau of Education for the Handicapped, Division of Research, Intramural Research Program, in conjunction with the Texas Education Agency, Department of Special Education and Special Schools, Division of Program Evaluation, 1973.

Lindvall, C. M., Yeager, J. L., Wang, M. & Wood, C. "Student Observational Form." In A. Simon & E. G. Boyer (Eds.), *Mirrors for Behavior II: An Anthology.* Volume A. Philadelphia: Research for Better Schools, Inc., 1970.

Minskoff, E. H. "An Analysis of the Teacher-Pupil Verbal Interaction in Special Classes for the Mentally Retarded." Unpublished doctoral dissertation, Yeshiva University, New York. Office of Education, U.S. Department of Health, Education, and Welfare, Project No. 6-8092, Grant No. 32-42-1700-6008, 1967.

Schmitt, J. K. S. "Modifying Questioning Behavior of Prospective Teachers of Mentally Retarded Children through a Computer-Assisted Teacher Training System (CATTS)." Unpublished doctoral dissertation, University of Michigan, Ann Arbor, 1969.

Semmel, M. I. "Toward the Development of a Computer-Assisted Teacher Training System (CATTS)." In N. A. Flanders & G. Nuthall (Eds.), *The Classroom Behavior of Teachers,* published by *International Review of Education,* XVIII, *4,* 1972.

Semmel, M. I., Sitko, M. & Kreider, J. "The Relationship of Pupil-Teacher Interactions in Classrooms for the TMR to Pupil Gain in Communication Skills." *Mental Retardation,* December, 1973.

Shuster, S. "A Proposed Preformance-Based Training Program for Special Education Teachers." In K. E. Stearns (Ed.), *Special Education in Search of Change,* published by *Viewpoints: Bulletin of the School of Education,* Indiana University, 49, *1*, 1973.

Simon, A. & Boyer, E. D. (Eds.). *Mirrors for Behavior II: An Anthology of Observation Instruments,* Volume A. Philadelphia: Research for Better Schools, Inc., 1970.

Soar, R. S., Soar, R. M. & Ragosta, M. *The Florida Climate and Control System (FLACCS).* Gainesville, Fla: Institute for Development of Human Resources, College of Education, University of Florida, 1971.

Van Every, H. J. F. "The Application of a Computer Assisted Teacher Training System to Speech Therapist Training." Unpublished doctoral dissertation, University of Michigan, Ann Arbor, 1971.

Hall has written an excellent companion chapter to the one authored by Semmel and Thiagarajan. Behavioral observation is a necessary but not sufficient ingredient in effective teaching. Observation must be part of a measurement system—as indicated in the Semmel article—and it must be used to evaluate teacher-devised instructional strategies. Hall has proposed that pupil performance measures be used to evaluate (research) the effects of instructional methods. The chapter describes the procedures which teachers can implement for the daily evaluation of instruction. It also includes examples of the evaluation system as implemented by practicing teachers of pupils. Hall labels the basic approach as "responsive teaching." But whatever the label, it is a system teachers can use to improve instruction and pupil performance.

Responsive Teaching:
Focus on Measurement and
Research in the Classroom
and the Home

R. Vance Hall
Juniper Gardens Children's Project, Kansas

A long needed revolution is occurring in the fields of psychology and educational research. One impact of this revolution is that psychological and educational research as we have known it is being altered. The emphasis in research is shifting from the investigation of general questions involving comparisons between experimental groups and control groups to investigations of specific procedures and their effects on classroom groups and individual children. The emphasis is also changing from experiments carried out by university level researchers to investigations carried out by teachers and parents in their own classrooms and homes. In addition, tools to observe and to understand behavior and learning problems are now available. Most important, this revolution offers new hope for scientifically evaluating the effects of programs and procedures dealing with behavior and learning problems, a point of special significance for teachers and parents of exceptional children.

NEW WAYS TO OBSERVE AND MEASURE BEHAVIOR

The keynote to the new approach centers around recently developed ways to observe and measure behavior.[1] Pavlov, Skinner and other researchers were able to look at behavior in the laboratory more closely than had their predecessors because they developed sophisticated measurement techniques and recording devices. In fact, their discoveries about the relationships of behavior to the environment were entirely dependent upon their ability to observe and measure behavior precisely. It can be forcefully argued that the main contributions of these men were due not to their theories of reflex and operant conditioning, but rather to their new methods of observing and recording behavior.

Unfortunately, the automatic recording devices used in the laboratory, such as Skinner's cumulative recorder, are not practical for general research in the classroom or home. They are too expensive, they are not generally available, and they will not measure many of the behaviors of interest to teachers and parents. Therefore, it remained for researchers who were interested in carrying out applied research in classrooms and home settings to develop techniques which could be used outside the experimental laboratory.

Recording by Outside Observers

The child development group at the University of Washington were among the early pioneers who developed observation and recording procedures which could be carried out by trained observers. Sidney Bijou, Don Baer, Montrose Wolf, Florence Harris and their colleagues developed interval recording procedures which made possible the preschool studies (e.g., Harris, Baer & Wolf, 1968) which have contributed so much to our understanding of the management of behavior. Many of the studies involving exceptional children which followed, such as those by Becker and by Hall and their colleagues (Thomas, Becker & Armstrong, 1968; Hall & Broden, 1967; Hall, Lund & Jackson, 1968), used adaptations of these interval recording procedures and outside observers.

While these studies were extremely important, they did require trained outside observers (Bijou, Peterson & Ault, 1968; Broden, 1971) and were supervised by skilled researchers rather than by teachers or parents. Therefore, the procedures themselves, and certainly the observation and measurement

---

1. Detailed explanations of the recording procedures mentioned in this section will be found in *Behavior Management Series, Part I*, Hall, 1971.

techniques, were of limited use to the busy classroom teacher or to the practicing parent.

Recording by Teachers, Parents and Pupils

The latest step in the progression which has taken research out of the laboratory and put it into the classroom and home has been the development of observation procedures to be used by teachers, parents and even the children themselves. Although it was impractical for teachers to use automatic recording devices or outside observers since they were too costly or unavailable, teachers can use other procedures that are practical and effective.

One procedure which can easily be adapted to the new research approach is the *direct measurement of permanent products*. Teachers have long been used to recording spelling scores, the number of problems worked correctly on math tests, and whether or not assignments have been completed and handed in. In these cases, the behavior of a pupil results in a permanent product which can be observed and counted and lends itself very well to repeated measures of behavior over time.

Event recording is also a useful tool for observing behavior. It has been found that there are many behaviors which teachers and parents can reliably count and record as they occur. In many instances, to do so does not interfere with ongoing teaching or parental tasks. Thus, a teacher can count the number of times a given event (such as a talk out, an argument, a fight, the number of pupils who come in late) occurs by tallying with a pencil on paper or by using a small hand or wrist counter.

Time sampling is another tool for observing behavior. It has been shown that teachers and parents can use a time sampling procedure (MacKenzie, Clark, Wolf, Kothera & Benson, 1968) to obtain an accurate estimate of the percentage of time children engage in ongoing behaviors, such as wearing an orthodontic device. In time sampling, the pupil is observed at given intervals to determine whether the behavior of concern is occurring. By dividing the number of times the behavior occurs by the number of observations, the level of the behavior can be determined.

Duration, another measure which can be used in applied research, is recorded when the time spent engaged in a behavior is an important dimension of the behavior—as it is in thumbsucking or in practice on a musical instrument. Wall clocks and stopwatches can be used to measure the duration of certain behaviors.

Recently, Risley (1972) developed *Placheck* (Planned Activity Check), an observation and recording procedure for measuring the ratio of pupils engaged in a scheduled activity which also shows promise for use by teachers and parents. At given intervals, the observer counts the number of pupils engaged in the planned activity and divides this by the number of pupils present. The result is a ratio or percent of children who are actually participating in the activity.

A NEW RESEARCH APPROACH

In the past almost all psychological and educational research sought to find correlations between certain factors or conditions and behaviors or performance by comparing one group with another. This was often difficult or impossible for the classroom teacher to do. For one thing, it involved equating a classroom with one or more similar classrooms and trying an experimental condition in one class but not the other. Not only was it difficult to find another similar classroom, but also one was never certain whether the classes were truly equated or whether the experimental condition caused any observed difference. A second problem for teachers and parents was that usually the behaviors and learning problems of concern involved individual children and not groups. Since group comparisons are not valid for individual children, teachers and parents could not experimentally determine whether or not the procedures they used with individual children were valid or effective. The development of ways for teachers and parents to accurately measure the levels of behavior of the children in their charge and the use of applied behavior analysis research designs (Baer, Wolf & Risley, 1968) makes it possible for each teacher and parent to become a researcher who could scientifically determine which programs and procedures help children with problems and which are ineffective.

Applied Behavior Analysis Research Designs

The two basic research designs available to the applied researcher have been labeled the *reversal* and the *multiple baseline* design. One characteristic of these designs is that both involve repeated measures of the behavior or performance of concern. That is, once the behavior or behaviors are defined, the level is measured over a period of days or weeks in order to determine its pre-experimental or baseline level.

The baseline record is usually graphed as a simple conventional graph so that a visual representation is available. It has been found that most people can easily interpret behavioral data in this form. Some have advocated the use of special graph paper, log scales, etc. Experience indicates, however, that using conventional graphs is simpler, cheaper, more valid, and results in better communication with a larger number of people.

New versus Old

The new approach to measurement and research contrasts with the old along the following dimensions:

1. The old focused on the past. Often the old approach sought to discover events or conditions that had occurred during the development of children which might be related to present behavior or learning problems. The new focuses on what is going on in the present and on events and conditions which exist *now* that affect behavior and learning.

2. The old approach focused on using various tests, attitude surveys and other devices designed to provide samples of behavior before and then after experimental programs and procedures were implemented. The new approach emphasizes measuring the behavior of concern more directly and precisely, repeating the measures over time so that a more accurate picture of performance can be obtained. In addition, changes in behavior can be seen as they occur.

3. The old focused on the group rather than the individual. Many valid statistical comparisons could be made only by comparing behavior or performance of an experimental group with that of a matched control group. The new approach allows comparisons of behavior and performance of individuals as well as groups, and eliminates the imprecision associated with attempts to match groups that may differ along many important dimensions.

4. The old approach dictates that research be carried out by researchers and statisticians who impose themselves upon the educational or home environment to investigate questions which may or may not seem valid or important to the teacher or parent. The results of the research have frequently failed to affect the practice of teachers and parents. The new approach allows the teacher or parent the opportunity to carry out research in the classroom or home. The experiments can be selected on the basis of their importance to the teacher or parent. Therefore, the results are much more likely to affect the practice of the teachers and parents involved as well as of those teachers and parents with the same or similar problems. Thus, the new approach allows teachers and parents to deal responsibly with learning and behavior problems of their children whether or not the children have been labeled exceptional.

Responsive Teaching Model

For the purpose of identification, we have labeled this approach the *Responsive Teaching Model*. Models incorporating similar strategies are Dr. Montrose Wolf's *Achievement Place Model* for delinquents and the University of Vermont's *Consulting Teacher Special Education Model* developed by Dr. Hugh McKenzie.

Three points are essential to the Responsive Teaching Model:

1. The behavior or academic task is objectively defined, and the level of the behavior is observed and recorded.
2. A method or procedure designed to improve or remediate the child's performance is introduced.
3. If a desired change occurs, it can be experimentally determined whether the procedures and materials used brought about the change. If no change occurs or if the problem worsens, feedback is available so that the teacher or parent can respond appropriately by altering the procedure or material until more effective ones are found.

Thus, Responsive Teaching and similar approaches featuring simple and effective measurement/recording procedures and research designs help to accomplish a revolution long needed in the areas of educational and psychological research. This revolution is shifting the emphasis of scientific investigation from general effects of procedures on groups in the laboratory to specific effects of procedures on individuals in the classroom and the home. As this revolution is accomplished it seems highly probable that in the future there will no longer be a fifty-year lag between the time research proven procedures developed in the laboratory are implemented in the classroom. Since teachers and parents now can see clearly and quickly whether or not the procedures and materials they are using are effective and since the most important applied research will be carried out by *them* in their own classrooms and homes, implementation of research findings will be almost immediate.

RESPONSIVE TEACHING STUDIES

The following studies,[2] utilizing the Responsive Teaching Model approach, were conducted by persons enrolled in the Responsive Teaching course at the University of Kansas Medical Center.

---

2. Other studies and a more complete description of the Responsive Teaching Model may be found in Hall and Copeland (1971), Hall, Fox, Willard, Goldsmith, Emerson, Owen, Davis, and Porcia (1971), Hall, Axelrod, *et. al.* (in press), Hall, Cristler, Cranston and Tucker (1971).

Increasing Face Wiping in a Cerebral Palsied Girl
As a Treatment for Drooling

Madelyn Regan

Drooling is a frequent problem of the mentally retarded and cerebral palsied. Swallowing therapy is usually prescribed as the treatment procedure in such cases. There are a few subjects, however, for whom such treatment seems ineffectual. The present study employed a face wiping procedure to decrease the high incidence of a wet face resulting from frequent drooling.

Subject and Setting

Marta was a nine-year-old, quadraplegic, cerebral palsied girl of normal intelligence enrolled in a special class for the orthopedically handicapped at the Children's Rehabilitation Unit, University of Kansas Medical Center. Marta had a long history of drooling and had been seen for two years by speech and occupational therapists who attempted to remediate the problem. Treatment included encouraging frequent swallowing and a token reinforcement program for a dry face. Although the treatment produced a temporary decrease in drooling, the decrease was not maintained. Marta had expressed a desire to reduce drooling because she was due to transfer to a regular public school classroom and because she was afraid her future classmates would not approve of drooling.

Observation

A practicum student assigned to the class observed Marta from 9:00 to 10:00 each morning. A five minute time sampling procedure was used. At the end of each five minute period, the student recorded whether there was any visible moisture on or about the area of Marta's chin. The regular classroom teacher made independent, simultaneous observations for 14 days during the study. Agreement between records ranged from 91% to 100% with a mean of 99%.

$Baseline_1$: During a 16-day baseline phase, it was found that Marta's chin was dry on an average of 32% of the time (see Figure 1).

$Reinforcement_1$: During the next 14 days, the teacher placed a chart on the child's desk and began recording the number of times she observed Marta wiping her face with a facial tissue. She also praised her for remembering to wipe her face. Under these conditions, the mean of dry face checks rose to 80%.

$Baseline_2$: The teacher then told Marta that she was doing so well that a face wiping chart was no longer necessary. She also withdrew her attention and praise. Over the next three days, the mean of dry face checks decreased to 53% and was trending downward.

231

Figure 1

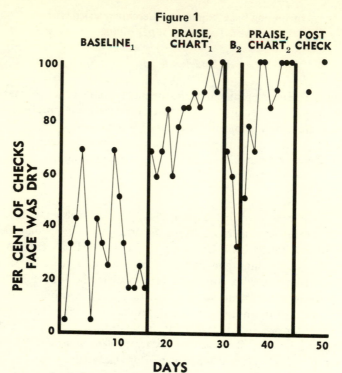

A record of the percentages of time that a 9-year-old cerebral palsied girl's face was dry during time sample checks during *Baseline₁*—prior to experimental procedures. *Praise and Chart₁*—teacher provided feedback by charting and gave praise for dry face. *Baseline₂*—charting and praise withdrawn. *Praise and Chart₂*—charting and praise reinstated. *Post Checks*—periodic post checks, 3 day intervals.

Reinforcement₂: When the teacher again began charting and praising face wiping, the mean level of dry face checks rose to 87%.

Post Checks: Two post checks taken at three day intervals after continuous observation was discontinued indicated that dry face behavior was being maintained at high levels.

At the end of the study, Marta was enrolled in a regular school classroom. By this time face wiping had been well established, and the regular classroom teacher reported that drooling (or at least a wet face) was not a problem.

Discussion

Although we cannot be certain that these data whether teacher praise, feedback provided by charting, or both were responsible for the observed change, it would seem that this simple procedure was effective. It is significant that the teacher and her practicum student succeeded in solving the problem of a wet face caused by drooling after other approaches involving special therapists proved ineffective. Furthermore, they were able to scientifically verify the causal relationship between their procedure and its effect on the behavior they observed by using a single subject reversal design.

Decreasing Talk Outs in Reading, Writing and Math: A Multiple Baseline Study

Zora Milne

Talking out in the classroom seems to be one of the most universal problems confronted by teachers (Hall, Fox, Willard, Goldsmith, Emerson, Owen, Davis & Porcia, 1971). In this study a special education teacher used a novel consequence and a multiple baseline research design in decreasing talk outs of an educable mentally retarded boy.

Subject and Setting

Jerry was an eight-year-old boy enrolled in a self-contained, special education classroom for 11 educable mentally retarded pupils in the Turner, Kansas, Public School District. Jerry, who had a Stanford Binet IQ of 80, had been excluded from a regular classroom because of his failure to achieve academically and because of high rates of disruptive behaviors. He continued to be disruptive in the special education classroom, frequently talking without raising his hand or respecting class rules about interrupting.

Observation Procedures

The teacher observed Jerry for 20-minute sessions during reading, writing, and math classes. The number of talk outs in each class was tallied with pencil and paper. Taling out was defined as (a) interrupting while another pupil was talking, (b) interrupting while the teacher was giving directions, (c) interrupting the teacher while the teacher was listening to another pupil read, and (d) talking out during assignment periods. An outside observer made an independent, simultaneous record in one class. There was 100% agreement with the teacher's record.

Experimental Procedures and Results

Baseline records of Jerry's talk outs were made prior to instituting experimental procedures. As can be seen in Figure 2, these baseline records revealed that the mean number of talk outs was 4.5 in both reading and writing, and 3.7 in math.

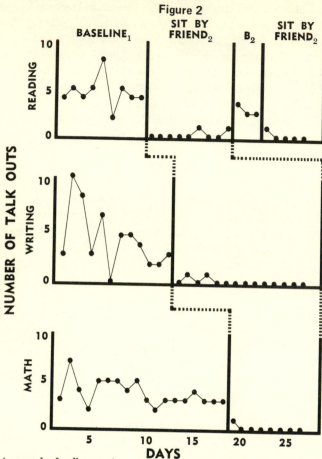

Figure 2

A record of talk outs by an 8-year-old boy enrolled in a special education classroom during reading, writing and math periods. *Baseline.*—prior to experimental procedures. *Sit by Friend*—Jerry was allowed to sit by a friend contingent on low talk out rates. *Baseline₂*—return to baseline conditions in reading only.

During baseline Jerry had frequently requested permission to move his desk to sit next to Donna. After 9 days of baseline the teacher gave him permission to sit next to Donna during reading, on the condition that he was not to talk out or disturb anyone. Each morning he was reminded that sitting next to his friend in reading was dependent on his behavior. On day 13 he was granted permission to sit next to Donna during writing class as well as during reading, contingent on low talk out rates. Beginning on day 19 Jerry was allowed to sit next to his friend during math period as well as writing, contingent on not talking out and disturbing the class. Under these conditions, there was an immediate decrease in talking out in each class when Jerry was allowed to sit next to Donna. The mean rate of talk outs for Jerry decreased from 4.5 to .2 in reading, from 4.5 to .1 in writing, and from 3.7 to .1 in math.

A brief reversal procedure was introduced during reading period on the 19th day. During this phase Jerry was told he could not sit next to Donna during reading, but he was encouraged not to disturb the class. Talk outs during reading increased over the next 3 days but decreased once he was allowed to sit next to Donna again. There was no corresponding change in talk outs during writing and math.

Discussion

This study showed that a contingency as simple as allowing a disruptive boy in a special education class to sit next to a friend was effective in decreasing talk outs. A multiple baseline procedure in which the same behavior was recorded in three different stimulus situations (Hall, Cristler, Cranston, & Tucker, 1970) with successive introductions of the experimental condition was used to demonstrate causality. A further verification was made by introducing a brief reversal during the reading period.

REFERENCES

Bijou, S.W., Peterson, R.F. & Ault, M.H. "A Method to Integrate Descriptive and Experimental Field Studies at the Level of Data and Empirical Concepts." *Journal of Applied Behavior Analysis,* 1968, 1, 175-191.

Broden, M. "Notes on Recording and Conducting a Basic Study." *Journal of Applied Behavior Analysis,* 1971, 4, 163-171.

Hall, R.V. Behavior Management Series. *Part I. The Measurement of Behavior.* Lawrence, Kansas: H & H Enterprises, 1971.

Hall, R.V., Axelrod, S., Tyler, L., Grief, E., Jones, F.C. & Robertson, R. "Modification of Behavior Problems in the Home with Parent as Observer and Experimenter." *Educational Technology,* 1972.

Hall, R.V. & Broden, M. "Behavior Changes in Brain Injured Children through Social Reinforcement." *Journal of Experimental Child Psychology,* 1967, 5, 463-479.

Hall, R.V. & Copeland, R. "The Responsive Teaching Model: A First Step in Shaping School Personnel as Behavior Modification Specialists." A Paper presented at the Third Banff International Conference on Behavior Modification, April 1971.

Hall, R.V., Cristler, C., Cranston, S.S. & Tucker, B. "Teachers and Parents as Researchers Using Multiple Baseline Designs." *Journal of Applied Behavior Analysis,* 1970, 3, 247-255.

Hall, R.V., Fox, R., Willard, D., Goldsmith, L., Emerson, M., Owen, M., Davis, F. & Porcia, E. "The Teacher as Observer and Experimenter in the Modification of Disputing and Talkingout Behaviors." *Journal of Applied Behavior Analysis,* 1971, 4, 141-149.

Hall, R.V., Lund, D. & Jackson, D. "Effects of Teacher Attention on Study Behavior." *Journal of Applied Behavior Analysis,* 1968, 1, 1-12.

Harris, F.R., Wolf, M.M. & Baer, D.M. "Effects of Adult Social Reinforcement on Child Behavior." *Journal of Applied Behavior Analysis,* 1968, 1, 1-12.

Thomas, D.R., Becker, W.C. & Armstrong, M. "Production and Elimination of Disruptive Classroom Behavior by Systematically Varying Teacher's Behavior." *Journal of Applied Behavior Analysis,* 1968, 1, 35-45.

While Brown and York have written this chapter with a focus upon teacher training, the reader will note that the content is also directly related to child-teacher interaction within instructional environments. The rationale for the association between training and subsequent teaching is that Brown and York have systematically developed training programs which are child-teacher centered. That is, if a teacher is expected to perform certain tasks with children subsequent to training, then the training curriculum should be a model for that future event. The training closely approximates the real world of the instructional process. Practicing teachers can learn a great deal from this chapter. It describes a procedure for teaching the severely handicapped pupil, a long neglected participant within the educational system.

Developing Programs for Severely Handicapped Students: Teacher Training and Classroom Instruction

Lou Brown, Robert York
University of Wisconsin, Madison

This paper is intended to relate to some of the problems confronting those persons who are attempting, through the preparation of personnel, to generate quality services for severely handicapped students. In the recent past there have been several events of vital importance to the nature of services available to severely handicapped students. These events may be referred to as judicial-legislative actions. For a more historical and technical treatment of these judicial-legislative actions, the reader is referred to Gilhool (1973), Lippman and Goldberg (1973), and Schwartz (1973). Our admittedly unsophisticated interpretation of these events goes something like this. Children need to be included in, not excluded from, public school programs *because* they are "too something or other." That is, too custodial, too retarded, too disturbed, too autistic, too nonambulatory, too sick, etc. The parents and friends of severely handicapped children realized this, obtained counsel, and asked a group of judges for reasons why some children should go to school and other children could not. The judges found the reasons offered by others inadequate (e.g., no money, no room, no teachers, can't benefit) and ruled that *all* children should have *equal* access to public services. That is, if one child is entitled to a free public education, then all children are entitled to such a service.

Once one group of judges decided that all children had a right to the same public services, it became apparent that other judges in similar cases would probably reach the same conclusion. Thus, many state legislatures, involved in or anticipating similar litigation, enacted laws providing for free public education for all children within their borders (e.g., Washington, Wisconsin, and Michigan). Our purpose here is not to delineate the important and at times devastating implications of such comprehensive legislative and judicial actions. Rather we are assuming that in the very near future *all* children in the nation, regardless of level of functioning, will have access to a free public education. Thus, in our judgment, the issue now becomes *how* can we provide the best possible developmental services to the lowest functioning children in our society.

Obviously, if a large number of severely handicapped children will be provided for in public school settings, a large number of special educators will be needed to develop and implement instructional programs for these newly acknowledged students. For the past several years, the writers and their colleagues have been attempting to prepare teachers who have the technological repertoires necessary to provide reasonable instructional services to these students both in public school and in residential settings. In the sections that follow we will attempt to delineate several of the basic components of an evolving teacher training model that we have found useful.

WHO ARE SEVERELY HANDICAPPED STUDENTS?

The generic term "severely handicapped" as it is used here refers to children who have been given such labels as "low functioning," "trainable retarded," "severely emotionally disturbed," "severely retarded," "psychotic," "autistic," "custodial," "developmentally young," "schizophrenic," "subtrainable," "dependent," "multiply handicapped," "vegetables," and the like. Many of these children, until recently, have been excluded from public school programs because of various social, sensory-motor, behavioral, and intellectual deficits. Perhaps, more specifically, "severely handicapped"

...includes students who are not toilet trained; aggress toward others; do not attend to even the most pronounced social stimuli; self-mutilate; ruminate; self-stimulate; do not walk, speak, hear, or see; manifest durable and intense temper trantrums; are not under even the most rudimentary forms of verbal control; do not imitate; manifest minimally controlled seizures; and/or have extremely brittle medical existences. [Sontag, Burke, and York, 1973]

It should be noted that the term severely handicapped, as it is used here, did not emanate from a scholarly treatment of complex and dynamic categorical parameters germane to the categorization of children, but as a result of other more banal experiences. Namely, if students do not speak, follow directions, imitate, play with peers, control their own behavior, etc., they are severely handicapped in their ability to function in society and need to be taught such skills to do so. Given the developmental level of current assessment instruments and inferential measurement, we find little instructional validity in such terms as autistic, severely retarded, or low functioning. Therefore, we have chosen to refer to such individuals as "severely handicapped." It should be realized that the term is for the most part irrelevant to instructional programming and simply provids a generic name for the population of individuals discussed here. In the public school classrooms in which we are involved, almost every diagnostic label imaginable can be found by searching students' cumulative records. In addition, these individuals have spent time in nearly every type of service delivery system available (e.g., institutions for the mentally retarded, mentally ill, and emotionally disturbed; local ARC programs; private schools for exceptional children).

Thus, we have found it expedient to classify students into two social and academic functioning levels: mild and severe. The discrimination problems attendant to delineating the presumed differences between "emotionally disturbed," "mentally retarded," or "learning disabled" students can now be focused upon the differences between "mild" and "severe." However, such problems are in the hands of school psychologists, social workers, and administrators—with teacher attention being focused upon grouping and instructing children along relevant educational dimensions.

THE PROBLEM OF SELECTION AND RECRUITMENT

When attempting to develop a college or university based training program for teachers of severely handicapped students, there are several inherent impediments that must be confronted.

First, extremely few college students have had exposure to severely handicapped children prior to entering college. Unfortunately, this lack of exposure in many cases results in people not even knowing that such children exist. Second, there are very few college students who start their careers with a strong inclination toward becoming teachers of severely handicapped students. Third, there seems to be a pecking order within special education. That is, it is apparently more glamorous for college students to manifest interest in becoming teachers of emotionally disturbed students or children with special learning disabilities than it is for them to declare interest in becoming teachers. of severely handicapped students. Fourth, even though a person does manifest an interest in working with severely handicapped students, it does not necessarily mean that he or she will be an effective teacher. That is, there are people who have a mongoloid uncle or who have heard that there are going to be jobs open in the future for teachers of severely handicapped children and base their career decisions accordingly. We have found very little predictive validity in such factors.

Obviously, we have encountered such barriers and over a period of years have evolved compensatory actions that might be of interest to others. First, we offer a relatively large lecture course entitled "Introduction to Mental Retardation." Usually about 75-100 students enroll in this course each semester. The course is structured in such a way that students have an option of working with severely handicapped persons or taking standard university type tests. Over the past 8 semesters, 99.9 percent of the students who have taken the course have chosen to work with severely handicapped persons. Some of the settings in which these students work are in schools operated by the Madison Area Association for Retarded Citizens (programs for preschool and postschool age persons), Central Wisconsin Colony (a residential facility for severely and profoundly retarded persons ranging in age from birth to ages 50-60), the Madison Public Schools, and a local nursing home for retarded adults.

Two of the few criteria of these practicum placements are (1) that the students work with professionals at the various facilities, and (2) that they make at least 2 trips per week for at least 1½ hours per trip. After these practicum placements are arranged, those responsible for teaching the course visit the various facilities and talk to the professionals about the performance and capabilities of the university students under their supervision. The basic question asked of the professionals in the various facilities is "Who do you have that in your judgment will be a good teacher of severely handicapped students?" Responses to such a question usually result in a list of about 40-45 students. The professor in charge of the course then invites those delineated individually or in small groups to his office for coffee, etc., to discuss the possibilities of pursuing a career as a teacher of severely handicapped students. Usually, about 15 students per semester come to realize that what they have always wanted was a career teaching severely handicapped students. Obviously, the interaction between the recruiting professor and the student is crucial. However, the exact content of the conversations is perhaps inappropriate for presentation here. The point is that this is one vehicle that might be used to select and recruit potential teachers. Certainly there are other approaches, and we are sure that as preparation programs designed to train teachers of severely handicapped students develop over the country other vehicles will evolve.

THE NEED FOR PRE-LICENSE PRACTICUM INVOLVEMENT

Most children, even mildly handicapped children (i.e., children with learning disabilities, educably mentally retarded, and mildly emotionally disturbed children), come to school with reasonably well developed behavioral repertories. That is, most students come to school toilet trained, with the ability to speak in varying degrees of fluency, with the ability to follow complex verbal directions, with the ability to play with peers with minimal supervision, with relatively complex receptive language skills, and with some ability to work alone in a constructive manner. Thus, teachers of normal and mildly handicapped children have many valuable social and emotional foundations upon which they can base their instructional systems. In addition, as teachers have usually been playing with and otherwise relating to children throughout their lives, there are many skills that teachers have acquired that are directly relevant to the job requirements needed for teaching mildly handicapped or normal children.

Obviously, all children are alike in some ways and, obviously, all children are uniquely individual in some ways. Unfortunately, severely handicapped children in many ways are dramatically different from their age peers. Thus, teachers of severely handicapped children require different teacher-child interaction skills. For example, such general approaches like "He'll grow out of it." "She'll learn to do it another way." "Just leave him alone." "You have to give her time," etc., are simply not applicable. Severely handicapped children may never "grow out of it," and they may never "try another way." Thus, we have found it necessary to provide teachers in training with intense and durable experiences with severely handicapped children. Several of the specifics related to these experiences are presented in another section of this paper. Perhaps it is appropriate here to present in outline form the structure of a typical pre-license practicum sequence.

First, a student will spend at least 3 hours per week working under professional supervision, usually in a nonpublic school setting, for 16 weeks or a total of 48 contact hours. Subsequently, students will spend 4 hours per day, 5 days per week for 16 weeks or a total of 320 contact hours in a public school classroom for severely handicapped students as a part of pre-practice teaching "methods course." Finally, students will spend 4 hours per day, 5 days per week for 16 weeks as a "practice teacher" in a public school classroom for severely handicapped students. Thus, across 3 semesters a student will spend approximately 680 contact hours with severely handicapped students under the supervision of various professionals.

Such a durable and intense practicum sequence is certainly not unique to special education nor is it a guarantee that a student will acquire the skills necessary to perform well as a teacher. However, in our judgment this kind of sequence and involvement is at least necessary, however insufficient.

A WORKING DEFINITION OF TEACHING

In an attempt to deemphasize the tendency to focus on aspects of severely handicapped students that classroom instructional personnel can do little if anything about (e.g., genes, brains, prenatal experiences, poor protoplasm), we have evolved a tentative definition of teaching.

Severely handicapped children are considered severely handicapped because they cannot perform skills that other children can perform. The dependent variables in an instructional setting are changes in the behavioral repertoires of the students. Thus, teaching refers to or may be defined as the *creation or arrangement of an environment that produces specified changes in the behavioral repertoires of the students.* This definition, of course, is an extreme oversimplification of a complex and dynamic construct and may have little if any utility for someone teaching poetry to gifted adolescents. Nevertheless, we have found substantial practical value in such a definition for at least the following reasons:

1. This definition requires that a teacher delineate or specify precisely the responses the students will perform that they are not now performing in the presence of the teacher. In effect, the teacher becomes an instructional determinist.

2. This definition requires that a teacher delineate or specify precisely the activities or behaviors in which he or she will engage that are expected to enhance the behavioral repertoires of the students. In effect, the teacher becomes an instructional environmentalist in that attention is focused almost exclusively on factors in the instructional environment (outside the body of the student) that the teacher can in some degree manipulate.

3. This definition requires that a teacher verify the existence of changes in the behavioral repertoires of the students. In effect, the teacher becomes an instructional empiricist in that changes in the students must be operationally defined and sensed.[1]

Thus, in our view, it seems reasonable to require a teacher of severely handicapped students (1) to specify *what* responses, skills, concepts, etc., he or she intends for the student to acquire, (2) to specify *how* he or she intends to impart such responses, skills, concepts, etc., and (3) to *measure* whether or not the students have the responses, skills, concepts, etc., in their behavioral repertoires.

On the other hand, the reader should be forewarned that when teachers of severely handicapped students attempt to adhere to the criteria of this

---

1. For a further discussion of instructional determinism, environmentalism, and empiricism, the reader is referred to Brown, 1973.

particular definition of teaching they are assuming an unusual instructional responsibility. That is, they cannot claim or continue to claim the title of teacher until they have demonstrated that they have induced students to acquire skills or continue to induce students to acquire skills that they have not manifested previously. In other words "if I cannot engage in activities that result in changes in the repertoires of may students, I cannot claim to be a teacher."

INSTRUCTIONAL COMPETENCIES

If a teacher adheres to the criteria of the definition of teaching presented above (i.e., teaching is changing students in demonstrable ways), then an instructional repertoire of behavioral competencies becomes crucial. Potential teachers can accrue grade point averages of 4.0, they can talk in university seminars for hours about changing society, changing schools, relating to children, grasping the fundamentally transcendental nature of emotive child-teacher interactions, etc., but they cannot claim to be teachers until they have changed students in demonstrable ways.

While the quest for competency based models of instruction has been present in education for centuries, several factors have contributed to unusual recent concern. First, there is less of a shortage of licensed teachers now than ever before. Thus, many persons are less concerned with quantity and filling orders. Second, recent conceptual and empirical developments in the business community and in certain federal government programs (e.g., the space program) related to systems analysis approaches to problem solving have permeated the thinking of many school administrators in the form of "management by objective contracts" (Vergason, 1973). This management by objectives approach is now becoming discernable in relation to the performance of teachers in classrooms. Third, the general mood of the country in the 1970s both politically and economically has shifted to the right of the general mood of the 1960s. This mood swing has brought to the fore ideas that many educators find disconcerting to say the least. Such concepts as cost-effectiveness, accountability, behavioral objectives, and long range manpower needs have put new pressures upon school administrators, teachers, and teacher training institutions. Competency based teacher training models are but one of the manifestations of these new pressures.

One view of an instructional competency is as follows: an instructional competency is a set of behaviors a teacher engages in that result in empirically verifiable changes in the behavioral repertoires of the students in his or her charge. For example, assume that a teacher determines that a student should demonstrate the skill of correctly adding any 2 numerals that total 10 or less (predictable change). The teacher then must arrange an instructional environment (engage in behaviors) that results in the student's performing such skills. If the student does not perform the skills, then it must be assumed that the teacher does not have the competencies necessary to teach them. Stated another way, "the person cannot claim to have taught because it has not been demonstrated that anything was changed."

If this view of instructional competencies is imposed upon teacher training institutions, several interesting phenomena might occur. It is the rare teacher training institution indeed that claims to produce incompetent teachers. If the training institution claims to produce competent teachers, then it is responsible for empirically verifying the specific competencies a particular teacher has acquired. If training institutions opt for competencies as they have been described here, then most paper-pencil tests of competencies are irrelevant. Thus, potential teachers must be able to demonstrate that they can change public school students in prescribed ways *before* they receive a license to teach. Just as parents have the right to except that physicians have demonstrated skills necessary to cure certain ailments *before* they physician is exposed to their children, parents have the right to expect that teachers have demonstrated skills necessary to teach *before* the teacher is exposed to their children.

The position proposed here is that severely handicapped students are often dramatically different, if only in degree, from mildly handicapped students and thus need teachers with different competencies. For example, most severely handicapped students manifest severe speech and language deficits, severe behavioral management problems, severe imitation deficits, severe academic skill acquisition deficits. Thus, a competency based training model must require that potential teachers have demonstrated that they have taught severely handicapped students to speak, to communicate, to imitate, to perform basic adademic skills, to behavior appropriate, etc., *prior* to obtaining a teaching license.

Perhaps a quote from Sontag, Burke, and York (1973) is appropriate here:

> In our view, there is a direct relationship between the level of the students' disability and the competencies of the teachers, i.e., the more pronounced the level of disability, the more specific and precise are the competencies required of the teachers. Most nonhandicapped and mildly handicapped students acquire information and skills from many diverse and nebulous sources: parents, teachers, siblings, peers, TV, toys, etc. These children can develop in spite of a poor teacher or an unconcerned parent. However, severely handicapped students have not been able to acquire the general basic skills and information in any way, from anyone, or anything. Therefore, unless drastic environmental manipulations are engineered, severely handicapped students will not be able to acquire the needed general basic skills and information. Procedures that are typically used by parents, TV producers, siblings, and most classroom teachers to impart skills and information to nonhandicapped and mildly handicapped students are of little utility with severely handicapped students.

The issue then becomes "What competencies are needed by the teachers of severely handicapped students?" In our view, the teachers' competencies are directly related to the instructional problems and acquisition deficits presented by the students. Thus, if the students are not toilet trained, but are physically capable of becoming so, the teacher must have within her instructional repertoire an applicable technology which will result in such students becoming toilet trained. If students are nonimitative, nonverbal, and/or do not attend or respond to social stimuli, then the teacher must be able to teach the students to speak, imitate, and/or relate to social stimuli.

Concomitantly, the teachers must be able to do away with self-mutilating behavior, stereotypes, temper tantrums, and various escape and avoidance behaviors. In addition, the teachers must be able to teach the students to play with and acquire information from materials, self-feed, self-dress, ambulate, write, read, compute, etc. Finally, it is the teacher who will be the major source of practical information for the parents of the students in her charge. Thus, the teacher must be able to function as an effective parent-trainer.

At this point in time, it is a rare teacher who has been able to acquire all the skills needed to teach severely handicapped students merely from the experiences obtained in his or her college level special education training program. Assuming that the previous statement is accurate, then it seems logical that there are very few teachers in the field who have the competencies to teach severely handicapped students and that there are very few, if any, teacher training programs producing teachers with these needed competencies. Thus, most of the new classes arranged for these students will be staffed by untrained teachers."

During the past five years, the writers and their colleagues have at various times drafted lists of behavioral competencies without which a teacher of severely handicapped students presumably could not succeed. A detailed presentation of these lists is obviously inappropriate for inclusion here. However, it might be fruitful to delineate several of the categories that were articulated:

1. Techniques of managing severe behavior problems
2. Procedures for the development of teacher made instructional materials
3. The engineering of physical properties of classrooms
4. Basic principles of acquisition and performance
5. Basic principles and techniques of instructional measurement
6. Basic principles of imitation training, generalization, discrimination, and maintenance
7. Basic principles of task analysis
8. Development and implementation of instructional programs
9. Procedures used to develop curriculum sequences

It should be noted and emphasized that this is only a partial list of categories and that within each category substantial listings of behavioral competencies are mandatory. Thus, it was our objective to produce teachers with demonstrated behavioral competencies in each of the categories listed above. In all honesty we have found this task to be impossible. That is, we have been incompetent teacher trainers in that we have not demonstrated that our students could perform all the required competencies necessary for the provision of quality instructional services to severely handicapped children. Unfortunately, we have had to resort to paper-pencil and verbal ("Tell us what you would do if...") indications of potential classroom instructional performance (i.e., inferential measurement).

COMPONENTS OF AN INSTRUCTIONAL PROGRAM

We realize that in presenting this model of teaching severely handicapped students we are oversimplifying complex multi-person interactions. Nevertheless, we have found it advantageous to attempt to conceptualize many classroom activities into what may be referred to as instructional programs. An instructional program in our view may be conceptualized as consisting of at least 4 not necessarily mutually exclusive components: *content, method, materials,* and *measurement.*

Content

Content refers to the *what* of instruction. That is, if the teacher asks the question "What do I want a student to be able to do that he could not do in the past?" he or she is asking a *content* question. Content refers to specific responses students might make when presented with specified stimuli. Most available "curriculum guides" are composed primarily of instructional content or information related to *what* a teacher might decide to attempt to teach. However, rarely do curriculum guides contain the precision in content delineation mandatory for instructing severely handicapped students. That is, such guides rarely specify the specific responses to specific stimuli that a student is supposed to emit and what criteria or acceptable level of performance the child must achieve to be considered to have learned a task. Such precision in curriculum delineation is not new to education (Mager, 1962, p. 12), it simply has not been utilized in the vast majority of curriculum guides.

In an attempt to realize precision in content delineation, we have found a task analysis approach quite useful. By a task analysis approach we mean that at some point in time a teacher takes the responsibility of determining what responses the students should make. This determination may be labeled the terminal objective. Once a teacher has specified a terminal objective, it is necessary that he or she divide the objective into steps or components that lead from responses in the student's present behavioral repertoire to the terminal objective. The teacher then arranges these steps in a series so that the student's progress through the series culminates in the performance of the terminal objective. These components may be extremely small bits of behavior taught separately and then chained together into the terminal objective, or they may become part of a more complex response as soon as they are acquired. If, for example, a child cannot move easily from step 5 to step 6, then step 6 may be too demanding and perhaps there should be a step 5½. Increasingly finer breakdowns (slicing) of the curriculum or the elimination of unnecessary steps are constant aspects of the task analysis process as one goes from the teacher constructed task analysis to the task analysis required by the student to achieve the terminal objective. Bateman (1971) describes this process as a progression from a logical task analysis (that constructed initially by the teacher) to an empirical task analysis that actually necessary for the student to perform the terminal objective). Thus, a task analysis approach is always a dynamic process in which it is most likely that any given task analysis will be modified for individual students.

The following is an example of a task analysis currently being developed for use in a public school classroom for young severely handicapped students (Swetlik, 1974). This task analysis emanated from two teacher observations. First, it was observed that in many situations requiring expressive or receptive verbal language the students were not using or comprehending personal pronouns appropriately. Second, the students did not appear to comprehend personal pronouns when they were included in reading material. Thus, the appropriate use and comprehension of personal pronouns were judged crucial longitudinal language and reading skills. The teacher then attempted to develop an instructional program that would result in the development of selected uses of personal pronouns. What follows is the task analysis component of that program.

TEACHING LOW FUNCTIONING STUDENTS (*Ss*) SELECTED FIRST, SECOND, AND THIRD PERSON SINGULAR PRONOUN EXPRESSIVE LANGUAGE RESPONSES TO "WHO-DOING" QUESTIONS

Task Analysis II

Phase I: Verifying that *S*s could imitate selected 1, 2, and 3 word verbal responses.

Part 1 — Verifying that *S*s could imitate one word verbal responses (e.g., I).

Part 2 — Verifying that *S*s could imitate 2 word verbal responses (e.g., I am.).

Part 3 — Verifying that *S*s could imitate 3 word verbal responses (e.g., I am sitting.).

Phase II: Teaching Ss to perform actions in response to verbal cues, to visually discriminate actions, and to label actions.

Part 1 — Teaching Ss to perform actions in response to verbal cues (e.g., Show me standing.).

Part 2 — Teaching Ss to visually discriminate actions (e.g., Touch someone standing.).

Part 3 — Teaching Ss to label actions (e.g., What is Joe doing?).

Phase III: Teaching Ss to visually discriminate (touch) self, teacher (T) and peers in response to name cues.

Part 1 — Teaching Ss to visually discriminate (touch) self in response to a name cue.

Part 2 — Teaching Ss to visually discriminate (touch) T in response to a name cue.

Part 3 — Teaching Ss to visually discriminate (touch) peers in response to name cues.

Part 4 — Teaching Ss to visually discriminate (touch) self, T, and peers in response to name cues.

Phase IV: Teaching Ss to visually discriminate males and females using 3rd person singular subject pronoun cues (e.g., Touch a he; Touch a she).

Part 1 — Teaching Ss to visually discriminate males using the 3rd person singular subject pronoun cue *he* (e.g., Touch a he.).

Part 2 — Teaching Ss to visually discriminate females using the 3rd person singular subject pronoun cue *she* (e.g., Touch a she.).

Part 3 — Teaching Ss to visually discriminate males and females using the 3rd person singular subject pronoun cues *he* and *she* (e.g., Touch a he. Touch a she.).

Phase V: Teaching Ss to make identity responses (proper name responses) to "who" questions containing 1st, 2nd, and 3rd person singular subject pronouns.

Part 1 — Teaching Ss to label T in response to "who" questions containing the 1st person singular subject pronoun *I* (e.g., Who am I?).

Part 2 — Teaching Ss to label self in response to "who" questions containing the 2nd person singular pronoun *you* (e.g., Who are you?).

Part 3 — Teaching Ss to label *T* and self in response to "who" questions containing the 1st and 2nd person singular subject pronouns *I* and *you* (e.g., Who am I? Who are you?).

Part 4 — Teaching *S* to label male peers in response to "who" questions containing the 3rd person singular subject pronoun *he* (e.g., Who is he?).

Part 5 — Teaching Ss to label female peers in response to "who" questions containing the 3rd person singular subject pronoun *she* (e.g., Who is she?).

Part 6 — Teaching Ss to label male and female peers in response to "who" questions containing the 3rd person singular subject pronouns *he* and *she* (e.g., Who is he; Who is she?).

Part 7 — Teaching Ss to label themselves, *T*, and male and female peers in response to "who" questions containing the 1st, 2nd, and 3rd person singular subject pronouns (e.g., Who am I? Who are you? Who is she/he?).

Phase VI: Teaching Ss to respond to "Who-doing?" questions with the 1st person singular subject pronoun and present progressive verbs (e.g., Q: Who is standing? A: I am standing.).

Phase VII: Teaching Ss to respond to "Who-doing?" questions with the 2nd person singular pronoun and present progressive verbs (e.g., Q: Who is standing? A: You are standing.).

Phase VIII: Teaching Ss to respond to "Who-doing?" questions with 3rd person singular subject pronouns and present progressive verbs (e.g., Q: Who is standing? A: He/She is standing.).

Part 1 — Teaching Ss to respond to "Who-doing?" questions with the 3rd person singular pronoun *he* (e.g., He is standing.).

Part 2 — Teaching Ss to respond to "Who-doing?" questions with the 3rd person singular pronoun *she* (e.g., She is standing.).

Part 3 — Teaching Ss to respond to "Who-doing?" questions with the 3rd person singular pronouns *he* or *she*.

Phase IX: Teaching *S*s to respond to "Who-doing" questions with singular subject pronouns (1st, 2nd, and 3rd person) and present progressive verbs (e.g., Q: Who is standing? A: I am standing. Q: Who is standing? A: You are standing. Q: Who is standing? A: He is standing. Q: Who is standing? A: She is standing.).

Another aspect of task analysis crucial to the teacher of severely handicapped students that should be made salient is its relationship to assessment. A teacher confronting a severely handicapped student for the first time can learn little about the new student from the information obtained from traditional asssessment instruments (IQ tests, achievement tests, etc.). A technique of much greater instructional relevance is that of individual assessment on components of specific task analyses. This approach requires that the teacher proceed through each of the steps of the analysis he or she has developed for each of the tasks being taught in the classroom. Instruction would then being on those steps performed incorrectly by the student and proceed sequentially through more difficult steps. Students might be grouped according to the steps to be taught and proceed in accordance with the attainment of criterion level performance on those steps rather than on the mean performance of the group or as a function of the passage of time. Presently, all of the necessary task analyses are not available for an ideal assessment system (all necessary skills analyzed from zero competence in an area to complete competence in that area). However, rapid progress is being made in some areas (e.g., math, see Resnick, Wang & Kaplin, 1973); and it is the rare teacher who cannot do better than traditional inferential measurement devices.

Finally, before leaving this cursory treatment of instructional content, a note concerning the direction we feel content delineation should take might be in order. Whenever possible, we have chosen to emphasize the areas traditionally known as academic—i.e., speech and language, reading, math, and writing. Thus, we find ourselves in agreement with the 1967 position of Cawley and Pappanikou:

> However, the success or failure of a human being in Western civilization has, is, and apparently will continue to be based upon one's ability to express oneself orally, to read, to write, to deal with number concepts, and to handle money.

> With this in mind, then, it is indeed quite perturbing to the special educator who from time to time has to witness programs and discount academics on the pretense that birthday parties and craftwork are more important to the final integration, habilitation, and/or rehabilitation of the regarded in society. This is usually done in the name of personal and social adequacy. Such a change in curricular emphasis is looked upon by these authors more as an inability of that particular teacher to adapt methods of instruction appropriate to the aforementioned characteristics of her pupils, than as an inherent inability in the particular retardate to learn academics.

The reader interested in securing further information regarding instructional content that might be relevant to instruction programs might find the following selected references of interest: Becker, Englemann, and Thomas (1971); Bricker and Bricker (1972); Bricker and Bricker (1973); Bricker, Dennison, Watson, and Vincent-Smith (1973); Sheperd, Wyrick, and Bilyou (1970); and Thiel (1972).

Method

Method refers to the *how* of instruction. If a teacher asks the question "How do I get a student to do what he could not do in the past?" he or she is asking a method question. Specifically, method is concerned with how a teacher arranges the instructional environment, including his or her own behavior, so that enhancement of the behavioral repertoires of the students can be empirically verified.

Teaching students to make the responses that were delineated and sequenced in a task analysis is in our judgment the most difficult function the teacher performs. That is, a teacher can develop or purchase a precise and logical task analysis, utilize beautiful and relevant materials, and generate creative measurement systems; but if the teacher cannot teach the student to perform new responses, all is for naught. The techniques, tactics, procedures, principles, etc., that we employ related to the *how* of instructing severely handicapped students have been taken from the contributions of such persons as Itard, Sequin, Montessori, Descoeudres, Fernald, Strauss and Lehtinen, and Skinner.

Recently, however, we have found it useful to generate instructional methods from the conceptual framework of what is referred to as *applied behavior analysis* (Baer, Wolf & Risley, 1968; Bandura, 1969). More specifically, we make conscientious attempts to systematically utilize such principles, tactics procedures, etc., as response priming, imitation training, escape training, avoidance training, stimulus fading, stimulus discrimination and generalization, contingent consequation, overcorrection, errorless learning, and response chaining. Unfortunately, space does not permit a more detailed presentation of how the principles delineated above are converted for use in classroom instructional programs. The reader interested in such a presentation is referred to Brown, Bellany, and Sontag (1971); Brown and Sontag (1972); and Brown, Scheuerman, Cartwright, and York (1973).

Materials

Once teachers determine the specific responses they intend to teach (i.e., what to teach), they then must determine the materials (persons, places, printed words, physical objects, etc.) to which those responses should be made. In other words, instructional materials should be generated subsequent to the delineation of instructional objectives. Unfortunately, there is an extreme dearth of sequenced instructional materials that have either been developed or empirically verified for classroom use with severely handicapped students. In general, it has been our experience that commercially available sequenced materials are not sufficiently concrete, precise, redundant, or relevant for use with most severely handicapped students. Thus, the teacher is forced to rely on his or her ingenuity to generate new or adapt existing materials.

It is expected that in the near future, because of the appearance of large numbers of severely handicapped students in public schools, a concerted effort on the part of commercial publishers and others will be made to develop much needed instructional materials. Hopefully, attempts will be made to empirically verify the validity of the materials *prior* to unrestricted dissemination. There is little doubt that the *"Wipple-dip language, reading, math, science, motor, and self-help contraption for delayed, low functioning, severely handicapped but needy children"* will appear and be purchased by many "because there is nothing else available." However, such a dilemma is still uncomfortable.

Measurement

In any empirical definition of teaching, instructional measurement is crucial. With normal and mildly handicapped students, inferences about populations of skills made from samples and inferences about generalization of skills across persons and places and materials are probably necessary and tenable. Unfortunately, inferential measurement, in our judgment, is an extremely questionable measurement orientation when applied to most severely handicapped students. The general rule that we try to follow may be stated as follows: If you determine that a particular response, skill, concept, etc., is important to the development of the student, then it is incumbent upon the teacher to *directly* measure the existence of the response, skill, concept, etc., of concern. A related aspect of direct measurement may be stated as follows:

> Direct measurement is particularly crucial in attempts to teach cumulative tasks. If the correct performance of the responses in component c of a task are dependent upon the correct performance of the responses in components a and b, then the teacher must guarantee that a and b responses are in the behavioral repertoire of the student before she even considers progression to component c. Since most developmental skills are in many ways cumulative (mathematics, reading, language, speech, practical arts), teachers of trainable-level retarded students must be prepared to spend relatively long periods of time and considerable effort developing basic behavioral repertoires. [Brown, 1973]

Thus, it is necessary that teachers be skilled in the use of measurement designs that allow for the frequent and direct measurement of relevant behavioral dimensions. Frequent measurement is crucial if only to delineate instructional failure as soon as possible. That is, assume that a teacher designs and implements an instructional program in September, continues to implement that program until December, and then measures how much of the information, etc., in the program the students acquired. If the students acquired 100% of the information, fine. If, however, the students acquired *none* of the information, the teacher has wasted a substantial amount of instructional time and energy. More frequent measurement would have allowed the teacher to delineate and adapt to instructional failure much sooner. On the other hand, direct and continuous measurement of all responses performed in the classroom through-out the entire school year is impractical, unnecessary, and irrelevant. Obviously, a balance has to evolve in each classroom with each student and each teacher.

In an attempt to provide teachers with a reasonable amount of flexibility regarding how much, how often, and what to measure directly, we have found it necessary to provide them with information, examples, and, in some situations, practice using some of the following subjects as their own controls paradigms and related measurement skills: reversal designs, learning set designs, trials to criterion and errors to criterion designs, multiple baseline and modifications of multiple baseline and modifications of multiple baseline designs, test-teach designs, and cumulative frequency designs.

Hopefully, if teachers have a sufficient number of measurement designs in their technological repertoires, they will apply these designs to the evaluation of the instructional programs in their classrooms—thus enabling themselves to base daily or weekly adaptations in the content and methods of instruction upon student performance.

In summary, an instructional program requires a teacher (1) to determine *what* to teach students by precisely delineating behavioral objectives, (2) to determine *how* to teach students by clearly specifying his or her instructional activities, (3) to select or generate *materials* that require responses delineated in the behavioral objectives, and (4) to *measure* directly the responses of the students in an attempt to evaluate instructional effectiveness.

THE POTENTIAL FOR BACKLASH

Thousands of severely handicapped children who were formerly accommo-dated at home, in private schools, in private and public residential institutions will now attend public schools. In the face of a restricting economic environment there are several potentially devastating reactions. It is extremely doubtful that many communities have at their disposal the *additional* economic resources necessary to secure the teachers, space, transportation, equipment, administrative personnel, etc., required to serve these *new* students. Most communities will have to reallocate resources currently assigned to other services.

If it can be demonstrated that a child who was once tied to a bed in an institution because he or she was self-mutilating can now read, write, compute, socialize, and in other ways behave more adaptively, few people will complain about giving up a new chemistry lab, new football uniforms, or small portions of their salary increases (Lovaas, 1974). If, on the other hand, a child who was tied to a bed in an institution is now tied to a bed in a public school classroom, it is doubtful that many persons will graciously accept the aforementioned economic adjustments. Obviously, the example of the child tied to a bed was used to dramatize a point. However, children sitting in classrooms finger painting for 10 months is less dramatic but will probably make the same point to the economically strapped taxpayer.

We believe the outcome of the placement of severely handicapped students in the school systems will be a function of the quality of the programs the school systems provide. Obviously, quality programs will be dependent upon the skills of the teachers hired to develop and maintain them. This, of course, makes the work of the trainers of these teachers extremely important.

Severely handicapped persons have not fared well in our society in the past. However, it seems that we now have an opportunity to create humane, tolerant, developmentally sound, and existentially relevant social and emotional environments that can replace the oppressive, rejecting, undignifying, and intolerant systems so long in operation. Hopefully, special education will supplement the activities of parents with varied contributions. Hopefully, among these contributions will be the production of aggressive and creative administrators capable of designing and engineering novel and flexible service delivery systems, and highly competent, dedicated, and efficient classroom teachers capable of providing quality instructional services over long periods of time. Finally, as we have so little in our technological repertories that has any empirical validity, special education will have to generate a substantial body of new information specifically applicable to the instruction of severely handicapped persons. Stated another way, "we have to get special, nothing else works."

REFERENCES

Baer, D. M., Wolf, M. M. & Risley, T. R. "Some Current Dimensions of Applied Behavior Analysis." *Journal of Applied Behavior Analysis, 1* (1), 1968 (91-97).

Bandura, A. *Principles of Behavior Modification.* New York: Holt, 1969.

Bateman, B. *The Essentials of Teaching.* San Rafael, Calif.: Dimensions in Early Learning Series, 1971.

Becker, W. C., Engelmann, S. & Thomas, D. R. *Teaching: A Course in Applied Psychology.* Chicago: Science Research Associates, 1971.

Bricker, D. & Bricker, W. *Toddler Research and Intervention Project: Report – Year II.* Nashville: IMRID Behavioral Science Monograph No. 21, 1972.

Bricker, W. & Bricker, D. "Early Language Intervention." Invited paper presented at NICHD Conference on Language Intervention with the Mentally Retarded, Wisconsin Dells, Wisconsin, June, 1973. Conference proceedings in press.

Bricker, D., Dennison, L., Watson, L. & Vincent-Smith, L. *Language Training Program for Young Developmentally Delayed Children: Volume 2.* Nashville: IMRID Behavioral Science Monograph No. 22, 1973.

Brown, L. "Instructional Programs for Trainable-Level Retarded Students." In L. Mann & D. A. Sabatino (Eds.), *The First Review of Special Education*, Vol. 2. Philadelphia: JSE Press, 1973.

Brown, L., Bellamy, T. & Sontag, E. "The Development and Implementation of a Public School Prevocational Training Program for Trainable Level Retarded and Severely Emotionally Disturbed Students." Part I. Madison Public Schools, Madison, Wisconsin, 1971.

Brown, L., Scheuerman, N., Cartwright, S. & York, R. "The Design and Implementation of an Empirically Based Instructional Program for Severely Handicapped Students: Toward the Rejection of the Exclusion Principle. Part III. Madison Public Schools, Madison, Wisconsin, 1973.

Brown, L. & Sontag, E. "Toward the Development and Implementation of an Empirically Based Public School Program for Trainable Mentally Retarded and Severely Emotionally Disturbed Students." Part II. Madison Public Schools, Madison, Wisconsin, 1972.

Cawley, J. & Pappanikou, A. J. "The Educable Mentally Retarded." In Haring, N. G. & Schiefelbusch, R. L. (Eds.), *Methods in Special Education*. New York: McGraw-Hill, 1967.

Engelmann, S. *Preventing Failure in the Primary Grades*. Chicago: Science Research Associates, 1969.

Gilhool, T. K. Education: "An Inalienable Right." *Exceptional Children, 39* (8), 1973 (597-609).

Lippman, L. & Goldberg, I. I. *Right to Education – Anatomy of the Pennsylvania Case and Its Implications for Exceptional Children*. New York and London: Teachers College Press, 1973.

Lovaas, I. "An Interview by Paul Chance." *Psychology Today, 7* (8), 1974 (76-84).

Mager, R. *Preparing Instructional Objectives*. Palo Alto, Calif.: Fearson Pub., 1962.

Molloy, J. *Trainable Children: Curriculum and Procedures*. New York: John Day Co., 1972.

Resnick, L. B., Wang, M. C. & Kaplan, J. "Task Analysis in Curriculum Design: A Hierarchically Sequenced Introductory Mathematics Curriculum." *Journal of Applied Behavior Analysis, 6* (4), 1973 (679-710).

Sailor, W., Guess, D. & Baer, D. M. "Functional Language for Verbally Deficient Children: An Experimental Program." *Exceptional Children, 11* (3), 1973 (27-35).

Schwartz, M. A. "The Education of Handicapped Children: Emerging Legal Doctrines." *Clearinghouse Review* (National Clearinghouse for Legal Services), 7 (3) 1973.

Sheperd, B. W., Wyrick, R. P. & Bilyou, D. *Curriculum Guide for Teachers of Trainable Mentally Retarded Children*. Jefferson City, Missouri: The Missouri State Department of Education Schools for Retarded Children, 1970.

Sontag, E., Burke, P. J. & York, R. "Considerations for Serving the Severely Handicapped in the Public Schools." *Education and Training of the Mentally Retarded, 8* (2), 1973 (20-26).

Swetlik, B. "Teaching Low Functioning Students Selected first, Second, and Third Person Singular Pronoun Expressive Language Responses to "Who-Doing" Questions." Unpublished manuscript, University of Wisconsin, 1974.

Thiel, E. A. *Design for Daily Living: A Framework for Curriculum Development for Children and Youth with Mental Retardation*. Qunicy, Fla.: Thiel Enterprises, 1972.

Vergason, G. A. "Accountability in Special Education." *Exceptional Children, 39* (5), 1973 (367-373).

This chapter provides the teacher a delineated system for organizing the physical environment of the classroom. More importantly, it describes the "what" and "how" instructional activities which should occur within the learning environment. One of the tests for any instructional strategy is its impact over time. While the notion of the Engineered Classroom is several years old, it has been adapted and used in many classrooms. As such, the system is still relevant and topical. It describes a way for a teacher to function with a group of pupils, the real world, yet move more and more toward the goal of individualized instruction. As with any effective teaching model, it places importance upon behavior observation, measurement, curriculum planning, and evaluation of instruction.

An Educational Solution:
The Engineered Classroom

Robert J. Stillwell, Alfred A. Artuso, Frank D. Taylor
Santa Monica School District, California

Frank M. Hewett
University of California, Los Angeles

Public school educators today have a growing concern about the ever-increasing number of inattentive, failure-prone, hyperactive children who cannot be contained within the usual classroom structure. Often all appropriate public school techniques have been exhausted and both teachers and administrators have been unable to find a suitable solution.

It is apparent that many of these students have the potential to achieve in school if some appropriate program could be developed for them. It has not been enough merely to label them as school failures or potential dropouts. Repeated student and parent conferences, transfers to other classrooms or schools, intervention from outside agencies, suspension, expulsion, and home instruction have all been utilized with little or no noticeable effect. At the same time it has not always been feasible to leave the disordered student in the regular classroom.

In an effort to find more appropriate solutions, education looked to the disciplines of medicine, psychiatry, and neurology for help. Such phrases as "neurologically impaired," "brain damaged," "perceptually handicapped," "school phobic," "neurotic," and "emotionally disturbed" were soon added to the vocabulary of many teachers, administrators, and parents. Often the only contribution this terminology made was to glamorize a diagnosis that was not always functional for the classroom teacher attempting to cope with problem students on a day-to-day basis.

What was needed was an instructional program that would be meaningful to a teacher, translatable to a classroom, and have promise of changing the behavior of the increasing number of students described earlier and often labeled educationally handicapped or emotionally disturbed.

Dr. Frank M. Hewett, Head of the Neuro-Psychiatric Institute School of U.C.L.A., envisioned a possible educational solution for the problem. He hypothesized that what was needed was basically an educational model—a developmental sequence—that would provide for the merging of sound individualized instructional techniques already in use in many classrooms with some aspects of behavior modification theory.

Dr. Alfred A. Artuso, Superintendent, and Dr. Frank D. Taylor, Director of Special Services, of the Santa Monica Unified School District cooperated with Dr. Hewett in evaluating this new model, now known as the Engineered Classroom.

This cooperative endeavor between a public school system and a major university has proven very productive. The University provides the creative talents of experts in learning theory and the knowledge for sound research studies. The public schools are a resource for personnel in developing classroom procedures and curriculum while providing the opportunity of testing an educational innovation in the reality of the "real world." In the final analysis the value of any educational innovation must not be decided until after it has stood the test of a genuine public school situation.

In the first four years of the project, there were as many as twelve classrooms in operation, from primary through junior high school grades. These classes are in schools in a typical urban community with all the concerns of public school teachers, administrators, P.T.A. organizations, and parents, while still encompassing the full spectrum of ethnic and socioeconomic backgrounds ideally structured for research.

The classrooms for educationally handicapped students as developed in Santa Monica provide the teacher with a carefully structured plan for assigning appropriate educational tasks to students, providing meaningful rewards for learning, and for maintaining student-like behavior within well-defined limits. Specific instructional materials already utilized by many school systems in individualizing instruction, the concept of the developmental sequence of educational goals (Hewett, 1968), and a pragmatic use of some aspects of behavior modification provide the foundation of the basic elements of the educational solution.

The first element of the educational solution is the developmental sequence.

A DEVELOPMENTAL SEQUENCE OF EDUCATIONAL GOALS

The developmental sequence mentioned earlier postulates six educational task levels. These goals or behavioral categories move from *attention, response, order, exploratory,* and *social* to *mastery* (see Figure 1). The implication is that we must gain a child's attention and make contact with him, get him to participate and respond in learning, aid him in adapting to routines and direction following, help him to accurately and thoroughly explore his environment through multisensory experience, learn to gain the approval of others and avoid their disapproval, and finally master academic skills of reading and arithmetic and gain knowledge in curriculum content areas.

Figure 1

DEFICITS ACCORDING TO A DEVELOPMENTAL
SEQUENCE OF EDUCATIONAL GOALS

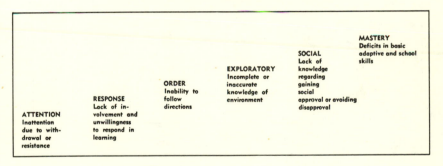

The child is taken where he is on this developmental sequence, his weaknesses bolstered and his strengths supported. While the ultimate goal of the teacher is to engage the student at the mastery level, children must first be considered in terms of their development at lower levels, and assignments in school must take this into account. In helping an educationally handicapped child get ready for intellectual training, the teacher can profitably use the behavior modification principle of shaping rather than hold out for the ultimate goal.

The second element of the structure is the classroom setting.

CLASSROOM SETTING

The typical elementary classroom is a 20' by 30', well lighted, portable classroom, with double desks (2' x 4') for each of the 9 to 12 pupils. The physical environment can be described according to four major centers, paralleling levels on the developmental sequence of educational goals. The Mastery Center consists of the student desk area where academic assignments are undertaken, and study booths or "offices" where the student continues his academic progress is another postural setting. An Exploratory Center is set up near the windows, and there are sink facilities for simple science experiments, arts, and crafts. A Communication Center where social skills are fostered is also located in the back of the room. The Order Center consists of tables where games, puzzles, exercises, and activities emphasizing attention, orderly response, and routine are kept (Figure 2).

Figure 2
ELEMENTARY SCHOOL CLASSROOM

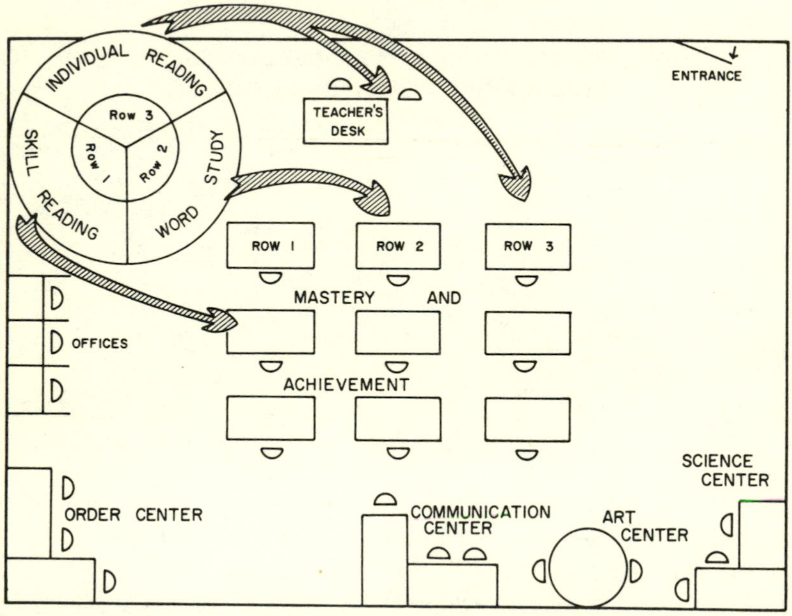

While the classrooms at the junior high school level are the same size and the same four centers are present, the room was designed to provide greater flexibility. The student "home base" in the room has armchair desks (Station One) exactly like those used in other classrooms in the school. Around this area are three additional work areas. Station Two has three study carrels, with soft upholstered chairs and reference materials such as a dictionary, telephone book, department store catalog and an almanac placed in each one. Station Three features three drafting tables with high stools to offer a marked shift in sitting and working position, as well as setting. Station Four has three large tables offering still another setting. The rationale for setting up these four stations within the Mastery Area is that frequent moving to a different setting or working position appears to facilitate interest and concentration with this action-oriented adolescent group. During the day the teacher may rotate the entire class or only selected members through these work stations. The Exploratory Center (Station Five) stresses appropriate junior high science content and may have a stand-up work counter for another setting. The Art Center (Station Six) and Communication Center (Station Seven) utilize many of the same types of tasks found effective with elementary age children, and the Order Center (Station Eight) often contains mechanical parts such as a simple one-cylinder engine which can be dismantled piece by piece and reassembled. Puzzles and other direction-following activities are also found here (Figure 3).

Figure 3
JUNIOR HIGH SCHOOL CLASSROOM

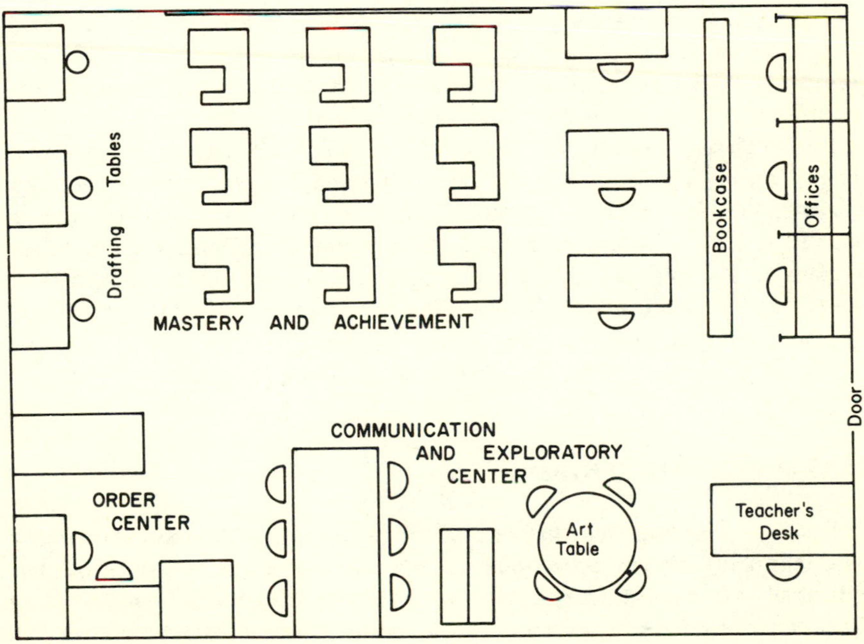

The classrooms are under the supervision of a regular teacher and a teacher aide. The aide need not be a credentialed or specifically trained individual. High school graduates and PTA volunteers have been employed.

The third element of the structure is the concept of the Work Record Card or the Checkmark System.

THE CHECKMARK SYSTEM

Mounted by the door is a Work Record Card Holder, much like a time card rack near the time clock in a factory. An individual Work Record Card for each student is in the holder. As each student enters the room in the morning, he picks up his individual Work Record Card which is ruled with approximately 190 squares. As the student moves through the day, the teacher and aide recognize his efficiency to function as a student by giving checkmarks on the Work Record Card. The student carries his card with him wherever he goes in the room. Checkmarks are given on a fixed interval basis with a possible 10 checkmarks for each 15 minutes (Figure 4).

This system attempts to provide rewards on a concrete, immediate basis for children who have not been responsive to the more typical kinds of rewards provided by school (e.g., long-range grades, praise, parental recognition, competition, etc.). The teacher attempts to convey the idea that the checkmarks are objective measures of accomplishment and literally part of a reality system in the classroom, over which the teacher has little subjective control. Student save completed Work Record Cards that can be exchanged for one of the exchange items available in Phases I, II, and III.

During Phase I students may exchange a completed Work Record Card for a simple trinket or a candy reward. Phases II and III provide opportunities to exchange the Work Record Cards for 15 minutes of free choice activity time at one of the centers within the room or a report card—complimentary note home to parents. As students approach reintegration into regular classrooms, they move from the more basic candy or trinket rewards of Phase I to the more typical school type reporting forms of Phase III.

The fourth element of the structure is the use of interventions.

CLASSROOM INTERVENTIONS

Earlier it was suggested that one of the essential ingredients in all learning situations was a suitable educational task—a task that made it possible for each individual student to succeed at all times. Thus, the teacher must be aware of each student's progress throughout the school day and be ready to intervene at

Figure 4
WORK RECORD CARD AND CHECK MARK SYSTEM

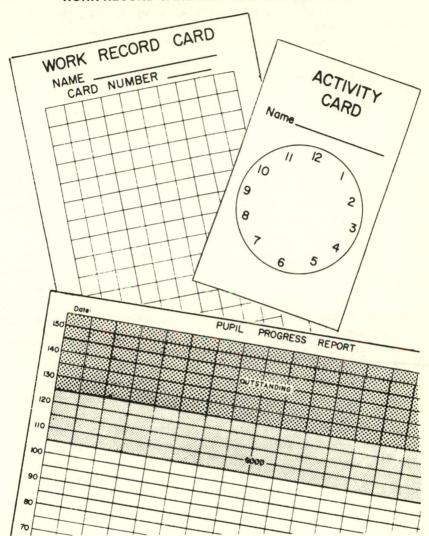

any time when a given task assignment proves inappropriate. Nine specific interventions have been developed which encompass the six levels on the developmental sequence of educational goals.

As long as the child is able to stabilize himself during any of the student interventions, he continues to earn checkmarks on a par with those students

261

successfully pursuing mastery level assignments. He is in no way penalized for the shift in assignment made by the teacher.

If, at any time during the school day, a student begins to display signs of maladaptive learning behavior (e.g., inattention, daydreaming, boredom, disruption), the teacher has appropriate resources in the form of interventions to meet the situation.

Figure 5 summarizes the interventions which may be utilized in an attempt to foster adaptive student functioning. The teacher may select any intervention seen as appropriate with a given student or may try the student at each intervention level until his behavior improves. Actual practice has shown that it is only on rare occasions that the teacher needs to employ a time-out or exclusion.

The fifth element of the structure is the daily instructional program.

DAILY INSTRUCTIONAL PROGRAM

The original daily schedule and curriculum of the Engineered Classroom has been constantly assessed and modified, not only in Santa Monica but in other school districts throughout the country. It should be obvious that although the following program suggests specific activities the students, facilities, community needs, and individual school may dictate considerable changes in time blocks and subject matter (Figure 6).

An attempt has been made to provide the classroom teacher with specific ideas that minimize the preparation of endless ditto masters while maximizing the individualization of instruction for each of the students. This is accomplished, in part, by utilizing commercially available self-correcting materials such as S.R.A. Reading Labs, Sullivan Programmed Arithmetic and Reading Materials, Write and See Phonics and Reader's Digest Materials, and by capitalizing on the teacher and teacher aides themselves as "instructional material." For example, during two of the three time blocks in both Reading and Arithmetic, the teacher and aide rely primarily on individual or small group instruction at the teacher's desk, the pupil's desk, or the chalkboard. Instruction at this time is largely personalized through participation on the part of the pupil with a library book, arithmetic at the chalkboard, or an immediate follow-up task assigned by the teacher or aide. Typical workbook ditto-type lessons are not utilized since the teacher becomes the "textbook."

At times during the day when worksheets are needed the teacher uses either commercially available materials or open-ended multilevel assignments developed by staff members of the Santa Monica Schools.

The initial assignment of the day, given during the order period, is designed to provide the students with a simple paper and pencil or a concrete

Figure 5

HIERARCHY OF INTERVENTIONS TO MAINTAIN STUDENT ROLE

Level	Student Interventions
1. Mastery	a. Assign student to study booth to pursue mastery work. b. Modify mastery assignment and have student continue at desk or in study booth.
2. Social	Verbally restructure expectation of student role (e.g., respect working rights of others, accept limits of time, space, activity).
3. Exploratory	Remove mastery assignment and reassign to Exploratory Center for specific science, art, or communication activity.
4. Order	Reassign to Order Center for specific direction following tasks (e.g., puzzle, exercise, game, work sheet).
5. Response	Remove child from classroom and assign him to a task he likes to do and can do successfully outside (e.g., running around playground, punching punching bag, turning specific number of somersaults on lawn).
6. Attention	Remove child from classroom, put on a one-to-one tutoring relationship with teacher aide, and increase use of extrinsic motivators to obtain cooperation, attention, and student behavior.
	Nonstudent Interventions
7. Time Out	Take away work record card and explain to child he cannot earn checkmarks for a specific number of minutes which he must spend in isolation in room adjacent to class.
8. Exclusion	If the child is not able to function in timeout room, immediately suspend him from class and, if possible, send him home.

Figure 6
DAILY SCHEDULE

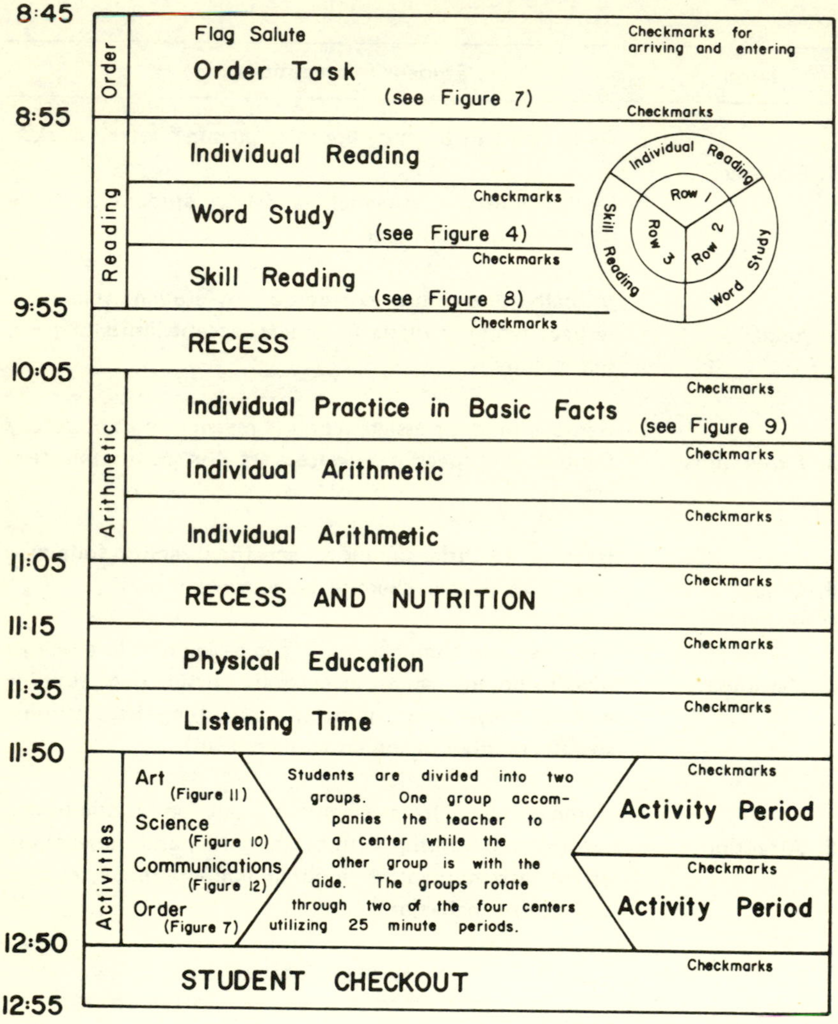

Time		Activity	
8:45	Order	Flag Salute **Order Task** (see Figure 7)	Checkmarks for arriving and entering Checkmarks
8:55	Reading	**Individual Reading**	
		Word Study Checkmarks (see Figure 4)	
		Skill Reading Checkmarks (see Figure 8)	Checkmarks
9:55		**RECESS**	
10:05	Arithmetic	**Individual Practice in Basic Facts** (see Figure 9)	Checkmarks
		Individual Arithmetic	Checkmarks
		Individual Arithmetic	Checkmarks
11:05		**RECESS AND NUTRITION**	Checkmarks
11:15		**Physical Education**	Checkmarks
11:35		**Listening Time**	Checkmarks
11:50	Activities	Art (Figure 11) Science (Figure 10) Communications (Figure 12) Order (Figure 7) — Students are divided into two groups. One group accompanies the teacher to a center while the other group is with the aide. The groups rotate through two of the four centers utilizing 25 minute periods.	Checkmarks **Activity Period** Checkmarks **Activity Period**
12:50		**STUDENT CHECKOUT**	Checkmarks
12:55			

Reading wheel: Individual Reading — Row 1; Word Study — Row 2; Skill Reading — Row 3

manipulative direction-following task that can be easily completed in a successful manner. Commercially available perceptual motor training work sheets are used along with other nonverbal tracing, design copying, or visual discrimination tasks (Figure 7).

The reading program is divided into three 15-minute periods. Individual reading is done at the teacher's desk with each child. The child brings his work reader (a basal or remedial text close to his actual functioning level) to the desk

Figure 7
ORDER TASKS

Simple paper and pencil tasks or concrete manipulative tasks of a direction following nature that can be completed by students with varying ability levels.

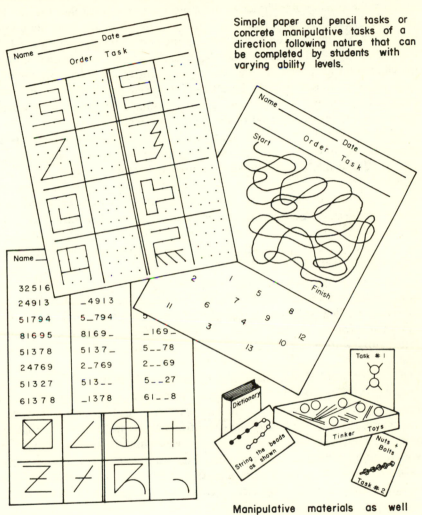

Manipulative materials as well as specific academic direction following tasks are utilized during the Order activities scheduled the last hour of the day.

and reads aloud with the teacher aide for a three-minute period. The three minutes are timed by a small hourglass which the child turns over when he is ready to start reading. As the child correctly completes each line of reading material the teacher aide dispenses an appropriate reward to the student. The aide also keeps a record of each word the child misreads, and these are printed on a 3" x 5" file care for later study. At the end of the 3-minute period the teacher aide and child work on tasks that help develop comprehension and then the child takes his reward and the new reading words back to his desk. Candy is used initially in this activity because of the high motivation it produces, exhibited by students when practicing their reading before going to the teacher aide's desk and their concentration during oral reading.

While the initial reward may have been candy (M & Ms), the students are soon working for checkmarks that can be exchanged for activity time, or plastic counters dropped into a cup and later counted and graphed.

After each child in a given group has had individual reading, an assignment wheel is turned; the teacher has all students put down their work and both teacher and aide circulate, giving children their checkmarks. This takes approximately three to five minutes, during which time the children also learn to wait quietly. The bonus checkmarks given for "being a student" will reflect such "waiting" behavior.

Next, the groups move to either word study or skill reading. *Word study* is done at the child's desk. The teacher circulates (while the aide continues individual reading with another group of three students) and works with individual students or small groups on reading skill. Spelling words acquired during story writing (discussed later) are also reviewed as spelling words at this time.

Following word study, the wheel is turned and checkmarks are given all students. It is important to point out that during the checkmark-giving period, not only is the previous assignment corrected and acknowledged with checkmarks, but the next assignment is introduced. It has been found that this type of individual transition period is very useful in maintaining the work-oriented atmosphere in the class. The teacher does not rely on verbal assignments in front of the class by repeatedly calling out, "Boys and girls! Boys and girls! That means you too, Henry! Give me your attention! I am waiting for two people in row three." etc.

Skill reading involves an independent vocabulary and comprehension building activity, and commercial materials, including programmed or individualized ones such as Sullivan Programmed Readers, S.R.A., Write and See, or Barnell Loft materials are used. The Santa Monica staff has also developed some open-ended multilevel word games and decoding exercises that can be used occasionally during this time (Figure 8).

Figure 8
SKILL READING TASKS

Multi-level tasks differ from regular
worksheets because teachers can easily
modify a task to meet the needs of
each individual student.

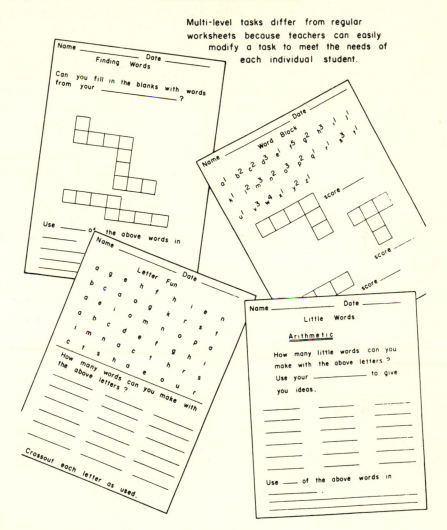

The interventions used to assist a child who is having difficulty with a reading assignment or any other assignment for a period of time utilize the centers around the room. Students may be assigned to do a simple puzzle at the Order Center, listen to the record player at the Communications Area, or complete an art or science task at one of the other centers.

Twice a week, *Story Writing* is done by the entire class rather than in small groups. The teacher usually makes a short motivation presentation in some area of interest to the class (e.g., knighthood, deep sea life), and the students are encouraged to write about the topic.

Following either reading or story writing, the class is dismissed for recess. This is taken outside the room, and as each child leaves he puts his Work Record Card away in its holder. Upon returning the card is picked up and the child receives up to a possible ten checkmarks for the recess period.

The *arithmetic* period occupies the next hour, which is divided into three periods of about 15 minutes each. The students are also divided into three groups based somewhat on their ability. One of the groups is working on arithmetic fundamentals, including basic addition, subtraction, division, and multiplication. The Santa Monica staff has adopted and developed multi-level arithmetic drill sheets (Figure 9) which can be quickly modified to fit a particular student's individual instructional needs. A second group of three to four students is working at the chalkboard or around a larger table at one of the centers with the teacher or teacher aide, learning new skills or getting help in problem-solving techniques. The third group may be using pages taken from a workbook, the SRA Computational Skills Kit, Junior Scholastic Materials, or solving problems put on the chalkboard by the teacher. Approximately every 15 minutes all work stops—assignments are corrected, checkmarks given, and students rotate to the next assignment.

During the next 20 to 25 minute period the students leave the classroom for physical education. Generally the teachers use low organized games that do not emphasize competitive skills but do have a lead-up value for games typically engaged in by their peers in regular classes. Work Record Cards are taken outside to the playground, and checks are given when students reach the play area, finish their play, and return to the room.

Following the lunch period a 10 to 15 minute group listening activity may be used to help students effect a transition from the active play on the playground to the more restricted behavior in the classroom. During this time the teacher reads aloud a portion of a continuing story.

The next period of the day is devoted to exploratory activities. The class is divided in half with one group going to a center with the teacher while the other group goes to a center with the aide. Students spend from 20 to 25 minutes working at the centers in the back of the room. At the end of this period the two groups either exchange centers or rotate to another center.

Each task is selected for its intriguing interest value rather than because it falls within any particular grade level curriculum. It may be recalled that the exploratory level falls below the mastery level; hence, science experiments are chosen for their multisensory rather than intellectual value. Nevertheless simple, accurate descriptions of all science experiments are given by the teachers to

Figure 9
ARITHMETIC TASKS

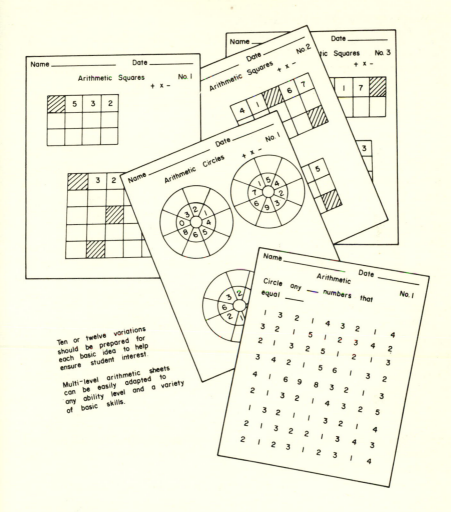

Ten or twelve variations should be prepared for each basic idea to help ensure student interest.

Multi-level arithmetic sheets can be easily adapted to any ability level and a variety of basic skills.

each group (Figure 10). Following the introduction of each day's science task, the card is filed at the center and is available for students during the interventions.

Art activities are varied and have been organized by the Santa Monica staff to include projects which allow the child self-expression. An attempt is made to keep these tasks simple so that they can be completed within a 25-minute work period. However, the children may continue them over from one day to the next. The art task cards are also filed at the art area for later reference and

Figure 10
EXPLORATORY TASKS—EXPLORING OUR ENVIRONMENT

Tasks are selected for their multisensory rather than intellectual value. Each task uses concrete manipulative materials in a situation with a predictable outcome that provides the student with an opportunity to explore his environment.

Many fine commercial materials and ideas are available.

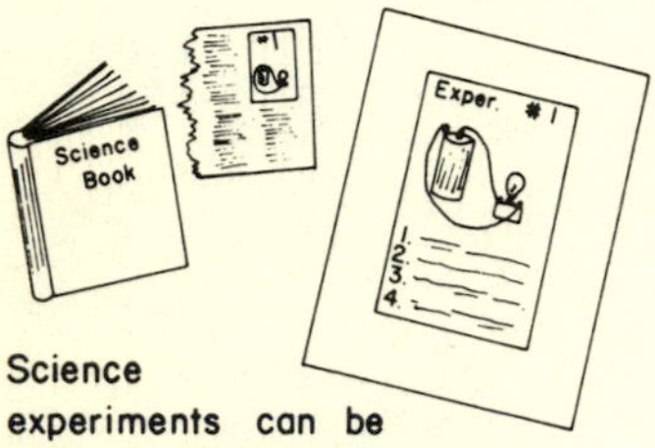

ED-U-CARDS

Science experiments can be cut out of Scott, Foresman or other science series and then mounted on cards.

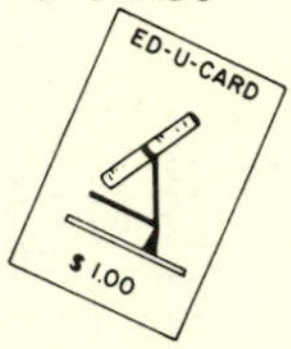

Sets of Science cards with experiments are inexpensive and available.

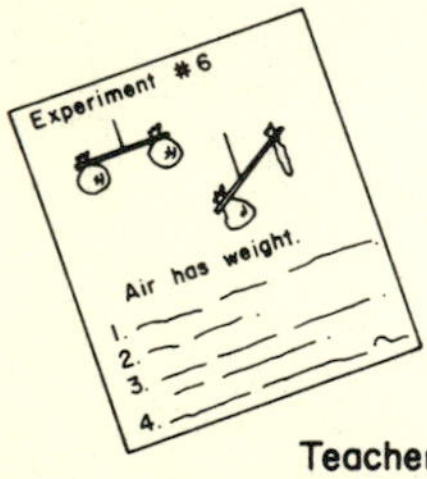

SILVER BURDETT SCIENCE LABORATORY

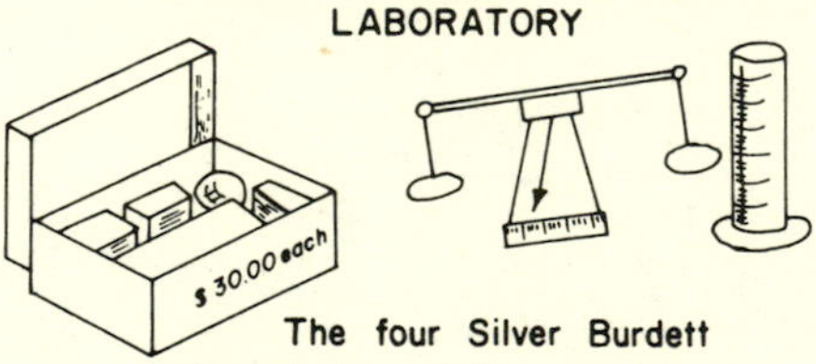

Teachers can collect science ideas from many sources and prepare cards with appropriate science tasks.

The four Silver Burdett Science Labs provide a total of more than 150 experiments and are ideal for the science area.

replication. Ideas from district guides, the *Instructor* and *Grade School Teacher* have been used (Figure 11).

Communication tasks for building social skills are introduced during the exploratory period and are also filed at the Communication Center for later usage. Since games entered into by two or more children inevitably involve a winner, those based more on chance rather than skill have proven most successful. Activities like Chinese checkers, chess, battleship, tic-tac-toe, hangman, etc., have also been used successfully (Figure 12).

Figure 11
EXPLORATORY TASKS—ART

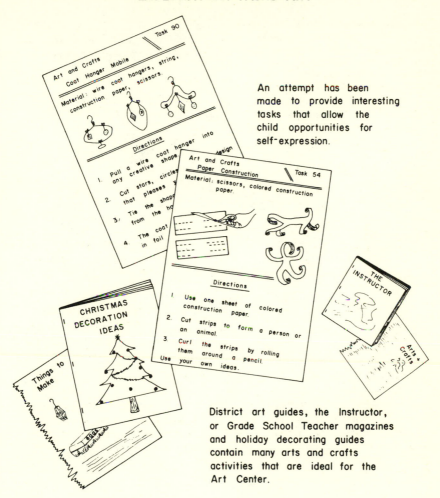

An attempt has been made to provide interesting tasks that allow the child opportunities for self-expression.

District art guides, the Instructor, or Grade School Teacher magazines and holiday decorating guides contain many arts and crafts activities that are ideal for the Art Center.

The teacher is in command of the classroom and has many resources to manipulate students creatively in a constant effort to insure the success of each student. However, it is still unrealistic to assume that the developmental sequence of educational goals, classroom organization, checkmark system, and interventions represent a foolproof formula for success with all educationally handicapped children. The guidelines do, however, offer sound educational, psychological, and developmental principles for training more effective teachers and establishing more adequate classrooms for disturbed children than is often

271

Figure 12
EXPLORATORY TASKS—COMMUNICATION

Communication tasks are designed to place two or more students in a structured situation with opportunities to build social skills, wait, take turns and share.

Since the games often involve a winner, activities based on chance rather than skill have proven most successful.

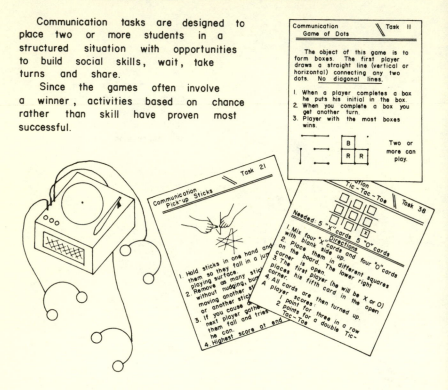

Ideas for Communication Tasks can be obtained from children's paper and pencil game books; adapting simple card games or modifying commercial puzzles and activities.

possible through reliance on subjective judgment, intuition, and "cafeteria" approaches.

EVALUATION

During the 1966-67 school year the first of two extensive evaluations supported by a U.S. Office of Education Grant #OEG-4-7-062893-0377, was conducted to determine the effectiveness of the Engineered Classroom design.

Four elementary schools and one junior high school were selected in the district and one or two project classrooms set up in each school. The junior high school class and one elementary class were not statistically compared but were used for innovative and demonstration purposes during the first year of the project. The junior high school class was evaluated during the 1968-1969 school year when a second class at the same grade level was added.

Six female elementary school teachers were selected from among new teaching applicants in the Santa Monica district for the project. Two additional teachers were selected to conduct the innovative and demonstration classes at the elementary and junior high level.

A two-week training program was conducted in order to acquaint the teachers with the developmental strategy and the Engineered Classroom design. At the close of the training program each project teacher's name was placed on a slip of paper, the slips shuffled, and then drawn one at a time in order to determine assignment to either an experimental classroom or a control classroom. Experimental teachers were to adhere rigidly to the engineered design, including the giving of checkmarks every fifteen minutes, while control teachers could use any aspect of the developmental strategy or engineered classroom design they chose *except* checkmarks or other token or tangible rewards.

Eight teacher aides without prior teaching experience, were selected for the project, including housewives and graduate students. They were given the same preliminary training as the teachers and then randomly paired with project teachers so that the nine students in both experimental and control classrooms were supervised by both a teacher and an aide.

The children were grouped into six classrooms of nine students each on the basis of IQ, age, and reading and arithmetic levels, in that order of priority. Some attempt was made to place children in classes which would be housed in or near their regular elementary schools, but no child was assigned a group because it was felt that he could profit more from the experimental, or control condition. The class groups were completed before any assignment of teachers or classroom condition was made.

The dependent variable in the project's experimental design included achievement testing three times over the year and daily task attention measurements. Task attention was recorded by two observers present in both experimental and control classrooms who clocked the number of seconds each child's eyes were on an assigned task during five-minute samples taken five times daily. In general, children in the experimental classrooms utilizing the engineered design enjoyed a five to twenty percent task attention advantage over children in the control classrooms not using the checkmark system. Experimental classes which abruptly withdrew the design at midyear showed no decrease in task attention—in fact they improved. While reading and spelling gains were not significantly different between experimental and control conditions, gains in arithmetic fundamentals were significantly correlated with presence of the engineered design. During the second federally funded project year 1968-69 it was found that academic emphasis in reading could be increased in the Engineered Classroom, producing statistically significant results.

As part of this second year project three groups of students were compared. Educationally handicapped (EH) students in Engineered Classroom, students identified as educationally handicapped but left in regular classroom, and "normal or average" students in regular classrooms. The EH students in the Engineered Classrooms outdistanced their EH counterparts in the regular classrooms and approached or exceeded the "normal" students both academically and behaviorally.

Evaluation of the Engineered Classroom design reveals its effectiveness for "launching" children into learning so that they are more susceptible to regular classroom instruction. The evaluation also indicated that a carefully controlled environment with flexible task assignments and a wide variety of rewards—in other words, true individualization of instruction coupled with a guarantee of success—does not promote prolonged dependency on "freeloading" but effectively gets the child ready for more traditional school learning.

REFERENCES

Hewett, F., Taylor, F. & Artuso, A. The Santa Monica Project: Demonstration and Evaluation of an Engineered Classroom Design for Emotionally Disturbed Children in the Public School, Phase 1: Elementary Level, *Final Report. Project No. 62839, Demonstration Grant No. OEG-4-7-062893-0377, Office of Education, Bureau of Research, U.S. Department of Health, Education and Welfare, 1967.*

Hewett, F., *The Emotionally Disturbed Child in the Classroom: A Developmental Strategy for Educating Children with Maladaptive Behavior.* Boston: Allyn and Bacon, Inc., 1968.

Hewett, F., Taylor, F. & Artuso, A., *The Engineered Classroom: An Innovative Approach to Education of Children with Learning Problems.* An unpublished report for Warren J. Aaronson, Director, Title III program, Project Centers Branch, Bureau of Education for the Handicapped, United States Office of Education, 1969.

Quay, Herbert C. & Peterson, Donald D. *Behavior Problem Checklist.* University of Illinois Children's Research Center, 1967.

Quay, Herbert C. & Werry, J. *Deviant Classroom Behavior Frequency Count.* University of Illinois Children's Research Center, 1967.

Several years before the recent but relevant emphasis upon "mainstreaming," Grosenick was conducting research on the placement or phasing of special class children into the regular classroom from which they came because they could not cope in that environment. Indeed, the maintenance of many handicapped children in regular classrooms, plus the return of others who require a period of small group classroom instruction, has been a goal of many teachers who, like Grosenick, interact with children usually labeled "emotionally disturbed." Because many of these children can learn to function within the mainstream does not mean that they have not been, at a point in time, severely handicapped. Indeed, they have—as exemplified by such labels as "childhood schizophrenia." Grosenick describes a method by which the regular and special education teachers can work together to facilitate the educational progress of children within various learning situations.

Integration of Exceptional Children into Regular Classes: Research and Procedure

Judith K. Grosenick
University of Missouri, Columbia

During the past decade, increasing emphasis has been placed on that segment of the school age population referred to as emotionally disturbed. As a result, schools, agencies, clinics and hospitals have sought to establish some form of educational experience for these children. In some instances, the provision of such services has been made mandatory by legislation. Consequently, public schools are forced, or at least encouraged, to provide some manner of education for the emotionally disturbed child. Following the procedure of educating children of other exceptionalities such as the mentally retarded or the sensory impaired, public schools have in most instances established special classes, either within the setting of the regular school or in an isolated segregated setting.

One of the most important objectives of a special education program for emotionally disturbed children is to return its pupils to the regular education program as soon as possible. In other words, special class placement is only a temporary intervention. In a sense, children in such classes are being prepared for integration into the regular education program from the very moment of their entry into the special classroom. To accomplish this, the special class must re-educate the child away from his effectual behavior and toward acceptable, satisfying behavior patterns necessary for functioning in society, i.e., the regular classroom (Richmond, 1964). If one accepts the position that behavior is learned, then one may expect that many emotionally disturbed children will be able to return to a normal setting when they have acquired and maintained acceptable behavior patterns.

Although return to the regular classroom appears to be of prime importance, meager information exists with regard to the process, procedure, or techniques for such integration. What little mention is made in the literature regarding the follow-up of disturbed children treats the generalities of the process rather than delineating specific steps. For example, Haring and Phillips (1962) advance the suggestion that ideally the process should be a gradual one.

Translated into procedure, this means that initially the child to be returned spends only part of the school day in the regular classroom. The time so spent would be determined by the child's ability to function adequately and appropriately in the regular class. Meanwhile, during those times in which special direction, structure, or programming is needed, he stays with the special class. Such a process begins on a limited basis and expands until the child functions the entire school day in the regular class. Integration is then complete. This procedure is most easily employed in settings where the special class is located within a regular public school building. In instances where the disturbed children are housed away from the regular building, alternate methods may need to be used.

Elsewhere (Haan, 1957) it has been emphasized that the integration procedure needs to involve a variety of professionals. Cooperation among teachers, principals, psychologists, and parents appears basic to successful integration.

Since the creation of special classes for emotionally disturbed children is of recent origin, the problem of delineating specific steps for integration is also new. The lack of information regarding integration may in reality be an accurate reflection of the actual use of such practices and procedures. Morse, Cutler, and Fink (1964) suggest that two reasons for this lack of information are (a) follow-up procedures are left solely to the special class teacher to be performed on the basis of his own interest and initiative and (b) in a greater percentage of cases continued special education placement occurs. This second explanation suggests that many teachers of emotionally disturbed children consider special classes as a "dead end" for these children.

CLASSROOM PRACTICES INFLUENCING INTEGRATION

There are, of course, a multitude of variables affecting the successful placement of exceptional children into regular classes. Two bear particular attention—since they may serve to actually deter integration. Moreover, they have been observed operating in other fields of rehabilitation.

One of these variables is the length of stay in the special class. Rehabilitation personnel refer to this problem as the syndrome of *institutionalism*. In practice this means that the longer a person remains in the special setting, the less possibility exists of his wanting to leave or for realistic planning for a future outside of the special placement (Wing, 1963). Translated into special education, this suggests that integration into the regular setting may become more difficult with increasing length of stay within the special setting. This is of particular significance when viewed in conjunction with the previously mentioned fact regarding the large percentage of teachers who consider special class placement as the last resort for emotionally disturbed children. Such a belief is contrary to the goals of a special class. If the child is to be returned to adequate functioning in the regular class setting, such integration must occur as soon as it is legitimately possible.

A second problem closely allied to re-education and reintegration is one of providing experiences that are an integral part of everyday functioning in the "outside world." Although this difficulty is perhaps more characteristically encountered in a segregated special education placement, it certainly cannot be overlooked by the special class teacher located within the regular school. If the child is to be successfully re-settled, a set of experiences commonly practiced in a regular school setting must be provided. Such a list of experiences may include practice fire drills and storm weather warnings, independent use of free time, and appropriate behavior in the cafeteria, library, etc. In other words, for subsequent adjustment to be successful, the special class teacher must be acutely aware of the behaviors expected and experiences encountered in the specific regular class environment receiving the child. The child must be given the opportunity to learn these behavior patterns so they become a part of his functional repertoire. If the special class provides experiences approximating those required in the regular class, *hopefully* the probability of the child's performance generalizing to and maintaining itself in the regular setting will increase.

METHODS FOR ASSESSING INTEGRATION

If one assumes that the previous variables have been taken into consideration, the next question that arises focuses on the assessment of the integration. How does one evaluate the success of emotionally disturbed children's integration and the degree of maintenance of the new behaviors? Until recently this had been an overwhelming problem. As a result, integrations that have occurred may have been noted anecdotally in global terms, i.e., the child made it or he didn't. Changes in performance between the two different environments (special and regular class) often have not been readily identified. Sometimes subtle changes have proceeded undetected until becoming so disruptive that the regular class teacher has asked to have the child returned to the special class permanently.

One method of assessment that appears to offer a fruitful avenue of approach involves the direct observation of classroom behaviors. In other wirds, the teacher observes a child's adjustment and performance in the regular class and compares it to the child's pre-integration behavior. In such a procedure the child becomes his own control. His performance in the regular class is evaluated in terms of what is educationally and behaviorally acceptable in that specific classroom rather than an ideal standard.

Following this idea, researchers such as Becker, Madsen, Arnold, and Thomas (1968) and Werry and Quay (1969) have employed a method involving direct frequency counts of numerous classroom behaviors. Their studies support the contention that this technique is applicable to the assessment of progress and rehabilitation both in special and regular classes. Other studies (Hall, Lund & Jackson, 1968; Hall, Panyon, Rabon & Broden, 1968) have substantiated that such behavioral procedures can be utilized within the structure of a public school classroom.

Most recently, Lovitt (1970) reinforces the use of behavioral measurement. He points out that one way measurement of behavior can aid in rehabilitation is by establishing behavioral norms. He explains that "unless the extent to which an individual's performance veers from normal standards is known, the rehabilitation process could be too long or too short."

In addition, Lovitt suggests that continuous measurement of behavior can help the teacher "detect minor deviations from the norm and quickly arrange the slight remediation tactic called for." This appears more realistic, efficient, and less costly than allowing the behavioral deviation to become greater in magnitide and intensity.

EVALUATION OF INTEGRATION: A SAMPLE STUDY

Based on this growing body of behavioral methodology and research within the regular and special classrooms, a study was conducted utilizing observations and recordings of academic and social behavior. These techniques were used to evaluate the process of integration of a group of emotionally disturbed children into a regular class. In addition, the sequential procedures used in placing each child were delineated.

Subjects

The subjects selected for this investigation ranged in chronological age from seven to eleven years. All were enrolled in second or third grade. The children were divided into three groups.

The first group consisted of five boys previously enrolled in a special class for emotionally disturbed, learning disabled children. These children had been evaluated by the special class teacher and school psychologist as ready to resume attendance in the regular classroom. This determination was based on the fact that the subjects were performing on or near grade level in the academic areas and demonstrated appropriate social behaviors necessary for functioning adequately in the regular education program. The average length of enrollment in the special class for these boys was 16 months. The length of time the boys spent in the regular classroom after integration ranged from three weeks to two months.

The second group of children were the pupils enrolled in the five regular public school classrooms into which the five special class children were to be integrated.

The third group involved in this study consisted of twenty children, four from each of the five regular classrooms comprising group two. Each classroom teacher selected two students exhibiting what she considered very good study habits and two children lacking good study habits. The rationale supporting the selection of this subgroup was that there was a high probability that each regular class teacher would evaluate the study habits of the special class students being integrated into her class in relation to the standards she established for the rest of the class.

Procedures

Two major categories of behavior were recorded: social and academic. In addition, three specific sociometric measures (Class Play, Incentive Orientation and Locus of Control) were also administered. All behaviors were observed and recorded pre- and post-integration.

The academic behaviors included arithmetic, study time, and oral reading performance. The first two behaviors were recorded for each of the special class boys and the teacher-selected students. Oral reading performance was measured only for the special class boys.

Specifically, arithmetic performance was defined as rate correct per minute. This information was gathered by the teacher on daily arithmetic work as well as on a series of weekly five-minute timed tests.

Because of the difficulty encountered in quantifying written reading responses, correctness in oral reading was selected as an indication of reading performance. This data was obtained by a frequency count of words missed (omitted or mispronounced) in comparison to the total number of words read in an oral reading situation. The teachers gathered this information at least twice a week.

Study behavior was observed during those times designated by the teacher as independent academic study time. Usually the information was collected during arithmetic study time. Study behavior was defined as the child's being oriented toward his paper and moving his pencil across the paper. This data was collected by an independent observer using a 15-second interval time check to compare the proportion of time spent studying to the total time observed.

Four social behaviors were also considered.

1. Talking out—observable verbal interaction, audible or nonaudible between students or by an individual student. Examples: whispering, unsolicited remarks, whistling, shouting, crying, laughing.
2. Out of seat—buttocks of the chair and both feet on floor, without direct teacher permission. This included walking, running, skipping, or simply standing up.
3. Hand raising—having one's hand off his desk and in the air beside or above his head (not stretching).
4. Teacher response to 1, 2, or 3—any response verbal or nonverbal, positive or negative.

All of these behaviors were recorded by an independent observer on the basis of a direct frequency count. The data was collected while the class was engaged in independent activities. These behaviors were recorded for each entire class as well as the special education child.

The specific academic and social behaviors were chosen because they represent the types of problems the boys had demonstrated when they were originally referred to the special class. Because these behaviors had been cited as critical to the original decision to place these boys in special classes, it was felt these problems might be the first to recur when the boys were integrated into regular classes.

280

Results

Conclusions and results obtained from an analysis of the acdemic and social data showed scattered occurrences of significant changes.

When comparing the special class boys and teacher selected students on arithmetic performance, no significant differences were noted as a result of the move. However, it was observed that all special class boys either maintained or improved their arithmetic performance after integration. This was also true of the oral reading performance. On the other hand, after integration all the special class boys began to spend a significantly greater percentage of their independent activity time in study behavior. Three of the twenty teacher-selected students also increased their study behavior significantly.

The second major set of comparisons was made between the special class boys and the regular class students regarding the social behaviors. No differences on any of the four behaviors were noted in the regular class students when pre- and post-integration scores were compared. This also held true with the special class boys with one exception. The rate of hand raising by special class boys decreased significantly after integration into the regular public school class. Both before and after integration the special class students demonstrated significantly lower scores on all the social behaviors.

Little significant statistical information was gained from the sociometric measures. It was felt that this was due in part to the short period of time over which the study extended.

Conclusions

In general this study supported the previous belief that measurement of observable performance and behavior is an effective means of assessing the effects of movement from one environment to another. According to the behavioral standards set for this study, the five special class boys were integrated successfully into the regular class. Using the same standards, the integration of special students did not produce any significant effects on the performance of the regular class students. Any changes that did occur were in a positive direction.

SEQUENTIAL INTEGRATION PROCEDURES

In the course of conducting this study an outline of integration procedures was formulated, delineating the actual step by step process and personnel involved in the integration. Although developed as a result of a specific investigation, the outline could be used as a guideline by any school system or teacher who wishes to integrate special class students into a regular program. It should be noted that the initial guidelines were based on the integration of children located in a segregated special setting. Thus the actual integration occurred on a specified day, and each child completed total integration on that day. For those special class teachers housed within a regular public school building, the integration could be implemented gradually as previously described. Some of the preparations to be described would need to be adjusted accordingly if gradual integration were to be used. However, many of the steps and personnel contacted would be similar regardless of the setting of the special class.

Pre-Integration: Determining Readiness

Each special class child was individually tested to determine his readiness to return to the regular classroom. A psychological and an educational evaluation were conducted. Sociometric measures were also administered. Observation and recording of arithmetic performance, oral reading performance, study time behaviors, and social behaviors were initiated. The behaviors chosen by a teacher to be recorded will, of course, depend on each individual case. The important point to note is that if the teacher has not already been continuously recording the target behaviors she should begin such recording prior to integration. Such information then provides a reference point against which to compare post-integration performance. The comparison of the pre- and post-integration data will allow evaluation of the success of behavior maintenance in the new setting. In addition, this pre-integration information may be of value to the receiving teacher.

Once a child's readiness to integrate was ascertained, the special class teacher then notified all appropriate personnel. In this investigation the people with whom she communicated included the director of the special school in which the child was enrolled, the director of special education services for the public school district, and the special school's social worker who served as liaison between the school and the child's family. The special education teacher suggested the order in which each child was to be integrated. If a teacher was pursuing gradual integration, a list of preferred subjects or activities into which the child could be integrated would need to be recommended.

The special education director gave the teacher a list of possible classes into which each child might be integrated. The special teacher visited each of the proposed classes and discussed possible integration with the principal. The teacher then met with the special school's personnel and the investigator to discuss the results of the visits, evaluate the alternatives, and select the classroom most appropriate for the child.

Pre-Integration: Preparing for the Change

The special class teacher worked to prepare each child for the integration. Each boy was told about the move. Experience charts conveying information about the new school were prepared. Names of some of the students and personnel (music teacher, physical education teacher, etc.) in the regular school program with whom the child would come in contact were woven into such charts. Mention was also made of some of the activities in the regular class which the special child might anticipate.

After the appropriate class was chosen, a meeting with the regular school personnel was held. The special class teacher, a representative of the special school unit, the regular class teacher, the school principal, and any other persons whose services might be utilized in integrating the child, e.g., the school psychologist, speech therapist, etc., attended the meeting. The purpose of this meeting was to acquaint the school personnel with the child's background and to enlist their cooperation in continuing the collection of data as a means of determining successful integration. Actual date of placement was also established. The regular class teacher was asked to select the four students from her class whom she thought had the best and worst study skills.

In each of the regular classes, pre-integration tests (sociometric, timed arithmetic, and social behaviors) were administered to all the students. Observations and recordings of the teacher-selected students' arithmetic performance and study time behavior were initiated.

The investigator served as liaison between the regular class and special class. Current regular class activities were relayed to the special class teacher, and any necessary implementation or adjustment was made in the special class program to better prepare the child for integration. For example, in one regular classroom the daily schedule included an arithmetic computation competition at the chalkboard by opposing teams of class members. Such an activity was not part of the special class environment. It was necessary to adjust the special program to allow for such a game, thus providing the child with an opportunity to learn the appropriate behavior for such an occasion. Obviously, not every program difference could be anticipated and handled in the aforementioned manner. However, any major deviation which might upset the child was presented in the special class prior to integration.

In the meantime, the regular class teacher prepared her class for the new arrival, following procedures normally employed for the enrollment of a new student. The parents and the child registered at the school, met the receiving teacher, and saw the classroom into which the child would move on integration day.

Integration: Managing Initial Placement

An attempt was made to have the investigator in the regular classroom on the day of integration. If this was not possible, she communicated with the regular class teacher at the end of the integration day to learn the teacher's assessment of the actual integration. In this study, the integration of all five males was not made at the same time. Transfers were spread approximately two weeks apart to allow adequate intensive pre-integration and post-integration observation.

Post-Integration: Assessing Behavior Maintenance

Ongoing recording of arithmetic performance, oral reading performance, study time behavior, and social behavior continued. These results were communicated regularly to the receiving teacher. The investigator maintained a communication link between the regular class and the special class with regard to each child's progress. In addition, the parents were kept informed of the child's progress through the efforts of the special class teacher, the regular class teacher, and the special school's social worker.

The frequency of observation and contact with the special class gradually decreased as the data indicated each child was maintaining himself. After continuous observation of the child had ceased, the investigator maintained periodic communication with the regular class teacher. Occasional observations to spot check the child's behavior were also made. At the end of the academic year post-tests were administered in each class.

A final staffing at the special school was held to evaluate the success of each integration. Involved in this meeting were the investigator, the special class teacher, social worker, and other personnel. The investigator also met with each regular class teacher to discuss recommended placement for the next school year.

CONCLUSIONS

From this sample investigation of integration, several findings resulted. In general these focused upon (1) the use of behavior measurement techniques and (2) the actual integration procedures.

Several practical applications of the measurement techniques occurred. In some instances these were not necessarily an expected or anticipated result of the initial research but happened more as a side effect.

One aspect of the measurement data that appeared of high interest to the regular class teachers was the rate correct of the daily arithmetic performance. Initially, it was anticipated that the collection of this information could prove to be bothersome and cumbersome to the teachers. Consequently, much encouragement and aid was given to the regular teachers prior to and during the initial collection of this data. It was decided to have the children record their own beginning and ending times for the daily arithmetic assignments. In all but one class, the teachers announced the time at which the arithmetic assignment was started; class members recorded this information on their papers. Each student was responsible for recording the time which he completed his work. These directions were given to the entire class so as not to call attention to the children actually involved in the study.

The teachers regarded the opportunity for their children to practice needed time-telling skills very positively. Several ambitious students independently calculated their own performance rates. The teachers viewed this as valuable because it not only provided additional arithmetic practice but also involved the child with measuring and evaluating his own performance. Students not directly involved in the study approached the teacher regularly with evaluative statements like "I did much better today because I got more right in less time than I did yesterday."

In one classroom, however, many of the children were unable to tell time. In this class each child was provided with a small pad of paper, each sheet of which was stamped with a blank clock face and the date. The children were instructed to draw in the hands of the clock on the first sheet to designate the time they began the arithmetic assignment. The same procedure was followed on the next sheet upon completion. Once again all children were involved in the data recording. The regular teacher in this classroom was very enthusiastic about the motivation this approach provided for initiating telling time. The children became attentive to details such as the numbering on the face of the clock and the difference in size and the relative speed of movement of the clock hands.

A second behavioral observation instrument which provided a valuable source of feedback to the teachers was one utilized for recording the social behaviors. On a chart showing the classroom seating arrangement, the investigator recorded the frequency of the four behaviors under consideration (Figure 1). Such graphic pictures were shown to each teacher regularly. The data from these charts served to guide the teachers to rearrange seating, to be aware of active areas in the classroom, and to be cognizant of their own patterns of responding to the children. Several of the teachers became interested enough to do recording of other behaviors. Additional uses of this particular recording form and behavioral measurement in general have been suggested elsewhere (Grosenick, 1970).

As described previously, one of the early steps vital to the success of the integration process is the selection of a regular classroom. Ideally one might hypothesize that, if each regular classroom had its own set of behavioral norms recorded and established, the special teacher could match the special child's

Figure 1
CLASSROOM SEATING CHART RECORDING FORM

Teacher: ———————————

Date: ———————————

Time: ———————————

Code

H = Handraising
T = Talking Out
O = Out of Seat
R = Teacher Response

Classroom Seating						
H T	O R				H H R	
H	O O H R				T H R	
	T T T	H R				T O
O R			O O T			H R
	O		H R		T O O	

performance to these norms. Thus integration would become a matter of locating a regular classroom with behavioral norms which coincide with the behavioral functioning of the special child. Presently, however, regular classrooms are chosen on a more subjective, intuitive basis which suggests that it is necessary for the special class teacher to have the opportunity to observe the regular classroom and to talk to the potential receiving teacher.

In this investigation, three prime considerations in the selection of a regular classroom included:

1. Cooperativeness of the regular classroom teacher—that is, was she willing to accept a special class child. Many teachers expressed reluctance to assume this responsibility partly because they had little knowledge about the particular child, his problems and needs, and the amount of work involved. Some teachers, though quick to express their hesitance, were willing to accept the child as long as communication and supportive help from the special teacher was assured.

2. Personality of the receiving teacher as compared to the special child and his needs. This is one factor that involved a great deal of subjectivity on the part of the special class teacher. Apparently the special class teacher

attempted to evaluate each child's needs for factors such as structure, limitations, affection, etc., and then proceeded to select a receiving teacher who outwardly seemed to meet these needs.

3. Special academic needs of the child. For example, by utilizing a school with an ungraded primary plan it was possible to integrate a child who needed reading instructions at the second grade level yet functioned at a third grade level in other subject areas. Readers or tutors were used to help with science and social studies which the child could comprehend at a third grade level but did not have the reading skills to attack. Such programming flexibility permitted the successful integration of a child sooner than if it had been necessary to wait until his reading advanced commensurate with his other skills. If the special class had been located in the regular building, it might have been possible to program the child into the regular class for all the subject areas except reading which could have been handled by the special class teacher. In general, however, successful integration will be influenced by the range of flexibility available in the academic programming.

The order in which the above factors were discussed by no means infers order of importance. The factor given chief consideration was different from case to case, although certainly the cooperativeness of the regular teacher was paramount in each instance.

Closely allied to, if not underlying, the need for cooperation from the regular class teacher was the entire aspect of public relations. Much preliminary preparation time was spent meeting with the regular school personnel in an attempt to *sell* the idea of integration. The reluctance to accept an exceptional child was not a feeling confined solely to the regular class teacher. Other public school personnel expressed similar hesitancy. A great deal of time and effort was expended explaining the child, his needs, and the role of the regular public school program. Frequent reassurances of intensive contact with the investigator and the special teacher during integration were necessary.

Apparently, patience and tact are prime prerequisites if integration is to succeed. In addition, the person responsible for initiating integration (usually the special education teacher) must strongly believe that integration is necessary. If special education personnel believe, as inferred by some research, that special classes are the final placement for emotionally disturbed children, integration procedures will probably not be initiated. If such personnel are uncertain as to the efficacy of integration, they may not be able to penetrate the reluctance shown by the regular school personnel. Hence, integration is not a process to be undertaken halfheartedly.

Numerous minor findings also proved valuable. For example, the day chosen for actual integration was an important variable. At first glance, Monday seemed the most obvious choice to the professional personnel involved. It was not, however, the day preferred by the child and his parents. Placement in the regular class on Monday was preceded by a weekend of worry and nervous anticipation of the "big day" by the child. Similarly, integration on the first day following vacation was preceded by anxiety. In these instances, parents did not hesitate to recommend change. Integrating the child into the regular class nearer the end of the school week enabled the child to familiarize himself with the school routine and begin the next week with greater confidence while the special school personnel, parents, and regular school personnel utilized the extra time to confer and make program or procedural adjustments.

In addition to the value of releasing the special class teacher during school time to observe the potential regular class, it was found that freeing the regular class teacher to make a similar observation in the special classroom prior to integration proved equally beneficial. In this study, the investigator substituted for the regular teacher allowing her to make the observation at no expense to the school. Observation of the child in the special class also contributed to a better understanding of the child, his problems and his performance and reduced the regular teacher's anxiety and reluctance. Ideally, it is suggested that such an exchange of observations by all teachers regardless of whether they will receive a special child would serve to reduce reluctance to accept a special child and to improve communication between special and regular education.

In conclusion, special education class placement must not be viewed as a dead end for all exceptional children. Since the responsibility for integrating children from special classes into regular classes falls primarily on the shoulders of the teachers, it is imperative that teachers use tools, techniques and procedures which provide effective means of assessing the acquisition and maintenance of desirable behavior patterns as well as implementing the integration itself, thereby reducing the haphazardness previously associated with transferring children from one environment to another.

REFERENCES

Becker, W.C., Madsen, C. H., Arnold, Carole R. & Thomas, D.R. "The Contingent Use of Teacher Attention and Praise in Reducing Classroom Behavior Problems." *The Journal of Special Education,* 1967, 1, 287-307.

Grosenick, Judith. "Assessing the Reintegration of Exceptional Children into Regular Classes." *Teaching Exceptional Children,* 1970, 2, 113-119.

Haan, Norma. "When the Mentally Ill Child Returns to School." *The Elementary School Journal,* 1957, 57, 379-385.

Hall, R.V., Lund, Diane & Jackson, Deloris. "Effects of Teacher Attention on Study Behavior." *Journal of Applied Behavior Analysis,* 1968, 1, 1-12.

Hall, R.V., Panyon, Marion, Rabon, Deloris & Broden, Marcia. "Instructing Beginning Teachers in Reinforcement Procedures Which Improve Classroom Control." *Journal of Applied Behavior Analysis,* 1968, 1, 315-322,

Haring, N.G. & Phillip, E.L. *Educating Emotionally Disturbed Children.* New York: McGraw-Hill Book Company, 1962.

Lovitt, T. "Behavior Modification: Where Do We Go From Here?" *Exceptional Children,* 1970, 37, 157-167.

Morse, W.C., Cutler, R.L. & Fink, A.H. *Public School Classes for the Emotionally Handicapped: A Research Analysis.* Washington, D.C.: Council for Exceptional Children, 1964.

Richmond, S. "The Vocational Rehabilitation of the Emotionally Handicapped in the Community." *Rehabilitation Literature,* 1964, 25, 194-202.

Werry, J.S. & Quay, H.C. "Observing the Classroom Behavior of Elementary School Children." *Exceptional Children,* 1969, 35, 461-467.

Wing, J.K. "Rehabilitation of Psychiatric Patients." *British Journal of Psychiatry,* 1963, 109, 635-641.

The authors of this chapter, as was true with Grosenick, were pioneers in the initial stages of the movement that has now become known as "mainstreaming." The systematic procedure for maintaining and intergrating handicapped students in regular classrooms is a direct and actual outgrowth of the Engineered Classroom described in a previous chapter. The Plan requires the abandonment of the traditional, often stigmatic, labels assigned to children and the acceptance of handicapped children as **learners.** *The Plan also emphasizes that children should be placed in the least possible restrictive learning environment, i.e., one in which learning is facilitated at an appropriate level. This chapter provides very specific and systematic procedures which a school district can adopt and adapt in order to provide appropriate educational services for all learners.*

A Learning Center Plan
for Special Education

Frank D. Taylor, Alfred A. Artuso, Robert J. Stillwell,
   Michael M. Soloway
Santa Monica School District, California

Frank M. Hewett
University of California, Los Angeles

Herbert C. Quay
Temple University, Philadelphia

Past and present efforts to evaluate, classify, describe, and provide educational programs for exceptional children are being seriously questioned by many in the field of education. The specialized, self-contained classes that have evolved for handicapped students, the degree of specialization found in graduate courses, state credential requirements, and public school financing may be operating to the detriment of the students we are ostensibly seeking to help (Dunn, 1968). Questions about the possible limited effectiveness of special

290

education curriculum and instructional techniques, and doubts about cost effectiveness along with more profound doubts about the social-psychological impact of the traditional special classes have increased (Blackman, 1967; Connor, 1968; Quay, 1968; Lilly, 1970). A recent survey of fifty-seven special education researchers, conducted by the Council for Exceptional Children Information Center, identified behavior modification, alternatives to traditional disability groupings, and special class placement as the principal current issues in the field of special education (Jordan, 1971).

Many parents, as well as educators, question the desirability of traditional self-contained classrooms for many exceptional children. Labeling, damage to self-concept, compartmentalization, concerns by minority groups, and loss of stimulating opportunities, as well as questions about the constitutionality of some current testing and grouping practices are matters of increasing concern. Furthermore, some school districts are unable to offer a full range of programs for handicapped students because of the demand for special classes each with its own specially trained teacher.

The decade of the seventies will certainly be marked by the search for, and widespread adoption of, new methods of instruction and new models for service delivery. The emphasis may well shift from the medico-psychological model to educational models whose philosophical and empirical foundations lend themselves to objective results that can be combined with an opportunity to evaluate cost-effectiveness.

Philosophical Premises

The authors share two basic premises about exceptional children. The first belief is that all exceptional children are, first and foremost, *learners*—learners who have often been labeled and placed in separate, self-contained rooms because of handicaps. Viewing the child as a learner rather than labeling him may create an optimism and open-mindedness that will result in a more favorable atmosphere for the actual instructional situation. The educational program and teacher must now assume the responsibility for providing productive instructional experiences. This shift in emphasis from labels to learners may help avoid some of the self-fulfilling prophecy effect of traditional, self-contained rooms of categorized handicapped students.

The second belief is that it is desirable to remove as many exceptional children as possible from separate self-contained rooms and integrate them for optimum periods of time in regular classrooms. This assumes, of course, that the exceptional children are prepared for, and supported during, the time they are in regular classrooms.

291

THE MADISON SCHOOL PLAN

With these two philosophical premises in mind and as an outgrowth of an earlier program which was based on an engineered classroom concept of behavior modification (Hewett, 1967), the authors began to conceptualize an operational learning center that would facilitate the grouping of students according to their learning deficts as opposed to traditional grouping by exceptionality and/or diagnostic categories (Soloway, 1970). In the past students often were tested, classified, and grouped according to how well they perform or rate on a variety of measures that evaluate such factors as vision, hearing, motor coordination, intelligence, and perceptual ability. If a child scores from 88 to 112 on the intelligence scale or continuum, he is rated "average or normal" and is placed in the regular classroom. If another child scores significantly higher or above 132 on the intelligence continuum, he may be classified "gifted" and be given "enrichment opportunities." Still another child may score below 70 and be placed in a special classroom for the educable mentally retarded (EMR). In the special classroom for the educable mentally retarded, he will be seen as a different kind of student, taught in a different way, with different expectations; and, sadly enough, he will often become different. The same can be true of students who have auditory, visual, motoric, physical, or perceptual handicaps.

With these facts in mind, the authors were confronted with the task of organizing an education program with instructional settings for several traditional disability categories into one learning center that could serve a typical elementary school. It was decided that one scale or dimension that is common to all children regardless of possible handicaps, is their *readiness for regular classroom functioning*. This common dimension seemed to encompass four basic behaviors or abilities that all children must have in order to succeed in school.

1. The first set of behaviors includes the ability to pay attention, respond, and follow directions as formulated in a developmental sequence (Hewett, 1964). In the Madison School Plan, this has been expanded to include the additional pre-academic skills of taking part verbally or orally and doing what one is told in terms of reasonable class limits. These skills are basic to succeeding in a regular classroom, regardless of the student's visual, intellectual, or physical abilities.
2. The second set of behaviors includes the academic abilities of being neat, being correct, being able to read, spell, write, and do arithmetic.
3. The third set of behaviors requires that the child must be able to function in the instructional settings that occur in the regular classroom—when the teacher is giving directions from the front of the room, when the child is

working in a small group, or when the child is working independently. Different kinds of concentration or attention are required when the entire class is reading silently for information than when the teacher is explaining a new concept at the chalkboard.

4. The fourth area is related to the student's susceptibility to regular classroom rewards or reinforcers. While some children are motivated by report card grades, others are encouraged by a smile or word of praise from the teacher; a few may respond better, at least initially, when given candy, tokens, or checkmarks that can be exchanged for a small prize.

The authors felt that an instructional program, encompassing the above concepts in a learning center environment, would offer optimum opportunities for children to learn the skills necessary to facilitate maximum regular classroom integration. The operational model provided an instructional program for exceptional children based on their specific learning strengths or weaknesses rather than traditional categories for the handicapped. Identified as the Madison School Plan, the project was initiated in September 1968 and was made possible through a California State Department of Education Title VI-B Grant.

The project was directed toward the demonstration and evaluation of a plan for the education of a group of handicapped children who would have been labeled educable mentally retarded, emotionally disturbed, learning disabled, and visually or auditorily impaired. This plan, to be described in detail below, provides for the education of these children in a setting that allows free flow of children between the regular classes and the specialized facility (learning center). The plan permits the elimination of traditional disability grouping for all but administrative purposes and provides an instructional program that is linked to a continuous assessment of those educational variables that have hindered the performance of the exceptional child in the regular classroom in the past.

The grouping framework utilized in the Madison School Plan was organized by creating four points along the dimension of readiness for regular classroom functioning: Pre-Academic I, Pre-Academic II, Academic I, and Academic II (the regular classroom). Each of these sections in the learning center sets an expectancy according to the four areas of behavior that were mentioned above.

Pre-Academic I

This section of the learning center was conceived as a largely self-contained class grouping of six to twelve students and is essentially an engineered classroom (Stillwell et al., 1970). The strongest instructional setting, teacher-child or child-independent, is used since students in this section need to learn to sit still, pay attention, respond appropriately, take turns, follow simple directions, get along with others, and begin to develop the ability to function in small groups (see Figure 1). While the emphasis is on the pre-academic skills discussed above in the first set of behaviors, academic written exercises in reading, spelling, handwriting, and arithmetic represent the major experiences during the day. It is while working on these academic materials that the students learn to ask for help and finish a task. All of these behaviors are appropriately rewarded. Many of the open-ended, multi-level tasks in use were developed or evaluated by the teachers in the original engineered classroom project and are now commercially available (Taylor, Artuso & Hewett, 1970). The highest level of reinforcement for each student is used. This is a continuation of the checkmark system, backed up with candy, food, free time, or a free chance which is patterned after the Monopoly game's "Take-A-Chance" card.

Figure 1
TWO TYPICAL LEARNING CENTER CLASSROOMS
WITH CONNECTING DOOR

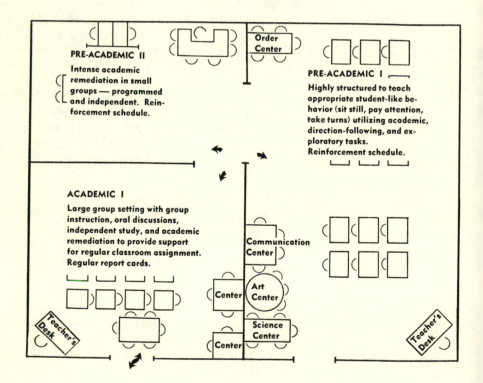

Pre-Academic I is a launching experience in this learning center concept in much the same manner the engineered classroom was originally intended. The students do not spend any time in the regular classroom. The visually and auditorily impaired, as well as the mentally retarded or emotionally disturbed students who need to master the pre-academic skills necessary to function in the regular classroom, would start in this section of the center. They are children who need the experience of the Pre-Academic I learning environment. The environment is labeled, not the student; and in this way we attempt to avoid the negative effects that sometimes occur with student labels.

Pre-Academic II

At this level the emphasis shifts from pre-academic skills to academic skills. However, the big shift is in the kind of work setting. In Pre-Academic I the children work individually at self-contained units with a teacher or aide. Little or no group work or interaction occurs. In Pre-Academic II, six to eight children sit at a cluster of tables, getting all of their instruction from the teacher who is in the middle of the cluster. The children work together, cooperate, are paired off, and encouraged to raise their hands and participate verbally. This section is designed to foster social interaction and verbal participation in group lessons, which was missing in the original engineered classroom design. In terms of reinforcement, the checkmark system is still used; but students usually are limited to trading their completed Work Record Cards for fifteen to twenty minutes of free time. Beginning with Pre-Academic II, each student is integrated into a regular classroom for at least a few minutes during the day.

Academic I

This section of the learning center is a simulated regular classroom setting for twelve to twenty-five children who have primary academic problems that can be dealt with in a large teacher-class setting. These students have the ability to spend increasing amounts of time in the regular classroom and have a readiness for the more traditional system of grading in terms of effort, quality of work, and citizenship. In this setting, the teacher leads class discussions and presents lessons to the large group in reading, arithmetic, spelling, social studies, and English. Students are grouped within this setting in the same manner expected by a regular classroom teacher; opportunities for silent, independent study are also present. Emphasis is placed on helping each student with the specific skills needed to increase the amount of time spent in a regular classroom.

Academic II

This is the regular classroom in the school composed of twenty-eight to thirty-five students. It follows the typical public school program. All handicapped students in the program are assigned to one of the Pre-Academic I, Pre-Academic II, or Academic I settings. Those in the latter two groups are integrated for varying periods of time in Academic II.

Background Procedures

The existing six elementary and two secondary learning centers are located in regular public schools in Santa Monica, California. They serve the exceptional students as well as numerous regular students in the individual schools where they are located. Transportation of students is held to a minimum since the problems of having separate self-contained classrooms for each area of exceptionality have been dramatically reduced.

Students with auditory or visual handicaps are assigned to an appropriate setting within the center and are integrated into regular classrooms for varying lengths of time, depending on their abilities. These students, as well as other students in the center, have the services of specialists in oral communications, lip reading, braille, mobility instruction, and speech therapy. It is not unusual to see several mentally retarded or visually impaired children profiting from participation in an oral communication lesson that is designed primarily for the hearing handicapped. The same might be true for lessons in mobility or speech articulation.

Usually two classrooms that are next to each other, with or without a door between them, are converted into a center. It is important to keep in mind the needs of the students to be served and the composition of the groups before arbitrarily setting up the rooms within the center. It has been found that, although the room arrangement described in Figure 1 is generally in use in the operational centers in Santa Monica, there must be flexibility. Several other variations have been utilized when the particular needs of the students in any one school require different instructional emphasis (see Figure 2).

A daily schedule for the three settings within the learning center is carefully planned to provide individual, independent, and group lessons that relate to specific student needs. Commercially available materials are utilized, programed instructional techniques are employed, and teacher preparation time is kept to a minimum (see Figure 3).

The model implies, in essence, that first you assign children to a grouping category based on a pre-placement inventory and that once this assignment has been made you zero in on a continual detailed assessment over a period of time,

Figure 2
VARIATIONS OF THE LEARNING CENTER CLASSROOM MODEL

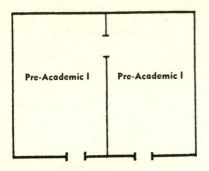

All of the students need to learn how to sit still, follow directions, take turns, and raise their hands. As some students progress, they will move into the Pre-Academic II and Academic I portion of the center, which will evolve as one of the Pre-Academic I settings is converted. This is the most widely used variation when starting a new center and may be the best starting model.

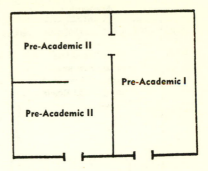

Some of the students are beyond Pre-Academic I and can function in Pre-Academic II settings, but are not ready for Academic I. This will evolve later as one Pre-Academic II setting is converted into an Academic I.

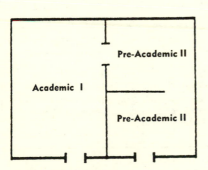

None of the children in this model need the experiences of Pre-Academic I since they can all follow directions, raise their hands, and take turns.

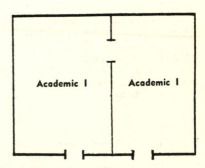

All of the children can be integrated into regular classrooms during the day and need only occasional supportive instructional assistance.

rather than stop with just an initial assessment which is often the case in traditional programs.

In order to maintain a continuous assessment of each child's progress and provide data for reassignment to different groupings, two types of procedures

Figure 3
DAILY SCHEDULE OF ACTIVITIES IN THE LEARNING CENTER

	Academic I	Pre-Academic II	Pre-Academic I
8:45	Typical Class Opening Exercises		Direction-following Task
9:00	Reading — Typical large class reading program. Group and individual reading. Basal Readers, SRA, etc.	Reading — Remedial-reading instruction or motivation for story writing.	Reading — Individual Reading
		Story writing or remedial follow-up task.	Word Study
		Word study. Individual reading, programmed material.	Skill Reading
10:00	.... Recess .... Recess .... Recess		
10:15	Arithmetic — Typical large class program. Discussions. Group and independent work.	Arithmetic — Arithmetic instruction. Specific follow-up tasks. Remedial opportunities.	Arithmetic — Arithmetic Drill
			Instruction
			Follow-Up
10:55	Spelling	Language Development and/or Spelling.	Language Skills
11:25	.... Lunch .... Lunch .... Lunch		
12:25	Read to Class.		
12:40	Social Studies / English / Art	Pre-Academic II students join ←— either —→ group according to their individual needs.	Exploratory — Art / Science / Order / Communication
1:50	.... Recess .... Recess .... Recess		
2:00	Physical Education		Opportunities for individualized remedial instruction.
2:30	Individual Tutoring		
3:00			

are utilized—a checkmark system in Pre-Academic I and II, and a numerical rating system in Academic I and II. In the checkmark system, the teacher gives each child a maximum of ten checkmarks, in the form of alphabet letters that represent attending to work, following directions, etc., *every twenty minutes* during the day. These checkmarks are given in two categories; a possible five are given for the child's performance with the instructional tasks and five for his classroom behavior. When giving checkmarks, the teacher may give all ten checkmarks to bolster strengths or elect to withhold several checkmarks in either category to alert the child to an area where he needs to improve.

At the beginning of the school year, as many of the educationally handicapped children with learning disabilities as possible are assigned to regular classrooms. As students are referred out to the special program because they cannot handle the behavioral and academic demands of the class, an attempt is made to preserve some link with the regular class by having the child return for morning exercises, P.E., music, etc. As they demonstrate academic and/or behavioral improvement, an effort is made to increase their time in the regular class until optimum placement is reached. The evaluation procedures aid in determining this reassignment. The EMR children start in the special program, but early in the school year efforts are made to establish a regular classroom link for them. During the year, their progress on the evaluation ratings is noted and integration increased whenever possible.

During the 1970-71 school year, 73% of the educable mentally retarded students and 85% of the emotionally disturbed students from the six learning centers were integrated into regular classrooms for one hour or more each day. By the beginning of the 1971-72 school year, 36% of the educable mentally retarded students and 41% of the emotionally disturbed students were integrated full time into regular classrooms.

The authors are aware that any attempt to overhaul practices in special education has to take two things into account. *First,* one must be able to demonstrate that what is to be done has more in it for the exceptional child than what was being done before. One is accountable to show that this child is, indeed, better off in Pre-Academic I or II than he was in the EMR or EH class. The *second* thing one must do is answer the questions of practicality and ease of replication. If the program costs two or three times as much as existing programs and if it requires more teachers and additional facilities, it's probably not going to be replicated very many places. In sum, the child has to be given something more than he is given in the traditional framework, and the field of special education should not be encumbered with costs beyond any reasonable level.

SUMMARY

The Madison School Plan, developed over a three-year period, attempts to combine traditional categories of exceptionality along a dimension of readiness for regular classroom functioning and provide for the instruction of educable mentally retarded, emotionally disturbed, and learning disabled students in a setting allowing an increased flow of children between regular classrooms and a specialized resource facility. The plan permits the elimination of traditional disability grouping and the resultant self-contained classrooms. The exceptional students are not labeled, but considered to be learners in various stages of preparation for return to the regular classroom. Assessment and evaluation of the children is based on academic and behavioral functioning, and a major goal of the plan is to increase the amount of time the exceptional child participates in a regular classroom program.

REFERENCES

Blackman, L. "The Dimensions of a Science of Special Education." *Mental Retardation, 5,* 1967, 7-11.

Connor, L. "The Heart of the Matter." *Exceptional Children*, 34, 1968, 579.

Dunn, L. M. "Special Education for the Mildly Retarded—Is Much of It Justifiable?" *Exceptional Children, 35,* 1968, 5-22.

Hewett, F. M. "Educational Engineering with Emotionally Disturbed Children." *Exceptional Children,* March, 1967, 459-467.

Hewett, F. M. "A Hierarchy of Educational Tasks for Children with Learning Disorders." *Exceptional Children,* 31, 1964, 207-214.

Jordan, J. B. "The Now Way to Know." *Education and Training of the Mentally Retarded,* February, 1971, 29-41.

Lilly, M. S. "Special Education: A Teapot in a Tempest." *Exceptional Children,* 37, 1970, 43-48.

Quay, H. C. "The Facets of Educational Exceptionality: A Conceptual Framework for Assessment, Grouping and Instruction." *Exceptional Children,* 35, 1968, 25.

Soloway, M. M. "A Descriptive Study of the Madison School Plan." Unpublished master's thesis, University of California at Los Angeles, 1970.

Stillwell, R. J. et al. "An Educational Solution." *Focus on Exceptional Children, 2,* No. 1, 1970, 1-15.

Taylor, F. D., Artuso, A. A., & Hewett, F. M. *Creative Art Tasks for Children.* Denver, Colo.: Love Publishing Company, 1970.

Taylor, F. D. et al. *Individualized Arithmetic Instruction.* Denver, Colo.: Love Publishing Company, 1970.

Taylor, F. D. et al. *Individualized Reading Skills Improvement.* Denver, Colo.: Love Publishing Company, 1970.

Many special educators have questioned the effectiveness and efficiency of a dualistic service delivery system or administrative arrangements, e.g., the regular class and the special class. This dual approach often operated in isolated segments; the expected flow of communication between the operatives of this system and the natural flow, based upon learning needs, of children between the two types of instructional settings did not occur. Like the authors of the previous two chapters, Wiederholt has developed an alternative model to serve the learning needs of pupils. The model is based upon sound educational concepts and, therefore, can function without reliance upon nonfunctional child labeling. The author presents a careful plan for school administrators and teachers to follow in developing a "resource room." As with any system, Wiederholt cautions, its success in assisting children is dependent upon the competencies of those who implement it.

Planning Resource Rooms
for the Mildly Handicapped

J. Lee Wiederholt
University of Texas, Austin

Historically, children with learning problems have received two distinct types of service arrangements in public schools—regular education or special education. For the most part if a child's learning problem was viewed as significantly interfering with his school achievement, he was labeled "mentally retarded," "emotionally disturbed," "learning disabled," "deaf," "blind," etc., and placed in a self-contained special education classroom. If on the other hand the learning problem was viewed as mild, the child would remain in the regular classroom, in most cases without special education support. Unfortunately, this "either/or" situation did not account for those children who might be able to profit from the services of both the special and regular education programs.

Recently, however, an addition that attempts to bridge the gap between special and regular education has been added to this service system. This variation is most often called a "resource room." A resource room is basically any special education instructional setting to which a child comes for specific periods of time on a regularly scheduled basis for remedial instruction. The key difference between a resource room and a self-contained special class is that the child attends the resource room only on a part-time basis, remaining for at least a portion of the day in his regular classroom. The type of remedial instruction the pupil receives is based upon his identified learning weaknesses, an individually planned and implemented instructional program geared to ameliorate or minimize his problems, and/or consultant support to the child's regular classroom teacher regarding his instruction in that system.

The growth of these resource rooms in the last few years has been phenomenal; yet many teachers and administrators remain uncertain regarding the implementation and operation of these programs in the schools. In this article, some suggestions are made concerning start-up practices and daily operation procedures.

START-UP PRACTICES

Careful pre-planning is necessary for the successful implementation of a resource program in an individual school. The following matters need to be considered:

1. Preparing the school staff
2. Selecting a resource model
3. Selecting a resource teacher
4. Establishing communication channels

Some general guidelines are suggested relative to these points.

Preparing the School Staff

As with most innovations, there will be some resistance to this "new" program. Regular classroom teachers may be somewhat hesitant to accept problem children in their classrooms; special education teachers may be resistant to changing their roles; and administrators may cast a somewhat jaundiced eye at this new "panacea." In addition, some parents may be unwilling to expose their children to the program. This includes not only the parents of mildly handicapped children who desire extensive special help but also some parents of "normal" children who may be reluctant to have their child educated with "deviant children." For this reason, professionals implementing the resource programs must be equipped with objective information to present to resistant people regarding the rationale of this particular type of service system.

Well-documented rationales for change within special education have been presented by Dunn (1968), Lilly (1970), Iano (1972), Christopolos and Renz (1969), Ross, De Young and Cohen (1971), Hammill and Wiederholt (1972), and Garrison and Hammill (1971) among others. These authors have expressed concern regarding a variety of inadequacies in special education which include inappropriate and invalid testing, the lack of positive efficacy research regarding self-contained special classes, the mislabeling and misplacing of many exceptional children, the fact that minority discrimination practices exist in special education, and the lack of alternatives in providing educational support to exceptional children.

After becoming familiar with these references, someone must be selected to "present the case for the resource room" to staff and parents. In most cases, it is preferable to choose someone from within a given school rather than an outside "expert." As outsiders will not be around to confront the daily problems that arise from instituting changes, teachers are justifiably concerned about receiving continuing support in the endeavor. For the most part the building principal is a logical choice, and enlisting his aid also insures his administrative understanding and cooperation in the endeavor.

Those advocating this change must stress that resource rooms are not meant to supplant all self-contained special classes. While some special classes may be disbanded and resource rooms established in their place, some self-contained units must continue to operate to serve those children who are not able to profit from even part-time placement in a regular classroom. However, as Deno (1970) and Reynolds (1962) have pointed out, there is a need for more resource rooms than self-contained classes because there are more children with mild handicaps who can profit from regular classroom placement with support than there are those with more severe disabilities who require isolated settings.

Objective information, therefore, needs to be presented to those involved with any changes in the special education system. In the case of the resource room, this would include both regular and special education teachers and parents. The person selected to share this information should be someone who will continue to be directly responsible for the operation of the resource rooms other than the resource teacher. In addition to presenting the rationale for the resource rooms, the discussion should also include information concerning the type of resource rooms to be implemented.

Selecting a Resource Model

Prior to implementing a resource room, decisions must be reached on the nature of that model. Two very different models currently exist—the categorical model and the noncategorical model.

When using the *categorical* model, the resource room services are reserved for children who satisfy a particular disability label. For example, one resource room may be set up for educable mentally retarded youngsters. This room provides support in a given school for children with "borderline intelligence" who have some skills which allow them to function in the regular classroom with supportive help. The stated purpose of this "mentally retarded resource room" is to aid and support mentally retarded children in the regular classroom.

On the positive side, the categorical model conforms fairly well to existing state laws and regulations as well as historical precedence in special education. Many educators, administrators, teachers, parents, and legislators are simply more comfortable with this model. Programs of this nature have been described by Barksdale and Atkinson (1971) for the educable mentally retarded and by Glavin, Quay, Annesley, and Werry (1971) for the emotionally disturbed.

However, the categorical resource room has several drawbacks. First, since resource rooms are for the mildly handicapped, the necessity of labeling children with socially stigmatizing terms such as "mentally retarded," etc., is questionable and probably harmful as well. Second, the resource room continues to bear the same stigma as the special self-contained classes. It is still known as the "retarded" or "disturbed" room, or even by more derogatory names. Third, it is extremely difficult to diagnose accurately children who evidence mild to moderate problems. The learning disabled, emotionally disturbed, disadvantaged, nonmotivated, borderline intelligent, and poorly taught children all appear pretty much alike. Finally, all categorical resource teachers teach reading, math, spelling, handwriting and acceptable behavior regardless of the disability group they serve. Therefore, the categorical resource rooms appear to be more of an administrative convenience than an actual benefit to mildly handicapped pupils.

The *noncategorical* resource room, however, is designed to meet the educational needs of all pupils in a school, not just those who can "fit" a special education label. Any child from a regular or another special education class who is having difficulty in school work or adjustment can be referred to this setting for periods of time without having to satisfy any existing category. Psychological evaluations are not necessary to make a placement, thereby freeing the psychologists to work with the more severe cases. As a result, the focus of evaluation in the noncategorical resource room is educational. Specific disabilities in reading, spelling, behavior, etc., are pinpointed; and remedial programs are planned to aid the child in successful school performance.

Stigmatization is minimized as children are not given a label, such as "mentally retarded," which may follow them through life. Children coming to the resource rooms may be mildly mentally retarded, emotionally disturbed, or learning disabled who need individualized education for a period of time. In addition the gifted child, an unfortunately largely ignored population, is also eligible for resource help, thus diminishing the negative connotation that could accompany this special service. Reger and Koppmann (1971) and Hammill and Wiederholt (1972) have described models of the noncategorical variety.

In the noncategorical model, decisions regarding who needs resource support remains with the individual school personnel. Referrals for outside testing are not essential, thereby diminishing the time between referral and service. Resource support is planned to some extent using the viewpoints and opinion of the personnel who are most familiar with the individual child.

Funding is a problem in the noncategorical model. As children are not given psycho-medical labels, there is in reality no special funding base. Some of these programs can be funded as "experimental," but every effort should be made to reorganize funding procedures so that this model will be reimbursable in the regular budgeting procedure.

Responsibility for financial reimbursement for resource support for children with mild problems is currently being assumed in most cases by special education. Funding, however, should be assumed by regular education alone, or at least jointly with special education. First-hand experience has indicated that children being served by resource personnel are more "normal" than they are "deviant." A child who has a reading disability, for example, may or may not be handicapped. His problem may be more in areas of teacher incompetency, lack of flexibility in regular educational programming, or other "system defects" rather than "child defects."

Once funding is changed, teachers who are selected as resource teachers need not be special educators. There are many regular classroom teachers who, with some in-service, would be able to function as resource teachers. The same holds true for reading teachers, speech therapists, etc. Some criteria for selecting a resource teacher are discussed in the next section.

Selecting a Resource Teacher

In many cases, self-contained special classes are being disbanded and resource rooms are being instituted in their place. In other cases where special services are minimal or nonexistent (such as in the case of children with learning disabilities), resource rooms are being developed rather than self-contained classes.

In the first instance, the teacher simply changes his focus and becomes a resource teacher. Some in-service is usually made available to these teachers to help in their transition. The success of this practice depends upon the initial competence and the acceptance of the new role by the teachers as well as upon the effectiveness of the in-service training. In the second case, where a new teacher is selected, he probably will not have had prior training to operate in this role but with some in-service training is viewed as being capable of functioning in this role. There are a few teachers who have had resource experience or university training, but the rapid expansion of this model has not yet been met with equal growth in training programs.

Regardless of how the resource teacher is selected, he must possess several competencies and have at least one important "personality characteristic." This characteristic is the ability to work effectively with colleagues. In the past, we have noted some of the difficulties in communication that arise between the resource teacher and the regular education teachers concerning children who are shared. Classroom teachers in the past have been rather autonomous regarding individual children's total curriculum or at least regarding one aspect of their education, such as reading, arithmetic, social studies, etc. Because of the shared responsibility in some content areas, the resource teacher must be able to efficiently communicate the need for and facilitate change in programming in the regular classroom.

Resource teachers must also be able to deal with specific requests from regular classroom teachers regarding the instruction of individual pupils. In cases where these requests are logical, there is little problem; however, any resource teacher will experience some illogical requests. For example, in my experience one elementary regular education teacher insisted that a child be taught "algebra" in the resource room because his peers in the regular classroom were learning algebra. Unfortunately, the child in question did not know his basic addition and subtraction facts. In another case, a junior high teacher requested that a child write a paper on "Corinthian Columns" in the resource room despite the fact that his reading level was at the first grade level. In both cases, explanations to the regular classroom teacher did not result in a change of attitude; rather they became even more adamant. The resource teachers had to change their planned remedial programs and help the pupils complete the requests in as short as time as possible and then teach them what they thought was more important.[1] This, of course, frustrated the resource teacher.

As a result the resource room teacher will have to be highly skilled in public relations, as the success of his program depends in no small part on the support of the regular classroom teachers. Where this support is absent, the resource teacher will have to overcome many problems before the operation can be successful.

In addition to the ability to work effectively with colleagues, the resource teacher needs to be competent in at least two other areas. First, he must be able to do most of his own educational and behavioral assessment. Second, he must be able to successfully develop and implement individualized programs.

---

1. It is interesting to note that even with the resource teacher's help the junior high student received a "C" on his "Corinthian Columns" paper.

Some general guidelines regarding these skills are discussed later in this article under *Assessment and Remediation.*

In summary, to perform adequately in the resource model, the teacher must possess three particular kinds of ability. First, he must be able to work closely and harmoniously with other teachers and ancillary staff. Second, he must be able to assess specific educational and behavioral problems and needs. Third, he must be able to design and implement individualized instruction for children referred to the resource room. The most effective resource teachers will be those who have these basic skills. In addition, these necessary skills can be markedly enhanced if proper communication channels have been established in the school prior to implementing the resource room.

Establishing Communication Channels

Once the staff has been informed that resource rooms are to be set up in the school, there is a need for insuring initial and continuing communication flow. In the beginning there is always some confusion regarding such policy matters as referrals and scheduling. How the child is referred and to whom he is referred often are confusing when there are other ancillary personnel in a given school (such as a counselor, nurse, reading teacher, team leaders, vice-principals, speech therapist, etc.), and remedial roles become confused. In other schools the resource room may be the only available supplemental support, and as a consequence the confusion will be somewhat diminished.

As a supervisor and coordinator of resource rooms for Temple University and the Philadelphia Public Schools, I found that appointing a *resource team* was of benefit in facilitating communication flow. One hour was set aside for a team meeting once a week. Members of the team meet before or after school, during lunch (brown-bagging it) or, if aides are available, during the school day. Members of this team include the resource teacher, any regular classroom teacher who has a child to be discussed during that specific meeting, and all other ancillary personnel such as those previously specified. Two points regarding team members are most important. First, the principal of the school should probably be the resource team chairman. He is the one to make the final decision regarding the type of resource service an individual child is to receive. If the resource teacher acts as team chairman, then he becomes the final decision-maker and the one who takes the responsibility for making unpopular decisions. Because of the necessity of his being able to work efficiently on a one-to-one basis with other teachers in the school, he would be an unwise choice as a team chairman. In addition, some decisions ultimately need to be made and supported by the principal; and his being team chairman necessitates that he attend each meeting.

307

The specific purposes of these meetings are to discuss the treatment of children for resource support, a periodic progress report on the success of individual children, and other problems that arise from time to time. Usually, children who have been referred by the regular classroom teacher are discussed. These referrals should go to the principal who, in turn, gives the referral to the resource teacher who then makes a classroom visit to observe the child functioning in the regular grade. Giving the referral to the principal first enables him to keep track of who is referring children and who is not, as well as who is over-referring children (the over-referring teacher will probably need some help of a consulting nature). The specific steps in implementing this team approach are as follows:

1. A team consisting of the school principal, regular classroom teachers, resource teacher, and ancillary school personnel is appointed. The team is made up of in-house rather than district personnel, as the purpose is not labeling children but rather working out an individualized program based upon existing school resources. Initially, this resource team meets weekly. When the resource teacher achieves a full caseload and the resource room is fully operational, meetings may be less frequent.

2. Three copies of the referral form are given to each teacher in the school together with specific instructions regarding completing the form and sending it to the principal. During the initial implementation of the program, the form should be clear, concise, easy to fill out and should include factors such as the child's level of performance of basic academic skills, his ability to profit from group instruction, his classroom behavior, and any additional comments the referring teacher may care to make. As the resource model becomes better understood and operational, more detailed information on the referral form may be requested.

3. The principal records, makes written comments, and passes along the referral form with the school records of the child to the resource teacher.

4. The resource teacher observes the child in the regular classroom and compiles information regarding his present and past performance.

5. The team meets and decides upon the best program for the child. Some decisions that may be made are as follows:

- Should a psychological or medical examination be given?

- Is the child's problem of such a mild nature that the resource teacher can do an assessment, e.g., informal arithmetic inventory?

- Is the child's problem of such a nature that his program should be implemented by other than the resource teacher, e.g., reading teacher, counselor, social worker, speech therapist?

- What type of support does the regular classroom teacher need?
- Periodic reviews of the achievement of individual children.
- Any additional problem that needs a team decision.

The success of these team meetings rests for the most part on the resource teacher. He needs to be aware of the existing resources, to plan the agenda for the meetings, and to be able to offer pragmatic suggestions regarding placement and programming decisions.

This group decision-making removes much of the conflict that a resource teacher might encounter if he dealt directly with regular classroom teachers regarding the programming for individual children. In addition both the resource and regular classroom teachers are "peers" in making contributions regarding individual children, and plans are made by the group concerning their specific interaction for a given pupil in the future.

Personal experience has indicated that the team, in addition to making decisions about mildly handicapped children, also begins to deal with issues such as inadequate resources available within a school, modifications of existing curriculum in the classroom, parents' support, etc. The resource room then becomes the center for educational support for problem pupils as well as for changing a variety of school practices.

Summary

The advantages of the resource room approach for mildly handicapped pupils, the school, and the teachers can be enumerated as follows (1 to 6 pertain to resource rooms in general; the remainder are more likely to be associated with noncategorical resource rooms):

1. Mildly handicapped pupils can benefit from specific resource room training while remaining *integrated* with their friends and age-mates in school.
2. Pupils have the advantages of a *total remedial program* which is prepared by the resource teacher but may be implemented in cooperation with the regular class teacher.
3. Resource rooms are *less expensive* as the teachers are able to serve a greater number of children than special class programs.
4. More children's needs can be served under the resource room arrangement than can be served by the present system.
5. Since the resource teacher is assigned to a particular school (unlike some school psychologists, remedial reading therapists, speech correctionists, or other itinerant staff), he is less likely to be viewed as an "outsider" by other teachers

in the school. In addition, he probably better understands the programming problems in a particular school.

6. Because young children with mild, though developing, problems can be accommodated, later severe disorders may be *prevented*.

7. Because disability diagnoses are not necessary for placement purposes, pupils are *not labeled* in *any* way as handicapped.

8. Because labeling and segregation are avoided, the stigma invariably associated with receiving special attention is *minimized*.

9. Since most schools are large enough to accommodate one or more resource rooms, pupils can receive help in their *neighborhood school*.

10. Pupils are the recipients of *flexible scheduling* in that remediation can be applied entirely in their classrooms by the regular teacher with some resource teacher support or in the resource room itself when necessary; also the schedule can be quickly altered to meet the children's changing situations and needs.

11. Because placement in the resource room is an individual school matter involving the principal, the teachers, and the parents, *no appreciable time lapse* need occur between the teacher's referral and the initiation of special services for the child.

12. Under this alternative, medical and psychological work-ups are done only at the school's request rather than on a screening-for-placement basis; thus, the school psychologist is freed to do the work he was trained to do instead of being relegated to the role of psychometrist.

13. Since the resource room will absorb most of the "handicapped" children in the schools, the special classes will increasingly become instructional settings for "truly" handicapped pupils, i.e., the children for whom the classes were originally intended.

14. Because of the resource teacher's broad training and experience with many children exhibiting different educational and behavioral problems and varying maturational levels, he is likely to become an "in-house" consultant to his school.

To conclude, the resource room model appears to be a promising instructional alternative deserving of the continued interest of educators. Its use may well enhance the education of both handicapped and nonhandicapped children with learning and behavior problems, especially those with mild to moderate difficulties. However, as anyone with first-hand experience in this area can avidly testify, the model is no panacea or "Promised Land." For the resource room model to work successfully, considerable public relations, tact, administrative support and, most of all, teacher competence are required. Neither is the model a substitute for special education disability classes. Some children are so unmanageable or have such commanding instructional problems that their assignment to a regular class would be inadvisable. In any event, we are likely to witness the widespread growth of resource rooms in one form or another within the next few years; hopefully, many of them will be implemented on a noncategorical basis (Hammill & Wiederholt, 1972).

OPERATING PROCEDURES

Once the individual school staff has been prepared for the resource program, the model and teachers selected, and communication channels clearly established, some additional daily operating procedures are recommended. These include assessment and remediation and the organization of the resource rooms.

Assessment and Remediation

Screening for admission into the resource room has been described earlier in this article under *Establishing Communication Channels.* Referral forms that are clear, concise, and easy to fill out are given to regular classroom teachers who submit the referral forms to the principal. A team of school personnel meets to discuss the next step in providing service to an individual child. If financial reimbursement rests upon the fact that a child must fit a given special education category, psychological and/or medical exams might be requested. Hopefully, for the mildly handicapped, this process can be circumvented; and educational assessment and scheduling can be the focus of the decision making.

When educational assessment is viewed as the next step in planning a remedial program, the resource teacher is the logical choice to administer and interpret selected tests. It is important that a battery of standardized tests *not* be routinely administered to children in educational assessment. This process represents an expensive and inefficient use of the resource teacher's time, increases the interval between referral and services and, in many cases, yields educationally useless information. For example, if the team agrees that the child's major problem appears to be reading, then an appropriate reading test should be administered. If, as in the case of younger children, reading is taught as a formal curriculum process, then the reading test employed should tap out those skills the child is expected to have in the reading series employed in the regular classroom, e.g., *Banks Basic Reading Series, Ginn 360* etc. It is important to remember that the purpose of the resource room is to keep children in the regular classroom, and it is simply ineffective not to consider the curriculum of the regular classroom in selecting assessment techniques. If reading is taught by phonics in the regular classroom, then a phonics test should be given, not a word-recognition test. The same holds true for the other curriculum categories.

In assessing behavior disabilities, the regular classroom teacher needs to be consulted regarding what he views as the individual child's most severe specific behavior problem (e.g., talking out, fighting, inattention, passivity, etc.). The more specifically the problem can be stated, the more specifically the remedial program can be developed and implemented. As in educational assessment, the resource teacher needs to keep in mind that the purpose of the resource room is to keep the child in the regular classroom.

The second step is to utilize the specific assessment information derived and plan an individualized program of remediation to be implemented by the regular classroom teacher, the resource teacher, or a combination of both. As in assessment, this plan should be directed toward helping the child secure information he needs to successfully remain in the regular classroom. If, as in the previously mentioned case, the child is being taught phonics, the remedial program should be phonic in nature, possibly even with existing regular classroom materials presented again, individually, to the child.

Careful analysis of the daily or weekly progress of the child in the remedial activities should be noted. Where progress is *not* being made, additional manipulation of the curriculum should be made, such as the use of more specific and smaller instructional units presented with reinforcement. If the child still does not make progress, more detailed assessment of reading difficulties will need to be made. Informal standardized reading tests such as the *Durrell Analysis of Reading Difficulties* or other devices can be given. If through continual testing/remediation the child still is not making progress and if the resource teacher believes he needs a very specific, different-from-the-regular classroom reading instruction (e.g., the Gillingham or Fernald program), then a referral to another service class possibly should be considered, as these latter highly-structured programs take a great deal of time and expertise to teach. However, a resource teacher should not conclude that because a child is referred he *cannot* learn and progress in the existing regular classroom curriculum.

Regarding educational assessment/remediation, many resource teachers are extremely concerned about auditory and visual perceptual disabilities as well as psycholinguistic dysfunctions. This is hardly surprising considering the preoccupation of some educators, psychologists, physicians, optometrists, and parents with these processes. This interest is one of the most remarkable phenomena occurring in special education during the last 15 years. As a consequence, many perceptual-motor and psycholinguistic tests and training programs, ranging from highly standardized tests and sequenced instructional packages to informal assessment procedures and loosely structured collections of activities, have been developed.

After a decade and a half of extensive testing, instruction and research, some professionals have begun to question if the allocation of time, the expenditure of funds, and the untold efforts of children and teachers have been worthwhile.

After careful examination of the literature that has accumulated over the last several years on the relationship of selected auditory perceptual skills and reading ability (Hammill & Larsen, 1974), on the efficacy of psycholinguistic training (Hammill & Larsen, 1973), on the success of training visual-motor perceptual processes (Hammill, Goodman & Wiederholt, 1974), and on the effect of learning meaningful and nonmeaningful material by auditory and visual learners (Newcomer & Goodman, 1974), these authors have concluded that the validity of these techniques simply have never been clearly established. As a result, the usefulness of process and perceptual programs by resource teachers is questionable. Adding to the efficacy research the fact that the purpose of the resource room is to maintain children in the regular classrooms makes such programs as an integral part of mainstreaming instruction for most mildly handicapped children extremely inadvisable. Curriculum in the resource room for individual children should be as closely related as possible to the curriculum in the regular classroom, which is rarely of a structured perceptual or process nature.

Therefore, the assessment/remediation process by resource teachers needs to focus upon what skills the child needs to know in order to function in a specific regular classroom. Criteria for selection of assessment techniques and remedial programs are based upon the regular classroom instruction. Only if a child continues to fail after adaptations of the existing curriculum are other assessment/remediation procedures selected. For a few children it is possible that the remediation program ultimately chosen will be far removed from the regular curriculum, but every attempt should be made to move the pupils as quickly as possible to those activities utilized by the regular classroom teacher. In order to accomplish this assessment/remediation process efficiently, there needs to be a carefully planned organization of the resource room.

Organization of the Resource Room

Inherent in the discussions throughout this article is the need for a set plan in the organization of the resource teacher's time and classroom. As noted throughout, the resource teacher needs periods of time for assessment, remediation, and consultation in order to be effective. During the initial stages of program development, at least one hour per day should be set aside for consultation, one hour for assessment, and one hour for program planning. In total, approximately half of the school day is *not* devoted to actual remedial instruction with individual pupils. In addition, Hammill and Wiederholt (1972) have recommended that during the first two or three weeks of school no pupils should be assigned to the resource room. This delay allows for (1) reevaluation of pupils who have been designated as handicapped the previous year and are likely to need resource support, (2) the regular classroom teachers to modify

313

their programs to accommodate the mildly handicapped pupils, and (3) the resource teacher to analyze the regular classroom programs with emphasis on acquiring and/or developing related assessment and remediation devices.

After the first few weeks, children can begin to be slowly scheduled into the resource room. As the assessment and remediation programs are planned and implemented and evaluated as successful, more mildly handicapped youngsters can be added from time to time to the resource room program.[2] Aides (paraprofessionals, parents, or bright pupils) are extremely beneficial in increasing the number of children who are served in the resource room. They should be considered quite seriously whenever possible.

These recommendations should be considered in planning the time allocations for the resource teacher during the initial stages of the program. However, as the program becomes operational, more flexible scheduling of time will develop naturally. For example, the resource teacher may be so skilled at consultant support that it may be simply more profitable for the mildly handicapped pupils that he work closely with the regular classroom teachers. Another resource teacher may find for a variety of reasons that there is some resistance by the regular education staff to consultant support and may find it more expedient to work in the resource room with selected students.

The beauty of the resource room program is its inherent flexibility. This flexibility allows these programs to integrate into a school rather than requiring the school staff to adjust their programs to this new model. The scheduling of the resource teacher's time is based upon an individual school's actual needs and assets rather than a global preconceived notion of that school's need in the form of resource support.

While this flexibility may appear to allow the resource teacher to be unaccountable for his time and activities, this is far from the truth. He is being watched and monitored carefully by the regular classroom teachers, and they will be the first to note his success (or failure) in aiding the education of handicapped children within the mainstream. When problems arise, ways should be found to reallocate the resource teacher's time to better meet the needs of problem children.

The accountability of the resource teacher to regular classroom teachers may present a problem during the initial implementation of the program. This is particularly true when the resource program has been introduced in glowing

---

2. The number of children served will vary from teacher to teacher. Some teachers will be able to deal successfully with a great number of students because of his skill, the regular classroom teachers' support, and the mild nature of the referred children. In other cases, a much smaller number of students will be able to be successfully supported because of the absence of one or more of the above factors. The focus should be upon the words "successful support," and this should not be sacrificed for specified quantity.

terms and offered as the "Promised Land." Educators, particularly those planning the changes, have a tendency to approach innovations with a missionary-like zeal. The resource room, despite the claims of some of its proponents, is not a panacea. It is simply an administrative arrangement that appears necessary and viable for the 1970s in the American educational system. The point here is that because of the accountability of the resource teacher to the regular classroom teachers the proponents of this approach should not promise too much when introducing this system. When expectations are too high, only disappointment and dissatisfaction can result.

In addition, the variety of activities as well as the numbers of children served necessitates some planning as to the organization of the resource room itself as well as the equipment that facilitates efficient instruction. Note some of the following equipment and its general uses:

1. *Desks for group activities and individual study areas.* While the focus of the resource room is on individualized instruction, seldom will it be occupied only by the teacher and one child. Some children may be receiving direct help from the teacher, while others may be involved in independent activities that reinforce individual instruction. As a result, a place should be set aside for one-to-one instruction, one-to-three or five instruction, and individual study areas. Usually, the pupil's desks found in any school will suffice with the addition of large tables. Booths are excellent but sometimes too expensive for individual study areas. Creativity by utilizing existing materials can be applied in establishing these areas. Regular classroom desks partitioned off by bookcases, portable chalkboards, etc., are easy to create and arrange. Also, large pieces of cardboard may be taped to desks to insure privacy and to enhance attending behavior.

2. *File cabinets.* The organization of a number of worksheets, pupil folders, testing materials, etc., is facilitated by a file cabinet where teachers can efficiently store and retrieve necessary materials. Where monies are not available for file cabinets, cardboard boxes can be utilized. Any materials developed by the teachers then can be copied and filed for future use when appropriate.

3. *Tape recorder and headsets.* In facilitating individualized instruction, it is helpful for the resource teacher to record stories, questions, or directions that a pupil can listen to while doing his assignment. As any resource teacher can attest, most commercial materials need to be manipulated for independent work. The headsets serve a dual purpose—listening to teacher made or commercially made tapes and screening out extraneous noise.

4. *Regular classroom texts and materials.* As the purpose of the resource room is to maintain problem children in the regular classroom, the resource teacher needs to have a complete set of the materials utilized in the regular

system. This includes the reading, arithmetic, etc., materials which, in turn, are utilized in an individualized manner.

5. *Supplemental materials.* It is assumed, of course, that the resource room will be equipped with paper, pencils, etc. In addition, the teacher will probably want to supplement all of the previously mentioned materials and equipment with his own preferred programs and devices. Word cards, alphabet letters, and other materials can be selected from any number of school catalogs. The resource teacher should examine carefully the constraints of the budget and select those materials that are the cheapest and that cannot be teacher-made as well as those materials that promote mainstream success. Three-by-five cards, paper, magic markers, and creativity can and should be used where possible instead of purchasing attractively packaged, expensive commercial materials.

In this section on the organization of the resource teacher's time and classroom, some general suggestions were posited. The scheduling of time for activities focus upon flexibility and fitting into the needs of the school and the mildly handicapped pupils. The resource room should promote individualized instruction and mainstream programming. In most cases, this demands creativity by the resource teacher. Overall, the room should present an attractive, well-organized appearance that reflects well upon the resource program for both the other school staff members and the resource pupils.

CONCLUSION

In this article, some suggestions have been made concerning initial procedures for establishing resource rooms along with some general operational guidelines. Reiterated throughout has been the premise that resource rooms should be established in a flexible manner in order to meet the needs of the mildly handicapped youngsters in a specific school and that there are no hard-and-fast rules regarding their implementation and operation. This, however, demands a constant in-house check to determine the efficacy of the individual approaches selected.

Professionals who are interested in the possibility of establishing resource rooms should read at least some of the references cited and should visit on-going programs to see them at first hand in practical operation. They should talk with regular classroom teachers, the building principal, and some pupils as well as with the resource teacher. In particular, they should be on the lookout for shortcomings as well as the advantages of the programs visited. In so doing, they can obtain a fair picture, thereby determining just which aspects of the program it would be wise to attempt to adapt for their own schools and identifying potential difficulties that could be prevented.

As with all educational enterprises, the success of the resource room model does not depend entirely upon its inherent superiority over other approaches; the adoption of the model will not in and of itself mandate pupil achievement. Effective operation of the model depends upon the competency of the resource teacher, the cooperation and abilities of the regular teachers, the enthusiastic support of the building principal, and the availability of adequate space and materials. Where these elements are absent, failure is unavoidable; where they are present, the success of the effort will be insured.

REFERENCES

Barksdale, M. W. & Atkinson, A. P. "A Resource Room Approach to Instruction for the Educable Mentally Retarded." *Focus on Exceptional Children, 3,* 1971 (12-15).

Christopolos, F. & Renz, P. A. "A Critical Examination of Special Education Programs." *Journal of Special Education, 3,* 1969 (371-379).

Deno, E. "Special Education as Developmental Capital." *Exceptional Children. 37,* 1970 (229-237).

Dunn, L. M. "Special Education for the Mildly Retarded—Is Much of It Justifiable?" *Exceptional Children, 35,* 1968 (5-22).

Garrison, M. & Hammill, D. D. "Who Are the Retarded?" *Exceptional Children, 38,* 1971 (13-20).

Glavin, J. P., Quay, H. C., Annesley, F. R. & Werry, J. S. "An Experimental Resource Room for Behavior Problem Children." *Exceptional Children, 38,* 1971 (131-137).

Hammill, D. D. & Larsen, S. C. "The Relationship of Selected Auditory Perceptual Skills and Reading Ability." *Journal of Learning Disabilities, 7,* 1974 (40-46).

Hammill, D. D. & Larsen, S. C. "The Efficacy of Psycholinguistic Training." Unpublished manuscript (University of Texas-Austin, 1973).

Hammill, D. D., Goodman, L. & Wiederholt, J. L. "Visual-Motor Processes: What Success Have We Had in Training Them." *The Reading Teacher, 27,* 1974 (469-478).

Hammill, D. D. & Wiederholt, J. L. *The Resource Room: Rationale and Implementation.* Fort Washington, Pennsylvania: Journal of Special Education Press, 1972.

Iano, R. P. "Shall We Disband Our Special Classes?" *Journal of Special Education, 6,* 1972 (167-177).

Lilly, S. M. "Special Education: A Teapot in a Tempest." *Exceptional Children, 37,* 1970 (43-48).

Newcomer, P. & Goodman, L. "Effects of Modality of Instruction on the Learning of Meaningful and Nonmeaningful Material by Auditory and Visual Learners." *Journal of Special Education,* 1974.

Reger, R. & Koppmann, M. "The Child-Oriented Resource Room." *Exceptional Children, 37,* 1971 (460-462).

Reynolds, M. C. "A Framework for Considering Some Issues in Special Education." *Exceptional Children, 7,* 1962 (367-370).

Ross, S. L., De Young, H. G. & Cohen, J. S. "Confrontation: Special Education Placement and the Law." *Exceptional Children, 38,* 1971 (5-12).

At first glance, the title of this chapter may elicit a response such as "What's new? Of course the classroom consists of interaction patterns." However, the reader is cautioned not to stop with the title, but to read further. Carroll does an outstanding job of presenting what all educators believe to be important but do not, as a rule, conceptualize as a fundamental part of instruction. Carroll has provided educators with a conceptual model for viewing the classroom as a ecosystem. In the first and final analysis, the success of any instructional program is contingent upon the recognition that interaction does occur between the pupil and the environment. Without interaction, there can be no learning or behavior change. Educators often neglect the obvious, but Carroll has brought it back into focus again so that it can be used continuously to plan more functional learning environments for children.

The Classroom as an Ecosystem

Anne W. Carroll
University of Denver

The trend toward an increased awareness of the needs and rights of the handicapped has resulted in

—a decreased emphasis upon the more traditional categorical approach to labeling the handicapped and an increasing tendency to view all children as learners with varying degrees of readiness.

—momentum to increase the availability of instructional options for all handicapped children.

—the emergence of an increased partnership between the special educator and the classroom teacher.

—less reliance on traditional standardized tests and more emphasis on actual teaching/learning assessment and careful observation of the learner's behavior as expressed in as natural a setting as possible.

—the need for a systematic approach to viewing the learner and the learning environment.

> To instruct men is nothing more than to help human nature to develop in its
> own way, and the art of instruction depends primarily on harmonizing our
> messages and the demands we make upon the child with his powers at the
> moment. [Swiss Educator, 1802]

Thus, the learner affects and is affected by his environment. This reciprocal
relationship must be considered in any attempt to describe the learner's
behavior systematically.

THE ECOLOGICAL MODEL

An ecological model is proposed in order to provide a conceptual framework
within which to discuss the dynamic interaction of the environment and the
learner (the ecosystem).

The ecological viewpoint tries to integrate the individual and the
environment into a single whole rather than to view them separately.

> Man is in the world and his ecology is the nature of his "inness" . . . what
> does he do there in nature? What does nature do in him? What is the nature
> of the transaction? [Shepard & McKinley, 1969, p.1]

It is not only the student and the teacher who act and react, but the total
ecosystem "behaves" as a whole. The child is a contributor as well as a reactor
to the learning process.

How Is the Ecological Model Applied to the Classroom?

The ecological model may be applied through a personalized education
approach, which is an attempt to achieve a balance between the characteristics
of the learner and the learning environment. It is the match of the learning
environment with the learner's information, processing strategies, concepts,
learning sets, motivational systems achieved, and skills acquired.

It is based upon the dynamic interaction of the student and the learning
environment and includes a congruence within the learning environment,
providing for adaptive growth within the accommodative capacity of the child.
The child's ongoing informational interaction with his environment is the basis
for program planning.

Teaching is viewed as the process by which accommodation and assimilation
are *facilitated* in the effort to control the match between the environmental
circumstances the pupil encounters and the schemata he has already assimilated
(Adelman, 1973).

Hunt (1972) suggested that adaptive growth takes place in a situation which
contains information, models, and challenges just discrepant enough from those

already stored and mastered to produce interest and call for adaptive modification in the structure of his "intellectual coping" which are not beyond his accommodative capacity at the time.

It may be inferred that "appropriate learning" is dependent upon

1. discrepancy being within the limits of an individual's capacity for accommodation.

2. the appropriate operation of the accommodative and assimilative processes.

An "appropriate match" for successful learning is one where there is an accountable discrepancy between one's adaptive assimilated schemata and the environmental circumstances one encounters (Hunt, 1972).

In contrast, the absence of the discrepancy between environmental circumstances one encounters and one's adaptive assimilated schemata is viewed as resulting in "arrested learning" (Adelman, 1973). In some situations it may be that there is nothing to accommodate, such as in the case where there is inadequate stimulation or when the stimulation is beyond one's accommodative capacity. If the student cannot avoid the circumstance, the result may be inappropriate learning or disruptive learning.

The absence of the "match" may result in a state of disequilibrium on the part of both the teacher and the learner.

THEORY OF COGNITIVE DISSONANCE

Cognitive dissonance as viewed by Festinger (1957) is an antecedent condition which leads to activity oriented toward dissonance reduction. The demands of the environment upon the student may disrupt his equilibrium, forcing him perhaps to display avoidance behaviors which may then disrupt the equilibrium of the teacher's cognitive structure, thus causing a state of dissonance or "level of uncomfortableness." Since the mind is continuously active, it may attempt to reconcile this state by rationalizing the position, discounting the source, or insulating one's beliefs by closing them. Such reconciliation often leads to frustration for many classroom teachers as their desire to help the children in their rooms develop to their greatest potential is hampered by a lack of preventive intervention strategies.

It has been theorized that each individual has formed latitudes of acceptance and rejection on those subjects with which he is involved. There are other subjects with which he chooses to remain noncommitted; this does not mean he remains uninvolved.

According to Sherif and Sherif (1969), norms have been established within one's cognitive structure around which he evaluates incoming information to see if he can tolerate it. If he cannot, he will reject it or let it lie dormant as a noncommitment.

How Much Dissonance Can One Tolerate?

If one examines his own thought processes, he will probably see that he has built up a cognitive buffer to insulate him from much of the dissonance-producing information that he receives on a daily basis. Referring to Festinger's concept, one can see that he could naturally avoid environments that cause a "state of uncomfortableness." Most people seek reinforcing situations and shy away from those that are dissonance-producing. In order to maintain some semblance of mental balance, one may attempt to avoid uncomfortable situations or keep them to a minimum. This is usually not diagnosed as passivity, but rather as a means of survival. The more disequilibrium existing in the mental state, the more mental activity one must generate to decrease the dissonance. Since man is a self-regulating system, he must have some type of gyro to keep him on course. Therefore, when the system is pushed too fast one tends to slow it down or block the input.

How Does the Theory of Cognitive Dissonance Apply to the Classroom?

Most teachers actively seek to attain a state of balance in the classroom. Of course, some people can live with more dissonance than others. Thus, some may disregard information that makes others upset. The theory of cognitive dissonance is built upon the premise that, after one has built a reactive system, one evaluates information in such a way that it fits into his prescribed format for decision making.

How Does One Decrease the Dissonance Level When the Learning or Behavior Problems Manifested within the Classroom Are Contradictory to One's Expectations of Class Behavior?

One approach is to avoid information which might increase the dissonance; the other is an attempt to achieve consonance with the learner and the environment.

The teacher's tolerance range for the acceptance of differences of behaviors in the classroom may be increased through a better assessment of the environment and, through this information, may decrease the range of dissonance. Thus, the state of disequilibrium on the part of the teacher in the classroom may be reduced by the utilization of a systematic approach to assessing the learner and the learning environment.

ASSESSMENT

Hunt (1972) suggested that assessment "should provide information to guide the educational process." The teacher should know what strategies of information processing, what motor habits, and what motivational interests are required before a child can respond with "productive accommodation" to a given curriculum or teaching situation. For example, what motor abilities, symbolic linguistic skills, cognitive abilities, and interests are required before a child can learn to read? Master teachers have usually taught with an intuitive approach to assessing a student's response to a problem; however, little has been organized into a helpful systematic approach.

What Is the Approach to Assessment?

Assessment is not a one-shot kind of process, but rather *an integral and ongoing part of the instructional strategy*. If an activity proves ineffective, it must be recognized as such and replaced; and this data must become a part of the cycle. No assessment is infallible and no one activity helps all children, but rather ongoing evaluation attests to the accuracy of the initial assessment and the effectiveness of the instructional program (Figure 1). Hopefully, in the next few years, specifics in teaching systems relevant to the learning characteristics of children can be identified. "Differential treatment should be a natural outgrowth of differential assessment" (Binet, 1918).

SYSTEM FOR ASSESSING THE LEARNER
AND THE LEARNING ENVIRONMENT

The six major steps in assessing a learner and his environment within the classroom setting are as follows:

Step 1. *Determine the goal* of assessing the learner and his environment.

Step 2. *Develop a conceptual framework* for assessing the learner and his environment.

Step 3. *Implement the assessment plan* based upon the above conceptual framework.

Step 4. *Evaluate the results* of step 3 and determine the primary learner goals.

Step 5. *Develop a set of hypotheses* about the student's learning and emotional characteristics.

Step 6. *Develop a learning plan* based upon Step 5, the learner characteristics and the learning environment.

Figure 1
CYCLICAL MODEL OF ASSESSMENT

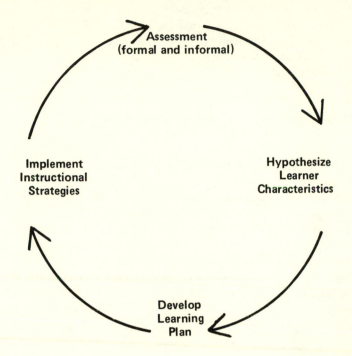

Steps 1, 2, and 3 are discussed in this article. Discussion and application of all six steps may be found in *Personalizing Education in the Classroom* (Carroll, 1975).

Step 1. Determine the Goal of Assessing the Learner and His Environment.

The following should be determined prior to the initiation of assessment:

1. What is the purpose of the assessment?
2. What information is necessary to attain the goal?
3. What is the known information about the student and the learning environment?
4. What additional information is necessary to gather?
5. Who will be responsible for the assessment?
6. How will the information be obtained?
7. How will the information be utilized, once obtained?

Step 2. Develop a Conceptual Framework for Assessing the Learner and the Learning Environment.

In assessing the learning environment, the teacher attempts to become aware of the options available within the teaching situations, and which combination of options elicits the most appropriate response from the student. It is through the assessment of the total situation that the teacher will attempt to achieve the match that is satisfactory for the learner. (See Figure 2.)

FRAMEWORK FOR ASSESSING THE LEARNING ENVIRONMENT

> Facility
> Personnel Analysis
> Process Analysis
> (Input response reinforcement)
> Task Analysis
> Curriculum Analysis
> Climate Analysis
> Time Analysis
> Group Analysis
> Data Analysis
> Resource Analysis

Facility Analysis

Questions to be answered about the facility:

1. Are facilities available to provide for large and small group interaction within the classroom?
2. Are individual study areas available (i.e., portable bookshelves or bulletin boards that can be used to divide the areas)?
3. Are learning carrels available (i.e., portable desk top carrels)?
4. Are activity centers available (i.e., communication centers, science centers, etc.)?
5. Are book corners readily accessible to students?
6. Does the student have his own desk or cupboard where he can store his personal material?
7. Are there facilities available in the room or in the school for crisis intervention (i.e., a time-out room)?

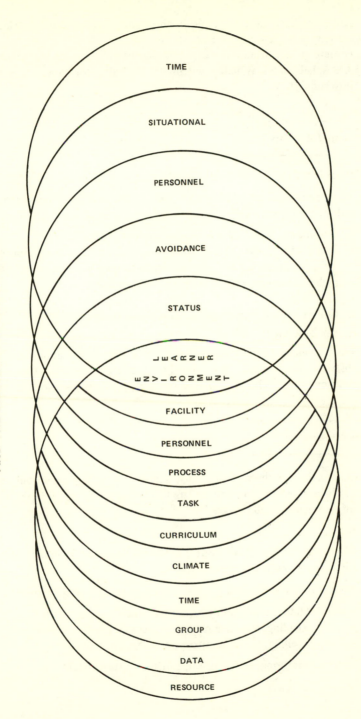

Figure 2

CONCEPTUAL FRAMEWORK FOR ASSESSING THE LEARNER
AND THE LEARNING ENVIRONMENT

TIME

SITUATIONAL

PERSONNEL

AVOIDANCE

STATUS

LEARNER
ENVIRONMENT

FACILITY

PERSONNEL

PROCESS

TASK

CURRICULUM

CLIMATE

TIME

GROUP

DATA

RESOURCE

8. Are there large areas available in the building or outside that can be used for play activities, drama presentations, etc.?
9. Is there an area around the building that can be used for exploration?
10. Are small rooms available within the building for subdividing the class into subunits?

Personnel Analysis

1. What is the ratio of students to teachers?

2. What personnel are available to help in the personalizing approach (i.e., within the classroom)?

    a. Community volunteers or senior citizens groups?
    b. Peers within the classroom for additional teaching? For example, intra-peer tutoring or older students to help younger students such as high school, junior high, fifth and sixth graders.
    c. Paid aides?
    d. College interns in preservice educational programs?
    e. Interested parent groups?

3. What ancillary support personnel are available in the building and school district (i.e., music, P.E. teachers, curriculum specialists, resource teachers, speech clinicians, social workers, psychologists and nurses)?

Process Analysis

Process analysis is the procedure for examining the task presented according to the skills required to complete it. The following questions on input, response, and reinforcement should be asked.

Input:

1. What type of stimuli or input is given to students throughout most of the day? Visual, auditory, crossmodal?

2. What is the type of input generally used in specific subject areas—i.e.,

        Math: visual, auditory, crossmodal?
        Reading: visual, auditory, crossmodal?
        Spelling: visual, auditory, crossmodal?

3. In social-emotional areas—visual, auditory, crossmodal?

4. What is the cognitive level of input?

    a. Concrete—i.e., How are a pear and an apple alike? They are round.

    b. Functional—i.e., They are edible.

    c. Abstract—i.e., They are both fruit.

5. What is the rate of input—i.e., fast, slow?

6. What is the amount of input—i.e., number of directions given?

7. What is the sequence of input—i.e., sensory, perceptual, memory, language?

Response:

1. What is the most frequent type of *response* requested of the students *throughout most of the day?* Oral, graphic, crossmodal?

2. What is the most frequent *response requested* of students in *specific subject areas*—i.e.,

        Math: oral, graphic, crossmodal?

        Reading: oral, graphic, crossmodal?

        Spelling: oral, graphic, crossmodal?

3. What is the most frequent *response* requested of students in *social-emotional areas?*

4. Are responses sequenced in the order of their difficulty?

    a. For example, the student affirms or negates the selection of the response by the teacher.

    b. The student sorts (pictures, objects) according to the categories which correspond to models presented by the teacher. Categories may be size, shape, color, function.

    c. The student compares and selects or points to a picture, object, or form to correspond to the model presented by the teacher.

    d. The student sorts as mentioned above, but without a model.

    e. The student matches pictures, objects, forms, or sounds which are alike.

    f. The student selects one of a series which is different from the rest of the series.

    g. The student arranges in series according to gradation in size, color, or some other standard.

    h. The student verbalizes his thoughts as to any of the above.

    i. The student responds in multiple-choice.

    j. The student responds in a short essay answer.

Reinforcement:

1. *What reinforcement strategy is used by the classroom teacher?*
   a. Oral, graphic?
   b. Immediate or delayed?
   c. Social or tangible?

2. What is the type of reinforcement usually given to students in math? in reading? in spelling?

3. What is the type of reinforcement usually given to students in social-emotional areas?

Task Analysis

1. What skills are involved in the performance of the task?

2. What is the main skill to be acquired?

3. What are the necessary subskills to complete the task?

Curriculum Analysis

Program Analysis:

1. Are there programs available in reading, math, and spelling which provide a variety of input stimuli for students?

2. Who gives the input? The teacher, other student, peer? This input can be on an individual basis or on a group basis. For example, the individual giving himself input through reading, etc.

Materials Analysis:

1. List the materials used in the classroom and inspect the responses required of students; such as graphic writing response; oral response; rhetoric, such as gestures or pointing, matching, etc.

2. List materials used in the classroom which provide variety of activities; such as the visual auditory, manipulative, and creative.

3. What materials in the classroom lend themselves to individual study?

4. What hardware is available to supplement the curricula, such as language master, overhead, tape recorder?

Behavior may be observed by considering specified characteristics operating within the classroom environment. According to research on classroom processes, there are four characteristics of the educational setting which may be observed informally by teacher-peer or teacher-administrator to assess the educational climate. These characteristics are creativity, individualization, group activities, and interpersonal relations (Galloway, 1970). Both teacher and student behaviors may be observed using the four-area framework (Figure 3).

Such behavioral observation may provide data for answering the following questions:

1. What type of leadership does the teacher, himself, exhibit—i.e.,

    a. Democratic (effective guide)?
    b. Persuasive (encourages spontaneity)?
    c. Authoritarian (efficiency is good)?
    d. Leadership (grouping for learning tasks)?

2. Is there interpersonal sensitivity on the part of both the teacher and the children to one another's needs?

3. Is the approach in the classroom problem solving vs. problem finding?

Time Analysis

1. What percentage of time is spent on academic tasks? What percent on social-emotional activities?

2. Is there time set aside for individual conferences?

Group Analysis

1. Is majority of the classroom work in large group settings? in small groups? in individual settings?

2. How are decisions made for groupings?

3. Who is involved in this decision making?

4. Are instructions for the group task already given to the students prior to the formation of the groups?

Figure 3
CLASSROOM OBSERVATION CHECKLIST

Date _____ Time _____ Teacher _____ Observer _____ Lesson _____
                    Date & Time   Date & Time   Date & Time

1st Observation (10 min.)_____ 2nd Observation _____ 3rd Observation_____

Checklist may be used for the following: a) math lesson   b) reading   c) spelling   d) social studies
Rating scale: 1) None   2) Little   3) Some   4) Occasionally   5) Usually   6) To a great extent

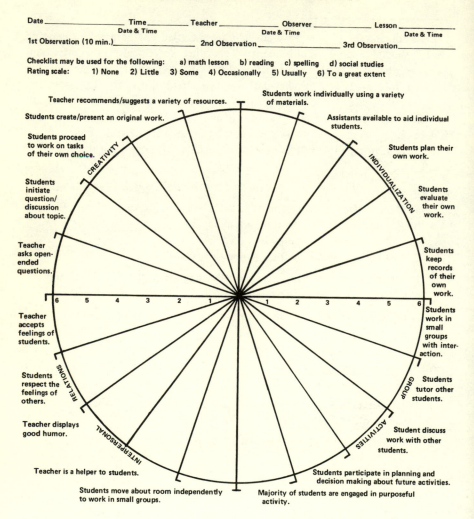

5. What types of activities lend themselves best to small group solutions vs. individual vs. large group?

| **Program Management Data Analysis** |

1. How is data recorded?

2. What data is recorded?

3. By whom is the data recorded?

4. When is the data recorded?

   a. Before the teaching technique is employed?

   b. During its use?

   c. After the teaching procedure has been modified or discontinued?

5. Is the data recorded in retrievable form? (See Figure 4.)

Figure 4
RECORD FORM FOR RECORDING BEHAVIORAL CHANGE

Name of Child: _____ Teacher: _____

Behavior Recorded:

Day	Date	Total Time Behavior Recorded	Time of Day	Number of Behaviors Observed	Percent of Work Completed	Percent of Work Correct	Comments

---

Resource Analysis

1. Building Resources

   What resources are available to the classroom teacher?

   a. Health resources—nurses, school physicians?

   b. Psychological resources—psychologists, consulting psychiatrists, social worker?

   c. Parent involvement?

   d. Instructional resource materials?

   e. Resource room?

   f. Human resources available within the building—reading specialist, counselor, etc.?

2. District Resources.

3. Community Resources.

4. State Resources.

5. National Resources.

ASSESSING THE LEARNER

Status Analysis
Avoidance Analysis
Personnel Analysis
Situational Analysis
Time Analysis

Status Analysis

Should attempt to answer the question: What does he know?

1. What is the level of achievement in the basic academic areas—in math, reading, and spelling?

2. Is there a discrepancy in his achievement and social-emotional behavior based upon the input and response modes?

Avoidance Analysis

1. Are there *specific subjects* he avoids? For example, during reading time does he drop his books on the floor and get a drink of water? During spelling tests does he have to sharpen his pencil? In math does he rarely complete his assignments? Possibly, he is more fearful of receiving an "F" than an incomplete, which he can rationalize.

2. Are there *specific tasks* he avoids—e.g., written language, copying activities, word problems in math, or specific types of homework assignments?

3. Are there *specific settings* he avoids? Is there anything in common for them?

4. Are there *specific people* he avoids—e.g., in terms of adults or other students?

Personnel Analysis

1. Does he learn best with an adult—e.g., a teacher, a volunteer, an aide, an intern?

2. Does he learn best with peers or older students?

3. Does he appear to learn best through group activities or individual activities?

4. What types of activities does he do best in small groups? What type of learning does he accomplish best with adults? With peers?

Situational Analysis

Should attempt to answer the question: Where does he learn?

1. In the classroom.
   a. Large group activities?
   b. Small group activities?
   c. Individually oriented activities?
   d. Activity centers?

2. On the playground.
   a. Parallel play activites?
   b. Team activities?

3. Special room.
   a. Reading room?
   b. Library?
   c. Resource teacher?
   d. Media centers?

Time Analysis

Should attempt to answer two questions.

1. What time of the day does he appear to learn best?
   a. Before mid-morning?
   b. Before lunch?
   c. Before mid-afternoon?

2. How long can he stay with an activity, and what type of activity?

Step 3. Implement the Assessment Plan Based upon the Above Conceptual Framework.

How can conceptual framework be implemented? Observations of behavior might be

1. *Continuous recording.* Behavior being recorded is easily observed. It occurs in a variety of settings and, particularly, occurs less than twenty five times per day. It is usually wise to record each instance of the behavior.

2. *Time sample recording.* When the behavior being recorded occurs only in a specific setting, such as reading instruction or on the playground, when it is difficult to observe, or when it occurs more than twenty five times per day, a time sampling recording technique is usually advisable.

3. *Duration recording.* Some behaviors are a concern to teachers, not because of their frequency, but because of their duration. A simple recording technique might be to observe the child when he is given a book to read and record the number of seconds or minutes he spends actually pursuing the book during a period of three to ten minutes using a stopwatch.

4. *Work records.* For some children, the behavior of greatest concern to the teacher may be the percent of the assigned work completed, percent of completed work correct, rate of work. Care should be taken to record work, age, academic subject separately to keep the number of possible responses approximately equal on successive days, and to make sure the assigned work requires discrete responses.

5. *Walk through the day.* One of the most advantageous approaches to observing a child's behavior is to select two or three children the teacher is most concerned about and spend one full day devoted to following them. This includes the playground and the lunchroom.

Who may give input?

1. *The child, himself,* through a conference approach is usually a viable source of information and one which is often overlooked. Conferences should include what the child himself views as being his strengths and areas in which he feels the need to improve. (See Figure 5.)

Figure 5

Esther M. Bearg, fifth grade teacher, Mt. Pleasant School, West Orange, New Jersey, states, "We educators have tried numerous grading systems over the years, but how far have we really progressed in our quest for sincere, explicit reporting? I finally had my students write their own report cards as auxiliaries to the official ones, encouraging them to write comments about themselves as though they were I. The result? Their comments were better than mine. Why? Because as you can see below, I was polite; my students were direct. Perhaps the task of reporting should belong to us both."

I said . . .	They said . . .
Donna needs firm yet gentle discipline to help her see what is appropriate both in her academic work and in interaction with her peers.	She should not make fun of people just because others do.
John means well. Firm, consistent, regular guidance will develop his ability to sustain his positive feelings and behavior toward school.	I think he needs a lot of improvement. He really does.
There has been some improvement in Bruce's work because his attitude toward school is better. However, he must keep after his daily work.	I think Bruce is doing so-so.
Basically Joe is capable and enthusiastic. Regular guidance and understanding will help him see the need for doing what is required.	He shouldn't talk so much. And he should have more self-control and respect everything in the room. And he should talk in turn.

Today's Education, NEA Journal, 1967

2. *The classroom teacher* may provide input through her observations of the child through formal assessment—such as achievement tests, etc.; through weekly achievement tests in the classroom; through criterion referenced testing; and through informal analysis.

Example: One example of a breakdown in communication between a teacher and child in assessing his learning problem was a youngster who said that he had been told by his teacher that if he did not understand his math to talk with her as soon as he had finished the page. However, this conversation took place in April, and he said that his teacher had told him that in October, but he could never talk with her about it because he had never completed a page of math.

3. *Parents* can provide valuable background information, help in the developmental history and rule out any interfering health factors, describe the child's behavior at home, etc.

4. *Ancillary personnel*, roving principals, other teachers, health nurses, social workers, school psychologists, special education teachers may also be available to give input into reaffirming the teacher's impressions of the child. Most, however, feel at this time that the classroom teacher has the best opportunity to observe the child and his behavior.

SUMMARY

Beliefs on assessing the learner and his environment.

1. Assessing the learner and his environment is a cyclical process.

2. Assessing the learner and his environment should be a flexible process.

3. Assessing the learner and his environment should include a multitude of resources.

4. Each measure of assessment should be carefully selected.

5. Assessment should include both formal and informal measures.

6. Assessment is a prerequisite to personalizing educational programs.

7. Assessment should include both the learner characteristics as well as the resources within the environment.

8. The assessment of the learner and his environment should result in a plan of action with strategies for program implementation.

9. The assessment should include a systematic way of recording the student's growth in the program.

10. The teacher as the learning facilitator has the primary responsibility for assessing a learner and his environment.

REFERENCES

Adelman, Howard. *Learning Problems and Classroom Instruction.* Special Project Grant #OEG-71-4152 (603), Division of Training, Bureau of Education for the Handicapped, U. S. Office of Education, August, 1973.

Barker, R. G. "Exploration in Ecological Psychology." *American Psychology, 20,* 1965 (1-14).

Carroll, Anne W. *Personalizing Education in the Classroom.* Denver: Love Publishing Company, 1975.

Festinger, L. A. *A Theory of Cognitive Dissonance.* Stanford, California: Stanford University Press, 1957.

Festinger, L. A. *Conflict, Decision and Dissonance.* Stanford, California: Stanford University Press, 1964.

Galloway, Charles M. "Teaching Is Communicating, Nonverbal Language in the Classroom." *Association for Student Teaching, Bulletin #29,* 1970.

Hunt, J. McVicker. "Psychological Assessment in Education and Social Class." *Proceedings in Special Education: Missouri Conference,* 1972.

Lewin, K. *Field Theory in Social Science: Selected Theoretical Papers.* D. Cartwright (Ed.). New York: Harper and Row, 1951.

Mann, Phillip H. & Suiter, Patricia. *Handbook In Diagnostic Teaching.* Boston: Allyn & Bacon, Inc., 1974.

Maryland State Department of Education. "Teaching Children with Special Needs." Owens Mills, Md., 1973.

Shepard, P. & McKinley, A. *The Subversive Science.* Boston: Houghton-Mifflin, 1969.

Sherif, Muzafer & Sherif, Carolyn W. *Social Psychology.* New York: Harper & Row, 1969.

"Today's Education." *NEA Journal, 5,* 1967 (3).

Beery, as Chaffin did in an earlier chapter, writes from a sound base of practical experience in mainstreaming efforts. He has been there. The reader will note that Beery is advocating a very humanistic approach to the issues and further insists that mainstreaming will be useful only if general educators are involved in the first stages of program development and throughout implementation. This is as it should be; if one is to change, one must be convinced that such change will be an improvement and will also participate in the process. Beery's chapter is an account of the insights gained in working with public school staff in carrying out a humanistic approach to mainstreaming. He is candid regarding the successes and failures of past efforts. More importantly, Beery provides hope for the eventual positive aspects of mainstreaming. He communicates a clear and articulate message to educators who are, whether aware of it or not, involved in the realities of providing educational services for handicapped children.

Mainstreaming:
A Problem and an Opportunity
for General Education

Keith E. Beery
Institute for Independent Educational
Research, San Rafael, California

Legislatures, courts, and others are pressing for "mainstreaming." What is it? Why do it? Who, how, when, where? Although I can only scratch the surface here, I *urge* that anyone who is considering participation in mainstreaming examine these questions in *depth* before starting. The greatest help I have to offer you are these questions.

This article is based on excerpts from *Models for Mainstreaming* (Beery, 1972a) and *The Guts to Grow* (Beery, et al., 1974) reprinted, with changes, by permission of the author and publisher.

What is mainstreaming? First of all, I think it is essential to discriminate between *philosophy* and *program*. Philosophically, to me mainstreaming means the valuing of human differences. It means that *everyone* is a teacher and that everyone is a learner. It means that all of us together are greater than any one of us or some of us. It means that heterogeneous grouping is more growth promoting, both academically and in the qualities that make us human, than is homogeneous grouping. It means the desirability of *in*clusion of people rather than *ex*clusion of people. These are the solid, philosophical goals which are finding increasing support in hard data. But they are goals which, by definition, one *strives* toward and never fully realizes.

Programmatically, to me mainstreaming means a *continuum* of services with a conscious, monitored thrust to include everyone as much as possible (in terms of each person's welfare) with everyone else. "Everyone" includes adults as well as children, a concept not yet recognized or implemented in most mainstreaming programs I've seen. Most current programs use a simplistic program definition limited to children, some to the extreme of requiring *full*-time participation of *all* handicapped children in regular classrooms. Such definitions do not make sense to me because many children and adults suffer under them.

Why mainstream? Hopefully, the answer is implicit in the foregoing. I would add that we should *not* mainstream if the basic motivations are pressure or anything smacking of faddism. I fear that we may already be into a "pendulum swing" that could result in regression rather than growth. The only justification for mainstreaming must be its promise as a way to *improve* upon the past. Personally, I believe that a healthy concept of mainstreaming, with sensible implementation, can prove to be the most far-reaching and productive educational movement in this century. It has the potential for health revolution in our troubled educational systems. But we must make haste slowly!

As to the who, when, how, and where questions, please read on. We are happy to share experiences that may be of help to you. All we ask is that you examine these ideas *critically* and that you share your ideas with us.

THE GENERAL EDUCATION APPROACH

There are three basic ways to include more children in the mainstream of educational life: (1) simply return them from pull-out programs, (2) have special education take the lead in identifying pupil needs and programs, and (3) have general education take the lead in increasing the individualization and personalization of instruction in regular classrooms. To me, the third alternative is the best route.

In order to support my belief that *organizational development*—with leadership coming from general education—is the best mainstreaming road to travel, I will need to backtrack and relate some professional history.

In *Remedialdiagnosis* (Beery, 1968) and *Teaching Triads* (Beery, 1972b), I reported our efforts over a period of several years to assist children with learning and behavioral difficulties in schools. Initially, we focused upon the children themselves, using various techniques for evaluating and generating learning programs for the children. We then realized that all the understanding of a child's educational needs was of little value if his teacher did not understand these needs and what to do about them. So we began to focus our work on teachers, particularly classroom teachers.

Successes and Failures

For two years, a sophisticated multidisciplinary team was transported by means of a large mobile classroom to elementary schools. The team worked on a daily basis with teachers of a school for one month before moving on to another school. The work was highly oriented toward practicum and seminar experiences. It was quite successful in many ways. The handicapped pupils with whom the teachers worked gained, on the average, six months in reading, mathematics, spelling, and other skills during a one-month period. These initial gains were maintained and built upon in subsequent months (O'Donnell, 1969). Teachers were highly enthusiastic about this basically "inservice" approach.

I became convinced that the multidisciplinary team was not really needed in order to achieve similar, even better results, having become terribly impressed by the talent that existed among each of the some 20 facilities with whom we worked. Perhaps all that was needed was a teacher on the staff who would have time and responsibility for being an ongoing inservice facilitator for the staff.

Therefore, during the next year, we worked with 11 elementary schools, each of which had one of their own employees (usually a special education teacher) devote 50 percent or more time to trying to be the facilitator for the "same" inservice program which our team had provided previously. The only assistance provided to each school was the part-time consultation of one of our teachers who had served as a facilitator of our mobile classroom project. We had a great deal of success with this new indirect approach. The learning rates of both handicapped and other pupils in regular classrooms increased significantly (Ohlson, 1972) and most teachers were pleased with the experience. *However*, we had a number of significant failures and semi-successes among these schools.

The "System"

In retrospect we realized that we had not paid enough attention to the importance of the school *system*. We learned that "diagnosis" and "prescription" for a child, no matter how knowledgeable, was of little value if the child's teacher did not understand or welcome this knowledge for some reason. Thus, we shifted the focus of our work from children to teachers. So far, so good. But as we worked with teachers, we began to realize that even this was of little value if the school system within which the child and teacher worked did not understand or welcome suggested innovations. We could have all kinds of insight about the child's needs, the teacher could be able and willing to do a first-class job, but to no avail, except frustration for all, if the school administration and/or other aspects of the "system" resisted needed change.

Bringing a large, high-powered outside team into a school for an intensive experience had *temporarily* freed the "system" in our earlier work. However, we discovered later that when the team left the scene things tended to return to "normal" within a relatively short period of time. We had been flushed with success that was not really success and had underestimated the dynamics of the system.

Thus, when we dropped the team and then went into some schools with (a) "our" project and (b) "only" a consulting teacher, we were sometimes absorbed and/or rejected by the system. In about half the schools the project was rather successful, but we were just "lucky" in these cases that certain system factors were in the project's favor.

One of the most important things that we had failed to do was to respect the principal! We had unthinkingly let our behavior say to the building leader, *"We* have this nifty approach; we'll appreciate your cooperation, but please don't insert your influence to change it — to make it *yours."* Unthinkingly, we were "saying" the same thing to the faculty.

In truth, we had always given a great deal more choice and participative planning in our work than was common in most inservice or other school projects. We just did not go far enough, probably because we were blinded by our short-term successes and because participants requested "structure." *Now we understand that considerable structuring by project leaders is usually required in short-term work, whereas lasting and in-depth work usually requires a great deal of participative planning.*

In short, we must individualize growth experiences for teachers, principals, and school "systems" as well as for children! If growth experiences are to be meaningful, lasting, and important, they must "belong" to the learner, not be "imposed" by someone else.

The School Environment

So there was our basic failure, the negative side of our experience coin. However, we probably would never have recognized it and would have simply blamed those "uncooperative" so-and-so's if it hadn't been for the more important positive side of our experiences. We dropped the outside team in our work, as I mentioned earlier, because we came to recognize the enormous wealth of talent and constructive motivation among the adults in schools—teachers, principals, special service personnel, and others. Our schools are chock-full of beautiful people—people who are trying very hard to make education an enjoyable and productive experience for children. I am truly awed by most of the educators I have met, as people and as professionals.

However, our experiences led us to believe that schools, as presently constituted, tend to be pretty lousy places for these fine people to work! I consider it no overstatement to say that our school systems unintentionally are *destroying* large numbers of these educators, as people and as professionals. This statement often shocks these very educators, which further saddens me because that says that they do not even realize what is happening to them. Yet look around with fresh eyes and see the large proportion of public school educators who came into the profession full of energy, idealism, and creativity, but who are now lethargic, depressed, even bitter, and certainly resistant to change. Some are doing the last thing that they want to do—making school a dull and unproductive, if not unhappy, experience for children. About three years in the system and the honeymoon is over for most teachers, right? This is not true for all, of course, but it is true for *many*; it should not be true for *any*!

Why does this happen? I don't pretend to know all the answers to that agonizing question, but I'm convinced for good reasons born of a great deal of intimate experience with dozens of schools and hundreds of teachers that most of it boils down to a very simple but sad oversight: schools have forgotten that educators are people too. People. Just like the kids are people—deserving of respect and love. By love, I mean more than "sentiment." I don't mean "liking," for one can love without that in my book. Love means, in part, effort—effort to know a person well—effort to help him or her to be successful, to grow, to enjoy. Love means coming to value another because of his differences as well as his similarities. People who are loved grow. People who are not loved disintegrate.

If that's too philosophical, let me put it this way—education consists of meaningful exchanges between human beings. Schools typically are rich in human resources, but these resources are wasted because meaningful exchanges are inhibited, almost by design. People (and I'm thinking of educators in particular now) are terribly isolated from one another in schools. We couldn't have planned this deprivation better if we had consciously tried! Physical walls isolate one professional from another. Time schedules isolate. Psychological barriers, particularly authoritarian hierarchies, divide and isolate and hold off. The cruel fact is that an educator, fresh from college, is "plugged into" the system like an appliance and treated like a cog in a wheel, a step in a factory assembly line. People atrophy under these conditions.

ORGANIZATIONAL DEVELOPMENT AND RENEWAL

People of any age need *growth* environments. Nowhere is this more true than in education. If a teacher is to provide stimulation and meaning and enjoyment for her pupils, then *she* must be working in a stimulating, meaningful, enjoyable environment—a *growth* environment. Yet how is one to grow if there is no ongoing provision for personal and professional growth, if instead there is isolation, indifference, even punitiveness?

Again, our schools are rich with fine adult people and professionals. Among them, they *have* all the potential for meeting the needs of our handicapped and other children. The only thing needed is a means for *pooling* these resources so that these fine people can grow and enjoy, so that they in turn can create better growth environments for children.

Industry has recognized the need for renewal systems for quite some time. A whole body of experience and knowledge has now been built for modifying organizations so that human potential and enjoyment is maximized. Schools are just now becoming aware of this critical field, but we have some excellent leadership to tap. Richard Schmuck and others at the University of Oregon (Schmuck & Miles, 1971) are outstanding examples in this regard.

To return to our personal experiences and to mainstreaming, I now believe that concepts of *organizational development* are our best hope, not only for handicapped children in the mainstream, but for all children and all adults who participate in this crucial endeavor we call education. In the spring of 1971 with invaluable consultation from Alfred Brokes, who is experienced in education as well as in organizational development work, and understanding support from the Bureau for Handicapped Children, U.S. Office of Education, we launched "Project Catalyst."

Our basic goal remains the same as in the past—helping handicapped children in mainstream settings as much as possible. However, having learned from our previous mistakes as well as positive learnings, we are approaching the problem quite differently. In essence, we are asking (not telling) the educators in a variety of elementary schools what *they* see as their personal needs as well as what they see as the pupils' needs. We are asking *them* to identify their own resources, their personal and group strengths. We are asking them to identify *their* personal and building goals. We are asking *them* to create their own means for meeting their professional and pupil goals. We are asking them, in short, to design their own growth environments.

Very importantly, we are focusing our consultation on building leaders—elementary school principals. Some people seem to think that a principalship is a diminishing role. We firmly believe that the elementary school principal is in one of the *most* important professional positions in our entire society. The building principal is in a position to be a tremendous positive influence upon the professional lives of the teaching staff and, therefore, upon the educational lives of children.

Process Overviews

At its simplest level graphically, the Catalyst process looks something like this:

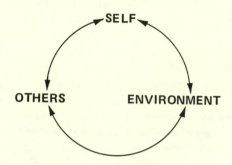

In words, two or more people agree to engage in a process of mutual growth. Each starts with *self* (as opposed to each trying to change the other) and asks others to provide information and moral support in this self-development effort. They create an environment (e.g., opportunities to interact constructively) which will enhance their efforts to growth together.

A little more specifically, the process looks like this:

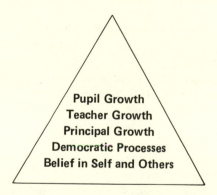

The foundation of the approach is a set of positive assumptions about people which the group will try to support in their day-to-day behaviors. *Belief in self and other* leads to creation of a *democratic environment* in which *principal growth* facilitates *teacher growth* which, in turn, facilitates *pupil growth*.

Finally, Figure 1 presents a somewhat expanded model of the Catalyst process showing major steps in a fairly sequentialized manner. In practice, activities often overlap one another.

Figure 1
CATALYST PROCESS

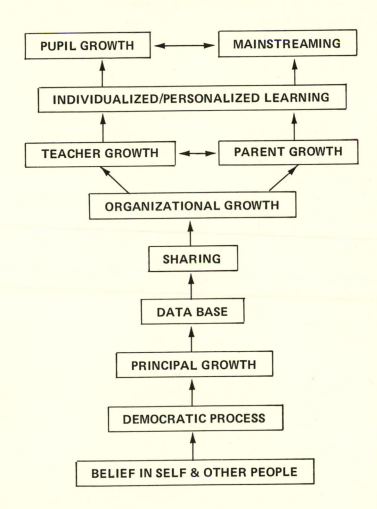

The Catalyst process might be dubbed "tough-minded humanism" because we think that love is very basic but is not enough. If we adults are to grow, just like the children, we need objectified information to help us know what we are

345

doing well and what needs to be worked on. *Data basis* for group decision-making is a critical need, as is data basis for individual decision-making in a democratic environment.

Meaningful data help us to (a) feel good about our successes and (b) set goals for further improvement. *Sharing,* the exchange of ideas and support among peers, becomes the major method for accomplishing individual and group goals. One of the outcomes of sharing is *organizational development,* procedures which facilitate goal attainment. The Catalyst process particularly emphasizes development or organizational procedures that promote ongoing *teacher growth.*

Parent growth is considered to be a very important area in the Catalyst process, but the *timing* of parental involvement is a point about which many people differ. Some individuals and schools believe that parents need to be brought into the process at the very beginning. Others feel that the school needs to get itself together "in house" before parents and other community members are involved extensively. Whatever the timing plan that is followed, we believe that parents *must* eventually become deeply involved in the life of the school if the professional staff is to maximize its effectiveness and enjoyment.

As teachers *and* parents grow in their abilities to *individualize* instruction, as they help children to individualize their own instruction, it becomes possible and very desirable to include a broader range of differences in "regular" classrooms, to include presently "sidetracked" children in the *mainstream* of life. When a teacher freely chooses to "mainstream" in the context of a relatively strong individualized program, we have found that the program for *all* children is enhanced and that the teacher experiences greater job satisfaction than when teaching to a narrow range of differences.

As the educators in the project define their own strengths, needs, goals, and means for meeting them through various forms of sharing and caring, we see a rapid growth in programs for individualizing and personalizing instruction in classrooms. To be sure, some of this movement existed previously on a piece-meal basis. People were trying before, without the help of Catalyst. However, I believe that it is fair to say that there is now an increasing *community* of effort and support and increasing encouragement of choice and creativity on the part of teachers, increasing interpersonal regard and more rapid individual as well as group growth.

Gains

Our initial prediction was that it would take two or three years before the indirect approach of "principal growth, leading to teacher growth, leading to pupil growth" would show any payoff for the children. But, like the adults, children showed significant growth in all three areas: skills, interpersonal relations, and enjoyment. For the total group of children (kindergarten through 6th grade), the average gain in *rate* of learning to read, according to state-mandated achievement testing, was 32%. Children who had scored in the lowest quartile in the fall of the first year, according to national norms, had an average increase in rate of learning to read of about 25%.

Very importantly, the schools which had become the most democratic made the greatest gains!

After two years of working together, our 10 schools had reduced the number of children who were being pulled out of "regular" classrooms for remedial work by over 50%. These children, in most cases, were doing better in "regular" classrooms than they had done before. It's not a 100% success story, to be sure. In fact, 2 of our 10 schools have not especially changed to date. Some of the children have *not* made it successfully in "regular" classrooms and continue to need "special" settings. However, strong beginnings, overall, have been made.

One of our schools, which has always had about 30 intermediate-aged children in self-contained classrooms for mentally retarded, now has *all* of the children functioning *more* successfully in "regular" classrooms. The "regular" pupils and classroom teachers are happier and more productive than they were three years ago because *they* have developed ways to pool their talents and support for one another. As one of the teachers recently told us, "A few years ago I was ready to quit teaching; I was so frustrated and tired by the end of the week. Now I feel so proud of what I'm doing and have lots of energy to devote to myself and my family." Sure, they still have problems, but it's a whole different world that they have created for *themselves!*

Insofar as mainstreaming organization is concerned, I see regular classrooms developing which look a great deal like the resource rooms which have been developing in special education. There will be a clearly stated continuum of academic and social skills toward which the teacher is working. There will be objective as well as subjective means for knowing what a child knows and needs to known on this continuum. There will be a variety of means by which a child can learn these skills and identification of the means which best suit his learning style at that point. There will be large group, small group, one-to-one and independent learning activities, peer teaching, learning centers, aides, team teaching, and inclusion of resource personnel *in* the classroom. Not all rooms will have all these features or any of them to the same degree, since each teacher is an individual and her differences *must* be respected. However, there will be an increase in individualization and personalization of instruction in the classroom coming from the *teacher* and from his or her colleagues in their efforts to create an enhanced learning environment for *themselves.*

Some handicapped pupils will be functioning in the classroom full time. Others will be functioning in a resource room on a full- or part-time basis, as *cooperatively* determined by the classroom teacher, the resource teacher, the

347

child, and others significant to such decisions. *Very* importantly, the resource teacher will be frequently working in regular classrooms as a teammate. The classroom teacher will be working in the resource room on occasion, with her entire class or with a few children.

Most importantly, teachers will be frequently and consciously learning from one another in various practica, much as *Teaching Triads* (Beery, 1972b).

Depending upon the particular school and its identified needs and desires, the Madison Plan, the Fail-Save plan, or some other plan modified or newly created by the staff may be utilized to assist in the mainstreaming and other processes. There is no one best mainstreaming organization for all schools. All I have been trying to say is that the organization should be generated by the entire staff, especially classroom teachers, based upon a self-created, ongoing staff and organizational development program for the building.

SUMMARY

Who do I think should "be mainstreamed"? *Everyone!* We cannot, in my opinion, successfully include children unless we include ourselves and all others who have a stake in the life of a school.

How should it be done? There are no programs "out there" that can provide more than a lead for you and your school. *You* must create the programs that you and your children need if success is to be yours. I believe that you need to help *general* education be in the forefront of any changes that are made, for the sake of *general* education as well as for handicapped kids! I think that you will need to have great respect for *data* in your efforts to plan, implement, and evaluate your progress.

When? I believe that all of us must make haste slowly, being sure that the field of general education has been plowed before seeds from "special" education are planted.

Where? Where ever there is a child, parents, professional, or other person who feels alone.

REFERENCES

Beery, Keith E. *Remedialdiagnosis.* San Rafael, California: Dimensions Publishing Company, 1968.

Beery, Keith E. *Models for Mainstreaming.* San Rafael, California: Dimensions Publishing Company, 1972a.

Beery, Keith E. *Teaching Triads.* San Rafael, California: Dimensions Publishing Company, 1972b.

Beery, Keith E. et al. *The Guts to Grow.* San Rafael, California: Dimensions Publishing Company, 1974.

O'Donnell, Patrick A. *Evaluation of the 1968-69 Remedialdiagnosis Implementation Study.* Sacramento, California: State Department of Education, Title VI A, Project Report, 1969.

Ohlson, Glenn A. *Evaluation of Project T. E. A. C. H.* Washington, D.C.: USOE Project Report, 1972.

Schmuck, Richard A. & Miles, Matthew E. *Organization Development in Schools.* Palo Alto: National Press Books, 1971.

Part 3
Approaches

Approaches for Alternative Programming: A Perspective

Nettie R. Bartel, Diane Bryen, Helmut W. Bartel
Temple University

With the increasing emphasis on equal opportunity for education for all children, educators have generated and applied, often desperately, a vast array of methods and approaches to meet the educational needs of all handicapped children. For the greater part of the last decade, this diversity in approaches and the resulting controversy in special education have focused primarily on finding the most effective administrative arrangement for delivering services to handicapped persons. Discussion has ranged from the pros and cons of special class placement to a number of alternatives including total integration of mildly handicapped youngsters into nongraded open school arrangements or partial integration of handicapped persons into traditional regular classrooms with the support of either itinerant teachers, resource rooms, or special class instructions. More recently, there has been a growing awareness among special educators that even the most "appropriate" administrative arrangement will not in and of itself create an equally appropriate model for instruction and learning. The controversy in special education has thus been extended to a description and analysis of various components of the instruction and learning process itself, as represented by the articles in this section.

When reading and evaluating these articles, the reader is confronted with a diversity of problems and issues. Some articles focus on one or more aspects of the content and goals of instruction (facts, cognitive skills, psycho-motor skills, creativity, etc.), others are directed toward a description of some of the necessary and more formal characteristics of the instructional process (assessment, evaluation, etc), while still others are meant to give guidance on the use of specific technological aids in the instructional process (e.g., the use of media).

As an aid in viewing these various problems and issues in some larger perspective we have found it useful to present a schematic description or model of the entire instructional process (Figure 1). The basic components of any instructional process variously involve a learner, a teacher, a curriculum, and a

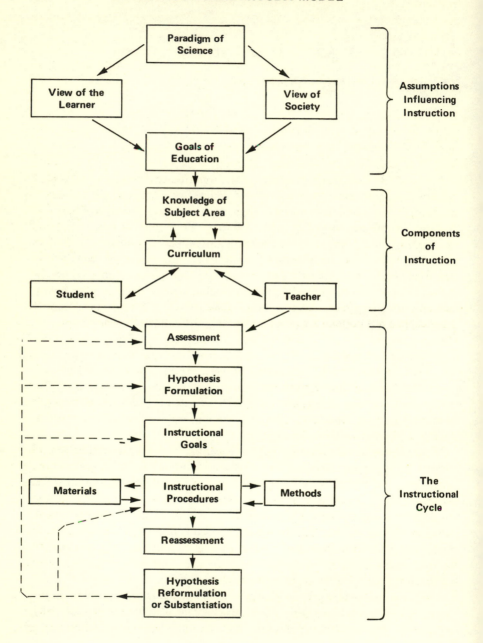

Figure 1
AN INSTRUCTIONAL PROCESS MODEL

knowledge base. The actual dynamic and sequential process of instruction, as effected by the various components, is characterized as a series of steps in an instructional cycle, including assessment, hypothesis formation, instructional goals, instructional procedures, reassessment, and hypothesis substantiation or reformulation.

ASSUMPTIONS INFLUENCING INSTRUCTION

Influencing all of these factors in an instructional process are a set of assumptions, stated either implicitly or explicitly, concerning one's view of the nature of knowledge, man, and society as well as one's assumptions about the overall, ultimate goals of education. These assumptions, we believe, are not only important but inevitable. The question is not whether the making of assumptions is permissible in science but rather, what kind of assumptions are made. Furthermore, and equally important, we wish to argue that these assumptions are not randomly or capriciously accepted by educators but reflect an overall "world view" or "paradigm of science" (Kuhn, 1962; Toulmin, 1967). It is a change of such a basic world view or "paradigm shift" (Segal & Lachman, 1972) in the sciences in general which we believe is beginning to be reflected in special education (Fisher & Rizzo, 1974) and as such may account not only for the current diversity of assumptions and approaches in aiding the handicapped but portend a new era of working with these persons.

The Paradigm of Science

Unlike the traditional mechanistic model of the natural science paradigm which used the basic metaphor of the machine, the organismic model of the new paradigm of science is based on the metaphor of the living organism (Matson, 1964; Overton & Reese, 1973).

Like a machine, the universe in the mechanistic world view was assumed to consist of discrete elements or particles (billiard balls) operating in a spatio-temporal field. Motion and relationships between such particles were explained as the application of forces, known as efficient and immediate causes. As a result it was assumed that in principle one could quantify and fully predict and control one's world. Science was seen as an objective method to accomplish these goals, divorced from the biases and active participation of the scientist or knower. Knowledge, as the product of this search, was seen as the progressive accumulation or accretion of objective facts.

The organismic world view, in contrast, perceives the world as an organic whole which is not equal simply to the sum of its parts (Cassirer, 1951). The essence of the world is not static and moved by efficient causes, but in continuous movement and in transition from one state to another by means of progressive differentiation and teleological causation. Strict quantification and prediction are thus seen as impossible in principle, to be approximated only in probabilistic terms. Knowledge in this paradigm is seen not as objective facts or as a passive copy of objective reality, but as constructive—thereby involving the knower. The process of science, like a game, is thus a process which involves the scientist and all of his assumptions. Furthermore, scientific progress is seen as a progressive qualitative transformation and reconstruction of scientific assumptions rather than a quantitative accumulation of objective facts. In short, the knower is now seen as central to the knowing process.

View of the Learner

As implied above, one's view of man is intimately related to one's overall view of the world and the assumed nature of knowledge. In a mechanistic world view the resulting model or metaphor of man is the reactive organism. Like the other parts of the universal machine, man is perceived as basically at rest and active only when activated by external forces; thus, all activities of man, whether behaving, perceiving, remembering, thinking, willing, or wishing, are viewed as phenomena which are ultimately reducible to simple units and efficient causes. Man as scientist, knower, or learner is only objectively and passively involved in the process of discovering objective reality.

In contrast, by viewing one's world as an organismic whole, dynamic and in process, one is led to perceive of man as an active organism actively engaged in the process of knowing. Knowledge is not seen as simply a passive copy of objective and static reality but rather as an active construction of reality.

Just as the scientist, as a living person, is perceived to engage in the process of scientific inquiry as a function of a certain set of assumptions and theoretical guidelines, so also is the individual learner seen as actively transforming all information in terms of encoding, constructing, and structuring his environment and his role in it. Viewed in this sense, a humanistic approach in psychology and education where the subject or learner and his perspective is taken into account (Giorgi, 1970) cannot simply be designated as soft-headed or altruistic but must be seen, in a very profound way, as basic to any scientific investigation.

The View of Society

Educators' view of man, as either an active or reactive organism, as well as their accepted goals of education are intimately related to their conception of the nature of society. There are at least two dimensions in one's view of society which can have dramatic implications for education. One can conceivably view society as either static or dynamic and as either unitary or pluralistic.

When espousing a relatively mechanistic world view, it is common for scientists and educators to perceive of society and culture as mechanistic and static. Moreover, since science and the process of knowledge acquisition are seen as resulting in a quantitative accumulation of objective facts, it is reasonable to perceive of society and culture as the socially structured guardian of this knowledge store. The goals of education are thus generated within the constraints of keeping the social order intact and indirectly preserving the knowledge base.

Within an organismic world view, society, like the world and man within it, is perceived of as dynamic and "in process." Society is qualitatively transformed, in this view, partly by the members in it. For man to live in such a society means not only to adjust to change but to take an active role in the very process of change.

The conception of society as either unitary or pluralistic in nature increases the complexity of the problem to be faced by educators. To perceive of society as essentially unitary in goals and function, or even as only ideally so, relegates education primarily to a conforming social-control function. A pluralistic conception of society, as implied by an organismic world view, cannot as easily espouse the simple knowledge transmission and conforming socialization functions of education. The educational process must instead direct itself to meeting the needs of, and perhaps creating, a pluralistic society.

The Goals of Education

An additional assumption influencing the instructional process concerns the goals of education. Even when schooling is custodial by nature (which precludes intentional instruction), education is influenced by the social and political changes experienced by the larger society. Education exists within a definite historical and social setting, and it can be said that education must meet the needs of a particular society in a particular time (Report of the Citizens Commission on Basic Education, 1973). It follows then that instruction will explicitly or implicitly reflect society's views of what people should do and know. Some may argue that the education process should promote competitiveness, because a democratic society is founded upon free enterprise and therefore implies the development of a "healthy" competitive spirit. Others may suggest that a goal of education is to prepare a pool of people with saleable skills so that they may join the established work force. The instructional process would therefore encourage the development of more passive skills or attitudes such as punctuality, following directions, deductive reasoning, etc. Still others may argue that the goal of education is to promote a lifelong interest in learning and social change and that both curriculum and instruction should promote curiosity, creativity, and participation by the child in decision making and problem solving.

While it is possible to list many alternative goals of education, Taba (1962) summarizes them by suggesting three main positions regarding the socio-political functions of education. Each of these functions has very direct implications for the instruction of handicapped children.

The first position views education as an agent for the preservation and transmission of the dominant culture. This position assumes the existence of a more formally absolute notion of what knowledge and skills are worth learning (a unitary curriculum), how that knowledge should be acquired (the instructional process), and a delineated set of criteria generated to assess when and to what degree a student has acquired that body of knowledge (assessment). The child, whether handicapped or not, is a relatively passive participant in the instructional process, his main role being to serve as the recipient of the knowledge, skills, and attitudes of his society. Not only does this goal of education imply a very restrictive concept of the child, the curriculum, and the instructional process, it can be argued that the more formally absolute the notions about learning and achievement, the greater are the chances of creating groups of "handicapped" persons. When measured against these formalized criteria, those who may have divergent learning or behavioral styles, expectations toward school, or linguistic patterns will have a high probability of being viewed and subsequently diagnosed as being deficient or deviant.

When the function of education is viewed as a potential transformer of society, then the process of instruction can be expanded to include a broader conception of what learning outcomes are acceptable. The child is viewed as more active, not only in acquiring knowledge, attitudes, and skills, but also in deciding the very nature of the educational experiences in which he will engage. Here the child is seen as a potential contributor to the society in which he will live in a way that cannot be predicted or prescribed in advance.

The third function of education described by Taba is that of emphasizing individual development. While the former positions view society as greatly important, this position relegates society's needs to lesser importance than the development and actualization of the child. The child is seen as actively initiating and participating in the instructional process, reconstructing his learning environment, and thereby "acting in accordance with the way he has constituted it" (Fischer & Rizzo, 1974). It therefore follows that the curriculum would be open and the instructional process characterized by the child initiating and the teacher responding (see Weikart, this volume). This view of education (as does the second position to a lesser extent) assumes that the handicapped child is responsible for his behavior, learning, and achievement, a view that educators have not widely held in relation to either the handicapped or nonhandicapped child.

COMPONENTS OF INSTRUCTION

We believe that there are four components of instruction which need to be considered in the overall process of instruction. They are the knowledge base, the curriculum, the student, and the teacher. The significance of each component, however, will be influenced by the assumptions described in the previous section.

The first component is the existence of a knowledge base. Instruction is not a contentless phenomenon. At its essence is some perception of what skills or knowledge are worth developing in students. While the nature and sequencing of this knowledge may not be unanimously accepted by all educators, instruction does not occur without some preconceived notion of what is worth knowing and how it is learned. Without a knowledge base reflecting a particular subject area, one is left with an empty technology of education. This is precisely what can occur when teachers are trained to utilize behavior modification or individualized/prescriptive teaching systems without integrating such systems with a knowledge of the content or skill area that reflects the desired outcome of the instructional effort. Once again, educators or epistemologists may not agree completely as to what knowledge is, or how it is acquired, or what skills within a particular subject area must be developed in the child. However, the instructional process cannot be isolated from a knowledge base, whether that base is commonly subscribed to or is controversial.

This knowledge base is then translated into a *curriculum* through the development of guidelines delineating the scope of a particular subject area and by sequencing the content into a hierarchy of concepts, facts, or strategies which will result in the acquisition, construction, or transformation of that knowledge base. Reflecting one's view of the child and of knowledge, the curriculum will either emphasize the learning of facts, concepts, or skills or will emphasize the active construction of knowledge by interacting with the environment.

Approaches to instruction must also include the *student* and a *teaching agent*. Johnson (1967) argues that it is the interaction between the teaching agent and an individual or individuals intending to learn that constitutes instruction. Not only does this argument stress the importance of the teacher in relationship to the student, but it also makes several assumptions about each partner in the teaching-learning process. The teacher is viewed as an agent or facilitator of learning, not a dispenser of knowledge. He participates in the process of instruction rather than determining it. While the teacher is seen as active, the child too is viewed as an active participant in the process, rather than a passive organism reacting to prearranged stimuli.

While it appears that maximum interaction among the four components of instruction would result in optimal learning by the student, different

359

approaches to instruction may relegate each component to greater or lesser significance. For example, some have argued that the scientific basis for viewing the nature of the child or the structure of knowledge is removed from the realities of teaching children and that this scientific knowledge base may be intercepted, modified, ignored, or denied by the teacher or may never reach the teacher. Therefore its effects may never be fully experienced in the instructional process. Educators and curriculum developers who are concerned with the huge gap which may exist between changes in knowledge and the integration of these changes by the teacher into the instructional process have argued for the development and use of "teacher-proof" curricula. This approach to curriculum establishes particular and specific instructional goals and their sequence, instructional procedures to be used to ensure that students attain these goals, and prescribed materials and methods to be used by the teacher along with criteria against which to measure the students' attainment of specified goals. All that is left for the teacher is the rigorous implementation of the prescriptions. The rationale for the development and use of teacher-proof curricula is that it minimizes teacher judgment and decision making, therefore "ensuring" that what is seen by the curriculum developers as the "truth" in the use of educational technology, modifications, developments in the knowledge base, or changes in the goals of education would bypass the active involvement of the teacher and be imparted directly to the student. While an analysis of proposed teacher-proof curricula is beyond the scope of this essay, the reader should carefully consider what assumptions this proposal makes about the roles and nature of both the child and the teacher as well as the validity of the entire instructional process. In contrast to teacher-proof curricula, Weikart's article in this section recommends that serious consideration be given to the interaction of the curriculum, the child, and the teacher.

THE INSTRUCTIONAL CYCLE

The instructional cycle, while treated separately in this section, is affected by both the assumptions and the components of the instructional process. Whether or not there is an established curriculum for a particular subject area, the teacher's initial task is one of assessing the student's development within a particular subject area. Which areas are assessed will depend upon what the goals of education are seen to be (by the teacher, by a curriculum committee, by a state legislature) in order to determine the extent to which a given student measures up to explicit or implicit educational goals. This *initial assessment* may actively involve the student in a structured situation such as answering questions, following directions, or performing particular tasks (reading a passage, solving a mathematical problem, or dressing). The assessment may also involve the student in a more naturalistic setting, where he is observed manipulating objects, playing in a group, or talking with his peers. Whether the assessment is conducted using norm-referenced techniques, criterion-referenced evaluation tools, direct behavioral observations, or information derived from the instructional cycle itself, the results of this assessment will generate a set of hypotheses concerning what the child is like, what he can do, and perhaps what strategies the student uses in attacking the particular tasks. *Hypothesis formulation* is used to describe this stage in the instructional cycle rather than the more commonly used term "diagnosis." This choice of terms is intentional, for at this stage of the cycle judgment about the child should be viewed as tentative and subject to reformulation as the student and teacher progress through the instructional cycle. Hypotheses about the child may also be dramatically altered with subsequent changes in either educational goals, knowledge of the subject area, or change (or perceived changes) concerning the roles of the teacher and the child in the instructional process.

On the basis of this set of hypotheses, *instructional goals* are developed. These goals may be established exclusively by the teacher in collaboration with resource persons such as an itinerant teacher or child study team, or the goals may be established utilizing the active input of the student. How these goals are established will be directly influenced by the teacher's conception of the nature of the child (active versus reactive) and by the perceived goals of education (societal preservation versus societal transformation versus individual development). The nature of these instructional goals will be additionally influenced by the knowledge base in a particular subject area as well as by conceptions about the nature of knowledge.

Once instructional goals have been developed, *instructional procedures* are utilized to facilitate the student's attainment of these goals. The procedures to be implemented, including methodology and materials, will implicitly or explicitly reflect assumptions about the nature of the teacher, child, knowledge, and goals of education. For example, use of task analysis procedures, behavior modification, drill, and lecture techniques all assume that if stimuli are properly arranged and presented the child will passively assimilate the material and integrate it into an already existing knowledge and behavioral repertoire. In contrast, when the child is viewed as an active, experiencing, and purposive being, instructional procedures will need to include activities which are child-initiated and determined. These procedures might include the use of manipulative, open-ended materials such as cuissannaire rods and geoboards as well as various teaching methods which encourage the child to reconstruct not only the solutions to problems but the problems themselves.

As the child engages in the instructional cycle, *assessment* of the child's performance will be reconsidered. This is not to imply that after every instructional interaction the teacher will formally administer or readminister a series of evaluative tests. What occurs is that the teacher observes what the child does when encountering a particular instructional task and how he arrives at his solutions, whether correct or incorrect. Jackson and Belford (1965) indicate that it is the continual flow of information provided by students during instruction that results in the evaluation of the instructional episode. On the basis of this *new* information, initial hypotheses about what the child can and cannot do, what reinforcers are most effective, or what strategies a child uses in attempting to solve a particular problem may result in either *hypothesis substantiation or reformulation.* Because the instructional cycle is a dynamic one, the teacher may feed back to any one of the previous stages in the cycle. Hypothesis reformulation may force the teacher to reconsider previous conceptions about the nature of the child, his role as a teacher, or the goals of education. Knowledge previously unknown to the teacher about reading or how children acquire language or mathematics concepts may result in a modification in any one of the stages of the instructional cycle. In some instances, changes in a particular stage of the cycle may be externally imposed on the teacher due to schoolwide, districtwide, or even statewide acceptance of a particular curriculum. Here, decisions influencing the instructional process may totally bypass the teacher. Within the instructional cycle itself, hypothesis reformulation may also result in changes in instructional goals or procedures. It may even require that the teacher return to the beginning stage of assessment, this time asking different questions about the child.

While this proposed instructional process model is not designed to reflect issues unique to the education of handicapped children, the factors previously considered and their influence on the instructional cycle may result in unique approaches to teaching handicapped youngsters. It may, however, duplicate approaches to teaching nonhandicapped children with only the administrative arrangement modified to accommodate the "special" educational needs of handicapped children. If the latter situation is a truer portrayal of reality, then special educators must seriously reconsider their role in educating the handicapped.

REFERENCES

Cassirer, E. *The Philosophy of the Enlightenment.* Boston: Beacon Press, 1951.

Fischer, C. T. & Rizzo, A. A. "A Paradigm for Humanizing Special Education." *The Journal of Special Education, 8,* 1974 (321-329).

Giorgi, A. *Psychology as a Human Science.* New York: Harper & Row, 1970.

Jackson, P. W. & Belford, E. "Educational Objectives and the Joys of Teaching." *The School Review,* 1965 (267-291).

Johnson, M. "Definitions and Models in Curriculum Theory." *Educational Theory, 17,* 1967 (24-31).

Kuhn, T. S. *The Structure of Scientific Revolutions.* Chicago: The University of Chicago Press, 1962.

Matson, F. *The Broken Image: Man, Science and Society.* New York: George Braziller, 1964.

Overton, W. & Reese, H. W. "Models of Development: Methodological Implications." In J. R. Nesselroade & H. W. Reese (Eds.), *Life-Span Developmental Psychology.* New York: Academic Press, 1973.

Report of the Citizens Commission on Basic Education to the Governor of Pennsylvania. Harrisburgh: Commonwealth of Pennsylvania, 1974.

Segal, E. M. & Lachman, R. "Complex Behavior of Higher Mental Processes: Is There a Paradigm Shift?" *American Psychologist, 27,* 1972 (46-55).

Taba, H. *Curriculum Development: Theory and Practice.* New York: Harcourt, Brace & World, 1962.

Toulmin, S. *The Philosophy of Science: An Introduction.* London: Hutchinson University Library, 1967.

In the following article are 12 guidelines for creating and modifying materials that are practical, easily understood, and applicable to all children, regardless of label. Teachers will find these guidelines most valuable. In addition, the article features a dimension often overlooked—evaluation. Specific steps are provided for teachers to employ to determine whether instructional practices are working and to what extent they are effective.

Creating and Evaluating Remediation for the Learning Disabled

Esther H. Minskoff
Groves School, Hopkins, Minnesota

Inasmuch as the learning disabled constitute one of the most heterogeneous populations of children, the learning disabilities teacher must be able to construct and utilize a great variety of teaching methods and materials. Although it is wondrously simple to do so, it is certainly educationally debilitating to use but one or just a few teaching methods and materials for all learning disabled children. Regrettably, for some types of learning disabilities there are few, if any, published methods and materials. Even if the many published methods and materials are to be used for a particular learning disabled child, they must be modified to his individual learning characteristics. Therefore, the primary purpose of this article is to guide the teacher in creating methods and materials where none exist and in modifying existing methods and materials so that the proper remediation can be provided for any learning disabled child.

Since there is presently a strong and justifiable emphasis on the effectiveness of remediation, a second purpose of this article is to aid the teacher in evaluating the adequacy of the remedial methods and materials she has created or modified for a specific child.

Fortunately, the research on the effectiveness of various remedial methods and materials is growing. The learning disabilities teacher, however, must learn to be a knowledgeable consumer of such research if the current trend of blanket acceptance or rejection of remedial techniques is to be avoided. Hence, a third objective of this article is to provide the learning disabilities teacher with certain criteria for realistically assessing research on the efficacy of remedial methods and materials.

GUIDELINES

The following 12 guidelines are to be used by the teacher as a basis for creating or modifying remedial methods and materials. These guidelines are based on the author's experiences in constructing the *MWM Program for Developing Language Abilities* (Minskoff, Wiseman & Minskoff, 1972). Although many of the examples cited are for learning disabilities in language, these guidelines are applicable to remedial methods and materials for all types of learning disabilities.

1. Direct Remediation to the Child's Learning Disabilities, Not His Learning Abilities

Remediation must be directed to a child's learning disabilities. If it is not, then the child will have certain areas of development in which he has not reached a basic level of competence. This, in turn, prevents him from mastering certain requirements for school and social adjustment.

Too often remediation is not directed to a child's disability areas because of tenuous assumptions about prerequisite learnings, lack of understanding of the nature of the disability areas, and inadequate diagnosis.

Example of tenuous assumptions: The frequent practice of having a reading disabled child walk a balance beam even though he has no apparent motor problem is tied to the unsupported premise that development of balance is a required skill for reading. After the child has mastered walking the balance beam, he is no more ready to learn to read than previously, and precious learning time has been lost.

Example of lack of understanding: Limited comprehension of the 12 ITPA areas and their relation to the ITPA communication model often leads to inappropriate remediation. The Judy "Sequee" materials, in which a child logically arranges a series of pictures, are often used for a child with a Visual Memory disability. There is no memory component involved in the use of these materials; rather, the associaton process is involved. Understanding of the ITPA processes would not result in such erroneous usage of materials.

Example of inadequate diagnosis: Remediation of a reading disability that is based solely on reading achievement tests such as the Wide Range Achievement Test (Jastak &

Jastak, 1965) cannot be adequate as there is no information obtained concerning the reading processes of the child. Such information must be ascertained from more comprehensive diagnostic reading tests such as the Spache Diagnostic Reading Scales (Spache, 1963) and from diagnostic teaching.

2. Provide Remediation That Fits the Specific Symptoms of a Child's Learning Disability

There are many different symptoms associated with each type of learning disability. The specific symptoms of each child's disability can be ascertained from diagnostic teaching and from an analysis of the results of screening instruments and standardized achievement and diagnostic tests.

Example: Two children may have disabilities in Auditory Reception. However, one child may have difficulty only in understanding lengthy material such as series of oral directions, while the other child may have difficulty only with specific speech sounds such as rhymes. Obviously, each of these children requires totally different programs of remedial methods and materials.

Example: Some teachers use one method exclusively—such as Fernald's Kinesthetic Method of Teaching Reading (1943) or the Gillingham-Stillman Multi-Sensory Approach (1965)—for all children who have reading disabilities even though some of the children have difficulties with the visual aspects of reading, others with the auditory aspects, and still others with auditory-visual integration. The category of "reading disabilities" is global and cannot be used as the basis for providing remediation without knowledge of the specific symptoms of a child's reading difficulty.

3. Use the Child's Learning Abilities as Aids in Remediating His Learning Disabilities

It is necessary to use a child's learning abilities as instructional aids; therefore, his abilities as well as his disabilities must be determined in the diagnosis. The child's learning abilities are used temporarily until he begins to develop some competence in his disability areas and, when possible, they are phased out. If reliance on his abilities is not gradually eliminated, the child will not learn to function independently in his disability areas.

Example: A 7-year-old has a disability in Auditory Reception (4 year level), but he has an ability in Visual Reception (8 year level). To present only auditory material to such a child is to repeat an approach which has already proven ineffective. Initially, pictures and other visual cues must be used as aids. Once the child progresses to a higher level of functioning in understanding what he hears, these visual cues are gradually dropped and only auditory materials are used.

Example: A 11-year-old boy who has a learning disability in Auditory Memory (6 year level) and a learning ability in the association process (about the 12-year level) can be taught to memorize nonmeaningful materials such as the months of the year with the aid of meaningful associations. The 12 months of the year may be separated into seasonal groupings with the meaning cue of weather added. To further aid recall of each month, other specific cues are used (e.g., November is the month with Thanksgiving).

As the child recalls the months in each grouping, they are combined. First, he is to recall 6 months, then 9 months, and finally 12 months. The meaning cues are dropped and only reintroduced when the child has difficulty recalling any month.

4. Provide Remediation at the Child's Level of Functioning in His Disability Area

The child's level of functioning in his disability area is the appropriate instructional level for remediation. This level is lower than his CA or MA. The instructional level can be obtained from diagnostic teaching and from the age scores on standardized tests, such as the PA of the Frostig Developmental Test of Visual Perception (Frostig, et al., 1964) and the PLA of the ITPA (Kirk, McCarthy & Kirk, 1968).

Example: If a 7-year-old obtained a 3-6 PLA on the Grammatic Closure subtest of the ITPA, then grammatic structures for a normal child of 3½ would be taught. These would include grammatic structures such as action and descriptive sentences, but not structures with the passive voice or the "if-then" construction which are mastered at higher age levels.

A knowledge of child development norms is necessary for determining which activities best fit at particular age levels.

Example: A knowledge of developmental norms for copying shapes would indicate that a child with a fine motor problem would be taught to draw a circle when he is functioning at the 3-year level, a square at 4, a triangle at 5, and a diamond at 8 (Beery, 1967).

5. Include Both Testing and Teaching in Remediation

Both testing and teaching are inherent components of remediation. Testing in remediation does not involve the use of formal tests; rather, it involves the clinical use of teaching activities to continuously determine what the child has learned and what he has not learned. Naturally, testing is necessary *before* teaching to discover what learnings the child has not mastered so these can be taught. Testing is also necessary *after* teaching to ascertain the degree to which the child has mastered the material that was presented.

In both testing and teaching, there is a presentation of a stimulus to which the child makes a response. In testing, nothing occurs between the stimulus and the child's response. In teaching, strategies are employed between the stimulus and the response. The purpose of these strategies is to build in the desired responses if they have not been acquired. If they have been acquired, these strategies then serve to strengthen the responses.

Strategies differ for each remedial method and set of materials.

Example: Two strategies used to train a child's Visual Memory are *tracing* and *labeling*. If a child's Visual Memory is being tested, the visual stimulus of the word "cat" is presented; then the child writes the word from memory. If he cannot recall it, this word is then taught. Teaching in this case differs from testing in that the visual stimulus of the word "cat" is presented, and the child traces each letter as he says the letter names. Then he writes the word from memory.

Example: When testing a child's Verbal Expression, the child is asked to describe objects he sees. If the child is being taught, he is trained to describe certain aspects of people, animals, and things (e.g., color, shape, label, function, action, etc.). Teaching in this instance differs from testing in that the teacher draws from specific categories of questions which she consistently asks the child. She gradually phases out each category as the child independently begins to use it. Her teaching is successful when the child spontaneously describes all stimuli using these categories as an internal model of self-questioning.

The essential ingredient of remediation involves these specific strategies. Learning disabled children cannot master what is to be learned without them. If methods and materials are presented without such strategies, then the children are being tested and not taught.

6. Gradually Increase the Difficulty Level of the Stimulus

Stimuli presented to the child should be structured in such a way as to start with an easy stimulus and gradually work to more difficult stimuli.

Example: When training a Visual Reception disability, concrete stimuli such as actual objects and people should be used initially. After these are mastered, more abstract materials such as pictures are used, then photographs and realistic color drawings, then black and white line drawings and, finally, stick figures. At the most abstract level, symbols such as letters and numbers are employed.

Remedial materials must be selected on the basis of where a particular child is functioning in terms of the difficulty level of the stimulus.

7. Gradually Increase the Difficulty Level of the Response

The response required from a child should be structured in such a way as to elicit easy responses at first, such as recognition responses, and gradually work to more difficult ones, such as recall responses.

Example: When training an Auditory Association disability, a recognition task such as the following is first used. "Which one doesn't fit—an apple, orange, hamburger, or banana?" The required response is relatively easy as the child must select the correct response from the 4 alternatives. After this is mastered, a recall task in which the child gives the category label is used. "What are an apple, an orange, and a banana?" This is more difficult as the child must produce from his response repertoire the one correct answer. At the most difficult level, a recall task where the child generates the members of a category is used. "What are all the fruit you can name?" This is the most difficult as the child must produce a number of correct answers from his response repertoire.

Most remedial materials require only one type of response. Therefore, the teacher must construct different levels of responses using the same teaching materials. Then she must determine the most appropriate level of response difficulty for a particular child.

8. Provide Small Steps in a Graduated Sequence of Learning

The child must be moved to higher levels of performance in his disability areas in very small steps. Therefore, it is necessary for the teacher to formulate the total learning sequence from the child's starting point to the child's final performance goal. She then must break this sequence of learning into small graduated steps. In this way the child will experience success and a firm foundation of learning will be established.

> *Example*: When training Visual Memory, the strategy of vanishing (Skinner, 1968) can be used to break the task into small steps. The complete visual stimulus such as the word "dog" is presented. Then the last letter is removed and the child must recall it (do_) This is the easiest letter for him to recall as it is the last letter he saw. After this is mastered, the first letter is removed (_og), and at a still higher level the middle letter is removed (d_g). Next, the 2 final letters are removed (d__). After this is learned, the initial 2 letters (__g) are removed. At the highest level, the child must recall all 3 letters he saw (___). Preceding the total recall task with 5 smaller steps ensures the solid development of the child's Visual Memory for letters.

9. Direct Remediation to the Child's Individual Rate of Progress

Regardless of whether a child is being given remediation in a group or on an individual basis, it must be geared to his own individual rate of progress. Therefore, the teacher must keep records of each child's progress so she can determine when each child is ready to move to a more difficult level. To do this, the teacher must establish a criterion level of mastery—that is, the number of correct responses required to define a child's mastery of a particular learning. It is suggested that a 90% criterion level of mastery be used. When a child correctly responds to a specific task 90% of the time (e.g., 9 out of 10 times, 18 out of 20, or 90 out of 100), the teacher moves the child to the next more difficult level in the sequence of learning. All learning disabled children vary in their rates of progress thereby making it necessary for the teacher to keep records of each individual's progress. Movement to a more difficult level should never be determined by the entire group's readiness or by a predetermined period of time.

> *Example*: A child with an Auditory Memory disability was taught to follow directions. Initially, he was taught to follow one direction at a time. He was able to do this 90% of the time after 16 trials. Then, series of 2 directions were given, and he reached the 90% mastery level after 37 trials. Finally, he was required to recall series of 3 directions, and it took him 112 trials to reach the 90% level.

10. Make the Content of the Remedial Methods and Materials of Social or Academic Value to the Child

The content of remediation should be of some social or academic significance. There is no logical reason for training a child's Auditory Memory for letters with nonsense words when actual spelling words that the child must learn can be used. This common practice has no academic value.

Most learning disabled children have a great deal of information to acquire because their disabilities have often prevented them from gaining this in school. Therefore, as much information as possible must be provided through the content of the remedial materials. The content of the remediation is primarily determined by the curricular demands of the child's grade placement and his own unique interests.

Example: A 9-year-old child with an Auditory Association disability should not be required to answer inferential, reasoning, and other types of association questions about fiction stories only. Rather, stories with content, such as those usually presented in the third grade, should be given (e.g., social studies units on transportation, communication, food, shelter, clothing, or the city).

Example: A 13-year-old boy in seventh grade who has a Visual Perception problem should not be given materials such as the Frostig Program for the Development of Visual Perception (Frostig & Horne, 1964). He should be receiving remedial instruction using maps, graphs, traffic signs, fractions, and other such academic material that ordinarily he would be expected to master in the seventh grade.

Although it is of utmost importance to stress academics, it is equally as important to stress the social aspects of learning. If a child has a problem in fine motor coordination, it is much more meaningful to teach him to tie his shoes, buckle his belt, button his shirt, cut with a knife, and other such social tasks than to make marble board designs or work with parquetry blocks.

11. Build Transfer into Remediation

It cannot be assumed that a child will automatically transfer learning from one type of material to other types of materials or situations. Remediation must be planned to provide for transfer to all types of materials and situations the child will encounter.

Unfortunately, this author has encountered learning disabilities teachers who state they are not responsible for effecting transfer from some singular type of remediation they may provide (e.g., perceptual motor training) to the child's work in the regular classroom. It is equally regrettable that some regular classroom teachers do not, or cannot, facilitate appropriate transfer from individual remedial sessions (with a learning disabilities teacher) to the child's regular classroom work. Remediation can never succeed in helping the child nor can the field of learning disabilities ever completely become a viable entity without a radical turnabout in the views as well as the skills of these teachers.

12. Restructure a Task When a Child Cannot Master It

The teacher must know how to restructure a task if a child does not master it in the way she tries to teach it. Restructuring strategies are probably one of the most important elements of remediation since few, if any, learning disabled children will automatically master all the tasks presented to them.

Naturally, restructuring strategies differ for each remedial method and set of materials. However, some of the more useful ways of restructuring are described.

Rearrange the stimulus. With this strategy, a visual stimulus may be rearranged or an auditory stimulus may be rephrased.

> *Example*: If a child with a Visual Reception disability could not determine which of 2 groups of blocks was bigger, one group might be placed under the other so that the child could match them.

> *Example*: If a child with a Verbal Expresson disability could not respond to the question, "Of all the children in your family, which one would you say is the oldest?" it might be rephrased to "Who's the oldest kid in your house?"

Give additional cues in the same channel. Here, more visual cues are added to a visual task and more auditory cues are added to an auditory task.

> *Example:* If a child with a Visual Closure disability could not tell that a tail was missing from an incomplete picture of a dog, a complete picture of another dog would be presented so that the child could make a visual comparison of the pictures.

> *Example*: If a child with an Auditory Association disability could not complete an unfinished story, the teacher might give a one-word auditory cue so that the child could build an ending around it.

Give additional cues in a different channel. With this strategy, auditory or kinesthetic cues might be added to a visual task. Or, for an auditory task, visual or kinesthetic cues might be added.

> *Example*: If a child with a Manual Expression disability could not pantomime the use of an object in a picture, the teacher might give verbal directions as to how to execute the pantomime.

> *Example*: If a child with an Auditory Reception disability could not execute a series of oral directions, the teacher might look or point toward each of the objects involved in the directions. If actions are involved in the directions, she might perform an abbreviated version of each of the actions expected of the child.

Lead the child to discover the correct response. With this strategy, the teacher asks certain questions that lead the child to discover the correct response. This strategy is derived from the inductive teaching method in which discovery of the correct response is a major component (Goldstein, Mischio & Minskoff, 1969; Mischio, 1973).

> *Example*: If a child with a Visual Association disability could not make up a picture to complete an unfinished series of 3 pictures, the teacher would ask questions about each of the pictures presented as well as inferential questions leading to the most likely picture to complete the series.

Use a cue at a lower difficulty level. Here, there is a return to a step at a lower difficulty level in the graduated sequence of learning.

> *Example*: If a child with an Auditory Reception disability could not recall the beginning sound of the word "boy," the teacher would use a recognition task which is at a lower difficulty level than a recall task (e.g., "Does *boy* begin with *b, g,* or *do*?").

> *Example*: If a child with a Grammatic Closure disability could not construct an action sentence about a picture of a boy running, the teacher would provide a sentence completion task that is at a lower difficulty level than the total production task. She would start a sentence and have the child complete it. "The boy..."

Give the correct response. This strategy should be used only as a last resort when there are no other restructuring strategies that can be used for the situation.

> *Example*: If a child with an Auditory Reception disability could not discriminate 2 environmental sounds as the same or different when he looks at the sound sources, then the correct response would be given by the teacher.

Giving the correct response is the least desirable strategy because it tends to add to the child's feelings of failure and his dependence upon the teacher or other students for getting the correct response.

TEACHER EVALUATION OF EFFECTIVENESS

Evaluation is a necessary step which follows the diagnosis and remediation of a child's learning disability. Such evaluation is too often unwittingly omitted from the diagnostic-remedial process. When the teacher should evaluate depends upon the severity of the child's learning disability and the frequency of the remedial sessions. The more severe the learning disability or the less frequent the remedial sessons, the longer the period of time necessary before the teacher can adequately evaluate the effectiveness of the remedial methods and materials she has been using with a particular child.

The data used for evaluation are the same as those used to make the original diagnosis of the child's learning disability. The sources of such data are shown in Figure 1.

Step I: Diagnostic Teaching

The teacher assesses the child's present performance in relation to his performance at the start of remediation. She analyzes his performance using some of the guidelines discussed in the previous section. Can the child function in his disability area without the aid of his learning abilities? Has the child progressed to a higher instructional level in remediation? Can the child function in his disability area without the aid of teaching strategies? Can the child

Figure 1
DATA FOR EVALUATING REMEDIATION

Step I: Diagnostic Teaching

Child has improved in remediation if he:	Child has NOT improved in remediation if he:	
a. can function without aid of learning abilities	a. cannot function without aid of learning abilities	Assess original diagnosis and alter accordingly.
b. has progressed to higher instructional level	b. has not progressed to higher instructional level	Assess adequacy of remediation on basis of following variables and alter accordingly:
c. can perform without aid of teaching strategies	c. cannot perform without aid of teaching strategies	a. subareas of remediation
d. has progressed to more difficult stimuli	d. has not progressed to more difficult stimuli	b. adequacy of child's learning abilities
e. has progressed to more difficult responses	e. has not progressed to more difficult responses	c. instructional level
f. has progressed to more advanced steps in sequence of learning	f. has not progressed to more advanced steps in sequence of learning	d. teaching strategies
g. has increased his rate of reaching mastery level	g. has not increased his rate of reaching mastery level	
h. requires fewer restructuring strategies	h. requires same number of restructuring strategies	

Step II: Testing

Child has improved on testing if he scores significantly higher on achievement and diagnostic tests used for original diagnosis.	Child has NOT improved on testing if he scores at same level on achievement and diagnostic tests used for original diagnosis.	
		Analyze tests and nature of remediation and minimize test results if child seems to have been helped by remediation.
		Assess adequacy of remediation on basis of following variables and alter accordingly:
		a. subareas of remediation
		b. transfer
		c. social and academic behaviors

Step III: Observation of Social and Academic Behaviors

Child has improved if he can adequately perform social and academic behaviors he could not do prior to remediation.	Child has NOT improved if he still cannot adequately perform social and academic behaviors he could not do prior to remediation.	
Treat other untreated learning disabilities.	Stop intensive remediation and give supportive remediation.	Assess remediation in terms of transfer and social and academic relevance, and alter accordingly.

respond to more difficult stimuli in his disability area? Can the child make more difficult responses in his disability area? Has the child progressed to more advanced steps in the graduated sequence of learning? Does the child reach his mastery level at a faster rate? Does the child require fewer restructuring strategies to master the task?

If the answers to most or all of these questions are affirmative, then the teacher may conclude that the child has profited from remediation and proceeds to Step II of evaluation.

If the answers to most or all of the above questions are negative, then the teacher would conclude that remediation has not been successful. The teacher then assesses the original diagnosis to determine if it is indeed appropriate to the child and whether a rediagnosis is in order. Should the original diagnosis prove to be appropriate, then the teacher evaluates the adequacy of the remediation on the basis of the following variables: Is the remediation centered on the most critical subareas or symptoms of the child's disability? Does the child have the learning abilities that are required as aids? Is the remediation at the suitable instructional level? Are the teaching strategies effective? On the basis of this analysis, the teacher should modify the remediaton.

Step II: Testing

If the child shows improvement in remediation, then the same achievement and diagnostic tests used in the original diagnosis are used to measure the child's progress. Should the child obtain significantly higher retest scores, the teacher would then move to Step III of evaluation.

If the child does not obtain significantly higher retest scores, the teacher must analyze the nature of the remediation in relation to the nature of the tests. Discrepant findings between Step I and Step II are often due to the different subareas or symptoms stressed in a particular test as opposed to those stressed in remediation. For example, in the diagnostic process the Visual Memory subtest of the ITPA uses nonmeaningful, unfamiliar symbols, while the remediation of a Visual Memory disability usually stresses symbols such as letters and numbers. Even though the child's Visual Memory for letters and numbers may have improved as a result of remediation, there may be no transfer to the nonmeaningful symbols of the ITPA. In such instances, the results of the test must be placed in proper perspective and minimized. In other cases, remediaton may have been inappropriate. For example, too few subareas or symptoms of the disability may have been stressed, or there was no attention to transfer or to the inclusion of relevant social and academic learnings. Remediaton must then be altered accordingly.

Step III: Observation of Social and Academic Behaviors

When a child has improved in remediation and in test scores, it must be determined if this improvement is being manifested in the child's social and academic performance. Thus, it is necessary for the teacher to channel and record her observations of social and academic behaviors through the use of screening instruments such as the Inventory of Language Abilities of the MWM Program (Minskoff, Wiseman & Minskoff, 1972).

If improvement in social and academic behaviors is found to corroborate the improvement found in diagnostic teaching and with tests, the teacher then proceeds to treat the child's other learning disabilities that have been given little or no instructional attention. If the child has no other disabilities, then intensive remediation is curtailed and supportive remediation is provided. After intensive remediation is stopped, most children cannot be expected to progress at a "normal" rate in their former disability areas (Balow, 1965; Lovell, Byrne & Richardson, 1963). If they are not given some form of special supportive attention at certain intervals, they may again evidence significant problems. For example, a 13-year-old may have had an Auditory Reception disability that made it difficult for him to learn to read by a phonic method when he was 7 years old. Remediation was given at that time, and he was able to master rudimentary phonics. Now he is enrolled in French where strong demands are made on his Auditory Reception. Specific remedial methods and materials must be designed and provided until he can meet the requirements of mastering French.

If there is no improvement noted in the child's social and academic behaviors, the teacher must analyze the remediation for transfer and for inclusion of relevant social and academic learnings. Then she must alter the remediation accordingly.

RESEARCH

To be a knowledgeable consumer of remedial methods and materials, the teacher must be able to assess the research concerned with remediation. She must be aware of certain relevant variables involved in assessing such studies. Although there are other variables that are important in terms of statistics and research design, only the variables relevant to the teacher are discussed here. These are shown in Figure 2.

Figure 2
VARIABLES FOR TEACHERS TO USE IN ASSESSING RESEARCH ON REMEDIATION

I. SAMPLE OF SUBJECTS
   A. Were the subjects learning disabled?
   B. How were the subjects' learning disabilities operationally defined?
   C. How severe were the subjects' learning disabilities?
   D. What were the background characteristics of the subjects (e.g., age, learning abilities, IQ, social class, and race)?

II. NATURE OF TREATMENT
   A. What time factors were involved (e.g., length of remedial sessions, frequency of sessions, and total number of sessions)?
   B. Was remediation given on an individual, small group, or large group basis?
   C. What was the theoretical basis of the remediation?
   D. What were the specific remedial methods and materials used in terms of each of the guidelines presented in this article (e.g., symptoms treated, abilities used as aids, instructional level, strategies, level of difficulty of stimulus and response, sequence of learning, mastery level, transfer, social and academic relevance, and restructuring strategies)?

III. NATURE OF TEACHERS PROVIDING REMEDIATION
   A. What was the nature of the teachers' training?
   B. What was the nature of the teachers' experience?

IV. EXPERIMENTAL DESIGN
   A. Was a control group used?
   B. If a control group was used, on what variables was it matched to the treatment group?
   C. If one subject was used, was adequate baseline data provided?

V. ANALYSIS OF RESULTS
   A. Were statistics used to analyze findings?
   B. Was reevaluation done "blind"?
   C. Were relevant tests used for reevaluation?
   D. Was reevaluation data from diagnostic teaching or social and academic behaviors obtained?

VI. CONCLUSIONS FROM DATA
   A. Were conclusions warranted on basis of results?
   B. Was there complete acceptance or rejection of remedial methods or materials?

Sample of Subjects

The subjects used in the study must be described in detail so that the teacher can determine the degree of generalizability possible from the children in the study to the groups of learning disabled children with whom she is working.

Whether the subjects in a study were actually learning disabled or not is an important factor. Despite titles of studies or labels assigned to the subjects, some studies are conducted with non-learning disabled children. In these cases, one must be cautious in inferring that similar findings would be obtained with learning disabled children.

The definition of learning disabilities used as the basis of forming the group of subjects in a study must be made explicit. In some studies no operational definitions are presented. Even when definitions are given, confusion often results because of the multiplicity of definitions of learning disabilities which abound in the field. Therefore, children defined as learning disabled in one study may bear little resemblance to other groups so labeled.

The degree of severity of the subjects' learning disabilities is very relevant. Obviously, the more severe the disability, the more difficult it is to remediate. Hence, results obtained from children with mild or moderate disabilities cannot necessarily be expected for children with severe disabilities.

It is imperative to analyze the background characteristics of the subjects in any study. The ages of the children are important since it is evident that the older the children, the more difficult it is to successfully remediate their disabilities. Therefore, if particular remedial methods or materials are found to be successful with younger children, it cannot be automatically assumed that similar results might be found with older children.

The learning abilities of the subjects are important and must be described. These are areas that often are used as instructional aids. If children do not have certain areas of learning ability, then these instructional aids cannot be effectively employed.

The general level of intellectual functioning may be a factor of significance. Generally, children at higher intellectual levels learn at a faster rate and have areas of superior ability which they can use to compensate for their disabilities. Thus, remedial methods and materials found to be effective with high IQ learning disabled children may not be as effective for the average or below average IQ learning disabled.

Social class and racial backgrounds of subjects are also relevant and must be made explicit. Research findings for middle class or white children do not necessarily hold for lower class or minority group children.

Nature of Treatment

It is essential that research studies specify in detail the nature of the educational treatment. In this way, the teacher can identify the critical elements that seem to be responsible for the success or failure of the remedial methods or materials under study. If remediation is not fully described, there may be modifications in its application by others; there may then be very different findings regarding its effectiveness.

The time factors involved in the remediation must be described. Obviously, the length of remedial sessions, the frequency of the sessions, and the total number of sessions provided greatly influence the likelihood of success for any method or materials. Studies such as Rejto's (1973) in which a small number of remedial music sessions over a relatively short period of time is reported to have resulted in substantial improvement in language, perception, and intelligence must be seriously questioned.

It must be determined if the remediation was done on an individual, small group, or large group basis as there is a greater probability of success for any remediation given on an individual basis than a group basis. It also follows that any remediation given to a small group will be more likely to succeed than the same remediation given to a large group.

The theoretical basis of the remediation (e.g., Frostig, Kirk, Orton, etc.) should be made explicit so that the teacher can judge the findings of a particular study in relation to the body of knowledge regarding that theory. In addition, knowing the theoretical basis of the remediation and the bias of the researcher often places the results in clearer perspective. It seems that researchers who favor a particular theory usually find research support for that theory. Conversely, those researchers opposed to a particular theory most often do not find support for it.

There should be a detailed description of the methods and materials in terms of the guidelines outlined earlier in this article. Such a description should include the specific symptoms treated, the learning abilities used as aids, the instructional level, the teaching strategies, the organization of the levels of difficulty of the stimulus and also of the response, the sequence of learning, the criterion for mastery level, transfer, the inclusion of social and academic behaviors, and restructuring strategies. The delineation of these variables is of utmost importance because changes in any of these may result in markedly different results for the same remedial methods and materials. Most studies do not describe these variables and, therefore, it is usually impossible to determine the critical elements that make for the success or failure of the methods and materials under study.

Nature of Teachers

It is necessary to describe the teachers who provided the remediation in order to determine whether specialized training or experience is necessary for the use of such remediation. It is important to know first the nature of the teachers' academic training and second the specific training necessary for using the remedial methods and materials under investigation.

The nature of the teachers' experiences should be given to determine whether experience with the handicapped is needed to utilize the remediation discussed.

Experimental Design

It should be noted whether a control group was employed as a basis for comparison with the experimental or treatment group. If no control group was used, then any improvement noted in the treatment subjects may have been due to any number of events including the passage of time or the extra attention subjects received rather than the actual remediation itself. Therefore, a control group serves a vital purpose and should be matched to the treatment group on relevant variables such as the nature of their learning disabilities and abilities, IQ, age, social class, and race.

In some studies there is an in-depth analysis of the remediation given to one child. With such an experimental design, it is mandatory to have adequate baseline or performance data for the child prior to the remediation. In this way, any changes noted following remediation can be directly attributed to the remedial treatment itself.

Analysis of Results

Any remediation study should include a statistical analysis of the data. Conclusions should not be drawn simply from a visual appraisal of the results. For example, Linn (1968) found that children who were given Frostig training were 2 to 4 months ahead in achievement as compared with control subjects. With no statistical analysis, she concluded that this relatively small difference supports the use of the Frostig materials with kindergarteners.

Reevaluation after remediation must be done "in the blind"—that is, the persons administering and scoring the tests should not be aware of whether the children were in the control or experimental groups. In this way, it is possible to avoid the natural inclination of many researchers to obtain favorable results.

Tests that are used for reevaluation after remediation must be relevant to the nature of the remediation. In a critical article concerned with training methods for disabilities in visual perception (especially the Frostig materials), Hammill

(1972) based his evaluations on tests of reading comprehension. Such reading tests are not relevant to visual perception as many other variables are more important than visual perception for understanding what is read. More relevant types of tests for evaluating remediation for visual perception disabilities are in word discrimination, word knowledge, or reversals since these are reading processes which rely heavily on visual perception.

In order to determine if the remediation has really been successful, however, it is necessary to use more than standardized tests. It is mandatory that information be obtained from diagnostic teaching and, most importantly, from an analysis of how children who were given certain remediation now perform in social and academic areas.

Conclusions from Data

The major issue here is whether or not the conclusions reached by the researcher are merited on the basis of the results of the study. Unfortunately, some researchers find that certain methods and materials work for only some children, yet they conclude that this form of remediation is appropriate for all learning disabled children. Conversely, if remediation is found not to be effective with children in a study, it should not follow that such remediation would be ineffective with all learning disabled children. Whenever there is complete acceptance or complete rejection of remedial methods or materials from the findings of one study, then one must seriously question the conclusions. The learning disabled are a heterogeneous population; therefore, some of these children will profit from certain methods and materials while others will not benefit from these same methods and materials.

The question to be answered by studies purporting to evaluate various kinds of remediation is, What type of learning disabled children will profit from what specific remedial methods and materials? This is, indeed, a complex and challenging question, but one designed to tighten and refine the nature of both research on remediation as well as evaluation of such research. Once the answers to this question are forthcoming, it will be possible to educationally meet each learning disabled child's unique needs.

REFERENCES

Balow, B. "The Long-Term Effect of Remedial Reading." *The Reading Teacher, 18,* 1965 (581-590).

Beery, K. E. *Developmental Test of Visual-Motor Integration.* Manual. Chicago: Follett, 1967.

Fernald, G. M. *Remedial Techniques in Basic School Subjects.* New York: McGraw-Hill, 1943.

Frostig, M. & Horne, D. *The Frostig Program for Development of Visual Perception.* Chicago: Follett, 1964.

Frostig, M., Maslow, P., Lefever, D. W. & Whittlesey, J. R. B. *The Frostig Developmental Test of Visual Perception.* 1963 Standardization. Palo Alto, Calif.: Consulting Psychologists Press, 1964.

Gillingham, A. & Stillman, B. *Remedial Training for Children with Specific Disability in Reading, Spelling, and Penmanship.* Cambridge, Mass.: Educators Publishing Service, 1965.

Goldstein, H., Mischio, G. S. & Minskoff, E. H. "A Demonstration-Research Project in Curriculum and Methods of Instruction for Elementary Level Mentally Retarded Children." Yeshiva University, Project #5-0395, U.S. Office of Education, 1969.

Hammill, D. "Training Visual Perceptual Processes." *Journal of Learning Disabilities, 5,* 1972 (552-559).

Jastak, J. F. & Jastak, S. R. *The Wide Range Achievement Test.* Wilmington, Del.: Guidance Associates, 1965.

Kirk, S. A. McCarthy, J. J. & Kirk, W. D. *Illinois Test of Psycholinguistic Abilities.* Revised Edition. Urbana, Ill.: University of Illinois Press, 1968.

Linn, S. H. "A Follow-up: Achievement Report of First-Grade Students after Visual-Perception Training in Kindergarten." *Academic Therapy Quarterly 3,* 1968 (179-180).

Lovell, L., Byrne, C. & Richardson, B. "A Further Study of the Educational Progress of Children Who Had Received Remedial Education." *British Journal of Educational Psychology, 33,* 1963 (3-9).

Minskoff, E. H., Wiseman, D. E. & Minskoff, J. G. *The MWM Program for Developing Language Abilities.* Ridgefield, N. J. 1972.

Mischio, G. S. "Inductive Teaching Techniques for the Mentally Retarded." *Focus on Exceptional Children, 4* (8), 1973.

Rejto, A. "Music as an Aid to the Remediation of Learning Disabilities." *Journal of Learning Disabilities, 6,* 1973 (286-295).

Skinner, B. F. *The Technology of Teaching.* New York: Appleton-Century-Crofts, 1968.

Spache, G. D. *Diagnostic Reading Scales.* Monterey, Calif.: California Test Bureau, 1963.

Research in the field of teaching has noted the overemphasis on rote learning and instruction which is teacher centered. Dr. Mischio's article emphasizes the inductive method of teaching. This method capitalizes on instruction illustrated by a complete example and subsequently reinforced by its application to partial examples. The author develops the method through numerous examples from which teachers can develop their own proficiency in the use of this approach.

Inductive Teaching Techniques for the Mentally Retarded

George S. Mischio
University of Wisconsin, Whitewater

Recent concern about the validity of special education for the mildly mentally retarded has often been concentrated upon the ineffectiveness of present categories for administrative policy, placement and/or funding purposes (Lilly, 1970). Furthermore, recommendations have been offered to revise current instructional programs to provide a more clinical and child oriented approach (Dunn, 1968); to offer alternative delivery systems (Lilly, 1970); or to follow new strategies and curriculum models (Meyen, Vergason & Whelan, 1972). The effectiveness of rote or inductive teaching styles for the mentally retarded has received considerably less attention in the literature and in practice. However, Gallagher (1967) emphasized that teacher-student interaction has become as significant a research and instructional variable as curriculum content, abilities of children or special education labels. Therefore, how a teacher presents content must receive equal scrutiny as special education continues its self-appraisal.

In search for a relevant teaching style suited for the retarded, the most discernible methods include rote, expository or discovery teaching. *Rote* teaching is the dispensing of facts or rules by the teacher. Only immediate recall of this information is required when the teacher questions the student about the contents of the lesson. If the child gives the correct answer, the teacher offers positive feedback. If the answer is incorrect, the teacher provides negative reinforcement and repeats the correct answer. It is a dependent relationship in which the student relies upon the teacher as the primary source of most stimulation, direction and feedback.

Expository teaching is the teaching of a rule which is illustrated by a complete example and subsequently reinforced by its application to partial examples. The expository approach is very frequently used in education as it is efficient, offers success and enables the learner to apply deductive reasoning to carefully selected situations or examples.

Discovery teaching is the presentation of a problem situation in which the learner must find or discover commonalities or relationships between the elements within this experience. Once the underlying rule, principle or concept is inductively derived, the learner is then required to assess other situations and try to apply the same principle whenever relevant.

An example of these teaching styles can be seen in the presentation of the following concept to a group of first graders. Concept: Measurement is the comparison of an object against a specific standard.

Rote Teaching

1. Teacher tells class that a yardstick is used to measure height or width of any object. She explains the differences between inches, feet and yards as measurement standards.
2. Students recite the information orally and/or may answer questions on a test.
3. Students may measure some object in art, shop, or other classes upon request of teacher.

Expository Teaching

1. Teacher presents the rule that rulers and yardsticks are standards of measurement against which any object can be compared. Then students are taught that there are 36 inches or three feet in a yardstick, twelve inches in a foot, etc.
2. Students and teacher measure varying length lines on chalkboard in order to apply the rule.
3. The children do measurement problems from their workbooks and compare answers.

Discovery Teaching

1. Teacher informs the class that the custodian's old basement workbench is available for their third floor classroom. However, the teacher claims that

she is not sure if it will fit through the doorway. She warns the class that the custodian will be very angry if he carries the bench up the stairs and then cannot fit it through the door frame. Thus, she asks the class to help solve the problem.

2. The class try visually to estimate the width of the bench and the doorway but disagree on whether it will fit.

3. Some students suggest using their arms as a standard or pacing off the width of the bench. After each method is tried, the class continue to disagree since they realized they slipped when using their arms or were not sure if their paces were always the same length.

4. Finally, through teacher questioning and structuring, the group decide to use a stick as a consistent standard. They measure the width of the bench and the door. Then, they compare and determine that the bench will fit through the door frame.

5. Teacher lets each child select a stick and use it as a guide for making columns on paper. After several error-filled trials, teacher introduces the ruler and yardstick. The children induce the value of inches and feet as a more precise standard for accurate measurement.

6. Children and teacher synthesize all these experiences and use inductive reasoning to discover the underlying concept.

While the superiority of either the expository or discovery methods for teaching mathematics (Shulman, 1970) or other content areas (Shulman & Keislar, 1966) have not yet been demonstrated for the normal child, the special educator is still faced with the decision of selecting a teaching style or styles most consonant with the intellectual limitations and verbal abilities of her mentally retarded students.

To facilitate such decision making, this paper will explore the utilization of a variation of the discovery method, e.g., inductive teaching, for educating the educable mentally retarded. By drawing upon a previous affiliation with Dr. Herbert Goldstein and his associates at Yeshiva University, the author will review our efforts to train special education teachers in the use of inductive teaching via preservice and inservice programs; to evaluate teacher-pupil interactions based upon inductive and other teaching styles; and to describe procedures for integrating inductive teaching strategies and techniques into a social learning curriculum.

Consequently, the purposes of this article will be:

1. To provide an overview of Discovery Learning.

2. To explore the research concerning the efficiency of inductive teaching for the retarded.

3. To analyze the elements of inductive teaching styles.

4. To discuss the problems related to introducing and maintaining inductive teaching within classes for the educable mentally retarded.

OVERVIEW OF DISCOVERY LEARNING

Discovery learning has received a considerable amount of investigation and appraisal concerning its implications for educational and psychological research, philosophical issues, curriculum innovations and theory building (Shulman & Keislar, 1966). When viewed from the broader perspective of productive thinking, discovery learning can be an integral part of the development of intelligence through training of productive and divergent thinking (Ashner & Blish, 1965). Consequently, these reviews suggest that discovery learning has become a potentially relevant approach. However, more systematic analysis and definition as well as innovative research and instruction techniques are required in order to establish the ultimate validity of discovery learning as a viable learning and teaching style.

Learning by discovery can be defined as uncovering or finding an association, a concept or a rule which explains the relationship between facts, experiences or events under investigation or consideration. Glaser (1966) characterizes discovery learning by two processes, i.e., induction or trial and error learning. *Induction* is the procedure of supplying examples and experiences of a more general to specific nature which permits the learner to induce the underlying proposition or rule involved. For example, a pre-schooler examining circles, triangles and squares can discover the concept that triangles, regardless of size, can be grouped together because they are three-sided. In the inductive teaching process, the teacher provides maximal structure by regulating the types of shapes studied and the order of presentation or exploration. *Trial and error* or errorful learning is a more unguided sequence of experiences in which the learner imposes his own structure and pace. In trial and error learning, the student is allowed to follow blind alleys, find negative instances and make wrong decisions before he discovers the underlying rule. For example, the student might manipulate triangles, cubes, balls, squares, irregular shapes and other objects before he discovers that he can separate the shapes by number of sides, size and other dimensions. In either procedure, the learner eventually discovers the relationship that binds the characteristics or facts together. The pedagogical difference between induction and trial and error learning is related to the amount of teacher structure, availability of resources and the amount of time required to discover the underlying generalization.

EFFICIENCY OF INDUCTIVE TEACHING
FOR THE MENTALLY RETARDED

The most efficient ways to develop discovery learning skills among the mentally retarded are most dependent upon the student's verbal skills and intellectual level, the length of the school day, physical limitations of materials and space as well as group behavioral problems. These factors as well as the retardate's limited ability for self-guidance and self-direction tend to mitigate against trial and error learning. Finally, due to the retardates' lower rates of learning, the time required to discover a principle through trial and error would be prohibitive if used consistently. Thus inductive learning, a variation of discovery learning, is probably more compatible with the needs and abilities of the mentally retarded because of the teacher-imposed structure and control.

Educability of Intelligence

Prior to an analysis of appropriate teaching methodology for the retarded, the concept of the educability of intelligence must be considered. Fernald (1943) viewed the retarded as incapable of conceptualization or abstract thinking whereby he proposed a rote teaching approach geared to the specific situations within their lives. Zigler (1966) tended to be pessimistic about the effective use of educational intervention in producing intellectual growth among the retarded. Blatt (1964) proposed that only the fact of intervention rather than the quality and type of intervention is significant. Thus, the intervention process is pessimistically viewed from their perspectives.

The possibility of the educability of intelligence has also rewarded positive support (Hunt, 1961, and Bruner, 1961). The importance of the special class teacher for enhancing cognitive development was stressed by Reynolds (1965), while Gallagher (1964) felt that consistently following a teaching style for the entire school year can help modify the intellectual operations and products of an exceptional child.

Specific research related to classroom attempts at educability of intelligence among the retarded have provided some positive findings. Katz (1963) developed and taught a problem-solving training program for high school educables. He found this style of instruction better prepared his students to handle new difficulties. Rouse (1965) disclosed that retarded children who had been given instruction on brainstorming techniques performed better on divergent thinking tasks than other retarded children.

It would appear that strong positive expectations about the educability of intelligence and systematic training can lead to significant growth of specific intellectual skills among the retarded.

Inductive Teaching Research

There is a scarcity of studies reporting on the efficacy of an inductive teaching method for the retarded. Dawe (1959) found only eight articles specifically related to teaching methodology for the retarded had been written between 1948 and 1958. None of the articles reviewed inductive teaching styles.

Tisdall (1962) reported that mentally retarded children in special classes who had been exposed to systematic inductive teaching and a consistent social studies curriculum were superior in performance to retardates in regular classes on tests of divergent thinking.

In a series of efficacy studies that utilized the same inductive teaching children, Goldstein and his associates disclosed the following findings:

1. In the Illinois study, carefully trained and supervised special educators could help Low IQ (below 80) retardates in special classes make significant academic, intellectual, personality, and divergent thinking gains over Low IQ retardates in regular classes. The converse was true for the High IQ group of retardates in regular classes who were superior to the retardates in special classes on these measures. (Goldstein, Moss & Jordan, 1965)

2. In the New Jersey Study, short term inservice training and two years of intensive field supervision in a replication of the Illinois Study could not sufficiently improve the competency of "typical" special educators in "typical" urban, suburban and rural settings to cause the student gains found in the Illinois Study. (Goldstein, Mischio & Minskoff, 1969)

3. In a supplementary study, the "typical" teachers of the New Jersey Study tended to ask mostly memory type questions rather than convergent, divergent, or evaluative questions; were more oriented to management and routine problems than to fostering productive thinking; and did not consistently use the elements of inductive teaching appropriately or effectively. (Minskoff, 1967)

To reduce the pedagogical problems found in their earlier efficacy studies, Goldstein and his associates (Goldstein, 1972) have begun construction of a Social Learning Curriculum that combines inductive teaching techniques with a very specific series of teaching "phases" or super units. Based upon the broad goals of developing the ability to think critically and act independently, the Curriculum is being nationally field tested in over eight hundred sites to determine whether the special class teacher can function more effectively with more specific content and imbedded inductive teaching strategies and techniques. These materials are specifically sequenced in a logical order based upon the retardates' "needs" to function successfully in the environment. Heiss and Mischio (1972) have extended the Social Learning Curriculum design to include academic, readiness and learning disabilities programs. Hopefully, these new curriculums, which have inductive teaching integrated appropriately with specific content, will be vehicles for conducting more appropriate research to test the validity of inductive instruction of the retarded.

Thus, the above review has lead to the following conclusions concerning the appropriateness of inductive techniques for the mentally retarded:

1. Discovery learning or inductive learning appears to be a viable approach, but it still requires more refinement of definition and research methodology.
2. Neither discovery nor expository teaching has been proven to be superior for educating normal or retarded children.
3. Inductive learning rather than trial and error learning is probably a more suitable style for the retarded due to the constraints of time, intellectual level and available resources.
4. Positive teacher expectancy regarding the educability of intelligence is essential if cognitive development oriented teaching methods are employed.
5. Limited progress has been made through incidental productive thinking training programs for the retarded.
6. The assessment of teacher competency and subsequent training are important if any teaching style is going to be consistently utilized in the special class.
7. Curriculums that attempt to integrate teaching style and substance in meaningful relationships offer a total program for testing the efficacy of inductive teaching.

INDUCTIVE TEACHING STYLES

Inductive teaching methodology is one means toward achieving a basic educational goal for the retarded (i.e., adequate adjustment in society). Essentially, this type of instruction improves evaluative and critical thinking and offers a candid and systematic procedure for appraising the environment. Such close scrutiny often provides guidelines for appropriate behavioral patterns. When a retarded person has been systematically instructed through inductive techniques, there is a greater probability that he will try independently to solve his problems, seek resources or assistance from other than the teacher, be more willing to encounter frustration to reach his goals, and be able to withstand a greater frequency of failure. In short, the retardate becomes less dependent upon the teacher and grows in self-direction and self-reliance.

Elements of Inductive Teaching

The inquiry nature of inductive teaching requires nimble verbal and nonverbal transactions between teacher and learner that are dependent upon the student's readiness, the teacher's knowledge and dexterity in consistently employing inductive techniques appropriately, the availability of suitable physical and printed resources (such as manipulative materials or books) and the type of content being taught. Thus, an inductive teaching paradigm would not be a static and unyielding diagram but rather a framework for many dynamic variations on the basic discovery theme. Therefore, it is more accurate to consider inductive teaching techniques and styles rather than a singular inductive teaching method.

The inductive approaches are variations of the discovery method which are based upon the following assumptions. A free and exciting learning atmosphere should be created to encourage experimenting, reasoning, and problem solving. The student requires a strong intrinsic motivation or desire to want to learn. The teacher is responsible for providing the necessary facts, information, and materials for the learner to discover a solution. Finally, the learner achieves a sense of closure and satisfaction in finding an answer or rule.

Based upon the underlying assumptions for discovery learning, the following elements should be present in every inductive teaching interaction: problem solving, structure, feedback and consistency.

Problem Solving

The essence of the inductive approach is the impetus to solve a problem or difficulty. The need to discover the answer has motivational as well as pedagogical properties. Therefore, every time a new generalization is designated to be discovered, the transactions are preceded by couching the experience in some type of problem theme. For example, if the teacher wants to develop the mathematical concept of one-to-one correspondence, she might challenge the class by saying, "I don't know if I have enough straws for everyone's chocolate milk at recess time. How can I find out?"

Structure

Structure is essential for teaching the retarded as they often lack the necessary self-guidance and self-direction to pursue the alternatives on their own. The teacher can start with tighter structure to insure many successful answers by carefully controlling the verbal questions and physical cues. To organize these cues, the teacher should have a thorough understanding of the student's experiential and conceptual background, limitations and assets, and general repertoire of knowledge. The most effective cues can then be selected on the basis of their appropriateness for the child's developmental level and their general relevancy to the problem. Therefore, the teacher might present the situation so that he could uncover the principle of one-to-one correspondence tasks, i.e., matching straws, milk cartons, place mats and/or children. For a verbal child, she might change her type of questioning to suit his vocabulary level. In such cases, prior knowledge of the child's experiences and style of learning is essential. As the student becomes more expert at inductive reasoning, the teacher reduces her external structure as he increases his internal structure and self-direction.

Feedback

The third and most crucial element is the nature of teacher feedback as it relates to the student's performance. If the child is correct, the teacher gives praise and encouragement. However, if incorrect, the teacher offers to help the child reappraise his answer and rerespond. Then, depending upon the answer, the teacher can continue the sequence by rephrasing the questions, restructuring the physical information, or calling upon other students to act as resources to supply additional information. If the child still persists in supplying the wrong information, the teacher should reevaluate her objectives to determine if the learner has sufficient information in his repertoire to respond correctly. If lack of readiness or knowledge is the case, the teacher then selects a less complex objective to solve the problem (e.g., have the child use rationale counting to determine if there are sufficient straws for each classmate).

It is very important for the student to realize the teacher will not supply the correct answer during the feedback interaction. Once this type of teacher-pupil relationship is established, the child becomes increasingly less dependent upon the teacher as the only source of stimulation and turns to other children, books, other adults and himself to find the answer.

Consistency

The final element—consistency—is often neglected if the teacher has trouble introducing or maintaining an inductive teaching style, associates induction with only one subject or provides random or sporadic usage. Figure 1 suggests a possible hierarchy of school subjects that lend themselves to induction.

Figure 1
HIERARCHY OF INDUCTIVE ORIENTED SUBJECTS

SOCIAL LEARNING
SCIENCE
HEALTH & SAFETY
ARITHMETIC
LANGUAGE ARTS
MUSIC
PHYSICAL EDUCATION

Those areas that deal primarily with concepts and principles (i.e., social studies or science) or those that deal with rules and relationships (i.e., health or arithmetic) can be more easily taught by searching for the underlying principles through induction. Similarly, rote or expository (rule first—followed by example) teaching may be more economical and efficient for teaching facts (e.g., the plus sign stands for addition *or* words can be divided into syllables at the point where two consonants are together). Once the child has quickly learned the rule or fact, he can then apply his time and energy to understanding the principles of place value in addition. Similarly, he can apply his syllabication rule to attack unfamiliar words when reading directions to assemble a model. Obviously, physical education and elementary music appreciation require more directed teaching in order to learn the lead-up skills or words of a song.

Consistent use of inductive reasoning is possible within nonacademic situations such as finding more efficient ways to do class chores or using lunch-room or after school situations to discover concepts (e.g., as the pupils wait for the school bus, they notice the appearance of the newly washed chalkboard is changing). Through inductive questioning, they soon discover the concept of evaporation.

Minskoff (1967) has diagrammed a comparison of rote and inductive teaching techniques based upon these elements (see Figure 2).

Information Building

One of the problems in preparing the retarded for the inductive approaches is the need to develop a classroom atmosphere conducive to inquiry and exploration. In addition to providing stimulating science corners, multimedia centers, exploration tables, and other manipulative and novel experiences, there is the necessity to foster each individual's attitude by creating a "learning to learn" set or perspective.

Figure 2
PROBLEM SOLVING INSTRUCTION SEQUENCE

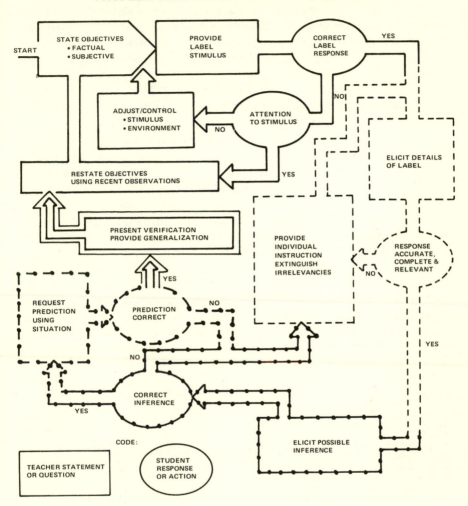

The following steps help to build an informational repertoire. *Labeling* helps identify gross or major aspects of a situation (e.g., who, what, what kind, where?). *Detailing* causes the learner to locate other significant but less important details or finer points (e.g., size, color, quantity, unusual features). *Inferring* requires the learner to synthesize the information obtained by labeling and detailing in order to make a judgment or interpretation of the situation (e.g., why, what do you think?) *Predicting* is the application of the accumulated

393

information to make a projection or statement regarding the probability of the next event occurring (e.g., what happens next, what would happen if?). On the basis of verification of the prediction and association with prior information and experiences, the student ends with *generalizing* in which he abstracts a principle, concept, or generalization that integrates or ties together all the elements of the experience (e.g., what is the reason, what could make this happen again?).

One of the most practical attempts to represent induction in teaching stages has been accomplished by (Goldstein & Boucher, 1972) and his staff who have evolved a Problem Solving Instruction Sequence that incorporates the five steps of information building with the elements of inductive teaching (see Figure 2). Using the systems approach of yes-no decision making, the teacher can evaluate the student's performance of each step, proceed to the next step if the child is correct (yes decision) or recycle through the step again if he is incorrect (no decision).

By studying the teacher-pupil interaction through Figure 2 for a social studies lesson, we can view a complete inductive sequence through the five steps since a yes decision was made at the end of each step. However, if a no decision had been made, if the child offered an incorrect label response, the teacher would have reexamined the verbal and physical stimulus and made the necessary changes and tried again. A second no decision at this step would lead the teacher to reevaluate his objectives. Similarly, an incorrect inference or prediction would lead to individual work in extinguishing irrelevancies that gave the student misleading or incorrect data.

SOCIAL STUDIES LESSON

Objective: People go to sports events to have fun and root for the favorite teams.

Atmosphere: The study of recreation has been established through a class discussion in which the junior high educables were complaining that there was "nothing to do in their town." The problem was stated as: How many ways can we have fun? Prior discussions have centered about amusement in the home. Now the teacher is ready to expand the discussion by showing a news clipping and an enlarged photo of Willie Mays hitting his first home run as a member of the New York Mets.

Code:

Yes-No Decision at Each Stage	Comments to Explain Inductive Process

Teacher-Announced Objective: "Today we are going to find out how people can enjoy themselves outside their homes. Look at this newspaper photo and see if you understand how and why these people are having fun away from their homes."

INDUCTIVE INTERACTIONS

Teacher	Student

LABELING

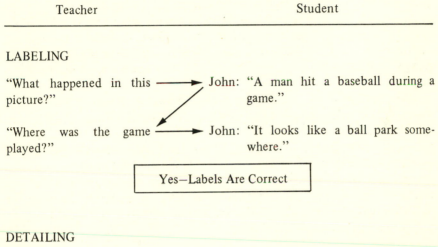

"What happened in this picture?" ——→ John: "A man hit a baseball during a game."

"Where was the game played?" ——→ John: "It looks like a ball park somewhere."

Yes—Labels Are Correct

DETAILING

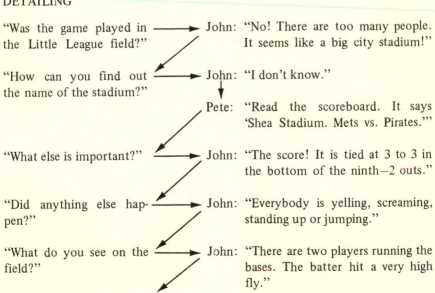

"Was the game played in the Little League field?" ——→ John: "No! There are too many people. It seems like a big city stadium!"

"How can you find out the name of the stadium?" ——→ John: "I don't know."

Pete: "Read the scoreboard. It says 'Shea Stadium. Mets vs. Pirates.'"

"What else is important?" ——→ John: "The score! It is tied at 3 to 3 in the bottom of the ninth—2 outs."

"Did anything else happen?" ——→ John: "Everybody is yelling, screaming, standing up or jumping."

"What do you see on the field?" ——→ John: "There are two players running the bases. The batter hit a very high fly."

395

Teacher	Student

"Very fine observations! ——→ John: "A New York Mets player because Who hit the ball?   ↓   it was their time up at bat."

Pete: "It's Willie Mays. That's his number! He just joined the team."

```
┌─────────────────────────┐
│  Yes—Details Are Correct │
└─────────────────────────┘
```

INFERRING

"What happened?" ——————→ John: "Willie Mays hit a homer or a triple."

"How do you know that?" ——→ John: "Look how high the ball is! It's heading for the stands."

"How do the fans feel?" ——→ John: "They are excited! They are cheering, yelling and jumping out of their seats. One man has a sign that says GO-WILLIE-GO."

```
┌─────────────────────────┐
│  Yes—Inference Is Correct │
└─────────────────────────┘
```

PREDICTING

"What happened?" ——————→ John: "The Mets won the game because they broke the tie."

"What if the fly ball was ——→ John: "At least one runner would have caught in the outfield?" scored. If it were a hit, maybe two runs would have scored. If it were a homer, Willie and the two guys on base would have scored to make it 6 to 3. Anyhow, Mets were the winners."

Teacher	Student
"What do you think the fans did?"	John: "I bet they went wild. Willie won the game."
"Why was it important for Willie?"	John: "It was first his game as a Met."

> Use Newspaper Article to Verify Prediction

"Let's see if we can find out what happened by reading the newspaper article. First, what does the headline say?"	John: " 'Mays saves his first game! Blasts homer to win 6 to 3.' "
"How did the fans like Willie?"	John: "It said they didn't let him leave the field for ten minutes. Everyone shook his hand, they gave him a beer bath and carried him off on their shoulders."

> Yes—Predictions Correct and Verified

GENERALIZING

"So, why do people go to a baseball game?"	John: "To have fun—to root for their team."
"Can't you do that by watching TV?"	John: "Sure, you can watch the game but you can't be with the people and cheer. When we go to a game, we walk across the field and sometimes get to talk to the players."
"Do you think it's a good idea to go to a ball game?"	John: "Yes—everybody has fun at the game. I enjoy the ride to the ball park. We always have pizza after the game. I have a ball. It is a good way to spend an afternoon."

INTRODUCTION, MAINTENANCE, AND FUTURE
OF INDUCTIVE TEACHING

A gradual transition from your present teaching style to induction can be accomplished through a series of readiness activities. Introduce problem solving through class games, a discovery corner, a science table or a mystery box containing puzzles, etc. Start giving each student more responsibility in your teacher-pupil interactions by staying with him when he does not know the answer and building information through the five steps. Develop your first inductive sequences with very concrete concepts and materials so that you can manipulate physical items if your rephrasing of questions gets confusing. Finally, explain to your pupils that you are teaching some problem solving techniques so they can function as detectives to help you unravel class problems or mysteries in their lessons.

Inductive teaching has been successful for many teachers provided they apply it appropriately and systematically. Our research has indicated that teacher expectation is a key factor in the success of inductive teaching. If the teacher has low expectations or is convinced that she cannot influence the performance of the retarded (Gozali, 1972), induction is doomed to fail. However, if a more positive and pragmatic approach permeates the entire situation (Boekel, 1972), the teacher is more likely to view the retarded as a potential problem solver if taught appropriately.

From a long range perspective, rote and directed teaching are probably most useful at the primary and early intermediate levels of school. As the child acquires the basic academic and social skills, he can apply them as problem solving tools. Consequently, inductive teaching will probably be used more frequently at upper intermediate and junior-senior high levels.

The future role of inductive instruction techniques for the retarded is uncertain but optimistic. As the new curriculums with imbedded inductive sequences are available, as teacher training institutions provide more systematic opportunities to develop these techniques, and as the retarded are given more opportunities for independence, we can further assess the validity of this approach.

REFERENCES

Ashner, M. J. & Blish, C.E. *Productive Thinking in Education.* Washington, D.C.: National Education Association, 1965.

Blatt, B. "Measuring and Modifying Behavior of Special Education Teachers." *Mental Retardation, 2,* 1964 (339-344).

Boekel, N. "The Influence of Teacher Expectations on the Performance Point of View." In Meyen, E., Vergason, G. & Whelan, R. (Eds.), *Strategies for Teaching Exceptional Children.* Denver, Colorado: Love Publishing, 1972 (233-243).

Bruner, J. *The Process of Education.* Cambridge, Mass.: Harvard University Press, 1961.

Dawe, A. "Progress in Curriculum and Methods for Mentally Handicapped Children." *American Journal on Mental Deficiency, 64,* 1959 (19-23).

Dunn, L. "Special Education for the Mildly Retarded—Is Much of It Justifiable? " *Exceptional Children, 35,* 1, 1968 (5-24).

Fernald, G. M. *Remedial Techniques in Basic School Subjects.* New York: McGraw Hill, 1943.

Gallagher, J. "New Directions in Special Education." *Exceptional Children, 33,* 7, 1967 (441-448).

Gallagher, J. *Teaching the Gifted Child.* Boston: Allyn & Bacon, 1964.

Glaser, R. "Variables in Discovery Learning." In Shulman, L. S. & Keislar, E. R. (Eds.), *Learning by Discovery: A Critical Appraisal.* Chicago, Illinois: Rand McNally, 1966.

Goldstein, H. "Construction of a Social Learning Curriculum." In Meyen, E., Vergason, G., & Whelan, R. (Eds.), *Strategies for Teaching Exceptional Children.* Denver, Colorado: Love Publishing, 1972 (94-114).

Goldstein, H. & Boucher, D. "Personal Communication—Describing an Inductive Teaching Flow Chart." Research and Development Center in Curriculum for the Mentally Retarded. Yeshiva University, New York, New York, October, 1972.

Goldstein, H., Mischio G., & Minskoff, E. *A Demonstration—Research Project in Curriculum and Methods of Instruction for Elementary Level Mentally Retarded Children.* USOE Final Report, Grant #32-42-1700-1010, 1969.

Goldstein, H., Moss, J., & Jordan L. *The Efficacy of Special Class Training on the Development of Mentally Retarded Children.* Final Report, Cooperative Research Project #619, 1965.

Gozali, Joav. "The Expectancy Phenomena: Implication for Educating the Mentally Retarded." In Meyen, E., Vergason, G., & Whelan, R. (Eds.), *Strategies for Teaching Exceptional Children.* Denver, Colorado: Love Publishing, 1972 (223-232).

Heiss, W. & Mischio, G. "Designing Curriculum for the Educable Mentally Retarded." In Meyen, E., Vergason, G., & Whelan, R. (Eds.), *Strategies for Teaching Exceptional Children.* Denver, Colorado: Love Publishing, 1972 (115-135).

Hunt, J. *Intelligence and Experience.* New York: Ronald Press, 1961.

Katz, P. "Discussion of the Possibilities of Using a Classroom as a Setting for Imparting a Strategy to Aid Educable Retardates to Transfer Learning and/or Solve Problems." Paper read at Council for Exceptional Children, Philadelphia, 1963.

Lilly, M. S. "Special Education: A Teapot in a Tempest." *Exceptional Children, 37,* 1, 1970 (43-48).

Meyen, E., Vergason, G., & Whelan, R. (Eds.). *Strategies for Teaching Exceptional Children.* Denver, Colorado: Love Publishing, 1972.

Minskoff, E. *An Analysis of the Teacher-Pupil Verbal Interaction in Special Classes for the Mentally Retarded.* Final Report, USOE Grant No. 32-42-1700-6008, 1967.

Reynolds, M. "The Capacities of Children." *Exceptional Children, 31,* 1965 (337-343).

Rouse, S. "Effects of a Training Program on the Productive Thinking of Educable Mentally Retarded." *American Journal on Mental Deficiency, 69,* 1965 (666-673).

Shulman, L. "Psychology and Mathematics Education" *National Society for Study of Education,* 69th Yearbook, Part I, 1970.

Shulman, L. & Keislar, E. (Eds.). *Learning by Discovery: A Critical Appraisal.* Chicago, Illinois: Rand McNally, 1966.

Tisdall, W. "Productive Thinking in Retarded Children." *Exceptional Children, 29,* 1962 (36-41).

Zigler, E. "Bruner and the Center for Cognitive Studies Discussion." In Garrison, M. (Ed.), "Cognitive Models and Development in Mental Retardation. Monograph. *American Journal on Mental Deficiency, 70,* 4, 1966 (7-25).

There are many frontiers and bandwagons in special education—some pass through as fads, while others make meaningful additions to serving children. Working with parents of handicapped and gifted children not only will be one of the "hottest" areas to develop, but stands to be one of the greatest advances in our efforts to help children. Dr. Kroth was involved in this movement long before it became fashionable and is responsible for having trained many of the parent trainers.

Facilitating Educational Progress by Improving Parent Conferences

Roger Kroth
University of New Mexico, Albuquerque

The question of whether or not to involve parents of exceptional children in the education of their own children is still somewhat controversial. Kelly (1973) has reviewed the literature relating to both sides of the issue and has concluded that "these studies and reviews confirm a growing consensus among professional educators that parental involvement is a necessary prerequisite to effective instruction in both general and special education" (p. 362). There seems to be little question that parents are a potent force in the lives of their children; therefore, the decision that educators must make is whether or not it is feasible or desirable to spend time in working with parents—i.e., is the effort worth the results?

Parents have been recognized as viable forces in the educational development of their children, but often the acknowledgment of their influence has been negative. Parents have been used as convenient scapegoats for the lack of success, rather than as facilitators for successful accomplishment, on the part of their children. Parents have not been able to escape the heredity vs. environment issue that is prominent in psychological literature. They are vilified or deified by proponents of either side of the issue depending upon the performance of their children.

In a success-oriented society such as the North American community, the excitement accompanying the birth of a child quickly can turn to dismay if the child is born handicapped. As Wolfensberger and Kurtz (1969) point out:

> The rearing of children is one of the most significant and demanding tasks most of us confront in our lifetime. Yet, paradoxically, this is a task for which the average citizen has received little or no formal preparation. Even when the child has an unimpaired growth potential, and even where parents are highly intelligent, well-educated, and possessed of abundant material resources, child rearing is typically fraught with error, and frequently marked by failure. How much more problematic the situation becomes when the child is handicapped! (pp. 517-518)

The parental reactions of mourning, denial, guilt, rejection, shame, and frustration as discussed by various authors (Buscaglia, 1971; Love, 1970; Ross, 1964) are neither unexpected nor surprising. The gap between the real situation and the ideal that was expected is frequently so large that initial efforts to cope with the handicapping situation necessitate outside help. Yet, where to turn for assistance can be perplexing. The family doctor, a minister, a psychologist, a psychiatrist, and a social worker represent some of the helping professionals that parents initially may come in contact with upon the discovery that their child is exceptional. As the child becomes older, other professionals may become involved in providing guidance for parents such as physical therapists, nurses, occupational therapists, speech therapists, audiologists, and school personnel, depending upon the nature of the handicap. It is conceivable that parents may be involved with a number of professional aides at the same period of time, all recommending various treatment procedures. In some cases the parents are faced with essentially no service when they reside far from large communities, while in other instances they may be overwhelmed by a panorama of services.

It is not the purpose of this paper to focus on the services or programs provided for parents by the various service personnel listed above, but rather to focus on programs for parents more clearly related to the educational environment.

Basically, there are two types of conferences that involve teachers and parents—information-sharing conferences, and problem-solving conferences. These are differentiated more by the stated purpose for the conference than by the actual content. In other words, the teacher and parents who come together to share information may find that a problem exists which can best be resolved by mutual action. On the other hand, a conference may be called by either the parents or teacher in which the successful resolution of a problem involves a program of information sharing. In either case the success or failure of the conference rests largely with the teacher, her preparation for the conferences and her techniques for problem solving.

It would be desirable if all teachers had the personal characteristics of "accurate empathy, nonpossessive warmth and therapeutic genuineness" which

401

Truax and Wargo (1966) associate with successful psychotherapists. While one recognizes these traits in a teacher and appreciates them, the behavioral components which compose the traits may be difficult to teach. On the other hand, there are organizational procedures, techniques and basic principles that teachers can follow which will enhance the parent-teacher relationship and facilitate both types of conferences.

INFORMATION-SHARING CONFERENCES

Under the general category of information-sharing conferences are the parent-teacher contacts that include an intake conference, an initial conference and group meetings. The rapport that is established in these contacts sets the stage for the quality of further interactions.

Beginning teachers often feel a great deal of uneasiness about parent conferences. "What if the parent questions what I'm doing for her child?" "What do I do with a crying parent, an angry parent, or one that is resentful of having to attend the session?" Parents, on the other hand, often come to the conferences with similar feelings. They recognize that the teacher holds in her hands strong consequences which can be used for or against the child. Because the teacher is professional, she should be the one to set the tone for the conference, structuring the context and placing the parent at ease.

Intake and Initial Conferences

The intake conference and the initial conference may be the same in many instances. In some school districts, the special education teacher has not been included in the intake conference. Her first contact is with the child when he appears in her classroom. This is unfortunate. When the decision is made for the child to be admitted to a special education program, both parents and teacher would be able to benefit from face-to-face contact. The teacher would be able to see the parents' concern and hear the condition of placement. The parents would be able to visit with the teacher and learn something of the educational objectives for the class.

Duncan and Fitzgerald (1969) investigated the effects of establishing a parent-counselor relationship prior to the child's entrance into junior high school and looked at such variables as (1) average daily attendance, (2) schedule changes, (3) dropouts, (4) disciplinary referrals, (5) grade point average, (6) overt parental interest and (7) communication between parent and child. Duncan and Fitzgerald found that the early contact group showed significantly greater parental contact with the school, better attendance, higher grade point average, lower dropout rate, and fewer disciplinary referrals than the group who did not have conferences prior to school.

If the teacher is making the initial contact, it is important for her to have in mind an outline of the kind of information she would like to have to help her work with the child and his parents (see Figure 1).

Not all of the information needs to be covered verbally. Some of it can be obtained by observation. There is nothing wrong with taking notes during the conference. Other professionals do, and it will show the parents that the teacher considers the information valuable in her work with the child.

Any information regarding physical limitations of the child which would suggest preferential seating or special materials or activities should be noted. Special attention should be paid to past educational experiences of the child, i.e., former teacher reports and observation, any special testing, samples of work, etc. Hobbies, preferred activities, likes and dislikes may furnish the teacher with clues as to potential reinforcers in the classroom, as well as planning programs between school and home. As one explores the family constellations, it is important to find out if there is a language other than English spoken in the home and to what extent it is spoken. If a second language is the predominant language in the home, it could have a pronounced effect on any standardized testing that had been carried out. Questions about socioeconomic level of the family may center around books, magazines, newspapers, radio and TV available to the child and family rather than the level of income. In this instance, the teacher is interested in the supplementary materials available for learning and how the family spends their money rather than the quantity of money available.

Since these conferences are considered information-sharing conferences, the teacher should be prepared to share information that she has available with the parents. Many teachers have found it valuable to prepare a handbook for parents, to be given to parents at the initial meeting. Usually the handbook will include the teacher's name, persons to contact concerning special problems, and a description of the class. The goals and objectives for the students help the parent understand *what* the teacher is trying to accomplish. A description of the structure of the classroom helps the parents understand *how* the teacher is going to accomplish her objectives. Any special procedures should be explained, such as time-out procedures, study carrels, lunch or dismissal that is contingent upon successful completion of work, etc. The fewer surprises that parents have in store for them during the year, the more productive later conferences can be.

Some teachers have found it valuable to include in the handbook sections on tips to parents, activities or management practices. Included might be a suggested list of books which parents might find helpful, such as *Parents Are Teachers* (Becker, 1971); *How To Parent* (Dodson, 1970); *Living with Children: New Methods for Parents & Teachers* (Patterson & Gullion, 1968); and *You Can*

Figure 1
INITIAL INTERVIEW GUIDE: GETTING A PICTURE OF THE CHILD

A. Present Status
   1. Age
   2. Sex
   3. Grade; class; last year's teacher's name

B. Physical appearance and history
   1. General impression made by child
   2. Obvious physical strengths and limitations
   3. General mannerisms, appearance, etc.

C. Educational Status
   1. Present school achievement; kind of work; any samples of work
   2. Promotions; accelerations, retardations; causes
   3. Relations with individual teachers—present and past
   4. Books, etc. used in last educational setting
   5. Tests, individual or group, types of measures used

D. Personal Traits
   1. Personality—general statement
   2. Attitudes toward home, friends, self, family, other students, school
   3. Hobbies, play life, leisure time activities
   4. Educational and vocational goals
   5. Marked likes and dislikes—foods, toys, TV programs, etc.

E. Home and Family
   1. Individuals in the home
   2. Socioeconomic level
   3. Relation with home—favorite brothers/sisters, parent/other relative
   4. Regular chores; pets, etc.
   5. Home cooperation
   6. Record at social agencies

F. Work Experience
   1. Part-time jobs (summer, after school)
   2. Attitude toward work, etc.

G. Additional Information Needed
   1. Sending school
   2. Outside agencies
   3. Private sources, doctor, mental health center, etc. (need release forms)
   4. Health information

Help Your Child Improve Study & Homework Behaviors (Zifferblatt, 1970). How detailed these sections will be is dependent upon the teacher's knowledge of the parents of the children in her classroom.

The handbook may be very inclusive (general school policies, special community agencies, vacations, dates of regularly scheduled meetings, dates of PTA meetings, special release forms for information and field trips, etc.) or merely a brief description covering the high points. At the very least, it does place something in the parents' hands that demonstrates the teacher's willingness to share as well as receive information.

Techniques for developing handbooks and handouts for parents have been discussed in more detail in *Communicating with Parents of Exceptional Children* (Kroth, 1975).

Grade-Reporting Conferences

Many school districts require conferences at the elementary school level to discuss pupil progress. Usually the time allotment for this type of conference is relatively short, often twenty to thirty minutes. Because of the time limits set for a progress-reporting conference, it is of utmost importance for the teacher to be well prepared. It is seldom the proper time for a problem-solving conference. If a problem-solving conference is indicated, schedule it for a later date, when time is available to explore possible strategies for dealing with the problem.

In preparing for a grade-reporting conference, the teacher should briefly review the period from the past conference to the present one for which she is preparing. Look over the records, graphs, and samples of work that have been accumulated. Select with care specific examples of the child's work to illustrate points that need to be made during the conference. A folder of all the child's work (while of interest to parents) is probably too much for the parents to assimilate in a short conference and may detract from the specific points that the teacher wants to make.

Generally it is best to show areas of growth first and then areas where additional concentration must take place. If one starts with deficiencies, the parents may never "hear" the areas of progress. As the deficient areas are brought up in the conference by the teacher, she should present the plan she has for remediation, i.e., "I'm going to try Julie on the 'Language Master' for the next two weeks to see if it will help her spelling." Secondly, when social behaviors are isolated as target areas it is important to describe them in behavioral terms followed by the intervention program the teacher has prepared. For instance, instead of saying, "Jimmy is out of his seat all of the time," the teacher might say, "Jimmy is out of his seat on the average of ten times an hour. I'm going to show him the graph that I'm keeping and see if he can't try to reduce the number of times during this next week." The behavioral statements provide the parents with specific knowledge and some assurance that the teacher is doing her job in a thoughtful, scientific manner. It may be wise at this point to set a date for a later conference to be conducted by phone or in person. Parents will appreciate some indication in the near future of whether the program outlined by the teacher is successful.

During the grade-reporting conference, it is desirable to elicit from the parents any questions that they would like answered about academic progress. Since special education classes are usually smaller than ordinary ones, there should be more opportunity to provide these parents with a greater amount of information. Daily or weekly progress reports may be helpful. These will be discussed in greater detail in the section on problem-solving conferences.

While it has usually been felt desirable from the teachers' point of reference to share information with parents, this has often not been done completely for various reasons. School personnel have regarded some information as confidential and, therefore, not to be shared with parents. Some information such as IQ scores and various other test scores have been felt to be so emotion laden or beyond the scope of parental understanding that they have been withheld even though parents have requested the data. Recent legislation, however, indicates that information obtained by school personnel will be shared with parents upon request. It also limits the sharing of this information with other individuals without parental permission ("Privacy Rights," 1975).

This recent development will be regarded by some with apprehension; however, it should be viewed as a healthy sign. In many ways it encourages a partnership between the significant adults in a child's life. From a Transactional Analysis frame of reference, the relationship between parent and teacher should become one of adult to adult, which should enhance child growth.

Group Conferences

During the course of the school year, school personnel have information which can be shared best with parents in a group setting. These meetings should not be construed as group therapy sessions but to impart specific information to parents. Topics for these meetings might include:

1. An orientation to special education.
2. Special testing programs.
3. An explanation of Adjunctive Therapies (physical and occupational therapy, speech therapy, psychological or psychiatric services, social work services, nursing services, etc.).
4. Occupational information (for older children).

5. Behavioral management techniques.
6. Christmas suggestions for special education children.
7. Summer programs available for special education children.
8. Recreational activities, etc.

These meetings should be informative, and some type of handout material should be made available to parents. Usually parents do not come to a meeting prepared to take notes; therefore, having available handouts, pencils, etc. will enhance the possibility of getting the information in the parents' hands.

In addition to the obvious advantage of presenting common information to a number of parents at the same time, parent group meetings have several additional benefits. By bringing together a number of parents with a common problem, each member realizes that he or she is not alone. If the group is small enough there can be an interchange of ideas. Parents are interested in how others have dealt with their own feelings and specific problem behaviors of their children. They are often receptive to suggestions by other members of the group.

By meeting together and holding open discussions, parents sometimes discover that they have a common problem that may be solved by joint action. They may decide to write letters to their legislators or meet with top school administrators to present their concerns.

Some activities can be conducted in a group as easily as with individuals. Recently, a few special education teachers in Albuquerque, New Mexico, decided they would like to get an idea of the perceptions that the parents of the children they had in their classes had of their children's classroom behaviors. Prior to the group meeting each teacher sorted a list of 25 classroom behaviors for each child (Kroth, 1972). These "sorts" reflected the teachers' perception of the child in the class. When the parents attended the regularly scheduled meeting they were asked to arrange the twenty-five behaviors on the form board as they thought their child behaved in the classroom and, secondly, as they wished their child would perform. The parents' perceptions were then compared to the teachers' perceptions. The ensuing discussion cleared up some perceptions, and the following meeting was scheduled to discuss ways of dealing with behaviors that both teachers and parents perceived as problems.

Probably the best public relations program the school community has at its disposal is a well organized and professionally conducted program of information-sharing conferences. Parents will view them as a joint effort involving the significant adults in their children's lives, established for the sole purpose of facilitating the education growth of their children. Through careful planning the teacher can make information-sharing conferences an event that the adults look forward to, and these conferences can serve as a firm foundation for conferences which may be regarded as problem-solving.

PROBLEM-SOLVING CONFERENCES

Problem-solving conferences can be an exciting cooperative venture between parents and professionals. Although both sets of individuals may approach the meeting with trepidation, the teacher can do a great deal to set the tone for a productive meeting or series of meetings. There are a number of considerations for the teacher to keep in mind in the successful resolution of what may be considered a problem situation. Some of the points that she might consider are (1) the location of the problem, (2) problem identification and pre-planning, (3) the timing of conferences, (4) the data needs of the parent, (5) the reinforcement needs of parents, and (6) the provision for a demonstration of techniques.

Who Has the Problem?

If one adheres to an environmentalist point of view which implies that the environment controls the behavior of an individual, then it is conceivable that the behavior emitted by the child in the classroom may be different than his behavior at home. Parents sometimes are surprised that their son, who will not pick up his clothes at home, offered to straighten the chairs in the classroom. The teacher who has a problem settling the class to practice for the all-school program is often pleased to see the event go smoothly. Therefore, when the teacher perceives a problem of either social or academic behavior, she should not assume that the same problem occurs in the home. When the teacher informs the parents that their child is acting out in the classroom, one should not be surprised if the parents regard the deviant behavior as the teacher's problem—because essentially it is.

When a behavioral problem occurs at school which the teacher has not been able to successfully cope with using traditional methods, the purpose of a parent-teacher conference may be to define the type and magnitude of the problem and to solicit help from the parents in the solution of the problem. It would be incorrect to assume that the behavior occurs with equal magnitude across environments or that it is caused by the parents. The teacher should be prepared to describe the problem with concrete data, to solicit suggestions from the parents for control techniques, and to outline a program that may require parental support or involvement.

Problem Identification and Pre-planning

Often during the course of the school year there are a select number of students who display excesses or deficits of behavior and who have not responded to conventional approaches of behavior modification. In addition, quite often each of the pupils has a number of behaviors which need specific attention.

If the parents are to be involved in an intervention program, the following steps should facilitate the conference:

1. Select the behaviors that are of concern by listing a number of observable behaviors or having the child select his own targets (Kroth, 1972).
2. Define the behaviors in observable terms so that they can be accurately measured.
3. Rank the behaviors according to priority. It is usually advantageous to rank academic behaviors ahead of social behaviors, because the successful modification of a deficiency in academics will often alleviate excessive social behaviors.
4. From the priority ranked list of behaviors, put a P (for parent) next to those you want to work on with the parents and a T (for teacher) next to those you feel you need to work on alone.
5. Keep an accurate record of the frequency, percent, duration of rate of occurence of the selected behavior(s) for a week.
6. Graph the data which have been collected to have a visual record to present to the parents.
7. Prepare an outline of a plan for intervention of what you are to do and what the parents are to do. This plan, of course, is subject to change depending upon what the parents can do or are willing to do.

The care that is taken by the teacher in identifying the problems that she feels are solvable through joint action can reduce the amount of random activity surrounding the parent-teacher conference. The specificity of the behavior in terms of frequency, etc., and the preparation of a graphic presentation indicates to the parents that the teacher has taken a methodical approach to the problem and, therefore, the foundation is established for a systematic remediation program.

Timing Conferences

The parents of exceptional children, particularly those whose children have been identified as emotionally disturbed or learning disabled, often have had conferences with school personnel dealing with problematic situations. In some instances, the major contacts between educators and parents have been traumatic. In order to set the stage for a positive working relationship, holding conferences prior to entry as suggested by Duncan and Fitzgerald (1969) seems desirable.

The timing of conferences can be crucial to the working relationship between parents and educator. If the teacher is attempting to work with the parents on a specific behavior, it is usually desirable to have regularly scheduled conferences as close as a week apart. The first or second conference can be used to identify the specific target or behavior and to develop techniques for measuring the behavior. When a baseline has been established, the teacher can begin to develop, with the parents' input, the type of consequences that will be effective to change the behavior. The regularly scheduled conferences provide the teacher with opportunities for careful monitoring of the procedures and give the teacher an opportunity to reinforce the parents at regularly scheduled intervals (fixed interval schedule) which should insure the building of the new behavior on the part of both child and parent. As the new behavior becomes established, the teacher and parent may schedule conferences further apart.

Another advantage of having regularly scheduled conferences is to eliminate the "crisis conference." From a behavioral point of view, holding a conference immediately following a crisis may reinforce crisis type behavior on the part of the pupil. In a classroom at the Children's Rehabilitation Unit (CRU) at the University of Kansas, a particular boy was being sent home on the average of once every two weeks for extremely disruptive behavior. There was usually a conference with the parents to discuss the event and to make plans to deal with the behavior. On occasion, both parents and teacher expressed dissatisfaction with the conferences. It was decided to hold regularly scheduled conferences instead of scheduling around an event. During these conferences, methods for handling excessive behavior at school and at home were discussed. Because children in the classroom were programmed for high degrees of success, both academically and socially, most of the discussions in the conferences centered around how well the boy was doing and the improvement (shown graphically) that he was making from day to day. The conferences became more pleasant and profitable. It was observed that there were considerably fewer disruptive episodes that resulted in the boy's being sent home before the end of the day. The parents and the teacher became a team with a common goal, and the boy could no longer enjoy the occurrences of parents and teacher in conflict. A greater consistency between management procedures at home and school resulted in a greater consistency in productive behavior at school during the ensuing months.

Another consideration in the timing of the conferences should be the time of day for the conference. If the purpose of the conference is merely to share data and consider slight modification procedures, then an open-ended time slot may hinder that objective. One set of parents tended to take every conference as an opportunity to discuss the other children in the family as well as the boy in the special class. While a discussion of the family dynamics was deemed desirable, the proper time for this was considered to be at a regularly scheduled group meeting of parents which was conducted by a social worker. In order to facilitate the data-sharing conference, it was decided to hold the conference thirty minutes before school began in the morning. The father needed to go on to work, and the teacher needed to go to class. Business was conducted in a precise and orderly fashion, and both teacher and parents were pleased with the progress.

One should consider the potentially positive effects of setting a limit on the number of conferences in a series. Various therapists have experimented with setting temporary termination dates to increase the pressure on the patient to take over his own management (Alexander & Selesnick, 1966; Shlien, Mosak & Dreikurs, 1962). In establishing a rationale for the structure Shlien, Mosak & Dreikurs (1962) say:

> In essence, the theory is that time limits place the emphasis where it belongs; on quality and process, rather than on quantity. Times does not heal because it cannot, only activity can heal; and the more activity, the shorter time required. This theory holds that limits, in effect, increase energy, choice, wisdom, and courage, and so they heighten the essential process while they reduce the largely unessential time. (p. 31)

Parents Need Data

Teachers sometimes comment on the ineffectiveness of report cards as behavior change agents. They point out the similarity of the grade point average from one marking period to the next.

One of the problems with the use of grade cards as modifiers is the long time span between the issuances of the reporting forms. In a sense, this strategy of reporting to parents may be considered as a fixed interval of reinforcement. In an attempt to alter the observed pattern of behavior associated with traditional home-school reports, various investigators have experimented with daily report card systems (Edlund, 1969; Fuller, 1971; Kroth, Whelan & Stables, 1970; Simonson, 1972).

Edlund (1969) described, in some detail, procedures for setting up a daily home-school communication list. Usually the teacher and parents establish in a conference a set number of social and academic behaviors to be communicated on a daily basis. They establish the nature of the symbols (percentages, check marks, Smiling Sams, letter grades) that will be recorded on a form, signed by the teacher, and conveyed by the child. In order to insure that the cards are received at home, a system (phone calls or consequences) is established to ensure that the card is brought home. At this point, teacher and parents usually agree on some reward system to be administered at home for improved performances at school.

When the school personnel informs parents of a problem relating to an excess or deficit of behavior on their child's part, some action will probably take place. This is often true even when teachers tell the parents not to concern themselves with the particular problem. For example, in the early grades, parents may be informed that their child is having problems with reading and at the same time are instructed not to do anything about it. Rare are the parents who can ignore a problem involving their child. When a problem area has been pinpointed, it is often far better to include the parents in plans for remediation. In the daily data system, they are provided with an active role. They can become a positive reinforcer for the child's growth. They have a specific plan of action and a key role, whereas if they are left alone they may punish the child or require long hours of nonproductive study time.

Edlund (1969) points out that "it is far more effective to arrange for teachers and parents to become directly involved in managing the child's behavioral learning progress than to simply tell them how behavior is learned" (p. 127). In order to effect change in the classroom, though, parents need data. They cannot rely on the child's verbal report.

Parents Need Reinforcement

Improved study habits, academic behavior, and social behavior on the part of the child are usually contingent upon reinforcement from parents. The parents must alter their schedule in such a way to insure that consistent rewards follow improved behavior. What guarantees that the parents will continue to maintain these new behavioral patterns after the initial program has been laid out?

Edlund (1969) states, "When a teacher or a parent rewards a child's desirable behavior, and that behavior is maintained, the teacher or the parent is, in turn, rewarded" (p. 127). While it is possible that behavioral change on the part of the child will be rewarding enough to maintain the reorganized patterns of behavior by parents, it is also a distinct possibility that the parents will revert to old familiar patterns of behavior when it appears that their problem has been solved. Adults have reinforcing events in their own world which may be incompatible with dispensing rewards to their child and providing the structure that is indicated. The cocktail hour, the bridge club, TV programs, or a good book may compete with listening to a child read, watching a child's graph go up, and providing milk and cookies after study time. In fact, the reordering of priorities may occur quite quickly as the child shows progress.

The teacher is probably well advised to provide some sort of systematic reinforcement to parents for successfully carrying out a planned program. The most common forms of providing reinforcement are letters and phone calls. However, some innovative teachers take the common approaches and make them unusual. One of the teachers in the Curriculum of Positive Emphasis (COPE) project in the Lincoln, Nebraska Public Schools had a child in a class for behaviorally disturbed children who successfully completed a difficult project. Rather than send a note or call the parents herself, she took the boy to the principal's office with the completed project and asked the principal to call the mother and inform the mother of her son's accomplishment. This procedure was extremely reinforcing to the parents, the child, and the administration. It also served to establish a different relationship between school and home. Often the contacts between school administrators and the parents of children who exhibit behavioral disorders have been precipitated by a crisis. As a result, calls to parents by school personnel may set up negative expectations on the part of parents.

Most parents never receive any personal communication from school other than notices of PTA meetings, quarterly report cards, occasional notices of pending failure or broken rules (smoking, tardiness, etc.) or a call from the nurse if the child is absent. The provision of data such as that mentioned earlier somewhat alleviates the communication void, but it does not solve the need for reinforcement for carrying out a planned program. Nielsen (1972) conducted a study to examine the effects of positive reinforcement on parents of behaviorally disturbed children. Twenty-three students and their parents were selected for the investigation. These children were divided into four groups. The parents of two of the groups were provided with academic activities in spelling and math to aid their children. The parents of the other two groups were provided with recommended games to improve their children's social behavior. One set of parents in each major group (academic and social) was reinforced periodically by notes, phone calls, and home visits for their children's academic achievement or for playing games with their children. Daily recording of scores in spelling and math and the pre- and post-scores on the Peterson and Quay Modified Behavior Checklist were used as measuring instruments. The pupils' teachers were the sources for the academic data and the behavioral ratings, and they were uninformed as to which of the parents were being reinforced.

The results of the study were as follows:

1. All six of the children whose parents were reinforced for playing games had improved behavioral rating scores, while only two of the five whose parents were not reinforced improved.

2. All six of the children whose parents were reinforced for academic assistance showed gain in both academic areas with the exception of one child who gained in spelling and maintained his math average. By contrast, only one child in the nonreinforced group improved in both spelling and math. One child decreased in both areas, while the other four children showed an increase in one area and a decrease in the other or maintained the same level.

Nielsen (1972) concluded that:

When targets are clearly specified and the parents are reinforced for working with their children, change takes place. It is not enough merely to identify a deficit and assume that parents will alter their methods of assisting their children at home. Parents, like children, need specific instruction and reinforcement for carrying out these planned programs. Furthermore, the present study indicates that notifying parents of their child's deficits and the failing to provide feedback may actually increase academic and behavioral problems. (p. 36)

To say that parents "ought to want" to change is an irrational idea. Learning to be a reinforcing parent is hard work. As such, it is necessary to provide parents with praise, letters, approval, and other signs of recognition for improved performance. Being a parent, like being a teacher, is a lonely profession. Approval for another significant adult can be highly rewarding.

Parents May Need a Demonstration

One does not learn to be a teacher by reading a book or by attending a series of lectures. Although a teacher can pick up some valuable ideas through these methods, usually the teacher is required to go through some form of internship. First there is the observation of children, then the observation of a master teacher, then teaching under supervision and finally the opportunity to teach alone. Obviously, during this process there is a certain amount of modeling behavior. When situations arise, the cadet teacher tends to try to respond as she saw the master teacher respond.

Parents, on the other hand, do not have the benefits of an internship. Even if they use their own parents as models, the advent of an exceptional child leaves them somewhat unprepared. Therapists with various philosophical orientations have advocated the use of parents in the treatment of children and have included them in the therapy sessions (Guerney, 1969). In some instances the parents act as passive observers, while, in other instances, therapists encourage the parent to take over the role of "teacher" under guidance.

Guerney (1969) reported a technique called *filial therapy* in which groups of parents of exceptional children are taught to conduct play sessions through a series of meetings. The beginning sessions are somewhat didactic, leading to an observation of other parents working with their children; then the parents conduct a play session with a child under supervision before they attempt the same procedures at home. The second stage involves having the parents use the techniques at home while having weekly discussion sessions with the group leaders. The final stage is concerned with phasing the parents out of the original parents group as their children reach levels of competence and obtain feelings of confidence.

A similar strategy of taking parents through a step-by-step procedure was used by Russo (1964), except that the skills which the parents learned were based on a behavior modification orientation rather than the Rogerian client-centered orientation. Through a shaping process, the mother observed the therapist interacting with her child; then a three-way interaction evolved, and finally the therapist began to withdraw from active participation in the sessions. A brief conference was held after each session to discuss the progress of the behavioral therapy, and an opportunity was provided for the therapist to reinforce the parent immediately for appropriate behavior.

Straughan (1964) reported a similar study in which the mother observed a therapist working with her child and was then phased into the therapist's role. The mother was reinforced for appropriate behavioral responses and inappropriate responses were ignored. Only five sessions were needed to bring about change in the mother-child relationship.

Not all parents need to go through the process described, and yet the opportunity for providing such a training session should be available to parents. The following case study reported by Simpson (1971) illustrates the point:

> A six year old boy, F, was referred to the CRU for a comprehensive evaluation to determine his functional levels and educational placement possibilities. Along with specific recommendations for educational placement and program, a behavior modification program was recommended to be carried out in the home by the parents to deal with F's negativism. F was described as "headstrong" and "set in his ways."
>
> Negative behavior was operationally defined, and an event-recording procedure was employed to measure the target daily. The procedures were to be carried out in the home. The baseline data was found to be fairly stable, although slightly ascending, with a median occurrence of 23 events a day (see Figure 2). Basic learning theory procedures were explained to the parents, and a two-point program was agreed upon. The parents were to ignore oppositional behavior while rewarding cooperative behavior, and they were to isolate F for 5 minutes following each instance of oppositional behavior.
>
> Oppositional behavior increased for the first two days of the modification program, and the mother reported that F was "uncontrollable." It became almost impossible physically to place F in the time-out room; and while he was there, he was destructive. F and his mother returned to the CRU and a telecoaching device was used whereby the mother wore an ear plug attached to a transistor radio. The teacher stood on one side of a one-way mirror and told the mother specifically when to reinforce, ignore and implement time-out procedures. After a single session, the mother implemented the procedure at home; and the median number of oppositional incidents was reduced to two.
>
> A follow-up conference with the mother a year later indicated that F was maintaining appropriate behavior and that the mother felt comfortable with the procedures, using them when needed.

Fortunately, in the preceding case, the mother called the teacher immediately to let her know the process was not working. One wonders how often parents leave the training session, try out the recommendations at home, find them ineffective, drop them without informing the teacher, and allow the teacher to think that the program was highly effective and to be recommended to the next set of parents.

Sometimes the language which is so familiar to the teacher is unfamiliar to parents. Instructions that seem clear are misinterpreted. The writer remembers one instance in which a parent was told to pinpoint a target and return with a

Figure 2
MODIFICATION OF NEGATIVE BEHAVIOR
USING TELECOACHING & TIME-OUT PROCEDURES

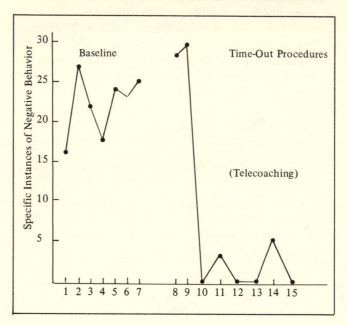

graph a week later. The parent came back with a graph with seven pins stuck on it. Perhaps a demonstration of the instructions would have helped.

Summary

The education of exceptional children is an exciting task. The teacher who accepts this responsibility should be well trained in programming for the special needs of her children and knowledgeable in special techniques for modifying behaviors. One area of her training that is sometimes neglected is the acquisition of specialized knowledge pertaining to working with parents.

Parents must be recognized as a powerful force in the success of any education program for children. Through their joint efforts, parents have been influential in gaining national, state, and local legislation in support of special education. Individually, they have contributed to or hindered the progress of their children in the classroom. Teachers who have recognized that parents are educators have found that well-planned conferences serve to facilitate the educational process.

Of the two major types of conferences outlined above, information-sharing conferences are the backbone of the home-school relationships. Initial efforts to establish a procedure for sharing knowledge sets the stage for further problem-solving situations. Teachers who are open about what goes on in their classroom and who share their techniques for change with parents will find it easier to gain information from parents that will help in the education of children. Parents have a right to know what the teacher knows about their children, and the teacher has an obligation to prepare the information in a manner that insures understanding. If this relationship is properly established, then problem-solving conferences become less traumatic and may be regarded as a joint effort rather than a conflict between what is and what should be in the eyes of the perceiver.

1. It is important in problem-solving conferences to decide who has the problem. Does the discrepancy between the "real" and "ideal" exist both in the classroom and the home, or is it strictly a school problem in which the parents' assistance is requested?

2. The teacher's skill in defining the problem in behavioral terms and preparing information to communicate to parents demonstrates the professional level of the teacher.

3. The teacher needs to consider the timing of the conferences. When conferences are held, the number and the length of the conferences play a part in the success or failure of the problem-solving process.

4. If parents are to become actively involved in the solution of a problem that is school based, then they need data to respond to in order to carry out their part of the program. Plans should be made to supply them with information or feedback from the classroom systematically.

5. Parents need to be reinforced for carrying out a home-school program. Although the area of parents programs has scarcely been researched, the evidence that exists suggests it is very important and should not be neglected.

6. To assume that parents understand their part of the problem-solving venture after a brief conference may be to assume too much. Occasionally, it is helpful to "walk parents through" a process. We all learn by having products and activities demonstrated to us. Industry considers it good salesmanship to show how a process works and education should consider the importance of using demonstrations when working with parents.

The education of children is a full-time job. To neglect the home environment and the influential effects of parents is unprofessional. The assumption that parents do not care is unwarranted. The successful special education teacher is "special" because she uses all resources available to facilitate the educational progress of her children.

REFERENCES

Alexander, F. G. & Selesnick, S. T. *The History of Psychiatry: An Evaluation of Psychiatric Thought and Practice from Prehistoric Times to the Present.* New York: Harper & Row, 1966.

Becker, W. C. *Parents Are Teachers.* Champaign, Ill.: Research Press, 1971.

Buscaglia, L. F. "Parents Need to Know: Parents and Teachers Work Together." In J. I. Arena (Ed.), *The Child with Learning Disabilities: His Right to Learn.* Pittsburg: Association for Children with Learning Disabilities, 1971.

Dodson, F. *How to Parent.* New York: New American Library, 1970.

Duncan, L. W. & Fitzgerald, P. W. "Increasing the Parent-Child Communication through Counselor-Parent Conferences." *Personnel and Guidance Journal,* 1969, 514-517.

Edlund, C. W. "Rewards at Home to Promote Desirable School Behavior." *Teaching Exceptional Children,* 1969, Summer, 121-127.

Fuller, J. M. "An Evaluation of the Home-School Behavioral Management Program Implemented in an Intermediate Classroom for the Emotionally Disturbed." Unpublished doctoral dissertation, University of Kansas, 1971.

Guerney, B. G., Jr. (Ed.) *Psychotherapeutic Agents: New Roles for Nonprofessionals, Parents, and Teachers.* New York: Holt, Rinehart & Winston, 1969.

Kelly, E. J. "Parental Roles in Special Education Programming—A Brief for Involvement." *Journal of Special Education, 7,* No. 4, 1973 (357-364).

Kroth, R. L. *Communicating with Parents of Exceptional Children.* Denver: Love Publishing, 1975.

Kroth, R. L., Whelan, R. J. & Stables, J. M. "Teacher Application of Behavior Principles in Home and Classroom Environments." *Focus on Exceptional Children, 3,* 1970, 1-10.

Kroth, R. L. *Target Behavior.* Olathe, Kansas: Select-Ed, 1972.

Love, H. D. *Parental Attitudes toward Exceptional Children.* Springfield, Ill.: Charles C. Thomas, 1970.

Nielsen, R. R. "The Influence of Reinforced Parents on Behaviorally Disturbed Children." Unpublished master's thesis, University of Kansas, 1972.

Patterson, G. R. & Guillion, M. E. *Living with Children: New Methods for Parents and Teachers.* Champaign, Ill.: Research Press, 1968.

"Privacy Rights of Parents and Students." *Federal Register, 40,* No. 3, Department of Health, Education, and Welfare, Jan. 6, 1975 (1208-1216).

Ross, A. O. *The Exceptional Child in the Family.* New York: Grune & Stratton, 1964.

Russo, S. "Adaptions on Behavioral Therapy with Children" *Behavior Research and Therapy, 2,* 1964, 43-47.

Shlien, J. M., Mosak, H. H., & Driekurs, R. "Effects of Time Limits: A Comparison of Two Psychotherapies." *Journal of Counseling Psychology, 9,* 1962, 31-34.

Simonson, G. "Modification of Reading Comprehensive Scores Using a Home Contract with Parental Control of Reinforcers." Unpublished master's thesis, University of Kansas, 1972.

Simpson, R. "A Telecoaching Approach to Behavior Modification: A Procedure For Decelerating Negative Behavior in an Emotionally Disturbed Child." Unpublished Paper, Kansas Federation CEC, 1971.

Straughan, J. H. "Treatment with Child and Mother in the Playroom." *Behavior Research and Therapy,* 1964, *2,* 37-41.

Truax, C. B. & Wargo, D. "Human Encounters that Change Behavior for Better or Worse." *American Journal of Psychotherapy,* 1966, *20,* 499-520.

Wolfensberger, W. & Kurtz, R. A. (Eds.) *Management of the Family of the Mentally Retarded: A Book of Readings.* Follett Educational Corporation, 1969.

Zifferblatt, S. *You Can Help Your Child Improve Study and Homework Behaviors.* Champaign, Ill.: Research Press, 1970.

One model of a program to train and assist the regular classroom teacher to provide meaningful learning experiences for children eligible for special education services is the consulting teacher. Such an approach applying individualized instruction and behavioral analysis seems imperative if "mainstreaming" is to be successful. The authors offer an in depth look at this approach, even to including how data should be collected and how the results of the program should be evaluated.

The Consulting Teacher Approach to Special Education: Inservice Training for Regular Classroom Teachers

Lu S. Christie, Hugh S. McKenzie, Carol S. Burdett
University of Vermont

In Vermont, consulting teachers train and assist regular classroom teachers to provide successful learning experiences for children eligible for special educational services. The rationale for consulting teachers (McKenzie, 1969; McKenzie et al., 1970; McKenzie, 1972; Fox, 1972) has been supported by Lilly (1971) and Martin (1972). Regular class placement for all but the profoundly handicapped is advocated. Inservice training to provide regular classroom teachers with special education skills is the fundamental approach.

The consulting teacher receives training in a two-year Master of Education program (McKenzie, 1972). During the program, the consulting teacher learns principles of applied behavior analysis, applying these principles to eligible children in regular classrooms, and learns to measure and monitor precisely a child's daily performance to ensure that applications are effective. The consulting teacher learns to individualize instruction, often adapting for use materials typically available in elementary schools. He learns to derive for classrooms and entire elementary schools a minimum set of objectives

419

which every child should achieve in language, arithmetic, and social behaviors. He learns procedures for training teachers, parents, aides, and other school personnel in behavior analysis, measurement, individualizing instruction, and deriving minimum objectives. When graduated and certified, the consulting teacher is employed full time by a Vermont school district and receives an appointment as an adjunct instructor in special education at the University of Vermont.

The successful consulting teacher trains all regular elementary classroom teachers who are his responsibility in the techniques of applied behavior analysis. As a result of this training, the teachers have derived minimum objectives for language, arithmetic, and social behaviors which all children in their classes are to achieve. The teachers regularly monitor the children's rates of achieving these objectives. Any child who is found not to be achieving objectives at the minimum rate needs the special skills the teacher has acquired. If these special skills fail to increase the child's rate of achievement, the teacher requests help from the consulting teacher, and together they develop teaching/ learning procedures effective for the child's successful learning.

This paper describes tactics which apparently have been successful in gaining the cooperation of regular teachers to provide special education in their classrooms, methods used for training these teachers, a summary outline of apparently critical tasks performed by consulting teachers, and a brief evaluation of the performance of consulting teachers over the past four years in Vermont.

GAINING AND MAINTAINING THE COOPERATION
OF THE CLASSROOM TEACHER

Within traditional administrative and philosophical approaches to special education, a teacher's major task is to identify a handicapped child and refer him for testing. Then he is either removed from the classroom and placed with other children with similar problems, or he remains in the classroom now labeled "dull normal," "retarded," "dyslexic," or "emotionally disturbed." Remaining in a regular class with a label can be another form of removal, perhaps more subtle but just as effective, as the teacher is often instructed to be "very understanding of the child's problem," not to "push" him, or not to ask him to do more than his "ability" will allow. Both alternatives can provide a teacher with acceptable reasons for no longer being accountable for the child's progress.

On the other hand, the consulting teacher insists that a referring teacher be accountable for every child's acquisition of important social and academic skills. The teacher must learn to apply special education skills in her classroom, though the required training process is a time consuming, challenging addition to her teaching responsibilities.

Because of this added burden, it is doubtful that the consulting teacher could gain the cooperation of *all* teachers without assistance. Several factors have apparently been instrumental in helping the consulting teacher gain teachers' cooperation, including support systems which have been developed at the state, university, and local levels. When a teacher does not participate in the training program despite these support systems, the consulting teacher may employ a variety of procedures which may involve the teacher or his supervising principal.

State Support

The Division of Special Educational and Pupil Personnel Services, Vermont State Department of Education, has been directly involved in the development of the consulting teacher approach to special education (McKenzie et al., 1970) and provides special certification for consulting teachers. The Division supports effective consulting teacher programs by providing 75% of the consulting teacher's and his aide's salaries, thus providing a considerable incentive for school districts to hire consulting teachers. The Division discourages the establishment of special classes for the moderately handicapped in districts where consulting teacher services are available or soon can be made available. The state approves workshops conducted by the consulting teacher for recertification credits for classroom teachers.

State program participation, financial support, endorsement, and certification provide incentives for local school districts and, thus, teachers to become involved in this approach to serving handicapped learners.

University Support

Before a consulting teacher is employed by a school district, representatives from the University describe to district administrators the objectives of the consulting teacher approach and the methods employed by the consulting teacher to achieve those objectives. Many hours of joint planning by district and university personnel transpire before a final decision is mutually made to initiate the consulting teacher approach to special education in that district. Such planning typically includes presentations by consulting teachers and consulting teacher interns to elementary school principals, teachers, and community groups as well as to school boards.

Once placed in a school district, the certified consulting teacher becomes an adjunct instructor at the University. In this role, he can offer graduate courses to teachers in his school district. Tangible rewards of certification and graduate credits result from a teacher's successful completion of these courses. Often such credits are required for continuation of employment and for salary increments. The offering of courses within the teacher's school district at convenient hours can represent a considerable savings in time and money for teachers who otherwise must travel some distance to attend classes during the school year or spend summers in graduate study. Moreover, such courses offer credit, in part, for on-the-job experience in teaching eligible children, meeting the demands of teachers who ask for "relevancy."

Local Support

The consulting teacher is not an "expert from the University." He is hired by the local school district after personnel of the district have been informed of the program's goals and methods for achieving them. During his second year of preparation to be a consulting teacher (see McKenzie, 1972), the student interns in a school district which has selected the consulting teacher approach, with financial support for this internship supplied partially through local funds. This financial investment enhances the commitment of administrators and school boards to this method of delivering special education services. Moreover, they respond positively to the accountability of the reliable measures of the behavioral approach.

Parents have also provided active support of the program, praising classroom teachers for their applications of new skills, praising principals for their encouragement of the program, and urging school boards and other administrators to continue and expand consulting teacher services. Parents sometimes say that this is the first time their child has ever received any "real" help.

Voluntary Teacher Cooperation

The foundation of state, community, and local support of the consulting teacher approach may both prompt and reward teacher cooperation in the inservice training program. However, many teachers appear to "voluntarily" cooperate.

Referrals for consulting teacher services from teachers who are not enrolled in formal training appear to be prompted by many different factors. The teacher may simply be curious about the program, interested in trying a new approach. Skepticism sometimes prompts a referral, a willingness to "try this nonsense for a while" to see if it has any merit. Sometimes a teacher becomes a consultee because she has tried every technique she knows with no results, and the consulting teacher represents one last chance to help a child. Often, a colleague who has had successful training experiences with the consulting teacher prompts another teacher who then initiates referrals. The referring teacher may have observed her colleague's success with a child, and she is at least partially convinced that the consulting teacher approach has merit.

Despite the differences in motivation, all of these consultees by their referrals, have approached a consulting teacher and indicated a willingness to at least attempt to provide a program for a child, thus learning some special education skills. For these approach responses the consulting teacher can provide consequences which, if effective, should result in increased involvement of each teacher in the program. The most effective consequence appears to be success with the child. When the teacher has been helped to create an environment which makes it possible for the nonreader to read or results in the classroom "terror" announcing from his desk that he "just loves school," it is difficult for her to return to or even tolerate the comfortable philosophies of the past.

An example was overheard in a teachers' room where one teacher was bemoaning the fact that "Sam" was learning nothing. Sam's previous teacher was sympathetic and offered the solution, "Well, what can you expect with an IQ that low?" A teacher who had been involved in the consulting teacher program for several years glanced up from her cup of coffee and quietly answered, "You'd be surprised!"

Gaining the Cooperation of the Reluctant Teacher

Unfortunately, not all referrals are initiated by the teacher. Sometimes they are forced by concerned parents, by a principal, or by another supervisor. In extreme cases, the teacher is told that she must work with the consulting teacher if she wishes to continue in the classroom. This teacher's referral does not represent an approach response, nor does it necessarily indicate concern for the child. Such a teacher is likely to be difficult to train. Often, this teacher's reluctance to work with the consulting teacher is coincidental with a minimal set of teaching skills and a feeling of aversion toward the child. This teacher may secretly and sometimes openly hope that the consulting teacher will fail to be of any help.

The first attempt with this reluctant consultee is to follow the training based model inherent in the consulting procedures. In this case, the consulting teacher's social skills are of the utmost importance. Often he must ignore a good many inappropriate verbal responses, while attending to all responses that approximate the appropriate. Success with this teacher often represents a large expenditure of time and effort on the part of the consulting teacher. However, the teacher may eventually respond with an excellent program for the child and become involved in a course or a workshop as a result.

If the teacher will not provide an effective program for the child, it is necessary to take other action. The consulting teacher may recommend the child's placement in another classroom or provide tutoring for the student by the consulting teacher aide, a peer, or a parent. Whatever the approach, if the teacher remains in the classroom an attempt is made to keep the channels of communication open in the hope that a later training attempt may be more successful.

There remains a group of teachers who either deny the existence of children in the classrooms who could benefit from their regular teachers' use of consulting teacher training or who are adamant in their refusal to work with the consulting teacher. These attitudes are not associated with any particular age group, appear to be the results of previous reinforcement and punishment associated with the education of handicapped learners, and may also represent a misunderstanding of applied behavior analysis. Whatever the reason, it is very difficult for the consulting teacher to provide for new learning to take place when the teacher avoids all contact with the program.

To date, this problem has been solved only when the building principal has insisted on total staff participation and has made working with the consulting teacher a condition under which new teachers are hired. While this may result in involving some teachers of the "reluctant" variety, it does at least provide for initial interaction.

Enlisting Administrative Support

The active support and enthusiasm of the building principal appears to be a crucial factor in both gaining and maintaining teacher involvement. The principal can provide encouragement for the teacher who is struggling to acquire new skills and can praise her when improvement in a child's behavior occurs. His suggestion that she should refer a child to the consulting teacher may be the deciding factor that prompts her first approach response.

The principal's endorsement of the zero-reject model (Lilly, 1971) and his insistence on special education services which result in measured increases in children's skills can insure the eventual total involvement of his faculty. This structure of administrative support must be built on a foundation of mutual trust between the principal and the consulting teacher. The consulting teacher assumes that the principal is a skilled professional who is concerned about the welfare and education of the children in his school. The principal cannot be expected to assume the consulting teacher possesses these same credentials. He must demonstrate professional skills and concern for children to earn the principal's respect and trust.

Trust cannot exist without communication. Formal monthly reports have their place as do lengthy statements of purpose and descriptions of procedures; but they cannot, in the authors' judgment, replace the more personal forms of communication and the sharing of reinforcers. A happy mother can be prompted to stop in at the principal's office or leave a note to tell him how pleased she is with her child's progress. A brief thank-you note hastily scribbled by the consulting teacher can be a meaningful consequence for a principal's contribution to a teacher's training. A five minute look at a child's data can prompt a principal to praise a teacher for her work on an individualized program.

The consulting teacher can arrange for requests from visitors to observe regular classroom teachers with special education skills. The principal's permission for these visits is always obtained; they are guests in his school. He is asked to greet the visitors and, whenever possible, to spend a few minutes talking with them about the program, answering their questions. These interviews provide valuable feedback for the consulting teacher. If the principal identifies with the program and can articulate its objectives, the communication system has been successful.

A principal has administrative skills. The consulting teacher is also an administrator and should earn the respect of the principal in that role as well. There are simple, courteous behaviors, such as promptness, meticulous concern for detail, and dependability which are indicators of administrative skills. The consulting teacher's administrative duties include establishing and maintaining such office procedures as efficient systems for collecting, recording, and filing data and other records. He must train an aide to take reliable measures of behavior and to carry out the office procedures. He must prepare and administer a budget.

An efficient referral and formal communication system must be established with district administrators, principals, teachers, and parents by the consulting teacher. That communication system becomes a vehicle for disseminating information and for prompting mutual support and reinforcement for effective services to children. The principal should be a key figure in that communication system, since he is the immediate supervisor who is often solely responsible for grade placement, referrals, and other crucial decisions about the education of an eligible child.

INSERVICE TRAINING OF TEACHERS

The consulting teacher approach is a teacher training based model of special education (Lilly, 1971). The consulting teacher provides three levels of training to regular elementary classroom teachers—consultation, workshops, and formal courses receiving University graduate credit. The training levels progress from specific and basic to complex and general special education skills, all involving applications within a trainee's classroom.

Consultation

The first level of teacher training is accomplished through consulting procedures undertaken with a teacher who has referred a child to a consulting teacher (see McKenzie, 1972, for an outline of the consulting steps employed to train consulting teachers).

Ideally, the consulting procedures are initiated by a teacher referral through the building principal. Together the consulting teacher and the referring teacher define the target behavior in observable and measurable terms and specify an instructional objective. The consulting teacher develops a simple measurement and recording procedure to be carried out by the teacher on a daily basis.

After the teacher has measured the behavior for a few days, she brings the data to the consulting teacher. If the data is determined to be reliable by a second observer (either the consulting teacher or his aide) and indicates that the child is performing below minimum objectives expected by the school, a parent conference is scheduled by the teacher. At this conference, the teacher and consulting teacher show and explain data which has been obtained, discuss general procedures which might be employed to help the child, and obtain written permission from the parent to serve the child through the consulting teacher. The consulting teacher then makes one or more classroom observations, confers with the teacher and often the child, and helps the teacher modify existing teaching/learning procedures. The parents and principal are informed of the planned procedures which then are implemented in the classroom. Daily measures of the target behavior are evaluated. If the child meets the instructional objective and achieves at acceptable rates, an exit interview is held with the parents. If not, further modifications of teaching/learning procedures are performed until the child achieves minimum objectives at acceptable rates.

Throughout this process the teacher is being informally trained to perform several tasks. She learns how a behavior is defined in observable and measurable terms; is trained to observe, reliably measure, record, and graph that behavior; and is shown how data is used to make educational decisions. When the modification procedure is implemented, she is trained to follow the prescribed program consistently. The procedure and the rationale for its use are described by the consulting teacher in terms of the principles of applied behavior analysis, thus initiating the teacher's understanding of these principles.

Throughout the consultation process, the consulting teacher provides the teacher with a great deal of attention and praise for her acquisition of new skills. As the child makes progress toward the instructional objective, that progress may become the reinforcer that maintains the teacher's behaviors. With prompts from the consulting teacher, if needed, the parent and principal also provide positive feedback for the teacher's service to the child.

426

Thus, the prompts, instructions and discussions of basic principles as well as the positive feedback provided by the consulting teacher, parents, and principal—all of which result from the consultation process—serve as effective initial training procedures for regular classroom teachers. What results from these initial training procedures is illustrated by the following case study.

P1 (Duval & Robinson, 1972)

P1 was referred to the consulting teacher because of severe academic deficits in his first grade work. He had scored low dull normal on an individual IQ test and would have been enrolled in a class for the mentally retarded had there been a place for him. Initially, the teacher felt that her skills were inadequate to provide for this child's educational needs.

The following *instructional* objective was specified:

Condition	Behavior	Criterion
Given 25 addition and subtraction equations written in vertical notation with sums and differences through 9 and an independent study time of at least 30 minutes,	the student will write the answers	with 90% accuracy.

Since entry level measures indicated that P1 could make correct oral responses to most equations with sums and differences through 5 (e.g., 3+2= , 2−1=), the consulting teacher prepared a series of daily worksheets on which P1 was expected to meet the following *enabling* objective:

Condition	Behavior	Criterion
Given 25 addition and subtraction equations written in vertical notation with sums and differences through 9 and an independent study time of at least 30 minutes,	the student will write the answers	with 90% accuracy.

P1 was assigned one of these worksheets per day. During baseline, P1's scores on these worksheets averaged 52%. The consulting teacher then asked the teacher to provide positive consequences for each sheet on which P1 met the 90% criterion. Consequences were teacher praise and a star pasted on the worksheet.

427

During the first 16 days these consequences were employed, P1's average correct rose to 96% (see Figure 1). The positive consequences were continued, and P1's high performance was maintained even though the difficulty of the worksheets steadily increased to include sums and differences through 6, 7, 8, and 9. The consulting teacher observed the arithmetic period and independently graded worksheets at least once each week to insure that measures were reliable and that positive consequences were delivered only when P1 met the specified criterion. P1's parents were happy to give permission for the use of consulting teacher services and were most pleased with the results.

Figure 1
PERCENTAGES CORRECT ON DAILY ARITHMETIC WORKSHEETS

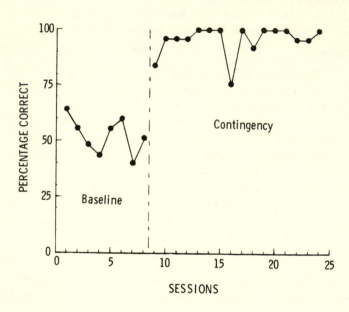

Summary. Through consultation, classroom teachers receive initial training in the following skills:

1. Defining target behavior in measurable terms
2. Measuring behavior reliably
3. Following teaching/learning procedures precisely
4. Collecting, recording, and graphing data daily
5. Identifying possible reinforcing consequences in the classroom
6. Writing instructional objectives
7. Responding to changes in the behavior of the child
8. Involving parents in the education process

Repeating this consultation process over time with several eligible children eventually would lead the teacher to acquiring complex and general special education skills. However, such skills appear to be more readily acquired by participation in the more formalized learning involved in workshops and courses conducted by the consulting teacher.

Workshops

Teachers who elect to take a consulting teacher workshop for three state recertification credits are required to read and respond to introductory readings on applied behavior analysis in the classroom and the rationale for the consulting teacher program. They also are required to carry out an individualized program for at least one child which may include verification of the procedures through either an ABAB or multiple baseline design (Baer, Wolf & Risley, 1968). Typically, teachers enrolled in workshops are asked to measure and graph more than one behavior. Again, the consulting procedures are followed. When the instructional objective has been met, the teacher must then describe in writing service to the child in case study form and orally present the study to a group of colleagues.

Thus, workshops add to the consultation process formal instruction in behavior analysis and the consulting teacher approach to special education. Moreover, the ability of teachers to verbally describe special education procedures is shaped through the writing of the case study and its presentation to other teachers participating in the workshop.

Graduate Courses

As previously noted, consulting teachers are appointed adjunct faculty of the Special Education Program of the University. In this role, consulting teachers can offer four courses of three hours each to teachers in their district.

The first two courses emphasize the analysis of behavior and individualizing instruction. These courses require both formal academic work and projects carried out in the teachers' classrooms. Teachers are required to do readings, take quizzes and make reports. They usually meet as a group with the consulting teacher for one to two hours a week throughout the semester. Here, assigned readings are discussed, reports are given and childrens' learning problems are resolved with other members of the class. In each of these courses, the teachers are required to improve the behaviors and individualize instruction for at least two students.

Teachers enrolled in the next two courses are required to write in specified form (Mager, 1962; Wheeler & Fox, 1972) terminal objectives that they expect their children to reach during the year in language, arithmetic, and social behaviors. For example, a teacher might state that the student must complete his spelling book by June with at·least 90% accuracy on all spelling tests. Teachers also may state their objectives in terms of tasks. For example, a teacher might list the following as some of the tasks a second grader must be able to complete by the end of the year, with 90-100% accuracy, with specified time limits for completing each tasks:

1. Add any two digit number with regrouping
2. Subtract any two digit number with borrowing
3. Tell time by 5 minute intervals
4. Know the multiplication facts through 5

The teacher is then required, with the help of the consulting teacher, to break down these terminal objectives into steps or enabling objectives and to put these enabling objectives on a time line which specifies the minimum amount each child must learn each month in order to complete required work by June. Students are checked monthly, and the teacher designs individualized instruction packets and applies consequences for those who have not met the monthly learning criteria set for the class.

As teachers progress through graduate courses, most become "turned on" by their increased special education skills and resulting successes with children with learning difficulties. These teachers generalize special procedures to their entire class, individualizing instruction in reading, writing, spelling, and arithmetic as well as developing instructional objectives in the area of social behaviors. Moreover, monthly checks are made on all children to insure that each child is achieving minimum objectives.

In each course, teachers are required to show scientific verification with at least one of their subjects—either by an ABAB or multiple baseline design. They must also write up the results of their studies and interpret the studies to parents, colleagues, and their immediate supervisor. The following case study shows the procedures one teacher used as a result of a course with the consulting teacher. The teacher individualized the student's entire language program. The study is an example of what she did in spelling.

P2 (Angney & Getsie, 1972)

P2 was chosen by his teacher as a subject for an individualized program because he seldom received adequate scores on his weekly spelling tests. P2 was an eight-year-old third grader who was experiencing difficulty in all areas of language arts. He was receiving special help from the remedial reading teacher and speech therapist and had been described as "perceptually handicapped."

The teacher's procedure was to present the words to the students on Monday, administer a pretest on Wednesday and a final test on Friday. No other formal spelling work was assigned during the week, although the children were allowed time to work on spelling independently. The teacher stated that P2 could spell with 90-100% accuracy on the final test if she spent time having him write the words with her during the week, but the time was not always available. During these baseline conditions, P2's scores averaged 64% (see Figure 2).

Figure 2
WEEKLY SPELLING TEST SCORES

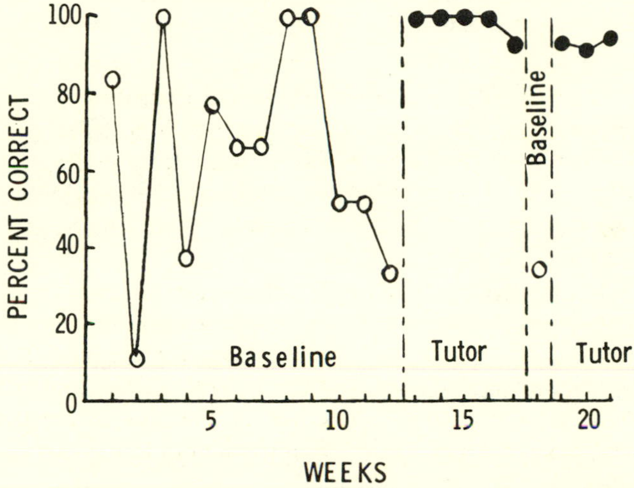

The teacher then established a peer tutor procedure. P2 was given a piece of paper folded lengthwise. The peer tutor would dictate P2's word, for example PENCIL. P2 would write it on his paper. When he finished the word, the tutor would ask, "Did you spell it, P-E-N-C-I-L?" If P2 wrote the word incorrectly, the tutor would spell it correctly, P2 would erase the word and rewrite it, and then turn his paper over and go through the same procedure again. This sequence was repeated with a new sheet of paper until P2 wrote the word correctly when it was dictated. If he wrote the word correctly the first time, he would mark it with a "C" and repeat the procedure with the next word. The tutor used this procedure with P2 daily. During this time, P2's scores on weekly spelling tests averaged 99%.

To test the procedure, that is, to see if the tutor was the variable affecting P2's grades, the teacher removed the tutoring procedure for one week. P2's score was 37% that week, and he asked to have his tutor again. The tutor was returned and again P2's test scores remained above the 90% criteria set by the teacher.

Thus, through graduate level courses, the consulting teacher extends teachers' training in the skills listed under *Consultation* above *and* trains teachers to . . .

1. Develop entry level measures of academic behaviors.
2. Establish minimum terminal objectives for a school year in language, arithmetic, and social behaviors.
3. Develop and sequence enabling objectives for school year terminal objectives.
4. Measure children's progress toward minimum objectives.
5. Develop materials and teaching/learning procedures needed to achieve objectives.
6. Evaluate effectiveness of procedures through ABAB or multiple baseline designs.
7. Write case studies of children served.
8. Interpret case studies to parents, colleagues, and administrators.

SUMMARY OF CONSULTING TEACHER TASKS

The major tasks of a consulting teacher may be briefly summarized as individualizing instruction, analysis of behavior, research, and consultation/training.

Individualizing Instruction. The consulting teacher helps teachers develop individualized sequences of instruction in language, arithmetic, and social behaviors. Sequences include measurement of entry level skills, derivation and specification of instructional objectives, selection of relevant learning materials, and measurement of pupil progress. Sequences of instruction are implemented with pupils eligible for special education. Written records, including reliable data, are kept for each implementation.

Analysis of Behavior. The consulting teacher shares his knowledge of the terminology and principles of the analysis of behavior by helping teachers and parents modify the behaviors of handicapped learners in the classroom setting as demonstrated by reliable measures of learners' behaviors. These applications of analysis of behavior focus on the principles of (1) reinforcement, (2) scheduling, (3) shaping, and (4) errorless discrimination.

Research. The consulting teacher *evaluates* research relevant to the education of handicapped learners according to the following criteria: applied, behavioral, analytic, technological, conceptual, effective, and generality (Baer, Wolf, and Risley, 1968).

The consulting teacher *adapts* research meeting the above evaluative criteria for application of the research procedures to handicapped learners.

Through consultees, the consulting teacher *applies* adapted research to handicapped learners with regular measures of learner's behaviors which reflect the effectiveness of the adaptation.

Consulting/Training. Each year the consulting teacher consults with teachers, parents, and administrators to help them serve 40 handicapped learners as demonstrated by measured behavioral changes in these learners.

The consulting teacher conducts workshops and courses on individualizing instruction and analysis of behavior for teachers in his district.

The consulting teacher makes formal and informal presentations describing the training of consulting teachers, the role of the consulting teacher in the school, data from service projects performed by the consulting teachers and teachers, and other related topics when appropriate. Presentations are made to various special interest groups, school personnel, and other professionals.

EVALUATION

The fundamental evaluative index to assess whether consulting teachers are successful in gaining cooperation and providing inservice training of teachers is the data depicting services to children (see P1 and P2 above). In the years that full-time consulting teachers have been employed in Vermont school districts, each has provided inservice training to 15-20 teachers per year. Through such training, each consulting teacher has yearly served at least 40 children eligible for special services (see Christie, Egner & Lates, 1973, for examples from the 1971-72 school year). Frequently, teachers trained in special skills independently apply these skills to children not eligible for special services.

Most teachers continue contact with consulting teachers once such contact has been initiated and, thus, the effects of inservice training cumulate. The cumulative effects of teacher training are illustrated by one regular class teacher who has worked with consulting teachers for four years and progressed through the training levels. She became a consultee during the first year consulting teacher services were available in her school, referring an eleven-year-old boy who was inattentive, disruptive, and a poor student (Humphreys and Seaver, 1969). Encouraged by her success with this child, the teacher enrolled in a workshop the following year during which she increased the attending behaviors and decreased the inappropriate social behaviors of three children (Seaver & Humphreys, 1970). She also measured and increased the attending behaviors of five additional children.

During her third year of inservice training, the teacher enrolled in a graduate course. Given a class of 16 boys who were all below grade level in reading, she measured their sight vocabulary entry levels, provided individualized programs to increase this skill, and retested them following instruction. She also measured and increased the attending behaviors of several boys and effected increases in weekly spelling scores by providing consequences for improvement. Her graduate studies continued during the fourth year when she developed comprehensive entry level measures for oral reading, sight vocabulary, spelling, written communication, and reading comprehension. These entry level measures provided the base for an individualized reading program, which incorporated procedures geared to the individual needs of each child. Monthly minimum objectives were developed and the progress of every child was monitored and graphed (Seaver, 1972). For two who were achieving at low rates, points contingent on work completed and correct were implemented throughout the day. One child exchanged his points for time with a peer tutor; the other accumulated his points to earn a basketball and net. The teacher also measured and increased the attending behavior of seven boys and eliminated thumb sucking in a girl who was engaged in this behavior throughout much of the school day.

During the four years of inservice training, this teacher has obtained reliable measures and effected improvements in the social and academic behaviors of a total of 48 children—one the first year, eight the second, 16 the third, and 23 the fourth. Her increasing special education skills have benefitted all of the children in her classroom, and she has prompted and encouraged the majority of the teachers in her school to become involved with the consulting teacher as consultees, workshop participants, or graduate students.

As a growing number of teachers are cumulating special education skills, so are a growing number of school administrators providing increasing support to consulting teachers. This support includes encouraging teachers to employ consulting teacher services as well as hiring only those teachers who will commit themselves to inservice training with the consulting teacher.

To date, 11 of Vermont's 54 supervisory school districts have employed consulting teachers, with an additional 14 of these districts having made firm plans to employ consulting teachers. Because of requests from school districts and the State Department of Education, the University now plans to begin graduating 16 rather than eight consulting teachers annually from its two-year Master of Education program preparing consulting teachers.

REFERENCES

Angney, A. & Getsie, R. "A Peer Tutor Procedure to Increase Spelling Accuracy." Unpublished manuscript, Special Education Program, College of Education, University of Vermont, 1972.

Baer, D., Wolf, M., & Risley, T. "Some Current Dimensions of Applied Behavior Analysis." *Journal of Applied Behavior Analysis, 1,* 1968, 91-97.

Christie, L., Egner, A., & Lates, B.J. (Eds.) *A Very Special Education for All Children.* Montpelier, Vermont: State Department of Education, Title III, ESEA, 1973.

Duval, J.K. & Robinson, L. "Increased Accuracy in Arithmetic in a First Grade Boy." Unpublished manuscript, Special Education Program, College of Education, University of Vermont, 1972.

Fox, W.L. "The Consulting Teacher Program." Unpublished manuscript, Special Education Program, College of Education, University of Vermont, 1972.

Humphreys, S. & Seaver, P. "Increasing Attending Behavior and Academic Performance in an 11-Year-Old Boy." In McKenzie, H.S. (Ed.), *The 1968-1969 Yearly Report of the Consulting Teacher Program: Volume II*. Burlington, Vermont: Special Education Program, College of Education, University of Vermont, 1969, 266-272.

Lilly, M.S. "A Training Based Model for Special Education." *Exceptional Children, 37,* 1971, 745-749.

Mager, R.F. *Preparing Instruction Objectives.* Palo Alto, California: Fearon Publishers, 1962.

Martin, E.W. "Individualism and Behaviorism as Future Trends in Educating Handicapped Children." *Exceptional Children, 38,* 1972, 517-527.

McKenzie, H.S. "Special Education and Consulting Teachers. In Clark, F., Evans, D., & Hammerlynk, L. (Eds.), *Implementing Behavioral Programs for Schools.* Champaign, Illinois: Research Press Company, 1972, 103-125.

McKenzie, H.S. (Ed.), *The 1968-1969 Yearly Report of the Consulting Teacher Program: Volume I.* Burlington, Vermont: Special Education Program, College of Education, University of Vermont, 1969.

McKenzie, H., Egner, A., Knight, M., Perelman, P., Schneider, B., & Garvin, J. "Training Consulting Teachers to Assist Elementary Teachers in the Management and Education of Handicapped Children." *Exceptional Children, 37,* 1970, 137-143.

Seaver, P. "An Adaptation of a Reading Procedure for Handicapped Learners to a Regular Classroom of Twenty-three Third Graders." Unpublished manuscript, Special Education Program, College of Education, University of Vermont, 1972.

Seaver, P. & Humphreys, S. "Increasing Study Behavior as a Result of Decreasing Inappropriate Responses." In Cleveland, M.D., Humphreys, S., Schneider, B.M., & Fox., W. L. (Eds.), *The 1969-1970 Yearly Report of the Consulting Teacher Program: Chittenden Central School District.* Burlington, Vermont: Special Education Program, College of Education, University of Vermont, 1972, 26-31.

Wheeler, A.H., & Fox, W.L. *Managing Behavior: Part 5, Behavior Modification: A Teacher's Guide to Writing Instructional Objectives.* Lawrence, Kansas: H & H Enterprises, Inc., 1972.

Regardless of whether a person is a "mainstreamer" or a "special classer," the success of a teacher will be determined by his or her ability to reinforce or not reinforce appropriate and inappropriate classroom behavior. Many a "good teacher" has had trouble on certain days when a particular child is present at school and she has lost control of her management repertoire. The following article tells it like it is in terms which regular or special class teachers can readily follow.

Teacher Attention to Appropriate and Inappropriate Classroom Behavior: An Individual Case Study

Hill M. Walker
University of Oregon, Eugene

Nancy K. Buckley
Spanish Peaks Mental Health Center, Pueblo, Colorado

A number of recent studies have demonstrated teacher attention, approval and praise to be effective reinforcers in increasing child behavior in the classroom setting (Becker et al., 1967; Hall, Lund & Jackson, 1968; Madsen, Becker & Thomas, 1968; O'Leary et al., 1969). Several studies have provided evidence that teacher disapproval, criticism and negative attention may also have reinforcing effects upon child behavior. A study by Lovaas et al., (1964) indicates that teacher attention, whether positive or negative, may be reinforcing. Studies by Madsen et al., (1968) and Thomas, Becker & Armstrong (1968) suggest that the teacher's use of disapproval, critical comments and warnings can actually strengthen the behaviors to which they are applied.

Experimental subjects in the above studies usually exhibited high rates of deviant classroom behavior. Systematic intervention procedures involved varying the teacher's behavior so as to produce changes in child behavior. In these studies, the teacher with experimenter supervision, produces behavior

436

change by substantially increasing the frequency and quality of social reinforcement for appropriate behavior. These studies have provided evidence that teacher attention may be instrumental in maintaining appropriate as well as inappropriate classroom behavior.

There is very little normative data available on the frequency with which classroom teachers attend to either appropriate or inappropriate child behavior. An additional question of interest is the amount of time teachers attend to the behavior of deviant versus nondeviant children in the same classroom. Also of interest is the ratio of teacher attention to the appropriate as well as inappropriate classroom behavior of deviant and nondeviant children.

The present study recorded the frequency with which a regular classroom teacher attended to the appropriate as well as inappropriate behavior of deviant and nondeviant children enrolled in her classroom. Specific objectives of the study were (1) to determine the proportion of overall teacher attention given to deviant versus nondeviant children, (2) to measure the amount of time the teacher attended to appropriate versus inappropriate classroom behavior of deviant and nondeviant children.

SETTING AND SUBJECTS

The setting for the study was a fifth grade classroom in a local elementary school. The classroom teacher was a university graduate with 3 years of reported successful teaching experience. Thirty-one children were enrolled in her classroom during the study.

The mean intelligence quotient for the class, as measured by the CTMM, was 101 with a standard deviation of 12. Individual scores ranged from 76 to 131. The mean achievement score on the California Achievement Test was grade level 5.1 with a standard deviation of 1.2. Achievement scores ranged from 2.7 to 7.6. The average chronological age for the class was 131 months with a standard deviation of 5.7 and a range from 124 to 147. Although there was considerable individual variation on the measures used, the class, as a whole, approximated age and grade level norms in academic achievement and intelligence quotient.

Subject Selection

The teacher was asked to complete the *Walker Problem Behavior Identification Checklist* (Walker, 1970) for each child in her class. Higher scores on the instrument indicate deviant behavior and lower scores indicate less deviant behavior. All 31 children were ranked from most deviant to least deviant based on their checklist scores.

The 5 most deviant children and the 5 least deviant children, according to checklist score, were selected for further observation and subsequent screening. Behavioral observation data were then used to select the 3 most deviant and the 3 least deviant subjects from this group.

These children served as experimental subjects throughout the remainder of the study. The classroom teacher was informed that the experimenters were conducting an observation study. However, she was not informed about the nature of the study nor which subjects were being observed until the study was concluded.

Observation and Recording

Observation of child behavior. Child behavior as well as teacher behavior was recorded in this study. Behavioral observation data were used in the process of screening and selecting deviant and nondeviant subjects at the beginning of the study. Observations of the deviant and nondeviant subjects' behavior were also recorded for the duration of the study.

A behavioral observation form (Ray, Shaw & Patterson, 1968) was used to record the classroom behavior of subjects in this study. The observation form provides a method of characterizing school situations for a child so as to facilitate understanding the determinants and consequences of his behavior. The 13 response codes on the form are divided into seven inappropriate and 6 appropriate categories.

The form also contains codes for the classroom setting, the social consequences of child behavior and the social agent supplying the consequence. During each 6-minute observation session, the activities of the classroom setting are coded as group, individual, transition or recess. The social consequences of child behavior are coded as no response, attention, praise, compliance, disapproval, noncompliance and physical (+ or -). The social agent supplying the consequence is coded as teacher, peer or observer.

The observation form is set up as a grid. Each horizontal line in the grid defines a 15-second interval. The 6-minute grid is further subdivided into 2-minute sections for observer convenience in reading the behavior codes. Using an observation clipboard, set for 15-second intervals, the observer moves down one grid line each time he receives a signal from the clipboard. During each 15-second interval, the observer records both the behavior of the subject and the social consequences of his behavior by placing the appropriate consequence and agent notation(s) in the space beneath the appropriate behavior code. More than one behavior category can be coded during a single 15-second interval; however, once coded, the same category cannot be recoded during the 15-second interval.

Two observers, graduate students in special education, were assigned to record child behaviors on a daily basis for the duration of the study. Observations were taken between 9 a.m. and 12 noon each day. Class activities during this period consisted of reading, language arts and mathematics. This instructional bloc was approximately evenly divided between group and individual activities. Group work consisted of the teacher lecturing, explaining assignments, giving instructions or holding group discussion sessions. Periods for individual work usually followed group activities. Observations were randomly taken across this 3-hour bloc throughout the study so as to sample all academic areas and class activities. Observers used a sampling without replacement procedure in taking observations. One subject was randomly selected for observation and not observed again until the remaining 5 subjects had been selected and observed. Approximately 12 minutes of observation data or six 2-minute observation sessions were taken daily on each subject during the study.

Observation of teacher behavior. The authors recorded interaction data between the teacher and the 6 experimental subjects between 9 a.m. and 12 noon for each day of a 2-week period. Each interaction between the teacher and any of the 6 subjects was timed with a stopwatch and recorded on a data sheet. The subject's behavior immediately prior to the interaction was coded as either appropriate or inappropriate. The authors coded whether the child continued the same activity or initiated a new activity immediately following termination of the interaction. If the subject changed his behavior within 15 seconds following the interaction, the authors coded initiation of a new activity. If the behavior did not change within this period, continuation of the same activity was coded.

The subject's behavior was again coded as appropriate or inappropriate following the interaction with the teacher. Each interaction was also coded as to whether it was a result of the child initiating to the teacher or a result of the teacher's independent initiation to the child.

Reliability

Approximately 1 month prior to the beginning of the study, the 2 observers were given the coding manual for the observation form developed by Ray, et al., (1968). The observers memorized the operational definitions for the response codes and familiarized themselves with the grid system, social agent and consequence codes. The observers were initially trained in an experimental classroom setting for behaviorally disordered children. Observer training was supervised by a graduate research assistant experienced in using the observation form in both the experimental and regular class setting. Observations were taken on subjects in the experimental classroom through one-way glass from an adjoining room. The observers were thus free to discuss differences in behavioral coding among themselves and with the training observer in the process of establishing reliability.

Inter-rater reliabilities were calculated by a percent agreement method in which number of agreements was divided by the total number of time intervals. Agreements were defined as 2 observers coding the same consequence and agent events under the appropriate behavior category in a given 15-second interval. Each observer was required to reach a criterion of .80 agreement with the training observer. The observers were then required to achieve the same criterion with one another. The observers then entered the regular classroom and re-established their reliability in this setting, according to the same criterion, prior to the beginning of systematic observation. Inter-rater reliabilities during the experimental class training sessions averaged .87 and ranged from .50 to 1.00. Inter-rater reliabilities during the training sessions in the regular class setting averaged .90 and ranged from .62 to 1.00.

The observation data collected by the 2 observers was used as a basis for validating the author's recordings of teacher-child interactions. Each time an interaction occurred, it was recorded by the authors as described earlier. The interaction was also recorded simultaneously by the observers. The subject's behavior prior to, during and following the interaction was coded as were the consequences supplied to the subject's behavior during the interactions.

During the study, each specific teacher-child interaction coded by the authors was also coded by the observers on the child behavior observation form. There was complete agreement on the two sets of recordings as to whether an interaction occurred and on whether it was initiated by the subject or the teacher.

RESULTS

Fifth grade subjects in the original standardization sample for the *Walker Problem Behavior Identification Checklist* (Walker, 1970) received an average score of 8.72. In contrast, the 3 deviant subjects selected for this study received an average score of 18 on the checklist while the nondeviant subjects received an average score of 1.

Rates of appropriate and inappropriate classroom behavior were computed for each subject from the observation data. During the study, the deviant subjects' rate of appropriate behavior averaged .44 per minute while their inappropriate behavior rate averaged .39 per minute. In contrast, the nondeviant subjects' rates of appropriate and inappropriate behavior were respectively .59 and .21.

There were 144 separate interactions between the teacher and the 6 subjects during the 2-week observation period. Seventy of the 144 interactions were a result of the child initiating to the teacher and 74 were a result of the teacher's independent initiation to the child.

The distribution of these interactions and the resulting teacher attention was quite unequal among the 6 subjects. For example, of the 74 interactions resulting from the teacher's initiation to the subjects, 57 (or 77%) involved the 3 deviant subjects and 17 (or 23%) involved the 3 nondeviant subjects. For the deviant subjects, 51 of the 57 interactions (89%) were a result of the teacher attending to their inappropriate behavior. For the nondeviant subjects, 14 of the 17 interactions (82%) were a result of the teacher attending to their appropriate behavior. The actual frequencies of teacher attention to the appropriate and inappropriate behavior of individual subjects is presented in Table 1.

Table 1

**Frequency of Interactions in Which Teacher
Attention Was Given to Appropriate
Versus Inappropriate Behavior for
Individual Subjects**

		Appropriate Behavior	Inappropriate Behavior
Deviant Ss	1	1	31
	2	4	11
	3	1	9
Nondeviant Ss	4	5	2
	5	5	1
	6	4	0

Inspection of Table 1 reveals there was a much higher frequency of interactions involving deviant subjects than nondeviant subjects. For the deviant subjects, there were nearly 9 times as many interactions involving teacher attention to inappropriate behavior as there were interactions involving teacher attention to appropriate behavior. In contrast, for the nondeviant subjects, there were approximately 5 times as many interactions involving teacher attention to appropriate behavior as there were interactions involving teacher attention to inappropriate behavior.

Across all subjects, the probability was .94 that interactions in which teacher attention was dispensed for appropriate behavior would be followed by appropriate behavior (in the post-interaction 15-second interval). Conversely, the probability was .58 that interactions in which teacher attention was dispensed for inappropriate behavior would be followed by inappropriate behavior. Thus, less than 50 percent of the time was the teacher's attention to inappropriate behavior effective in terminating or changing that behavior.

This held true for both deviant and nondeviant subjects. By subject classification, the probability was .59 for deviant subjects that the teacher's attention to inappropriate behavior would be followed by inappropriate behavior. For nondeviant subjects, the probability was .57. These probabilities suggest that the subjects in this study were negatively reinforcing the teacher's attempts at terminating their inappropriate behavior on an intermittent basis. That is, they sometimes reinforce the teacher immediately by terminating the inappropriate behavior. At other times, they would persist in the inappropriate behavior through several attempts by the teacher to terminate it.

DISCUSSION

The teacher-child interaction data indicate that the inappropriate behavior of the 3 deviant subjects was being maintained on a very dense schedule of teacher attention. In contrast, teacher attention to the appropriate behavior of the same subjects was relatively infrequent.

The imbalance in teacher attention to the appropriate versus inappropriate behavior of the deviant subjects is consistent with results of a prior study by Walker, Fiegenbaum and Hops (1971). In that study, 5 subjects exhibiting acting-out behavior in the classroom were selected for treatment in an experimental class setting. Pre-treatment observation data were collected on each subject over a 2-week baseline period. The subjects were enrolled in 5 different classrooms. As a group, they received teacher praise for appropriate behavior an average of 3 times per hour. Conversely, they averaged 45 teacher disapprovals to their inappropriate behavior during the same period.

In the above study, as in the present study, teacher attention to the deviant subjects' inappropriate behavior was designed to terminate that behavior. During these interactions, the teacher's verbal behavior was characterized by such comments as "sit down," "be quiet," "get back to work," "how many times have I told you to sit down," "stop talking," and so forth. Positive teacher attention or praise was never directed to inappropriate behavior in either of these studies.

Although the overall frequency of teacher attention was much lower for the nondeviant subjects, the imbalance in teacher attention to their appropriate versus inappropriate behavior was similar to that for the deviant subjects (89% to 11%—deviant Ss; 82% to 18%—nondeviant Ss). However, the behavior class to which teacher attention was directed was reversed for the 2 groups of subjects. For example, 89% of the teacher attention given to the deviant subjects was directed to their inappropriate behavior. In contrast, 82% of the teacher attention given to the nondeviant subjects was directed to their appropriate behavior.

In addition, teacher attention to the nondeviant subjects' appropriate behavior was consistently positive and was characterized by such comments as "nice work," "you're doing well," "good," etc. This held true for the deviant as well as nondeviant subjects. While teacher attention to inappropriate behavior was devoted to terminating that behavior, teacher attention to appropriate behavior was devoted to increasing its frequency. This also held true for both deviant and nondeviant subjects.

Although teacher attention covaried with the amount of appropriate and inappropriate behavior produced by the deviant and nondeviant subjects, this study did not establish cause and effect relationships between these two variables. However, there are studies which have demonstrated that teacher attention can be used to increase both appropriate and inappropriate classroom behavior. For example, studies by Becker et al., (1967), Hall, Lund & Jackson (1968), and Thomas, Becker & Armstrong (1968) have shown that an increased frequency of teacher attention to study behavior increases that behavior while a decrease in teacher attention is associated with a reduction in study behavior. A study by Madsen et al., (1968) demonstrated that out-of-seat frequency was increased by the teacher's use of "sit down" commands. The frequency was reduced when the teacher decreased her use of these commands. Thus, teacher attention, whether positive or negative, appears to have reinforcing properties which may be instrumental in maintaining both appropriate and inappropriate classroom behavior.

The relationship between the deviant subjects' inappropriate behavior and the teacher's efforts at consequating that behavior can be related to the reciprocity-coercion hypothesis developed by Patterson and Reid (1969). This hypothesis holds that coercive demands (mands) which are highly aversive are applied to a reinforcement dispenser (adult). The social interaction is usually terminated when the adult yields to the coercive manding. In this process, the behavior of the reinforcement dispenser is maintained through negative reinforcement (termination of the aversive manding); and the child's coercive manding is maintained through positive reinforcement (adult yielding to mands).

This process characterizes the teacher's interactions with the 3 deviant subjects. For example, the subjects would terminate the aversive mand (disruptive or deviant classroom behavior) only after 1 or more attempts by the teacher at consequating the inappropriate behavior. These attempts were almost exclusively verbal and included such comments as "sit down," "get to work," "I told you to be quiet," "stop disrupting the class." It is somewhat ironic that the attention dispensed by the teacher in consequating the subjects' inappropriate behavior appeared to be instrumental in maintaining it.

Moreover, the high frequency of teacher attention to the deviant subjects' inappropriate behavior appeared to be related to the intermittency with which they reinforced her by terminating their inappropriate behavior. The nondeviant subjects would usually terminate their inappropriate behavior on the first or second consequation attempt. However, the deviant subjects sometimes would not terminate the aversive behavior until the fourth, fifth, or even sixth attempt by the teacher to get them to do so. At other times, they would terminate the inappropriate behavior on the first or second attempt. Thus, it appeared the teacher's consequating behavior was partly under the control of a schedule furnished by the deviant subjects. The inappropriate behavior of the deviant subjects appeared to be maintained at a high rate by the teacher attention generated by this schedule.

The results of this study need to be cross-validated upon a large group of classroom teachers before they can be applied to teachers in general. If the results are replicated, they would suggest that classroom teachers respond to the behavior of deviant and nondeviant children in a very different fashion. The reasons for this are intriguing. If reinforcement schedules which are controlled and mediated by the deviant subjects account for this effect, then it would be interesting to know what the parameters of these schedules are. It would also be interesting to know how the inappropriate behavior of the deviant subjects develops and becomes strengthened while appropriate behavior is developed and strengthened for nondeviant subjects.

The teacher in this study appeared to be reasonably competent. She had 3 years of reported successful teaching, and her teaching lessons were usually well organized and clearly presented. There were several children in her class who were extremely difficult to manage, and she accepted this as a natural part of teaching. If she is representative of the average teacher, it would appear that teachers could benefit from training in behavior management techniques. Systematic training programs could reduce the deviant child's rate of inappropriate behavior while freeing the teacher to devote more of her time to instruction.

REFERENCES

Becker, W. C., Madsen, C. H., Arnold, R. & Thomas, D. R. "The Contingent Use of Teacher Attention and Praise in Reducing Classroom Behavior Problems." *Journal of Special Education, 1* (3), 1967 (287-307).

Hall, R. V., Lund, D. & Jackson, D. "Effects of Teacher Attention on Study Behavior." *Journal of Applied Behavior Analysis, 1,* 1968 (1-12).

Lovaas, O. I., Freitag, G., Kinder, M. I., Rubenstein, D. C., Schaeffer, B. & Simmons, J. B. "Experimental Studies in Childhood Schizophrenia–Establishment-Abolishment of Social Reinforcers." Paper delivered at Western Psychological Association, Portland, April, 1964.

Madsen, C. H., Becker, W. C. & Thomas, D. R. "Rules, Praise, and Ignoring: Elementary Classroom Control." *Journal of Applied Behavior Analysis, 2,* 1968 (139-150).

Madsen, C. H., Becker, W. C., Thomas, D. R., Koser & Plager. "An Analysis of the Reinforcing Function of "Sit Down" Commands." In R. K. Parker (Ed.), *Readings in Educational Psychology.* Boston: Allyn & Bacon, 1968.

O'Leary, K. D., Becker, W. C., Evans, M. B. & Saudargas, R. A. "A Token Reinforcement Program in a Public School: A Replication and Systematic Analysis." *Journal of Applied Behavior Analysis, 2,* 1969 (3-13).

Patterson, G. R. & Reid, J. "Reciprocity and Coercion: Two Facets of Social Systems." In C. Neuringer & J. Michael (Eds.), *Behavior Modification in Clinical Psychology.* New York: Appleton-Century-Crofts, 1969.

Ray, R. S., Shaw, D. A. & Patterson, G. P. "Observation in the School: Description of a Coding Form." *Oregon Research Institute Technical Report,* 1968.

Thomas, D. R., Becker, W. C. & Armstrong. "Production and Elimination of Disruptive Classroom Behavior by Systematically Varying Teacher's Behavior." *Journal of Applied Behavior Analysis, 1,* 1968 (35-45).

Walker, H. M. *Walker Problem Behavior Identification Checklist.* Test and Manual. Los Angeles, California: Western Psychological Services, January, 1970.

Walker, H. M., Fiegenbaum, E. & Hops, H. *Components Analysis and Systematic Replication of a Treatment Model for Modifying Classroom Behavior.* Report #5. Eugene, Oregon: Center at Oregon for Research in the Behavioral Education of the Handicapped, Special Education Department, University of Oregon, November 1971.

The development of creativity and divergent thinking in gifted children usually would not be questioned by most people. The development of the same skills in the handicapped is a new concept not often practiced in the field. Dr. Gallagher describes studies and provides practical suggestions for teachers to follow if they want to see the handicapped really express creativity.

Procedures for Developing Creativity in Emotionally Disturbed Children

Patricia A. Gallagher
University of Kansas Medical Center

Creativity is a highly valued human characteristic believed to be a natural phenomenon in all children (Anderson, 1959) and one which could be encouraged by special educators. For emotionally disturbed children, however, the development of creativity has often been neglected in the school environment. Educators appear to devote a major portion of their instructional hours to procedures designed to remediate the disturbed children's behavior deficits. These modification procedures and the inappropriate behaviors which disturbed children exhibit may function to disguise the presence of creative abilities. Torrance (1962) suggests that an individual's creativity is a potential resource in coping with life's problems and contributes to the acquisition of various skills. If special educators should attempt to mitigate the disabling effects of emotional disturbance by seeking procedures which strengthen creativity, personal adjustment in these children may improve.

One process associated with creativity is divergent thinking which implies inventiveness, innovation and the discovery of the unknown. Divergent production is believed to contain some of the most directly relevant intellectual abilities for creative thinking and creative production (Guilford, 1966). Our culture, however, generally associates divergency with delinquency and mental illness. These negative feelings can be conveyed to children who diverge from society's standards for conformity in behavior. When the disapproval placed on divergency is transmitted to a group of children whose handicaps are manifested by deviant behavior, the positive aspects of creativity may remain undetected. If the values of creative abilities in such children can be recognized, then the responsibility to guide, encourage and structure these abilities could be actively assumed by educators.

It is reasonable to assume and believe that creativity exists in emotionally disturbed children and that this ability is as uniquely differentiated in its personal meaning to them as it is to all children. In 1951, Berkowitz and Rothman reported an experimental art program conducted with children in Bellvue Hospital. The authors believed that disturbed children could be gradually directed in a therapeutic approach to creativity and originality. At first, exploring art media was threatening to the disturbed children; therefore, restrictive types of art activities were initially introduced and later replaced with free expressive art activities. Through specific activities, the children became less threatened and successful. In a recent publication, Rothman (1971) emphasized her belief that disturbed adolescent girls were truly creative. This is reflected in their divergent behavioral and verbal responses.

It has and continues to be this writer's belief that emotionally disturbed children are highly creative individuals frequently manifesting their talents with manipulative, inappropriate responses and in ways adults do not understand. If the talents are redirected, the children could have other appropriate and satisfying avenues for self expression. Although procedures designed to foster creativity in disturbed children have been limited, several studies (Gallagher, 1966; Norris, 1969; Auxier, 1971) explored the relevance of art, drama and writing activities designed to stimulate creative thinking in elementary age disturbed children. These procedures were introduced in four special classrooms where the Structured Approach, a psychobehavioral approach to the education of emotionally disturbed children, prevailed.

The purposes of the aforementioned three studies were (1) to provide planned activities as an educational procedure for the development of creativity in emotionally disturbed children, (2) to encourage and support the children's divergent thinking in their expression of creativity, and (3) to investigate the effects of the procedures on the children's scores in tests of creative thinking.

STUDY ONE

The subjects were ten emotionally disturbed children selected on the basis of their enrollment in the special classes of the Children's Rehabilitation Unit, University of Kansas Medical Center (Gallagher, 1966). Five of the subjects (Group 1) were assigned to the class for primary grade children. The remaining five (Group II) were students in the intermediate grade class.

Evaluation Instrument

An independent criterion delineating specific creative abilities was selected to measure the effects of the art media procedure to creativity. The Picture Construction Task, a nonverbal test, was chosen from the Minnesota Test of Creative Thinking. The scoring scheme for this test was based on a rationale presented in Yamamoto's (1964) experimental manual. Three abilities—originality, elaboration and activity (dynamic orientation)—were included in the test. This test is now a part of Torrance's Tests of Creative Thinking and available for use by teachers.

Procedure

The Picture Construction Task was individually administered to the subjects. This first testing session will be referred to hereafter as the Pretest. Following the Pretest session, Treatment I was initiated with the subjects for two weeks, one half hour daily. The treatment involved social interaction between the subjects and the writer. When the two weeks had elapsed, the Picture Construction Task was individually administered to the ten subjects. This test administration will be referred to as Posttest 1.

Art media, Treatment II, was then introduced to Group I and Group II, during half hour sessions for a four week period. Following the four weeks of art activities, the Picture Construction Task was individually administered to the subjects. This test will be referred to as Posttest 2.

Teaching Sessions—Treatment II

Since a universal approach to creativity has not been formulated, art media which are amenable to manipulations and are versatile in appeal to children were selected. Materials used for the art activities were those which normally would be found in an elementary school. Two lessons were selected from the *Instructor* magazine (Perrin, 1965; Wolpert, 1965), and the remaining eighteen lessons were selected from the writer's reserve of teaching materials. The teachers of the special classes selected an art period when the experimenter could present the lessons.

For each lesson, the subjects assembled as a group to receive the art media and to discuss the possible uses of the material. Then they took the art media to their desks where they were to execute their original ideas. Each subject was encouraged in his own techniques and self-expression of divergent thinking while he was manipulating the art materials. Freedom to follow through the original ideas was prevalent; however, structure and guidance were given to the subjects whose ideas appeared restricted. One subject perseverated on one particular monster creature during the first seven lessons. He was able to produce a monster regardless of the art media; therefore, he was strongly cajoled into producing other themes. With extra support and encouragement, the subject was able to break through his own barrier and began to freely express divergent thoughts.

The finished products were the results of the individual subject's endeavors and originality rather than reproductions of an adult's master copy. Too often great emphasis is placed on the finished product rather than the process of producing it. In this study, the creative process was of primary concern; therefore, productions were not evaluated.

Results

The Sign Test, a nonparametric statistical measure, was selected to analyze the data. The test requires that relevant independent variables be matched within each pair of related samples. This requirement was achieved by using each child as his own control.

Pretest and Posttest scores were used as matched pairs of observation. The Pretest scores served as initial measures while the Posttest scores served to indicate change. Negative and positive differences between the scores were determined by subtracting the Pretest score from each of the Posttest scores. The findings and levels of significance (Siegel, 1956) are summarized in Table 1.

Table 1
SUMMARY OF DIRECTION OF DIFFERENCES
IN PICTURE CONSTRUCTION TEST SCORES

Groups	Test Session	Sign Test p
Total Group	Pretest-Posttest 1	.50
Total Group	Posttest 1-Posttest 2	.05
Total Group	Pretest-Posttest 2	.01
Group I	Pretest-Posttest 1	NS
Group I	Posttest 1-Posttest 2	.18
Group I	Pretest-Posttest 2	.03
Group II	Pretest-Posttest 1	NS
Group II	Posttest 1-Posttest 2	NS
Group II	Pretest-Posttest 2	.18

Following the termination of Treatment 1, an increase in total group scores between Pretest and Posttest 1 was observed (p = .50). A significant level (p = .05) was reached when Posttest 2 was compared to Posttest 1. A greater increase in total group scores (p = .01) was observed when a comparison of Posttest 2 was made to the Pretest. This subsequent increase in Posttest 2 performance scores can be related to the effectiveness of the art media procedure. Although the writer was involved in the interaction activities with the subjects during the two treatment sessions, greater total group gain scores were obtained following the art media treatment.

Gain differences in the test scores for Group I were analyzed. There was no significant difference in the scores for Group I following the termination of the social interaction. Gains were observed between Posttest 1 and Posttest 2 (p = .18) and between Pretest and Posttest 2 (p = .03).

Factors contributing to the significance in gained scores were considered. The Pretest scores for Group I fell within the lower half of the test limits; therefore, the subjects' scores were more amenable to growth. Group I was composed of younger children (seven to ten years of age) who appeared to be more responsive than the older children to adult instruction. The younger children's enthusiasm and eagerness increased as they proceeded into their daily art activities.

Torrance's (1962) investigation relevant to a developmental curve of creative thinking abilities indicates a steady increase for children in the first through third grades. The subjects in Group 1 were in this grade range with the exception of one subject whose age exceeded the primary age. This subject was the only child in the younger group to obtain a lower Posttest score, which was a change in score in the negative direction.

Group II's differences in the Pretest and Posttest 2 scores (p = .18) did not approximate the significant results obtained for Group I's Pretest and Posttest 2 scores (p = .03). A factor contributing to the results found in Group II may have been the high Pretest scores achieved by four of the five subjects. These four scores fell within the upper half of the test limits. Consequently, the range for expansion for the four subjects was restricted. However, the greatest increase in their scores followed the art media treatment, thus adding evidence concerning the effectiveness of this treatment.

SAMPLE ART LESSONS

Wet Chalk Design

Materials

Newsprint, 12" x 18"
Construction paper, 12" x 18" in assorted colors

Drawing paper, 12" x 18"
Colored chalk, general assortment, broken pieces preferred
Black crayons
Paint brushes as found in water color paint boxes
Individual paint cups
Scissors
Paste
Fixatif in aerosol can

Procedure

Using a sheet of newsprint and a black crayon, have the children experiment with a free form design by circulating the crayon on the newsprint in a series of motions without lifting the crayon from the newsprint's surface. The final motion returns the crayon to the point of origin. After experimenting with several designs, the children should execute a free form design on a sheet of drawing paper and choose four pieces of chalk. The enclosed areas of the design should be painted with water, then immediately filled with chalk. The completed design is sprayed with the Fixatif. The dried, sprayed design should be cut and pasted into any position on a sheet of colored construction paper.

Geometric Shapes

Materials

Black construction paper, 9" x 12"
Assorted geometric shapes and sizes of colored construction paper
Paste
Scissors

Procedure

Prior to the art activity class, the colored construction paper is cut into assorted sizes and shapes. During the class activity, the children receive a 9" x 12" sheet of black construction paper and a portion of the assorted geometric shapes and sizes of colored paper. Although each child receives identical assortments, freedom to alter the shapes by cutting should be encouraged. The children construct a picture by pasting the geometric designs on the construction paper, using their own ideas as to composition.

Paper Strips

Materials

Construction paper in assorted colors, 9" x 12"
Gummed-backed paper strips in seven colors, approximately 3/8" x 4"

Procedure

Have the children count out six gummed-backed strips of seven colors, totaling forty-two strips. Bend, twist, pleat, or curl the strips to give a three dimensional effect. By attaching the strips to the sheet of construction paper, the children develop designs or pictures using as many of the strips as they wish.

Geometric Shapes

Materials

Drawing paper cut into geometric shapes
Crayons
Large grocery bag

Procedure

Cut the drawing paper into varying shapes, including ovals, circles, triangles and rectangles. During the art activity, have the children reach into a large paper bag and take one of the shapes. Encourage the children to imagine pictures which fit the paper shapes. For example, rectangular shapes might suggest a tree or giraffe; circle shapes might suggest a person's face or the earth's surface. An original picture should be completed with crayons.

Styrofoam Creations

Materials

Styrofoam balls, 1/2 inch and 2 inch diameters
Pipe cleaners in assorted colors, 6" lengths
Straight pins
Small gold beads
Scissors

Procedure

Each child receives three of the 1/2 inch styrofoam balls, one of the two inch balls, seven pipe cleaners, twelve gold beads and as many straight pins as needed. Encourage the children to create any figure or model from these materials.

STUDY TWO

The subject was a ten-year-old emotionally disturbed boy residing in a private mental health setting (Norris, 1969). A complete diagnostic evaluation revealed the child's inadequate emotional growth and deviant behavior. On the

Wechsler Intelligence Scale for Children, the subject achieved a verbal score of 143, a performance score of 127, and a full scale score of 138. The student worked on the fourth grade level which was commensurate with his chronological age; however, the IQ test scores indicated potential for a higher achievement level.

Evaluation Instrument

To study the effects of a creative writing approach to creativity, the Imaginative Stories Test was chosen from the Minnesota Tests of Creative Thinking. The scoring system for the test was based on Yamamato's (1964) rationale as presented in the experimental manual. The scoring scheme was divided into six main categories including organization, sensitivity, originality, imagination, psychological insight and richness. Five subcategories were assigned to each main category. This classification provided 30 terms which frequently define creativity.

Procedure

The Imaginative Stories Test consisted of Form A and Form B. Form A was used as the Pretest and Form B was used as the Posttest. Following the Pretest session, a series of creative writing lessons were introduced. Twenty to thirty minute lessons were presented daily to the subject for the first two weeks, thereafter once a week. At the end of the twenty-two lessons, the Posttest was given.

Teaching Sessions—Treatment

The creative writing lessons were selected from the *Experimental Scoring Manual for Minnesota Tests of Creative Thinking and Writing* (Yamamato, 1964), *Invitation to Speaking and Writing Creatively* (Myers & Torrance, 1965b), and the experimenter's file of materials. The directions for each lesson were given orally and in written form. The subject was given two specific topics from which he could choose the lesson. The student was also informed that the creative writing session was substituted for one of his regular daily academic assignments. The student needed reassurance that he was not expected to do extra work but he was to fulfill the lesson requirements. His creative writing productions were not graded. The boy's general fear of not being able to perform successfully was so intense that teacher comments were as supportive and reinforcing as possible. As the student became more comfortable with his creative writing endeavors, he volunteered evaluative comments and would discuss more easily some of the problems he encountered in the lessons. This type of evaluation was encouraged as it appeared to build objectivity and confidence in the boy relevant to his writing work.

Results

The Pretest score revealed the initial level of creativity while the Posttest score revealed the subsequent level of creative ability. The amount of change was determined by subtracting the Pretest subcategorical scores from the Posttest subcategorical scores. The Sign Test was selected to analyze the data.

The boy's scores revealed change in eleven pairs and no change in nineteen pairs of the 30 subcategories. There were 10 positive scores and one negative score (p = .006). The findings and level of significance (Siegel, 1956) are summarized in Table 2.

Table 2
SUMMARY OF DIRECTION OF DIFFERENCES
IN IMAGINATIVE STORIES TEST SCORES

		Summary of Signs	
Category	Negative	No Difference	Positive
Organization	0	5	0
Sensitivity	0	4	1
Originality	0	3	2
Imagination	0	2	3
Psychological Insight	1	3	1
Richness	0	2	3
	1	19	10
			p = .006

During the Posttest session the subject was under extreme stress in anticipation of a parental visit; however, he was able to function productively. The boy had been consistently structured and encouraged throughout the creativity sessions, especially when he showed anxiety and frustration. Perhaps this support was a variable contributing to the subject's productive Posttest behavior.

SAMPLE WRITING LESSONS

Write a story entitled "One Day on the Moon." Use your own imagination about what you think you would really find or what you would like to find. Your story can be about anything that happens to you "One Day on the Moon."

Read the beginning of the following story and then finish the story any way you choose. Make your story interesting and try to use as many words as you can. Try to make your story as vivid to me as it is to you.

In our science class at school we have been studying various kinds of animals. As a special treat, the teacher said each of us could bring a pet or animal to school to show the class. Most of us brought dogs, cats, birds, turtles, and a variety of spiders, and bugs. But everyone was very surprised when Linda brought a baby elephant. It really turned into the funniest day I can remember when . . . .

Pretend you are the top scientist for a large airplane plant. You have just finished designing a new airplane, and now you are sending your design with a letter to the Secretary of Defense at the Pentagon. In your letter explain your design, why it's special, what kind of crew will be needed, and why it is important for this plane to be added to our defense system.

Complete the following story in the most interesting way you can.

One day as I was walking to class I saw a strange oval object overhead. It was silver in color and the bottom appeared to be glass. As I observed this funny round vehicle, a sliding door opened and . . . .

Make up a tall tale, like the Paul Bunyan stories, which can be as funny or exaggerated as you like.

Draw a cartoon strip. The main character's name is Dandy. Dandy can be a person, an animal, an imaginery character, etc. You can use yourself in the cartoon and do whatever you wish.

455

STUDY THREE

The subjects for this study were six boys age 10 and one boy age 13 enrolled in a public school special education class in a small Kansas community (Auxier, 1971). They had been placed in the class for learning and behavior disorders based on teacher referrals, psychological examinations, and administrative decisions. All of these children were of average intelligence and had no serious physical handicaps.

Evaluation Instrument

To study the effects of the training procedures on creative thinking abilities, the Torrance Tests of Creative Thinking, Verbal Battery, Forms A and B (Torrance, 1966) were chosen. Seven activities comprise the verbal battery with comparable test items on the two alternate forms. The test was administered individually and orally under standardized conditions as specified in the test manual.

Procedure

The Verbal Form A of the Torrance Tests of Creative Thinking was administered as a Pretest. For the next 28 consecutive school days, training sessions were conducted for approximately 20 minutes each day. Following treatment procedures, the Posttest, Verbal Form B of the Torrance Test of Creative Thinking, was administered. The effects of the treatment procedure were assessed by comparing fluency, flexibility, originality and total test scores on Pre- and Posttest measures.

Teaching Sessions: Treatment

The 28 planned lessons were conducted for 20 minutes each school day at approximately the same hour. Some of the lessons were directly taken or adapted from Myers and Torrance (1964, 1965a, 1965b, 1966) teachers' guides; Cunnington and Torrance (1965) *Imagi/Craft Materials;* Dunn and Smith (1965, 1966, 1967) *Peabody Language Development Kits;* McCaslin (1968); and Wolff (1961a, 1961b). Other activities were developed by the investigator. All of the activities were designed to stimulate creative behavior. Students were encouraged to produce a large quantity of ideas, to use a variety of approaches to problems or situations, to think of ideas that were unusual, interesting and clever, and to work through their ideas in detail. The children were invited to view situations from different vantage points or to see things in many different ways. Many of the activities encouraged body movement or informal dramatization as a means of creative expression.

Results

All test results were scored by Personnel Press Scoring Service. This agency used professionally trained scorers. Tests were scored once and then independently checked, thus providing an interscorer reliability check.

The Wilcoxon Matched-Pairs Signed-Ranks Test, a nonparametric statistical test, was selected to analyze the data. The test requires that relevant independent variables be matched within each pair of related samples. This was accomplished in the present study by using each subject as his own control.

Each of the six subtests was scored for fluency, flexibility, originality, and total scores. Significant differences at the .02 level (Siegel, 1956) were found between pre- and postmeasures in the areas of fluency, flexibility, originality and total scores. These findings are summarized in Table 3.

Table 3
SUMMARY OF WILCOXON MATCHED-PAIRS SIGNED-RANKS TEST WITH TORRANCE TESTS OF CREATIVE THINKING

Pretest-Posttest Category	P value
Fluency	.02
Flexibility	.02
Originality	.02
Total + scores	.02

The subjects engaged enthusiastically in the creativity sessions, frequently asking to continue the activities. They explored the presented media in a variety of ways and generated new ideas. The quality of their responses visibly increased as the lessons progressed. However, it was not possible to determine which of the lessons—art, drama or writing—was most influential in the significant results.

SAMPLE DRAMA LESSONS

Round Robin Story from Pictures

Have each child contribute a sentence to the story taking turns around the group. Use stimulus pictures, such as motorcycle pictures, men-in-a-barn scene, etc.

Picnic Pantomine

Pass around a pretend picnic basket. Each child "chooses" the food he wants from the basket. He must show the other children what he has chosen by the way he handles it and pretends to eat it. The other students guess what food has been selected.

Story Suggested by an Object

Place an object in the center of the group. Have the children look at it for three or four minutes without speaking. Then give the following directions:

Try to think of a short story about this object. Where might it have come from? How did it get here? What did its owners do with it? What does it make you think of?

Use the following objects: a lantern, a mallet, a wooden box, a set of bells. Other objects may be substituted. Allow sufficient time for a short story from each child.

DISCUSSION

The emotionally disturbed children's responses to the creativity session were encouraging. By incorporating art, writing and/or drama lessons wherein creative thinking was stimulated and guided, many of the emotionally disturbed children were able to increase their scores on tests of creative thinking.

A salient feature of the three teaching procedures was the teacher's recognition and reinforcement of the children's original ideas. In Torrance's study (1965) the effects of the teacher's influence in rewarding student creative behavior was investigated. An assessment of teachers' evaluation behavior revealed that children tend to develop in areas where they are rewarded by teachers, even in the area of originality.

Permissiveness in the environment is often suggested for the development of creativity; however, Study II's subject revealed creative growth when the lessons were highly structured. As the subject understood the guidelines, his anxiety dissipated and his creativeness was expressed.

The Structured Approach to the education of emotionally disturbed children was amenable to the development of creativity in the children. One of the integral procedures for the implementation of the Structured Approach is programming for individual student needs. During the creativity session, each student explored, imagined, experimented and developed ideas in as interesting and meaningful a way as he desired. Thus, the same media presented to the subjects took on new meaning as each child became involved in or worked out productions at his level of creativity. Furthermore, the student was always successful because the process, not the product, was reinforced.

The results of the three studies suggest growth in creativity. Would the students continue to grow in their creativity abilities if creative activities were integrated into their academic programs? Would the teacher's value judgment placed upon the emotionally disturbed children's achievements in originality affect their perception of self and reality? If the self-image were altered, how would this change manifest itself in future creative ability? It is reasonable to assume that growth in one area of the self is contributory to the development of the whole personality? Future research concerning these possible implications is recommended.

SUMMARY

The underlying causes affecting the omission of creative experiences in classes for emotionally disturbed children are debatable; therefore, the three studies circumvented this issue by implementing teaching procedures designed to enhance creative abilities in disturbed children. Encouragement of divergency, a feature of creativity, may have been considered risky intervention; however, the children's responses to the experimental conditions were reassuring. Creative growth, as measured in the studies, was visible. It was demonstrated that the positive aspects of divergency were expressed when activities designed to promote creativity were planned and included in the academic program for emotionally disturbed children.

Note: All sample lessons were taken from the author's teaching files.

REFERENCES

Anderson, H. *Creativity and Its Cultivation*. New York: Harper, 1959.

Auxier, C. "Effects of a Training Program for Creative Thinking on the Creative Behavior of Emotionally Disturbed Children." Unpublished master's thesis, University of Kansas, 1971.

Berkowitz, P. & Rothman, E. "Art Work for the Emotionally Disturbed." *Clearing House,* *26,* 1951, 232-234.

Gallagher, P. "An Art Media Procedure for Developing Creativity in Emotionally Disturbed Children." Unpublished master's thesis, University of Kansas, 1966.

Guilford, J. "Intelligence: 1965 Model." *American Psychologist, 21',* 1966, 20-26.

Norris, M. S. "A Creative Procedure for Developing Creativity in a Gifted Emotionally Disturbed Child." Unpublished master's thesis, University of Kansas, 1969.

Rothman, E. *The Angel Inside Went Sour.* New York: McKay Company, 1971.

Siegel, S. *Nonparametric Statistics for the Behavioral Sciences.* New York: McGraw-Hill, 1956.

Torrance, E. P. *Guiding Creative Talent.* New Jersey: Prentice-Hall, 1962.

Torrance, E. P. *Rewarding Creative Behavior.* New Jersey: Prentice-Hall, 1965.

Torrance, E. P. *Torrance Tests of Creative Thinking.* New Jersey: Personnel Press, 1966.

Yamamato, K. *Experimental Scoring Manual for Minnesota Tests of Creative Thinking and Writing.* Kent, Ohio: Bureau of Educational Research, Kent State University, 1964.

Teaching Sessions

Cunnington, B. & Torrance, E. P. *Imagi/Craft Materials.* Boston: Ginn Company, 1965.

Dunn, L. & Smith, J. *Peabody Language Development Kit* (Level #1, Manual). Minneapolis: American Guidance Service, 1965.

Dunn, L. & Smith, J. *Peabody Language Development Kit* (Level #2, Manual). Minneapolis: American Guidance Service, 1966.

Dunn, L. & Smith, J. *Peabody Language Development Kit* (Level #3, Manual). Minneapolis: American Guidance Service, 1967.

McCaslin, N. *Creative Dramatics in the Classroom.* New York: McKay Company, 1968.

Myers, R. & Torrance, E. P. *Can You Imagine?* (Teacher's Guide) Boston: Ginn Company, 1965a.

Myers, R. & Torrance, E. P. *For Those Who Wonder.* (Teacher's Guide) Boston: Ginn Company, 1966.

Myers, R. & Torrance, E. P. *Invitation to Speaking and Writing Creatively.* (Teacher's Guide) Boston: Ginn Company, 1965b.

Myers, R. & Torrance, E. P. *Invitation to Thinking and Doing.* (Teacher's Guide) Boston: Ginn Company, 1964.

Perrin, J. "Space Animals." *Instructor, 75,* 1965, 62.

Wolff, J. *Let's Imagine Being Places.* New York: Dutton, 1961a.

Wolff, J. *Let's Imagine Thinking Up Things.* New York: Dutton, 1961b.

Wolpert, Elizabeth. "Crayon Impressions." *Instructor,* 1965.

Seldom has a trend in special education been so soundly based in research or as universally accepted as early childhood special education. The authors have operated one of the most successful programs in the country. Based on this, the authors give the reader a look into what they believe to be the main elements of curriculum and the kind of approach that can really produce change. Several practical examples are included to show how a systematic curriculum is applied.

Curriculum and Methods
in Early Childhood Special Education:
One Approach

Merle B. Karnes, R. Reid Zehrbach
University of Illinois, Urbana

Is the preschool teacher of a handicapped children's program an innovator or merely a caretaker? Recent developments indicate that precise planning can lead to important, even dramatic, changes in the development of young handicapped children. Basic to this precise planning is the involvement of the teacher in applied curriculum development.

The literature abounds with many definitions of curriculum; however, for the purpose of this article, curriculum is defined as those activities identified and used by the teacher to change/enhance a child's behavior to reach identifiable objectives and goals. In this sense, the activities may be implemented in the classroom, on the playground, on a field trip, on the school bus and in the home—the major characteristic being that it is a planned activity under the supervision of the teacher.

A variety of approaches to the process of teaching have been developed and described in the literature. A recent book, *Models of Teaching* (Joyce & Weil, 1972), provides a general overview of various ways of approaching the teaching-learning situation which have implications for curriculum development. In the early childhood area, the recent publication edited by Ronald K. Parker

(1972), *The Preschool in Action*, provides descriptions of 12 specific curriculums for the preschool classroom. While these approaches were developed with disadvantaged children, adaptions can be made for use with the handicapped.

PROBLEM AREAS

The development of any curriculum and selection of related teaching methods should be based on some rationale. One approach is to select a series of goals based on some philosophical orientation and then develop curricular materials to achieve these goals. Another approach, one adopted by the authors, is to select goals based on their relevance to problems identified through research and observation of individual children with handicaps. The following represent some common problems characteristic of handicapped children for which appropriate goals and objectives should be established and curriculum developed.

1. *Language*—One area critical to the total development of the young handicapped child is language. Language development is important because it is highly related to successful academic achievement, to the facilitation of social interaction and to the development of an adequate self-concept. There is also some basis for the belief that language can promote motor development.

Studies of children and groups of children often reveal deficits in one or more of the following language processing areas: reception, association, expression, sequential memory and closure. Frequently, patterns of deficits can be identified within groups of children. For example, many low income children are weak in Auditory Association and Verbal Expression. Educational programming to meet the needs of these children must be directed toward the amelioration of these deficits.

2. *Social Skills*—Studies of the handicapped reveal data to indicate that the handicapped most frequently fail to be successful on the job because of inadequate social skills rather than lack of competency to perform the task. Weak language development, poor social models by parents, overprotection by parents and rejection by peers and members of the family are frequent inhibitors of the development of appropriate social skills.

3. *Self-Concept*—Handicapped children frequently develop weak self-concepts. The development of a strong, positive self-concept is fostered when the child is able to interact successfully, but children who lag behind in language development have difficulty communicating their ideas to others.

When a child is provided with learning tasks where success is possible and where feedback is available, he feels good about himself. Conversely, when he encounters a preponderance of failures, his self-concept is undermined. Too often the handicapped child encounters failure because his teachers have not given due attention to what Hunt (1961) refers to as the match, that is, providing him with tasks compatible with his cognitive development so that he can interact with others and complete tasks successfully.

4. *Self-Help*—A basic concern of parents and teachers of young children is that they develop self-help skills particularly in the areas of toileting, eating and dressing. Immaturity, inappropriate training techniques including over-protection, and consequent lack of opportunity appear to be the major reasons for handicapped children lagging behind in this area. Successful development of self-help skills determines to a large extent the amount of acceptance of the handicapped by others.

5. *Motor Skills*—Many handicapped children lack motor skills in one or more areas. Good control over one's body tends to enhance self-confidence. A child with poorly developed motor skills tends to feel inadequate and is reluctant to attempt activities requiring well developed motor skills. A child with poor motor skills is likely to have problems in the Self-Help area. He may hesitate to work and play with other children who are more skillful motorically even though they are his same age.

6. *Cognitive Skills*—The development of cognitive skills influences all facets of the child's development. If he is retarded in cognitive development, he is usually retarded in other important facets of development—self-help, social, motor and language. Poorly developed cognitive skills is one major characteristic of the mentally retarded. Too often the handicapped child is given tasks more in keeping with his chronological age than his mental age. When this is the case, the handicapped child becomes frustrated and emotional problems may develop.

7. *Lack of Understanding from Parents*—Typically, parents of the handicapped have no preparation to understand or to cope with the problems of the handicapped child. They need guidance and support in learning the new techniques for fostering the development of their handicapped child. It is important that the school and the home combine forces and provide the child with a consistent and appropriate curriculum both in the school and in the home.

BASIC ASSUMPTIONS AND BELIEFS

A well conceptualized curriculum for young handicapped children has imbedded in its philosophy and procedures a set of basic assumptions. The following represent the basic beliefs underlying one model program for young handicapped children developed at the University of Illinois. After the assumptions are described, they are related to actual practice in the classroom through a variety of illustrations.

• A high adult-child ratio fosters frequent interaction between the adult and child in an organized manner when structure is basic to the approach. In addition, feedback to the child is more frequent when the adult-child ratio is high. To maintain a high adult-child ratio, paid paraprofessionals, volunteers and parents should be utilized. (Their use is viable because the inherent structure of the program permits the necessary preplanning and post-teaching evaluation.)

• Teamwork among the adults is required as a characteristic of the approach. Teamwork includes involvement in preplanning, goal selection and the formulation of objectives for obtaining the goals on a group and individual basis. Also, the adults need to be able to convey by look, gesture or other signal how to cope with or change strategy for handling a given child as smoothly and unobtrusively as possible as they implement their plans in the instructional program.

• The social structure of the adult-child interaction should be as carefully planned as the activities designed to promote intellectual processing and acquisition of concepts. (Movement of the child from small group to larger group activities must be preplanned. The transfer of the control of a child from adult to adult must be accomplished smoothly, consistently and unobtrusively as the child moves from activity to activity.)

• To cope with the vast amounts of individual programming required, the teacher must be careful to delineate and implement structure in the instructional setting.

• Since handicapped children require the services of ancillary personnel and agencies, their expertise must be incorporated into both the planning and operational phases of the program.

• Ongoing group evaluation both of the child and of the adults is essential for program implementation. Evaluation should have as its major goal the delineation of positive growth. Inherent in the evaluation process must be a built-in feedback system to the appropriate personnel.

• In general, the entire approach should be "orchestrated" so that the parts fit together harmoniously with no one portion being too dominant or illusive.

PREPARING A LEARNING ACTIVITY

Inherent in any structured program is the need to develop a variety of carefully designed activities to foster learning. Consider the following guidelines found to be useful in the preparation of appropriate activities:

An instructional model is useful in developing activities. A model derived from the clinical model of the Illinois Test of Psycholinguistics has been found to be particularly helpful in guiding the development of curriculum, especially for handicapped children. A rationale for the use of this model is derived from its language focus which is quite congruent with many of the identified needs of handicapped children. In addition, it is a model that is process oriented. Process refers to the abilities to perceive, organize, manipulate, synthesize and integrate information regardless of the content. These are skills an individual needs throughout life.

Although the ITPA model lends itself to the identification of areas in need of specific emphasis, additional assistance can be derived from developmental guidelines which help illustrate the sequence of mastery in an area—skill or knowledge. The use of developmental guidelines helps the teacher be realistic about expectations so activities will be in line with the child's stage of development.

The following 11 areas identifiable through the ITPA clinical model provide one of the bases for determining goals.

Auditory Reception—Understanding what is heard.

Visual Reception—Understanding what is seen.

Auditory Association—Mentally manipulating, organizing and relating concepts presented orally.

Visual Association—Mentally manipulating, organizing and relating concepts presented visually.

Verbal Expression—Expressing ideas verbally.

Manual Expression—Expressing ideas through gestures.

Auditory Memory—Remembering in proper sequence what is heard.

Visual Memory—Remembering in proper sequence what is seen.

Grammatic Closure—Using syntax and grammatical constructs appropriately.

Visual Closure—Perceiving/integrating physical units into a whole or in complete pictures.

Auditory Closure—Perceiving/integrating sounds into meaningful words.

465

Objectives are selected, delineated and organized based on their relevance to a particular goal. The sequence in which activities are presented is determined by the functioning of the child, the desired goal and the developmental difficulty of the task.

Pacing of activities should be such that the handicapped child is challenged. At the same time the activities should be at a level where the child is not frustrated and where success is frequently attained. Careful sequencing of materials from simple to complex provides the basis for achieving appropriate pacing.

While the development of processing skills is felt to be more important than content, the acquisition of specific knowledge or content is essential to the development of information processing skills. It is important to select content that is of interest to the child and relevant to both his present status and future needs. Careful selection of content will help bridge the gap between the limited knowledge of the young child and the demands made of him later in his schooling.

Young handicapped children can often be motivated to learn by embedding an activity in a game format. Such an approach can arouse basic curiosities, create a feeling of excitement and result in improved motivation and desire to learn.

Materials that are flexible lend themselves to the development of important processes since a handicapped child can learn to interact to the same materials in a variety of ways. Although a set of materials may encourage flexible usage, little is accomplished unless the teacher uses a flexible approach. Every teacher must be constantly aware of alternative uses for a set of materials and use this knowledge to meet the needs of the handicapped child.

The most effective materials are often those which stimulate a variety of senses—those which encourage each child to touch, taste, smell, see, hear. Often when one sensory modality is weak or yields distorted perceptions, input through another sense may provide feedback that compensates for the handicap and assists in the learning.

Regardless of the worth of the activity, the teacher must introduce the activity in such a way as to obtain the attention of the child and establish a set for learning. Many activities fail to motivate the child to learn because the teacher fails to understand the importance of promoting a set for learning or inadvertently establishes an inappropriate set.

Since preschoolers have yet to develop the ability to benefit from written materials, most of their instruction and learning occurs through oral directions and dialogue between the adult and child and between children. The teacher must anticipate appropriate dialogue with children and incorporate such preplanning in the curricular materials he is developing or adapting so that paraprofessionals and volunteers who are supplementing the curriculum will use appropriate dialogue.

Since the basic goals are concerned with the development of processing skills, the child must be stimulated in a variety of ways to process relevant content. Provision of a wide variety of experiences based on careful planning and selection will help insure learning.

Although the teacher may use appropriate dialogue, stimulate various modalities, use materials flexibly and be prepared to promote an appropriate learning set, the activity may be a failure unless it is also interesting to the child and to the teacher. Both must be enthusiastic to ensure maximum learning. Novelty and uniqueness help to make an activity interesting, especially when the objective is to provide an overlearning "experience."

Criterion activities help the teacher determine if she has taught what she intended to teach. Careful observations of the child's behavior as he engages in the criterion activity provides information the teacher can analyze and use to determine present attainments and future curricular needs.

To ensure permanency of learning, the teacher must carefully plan review and reinforcement activities. Such activities should occur both shortly after the original learnings and several weeks or months later.

In addition to providing for direct reinforcement of new learnings, the teacher needs to provide activities that are similar to but not the same as the original learnings. In this way the child will develop a more generalizable set of behaviors. Thus, he will be able to function more adequately in a broader variety of problem areas.

IMPLEMENTING A LEARNING ACTIVITY

The best teachers are those who are able to develop curriculum to meet the needs of the children in their classes. The foregoing section provides a series of guidelines to help the teacher organize her thinking as she prepares an activity and to help her evaluate the likely effect of the activity. To illustrate the application of the guidelines, selected lesson plans[1] are presented and analyzed using the guidelines.

MANUAL EXPRESSION #20

To pantomine action stated by teacher

Materials: None

---

1. Reproduced by permission of the Milton Bradley Company, Springfield, Massachusetts, from the *GOAL: Language Development* program by Merle B. Karnes, 1972.

Procedure:

1. "Today we are going to be actors. You see actors on television—the people who act out parts in plays and movies. I will whisper something I want you to do, and you will act out what I say. You will pretend you have the things you need. If I whisper to you to sweep, you'll pretend you have a broom. Like this."

Show children how you hold your hands and swish a pretend broom back and forth.

"When you have finished, the other children will raise their hands if they think they know what you are acting out. I will call on one of them."

2. Give each child several turns to perform simple actions: washing his face or hands, shoveling snow, raking, swimming, eating an ice-cream cone, hanging clothes on a line, cutting with scissors, putting on a hat and mittens, cutting with a saw, hammering, putting on socks and shoes.

3. Give help to children who are shy about performing in front of others or who cannot think of appropriate actions. Whisper "Could you do it this way?" (Demonstrate.) "Now you do it."

4. Help children be perceptive in interpreting the actions. "Watch how John moves his arms. Try to think what he might be holding." Commend children who wait to be called on after they have raised their hands to identify the action of another child.

Criterion Activity:

—Each child will pantomine two actions suggested by the teacher. These should be actions not previously demonstrated in this lesson.

—Have the other children guess what each performer is doing.

Reinforcement:

The above activity may be extended and reinforced through the use of the following:

1. "We'll pretend a boy named Johnny has asked all of you to come over to his house to play. For awhile you play outdoors. Then it begins to rain,

and you have to go inside. Johnny says to you, 'What can we do inside on a rainy day? What can we do with our feet? Say, I have an idea. We can jump with our feet. Let's jump with both feet.'"

2. "Let's do what Johnny says, 'jump with both feet.' Now Johnny says, 'What else can we do with our feet?'"

Ask a child for a suggestion. If he suggests an action that can be done with the feet, ask all children to perform it. If he cannot think of an activity, tap your foot. Say to the child, "What am I doing? Yes, tapping my foot. Let's all tap our feet."

3. Other appropriate activities to be performed with the feet include tiptoeing, galloping, running, stamping, skating, hopping on one foot, walking on heels, walking on the outside of the feet, walking with the feet pointed outward or inward.

It will be noted that the major goal of the lesson is an information processing skill derived from the ITPA. Thus, this lesson plan meets the first criterion that activities should be based on an instructional model. As stated previously, one of the identified needs of most handicapped children is help in improving their language functioning. Since the instructional model is language based, it is an appropriate type of activity for handicapped children who manifest deficits in language.

Children who do poorly in school have difficulty processing information. The ITPA based instructional model is a process oriented model. Further, since the lesson plan itself provides the opportunity to utilize a wide variety of content, it seems to fit well in the process domain.

Since the activities in the program were developed on a base population of children from 3 to 5 years of age, the lesson plan should be appropriate for some of the handicapped children in a class made up of similar ages. Analyses of the needs of the children and the developmental level of the activities contained in the lesson plan should permit selecting and presenting the activities at a time when it is an appropriate match for the stage of development of the children.

The specific objective in the example lesson plan is to have the child "pantomine action stated by the teacher." This objective is obviously relevant to the goal of Manual Expression.

Since the lesson plans in the *GOAL: Language Development* program are intended to be model lesson plans, only moderate attention has been given to the sequencing of activities in an area; thus, the activities within a lesson plan may be too complicated for some children and too simple for others. The teacher will need to assess the capabilities of each child carefully and sequence the lesson plans for each child. In the above lesson plan, for example, a young 3 year old might not be able to pantomime the action of sweeping a broom without initial cues. The teacher may cue him by having him watch her sweep with a broom; then sweep with the broom himself; then pretend to sweep along with her; and, finally, pretend to sweep when she whispers to him to sweep. This entire sequence of activities might take place over several days for one child; for another child, who doesn't need the task to be broken down in such simple steps, it might be accomplished in a single period.

If the teacher, through careful observations, is aware of the development of each child and sequences activities commensurate to his stage of development, frequent success will be possible. The child will not be frustrated, but will enjoy learning and develop further motivation to learn.

The acquisition of appropriate content is necessary for the growth of a child. This lesson offers a variety of opportunities for the selection of appropriate content. For example, children who need to improve their self-help skills might be asked to perform motor tasks such as washing their face or hands, hanging clothes on the line, putting on a hat or mittens, putting on shoes and socks. Similarly, children who need a broader understanding of vocational activities might be asked to pretend to do such things as rake, hammer, cut with a saw.

This lesson plan can be easily adapted to capitalize on current interests such as acting like certain zoo animals after a field trip to the zoo or like farm animals after a visit to the farm. Adaptations can also be made for different cultures. Indians, for example, might be asked to demonstrate activities appropriate to their culture such as dances, sign language, making pottery, weaving baskets.

Analysis of the lesson plan reveals that the game format is used to implement the activities in the lesson. Curiosity should be easily aroused by the feeling of secrecy introduced in the activity. Excitement can be generated by the attitude of the teacher who conveys to the children that the activity is fun and exciting.

The question as to whether or not the lesson plan meets the criterion of flexibility can receive an affirmative answer on at least two dimensions. First, as previously illustrated, the lesson plan is extremely flexible with regard to content since the choice of content is essentially unlimited. In addition, the materials are flexible in levels of difficulty since it can be introduced with something as simple as washing of the face or hands or as complicated as the teacher deems necessary.

Although the basic activity stresses manual expression for the target child, the fact that each child in the group has an opportunity to go through the cycle of hearing the command (Visual Reception), manually expressing the idea (Manual Expression), observing another child (Visual Reception), and reporting his observation (Verbal Expression) clearly brings into play more than one modality of learning.

470

The establishment of an appropriate set is important for getting the attention of the children, stimulating their interest and motivating them to engage in an activity. Contained in the lesson plan are some suggestions for promoting a learning set, i.e., "Today we are going to be actors. You see actors on television—the people who act out parts in plays and movies. I will whisper something I want you to do, and you will act out what I say." Similar suggestions should be included in any adequate curriculum materials.

Through their play activities children often show delight when role playing or mimicking others. Since it is very similar to the natural actions of children, role playing becomes an inherently interesting lesson.

A criterion activity is provided to give the teacher additional opportunities to observe the child and determine if he is making progress in manual expression as delineated by this lesson. In addition, the lesson plan provides suggestions for revision and reinforcement of the language processing skill.

ADAPTATIONS OF A LESSON PLAN TO TYPES OF HANDICAPS

In this section a lesson plan from the Visual Reception area of the *GOAL: Language Development* program is adapted for children with different handicapping conditions.

VISUAL RECEPTION #8

To distinguish two like items in a set of three

Materials:

1. Two cups and one plate (can be paper)
2. Two forks and one spoon
3. Two pencils and one piece of chalk
4. Buttons of various shapes and sizes (must have two of the same of some buttons)
5. Two large spools and one small spool
6. Two each of the geometric shapes—circles, squares, rectangles, and triangles

Procedure:

1. Have all the items in a large container beside you, but out of sight and reach of the children.

2. Say to the children, "Let's play a game called 'Just the Same.' I will put *three* things on the table. When I call your name, you are to hold up all the things that are just the same."

Demonstrate by beginning with very simple items, such as two cups and one plate. As the child holds up the two cups, encourage him to say, "These are just the same."

Continue the game using sets of:

Two forks and one spoon
Two pencils and one piece of chalk
Two large spools and one small spool
Two circles and one square
Two squares and one triangle
Two rectangles and one square
Two triangles and one circle

Criterion Activity:

—Put two different buttons on the table, saying, "Now I will give each of you a turn to find the one button on the table that looks just like the one I have in my hand."

—Hold up a button that matches one of those on the table and say, "Elizabeth, find the one that looks just the same as this."

—The child should hold up the matching button and say, "This is the same."

—Give each child a turn, changing the buttons each time.

Reinforcement:

The above activity may be extended and reinforced through the use of materials such as:

1. Picture Cards, Set 2, Alikes
   Place three pictures on the table. Have the child find the two that are alike and tell why. "These are alike. They are both roosters."

2. Use Playskool No. 702 Jumbo Beads.
   Place three beads on the table. The child is to hold up the two that are

472

alike and tell why. "These two are alike. They are both (red, round, square)."

This sample lesson meets the criteria of a good lesson plan in the following areas: It is model based and language processing oriented; the objective leads toward a goal; it is flexible in regard to sequence, pacing and content; the game format is used; the learning set is described and the dialogue provided; a criterion activity is included as well as review and reinforcement activities. The lesson plan as written tends to be limited to one modality—the visual; however, the child can manipulate the materials which stimulates a second set of senses. To adapt the lesson, the teacher might describe the objects, which would stimulate the auditory senses, if she felt some child needed special help in the Auditory Reception area.

The activity is highly flexible with regard to the relevancy variable; therefore, it will be up to the teacher to select materials appropriate to the needs of the children. Since the lesson is so adaptable, it is especially appropriate for use with retarded children.

By using the illustrated format but varying the content by selecting items that are markedly different, one can begin the teaching of the concepts of likenesses and differences. For example, markedly different items such as two pencils and a book or two oranges and a shoe would be used initially. When the children are successful with these activities, items with greater similarity could be used such as oranges and an apple.

This lesson plan is basically very appropriate for the young deaf child, but the initial instructions should be modified. Repeated nonverbal demonstration of what is expected of the child should be used until he shows that he understands the activity. Dramatic reinforcements of correct responses would foster learning.

Adaptation of this lesson plan for use with blind *or* partially seeing children is relatively easy. More emphasis would have to be placed on the children handling the materials. In fact, the children should be encouraged to feel each item in a set thoroughly before determining the two that are alike. Great ingenuity can be used by the teacher in finding what will be especially interesting and stimulating to the blind child; for example, feathers, cotton balls, sandpaper of varying grits, rocks of different weights, smoothness and contour, different textures of fabric.

Adaptation of this lesson for an involved orthopedically handicapped might require the child to point with a stick to the two alike items or even knock them off the table with a swipe of the hand. Similarly, some markedly physically handicapped child may have to verbally indicate the two items that are alike by saying "Yes" or "No" when the teacher points to the three items one after the other.

If a young child is blind *and* deaf, this activity might be used by having the child feel the objects and eventually hold the two that are alike in the palms of his hands. Undoubtedly, learning will be a slow process, so the items used should be markedly different. Reinforcement with a hug, pat or even a bit of candy will help foster learning.

For the child who has a learning disability in the Visual Reception area, the lesson may be adapted so that he becomes more aware of the likenesses and differences through a combination of tactile, auditory and visual stimulations. For example, when determining the two that are alike—two cups and one plate—he should hold a cup; label, or call it, a cup; associate it with milk or water. The teacher might call attention to the handle and say, "Put your finger through the handle." The same general procedure would be used with the plate—running the finger around the edge, holding it between the palm of the two hands to feel the flatness of it and associating the word "food" with it. Then the teacher might say, "Look at the objects. Now give me the two cups." Later, she could expect the child to give her the two that are the same. The extent to which the process is task analyzed will be determined by the extent of the child's learning disability.

This lesson plan might be very appropriate for use with a young emotionally disturbed child since it requires a low degree of social interaction with other children and with the teacher. Should some suggested objects prove to be too stimulating, the teacher might want to make substitutions. On the other hand, the teacher might wish to densitize the child by playing the game over and over again while providing the child with considerable support when disturbing objects are presented. If the process is approached appropriately, the teacher may be able to desensitize a child to disturbing stimuli and, at the same time, help him develop cognitive skills. In a similar vein, children with socially inappropriate behavior may be helped to gain social skills if they are appropriately reinforced during the playing of the game.

A LESSON PLAN AS A TEACHING AND/OR DIAGNOSTIC TOOL

One of the problems teachers of preschool children face is the development or selection of activities commensurate with the needs of the children they are teaching. Since the young child cannot prepare products such as a theme or a complex scientific project that can be carefully studied by the teacher, she must gather most of her information about a child as he engages in an actual activity. The problem of gathering relevant data is probably most acute in the Auditory Association area where the teacher must be aware of both the question the child asks and the quality and content of his answer. The use of lesson plans as a setting for observation will facilitate controlling the types of questions that are asked of the children. Then, the teacher can spend more time and care in making observations as to how the child responds to the demands of the activity.

Many teachers find the ITPA model useful for developing activities and organizing their instructional program but lack the time of a professional psychologist to evaluate the children on the ITPA test. The class analysis sheet (see Figure 1) derived from the *GOAL: Language Development* program provides one way a teacher might determine the strengths and weaknesses of the children in her class.

Since the Auditory Association area is extremely important for a child's growth and development yet difficult to evaluate, a sample lesson has been selected for discussion.

No one activity lends itself to observing children in all aspects of the guidelines under Auditory Associations; thus, it will be necessary to watch children as they engage in more than one activity. On the other hand, the teacher must begin with some activity, preferably one that provides an opportunity to observe children along several guidelines of the processing area. Consider the appropriateness of the following lesson plan.

AUDITORY ASSOCIATION #3

To associate something with auditory clue and respond with appropriate answer

Materials: None

Procedure:

1. "Today I am going to ask you some questions. I will find out what good thinkers you are. I know you are good thinkers, but today you will really have to prove it.

   "If I say that I am going to the bank, why do you think I am going?
   If I say I don't feel very well, what do you think is wrong with me?
   If I have a hole in my coat pocket, what do you think may happen?
   If your refrigerator stopped running, why would your mother be concerned about it?
   If your stove were broken, what might happen?
   If you were carrying a glass of jelly and fell, what might happen?
   If a dog ran after you, what would you do?
   If there were a big cloud in the sky, what do you think might happen?
   If you fell out of a tree, what might happen to you?
   If everyone threw his chewing gum on the sidewalk, what would happen?"

Figure 1
(Date)
ITPA—AUDITORY ASSOCIATION
Class Analysis

Guidelines	Names of Children								
1. Perceives same, different, and opposite relationships presented verbally.									
2. Understands complex directions.									
3. Makes inferences from verbal materials.									
4. Detects "foolish" statements about a familiar topic.									
5. Answers questions of a "What if?" or "Why does?" nature.									
6. Responds to questions requiring divergent thinking.									
7. Responds to questions or riddles requiring convergent responses.									
8. Makes a riddle about an object or setting.									
9. Gives "thoughtful" answers.									

To make a class analysis, observe and rate the child as "below average" = 1, "average" = 2, and "above average" = 3.

2. Encourage children to respond in complete sentences. You may need to encourage some children by asking other questions or making a few suggestions.

Criterion Activity:

—Ask the children to respond to the following question. Have each of them think of a different answer. "If it were your birthday and you could have anything you wanted, what would you ask for?"

Comparison of the lesson plan with the guidelines (see Figure 1) reveals that there will probably be little opportunity to observe the children on "perceiving same and different" (No. 1) and "making a riddle" (No. 8). On the other hand, it should be immediately obvious that observations can be easily made on "make inferences" (No. 3), "What if?" (No. 5), "divergent thinking" (No. 6), "convergent thinking" (No. 7) and "thoughtful answers" (No. 9). With some modification of the content of the lesson plans, information might be obtained appropriate to "understanding complex directions" (No. 2) and "detects 'foolish' statements" (No. 4).

Once the teacher has analyzed her lesson plan and decided upon which guidelines she wants to focus, she is ready to initiate the observation in an actual situation. One of the most practical ways is to take groups of six to eight children to a quiet area of the room, preferably around a table, and engage the children in a selected lesson plan. During the session, she might write an abbreviated record of responses given by the children. After the completion of the lesson, if possible, or immediately after the children have left for the day, the teacher should sit down and rate the children on their responses relative to the guidelines. Children who are above average for the group will be given a 3; children who are average for the group will be given a 2; children below average will be given a 1 on each guideline. For example, one child might be above average (3) on divergent thinking and below average (1) when thinking convergently. In the same way, the other children in the class should receive the same lesson plan and activities and be rated accordingly. During succeeding days, additional lesson plans should be selected covering the guidelines not evaluated by the initial lesson (same-different; riddle). After the teacher has completed her evaluations of all the children in the class on all the guidelines in an area she will want to consider carefully how to regroup in order to program for them. Analysis may reveal that a regrouping of the class into small working groups based on overall maturity—social, physical and intellectual—may constitute the best grouping. Nevertheless, some children may need to be assigned to different groups based strictly on social interactive problems as might be the case when two children seem to agitate each other. Once workable groups are established, careful attention can be given to the selection of the lesson plans and the adaptation of lesson plans to meet not only the needs of the group but of individuals within the group. Thus, for example, when the teacher asks the group, "If your stove were broken, what might happen?" she might expect one child to be able to say something like "Have to call a repairman," "Have to go out for dinner," and "Eat cold food." Another child might answer "No food," "No eat," "Hungry." Each child could be praised for responses commensurate with his stage of development. In this way a workable social group can be established, yet each child will receive more careful individualized attention than would be possible if the above procedure were not followed.

PACING OF LESSON PLANS

Within a class, some children learn more rapidly than others. Furthermore, some children will have had broader experiences and different backgrounds than others. As a consequence, it is necessary to present lesson plans which hold differing expectations for achievement within a lesson plan. To illustrate how a lesson plan can be paced to meet individual differences in learning, the following lesson plan is presented.

VISUAL SEQUENTIAL MEMORY #23

To name in order four articles of clothing placed in suitcase

Materials:

1. Suitcase

2. Clothes (shoes, socks, sweater, slacks, pajamas, necktie, cap, handkerchief, underwear, shirt, toothbrush, toothpaste, comb)

Procedure:

1. Put the suitcase and clothing articles on the table. "Today we are going to pack a suitcase to go on a trip. We will take turns putting two things in the suitcase. Watch so that you can tell us how the things are put in the suitcase. I'll start. I'm going on a trip. Watch what I put in the suitcase." Put in the shoes. "Now watch!" Put in the sweater. Close the suitcase. "Benjamin, what did I put in my suitcase first?" If the child does not name the articles in sequential order, review with him what you put in the suitcase first, then second.

2. Continue this same procedure, giving each child a turn to pack two articles. Another child should tell in sequence how the articles were packed.

3. After the children are able to recall a series of two articles, increase the series to include three, then four articles.

Criterion Activity:

—Open the empty suitcase. "Watch while I put four things in the suitcase. Then I will close the suitcase and ask you to name the things in the order I put them in the suitcase." Alter the sequence of four for each child.

—This same procedure can be used in the following ways. Play a game in which three to five animals go in and out of a barn. Ask the children to recall in order the animals that went in the barn. Then have a child bring the animals out of the barn in the same sequence they went into the barn. (Milton Bradley Picture Sequence Cards No. 7524 can be used following this same game format.)

—Have each child identify objects as they are put into and taken out of a purse. Begin with two objects and progress to five.

The above lesson plan provides for making the lesson easier and more difficult by changing the number of items a child is expected to recall. During the first session with this activity, the number of articles that a child is asked to remember might be increased until his ceiling is reached. During subsequent sessions, the teacher can more accurately set the goal for each child as one item above that which he was able to accomplish during the last session. Once the child has obtained a goal, a new goal can be established. Extremely careful observation may reveal a child can remember three articles of clothing if they are very familiar with the items (shoe, sock, shirt), but only two of the items are unfamiliar (necktie, robe). Expectations can be varied based on the degree of familiarity.

REFERENCES

Hunt, J. McVickers. *Intelligence and Experience.* New York: Ronald Press, 1961.
Joyce. B. & Weil, M. *Models of Teaching.* Englewood Cliffs, N.J.: Prentice–Hall, 1972.
Parker, R.K. (Ed.). *In the Preschools in Action: Exploring Early Childhood Programs.* Boston, Mass.: Allyn and Bacon, 1972.

In the following article, the author gives us a look at another approach to early childhood curriculum and also presents some data on the advantages of early childhood programs.

Curriculum for Early Childhood Special Education

David P. Weikart
High Scope Educational Research Foundation, Ypsilanti, Michigan

The place of special education in the early childhood education movement has been a source of confusion and embarrassment for the last decade. The basic problem is that the vast majority of youngsters qualifying for special education programs have been diagnosed as "mildly retarded" with no specific organic etiology. If this group of youngsters were distributed randomly throughout the social classes, as are most categories of other handicaps, there would be no problem; the diagnosis of mild mental retardation would be accepted in the same manner as a diagnosis of a mild hearing loss or vision problem – as unfortunate and without stigma. However, the distribution is extraordinarily skewed; that is, a disproportionate number of "mildly retarded" children come from low income and minority group families, the disadvantaged groups of our society. While this overlap was conveniently overlooked in a more naive era, it is impossible to do so today.

The diagnosis of retardation without specific organic etiology places a stigma on the child, his family, and his culture. What is more, its validity is highly suspect. The case demonstrating the fallibility of tests used for placing disadvantaged children in special education is best illustrated by research concerned with language development. Initially, a number of researchers using tests of language development with disadvantaged children found what they thought were major developmental differences between these children and middle-class children. When other researchers scrutinized these results, however, paying close attention to the items on the tests, it became apparent that what the tests were measuring was sophistication in the standard American dialect and not general language development. When the child was assessed for language development within his own dialect, the language "retardation" disappeared (Baratz & Baratz, 1970). It is recognized today that many items on intelligence scales and standardized achievement tests show a similar "culture bias."

One of the principal lessons of the civil rights ferment of the sixties was that the individual is a product not only of family and subculture but also of a system of economic distribution and opportunity. There is widespread recognition today that society must take major steps to remedy the problems that this social-economic "system" generates for individuals from low-income and minority groups. The implication of a diagnosis of non-organic retardation is that the problem of educability has originated *in the individual*, through deficiencies of intelligence, just as the problem with the deaf child has originated in his physical handicap or with the organically retarded child in the abnormality of his brain. However, the fact that the "mildly retarded" children in special education classes are generally from low-income or minority groups points to another conclusion: that such children, because of the environment in which they are growing up, lack the *skills* and *attitudes*, not the intelligence, needed to succeed in school. The "deficiency" is to be found in the social order, in its effects on disadvantaged children. From education's point of view, this means that equality of educational opportunity becomes paramount. More specifically, it means that schools must change to meet the special needs of children from poverty environments — environments that are "deprived" because of inequities in the social-economic system.

Any discussion of the relation between special education and early childhood curriculum, then, must clearly distinguish between the organically mentally handicapped child and the environmentally disadvantaged child. For the latter, there is some impressive evidence pointing to the efficacy of a *preschool* experience; compensatory efforts at the primary level have had little success in helping disadvantaged children do better in school (Jencks, 1972).

THE YPSILANTI-PERRY PRESCHOOL PROJECT

The Ypsilanti-Perry Preschool Project (Weikart, Deloria, Lawser & Wiegerink, 1970) assessed the longitudinal effects of a two-year preschool program designed to compensate for the "functional mental retardation" believed to have been found in some children from disadvantaged families. (The diagnosis was based on Stanford-Binet IQ scores.) The program consisted of daily cognitively oriented preschool classes accompanied by weekly home-teaching visits. The project was operated from September 1962 to June 1967. Children were assigned to either an experimental or a control group in an essentially random manner, except that the two groups were matched on socioeconomic status and Stanford-Binet scores.

The preschool curriculum that evolved during the five years of the project was derived in part from Piagetian theory and teacher observation, and focused on cognitive objectives (Weikart, Rogers, Adcock & McClelland, 1971). Emphasis was placed on making the curriculum flexible enough for the teacher to gear classroom activities to each child's level of development. Verbal stimulation and interaction, sociodramatic play, and the learning of concepts through activity were considered more important than social behavior and other traditional concerns of nursery schools. Weekly afternoon home-teaching visits provided each family with an opportunity for personal contact with the child's teacher. The parents were encouraged to participate in the instruction of their children, the goal being to improve their relationship with school and teachers and to involve them in the education process. The teacher's child management techniques indirectly suggested to the mother alternative ways of handling children. Group meetings were used to reinforce the changes in parents' views regarding the education of their children.

The following are the general findings from the project:

1. The children who participated in preschool obtained significantly higher scores on the Stanford-Binet IQ test than the control group children. This superior functioning disappeared by third grade, and (from preliminary data) by eight grade both group means returned to the scores obtained at the three-year-old level.
2. The children who participated in preschool obtained significantly higher scores on achievement tests in elementary school than the control group children. This difference attained significance in first, third, and fourth grades, but is irregular in higher grades where data are incomplete.
3. The children who participated in preschool received better ratings by elementary school teachers in academic, emotional, and social development than the control group children. This difference continued through third grade.

In general, these findings show a positive impact of preschool education on the performance of disadvantaged children in the elementary grades. One of the specific goals of the High/Scope Foundation projects has been to follow the development of participating children long enough to study the impact of preschool upon special education placement, retention-in-grade, drop-outs, and teenage crime rates, etc., at the junior and senior high levels. Using the most recent data from the original Ypsilanti-Perry project, Table 1 presents information on the current grade placement and special education enrollment for Waves 0 through 4, now enrolled in grades five through nine.

Table 1

**SPRING 1973 SCHOOL PLACEMENT INFORMATION
FOR COMPLETE PERRY PROJECT SAMPLE* (N=123)**

		Experimental Group				Control Group		
Wave	Expected Grade (Spring '73)	Number of Children	Children in Expected Grade	Children in Special Ed.	Children Retained a Grade, but no Special Ed.	Number of Children	Children in Expected Grade	Children in Special Ed.	Children Retained a Grade, but no Special Ed.
0	9th	13	8	1	4	13**	7	6	0
1	8th	8	4	4	0	9	5	3	1
2	7th	12	11	0	1	13***	7	4	2
3	6th	13	8	2	3	14	8	3	3
4	5th	12	11	0	1	13	10	1	2
TOTALS		58	42	7	9	62	37	17	8
%		100% =	72% +	12% +	16%	100% =	60% +	27% +	13%

*Of the original sample of 123 children, 90 children are still enrolled in the Ypsilanti school system, where full special education services are available. Of these, 13% of the High/Scope graduates are in special education classes as compared to 34% of the nongraduates.
**Two control group children lost from this wave.
***One control group child lost from this wave.

Regardless of the intellectual and achievement differences, the school "treats" the children of the experimental group much differently than the control group children. This difference is evident in the grade and class placement of the children in school. Using the most recent data (spring 1973) for the complete sample of 123, the school assigned 72% of the experimental group to grade level as compared to only 60% of the control group. However, the most striking figures are those regarding special education class placement. In the experimental group 12% have been placed in special education classes as compared to 27% for the control group. When we review the school placement for the 90 children still enrolled in the Ypsilanti Public School system where full special education services are available (the other 33 children have moved to other school districts), 13% of the experimental children are in special education classes as compared to an astounding 34% of the control group children.

Since special education costs are more than twice that of regular education, the actual cash savings to public education is almost sufficient to cover the costs of providing preschool education to these "high risk" youngsters. When the broader social costs of individuals with inadequate education and poor self-esteem are included, failure to provide preschool education to all children who need the service is financially irresponsible as well as morally objectionable.

THE RANGE OF PRESCHOOL CURRICULA

Since preschool can make a difference under certain conditions, it is important to know the wide range of preschool curricula that are available and in use at this time. Many of the programs that fall under the nontraditional categories discussed below were developed in major early childhood education experiments conducted by special educators (e.g., Karnes, Kirk, Hodges, Spicker) and psychologists (Gray, Weikart, among others) with groups of low-income minority-group children, some of whom were diagnosed as "mildly" (non-organically) retarded.

Most early childhood education programs may be placed in one of four categories[1]: Programmed, Open Framework, Child-Centered, or Custodial. In Figure 1, each of these program types is related to the way teachers and children in such programs participate and interact, in other words to the teachers' and children's "roles." If the teacher's predominant role is to initiate, she plans lessons, organizes projects, and develops activities; she decides what will be done or directly influences what will be done; she presents materials, programs, and ideas; she guides action and directs the efforts of the children. The initiating, or active, teacher usually follows a specific theoretical position, developing her classroom activities from its tenets or following specific procedures prescribed for her. Indeed, an "initiating teacher" can even be a programmed textbook or a sophisticated computer terminal from which a theory of instruction interpreted by a program developer may be supplied through carefully controlled materials. In general, the teacher who initiates is forceful in applying her talents and skills to accomplish specific instructional objectives.

If the teacher's predominant role is to respond, she watches the actions of both individual children and groups of children in the classroom environment. She responds to their needs and tries to facilitate their interaction with each other and with the materials in the classroom. While she will introduce materials and activities at specific points, she does this in response to what she feels are the expressed needs of the children. To ascertain these needs, the responding teacher applies the general knowledge of child and social development she has gained through training and experience. On the whole, the teacher responds carefully through her essentially intuitive understanding of the children's behavior.

---

1. Of course, any system of categorization is a deliberate simplification of the real world. Categories overalp in practice; many preschool programs are eclectic, mixing parts of various general approaches. These mixed models are to be found usually in situations removed from the requirements of a rigorous research design. For a discussion of these categories from a philosophical viewpoint, see Kohlberg and Mayer (1972).

When the child initiates, he is engaged in direct experience with various objects through manipulation and full use of all his senses; he is involved in role playing and other kinds of fantasy play; and he is active in planning his daily program, determining how he will work in the classroom environment. There is considerable physical movement by the child and a balance among teacher-child, child-child, and child-material interaction patterns. In general, the impetus for learning and involvement comes from within the child.

When the child responds, he is attentive or receptive; he listens to the teacher and carries out her requests; and he responds verbally to requests and demands. The responding child tends to move about the classroom less than the initiating child, since his predominant role is to wait for and attend to what is prepared and presented to him. In general, this child is working within a clear framework of acceptable behavior and progressing toward a specified goal. The impetus for learning and involvement comes from the teacher or other extrinsic forces.

Each of the four curriculum types discussed below — Programmed, Open Framework, Child-Centered, and Custodial — is, among other things, a particular combination of these styles of teacher-child interaction.

Programmed

This model combines *teacher initiates* and *child responds*. Several major innovative programs in the current wave of compensatory education projects are Programmed curricula. Most organized special education curricula also fall into this group. These curricula tend to be directed at clearly defined immediate educational goals, such as the teaching of reading, language skills, and mathematics skills. The goal of most of these programs is to equip the youngster with the skills necessary to manage the demands of traditional education. These curricula tend to be rigidly structured, with the teacher dominating the child and with a heavy emphasis on convergent thinking — "Say it the right way." — and learning through repetition and drill. The programs tend to be oriented to specific procedures, equipment, and materials, especially in those approaches that are heavily programmed, with technology ranging from a simple language master and tape components to major learning systems with computers and all the trimmings.

The key to the programs in this quadrant is that the curricula are teacher-proof; that is, the curricula are prepared scripts and not subject to extensive modification by the individuals presenting the instructions. As one major exponent of teacher-proof methods said: "If you use my program, 75% of everything you say will be exactly what I tell you to say!" Usually these programs are produced by a central group of program developers and then published or distributed for general use by interested school systems and parent groups. Since these programs assume that everything can be taught by the careful control of the student response, many of them use behavior modification techniques. Diagnosis of student skills and careful monitoring of progress in acquiring the prescribed goals are heavily utilized.

The major advantage of the curricula in this quadrant is their ease of distribution to the general field of education, as the performance of the child is keyed to the materials and not to the creative abilities of the teacher. This means that relatively untrained paraprofessionals as well as sophisticated and experienced professionals can effectively use these curricula with little difficulty. In addition, the teacher-proof characteristic appeals to angry parent groups who question the motives or commitment of teachers and who want full teacher accountability for the time their youngsters spend in school. These parents want their children to be taught to read and write and do arithmetic, and these programs do that job without any nonsense. Many school administrators also like these kinds of programs, as they provide effective control of their teaching staff and lend themselves to ordering equipment and supplies in logical units. The educational accountability fad sweeping state legislators as well as teacher groups almost demands that education be conducted in a programmed fashion with its clear focus on immediate and measurable objectives.

Another advantage of Programmed curricula is the ease with which new components may be added as they become necessary or identified. For example, another innovator in the Programmed area was criticized because of the failure of his methods to permit creative experiences for the children. He commented, "If you'll define what you mean by creativity, I'll develop a program to teach it." Then too, these curricula do not make a priori assumptions about the limitations of individual children. The challenge for the teacher is to find out the present limits of the child's knowledge in the area of concern and begin an instructional program to bring him to a well-defined point of competence.

In general, these curricula have clearly defined educational objectives, present a carefully designed and extensive program sequence to move children toward those objectives, and give the teacher explicit instructions as to how to behave during these learning sequences. Teaching is accomplished through the application of scripted materials supplied by the program developers. Learning is seen as the acquisition of correct responses as determined by the materials; anything can be taught to almost any child if the educational goals and behavioral objectives can be specified. The principles which support these programs tend to be drawn from learning theory, behavior management procedures, and language development theory.

Open Framework

In this quadrant, representing *teacher initiates—child initiates*, are programs which subscribe to specific theoretical goals, but which depend upon the teacher to create the particular curriculum in which the child participates. These curricula tend to focus upon underlying processes of thinking or cognition and to emphasize that learning comes through direct experience and action by the child. They omit training in specific areas, such as reading or arithmetic, treating these skills as inevitable outcomes of basic cognitive ability. These curricula accept the responsibility of developing the capacity of the child to reason and to recognize the relationship of his own action to what is happening about him. They tend to be skeptical of claims that solutions to problems or academic skills can be taught meaningfully to youngsters. Instead the child is challenged to utilize these developing cognitive processes to observe and record his environment, to generate concerns and content for his attention, and to apply this growing knowledge in his cooperative work with others.

These curricula are usually based upon a theory of child development, the most popular of which is that of Piaget. Using this theory, a curriculum framework is structured so that the teacher has clear guidelines as to how the program should be organized. The curriculum theory delimits the range of education activities, giving criteria for judging which activities are appropriate. The framework generally includes directions for structuring the physical environment, arranging and sequencing equipment and materials, and scheduling the day. The theory also gives the teacher a framework for organizing her perspectives on the general development of children. It is this open framework that provides discipline to the program.

These curricula tend to be oriented toward organizing and utilizing the people involved rather than any special equipment. They demand that the teacher create a transaction between the child and his environment to develop his abilities. And they demand that the child learn by forming concepts through activity, not by repeating what he has been told. The curriculum provides guidelines for establishing these conditions, but does not require special commercial materials or equipment.

One of the major advantages of the Open Framework curricula is that while the teacher must adopt a theoretical position and work within its limits, the specific program she creates is uniquely hers, developed as an expression of her attempt to meet the needs of the children in her group. This personal involvement on the part of the teacher means she becomes deeply committed to her program, and it is highly probable that she will continue to implement her program over a long period of time. At the same time, since the curriculum is based upon a specific theory, her expression of that curriculum can be closely examined by others, who know both the theory and children, to provide the teacher with guidance and assistance, facilitating quality control of the program.

Another advantage of Open Framework curricula is that, since the programs focus on the development of basic cognitive processes rather than on rote skills and since the specific curriculum is created by the teacher by carefully planning

487

activities according to the developmental levels of individual children, they are relatively free of cultural bias and untested assumptions about children's abilities. Thus they can be used effectively with youngsters with varying abilities and from diverse ethnic and socioeconomic backgrounds. The programs are also free of specific linguistic criteria and may be employed with non-English speaking children.

The learning process, structured by the teacher within the Open Framework, is usually paced by the child himself, with adaption of the activities by the teacher to match the child's needs and interests. In well-run Open Framework classrooms teachers frequently report their surprise at the minimal discipline and management problems, which would seem to reflect the range of adaptations the framework allows.

In general, these curricula are organized to accomplish cognitive and language development based upon a theory of intellectual development. An open framework is provided for the teacher as a context within which she develops a specific program for the children in her classroom. Learning by the child is the product of his active involvement within the environment structured by the teacher. The High/Scope Foundation's Cognitively Oriented Curriculum, developed during the Perry Preschool Project (discussed earlier), is an example of this approach.

Child-Centered

In this quadrant, representing *child initiates-teacher responds*, are the bulk of the traditional preschool programs as found on college campuses and in national projects such as Head Start and many of the programs of the "free school" movement. These curricula tend to focus on the development of the whole child, with emphasis on social and emotional growth. They are characterized by open and free environments with a generally permissive relationship between the teacher and the children and among the children themselves. Content revolves around things of interest or helpful to the child, such as the community, seasons of the year, and holidays. Academic skills are not stressed. There is a firm commitment to the idea that "play is the child's work" and recognition of the importance of the child's active involvement in his environment. Considerable attention is given to social adjustment and emotional growth through fantasy play, imitation of adult roles, rehearsal of peer relationships, and the careful development of the ability of the child to be independent of direct adult assistance. If theory is involved in one of these programs, it is usually a theory of emotional development. The actual curriculum developed by the teacher comes mainly from her own intuitive understanding of child development on the one hand and her observation of the needs of her children on the other. In general, the hallmark of the

Child-Centered curricula is an open classroom with children free to express their individual interests and to create their own environment, and with a careful response by an experienced and intuitive teacher who has developed a sense of how to support this creative environment.

The major advantage of the Child-Centered curricula is the complete openness to the needs of individual children. The program may be in harmony with the goals of both the parents and the professionals, reflecting the specific concerns of all involved. In addition, Child-Centered curricula are highly reflective of the values given considerable prominence in society as a whole: independence, creativity, self-discipline, constructive peer relationships, etc. Also, since this is the predominant program style at the preschool level, there is a vast reservoir of trained talent throughout the country, in colleges and universities, in organized national associations, and in the large number of programs currently utilizing these methods.

In general, these curricula attempt to assist the child in his overall development through careful attention to his individual needs. The teacher draws upon her knowledge of child development to create a supportive classroom where learning is the result of the child's interaction with the materials, his classmates, and his teacher. While there may be agreement on general goals in most Child-Centered programs, each teacher is responsible for the design of almost everything in her work.

Custodial

In this quadrant, representing *teacher responds-child responds*, are programs which are of minimal value to children. At best these programs protect the child from physical harm and may be some improvement over extraordinarily bad social conditions. Institutional programs often fall into this category. Some of these are described by Kirk (1958) and Skeels (1966). However, with the knowledge and resources available today, there is little excuse for maintaining custodial centers where teachers and children respond to little more than physical needs.

THE EFFECTIVENESS OF PRESCHOOL CURRICULA

Programmed, Open Framework, and Child-Centered approaches differ widely on a number of important theoretical and practical issues, including curriculum supervision for staff, adaptability of the program to specific educational needs of minority and regional groups, breadth of curriculum focus, recommended procedures for child management, acceptability of the curriculum to teachers, and assumptions about how children learn. The basic question is, however, how does the particular curriculum model affect the immediate and long-term intellectual, academic, and social performance of participating children? Unfortunately, there is little basic information about the relative effectiveness of particular preschool curricula.

There have been several efforts to examine this issue of differential effectiveness over the last five years (Karnes, 1969; Miller et al., 1971; Weikart, 1973). On the national level, Planned Variation Head Start (Smith, 1972) tested preschool intervention models in a range of sites throughout the country. In general the data from these projects raise more questions than they solve. Differences in population samples, degrees of program readiness for implementation, experience of staff, availability of carefully designed training programs, etc., have all conspired to make unclear the relation between a model's potential and its measured impact.

However, it is increasingly obvious from the comparative research projects that "you get what you pay for." Disorganized or badly run programs produce little gain on the part of the children participating in the day-to-day activities. Generally "bad" programs are the result of severe underfunding, unusual community or other political pressures, major conflict among staff members with no hope of reconciliation, and bureaucratic concentration upon form rather than upon the children and the purpose of the project.

Taken as a whole, the various comparative projects indicate general outcomes in the areas of academic skills, social competencies, and cognitive abilities that do reflect the intent of the models. Programmed models with directed teaching of academic skills tend to accomplish their specific goals even at the preschool level. However, there is little indication that performance above comparison groups on academic skills generalizes to improved performance in cognitive abilities or to social competencies such as locus of control perceived as internal. Indeed, there is evidence to suggest that programmed instruction introduces a bias in favor of attributing to others the power over the self. The Child-Centered models tend to score below their comparison groups on academic skills but above on general social competency. Usually there is no difference with comparison groups on general cognitive ability. The Open Framework programs tend to produce scores somewhat above their comparison groups in all areas with significant results in cognitive abilities tests such as the Stanford-Binet and Peabody Picture Vocabulary.

RECOMMENDATIONS

When special education considers the issue of curriculum, be it for preschool or the early primary grades, there is a strong obligation to think very clearly about the total impact of the curriculum selected. Each style has specific advantages and disadvantages. The problem of curriculum selection is broader now than it used to be. It must be acknowledged from the outset that the "mildly retarded" group, the vast majority of special education youngsters, is made up predominantly of youngsters from low-income minority populations whose school performance is a consequence of being *environmentally* handicapped. These children may benefit enormously from well run, clearly focused preschool programs.

It is important to recognize the value of having socioeconomic integration of the classroom, so that disadvantaged children will have an opportunity to work in an atmosphere where differences in attitudes, skills, abilities, and talents can be made into productive encounters. Any curriculum selected for application must permit children to progress at differential rates without being failed for slow progress. This means the criteria for success must reflect the wide range of potential accomplishment generated by each child.

Not only should the pace of children's learning vary with the individual, but the actual content should diverge as necessary to accommodate each child. This means the curriculum content should permit individual interests, skills, and achievements as defined by the child himself, not as imposed by arbitrary adult expectations.

Parent involvement should result in adjustment of the content of the curriculum to reflect the cultural and ethnic heritage of the children's families. It is not enough to follow one specific orientation drawn from the majority of families enrolled in the class or school.

The procedures adopted to assess the progress of the children in the program must reflect *long-term* accountability, not just immediate accountability. The quality of life that surrounds the child in school is actually more important for his total well-being than attaining immediate objectives forced by narrowly focused teaching.

The challenge we now face is to make our classrooms centers of learning for *all* children without the pressure to excel in some standard way to some standard mold. The importance of this shift cannot be overemphasized, for in it lies the hope of altering the most basic institution of our society, the school., and of opening up for many children avenues for development that are rightfully theirs. When it is accepted that large numbers of children currently placed in special education either do not belong there or need not have been put there had their educational requirements been recognized and cared for at an earlier age, special educators will have an opportunity to devote all of their energies and resources to those children who need special education by virtue of physical and organic handicaps.

REFERENCES

Baratz, S. S. & Baratz, J. C. "Early Childhood Intervention: The Social Science Base of Institutional Racism." *Harvard Educational Review, 40,* 1970 (29-50).

Jencks, C. *Inequality: A Reassessment of the Effect of Family and Schooling in America.* New York: Basic Books Inc., 1972.

Karnes, M. B., et al. *Investigations of Classroom and At-Home Interventions, Research and Development Program on Preschool Disadvantaged Children. Final Report. Volume I.* University of Illinois, Urbana: Institute of Research for Exceptional Children, May 1969.

Kirk, S. *Early Education of the Mentally Retarded.* Urbana: University of Illinois Press, 1958.

Kohlberg, L. & Mayer, R. "Development As the Aim of Education." *Harvard Educational Review, 42,* 1972 (449-496).

Miller, L. B. et al. "Experimental Variation of Head Start Curricula: A Comparison of Current Approaches." Progress Report No. 9. Psychology Department, University of Louisville, Louisville, Ky., 1971.

Skeels, H. M. "Adult Status of Children with Contrasting Early Life Experiences: A Follow-Up Study." *Monographs of the Society for Research and Child Development, 32* (2), 1966.

Smith, M. "Findings of the Planned Variation Study." Presented at the annual meeting of the National Association for the Education of Young Children, Seattle, November 1972.

Weikart, D. P. "Development of Effective Preschool Programs: A Report on the Results of the High/Scope Ypsilanti Preschool Projects." Presented at the High/Scope Educational Research Foundation Conference: Using the High/Scope Cognitive Approach to Learning in Infant, Preschool, and Early Elementary Education, Ann Arbor, Michigan, May 1973.

Weikart, D.; Deloria, D.; Lawser, S. & Wiegerink, R. *Longitudinal Results of the Ypsilanti Perry Preschool Project.* Ypsilanti, Mich.: High/Scope Educational Research Foundation, 1970.

Weikart, D.; Rogers, L.; Adcock, C. & McClelland, D. *The Cognitively Oriented Curriculum: A Framework for Preschool Teachers.* Washington, D. C.: National Association for the Education of Young Children, 1971.

Author Index

Agard, Judith A., 35
Artuso, Alfred A., 255, 290

Bartel, Helmut W., 353
Bartel, Nettie R., 353
Beery, Keith E., 338
Brown, Lou, 236
Bruininks, Robert H., 92
Bryen, Diane, 353
Buckley, Nancy K., 436
Burdett, Carol S., 419

Carroll, Anne W., 318
Chaffin, Jerry D., 173
Christie, Lu S., 419
Clark, Gary M., 135

Gallagher, Patricia A., 446
Gottlieb, Jay, 35
Grosenick, Judith K., 275

Hall, R. Vance, 225
Hewett, Frank M., 255, 290
Hurley, Oliver L., 122

Johnson, Richard A., 153

Karnes, Merle B., 461
Kaufman, Martin J., 35
Kroth, Roger L., 400
Kukic, Maurine B., 35

MacMillan, Donald L., 73
McKenzie, Hugh S., 419
Mercer, Jane R., 112
Meyen, Edward L., 9
Minskoff, Esther H., 365
Mischio, George S., 383

Quay, Herbert C., 290

Rynders, John E., 92

Semmel, Melvyn I., 205
Soloway, Michael M., 290
Stillwell, Robert J., 255, 290

Taylor, Frank D., 255, 290
Thiagarajan, Sivasailam, 205
Tilley, B. K., 23

Vergason, Glenn A., 9

Walker, Hill M., 436
Whelan, Richard J., 9
Weikart, David P., 480
Weintraub, Frederick J., 55
Wiederholt, J. Lee, 301

York, Robert, 236

Zehrback, R. Reid, 461